Complex Networks and Dynamic Systems

Volume 3

Series Editor

Terry L. Friesz
Pennsylvania State University
University Park, PA, USA

More information about this series at http://www.springer.com/series/8854

Terry L. Friesz • David Bernstein

Foundations of Network Optimization and Games

Springer

Terry L. Friesz
Department of Industrial
and Manufacturing Engineering
Pennsylvania State University
University Park, PA, USA

David Bernstein
Department of Computer Science
James Madison University
Harrisonburg, VA, USA

ISSN 2195-724X ISSN 2195-7258 (electronic)
Complex Networks and Dynamic Systems
ISBN 978-1-4899-7593-5 ISBN 978-1-4899-7594-2 (eBook)
DOI 10.1007/978-1-4899-7594-2

Library of Congress Control Number: 2015934441

Springer New York Heidelberg Dordrecht London

Printed on acid-free paper

Springer Science+Business Media LLC New York is part of Springer Science+Business Media (www.springer.com)

Preface

THIS BOOK IS ABOUT computable mathematical models of infrastructure networks in decision environments that are primarily static or steady state in nature. The models considered are either mathematical programs or noncooperative mathematical games. The numerical methods considered include steepest descent, feasible direction, projection, fixed point, gap function, and computational intelligence algorithms.

The book is a direct outgrowth of teaching and research we have done at Penn State, James Madison University, George Mason University, MIT, Princeton, and the University of Pennsylvania. It is meant for use by students in civil engineering, industrial engineering, systems engineering, and operations research as either a primary or secondary textbook. It is also a reference for researchers specializing in the design and operation of transportation, water resource, telecommunications, and/or energy infrastructure networks.

The book includes quite a large number of numerical examples which we have found instructive to students and scholars who are selecting numerical methods for specific applications. At the same time, the book emphasizes a theoretical core of foundation models, each of which is a point of departure in the descriptive and prescriptive modeling of real networks.

University Park and Harrisonburg

Terry L. Friesz
David Bernstein

Contents

List of Figures

List of Tables

1 Introduction

It is quite common these days to hear laments about the quality of both the world's public and private infrastructure. In some developing countries, the infrastructure needed for economic vitality is said not to exist at all. In many developed countries, public infrastructure is said to be crumbling. In almost every country and geographical region, there is at least one economic sector for which investments in private infrastructure are not keeping pace with technological progress. These lamentations mean that some or all of the relevant transportation, telecommunications, energy distribution, and water resource *networks* are inadequate for the tasks at hand. As a result, a great many hard scientists, social scientists, and engineers have begun to study infrastructure networks in a systematic way.

As a participant in the evolving discourse on infrastructure networks, this book presents a class of mathematical models and computational methods that inform scholarly inquiry pertinent to infrastructure network engineering from the perspectives of microeconomic theory and game theory with a heavy dose of computational methods. The class of models and methods emphasized herein has been referred to both as *network economics* and as *network engineering.* Regardless of the appellation employed, the branch of scholarly inquiry considered herein is concerned with the formulation of both descriptive and prescriptive mathematical models of infrastructure as network optimization problems and network games. Network economics and network engineering are also concerned with the theoretical properties of the principal infrastructure network models studied, especially the properties of existence and uniqueness of solutions; it is also concerned with algorithms for finding infrastructure network flows, prices, and designs.

Because both physical and conceptual networks are studied in a variety of different fields, it is fairly difficult to trace the history of network economics and network engineering. Nonetheless, it is clear that important results have been developed by researchers in both methodology-driven (e.g., operations research, mathematics) and problem-driven (e.g., transportation, telecommunications) disciplines.

T.L. Friesz, D. Bernstein, *Foundations of Network Optimization and Games*,
Complex Networks and Dynamic Systems 3,
DOI 10.1007/978-1-4899-7594-2_1

In this chapter we discuss some representative mathematical models that illustrate the kind of infrastructure network applications that can be addressed with the tools developed in subsequent chapters. In order to set the stage for those examples, we need to introduce certain terminology and notation, which will be the foundation for the mathematical language we use to model all forms of infrastructure. Because this terminology and notation can seem a bit overwhelming to the uninitiated reader with no prior background in network modeling, we first introduce the language of network modeling in a rather informal way, counting on the formal treatment in subsequent chapters to refine and make more precise the reader's understanding.

After discussing some fundamental notions, this chapter considers the following models classes in brief:

Section 1.2: Transportation Networks. The problems of transportation network equilibrium and transportation network design are, respectively, presented as Nash and Stackelberg mathematical games.

Section 1.3: Telecommunication Networks. The problems of quasi-static flow routing and flow control in telecommunication networks are presented as nonlinear programs.

Section 1.4: Electric Power Networks. Noncooperative competition among power-producing firms, which are attached to the electric power grid and overseen by a regulatory authority, is presented as a differential Stackelberg game.

Section 1.5: Water Resource Networks. Irrigation network capital budgeting and efficient municipal water allocation are modeled from the perspective of mixed-integer mathematical programming.

1.1 Fundamental Notions

We begin by noting that networks are comprised of arcs and nodes. An *arc* is conveniently thought of as an entity that connects two nodes, while a *node* is any junction, origin or terminus of the network. So in everyday language an example of a node can be the intersection of two or more streets, and the streets, connecting as they do such intersections, are the arcs. Network arcs are also sometimes referred to as *links*, and less frequently as *edges* – although this latter name is more commonly associated with *graph theory*. Unless otherwise stated every network arc will be *directed* from a *tail node*, where flow enters to a *head node* where flow exits the arc. Sometimes nodes are referred to by their graph-theoretic name: *vertices*. Associated with the arcs and nodes of a network are various attributes that take on numerical values. Typical of these are cost, delay, flow, capacity, distance, impedance, demand and supply.

Since we have brought up the subject of graph theory, it is useful to distinguish graph theory from network modeling: *graph theory* is concerned primarily with topological and other non-numerical properties of networks. In fact, a collection of network arcs and nodes is by itself called a graph and is typically denoted as: $\mathcal{G}(\mathcal{N}, \mathcal{A})$, where $\mathcal{A}$ is a set of arcs and $\mathcal{N}$ is a set of nodes associated with those arcs. Every network model begins with the articulation of such a graph describing the nature of the connections among the arcs and nodes.

We will have much cause to discuss and to mathematically describe paths, also known as routes, on the graphs used to model infrastructure networks. Simply put, a *path* is a sequence of consecutive arcs directed in a fashion that allows flow from a specified origin to a specified destination to occur. We encourage the reader to reflect on the fact that a network may have substantially more paths than arcs, an important fact that we discuss in detail in later chapters. Suffice it to say for the time being that this tendency of networks to have extremely large numbers of paths has a profound impact on the development of numerical algorithms for solving certain types of infrastructure network models.

In the next section we begin the presentation of an overview of some relatively advanced optimization problems and mathematical games that illustrate the types of models that the reader of this book, whether student or researcher, will be able to apply, enhance, and solve by the time he/she reaches the last page. Some of the models presented in summary form in this chapter are considered in substantial detail in subsequent chapters, along with other models not noted here.

1.2 Transportation Networks

The transportation network is one of the most visible infrastructure networks, and a great many network models have been developed by transportation planners and engineers. Illustrative examples include traffic prediction, static network design, and real-time traffic control.

1.2.1 Traffic Prediction

In order to evaluate highway construction projects and perform environmental impact assessments for new developments, it is necessary to be able to predict traffic levels on the road network. To do so, we must be able to model how people make their path choices when driving. The most-often used behavioral model of this kind was proposed by Wardrop (1952). It is an equilibrium model that assumes drivers will individually choose the path that is best for them. Hence, if no driver has any incentive to change paths in equilibrium, it must be true that all used paths are minimum-cost paths.

To present the Wardropian equilibrium model more formally, suppose that h_p denotes the flow of vehicles that use path p from their origin to their destination, $\mathcal{P}$ is the set of all paths of the network, $h = (h_p : p \in \mathcal{P})$ is the vector of all path flows, $c_p(h)$ is the generalized unit cost of using path $p \in \mathcal{P}$ under flow condition h, and Q_{ij} is the rate of flow between origin-destination pair $(i, j) \in \mathcal{W}$, where $i \in \mathcal{N}$ denotes an origin node and $j \in \mathcal{N}$ denotes a destination node, while $\mathcal{W}$ is the set of all origin-destination (OD) pairs considered. We will also have need for the set of all paths connecting (i, j), which we denote by $\mathcal{P}_{ij}$. Finally, $c(h)$ will be the vector of all path costs. That is, $c(h) = (c_p(h) : p \in \mathcal{P})$. Then, h is a Wardropian user equilibrium if and only if:

$$\left.\begin{array}{ll} h_p > 0,\, p \in \mathcal{P}_{ij} \Longrightarrow c_p(h) = \min\{c_r(h) : r \in \mathcal{P}_{ij}\} & \forall\,(i,j) \in \mathcal{W} \\ \displaystyle\sum_{p \in \mathcal{P}_{ij}} h_p = Q_{ij} & \forall\,(i,j) \in \mathcal{W} \\ h_p > 0 & \forall p \in \mathcal{P} \end{array}\right\} \tag{1.1}$$

Now let the set of all feasible path flows be presently denoted as

$$\Omega = \left\{ h : \sum_{p \in \mathcal{P}_{ij}} h_p = Q_{ij} \quad \forall\,(i,j) \in \mathcal{W},\; h_p > 0 \quad \forall p \in \mathcal{P} \right\} \tag{1.2}$$

We will subsequently learn that this problem may be profitably stated as the following variational inequality problem:

$$\left.\begin{array}{lll} \text{find} & h^* \in \Omega & \\ \text{such that} & [c(h^*)]^T (h - h^*) \geq 0 & \forall h \in \Omega \end{array}\right\} \tag{1.3}$$

Formulation (1.1) is an example of a nonextremal static network equilibrium problem that will be discussed in considerable detail in Chap. 8 of this book.

1.2.2 Static Network Design

The problem of adding additional roads to a highway network whose flows are described by the Wardropian user equilibrium introduced in the previous example is known as the discrete equilibrium network design problem. From a mathematical point of view, the discrete equilibrium network design problem is a bilevel, nonlinear, mixed integer mathematical program. As such, it is among the most computationally demanding of all mathematical models, yet the ability to solve it is fundamental to informed capital budgeting for any road network.

The mathematical articulation of this problem requires defining the set of network arcs $\mathcal{A}$, an arbitrary element of which set we denote by the specific arc name a, where arcs are of course individual roads of the network of interest. On any arc will be a flow of automobiles, denoted by f_a, which is related to the path flows of the previous example according to

$$f_a = \sum_{p \in \mathcal{P}} \delta_{ap} h_p \qquad \forall a \in \mathcal{A}$$

where δ_{ap} is an element of the so-called *arc-path incidence matrix* $\Delta = (\delta_{ap} : a \in \mathcal{A},\, p \in \mathcal{P})$ and

$$\delta_{ap} = \begin{cases} 1 & \text{if } a \in p \\ 0 & \text{if } a \notin p \end{cases} \tag{1.4}$$

where $a \in p$ means that arc a belongs to path p. Of course, the notation $a \notin p$ means that arc a does not belong to path p.

We also associate with every arc an average generalized cost $c_a(f)$ where $f = (f_a : a \in \mathcal{A})$ is the full vector of arc flows. We will say more in Chap. 8 about the reasons for this type of functional dependence of arc costs on arc flows, but for now it suffices to say that such cost functions depict the congestion externalities known to be present on urban road networks. As a consequence, it is possible to articulate the objective of the network design process as

$$\min \sum_{a \in \mathcal{A} \cup \mathcal{I}} c_a(f) f_a$$

for the case of fixed travel demands, where $\mathcal{I}$ is the set of arcs being considered for insertion into the network. This minimization is meant to be accomplished in light of the following constraints:

(1) A budget constraint:

$$\sum_{a \in \mathcal{I}} \beta_a y_a \leq B$$

where B is the total budget for arc additions, $\beta_a \in \Re^1_{++}$ is the cost of constructing arc $a \in \mathcal{I}$, and y_a is a binary decision variable obeying

$$y_a = \begin{cases} 1 & \text{if arc } a \in \mathcal{I} \text{ is constructed} \\ 0 & \text{otherwise} \end{cases}$$

(2) Logical constraints:

$$f_a \leq M y_a \quad \forall a \in \mathcal{I}$$

where M is a suitably large positive number in the sense that

$$M \gg Q_{ij} \quad \forall (i,j) \in \mathcal{W},$$

so that when arc $a \in \mathcal{I}$ is not constructed its flow has the upper bound of zero, and when constructed its flow has effectively no upper bound;

(3) Constraints ensuring a Wardropian user equilibrium flow pattern:

$$h = \Phi(c, Q)$$

where $\Phi(c, Q)$ is an abstract operator signifying solution of the Wardropian user equilibrium problem for the cost vector $c = (c_p : p \in \mathcal{P})$ and demand vector $Q = (Q_{ij} : (i,j) \in \mathcal{W})$;

(4) Flow conservation constraints from (1.1); and

(5) Nonnegativity constraints from (1.1).

That is, the complete equilibrium network design model, for the circumstances we have described, takes the following form:

$$\left.\begin{aligned}
&\min \sum_{a\in\mathcal{A}\cup\mathcal{I}} c_a(f)\,f_a \\
&\text{subject to} \\
&f_a = \sum_{p\in\mathcal{P}} \delta_{ap}h_p \qquad \forall a\in\mathcal{A} \\
&h\in\Omega \\
&h=\Phi(c,T) \\
&\sum_{a\in\mathcal{I}} \beta_a y_a \leq B \\
&f_a \leq M y_a \qquad \forall a\in\mathcal{I} \\
&y_a = (0,1) \qquad \forall a\in\mathcal{I}
\end{aligned}\right\} \tag{1.5}$$

Because $h = \Phi(c, T)$ refers to the Wardropian network user equilibrium problem, it is clear that (1.5) is a bi-level problem for which an equilibrium problem is embedded within a mathematical program. That is to say, (1.5) is a nonlinear, mixed-integer mathematical program with equilibrium constraints. It is easy to show that (1.5) generally has a nonconvex feasible region, making the determination with certainty of a globally optimal network design effectively impossible. We will study (1.5) and problems like it in some detail in this book.

1.2.3 Real-Time Traffic Control

The advent of technology that allows near real time dissemination of information and instructions to individual vehicles operating over the transportation network has made it clear to both traffic engineers and theorists that models must be constructed that allow transient traffic states to be managed and exploited to achieve minimum congestion. Any such model must contain either an explicit or an implicit description of the traffic dynamics, by which is meant a description of how traffic flows and perceptions of travel cost evolve over time. Let us consider abstract traffic dynamics of the following form for the network of interest:

$$\frac{dh}{dt} = H(h,u,v,t) \tag{1.6}$$

$$\frac{du}{dt} = G(h,u,v,t) \tag{1.7}$$

where

h	is once again a vector of path flows $(h_p : p \in \mathcal{P})$
u_{ij}	is the perceived cost of travel between origin-destination pair (i, j)
u	is a vector of perceived costs $(u_{ij} : (i, j) \in \mathcal{W})$
$\mathcal{S}$	is the index set for information variables
v	is a vector of information variables $(v_k : k \in \mathcal{S})$

and $H(., ., .)$ and $G(., ., .)$ are vector operators. Although not explicitly stated, all components of the vectors h, u, and v vary with time.

For computation, it is convenient to employ discrete time instead of continuous time. To do so, we introduce the interperiod time step

$$\Delta = \frac{t_f - t_0}{N - 1} \approx dt$$

where t_0 is the initial time, t_f is the terminal time, N is a positive integer equal to the number of time steps employed to describe the dynamic process of interest, and dt refers to an infinitesimal increment of time that Δ is meant to approximate. That is, continuous time is replaced by the discrete time steps

$$\begin{aligned}
\tau_0 &= t_0 \\
\tau_1 &= \tau_0 + \Delta \\
\tau_2 &= \tau_1 + \Delta \\
&\vdots \\
\tau_{N-1} &= \tau_{N-2} + \Delta \\
\tau_N &= t_f
\end{aligned}$$

In this scheme, a function of continuous time, such as $h(t)$, where $t \in [t_0, t_f] \subset \Re^1_+$, is replaced by the vector

$$\begin{pmatrix} h_{\tau_0} \\ h_{\tau_1} \\ \cdots \\ h_{\tau_{N-1}} \\ h_{\tau_N} \end{pmatrix} \tag{1.8}$$

where $h_{\tau_i} \in \Re^{|\mathcal{P}|}$ for all $i \in [0, N]$. Similar discrete-time variables and notation are easily formed for u and v. Since (1.8) is rather tedious to write repeatedly, we use the less complicated shorthand

$$\begin{pmatrix} h_0 \\ h_1 \\ \cdots \\ h_{N-1} \\ h_N \end{pmatrix} \tag{1.9}$$

so long as no confusion will result. As a consequence, (1.6) and (1.7) may be restated in discrete time as

$$h_{t+1} = h_t + H_t(h_t, u_t, v_t) \cdot \Delta \quad t \in [0, N-1] \tag{1.10}$$

$$u_{t+1} = u_t + G_t(h_t, u_t, v_t) \cdot \Delta \quad t \in [0, N-1] \tag{1.11}$$

where t is now understood to be a discrete index. Furthermore, $H_t(h_t, u_t, v_t)$ is understood to be the values of the continuous-time vector $H(h,u,v,t)$ at the start of each discrete period $t \in [0, N-1]$; a similar interpretation of $G_t(h_t, u_t, v_t)$ of course applies.

The vector of information variables v describes message content, message frequency, congestion tolls, and the like from a traffic information system and are the fundamental control variables for real-time traffic management. The vectors of path flows h and perceived costs u are the so-called state variables; they are completely determined by knowledge of the controls. The vector operators $H(.,.,.)$ and $G(.,.,.)$ are specified to reflect an adjustment process describing the transitions among disequilibrium and equilibrium traffic states that characterize the traffic network of interest. The states are constrained by physical properties of the network, such as conservation of flow and nonnegativity of flows and perceived costs; such state-space constraints are similar to those developed above for static traffic equilibrium and are represented abstractly as

$$\begin{pmatrix} h \\ u \end{pmatrix} \in \Gamma(t) \tag{1.12}$$

Similarly, the information variables obey regulatory, fiscal, and budgetary constraints, as well as physical constraints imposed by the information technology itself, such as bandwidth, range, and the like. These control constraints are represented abstractly as

$$v \in \Lambda(t) \tag{1.13}$$

This completes the statement of the dynamics and our attention now turns to specifying the criterion for our traffic control system.

It is reasonable, if traffic demand is elastic, to select maximization of net economic surplus as the criterion. That is, we seek to maximize the difference between consumers' surplus[1] and congestion costs. Net surplus for our problem setting is

$$\max J = \int_{t_0}^{t_f} \exp(-rt) \sum_{(i,j)\in\mathcal{W}} \oint_{u}^{u^0} Q_{ij}(y,v,t)\, dy_{ij} dt \tag{1.14}$$

[1] Consumers' surplus is unused willingness to pay.

where

r	is the nominal rate of interest
y	is a vector of dummy variables $(y_{ij} : (i,j) \in \mathcal{W})$
$Q_{ij}(u,v,t)$	is the elastic demand for travel between $(i,j) \in \mathcal{W}$
$c_p(h,t)$	is the unit path cost at time t under traffic conditions h
$t_f - t_0$	is the planning horizon
r	is the constant rate of discount

and

$$\sum_{(i,j)\in\mathcal{W}} \oint_0^{u^0} Q_{ij}(y,v)\, dy_{ij}$$

is a line integral.

We may construct a discrete-time approximation of (1.14); that approximation is

$$J = \sum_{t=0}^{N-1} \exp(-rt) \left[\sum_{(i,j)\in\mathcal{W}} \oint_u^{u^0} Q_{ij,t}(y_t,v_t)\, dy_{ij,t} \right] \Delta$$

Consequently, the model of real-time control of the traffic network becomes

$$\max J = \Delta \cdot \sum_{t=0}^{N-1} \exp(-rt) \left[\sum_{(i,j)\in\mathcal{W}} \oint_u^{u^0} Q_{ij,t}(y_t,v_t)\, dy_{ij,t} \right] \tag{1.15}$$

subject to

$$\left.\begin{aligned} h_{t+1} = h_t + H_t(h_t,u_t,v_t) \cdot \Delta t \in [0, N-1] \\ u_{t+1} = u_t + G_t(h_t,u_t,v_t) \cdot \Delta t \in [0, N-1] \\ (h_t,u_t) \in \Gamma_t \\ v_t \in \Lambda_t \end{aligned}\right\} \tag{1.16}$$

Sets, functions, and variables with t as a subscript, in the above, are the discrete-time counterparts of the corresponding continuous-time entities defined previously. Later, we will learn numerical methods for this and similar models.

1.3 Telecommunication Networks

One of the most visible infrastructure networks is the telecommunications network. Among the two most important telecommunications network problems are *flow routing* and *flow control*. Roughly speaking the problem of flow routing is that of finding an optimal routing pattern for message demands currently active on the telecommunications network, while the problem of flow control is that of managing demand by accepting or rejecting message routing requests. It is important to recognize that these two fundamental problems are viewed as static problems for each instant in time at which message demand is evaluated. As such, the static flow routing and flow control models we describe below are frequently referred to as *quasi-static* models to reflect the need to solve them in near real time, update the current message demand, and quickly re-solve the models.

1.3.1 Quasi-static Flow Routing

Suppose we know (with certainty) the message demand Q_{ij} to be transmitted between every origin-destination pair $(i, j) \in \mathcal{W}$, where $\mathcal{W}$ is the set of all origin-destination pairs with active message demands. (This set will change from moment to moment, as allowed for by the quasi-static modeling perspective we have adopted.) We also have associated with every arc $a \in \mathcal{A}$, where $\mathcal{A}$ is again the set of all arcs that comprise the network, a unit transmission delay function or latency $D_a(f_a)$, where f_a is the message flow on arc a.

We may want, as the operator of a telecommunications network, to know how to simultaneously best route the current message demands. When this is our interest we are concerned with optimal flow routing, and the optimal flow routing problem is expressed as:

$$\left.\begin{array}{lll} & \min \sum_{a\in\mathcal{A}} D_a(f_a) f_a & \\ \text{subject to} & & \\ & \sum_{p\in P_w} h_p = Q_{ij} & \forall (i,j)\in\mathcal{W} \\ & f_a = \sum_p \delta_{ap} h_p & \forall a\in\mathcal{A} \\ & h_p \geq 0 & \forall p \in P \end{array}\right\} \tag{1.17}$$

where h_p is the number of messages sent along path p and δ_{ap} has the same definition (1.4) given in our previous discussion of transportation network models. We shall find in Chap. 8 that a mathematically similar transportation network model is known as the system optimal traffic assignment model.

1.3.2 Flow Control

There is a model related to (1.17) for the management of message demand in telecommunications networks. Demand management is frequently referred to as flow control and depends on the articulation of a penalty function for each origin-destination pair $(i, j) \in \mathcal{W}$ which we denote as

$$E_{ij}(Q_{ij}) \tag{1.18}$$

The penalty function (1.18) is a strictly monotonically decreasing function of demand Q_{ij} and is meant to be appended to the routing objective function of (1.17) to create the following model:

$$\left.\begin{array}{lll} & \min \sum_{a\in\mathcal{A}} D_a(f_a)\,f_a & + \sum_{(i,j)\in\mathcal{W}} \sum_{p\in\mathcal{P}_{ij}} E_{ij}(Q_{ij}) \\ \text{subject to} & & \\ & \sum_{p\in\mathcal{P}_{ij}} h_p = Q_{ij} & \forall (i,j)\in\mathcal{W} \\ & f_a = \sum_p \delta_{ap} h_p & \forall a\in\mathcal{A} \\ & h_p \geq 0 & \forall p\in\mathcal{P} \end{array}\right\} \quad (1.19)$$

By penalizing demand, this model controls flow entering the network as well as determines the optimal routing of demands. As such, (6.193) is a *combined flow routing and flow control model.* Note that (1.19) is not a telecommunications analog of the equilibrium network design model used in transportation since message packets do not have the autonomy of automobile drivers in selecting their own routes; as a consequence, flow control does not have the bilevel structure of equilibrium network design and is, as a consequence, computationally much more tractable.

1.4 Electric Power Networks

Pricing electric power and assuring the electrical distribution grid or network is adequate to meet anticipated demands is a fundamental infrastructure decision problem that lends itself quite naturally to network modeling. To construct an electric power model for predicting prices, we introduce the set of firms $\mathcal{F}$ that own electric power-generating facilities. The power transmission network is based on the graph $\mathcal{G}(\mathcal{N},\mathcal{A})$. We think of each node $i\in\mathcal{N}$ as a market for electric power, which may be served not only by power-generating firms located at that node but also by firms located at other nodes via the transmission network. We denote by $\mathcal{N}_f$ the set of nodes (markets) where firm $f\in\mathcal{F}$ has power-generating facilities. The set of power-generating facilities that firm $f\in\mathcal{F}$ possesses at node $i\in\mathcal{N}$ is denoted by $G(i,f)$.

Electric power pricing is an intrinsically dynamic matter. We will employ the same notion of discrete-time approximation introduced in Sect. 1.3 above. In particular, we take the analysis horizon to be $t_f - t_0$, where t_0 is the initial time and t_f is the final time. Since the horizon is short (typically 1–30 days), no notion of discounting to determine present value is necessary. Recall that, in discrete time, flows and prices are computed at the start of each time period and assumed to hold through a given period. The interperiod time step will be

$$\Delta = \frac{t_f - t_0}{N-1}$$

where N, a positive integer, is the number of time steps used to describe the dynamic process of interest. Thus, the sequence of time-steps $t = 0, 1, \ldots, N-1$ will reach t_f when starting at t_0.

1.4.1 Modeling the Firms Generating Power

We will also need the notion of an *inverse demand function* for electric power. An inverse demand function determines price when demand is specified. For the circumstance considered here, we take the inverse demand function for market $i \in \mathcal{N}$ during period t to be

$$\pi_{it}\left(\sum_{g\in\mathcal{F}} s_i^g\right)$$

where π_{it} is the price of power per MWatt-hour at node $i \in \mathcal{N}$ and s_{it}^f is the flow of power sold at the same node during period t. Therefore, the expression

$$\sum_{i\in\mathcal{N}} \pi_{it}\left(\sum_{g\in\mathcal{F}} s_{it}^g\right) \cdot s_{it}^f \cdot \Delta$$

is the *revenue* that firm f generates during period t.

The costs that a generating firm $f \in \mathcal{F}$ bears are:

(1) *Generation cost* for power generation unit $j \in G(i, f)$ denoted by

$$V_{jt}^f\left(q_{jt}^f\right)$$

where q_{jt}^f is the rate at which generator unit $j \in G(i, f)$, located at node $i \in \mathcal{N}_f$, produces power. Generation cost typically has a fixed component and a variable component. For example, generation cost may be quadratic and take the form

$$V_{jt}^f\left(q_{jt}^f\right) = \mu_j^f + \tilde{\mu}_j^f \cdot q_{jt}^f + \frac{1}{2}\hat{\mu}_j^f \cdot \left(q_{jt}^f\right)^2$$

where $\mu_j^f, \tilde{\mu}_j^f, \hat{\mu}_j^f \in \Re_{++}^1$ for all $f \in \mathcal{F}$ and all $j \in G(i, f)$ are exogenous parameters.

(2) *Ramping cost* obtained from a generation unit's rotor fatigue, impacting rotor life span. Ramping cost is negligible if the magnitude of power change is less than some elastic range; that is, there is a range in which the generation rate can be adjusted that causes minimal wear on the rotors and is thus considered cost-free. Therefore, in general, we may use the function

$$\Phi_{jt}^f\left(r_{jt}^f\right) = \frac{1}{2}\gamma_j^f\left[\max\left(0, \left|r_{jt}^f\right| - \xi_j^f\right)\right]^2$$

to represent the ramping cost associated with some generation unit $j \in G(i,f)$ whose ramping rate is r_{jt}^f during period t, with corresponding elastic threshold $\xi_j^f \in \Re_{++}^1$ and cost coefficient γ_j^f. In general, there will be asymmetric ramp-up and ramp-down costs, causing the ramping cost to be expressed as

$$\Phi_{jt}^f\left(r_{jt}^f\right) = \frac{1}{2}\gamma_j^{f+}\left[\max\left(0, r_{jt}^f - \xi_j^{f+}\right)\right]^2 + \frac{1}{2}\gamma_j^{f-}\left[\max\left(0, -r_{jt}^f + \xi_j^{f-}\right)\right]^2$$

where γ_j^{f-} and γ_j^{f+} are the cost coefficients during ramp-up and ramp-down, respectively; naturally, ξ_j^{f+} and ξ_j^{f-} are the respective ramp-up and ramp-down elastic thresholds.

(3) *Wheeling fee* w_{it} paid to the so-called independent service operator (ISO) for transmitting 1 MW-h of power from its hub, through which all power flows, to market i in period t. The wheeling fee is set by the ISO to enforce market clearing (supply of power equal to demand for power).

In light of the above, we may express the profits of each power-generating firm $f \in \mathcal{F}$ as

$$\begin{aligned} J_f\left(s^f, q^f; s^{-f}\right) &= \sum_{t=0}^{N-1}\left\{\sum_{i\in\mathcal{N}}\pi_{it}\left(\sum_{g\in\mathcal{F}} s_{it}^g\right)\cdot s_{it}^f\right. \\ &\quad - \sum_{i\in\mathcal{N}_f}\sum_{j\in G(i,f)}\left[V_j^f\left(q_{jt}^f\right) + \Phi_j^f\left(r_{jt}^f\right)\right] \\ &\quad \left. - \sum_{i\in\mathcal{N}} w_{it}\cdot\left(s_{it}^f - \sum_{j\in G(i,f)} q_{jt}^f\right)\right\}\cdot\Delta \qquad (1.20) \end{aligned}$$

where the following vector notation is employed:

$$\begin{aligned} s^f &= \left(s_{it}^f : i \in \mathcal{N}, t \in [0, N-1]\right) \\ s^{-f} &= \left(s_{it}^g : i \in \mathcal{N}, g \in \mathcal{F}\backslash f, t \in [0, N-1]\right) \\ q^f &= \left(q_{it}^f : i \in \mathcal{N}, t \in [0, N-1]\right) \\ w &= \left(w_{it} : i \in \mathcal{N}, t \in [0, N-1]\right) \end{aligned}$$

We naturally assume that (1.20) is meant to be maximized by firm $f \in \mathcal{F}$ using those variables within its control.

There are also constraints that must be satisfied by each firm $f \in \mathcal{F}$. In particular:

(1) Each firm must balance sales and generation for all time periods, since we do not here consider the storage of electricity; therefore

$$\sum_{i \in \mathcal{N}} s_{it}^{f} = \sum_{i \in \mathcal{N}_f} \sum_{j \in G(i,f)} q_{jt}^{f} \qquad \forall t \in [0, N-1] \tag{1.21}$$

(2) The sales of power at every market must be nonnegative in each time period; thus

$$s_{it}^{f} \geq 0 \qquad \forall i \in \mathcal{N}_f, t \in [0, N-1] \tag{1.22}$$

(3) The output level of each generating unit is bounded from above and below for each time period; thus

$$0 \leq q_{jt}^{f} \leq CAP_j^f \qquad \forall i \in \mathcal{N}_f, j \in G(i,f), t \in [0, N-1] \tag{1.23}$$

where $CAP_j^f \in \Re_{++}^1$ is the relevant upper bound on output from generator $j \in G(i,f)$. Each such bound is a physical characteristic of the corresponding generator.

(4) Total sales by all the firms at a particular market is bounded from above by a regulatory authority. This feature is represented by the following constraint that holds for each node and each time period:

$$\sum_{f \in \mathcal{F}} s_{it}^{f} \leq \sigma_i \qquad \forall i \in \mathcal{N}, t \in [0, N-1] \tag{1.24}$$

where $\sigma_i \in \Re_{++}^1$ is an exogenous market sales cap for every node $i \in \mathcal{N}$.

(5) The ramping rate for every generation unit is bounded from above and below, which again expresses a physical characteristic of the unit; consequently, we write

$$R_j^{f-} \leq r_j^f(t) \leq R_j^{f+} \qquad \forall i \in \mathcal{N}_f, j \in G(i,f), t \in [0, N-1] \tag{1.25}$$

where $R_j^{f+} \in \Re_{++}^1$ and $R_j^{f-} \in \Re_{++}^1$ are, respectively, the upper and lower bounds on the ramping rate of generation unit $j \in G(i,f)$.

We may now state the set of feasible solutions for each firm $f \in \mathcal{F}$ as

$$\Omega_f(s^{-f}) = \left\{ \begin{pmatrix} s^f \\ q^f \end{pmatrix} : (1.21), (1.22), (1.23), (1.24), \text{ and } (1.25) \text{ hold} \right\}$$

Note that the set of feasible solutions for each firm depends on the power flows sold by its competitors.

If we take the wheeling fees as exogenous, we have a collection of simultaneous, coupled mathematical programs that represent oligopolistic competition among power-providing firms. With w and s^{-f} exogenous and using s^f and q^f as decision variables, each firm $f \in \mathcal{F}$ seeks to solve

$$\max J_f\left(s^f, q^f; s^{-f}\right) \quad \text{subject to} \quad \begin{pmatrix} s^f \\ q^f \end{pmatrix} \in \Omega_f(s^{-f}) \tag{1.26}$$

We will learn in subsequent chapters to call (1.26) a generalized Nash game; we will also learn how to reformulate (1.26) as a variational inequality in order to facilitate its analysis and computation.

1.4.2 Modeling the ISO

We turn now to modeling the *independent service operator* (ISO). The job of the ISO is to clear the market for power transmission. Let us assume the vector of wheeling fees w is exogenous so that, in every period $t \in [0, N-1]$, the ISO solves a linear program to determine the transmission flow vector

$$y = (y_{it} : i \in \mathcal{N}, t \in [0, N-1])$$

where y_{it} denotes an actual power flow from a specific hub to node $i \in \mathcal{N}$ for period $t \in [0, N-1]$. The ISO's linear program for period $t \in [0, N-1]$ is

$$\max J_0 = \sum_{i \in \mathcal{N}} y_{it} w_{it} \tag{1.27}$$

subject to

$$\sum_{i \in \mathcal{N}} PTDF_{ia} \cdot y_{it} \leq T_a \ \forall a \in \mathcal{A} \tag{1.28}$$

where $\mathcal{A}$ is the arc set of the electric power network, the T_a are transmission capacities for each arc $a \in \mathcal{A}$, and the $PTDF_{ia}$ are *power transmission distribution factors* (PTDFs) that determine the flow on each arc $a \in \mathcal{A}$ as the result of a unit MW injection at the hub node and a unit withdrawal at node $i \in \mathcal{N}$. The PTDFs allow us to employ a linearized DC approximation for which every $PTDF_{ia}$, where $i \in \mathcal{N}$, is considered constant and unaffected by the transmission line loads. The DC approximation employed here means that the principle of superposition applies to arc and path flows, thereby dramatically simplifying the model. In the ISO formulation presented above, we ignore transmission loss, although such could be introduced without any complication other than increased notational detail.

To clear the market, the transmission flows y must balance the net sales at each node (market); thus

$$y_{it} = \sum_{f \in \mathcal{F}} \left(s_{it}^f - \sum_{j \in G(i,f)} q_{jt}^f \right) \qquad \forall i \in \mathcal{N}, t \in [0, N-1] \tag{1.29}$$

It is immediate that the ISO's set of feasible solutions is

$$\Omega_0 = \left\{ y : \sum_{i\in\mathcal{N}} PTDF_{ia} \cdot \sum_{f\in\mathcal{F}} \left(s_{it}^f - \sum_{j\in G(i,f)} q_{jt}^f \right) \leq T_a \ \forall a \in \mathcal{A} \right\}$$

As a consequence, the ISO's linear program may be restated as

$$\max J_{\text{ISO}}(t) = \sum_{i\in\mathcal{N}} \sum_{f\in\mathcal{F}} \left(s_{it}^f - \sum_{j\in G(i,f)} q_{jt}^f \right) \cdot w_{it} \quad \text{subject to} \quad y \in \Omega_0 \tag{1.30}$$

1.4.3 The Complete Electric Power Model

Taken together, (1.26) and (1.30) constitute a generalized Nash game that determines the power generated and sold by each power-producing oligopolist, as well as the power transmission facilitated by the ISO. Through the inverse demand functions, the price of power is also determined. Alternative formulations exist, including that for which the ISO is the leader of a Stackelberg game and the model becomes a *mathematical program with equilibrium constraints* (MPEC).

1.5 Water Resource Networks

There are several important infrastructure networks related to water resources, including water pipelines, sewer pipelines, and irrigation systems. As a result, many important water resource planning problems are problems in network analysis.

1.5.1 Irrigation Network Capacity Expansion Planning

We consider now a water supply system comprised of streams feeding reservoirs that are sources of water supplied to an urban area. Our focus is on the operation of interdependent reservoirs so we do not consider the detailed water delivery network after water is diverted from the reservoirs for urban use. Instead we will be concerned with how much yield can be taken from a network of reservoirs in order to obtain the upper bound on water yield from the system, which information can in turn be used to forecast when new sources of water supply or water conservation will be needed to accommodate growing demands for water.

It has become traditional to refer to specific segments of streams that comprise a river basin as *reaches*. A *reach* is defined when it is necessary to identify specific hydrological properties of a portion of some waterway or when there are head and tail nodes, like reservoirs and conjunctions with other streams, which naturally define the reach. We consider each reach to be an arc (i, j) of the water supply system; the tail and head nodes of the reaches are considered to be nodes of the network. Of course, reservoirs and the drainage areas from which the streams originate are nodes associated with appropriately defined reaches. Because our focus is reservoir yield, we are able to treat the reservoirs as the locations of final urban water demands. In this way the water supply system is viewed as a graph $\mathcal{G}(\mathcal{N}, \mathcal{A})$ where $\mathcal{A}$ is the set of arcs corresponding to reaches and $\mathcal{N}$ is the set of nodes associated with the reaches.

We begin formally by stating inter-temporal flow conservation equations for water at individual nodes of the irrigation network in the form

$$I_j^t + \sum_{i:(i,j)\in\mathcal{A}} f_{ij}^t (1 - a_{ij}) - \sum_{i:(j,i)\in\mathcal{A}} f_{ji}^t - d_j^t = 0 \qquad \forall j \in \mathcal{N},\, t \in [1, N] \quad (1.31)$$

where the following definitions obtain:

i, j	subscripts referring to nodes of the irrigation network
t	superscript referring to season
N	the total number of discrete seasons
I_j^t	water intake to the irrigation system at node j in season t
f_{ij}^t	water released from node i to node j in season t
a_{ij}	water evaporation and seepage loss coefficient
d_j^t	water demand at node j in season t.

For simplicity we have assumed in (1.31) that water intakes exist at every node; this assumption is easily relaxed. We must also impose constraints that assure that a priori levels of drainage reclamation are met, ground water potentials are never exceeded, intakes are never negative, link-carrying capacities are not violated, releases are bounded from above and below, and the total budget is not violated. That is,

$$d_j^t - \sum_{i:(j,i)\in\mathcal{A}} f_{ji}^t = 0 \qquad \forall j \in \mathcal{N},\, t \in [1, N] \quad (1.32)$$

$$0 \le I_j^t \le P_j^t \qquad \forall j \in \mathcal{N},\, t \in [1, N] \quad (1.33)$$

$$0 \le f_{ij}^t \le g_{ij}^t + g_{ij}^e \qquad \forall (i,j) \in \mathcal{A},\, t \in [1, N] \quad (1.34)$$

$$\sum_{(i,j)\in\mathcal{A}} \Psi_{ij}(g_{ij}) \le B \quad (1.35)$$

where

P_j^t	maximum water available at node j in season t
g_{ij}	increment to capacity of arc (i, j)
g_{ij}^e	existing capacity of arc (i, j)
B	the total budget for irrigation capacity expansion
$\Psi_{ij}(g_{ij})$	the cost of irrigation capacity expansion g_{ij} of arc (i, j)

It is also convenient to define the following decision vectors

$$f = \left(f_{ij}^t : (i,j) \in \mathcal{A},\, t \in [1,N]\right) \tag{1.36}$$

$$I = \left(I_j^t : j \in \mathcal{N},\, t \in [1,N]\right) \tag{1.37}$$

$$g = \left(g_{ij} : (i,j) \in \mathcal{A}\right) \tag{1.38}$$

so that

$$\Omega = \left\{ \ (f,I,g) : \ \text{constraints (1.31)–(1.35) are satisfied} \ \right\}$$

is the set of all feasible capacity expansion plans for a single year comprised of N seasons. It should be noted that the cost functions $\Psi_{ij}(g_{ij})$ reflect the capital costs of new and improved infrastructure (new pumping stations, improved pumping stations, new or improved canals and pipelines, and the like). These capacity expansion costs are known to be nonlinear in many circumstances. In fact, one possible arc cost model for capacity expansion is

$$\Psi_{ij}(g_{ij}) = K_{ij}^1 + K_{ij}^2 \left(g_{ij} - g_{ij}^e\right)^{n_{ij}} \tag{1.39}$$

where g_{ij}^e is the existing capacity, K_{ij}^1 is a parameter reflecting initial costs, K_{ij}^2 is a parameter reflecting scale costs, and n_{ij} is an exponent describing the degree of nonlinearity of arc (i,j). Generally speaking, capacity expansion functions will exhibit economies and diseconomies of scale for different levels of added capacity g_{ij}, as occurs when n_{ij} equals 3 in (1.39).

If we assume demand for irrigation is price inelastic, then it is appropriate to take the objective of capacity expansion to be the minimization of costs associated with irrigation. In this case, the short-run irrigation network planning problem may be stated as

$$\left.\begin{array}{ll} & \min \displaystyle\sum_{t=1}^{N} \sum_{(i,j)\in\mathcal{A}} C_{ij}^t f_{ij}^t \\ \text{subject to} & \\ & (f,g,I) \in \Omega \end{array}\right\} \tag{1.40}$$

where C_{ij}^t is the unit cost of irrigation over arc (i,j) in season t, which cost we take to be constant. A fundamental component of the unit cost C_{ij}^t is the cost of energy needed to effect water delivery and reclamation on arc (i,j); were that consideration taken into account the unit irrigation costs would be nonlinear functions of flow. Evidently (1.40) is a nonlinear mathematical program, which is potentially nonconvex owing to the budget constraint (1.35), even when the unit irrigation costs $C = \left(C_{ij}^t : \forall (i,j) \in \mathcal{A},\, t \in [1,N]\right)$ are taken to be constants as we have done here.

1.5.2 Municipal Water Supply

Municipal water supply networks can be modeled in much the same fashion as the irrigation network of the preceding example. However, for the purpose of this example, our focus will be on operation of the reservoirs connected to the water supply network in a fashion which meets prespecified, known demands without capacity expansion considerations. It is convenient to use much of the same notation of the previous example with the appropriate re-interpretation of key variables and parameters to fit the new setting; we shall also need some new definitions. We begin by distinguishing the nodes that are reservoirs from the other nodes of the network; specifically, we define $\mathcal{N}_R$ to be the set of reservoir nodes so that $\mathcal{M} = \mathcal{N} \backslash \mathcal{N}_R$ is the set of all other nodes. We also employ a different time scale: instead of seasons, we speak of a sequence of days spanning a season or a even a year. Consequently, we have two conservation equations:

$$I_j^t + \sum_{i:(i,j)\in\mathcal{A}} f_{ij} - \sum_{i:(j,i)\in\mathcal{A}} f_{ji}^t - d_j^t = 0 \qquad \forall j \in \mathcal{N}_R,\ t \in [1, N] \tag{1.41}$$

$$\sum_{i:(i,j)\in\mathcal{A}} f_{ij} - \sum_{i:(j,i)\in\mathcal{A}} f_{ji}^t - d_j^t = 0 \qquad \forall j \in \mathcal{M},\ t \in [1, N] \tag{1.42}$$

where now the following definitions obtain:

i, j	subscripts referring to nodes of the municipal water supply network
t	superscript referring to a given period
N	the total number of periods considered
I_j^t	water intake to the network from reservoir at node j in period t
f_{ij}^t	water released to node j from node i in period t
d_j^t	water demand at node j in period t

We have also to write conservation equations for the reservoirs; ensure that intakes by the municipal water network are never negative and do not exceed reservoir storage less a predetermined reserve; and that reservoir capacities are not exceeded. These considerations take the form

$$S_j^{t+1} = S_j^t + W_j^t - w_j^t - I_j^t \qquad \forall j \in \mathcal{N}_R,\ t \in [1, N] \tag{1.43}$$

$$0 \leq I_j^t \leq S_j^t - R_j \qquad \forall j \in \mathcal{N}_R,\ t \in [1, N] \tag{1.44}$$

$$S_j^t \leq K_j \qquad \forall j \in \mathcal{N}_R,\ t \in [1, N] \tag{1.45}$$

where the following additional definitions also obtain:

S_j^t	storage of the node j reservoir at the end of period t
W_j^t	naturally occurring stream intake at node j during period t
w_j^t	release by the node j reservoir during period t
R_j	prespecified reserve storage for the node j reservoir
K_j	known capacity of the node j reservoir

In (1.43), I_j^t describes the release during period t from the node j reservoir to assist in servicing municipal water demand and recognizes that release to be identical to the intake defined previously. Note that each reservoir has the option to release water not only to satisfy municipal demand, but also to directly release to prevent its capacity from being exceeded. It remains to stipulate that municipal water demands are satisfied and that releases are non-negative and do not exceed arc capacities; these considerations are stated as

$$d_j^t - \sum_{i:(j,i)\in\mathcal{A}} f_{ji}^t = 0 \qquad \forall j \in \mathcal{M},\, t \in [1, N] \tag{1.46}$$

$$0 \leq f_{ij}^t \leq g_{ij}^e \qquad \forall\,(i,j) \in \mathcal{A},\, t \in [1, N] \tag{1.47}$$

where g_{ij}^e is, of course, the existing capacity of arc (i,j).

Defining f and I as in (1.36) and (1.37), we have the feasible set

$$\Lambda = \left\{\ (f,I) : \text{constraints (1.41)–(1.47) are satisfied}\ \right\}$$

Our model for the coordination of reservoirs releases and municipal water supply activities is

$$\left.\begin{array}{ll} & \min \displaystyle\sum_{t=1}^{N} \sum_{(i,j)\in\mathcal{A}} C_{ij}^t f_{ij}^t \\ \text{subject to} & \\ & (f,I) \in \Lambda \end{array}\right\} \tag{1.48}$$

where the cost coefficients C_{ij}^t are assumed to be constant and describe the unit cost of providing water service on each arc (i,j) during period t. We have of course assumed that the demands d_j^t are inelastic at every node $j \in \mathcal{M}$. Note that (1.48) is an entirely linear program

1.6 The Way Ahead

We have seen in this chapter some examples of infrastructure network models that give a flavor of the types of models considered in subsequent chapters devoted to specific infrastructures. However, we must first build some new mathematical and numerical analysis skills. Accordingly, Chap. 2 immediately ahead is devoted to a review of basic linear and nonlinear programming, while Chap. 3 quickly reviews some basic notions from graph theory. In subsequent chapters, we explore a variety of network optimization models, the foundations of game theory, and a number of network games arising in applications.

1.7 References and Additional Reading

Bertsekas, D. P. (1982). Optimal routing and flow control methods for communication networks, in analysis and optimization of systems. (In A. V. Balakrishnan & M. Thoma (Eds.), *Analysis and optimization of systems*, (Lecture notes in control and information science, Vol. 44, pp.613–643). New York: Springer.

Chen, Y., Hobbs, B. F., Leyffer, S., & Munson, T. S. (2006). Leader-follower equilibria for electric power and NO_x allowances markets. *Computational Management Sciences, 3*, 307–330.

Fernandez, J. E., & Friesz, T. L. (1983). Travel market equilibrium: the state of the art. *Transportation Research B, 17*(2), 155–172.

Friesz, T. L. (1985). Transportation network equilibrium, design and aggregation. *Transportation Research A, 19*(5/6), 413–427.

Hobbs, B. F., & Pang, J. S. (2007). Nash-Cournot equilibria in electric power markets with piecewise linear demand functions and joint constraints. *Operations Research, 55*(1), 113–127.

Metzler, C., Hobbs, B. F., & Pang, J.-S. (2003). Nash-Cournot equilibria in power markets on a linearized DC network with arbitrage: formulations and properties. *Networks and Spatial Economics, 3*(2), 123–150.

Mookherjee, R., Hobbs, B. F., Friesz, T. L., & Rigdon, M. (2008). Dynamic oligopolistic competition on an electric power network with ramping costs and sales constraints. *Journal of Industrial and Management Optimization, 4*(3), 425–452.

Ramos, F. (1979). *Formulations and computational considerations for a general irrigation network planning model.* S.M. thesis, Massachusetts Institute of Technology.

Ramos, F. (1981). *Capacity expansion of regional urban water supply networks.* Ph.D. dissertation, Massachusetts Institute of Technology.

Rigdon, M. A., Mookherjee, R., & Friesz, T. L. (2008). Multiperiod competition in an electric power network and impacts of infrastructure disruptions. *Journal of Infrastructure Systems, 14*(4), 3–11.

Schulkin, J. Z., Hobbs, B. F., & Pang, J. S. (2008). Long-run equilibrium modeling of alternative emissions allowance allocation systems in electric power markets. *Operations Research, 58*(3), 529–548.

Wardrop, J. G. (1952). Some theoretical aspects of road traffic research. In *ICE proceedings: Engineering divisions* (Vol. 1, No. 3, pp. 325–362). Thomas Telford.

2

Elements of Nonlinear Programming

THE PRIMARY INTENT OF this chapter is to introduce the reader to the theoretical foundations of nonlinear programming. Particularly important are the notions of local and global optimality in mathematical programming, the Kuhn-Tucker necessary conditions for optimality in nonlinear programming, and the role played by convexity in making necessary conditions sufficient. The following is an outline of the principal topics covered in this chapter:

Section 2.1: Nonlinear Program Defined. A formal definition of a finite-dimensional nonlinear mathematical program, with a single criterion and both equality and inequality constraints, is given.

Section 2.2: Other Types of Mathematical Programs. Definitions of linear, integer and mixed integer mathematical programs are provided.

Section 2.3: Necessary Conditions for an Unconstrained Minimum. We derive necessary conditions for a minimum of a twice continuously differentiable function when there are no constraints.

Section 2.4: Necessary Conditions for a Constrained Minimum. Relying on geometric reasoning, the Kuhn-Tucker conditions, as well as the notion of a constraint qualification, are introduced.

Section 2.5: Formal Derivation of the Kuhn-Tucker Conditions. A formal derivation of the Kuhn-Tucker necessary conditions, employing a conic definition of optimality and theorems of the alternative, is provided.

Section 2.6: Sufficiency, Convexity, and Uniqueness. We provide formal definitions of a convex set and a convex function. Then we show formally how those notions influence sufficiency and uniqueness of a global minimum.

Section 2.8: Key Results from Nonlinear Programming Sensitivity Analysis. We provide a succinct review of nonlinear programming sensitivity analysis.

T.L. Friesz, D. Bernstein, *Foundations of Network Optimization and Games*,
Complex Networks and Dynamic Systems 3,
DOI 10.1007/978-1-4899-7594-2_2

Section 2.9: Numerical and Graphical Examples. We provide graphical and numerical examples that illustrate the abstract optimality conditions introduced in previous sections of this chapter.

Section 2.10: One-Dimensional Optimization. We provide a brief discussion of numerical techniques (sometimes called line-search methods) for solving one-dimensional minimization problems.

Section 2.11: Descent Algorithms in $\Re^n$. We consider a generic feasible descent algorithm for convex mathematical programs with a differentiable objective function and differentiable constraints.

2.1 Nonlinear Program Defined

We are presently interested in a type of optimization problem known as a finite-dimensional mathematical program, namely: find a vector $x \in \Re^n$ that satisfies

$$\left.\begin{array}{r} \min f(x) \\ \text{subject to} \qquad h(x) = 0 \\ g(x) \leq 0 \end{array}\right\} \tag{2.1}$$

where

$$x = (x_1, \ldots, x_n)^T \in \Re^n$$

$$f(\cdot) : \Re^n \longrightarrow \Re^1$$

$$g(x) = (g_1(x), \ldots, g_m(x))^T \ : \ \Re^n \longrightarrow \Re^m$$

$$h(x) = (h_1(x), \ldots, h_q(x))^T \ : \ \Re^n \longrightarrow \Re^q$$

We call the x_i for $i \in \{1, 2, \ldots, n\}$ decision variables, $f(x)$ the objective function, $h(x) = 0$ the equality constraints and $g(x) \leq 0$ the inequality constraints. Because the objective and constraint functions will in general be nonlinear, we shall consider (2.1) to be our canonical form of a nonlinear mathematical program (NLP). The *feasible region* for (2.1) is

$$X \equiv \{x : g(x) \leq 0, \ h(x) = 0\} \subset \Re^n \tag{2.2}$$

which allows us to state (2.1) in the form

$$\left.\begin{array}{r} \min f(x) \\ \text{subject to} \qquad x \in X \end{array}\right\} \tag{2.3}$$

The pertinent definitions of optimality for the NLP defined above are:

Definition 2.1 (Global minimum) Suppose $x^* \in X$ and $f(x^*) \leq f(x)$ for all $x \in X$. Then $f(x)$ achieves a global minimum on X at x^*, and we say x^* is a global minimizer of $f(x)$ on X.

Definition 2.2 (Local minimum) Suppose $x^* \in X$ and there exists an $\epsilon > 0$ such that $f(x^*) \leq f(x)$ for all $x \in [N_\epsilon(x^*) \cap X]$, where $N_\epsilon(x^*)$ is a ball of radius $\epsilon > 0$ centered at x^*. Then $f(x)$ achieves a local minimum on X at x^*, and we say x^* is a local minimizer of $f(x)$.

In practice, we will often relax the formal terminology of Definitions 2.1 and 2.2 and refer to x^* as a global minimum or a local minimum, respectively.

2.2 Other Types of Mathematical Programs

We note that the general form of a continuous mathematical program (MP) may be specialized to create various types of mathematical programs that have been studied in depth. In particular, if the objective function and all constraint functions are linear, (2.1) is called a *linear program* (LP). In such cases, we normally add slack or surplus variables to the inequality constraints to convert them into equality constraints. That is, if we have the constraint

$$g_i(x) \leq 0 \tag{2.4}$$

we convert it into

$$g_i(x) + s_i = 0 \tag{2.5}$$

and solve for both x and s_i. The variable s_i is called a *slack variable* and obeys

$$s_i \geq 0 \tag{2.6}$$

If we have an inequality constraint of the form

$$g_j(x) \geq 0 \tag{2.7}$$

we convert it to the form

$$g_j(x) - s_j = 0 \tag{2.8}$$

where

$$s_j \geq 0 \tag{2.9}$$

is called a *surplus variable*. Thus, we can convert any problem with inequality constraints into one that has only equality constraints and non-negativity restrictions. So without loss of generality, we take the canonical form of the linear programming problem to be

subject to

$$\left.\begin{aligned} \min \sum_{i=1}^{n} c_i x_i \\ \sum_{j=1}^{n} a_{ij} x_j = b_i \qquad i = 1, \ldots, m \\ U_j \geq x_j \geq L_j \quad j = 1, \ldots, n \\ x \in \Re^n \end{aligned}\right\} \tag{2.10}$$

where $n > m$. This problem can be restated further, using matrix and vector notation, as

subject to

$$\left.\begin{aligned} \min c^T x \\ Ax = b \\ U \geq x \geq L \\ x \in \Re^n \end{aligned}\right\} \text{LP} \tag{2.11}$$

where $c \in \Re^n$, $b \in \Re^n$, and $A \in \Re^{m \times n}$.

If the objective function and/or some of the constraints are nonlinear, (2.1) is called a *nonlinear program* (NLP) and is written as:

subject to

$$\left.\begin{aligned} \min f(x) \\ g_i(x) \leq 0 \quad i = 1, \ldots, m \\ h_i(x) = 0 \quad i = 1, \ldots, q \\ x \in \Re^n \end{aligned}\right\} \text{NLP} \tag{2.12}$$

If all of the elements of x are restricted to be a subset of the integers and I^n denotes the integer numbers, the resulting program

subject to

$$\left.\begin{aligned} \min f(x) \\ g_i(x) \leq 0 \quad i = 1, \ldots, m \\ h_i(x) = 0 \quad i = 1, \ldots, q \\ x \in I^n \end{aligned}\right\} \text{IP} \tag{2.13}$$

is called an *integer program* (IP). If there are two classes of variables, some that are continuous and some that are integer, as in

$$\left.\begin{array}{rll} & \min f(x,y) & \\ \text{subject to} & & \\ & g_i(x,y) \leq 0 & i = 1,\ldots,m \\ & h_i(x,y) = 0 & i = 1,\ldots,q \\ & x \in \Re^n & y \in I^n \end{array}\right\} \text{MIP} \tag{2.14}$$

the problem is known as a *mixed integer program* (MIP).

2.3 Necessary Conditions for an Unconstrained Minimum

Necessary conditions for optimality in the mathematical program (2.1) are systems of equalities and inequalities that must hold at an optimal solution $x^* \in X$. Any such condition has the logical structure:

If x^* is optimal, then some property $\mathbf{P}(x^*)$ is true.

Necessary conditions play a central role in the analysis of most mathematical programming models and algorithms.

We begin our discussion of necessary conditions for mathematical programs by considering the general finite-dimensional mathematical program introduced in the previous section. In particular, we want to state and prove the following result for mathematical programs without constraints:

Theorem 2.1 *(Necessary conditions for an unconstrained minimum) Suppose* $f : \Re^n \longrightarrow \Re^1$ *is twice continuously differentiable for all* $x \in \Re^n$*. Then necessary conditions for* $x^* \in \Re^n$ *to be a local or global minimum of* $\min f(x)$ *subject to* $x \in \Re^n$ *are*

$$\nabla f(x^*) = 0 \tag{2.15}$$

$$\nabla^2 f(x^*) \equiv \left(\frac{\partial^2 f(x^*)}{\partial x_i \partial x_j}\right) \text{ must be positive semidefinite} \tag{2.16}$$

That is, the gradient must vanish and the Hessian must be a positive semidefinite matrix at the minimum of interest.

Proof. Since $f(.)$ is twice continuously differentiable, we may make a Taylor series expansion in the vicinity of $x^* \in \Re^n$, a local minimum:

$$f(x) = f(x^*) + [\nabla f(x^*)]^T (x - x^*) + \frac{1}{2}(x - x^*)^T \nabla^2 f(x^*)(x - x^*) + \|x - x^*\|^2 \mathcal{O}(x - x^*)$$

where $\mathcal{O}(x - x^*) \longrightarrow 0$ as $x \longrightarrow x^*$. If $\nabla f(x^*) \neq 0$, then by picking $x = x^* - \theta \nabla f(x^*)$ we can make $f(x) < f(x^*)$ for sufficiently small $\theta > 0$ thereby directly contradicting the fact that x^* is a local minimum. It follows that condition (2.15) is necessary, and we may write

$$f(x) = f(x^*) + \frac{1}{2}(x - x^*)^T \nabla^2 f(x^*)(x - x^*) + \|x - x^*\|^2 \mathcal{O}(x - x^*)$$

If the matrix $\nabla^2 f(x^*)$ is not positive semidefinite, there must exist a direction vector $d \in \Re^n$ such that $d \neq 0$ and $d^T \nabla^2 f(x^*) d < 0$. If we now choose $x = x^* + \theta d$, it is possible for sufficiently small $\theta > 0$ to realize $f(x) < f(x^*)$ in direct contradiction of the fact that x^* is a local minimum. ■

2.4 Necessary Conditions for a Constrained Minimum

We comment that necessary conditions for constrained programs have the same logical structure as necessary conditions for unconstrained programs introduced in Sect. 2.3; namely:

If x^* is optimal, then some property $\mathbf{P}(x^*)$ is true.

For constrained programs obeying certain regularity conditions, we will shortly find that $\mathbf{P}(x^*)$ is either the so-called Fritz John conditions or the Kuhn-Tucker conditions. We now turn to the task of providing an informal motivation of the Fritz John conditions, which are the pertinent necessary conditions for the case when no constraint qualification is imposed.

2.4.1 The Fritz John Conditions

A fundamental theorem on necessary conditions is:

Theorem 2.2 *(Fritz John conditions) Let x^* be a (global or local) minimum of*

$$\left.\begin{array}{ll} & \min f(x) \\ \text{subject to} & \\ & x \in \mathcal{F} = \{x \in X_0 : g(x) \leq 0, h(x) = 0\} \subset \Re^n \end{array}\right\} \quad (2.17)$$

where X_0 is a nonempty open set in $\Re^n$, $g : \Re^n \longrightarrow \Re^m$, and $h : \Re^n \longrightarrow \Re^q$. Assume that $f(x)$, $g_i(x)$ for $i \in [1, m]$ and $h_i(x)$ for $i \in [1, q]$ have continuous first derivatives everywhere on $\mathcal{F}$. Then there must exist multipliers $\mu_0 \in \Re^1_+$, $\mu = (\mu_1, \ldots, \mu_m)^T \in \Re^m_+$, and $\lambda = (\lambda_i, \ldots; \lambda_q)^T \in \Re^q$ such that

$$\mu_0 \nabla f(x^*) + \sum_{i=1}^{m} \mu_i \nabla g_i(x^*) + \sum_{i=1}^{q} \lambda_i \nabla h_i(x^*) = 0 \quad (2.18)$$

$$\mu_i g_i(x^*) = 0 \quad \forall\, i \in [1, m] \quad (2.19)$$

$$\mu_i \geq 0 \quad \forall\, i \in [0, m] \tag{2.20}$$

$$(\mu_0,\ \mu,\ \lambda) \neq 0 \in \Re^{m+q+1} \tag{2.21}$$

Conditions (2.18)–(2.21) together with $h(x) = 0$ and $g(x) \leq 0$ are called the Fritz John conditions. We will give a formal proof of their validity in Sect. 2.5.3. For now our focus is on how the Fritz John conditions are related to the Kuhn-Tucker conditions, which are the chief applied notion of a necessary condition for optimality in mathematical programming.

2.4.2 Geometry of the Kuhn-Tucker Conditions

Under certain regularity conditions called *constraint qualifications*, we may be certain that $\mu_0 \neq 0$. In that case, without loss of generality, we may take $\mu_0 = 1$. When $\mu_0 = 1$, the Fritz John conditions are called the *Kuhn-Tucker conditions* and (2.18) is called the *Kuhn-Tucker identity*. In either case, (2.19) and (2.20) together are called the *complementary slackness conditions*. Sometimes it is convenient to define the Lagrangean function:

$$L(x,\lambda,\mu_0,\mu) \equiv \mu_0 f(x) + \lambda^T h(x) + \mu^T g(x) \tag{2.22}$$

By virtue of this definition, identity (2.18) can be expressed as

$$\nabla_x L(x^*, \lambda, \mu_0, \mu) = 0 \tag{2.23}$$

At the same time (2.19) and (2.20) can be written as

$$\mu^T g(x^*) = 0 \tag{2.24}$$

$$\mu \geq 0 \tag{2.25}$$

Furthermore, we may give a geometrical motivation for the Kuhn-Tucker conditions by considering the following abstract problem with two decision variables and two inequality constraints:

$$\left.\begin{array}{ll} & \min f(x_1, x_2) \\ \text{subject to} & g_1(x_1, x_2) \leq 0 \\ & g_2(x_1, x_2) \leq 0 \end{array}\right\} \tag{2.26}$$

The functions $f(.)$, $g_1(.)$, and $g_2(.)$ are assumed to be such that the following are true:

(1) all functions are differentiable;

(2) the feasible region $\mathcal{F} \equiv \{(x_1, x_2) : g_1(x_1, x_2) \leq 0,\ g_2(x_1, x_2) \leq 0\}$ is a convex set;

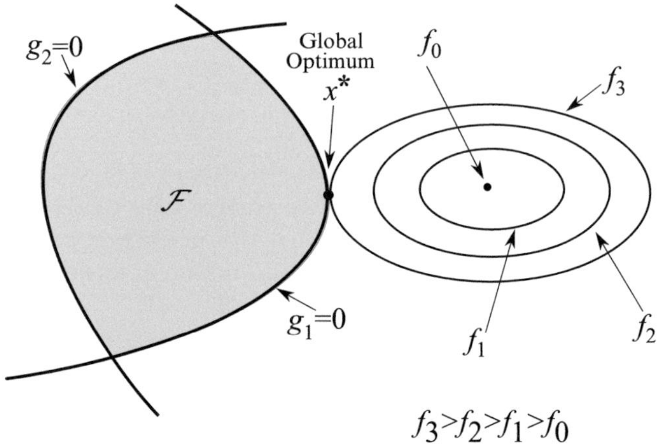

FIGURE 2.1: GEOMETRY OF AN OPTIMAL SOLUTION

(3) all level sets $S_k \equiv \{(x_1, x_2) : f(x_1, x_2) \leq f_k\}$ are convex, where $f_k \in [\alpha, +\infty) \subset \Re^1_+$ is a constant and α is the unconstrained minimum of $f(x_1, x_2)$; and

(4) the level curves

$$C_k = \left\{(x_1, x_2) : f\,(x_1, x_2) = f_k \in \Re^1\right\}$$

for the ordering

$$f_0 < f_1 < f_2 < \cdots < f_k$$

do not cross one another, and C_k is the locus of points for which the objective function has the constant value f_k.

Figure 2.1 is one realization of the above stipulations. Note that there is an uncountable number of level curves and level sets since f_k may be any real number from the interval $[\alpha, +\infty) \subset \Re^1_+$. In Fig. 2.1, because the gradient of any function points in the direction of maximal increase of the function, we see there is a $\mu_1 \in \Re^1_{++}$ such that

$$\nabla f(x_1^*, x_2^*) = -\mu_1 \nabla g_1(x_1^*, x_2^*), \tag{2.27}$$

where (x_1^*, x_2^*) is the optimal solution formed by the tangency of $g_1(x_1^*, x_2^*) = 0$ with the level curve $f(x_1^*, x_2^*) = f_3$. Evidently, this observation leads directly to

$$\nabla f(x_1^*, x_2^*) + \mu_1 \nabla g_1(x_1^*, x_2^*) + \mu_2 \nabla g_2(x_1^*, x_2^*) \;=\; 0 \tag{2.28}$$

$$\mu_1 g_1(x_1^*, x_2^*) \;=\; 0 \tag{2.29}$$

$$\mu_2 g_2(x_1^*, x_2^*) \;=\; 0 \tag{2.30}$$

$$\mu_1, \mu_2 \;\geq\; 0, \tag{2.31}$$

Note that $g_1(x_1^*, x_2^*) = 0$ allows us to conclude that (2.29) holds even though $\mu_1 > 0$. Similarly, (2.27) implies that $\mu_2 = 0$, so (2.30) holds even though $g_2(x_1^*, x_2^*) \neq 0$. Clearly, the nonnegativity conditions (2.31) also hold. By inspection, (2.28)–(2.31) are the Kuhn-Tucker conditions (Fritz John conditions with $\mu_0 = 1$) for the mathematical program (2.26).

2.4.3 The Lagrange Multiplier Rule

We wish to give a statement of a particular instance of the Kuhn-Tucker theorem on necessary conditions for mathematical programming problems, together with some informal remarks about why that theorem holds when a constraint qualification is satisfied. Since our informal motivation of the Kuhn-Tucker conditions in the next section depends on the Lagrange multiplier rule (LMR) for mathematical programs with equality constraints, we must first state and motivate the LMR. To that end, take x and y to be scalars and $F(x, y)$ and $h(x, y)$ to be scalar functions. Consider the following mathematical program with two decision variables and a single equality constraint:

$$\left.\begin{array}{lc} & \min F(x,y) \\ \text{subject to} & \\ & h(x,y) = 0 \end{array}\right\} \tag{2.32}$$

Assume that $h\,(x, y) = 0$ may be manipulated to find x in terms of y. That is, we know

$$x = H\,(y) \tag{2.33}$$

so that

$$F\,(x, y) = F\,[H\,(y)\,, y] \equiv \Phi\,(y) \tag{2.34}$$

and (2.32) may be thought of as the one-dimensional unconstrained problem

$$\min_{y} \Phi\,(y) \tag{2.35}$$

which has the apparent necessary condition

$$\frac{d\Phi\,(y)}{dy} = 0 \tag{2.36}$$

By the chain rule we have the alternative form

$$\frac{d\Phi\,(y)}{dy} = \frac{\partial F\,(H, y)}{\partial y} + \frac{\partial F\,(H, y)}{\partial H}\frac{\partial H}{\partial y} = 0 \tag{2.37}$$

Applying the chain rule to the equality constraint $h\,(x, y) = 0$ leads to

$$dh(x, y) = \frac{\partial h}{\partial x}dx + \frac{\partial h}{\partial y}dy = 0 \tag{2.38}$$

from which we obtain

$$\frac{\partial x}{\partial y} = (-1)\frac{\partial h/\partial y}{\partial h/\partial x} \tag{2.39}$$

The necessary condition (2.37), with the help of (2.33) and (2.39), becomes

$$\begin{aligned}\frac{\partial F}{\partial y}+\frac{\partial F}{\partial x}\frac{\partial x}{\partial y} &= \frac{\partial F}{\partial y}+\frac{\partial F}{\partial x}(-1)\frac{\partial h/\partial y}{\partial h/\partial x}\\ &= \frac{\partial F}{\partial y}+(-1)\frac{\partial F/\partial x}{\partial h/\partial x}\frac{\partial h}{\partial y} \qquad (2.40)\\ &= \frac{\partial F}{\partial y}+\lambda\frac{\partial h}{\partial y}=0\end{aligned}$$

where we have defined the Lagrange multiplier to be

$$\lambda=(-1)\frac{\partial F/\partial x}{\partial h/\partial x} \qquad (2.41)$$

The LMR consists of (2.40) and (2.41), which we restate as

$$\frac{\partial F}{\partial x}+\lambda\frac{\partial h}{\partial x} = 0 \qquad (2.42)$$

$$\frac{\partial F}{\partial y}+\lambda\frac{\partial h}{\partial y} = 0 \qquad (2.43)$$

Recognizing that the generalization of (2.42) and (2.43) involves Jacobian matrices, we are not surprised to find that, for the equality-constrained mathematical program

$$\left.\begin{array}{r}\min f(x)\\ \text{subject to} \qquad h(x)=0\end{array}\right\} \qquad (2.44)$$

where $x\in\Re^n$, $f:\Re^n\longrightarrow\Re^1$, and $h\in\Re^q$, the following result holds:

Theorem 2.3 *(Lagrange multiplier rule) Let $x^*\in\Re^n$ be any local optimum of $f(x)$ subject to the constraints $h_i(x)=0$ for $i\in[1,q]$, where $x\in\Re^n$ and $q<n$. If it is possible to choose a set of q variables for which the Jacobian*

$$J[h(x^*)]\equiv\begin{bmatrix}\frac{\partial h_1(x^*)}{\partial x_1} & \cdots & \frac{\partial h_1(x^*)}{\partial x_q}\\ \vdots & \ddots & \vdots\\ \frac{\partial h_q(x^*)}{\partial x_1} & \cdots & \frac{\partial h_q(x^*)}{\partial x_q}\end{bmatrix} \qquad (2.45)$$

has an inverse, then there exists a unique vector of Lagrange multipliers $\lambda=(\lambda_1,\ldots,\lambda_q)^T$ satisfying

$$\frac{\partial f(x^*)}{\partial x_j}+\sum_{i=1}^{q}\lambda_i\frac{\partial h_i(x^*)}{\partial x_j}=0 \quad j\in[1,n] \qquad (2.46)$$

The formal proof of this classical result is contained in most texts on advanced calculus. Note that (2.46) is a necessary condition for optimality.

2.4.4 Motivating the Kuhn-Tucker Conditions

We now wish, using the Lagrange multiplier rule, to establish that the Kuhn-Tucker conditions are valid when an appropriate constraint qualification holds. In fact we wish to consider the following result:

Theorem 2.4 *(Kuhn-Tucker conditions) Let $x^* \in \mathcal{F}$ be a local minimum of*

$$\left.\begin{array}{ll} & \min f(x) \\ \textit{subject to} & \\ & x \in \mathcal{F} = \{x \in X_0 : g(x) \leq 0, h(x) = 0\} \subset \Re^n \end{array}\right\} \quad (2.47)$$

where X_0 is a nonempty open set in $\Re^n$. Assume that $f(x)$, $g_i(x)$ for $i \in [1,m]$ and $h_i(x)$ for $i \in [1,q]$ have continuous first derivatives everywhere on $\mathcal{F}$ and that a constraint qualification holds. Then there must exist multipliers $\mu = (\mu_1, \ldots, \mu_m)^T \in \Re^q$ and $\lambda = (\lambda_i, \ldots, \lambda_q)^T \in \Re^m$ such that

$$\nabla f(x^*) + \sum_{i=1}^{m} \mu_i \nabla g_i(x^*) + \sum_{i=1}^{q} \lambda_i \nabla h_i(x^*) = 0 \quad (2.48)$$

$$\mu_i g_i(x^*) = 0 \quad \forall\, i \in [1,m] \quad (2.49)$$

$$\mu_i \geq 0 \quad \forall\, i \in [1,m] \quad (2.50)$$

Expression (2.48) is the Kuhn-Tucker identity and conditions (2.49) and (2.50), as we have indicated previously, are together referred to as the complementary slackness conditions. Do not fail to note that the Kuhn-Tucker conditions are necessary conditions. A solution of the Kuhn-Tucker conditions, without further information, is only a candidate optimal solution, sometimes referred to as a "Kuhn-Tucker point." In fact, it is possible for a particular Kuhn-Tucker point not to be an optimal solution.

We may informally motivate Theorem 2.4 using the Lagrange multiplier rule. This is done by first positing the existence of variables s_i, unrestricted in sign, for $i \in [1,m]$, such that

$$g_i(x^*) + (s_i)^2 = 0 \quad \forall\, i \in [1,m] \quad (2.51)$$

so that the mathematical program (2.1) may be viewed as one with only equality constraints, namely

$$\left.\begin{array}{ll} & \min f(x) \\ \text{subject to} & h(x) = 0 \\ & g(x) + \mathrm{diag}(s) \cdot s = 0 \end{array}\right\} \quad (2.52)$$

where $s \in \Re^m$ and

$$\text{diag}\,(s) \equiv \begin{pmatrix} s_1 & 0 & \cdots & 0 & 0 \\ 0 & s_2 & \cdots & 0 & 0 \\ \vdots & \vdots & \ddots & \vdots & \vdots \\ 0 & 0 & \cdots & s_{m-1} & 0 \\ 0 & 0 & \cdots & 0 & s_m \end{pmatrix} \tag{2.53}$$

To form the necessary conditions for (2.51), we first construct the Lagrangean

$$\begin{aligned} L\,(x,s,\lambda,\mu) &= f(x) + \lambda^T h(x) + \mu^T \left[g(x) + \text{diag}\,(s) \cdot s\right] \\ &= f(x) + \sum_{i=1}^{q} \lambda_i h_i\,(x) + \sum_{i=1}^{m} \mu_i \left[g_i\,(x) + s_i^2\right] \end{aligned} \tag{2.54}$$

and then state, using the LMR, the first-order conditions

$$\frac{\partial L\,(x,s,\lambda,\mu)}{\partial x_i} = \frac{\partial f(x)}{\partial x_i} + \sum_{j=1}^{q} \lambda_j \frac{\partial h_j\,(x)}{\partial x_i} + \sum_{j=1}^{m} \mu_j \frac{\partial g_j\,(x)}{\partial x_i} = 0$$

$$i \in [1,n] \tag{2.55}$$

$$\frac{\partial L\,(x,s,\lambda,\mu)}{\partial s_i} = 2\mu_i s_i = 0 \quad i \in [1,m] \tag{2.56}$$

Result (2.55) is of course the Kuhn-Tucker identity (2.48). Note further that both sides of (2.56) may be multiplied by $-s_i$ to obtain the equivalent conditions

$$\mu_i \left(-s_i^2\right) = 0 \quad i \in [1,m] \tag{2.57}$$

which can be restated using (2.51) as

$$\mu_i g_i\,(x) = 0 \quad i \in [1,m] \tag{2.58}$$

Conditions (2.58) are of course the complementary slackness conditions (2.49).

It remains for us to establish that the inequality constraint multipliers μ_i for $i \in [1,m]$ are nonnegative. To that end, we imagine a perturbation of the inequality constraints by the vector

$$\varepsilon = \begin{pmatrix} \varepsilon_1 & \varepsilon_2 & \cdots & \varepsilon_m \end{pmatrix}^T \in \Re^m_{++},$$

so that the inequality constraints become

$$g(x) + \text{diag}\,(s) \cdot s = \varepsilon$$

or

$$g_i\,(x) + s_i^2 - \varepsilon_i = 0 \quad i \in [1,m] \tag{2.59}$$

There is an optimal solution for each vector of perturbations, which we call $x(\varepsilon)$ where $x^* = x(0)$ is the unperturbed optimal solution. As a consequence, there is an optimal objective function value

$$Z(\varepsilon) \equiv f[x(\varepsilon)] \tag{2.60}$$

for each $x(\varepsilon)$. We note that

$$\frac{\partial Z(\varepsilon)}{\partial \varepsilon_i} = \sum_{j=1}^{n} \frac{\partial f(x)}{\partial x_j} \frac{\partial x_j(\varepsilon)}{\partial \varepsilon_i} \tag{2.61}$$

by the chain rule. Similarly for $k \in [1, m]$

$$\frac{\partial g_k(x)}{\partial \varepsilon_i} = \frac{\partial \left[\varepsilon_k - s_k^2\right]}{\partial \varepsilon_i} = \begin{cases} 1 & \text{if } i = k \\ 0 & \text{if } i \neq k \end{cases} \tag{2.62}$$

and for $k \in [1, q]$

$$\frac{\partial h_k(x)}{\partial \varepsilon_i} = \sum_{j=1}^{n} \frac{\partial h_k(x)}{\partial x_j} \frac{\partial x_j(\varepsilon)}{\partial \varepsilon_i} \tag{2.63}$$

Furthermore, we may define

$$\Phi_i \equiv \frac{\partial Z(\varepsilon)}{\partial \varepsilon_i} + \sum_{k=1}^{q} \lambda_k \frac{\partial h_k(x)}{\partial \varepsilon_i} + \sum_{k=1}^{m} \mu_k \frac{\partial g_k(x)}{\partial \varepsilon_i} \tag{2.64}$$

and note that

$$\Phi_i = \frac{\partial Z(\varepsilon)}{\partial \varepsilon_i} + \mu_i \tag{2.65}$$

With the help of (2.61)–(2.63), we have

$$\begin{aligned}
\Phi_i &= \sum_{j=1}^{n} \frac{\partial f(x)}{\partial x_j} \frac{\partial x_j(\varepsilon)}{\partial \varepsilon_i} + \sum_{k=1}^{q} \lambda_k \sum_{j=1}^{n} \frac{\partial h_k(x)}{\partial x_j} \frac{\partial x_j(\varepsilon)}{\partial \varepsilon_i} \\
&\quad + \sum_{k=1}^{m} \mu_k \sum_{j=1}^{n} \frac{\partial g_k(x)}{\partial x_j} \frac{\partial x_j(\varepsilon)}{\partial \varepsilon_i} \\
&= \sum_{j=1}^{n} \left[\frac{\partial f(x)}{\partial x_j} + \sum_{k=1}^{q} \lambda_k \frac{\partial h_k(x)}{\partial x_j} + \sum_{k=1}^{m} \mu_k \frac{\partial g_k(x)}{\partial x_j} \right] \frac{\partial x_j(\varepsilon)}{\partial \varepsilon_i} = 0
\end{aligned} \tag{2.66}$$

by virtue of the Kuhn-Tucker identity (2.55). From (2.65) and (2.66) it is immediate that

$$\mu_i = (-1) \frac{\partial Z(\varepsilon)}{\partial \varepsilon_i} \qquad i \in [1, m] \tag{2.67}$$

We now note that, when the unconstrained minimum of $f(x)$ is external to the feasible region

$$X(\varepsilon) = \{x : g(x) \leq \varepsilon, h(x) = 0\},$$

increasing ε_i can never increase, and may potentially lower, the objective function for all $i \in [1, m]$; that is

$$\frac{\partial Z(\varepsilon)}{\partial \varepsilon_i} \leq 0 \quad i \in [1, m] \tag{2.68}$$

From (2.67) and (2.68) we have the desired result

$$\mu_i \geq 0 \quad \forall i \in [1, m] \tag{2.69}$$

ensuring that the multipliers for inequality constraints are nonnegative.

2.5 Formal Derivation of the Kuhn-Tucker Conditions

We are next interested in formally proving that, under the linear independence constraint qualification and some other basic assumptions, the Kuhn-Tucker identity and the complementary slackness conditions form, together with the original mathematical program's constraints, a valid set of necessary conditions. Such a demonstration is facilitated by Gordon's lemma, which is in effect a corollary of Farkas's lemma of classical analysis. The problem structure needed to apply Gordon's lemma can be most readily created by expressing the notion of optimality in terms of cones and separating hyperplanes. Throughout this section we consider the mathematical program

$$\min f(x) \quad \text{subject to} \quad x \in \mathcal{F} \tag{2.70}$$

where, depending on context, either $\mathcal{F}$ is a general set or

$$\mathcal{F} \equiv \{x \in X_0 : g(x) \leq 0\} \subset \Re^n \tag{2.71}$$

and

$$f \;:\; \Re^n \longrightarrow \Re^1 \tag{2.72}$$

$$g \;:\; \Re^n \longrightarrow \Re^m \tag{2.73}$$

where X_0 is a nonempty open set in $\Re^n$. Note that we presently consider only inequality constraints, as any equality constraint

$$h_k(x) = 0$$

may be stated as two inequality constraints:

$$\begin{aligned} h_k(x) &\leq 0 \\ -1 \cdot h_k(x) &\leq 0 \end{aligned}$$

2.5.1 Cones and Optimality

A cone is a set obeying the following definition:

Definition 2.3 (Cone) A set C in $\Re^n$ is a cone with vertex zero if $x \in C$ implies that $\theta x \in C$ for all $\theta \in \Re^1_+$.

Now consider the following definitions:

Definition 2.4 (Cone of feasible directions) For the mathematical program (2.70), provided $\mathcal{F}$ is not empty, the *cone of feasible directions* at $x \in X$ is

$$D_0(x) = \{d \neq 0 : x + \theta d \in \mathcal{F} \ \forall \theta \in (0, \delta) \text{ and some } \delta > 0\}$$

Definition 2.5 (Feasible direction) Every nonzero vector $d \in D_0$ is called a *feasible direction* at $x \in \mathcal{F}$ for the mathematical program (2.70).

Definition 2.6 (Cone of improving directions) For the mathematical program (2.70), if f is differentiable at $x \in \mathcal{F}$, the *cone of improving directions* at $x \in \mathcal{F}$ is

$$F_0(x) = \{d : [\nabla f(x)]^T \cdot d < 0\}$$

Definition 2.7 (Feasible direction of descent) Every vector $d \in F_0 \bigcap D_0$ is called a *feasible direction of descent* at $x \in \mathcal{F}$ for the mathematical program (2.70).

Definition 2.8 (Cone of interior directions) For the mathematical program (2.70), if g_i is differentiable at $x \in X$ for all $i \in I(x)$, where

$$I(x) = \{i : g_i(x) = 0\} \ ,$$

then the *cone of interior directions* at $x \in \mathcal{F}$ is

$$G_0(x) = \{d : [\nabla g_i(x)]^T \cdot d < 0 \ \forall \ i \in I(x)\}$$

Note that in Definition 2.4, if $\mathcal{F}$ is a convex set, we may set $\delta = 1$ and refer only to $\theta \in [0, 1]$, as will become clear in the next section after we define the notion of a convex set. Furthermore, the definitions immediately above allow one to characterize an optimal solution of (2.70) as a circumstance for which the intersection of the cone of feasible directions and the cone of improving directions is empty. This has great intuitive appeal for it says that there are no feasible directions that allow the objective to be improved.

In fact, the following result obtains:

Theorem 2.5 *(Optimality in terms of the cones of feasible and improving directions) Consider the mathematical program*

$$\min f(x) \quad \text{subject to} \quad x \in \mathcal{F} \tag{2.74}$$

where $f : \Re^n \longrightarrow \Re^1$, $\mathcal{F} \subseteq \Re^n$ *and* $\mathcal{F}$ *is nonempty. Suppose also that* f *is differentiable at the local minimum* $x^* \in \mathcal{F}$ *of (2.74). Then at* x^* *the intersection of the cone of feasible directions* D_0 *and the cone of improving directions* F_0 *is empty:*

$$F_0(x^*) \cap D_0(x^*) = \emptyset$$

That is, at the local solution $x^* \in \mathcal{F}$*, no improving direction is also a feasible direction.*

Proof. The result is intuitive. For a formal proof see Bazarra et al. (2006). ■

Theorem 2.6 *(Optimality in terms of the cones of interior and improving directions) Let* $x^* \in \mathcal{F}$ *be a local minimum of the mathematical program*

$$\min \; f(x) \quad \text{subject to} \quad x \in \mathcal{F} = \{x \in X_0 : g(x) \leq 0\} \subset \Re^n \tag{2.75}$$

where X_0 *is a nonempty open set in* $\Re^n$*, while* $f : \Re^n \longrightarrow \Re^1$ *and* $g : \Re^n \longrightarrow \Re^m$ *are differentiable at* x^**, and the* g_i *for* $i \in I$ *are continuous at* x^**. The cone of improving directions and the cone of interior directions satisfy*

$$F_0(x^*) \cap G_0(x^*) = \emptyset$$

Proof. This result is also intuitive. For a formal proof see Bazarra et al. (2006). ■

2.5.2 Theorems of the Alternative

Farkas's lemma is a specific example of a so-called *theorem of the alternative*. Such theorems provide information on whether a given linear system has a solution when a related linear system has or fails to have a solution. Farkas's lemma has the following statement:

Lemma 2.1 *(Farkas's lemma) Let* A *be an* $m \times n$ *matrix of real numbers and* $c \in \Re^n$*. Then exactly one of the following systems has a solution: System 1:* $Ax \leq 0$ *and* $c^T x > 0$ *for some* $x \in \Re^n$*; or System 2:* $A^T y = c$ *and* $y \geq 0$ *for some* $y \in \Re^m$.

Proof. Farkas's lemma is proven in most advanced texts on nonlinear programming. See, for example, Bazarra et al. (2006). ■

Corollary 2.1 *(Gordon's corollary) Let A be an $m \times n$ matrix of real numbers. Then exactly one of the following systems has a solution: System 1: $Ax < 0$ for some $x \in \Re^n$; or System 2: $A^T y = 0$ and $y \geq 0$ for some $y \in \Re^m$.*

Proof. See Mangasarian (1969). ■

2.5.3 The Fritz John Conditions Again

By using Corollary 2.1 it is quite easy to establish the Fritz John conditions introduced previously and restated here without equality constraints:

Theorem 2.7 *(Fritz John conditions) Let $x^* \in \mathcal{F}$ be a minimum of*

$$\min\ f(x) \quad \text{subject to} \quad x \in \mathcal{F} = \{x \in X_0 : g(x) \leq 0\}$$

where X_0 is a nonempty open set in $\Re^n$ and $g : \Re^n \longrightarrow \Re^m$. Assume that $f(x)$ and $g_i(x)$ for $i \in [1, m]$ have continuous first derivatives everywhere on $\mathcal{F}$. Then there must exist multipliers $\mu_0 \in \Re^1_+$ and $\mu = (\mu_1, \ldots, \mu_m)^T \in \Re^m_+$ such that

$$\mu_0 \nabla f(x^*) + \sum_{i=1}^{m} \mu_i \nabla g_i(x^*) = 0 \tag{2.76}$$

$$\mu_i g_i(x^*) = 0 \quad \forall\, i \in [1, m] \tag{2.77}$$

$$\mu_i \geq 0 \quad \forall\, i \in [1, m] \tag{2.78}$$

$$(\mu_0,\ \mu) \neq 0 \in \Re^{m+1} \tag{2.79}$$

Proof. Since $x^* \in \mathcal{F}$ solves the mathematical program of interest, we know from Theorem 2.6 that $F_0(x^*) \cap G_0(x^*) = \emptyset$; that is, there is no vector d satisfying

$$[\nabla f(x^*)]^T \cdot d \ < \ 0 \tag{2.80}$$

$$[\nabla g_i(x^*)]^T \cdot d \ < \ 0 \quad i \in I(x^*) \tag{2.81}$$

where $I(x^*)$ is the set of indices of constraints binding at x^*. Without loss of generality, we may consecutively number the binding constraints from 1 to $|I(x^*)|$ and define

$$A = \begin{pmatrix} [\nabla f(x^*)]^T \\ [\nabla g_1(x^*)]^T \\ [\nabla g_2(x^*)]^T \\ \vdots \\ [\nabla g_{|I(x^*)|}(x^*)]^T \end{pmatrix}$$

As a consequence we may state (2.80) and (2.81) as

$$A(d) < 0 \tag{2.82}$$

According to Corollary 2.1, since (2.82) cannot occur, there exists

$$y = \begin{pmatrix} \mu_0 \\ \mu_i : i \in I(x^*) \end{pmatrix} \geq 0$$

such that

$$A^T y = A^T \begin{pmatrix} \mu_0 \\ \mu_i : i \in I(x^*) \end{pmatrix} = 0 \tag{2.83}$$

Expression (2.83) yields

$$\mu_0 \nabla f(x^*) + \sum_{i=1}^{|I(x^*)|} \mu_i \nabla g_i(x^*) = 0 \tag{2.84}$$

We are free to introduce the additional multipliers

$$\mu_i = 0 \quad i = |I(x^*)| + 1, \ldots, m \tag{2.85}$$

which assure that the complementary slackness conditions (2.77) and (2.78) hold for all multipliers. As a consequence of (2.84) and (2.85), we have (2.76), thereby completing the proof. ■

2.5.4 The Kuhn-Tucker Conditions Again

With the apparatus developed so far, we wish to prove the following restatement of Theorem 2.4 in terms of the linear independence constraint qualification:

Theorem 2.8 *(Kuhn-Tucker conditions) Let $x^* \in \mathcal{F}$ be a local minimum of*

$$\min f(x) \quad \text{subject to} \quad x \in \mathcal{F} = \{x \in X_0 : g(x) \leq 0, h(x) = 0\}$$

where X_0 is a nonempty open set in $\Re^n$. Assume that $f(x)$, $g_i(x)$ for $i \in [1, m]$ and $h_i(x)$ for $i \in [1, q]$ have continuous first derivatives everywhere on $\mathcal{F}$ and that the gradients of binding constraint functions are linearly independent. Then there must exist multipliers $\mu = (\mu_1, \ldots, \mu_m)^T \in \Re^m$ and $\lambda = (\lambda_i, \ldots, \lambda_q)^T \in \Re^q$ such that

$$\nabla f(x^*) + \sum_{i=1}^{m} \mu_i \nabla g_i(x^*) + \sum_{i=1}^{q} \lambda_i \nabla h_i(x^*) = 0 \tag{2.86}$$

$$\mu_i g_i(x^*) = 0 \quad \forall\, i \in [1, m] \tag{2.87}$$

$$\mu_i \geq 0 \quad \forall\, i \in [1, m] \tag{2.88}$$

Proof. Recall that a constraint qualification is a condition that guarantees the multiplier μ_0 of the Fritz John conditions is nonzero. We again use the notation

$$I(x^*) = \{i : g_i(x^*) = 0\}, \tag{2.89}$$

for the set of subscripts corresponding to binding inequality constraints. Note also that by their very nature equality constraints are always binding. Linear independence of the gradients of binding constraints means that only zero multipliers

$$\mu_i = 0 \quad \forall\, i \in I(x^*) \tag{2.90}$$

$$\lambda_i = 0 \quad \forall\, i \in [1, q] \tag{2.91}$$

allow the identity

$$\sum_{i \in I(x^*)} \mu_i \nabla g_i(x^*) + \sum_{i=1}^{q} \lambda_i \nabla h_i(x^*) = 0, \tag{2.92}$$

to hold. We are free to set the multipliers for nonbinding constraints to zero; that is

$$g_i(x^*) < 0 \Longrightarrow \mu_i = 0 \quad \forall\, i \notin I(x^*)$$

which assures (2.87) and (2.88) hold for $i \in [1, m]$. Consequently, linear independence of the gradients of binding constraints actually means that there are no nonzero multipliers assuring

$$\sum_{i=1}^{m} \mu_i \nabla g_i(x^*) + \sum_{i=1}^{q} \lambda_i \nabla h_i(x^*) = 0 \tag{2.93}$$

That is, either all $\lambda_i = 0$ and all $\mu_i = 0$ or

$$\sum_{i=1}^{m} \mu_i \nabla g_i(x^*) + \sum_{i=1}^{q} \lambda_i \nabla h_i(x^*) \neq 0 \tag{2.94}$$

In the latter case, the Fritz John identity

$$\mu_0 \nabla f(x^*) + \sum_{i=1}^{m} \mu_i \nabla g_i(x^*) + \sum_{i=1}^{q} \lambda_i \nabla h_i(x^*) = 0 \tag{2.95}$$

immediately forces

$$\mu_0 \neq 0 \tag{2.96}$$

unless $\nabla f(x^*) = 0 \in \Re^n$; in this latter case (2.93) must hold and so we may still enforce (2.96) without contradiction or loss of generality. ■

2.6 Sufficiency, Convexity, and Uniqueness

Sufficient conditions for optimality in a mathematical program are conditions that, if satisfied, ensure optimality. Any such condition has the logical structure:

If property $\mathbf{P}(x^*)$ is true, then x^* is optimal.

It turns out that convexity, a notion that requires careful definition, provides useful sufficient conditions that are relatively easy to check in practice. In particular, we will define a convex mathematical program to be a mathematical program with a convex objective function (when minimizing) and a convex feasible region, and we will show that the Kuhn-Tucker conditions are not only necessary, but also sufficient for global optimality in such programs.

2.6.1 Quadratic Forms

A key concept, useful for establishing convexity of functions, is that of a quadratic form, formally defined as follows:

Definition 2.9 (Quadratic form) A *quadratic form* is a scalar-valued function defined for all $x \in \Re^n$ that takes on the following form:

$$Q(x) = \sum_{i=1}^{n} \sum_{j=1}^{n} a_{ij} x_i x_j \tag{2.97}$$

where each a_{ij} is a real number.

Note that any quadratic form may be expressed in matrix notation as

$$Q(x) = x^T A x \tag{2.98}$$

where $A = (a_{ij})$ is an $n \times n$ matrix. It is well known that for any given quadratic form there is a symmetric matrix S that allows one to re-express that quadratic form as

$$Q(x) = x^T S x \tag{2.99}$$

where the elements of $S = (s_{ij})$ are given by $s_{ij} = s_{ji} = (a_{ij} + a_{ji})/2$. Because of this symmetry property, we may assume, without loss of generality, that every quadratic form is already expressed in terms of a symmetric matrix. That is, whenever we encounter a quadratic form such as (2.98) or (2.99), the underlying matrix generating that form may be taken to be symmetric if doing so assists our analysis.

A quadratic form may exhibit various properties, two of which are the subject of the following definition:

Definition 2.10 (Positive definiteness) The quadratic form $Q(x) = x^T S x$ is *positive definite* on $\Omega \subseteq \Re^n$ if $Q(x) > 0$ for all $x \in \Omega$ such that $x \neq 0$. The quadratic form $Q(x) = x^T S x$ is *positive semidefinite* on $\Omega \subseteq \Re^n$ if $Q(x) \geq 0$ for all $x \in \Omega$.

Analogous definitions may be made for negative definite and negative semidefinite quadratic forms. Frequently, we will say that the matrix S is positive (semi)definite when it is actually the quadratic form induced by S that is positive (semi)definite.

An important lemma concerning quadratic forms, which we state without proof, is the following:

Lemma 2.2 *(Properties of positive definite matrix) Let the symmetric $n \times n$ matrix S be positive (negative) definite. Then*

(1) The inverse S^{-1} exists;

(2) S^{-1} is positive (negative) definite; and

(3) $A^T SA$ is positive (negative) semidefinite for any $m \times n$ matrix A.

In addition, we will need the following lemma, which we also state without proof:

Lemma 2.3 *(Nonnegativity of principal minors) A quadratic form $Q(x) = x^T Sx$, where S is the associated symmetric matrix, is positive semidefinite if and only if it may be ordered so that s_{11} is positive and the following determinants of the principal minors are all nonnegative:*

$$\begin{vmatrix} s_{11} & s_{12} \\ s_{21} & s_{22} \end{vmatrix} \geq 0, \quad \begin{vmatrix} s_{11} & s_{12} & s_{13} \\ s_{21} & s_{22} & s_{23} \\ s_{31} & s_{32} & s_{33} \end{vmatrix} \geq 0, \ \ldots \ , |S| \geq 0$$

2.6.2 Concave and Convex Functions

This section contains several definitions, lemmas, and theorems related to convex functions and convex sets that we need to fully understand the notion of sufficiency. First, consider the following four definitions:

Definition 2.11 (Convex set) A set $X \subseteq \Re^n$ is a *convex set* if for any two vectors $x^1, x^2 \in X$ and any scalar $\lambda \in [0, 1]$ the vector

$$x = \lambda x^1 + (1 - \lambda)x^2 \tag{2.100}$$

also lies in X.

Definition 2.12 (Strictly convex set) A set $X \subseteq \Re^n$ is a *strictly convex set* if for any two vectors x^1 and x^2 in X and any scalar $\lambda \in (0, 1)$ the point

$$x = \lambda x^1 + (1 - \lambda)x^2 \tag{2.101}$$

lies in the interior of X.

Definition 2.13 (Convex function) A scalar function $f(x)$ is a *convex function* defined over a convex set $X \subseteq \Re^n$ if for any two vectors $x^1, x^2 \in X$

$$f(\lambda x^1 + (1-\lambda)x^2) \leq \lambda f(x^1) + (1-\lambda)f(x^2) \quad \forall\, \lambda \in [0,1] \tag{2.102}$$

Definition 2.14 (Strictly convex function) In the above, $f(x)$ is a *strictly convex function* if the inequality is a strict inequality ($<$) for all $\lambda \in (0,1)$.

Note that concave and strictly concave functions are defined by reversing the inequalities in the preceding definitions.

We are now ready to state the following theorems:

Theorem 2.9 *(Sum of convex functions) The sum of any two convex functions is convex.*

Theorem 2.10 *(Convexity of linear functions) Any linear function is both convex and concave.*

Theorem 2.11 *(Convexity of quadratic form) For any positive semidefinite and symmetric matrix S, the quadratic form $Q(x) = x^T Sx$ is a convex function over all of $\Re^n$.*

The proofs of the preceding results are straightforward and are left to the reader. Another important result is the following that relates convex level sets and convex functions:

Theorem 2.12 *(Level sets of convex function) If $f(x)$ is a (strictly) convex function over $\Re^n$, then the set of points*

$$S \equiv \{x : f(x) \leq b\}, \tag{2.103}$$

where b is any real number, is a (strictly) convex set.

Proof. The definition of convexity tells us that

$$\begin{aligned} f(\lambda x^1 + (1-\lambda)x^2) &\leq \lambda f(x^1) + (1-\lambda)f(x^2) \\ &\leq \lambda b + (1-\lambda)b = b \end{aligned}$$

A strict version of this inequality is obtained for strictly convex functions, thereby completing the proof. ■

We will also need the following lemma:

Lemma 2.4 *(Intersection of convex sets) The intersection of any two convex sets is itself a convex set.*

Proof. Take x^1 and x^2 within the intersection $X^1 \cap X^2$, where X^1 and X^2 are convex sets. Join these points by a line segment. That line segment and all the points on it are both in X^1 and X^2. ■

It is now trivial to establish the following result:

Theorem 2.13 *(Convex feasible region) The feasible region X of the mathematical program (2.3) is a convex set if the following two conditions are met:*

(1) the equality constraint functions $h_i(x) : \Re^n \longrightarrow \Re^1$ for $i \in [1, q]$ are all linear on X; and

(2) the inequality constraint functions $g_i(x) : \Re^n \longrightarrow \Re^1$ for $i \in [1, m]$ are all convex on X.

Proof. For the given, the sets

$$\begin{aligned} S_h &= \{x : h(x) = 0\} \\ S_g &= \{x : g(x) \leq 0\} \end{aligned}$$

are convex. The feasible region X obeys

$$X = S_h \cap S_g$$

Hence, X is convex, since the intersection of two convex sets is a convex set. ■

Now we are ready to deal with the following key result:

Theorem 2.14 *(Global minimum of a convex program) If the function $f(x) : \Re^n \longrightarrow \Re^1$ is defined and convex on the closed convex set $X \subseteq \Re^n$, then any constrained local minimum of $f(x)$ for $x \in X$ is a global minimum on X. Similarly, if $f(x)$ is concave on the closed convex set X, then any constrained local maximum of $f(x)$ for $x \in X$ is a global maximum on X.*

Proof. Suppose $x^0 \in X$ is a constrained local minimum but not a global minimum, so that there exists some $x^* \in X$ such that $f(x^*) < f(x^0)$. Then for any $\lambda \in [0, 1]$ the convexity of $f(x)$ tells us that

$$\begin{aligned} f(\lambda x^* + (1 - \lambda)x^0) &\leq \lambda f(x^*) + (1 - \lambda) f(x^0) \\ &< \lambda f(x^0) + (1 - \lambda) f(x^0) = f(x^0) \qquad (2.104) \end{aligned}$$

Now, consider a straight line segment from x^0 to x^* which must lie entirely in X (by convexity). For any small positive δ (a scalar), there exists $\lambda > 0$ such that

$$x = \lambda x^* + (1 - \lambda)x^0 \tag{2.105}$$

lies in X at a distance δ away from x^0. However, we have already shown in (2.104) that

$$f(x) < f(x^0) \tag{2.106}$$

Since δ may be infinitesimally small, x^0 cannot be a local minimum. Hence, we have a contradiction. ■

Another important result is the following:

Theorem 2.15 *(Tangent line property of a convex function) Let $f(x)$ have continuous first partial derivatives. Then $f(x)$ is convex over the convex region $X \subseteq \Re^n$ if and only if*

$$f(x) \geq f(x^*) + [\nabla f(x^*)]^T (x - x^*) \tag{2.107}$$

for any two vectors x^* and x in X. Moreover, $f(x)$ is concave over the convex region $X \subseteq \Re^n$ if and only if

$$f(x) \leq f(x^*) + [\nabla f(x^*)]^T (x - x^*) \tag{2.108}$$

for any two vectors x^* and x in X.

This result may be proven by taking a Taylor series expansion of $f(x)$ about the point x^* and arguing that the second and higher terms sum to a positive number. Theorem 2.15 expresses the geometric property that a tangent to a convex function will underestimate that function. Still another related result is:

Theorem 2.16 *(Convexity and positive semidefiniteness of the Hessian) Let $f(x)$ have continuous second partial derivatives. Then $f(x)$ is convex (concave) over the region $X \subseteq \Re^n$ if and only if its Hessian matrix*

$$H(x) \equiv \begin{bmatrix} \dfrac{\partial^2 f}{\partial x_1^2} & \dfrac{\partial^2 f}{\partial x_1 \partial x_2} & \cdots & \dfrac{\partial^2 f}{\partial x_1 \partial x_n} \\ \dfrac{\partial^2 f}{\partial x_2 \partial x_1} & \dfrac{\partial^2 f}{\partial x_2^2} & \cdots & \dfrac{\partial^2 f}{\partial x_2 \partial x_n} \\ \vdots & \vdots & \ddots & \vdots \\ \dfrac{\partial^2 f}{\partial x_n \partial x_1} & \dfrac{\partial^2 f}{\partial x_n \partial x_2} & \cdots & \dfrac{\partial^2 f}{\partial x_n^2} \end{bmatrix} \tag{2.109}$$

is positive (negative) semidefinite on X.

Proof. We give the proof for concave functions, although the case of convex functions is completely analogous.

(i) [negative semidefiniteness $\Longrightarrow$ concavity] First note that the Hessian H is symmetric by its very nature. We may make a second-order Taylor series expansion of $f(x)$ about a point $x^* \in X$ to obtain

$$f(x) = f(x^*) + [\nabla f(x^*)]^T (x - x^*) + \frac{1}{2}(x - x^*)^T H[x^* + \theta(x - x^*)](x - x^*) \tag{2.110}$$

for some $\theta \in (0, 1)$. Because X is convex we know that the point

$$x^* + \theta(x - x^*) = \theta x + (1 - \theta)x^* \ , \tag{2.111}$$

a convex combination of x and x^*, must lie within X. Now suppose that H is negative definite or negative semidefinite throughout X, so that the last term on the righthand side of the Taylor expansion is clearly negative or zero. We get

$$f(x) \leq f(x^*) + [\nabla f(x^*)]^T (x - x^*) \tag{2.112}$$

It follows from the previous theorem that $f(x)$ is concave.

(ii) [concavity $\Longrightarrow$ negative semidefiniteness] Now assume $f(x)$ is concave throughout X, but that the Hessian matrix H is not negative semidefinite at some point $x^* \in X$. Then, of course, there will exist a vector y such that

$$y^T H(x^*)y > 0 \tag{2.113}$$

Now define $x^0 = x^* + y$ and rewrite this last inequality as

$$(x^0 - x^*)^T H(x^*)(x^0 - x^*) > 0 \tag{2.114}$$

Consider another point $x = x^* + \beta(x^0 - x^*)$ where β is a real positive number, so that

$$(x^0 - x^*) = \frac{1}{\beta}(x - x^*) \tag{2.115}$$

It follows that for any such β

$$(x - x^*)^T H(x^*)(x - x^*) > 0 \tag{2.116}$$

Since H is continuous, we may choose x so close to x^* that

$$(x - x^*)^T H[x^* + \theta(x - x^*)](x - x^*) > 0 \tag{2.117}$$

for all $\theta \in [0, 1]$. By hypothesis $f(x)$ is concave over $\Re$ so that

$$f(x) \leq f(x^*) + [\nabla f(x^*)]^T (x - x^*) \tag{2.118}$$

holds, together with the Taylor series expansion (2.110). Subtracting (2.118) from (2.110) gives

$$0 \geq \frac{1}{2}(x - x^*)^T H[x^* + \theta(x - x^*)](x - x^*) \tag{2.119}$$

for some $\theta \in (0, 1)$. This contradicts (2.117). ■

Note this last theorem cannot be strengthened to say a function is strictly convex if and only if its Hessian is positive definite. Examples may be given of functions that are strictly convex and whose Hessians are not positive definite. However, one can establish that positive definiteness of the Hessian does imply strict convexity by employing some of the arguments from the preceding proof. Furthermore, the manner of construction of the preceding proofs leads directly to the following corollary:

Corollary 2.2 *(Convexity of solution set) If the constrained global minimum of $f(x)$ for $x \in X \subset \Re^n$ is α when $f(x) : \Re^n \longrightarrow \Re^1$ is convex on X, a convex set, then the set*

$$\Psi = \{x : x \in X \subset \Re^n, \;\; f(x) \leq \alpha\} \tag{2.120}$$

is the set of all solutions and is itself convex.

We now turn our attention to the question of additional regularity conditions that will assure that the set Ψ is a singleton. In fact, we will prove the following theorem:

Theorem 2.17 *(Unique global minimum) Let $f(\cdot)$ be a strictly convex function defined on a convex set $X \subset \Re^n$. If $f(\cdot)$ attains its global minimum on X, it is attained at a unique point of X.*

Proof. Suppose there are two global minima: $x^1 \in X$ and $x^2 \in X$. Let $f(x^1) = f(x^2) = \alpha$. Then, by the previous corollary the set Ψ is a convex set and is the set of all solutions. Therefore

$$x^1, \; x^2, \; x^3 \in \Psi \tag{2.121}$$

where $x^3 = \lambda x^1 + (1 - \lambda)x^2$, and

$$\alpha = f(x^3) = f(\lambda x^1 + (1 - \lambda)x^2) < \lambda f(x^1) + (1 - \lambda)f(x^2) = \alpha.$$

This is a contradiction and therefore there cannot be two global minima. ■

2.6.3 Kuhn-Tucker Sufficient Conditions

The most significant implication of imposing regularity conditions based on convexity is that they make the Kuhn-Tucker conditions sufficient as well as necessary for global optimality. In fact, we may state and prove the following:

Theorem 2.18 *(Kuhn-Tucker conditions sufficient for convex programs) Let*

$$\begin{aligned} f &: X \subset \Re^n \longrightarrow \Re^n \\ g &: X \subset \Re^n \longrightarrow \Re^m \\ h &: X \subset \Re^n \longrightarrow \Re^q \end{aligned}$$

be real-valued, differentiable functions. Suppose X_0 is an open convex set in $\Re^n$, while f is convex, the g_i are convex for $i \in [1, m]$, and the h_i are linear affine for $i \in [1, q]$. Take x^* to be a feasible solution of the mathematical program

$$\left.\begin{array}{ll} & \min f(x) \\ \textit{subject to} & \\ & h_i(x) = 0 \quad (\lambda_i) \quad i \in [1, q] \\ & g_i(x) \leq 0 \quad (\mu_i) \quad i \in [1, m] \\ & x \in X_0 \end{array}\right\} \tag{2.122}$$

If there exist multipliers $\mu^* \in \Re^m$ and $\lambda^* \in \Re^q$ satisfying the Kuhn-Tucker conditions

$$\nabla f(x^*) + \sum_{i=1}^{m} \mu_i^* \nabla g_i(x^*) + \sum_{i=1}^{q} \lambda_i^* \nabla h_i(x^*) = 0$$

$$\mu_i^* g_i(x^*) = 0 \quad \mu_i^* \geq 0 \quad i \in [1, m] \ ,$$

then x^* is a global minimum.

Proof. To simplify the exposition, we shall assume only constraints that are inequalities; this is possible since any linear equality constraint

$$h_k(x) = 0$$

for $k \in [1, m]$ may be restated as two convex inequality constraints in standard form:

$$\begin{aligned} h_k(x) &\leq 0 \\ -h_k(x) &\leq 0 \end{aligned}$$

and absorbed into the definition of $g(x)$. The Kuhn-Tucker identity is then

$$\nabla f(x^*) + \sum_{i=1}^{m} \mu_i^* \nabla g_i(x^*) = 0 \tag{2.123}$$

Postmultiplying (2.123) by $(x - x^*)$ gives

$$[\nabla f(x^*)]^T (x - x^*) + \sum_{i}^{m} \mu_i^* [\nabla g_i(x^*)]^T (x - x^*) = 0 \tag{2.124}$$

where x^* is a solution of the Kuhn-Tucker conditions and

$$x, x^* \in X = \{x \in X_0 : g(x) \leq 0\}$$

We know that for a convex, differentiable function

$$g(x) \geq g(x^*) + [\nabla g(x^*)]^T (x - x^*) \tag{2.125}$$

From (2.124) and (2.125), we have

$$[\nabla f(x^*)]^T (x - x^*) = -\sum_i^m \mu_i^* [\nabla g_i(x^*)]^T (x - x^*)$$

$$\geq \sum_i^m \mu_i^* [g_i(x^*) - g_i(x)] \tag{2.126}$$

$$= \sum_i^m \mu_i^* [-g_i(x)] \geq 0$$

because $\mu_i^* g_i(x^*) = 0$, $\mu_i^* \geq 0$ and $g_i(x) \leq 0$. Hence

$$[\nabla f(x^*)]^T (x - x^*) \geq 0 \tag{2.127}$$

Because $f(x)$ is convex

$$f(x) \geq f(x^*) + [\nabla f(x^*)]^T (x - x^*) \tag{2.128}$$

Hence, from (2.127) and (2.128) we get

$$f(x) - f(x^*) \geq [\nabla f(x^*)]^T (x - x^*) \geq 0 \tag{2.129}$$

That is

$$f(x) \geq f(x^*) ,$$

which establishes that any solution of the Kuhn-Tucker conditions is a global minimum for the given. ■

Note that this theorem can be changed to one in which the objective function is strictly convex, thereby assuring that any corresponding solution of the Kuhn-Tucker conditions is an unique global minimum. The given of Theorem 2.18 may also be relaxed if certain results from the theory of generalized convexity are employed.

2.7 Generalized Convexity and Sufficiency

There are generalizations of the notion of convexity that allow the sufficiency conditions introduced above to be somewhat weakened. We begin to explore the notion of more general types of convexity by introducing the following definition of a quasiconvex function:

Definition 2.15 (Quasiconvex function) The function $f : X \longrightarrow \Re^n$ is a *quasiconvex function* on the set $X \subset \Re^n$ if

$$f\left(\lambda_1 x^1 + \lambda_2 x^2\right) \leq \max\left[f\left(x^1\right), f\left(x^2\right)\right]$$

for every $x^1, x^2 \in X$ and every $(\lambda_1, \lambda_2) \in \{(\lambda_1, \lambda_2) \in \Re^2_+ : \lambda_1 + \lambda_2 = 1\}$.

We next introduce the notion of a pseudoconvex function:

Definition 2.16 (Pseudoconvex function) The function $f : X \longrightarrow \Re^n$, differentiable on the open convex set $X \subset \Re^n$, is a *pseudoconvex function* on X if

$$\left(x^1 - x^2\right)^T \nabla f\left(x^2\right) \geq 0$$

implies that

$$f(x^1) \geq f(x^2)$$

for every $x^1, x^2 \in X$.

Pseudoconcavity of f occurs of course when $-f$ is pseudoconvex. Furthermore, we shall say a function is pseudolinear (quasilinear) if it is both pseudoconvex (quasiconvex) and pseudoconcave (quasiconcave).

The notions of generalized convexity we have given allow the following theorem to be stated and proved:

Theorem 2.19 *(Kuhn-Tucker conditions sufficient for generalized convex programs) Let*

$$\begin{aligned} f &: X \subset \Re^n \longrightarrow \Re^n \\ g &: X \subset \Re^n \longrightarrow \Re^m \\ h &: X \subset \Re^n \longrightarrow \Re^q \end{aligned}$$

be real-valued, differentiable functions. Suppose X_0 is an open convex set in $\Re^n$, while f is pseudoconvex, the g_i are quasiconvex for $i \in [1, m]$, and the h_i are quasilinear for $i \in [1, q]$. Take x^* to be a feasible solution of the mathematical program

$$\left.\begin{array}{ll} & \min f(x) \\ \textit{subject to} & \\ & h_i(x) = 0 \quad (\eta_i) \quad i \in [1, q] \\ & g_i(x) \leq 0 \quad (\lambda_i) \quad i \in [1, m] \\ & x \in X_0 \end{array}\right\} \tag{2.130}$$

If there exist multipliers $\mu^* \in \Re^m$ and $\lambda^* \in \Re^q$ satisfying the Kuhn-Tucker conditions

$$\nabla f(x^*) + \sum_{i=1}^{m} \mu_i^* \nabla g_i(x^*) + \sum_{i=1}^{q} \lambda_i^* \nabla h_i(x^*) = 0$$

$$\mu_i^* g_i(x^*) = 0 \quad \mu_i^* \geq 0 \quad i \in [1, m],$$

then x^* is a global minimum.

Proof. The proof is left as an exercise for the reader. ■

We close this section by noting that if, in addition to the given of Theorem 2.19, an appropriate notion of strict pseudoconvexity is introduced for the objective function f, then the Kuhn-Tucker conditions become sufficient for a unique global minimizer.

2.8 Sensitivity Analysis

In this section the sensitivity analysis of nonlinear programs in the face of parameter perturbations is emphasized. The foundations of the theory of sensitivity analysis for nonlinear programs is largely the product of collaboration between Anthony Fiacco and Garth McCormick; their theory, reported in the celebrated book *Nonlinear Programming: Sequential Unconstrained Minimization Techniques*, first published in 1968, has withstood the test of time and remains the dominant perspective on NLP sensitivity analysis. A key result needed for the derivation of sensitivity analysis formulae for nonlinear programs is the implicit function theorem. In the exposition that follows $C^k\left[N_\epsilon\left(\xi^0\right)\right]$ will denote the space of k-times continuously differentiable functions defined on an ϵ-neighborhood of ξ^0. We will use the following version of the implicit function theorem employed by Fiacco (1983) in studying sensitivity analysis:

Theorem 2.20 *(Implicit function theorem) Suppose $\Phi : \Re^{n+m} \longrightarrow \Re^n$ is a k times continuously differentiable mapping whose domain is D. Further suppose that*

$$\begin{pmatrix} x^0 \\ \xi^0 \end{pmatrix} \in D \tag{2.131}$$

$$\Phi(x^0, \xi^0) = 0 \tag{2.132}$$

and that the Jacobian

$$J_x\left(x^0, \xi^0\right) = \left(\nabla_x \Phi(x^0, \xi^0)\right)^T \tag{2.133}$$

is nonsingular. Then there exists a neighborhood $N_\epsilon\left(\xi^0\right) \subset \Re^m$ and an unique function $\Psi \in C^k\left[N_\epsilon\left(\xi^0\right)\right]$ such that

$$\Psi : N_\epsilon\left(\xi^0\right) \longrightarrow \Re^n \tag{2.134}$$

$$\Psi\left(\xi^0\right) = x^0 \tag{2.135}$$

$$\Phi\left[\Psi\left(\xi\right), \xi\right] = 0 \quad \forall \xi \in N_\epsilon\left(\xi^0\right) \tag{2.136}$$

Proof. See Hestenes (1975). ■

We will ultimately be applying Theorem 2.20 to the following mathematical program, that will be denoted by MP(ξ):

$$\left.\begin{array}{l} \min f(x) \\ \text{subject to} \\ x \in \mathcal{F}(\xi) = \{x \in \Re^n : g(x,\xi) \leq 0, h(x,\xi) = 0, h(x) = 0\} \end{array}\right\} \quad (2.137)$$

where

$$f : \Re^n \times \Re^s \longrightarrow \Re^1$$

$$g : \Re^n \times \Re^s \longrightarrow \Re^m$$

$$h : \Re^n \times \Re^s \longrightarrow \Re^q$$

and

$$\xi \in \Re^s$$

is a vector of parameter perturbations. It will also be helpful to define the associated Lagrangean

$$L(x^*, \mu^*, v^*, \xi) = f(x^*, \xi) + \sum_{i=1}^{m} \mu_i^* g_i(x^*, \xi) + \sum_{j=1}^{q} v_j^* h_j(x^*, \xi)$$

When there are no perturbations, the program of interest, MP(0), is understood to be

$$\min \ f(x,0) \quad \text{subject to} \quad x \in \mathcal{F}(0) \tag{2.138}$$

and its Lagrangean is denoted by $L(x^*, \mu^*, v^*, 0)$. In our subsequent discussion of sensitivity analysis, we will have need for the following second-order sufficiency result:

Theorem 2.21 *(Second-order sufficient conditions for a strict local minimum of MP(0)) Suppose f, g, and h are twice continuously differentiable in a neighborhood of $x^* \in \mathcal{F}(0)$. Also suppose that x^* is a Kuhn-Tucker point; that is, there exist vectors $\mu^* \in \Re^m$ and $v^* \in \Re^q$ such that*

$$\nabla L(x^*, \mu^*, v^*, 0) = \nabla f(x^*, 0) + \sum_{i=1}^{m} \mu_i^* \nabla g_i(x^*, 0) + \sum_{j=1}^{q} v_j^* \nabla h_j(x^*, 0) = 0 \tag{2.139}$$

$$\mu_i^* g_i(x^*, 0) = 0 \quad \forall i \in [1, m] \tag{2.140}$$

$$\mu_i^* \geq 0 \quad \forall i \in [1, m] \tag{2.141}$$

Further assume that

$$z^T \left[\nabla^2 L(x^*, \mu^*, v^*, 0)\right] z > 0 \tag{2.142}$$

for all $z \neq 0$ such that

$$[\nabla g_i(x^*, 0)]^T z \leq 0 \quad \text{for all } i \in I^* \tag{2.143}$$

$$[\nabla g_i(x^*, 0)]^T z = 0 \quad \text{for all } i \in J^* \tag{2.144}$$

$$[\nabla h_i(x^*, 0)]^T z = 0 \quad \text{for all } i \in [1, q] \tag{2.145}$$

where

$$I^* = \{i : g_i(x^*, 0) = 0\}$$

$$J^* = \{i : \mu_i^* > 0\}$$

Then x^* is a strict local minimum of MP(0). That is, there exists a neighborhood of x^* such that there does ***not*** *exist any feasible $x \neq x^*$ with the property*

$$f(x, 0) \leq f(x^*, 0)$$

Proof. We follow Fiacco and McCormick (1968) and first assume that x^* is not a strict local minimum. As a consequence, there exists a sequence of points $\{y^k\}$ with the following properties:

$$\text{Property A: } \lim_{k \longrightarrow \infty} y^k = x^*$$

$$\text{Property B: } y^k \in \mathcal{F}(0)$$

$$\text{Property C: } f(y^k, 0) \leq f(x^*, 0)$$

We may rewrite every y^k as follows:

$$y^k = x^* + \delta_k s^k$$

where $\delta_k \in \Re^1_{++}$ and $\|s^k\| = 1$ for every k. Thus, any limit point of the sequence $\{\delta_k, s_k\}$ is of the form $(0, \bar{s})$, where $\|\bar{s}\| = 1$. By Property B we have

$$g_i(y^k, 0) - g_i(x^*, 0) \leq 0 \quad \forall i \in I^* \tag{2.146}$$

$$h_i(y^k, 0) - h_i(x^*, 0) = 0 \quad \forall i \in [1, q] \tag{2.147}$$

Furthermore, Property C requires

$$f(y^k, 0) - f(x^*, 0) \leq 0 \tag{2.148}$$

Dividing expressions (2.146)–(2.148) by δ_k and taking the limit as $k \longrightarrow \infty$, we have, by Property A and the given differentiability of the functions involved, the following results:

$$[\nabla g_i(x^*,0)]^T \bar{s} \le 0 \quad \forall i \in I^* \tag{2.149}$$

$$[\nabla h_i(x^*,0)]^T \bar{s} = 0 \quad \forall i \in [1,q] \tag{2.150}$$

$$[\nabla f(x^*,0)]^T \bar{s} \le 0 \tag{2.151}$$

Now consider the following two cases:

(1) For the unit vector $\bar{s}$ defined above

$$[\nabla g_i(x^*,0)]^T \bar{s} < 0$$

for at least one $i \in J^*$. In that case

$$0 \ge [\nabla f(x^*,0)]^T \bar{s} = -\sum_{i\in J^*} \mu_i^* \nabla g_i(x^*,0)\bar{s} - \sum_{j=1}^{q} v_j^* \nabla h_j(x^*,0)\bar{s} > 0$$

which is a contradiction; thus x^* must be a strict local minimum.

(2) For the unit vector $\bar{s}$

$$[\nabla g_i(x^*,0)]^T \bar{s} = 0$$

for all $i \in J^*$ or $J^* = \emptyset$. Inequality (2.148) still applies, so that by the mean value theorem

$$\begin{aligned} 0 &\ge f(x^* + \delta_k s^k, 0) - f(x^*,0) \\ &= \delta_k \nabla f(x^*,0)s^k + \frac{(\delta_k)^2}{2} s^k \left[\nabla^2 f(a_0^k,0)\right] s^k \end{aligned} \tag{2.152}$$

where

$$a_0^k = \omega_0 x^* + (1-\omega_0)\left(x^* + \delta_k s^k\right) \qquad \omega_0 \in (0,1)$$

Furthermore

$$\begin{aligned} 0 &\ge g_i(y^k,0) = g_i(x^* + \delta_k s^k, 0) \\ &= g_i(x^*,0) + \delta_k \nabla g_i(x^*,0)s^k + \frac{(\delta_k)^2}{2} s^k \left[\nabla^2 g_i(b_i^k,0)\right] s^k \quad \forall i \in I^* \end{aligned} \tag{2.153}$$

$$\begin{aligned} 0 &= h_j(y^k,0) = h_j(x^* + \delta_k s^k, 0) \\ &= h_j(x^*,0) + \delta_k \nabla h_j(x^*,0)s^k + \frac{(\delta_k)^2}{2} s^k \left[\nabla^2 h_j(c_j^k,0)\right] s^k \quad \forall j \in [1,q] \end{aligned} \tag{2.154}$$

where

$$b_i^k = \eta_i x^* + (1-\eta_i)\left(x^* + \delta_k s^k\right) \qquad \eta_i \in (0,1) \qquad \forall i \in I^*$$

$$c_i^k = \sigma_j x^* + (1-\sigma_j)\left(x^* + \delta_k s^k\right) \qquad \sigma_i \in (0,1) \qquad \forall j \in [1,q]$$

Note also that

$$\lim_{k\longrightarrow\infty} a_0^k = \lim_{k\longrightarrow\infty} b_j^k = \lim_{k\longrightarrow\infty} c_i^k = x^*$$

From (2.153), (2.154), and (2.152) we have

$$0 \geq \delta^k \left[\nabla f\left(x^*, 0\right) + \sum_{i\in J^*} \mu_i^* \nabla g_i(x^*, 0) + \sum_{j=1}^{q} v_j^* \nabla h_j(x^*, 0)\right] s^k$$

$$+ \frac{\left(\delta_k\right)^2}{2}\left(s^k\right)^T \left[\nabla^2 f(a_0^k, 0) + \sum_{i\in J^*} \mu_i^* \nabla^2 g_i(b_i^k, 0) + \right. \qquad (2.155)$$

$$\left. \sum_{j=1}^{q} v_j^* \nabla^2 h_j(c_i^k, 0)\right] s^k$$

Taking the limit of (2.155) as $k \longrightarrow \infty$, we obtain

$$\left(\bar{s}\right)^T \nabla^2 L\left(x^*, \mu^*, v^*, 0\right) \bar{s} \leq 0 \qquad (2.156)$$

Thus, we have shown that, if x^* is not a strict local minimum, a contradiction of (2.142) results. As a consequence, enforcement of (2.142) assures x^* is a strict local minimum.

■

We are now in a situation to present and prove our main result on sensitivity analysis:

Theorem 2.22 *(Sensitivity analysis of the perturbed mathematical program MP(ε)) Suppose that in a neighborhood of $(x^*, \xi = 0)$: (i) The functions f, g, and h defining MP(ξ) are twice continuously differentiable with respect to x; the gradients of f, g and h with respect to x are once continuously differentiable with respect to ξ; and the constraint functions g and h are themselves once continuously differentiable with respect to ξ. (ii) The second-order sufficient conditions for a local minimum of MP(0) hold at (x^*, μ^*, v^*). (iii) The gradients $\nabla g_i\left(x^*, 0\right)$ for all $i \in I^* = \{i : g_i(x^*, 0) = 0\}$ are linearly independent, while the gradients $\nabla h_i\left(x^*, 0\right)$ for all $i \in [1, q]$ are also linearly independent. (iv)*

The strict complementary slackness condition

$$\mu_i^* > 0 \text{ when } g_i(x^*, 0) = 0 \tag{2.157}$$

is satisfied. Then the following results obtain:

(1) The point x^* is a local isolated minimum of MP(0) and the associated multipliers $\mu^*(0) \in \Re_+^m$ and $v^*(0) \in \Re^q$ are unique.

(2) For ξ near zero, there exists a unique once continuously differentiable function

$$y(\xi) = \begin{pmatrix} x(\xi) \\ \mu(\xi) \\ v(\xi) \end{pmatrix} \tag{2.158}$$

satisfying the second-order sufficient conditions for a local minimum of MP(ξ) such that $x(\xi)$ is a locally unique solution of MP(ξ) for which $\mu(\xi)$ and $v(\xi)$ are unique multipliers associated with it. Moreover

$$y(0) = \begin{pmatrix} x^* \\ \mu^* \\ \pi^* \end{pmatrix}$$

Furthermore, a first-order differential approximation of $y(\xi)$ is given by

$$y(\xi) = \begin{pmatrix} x^* \\ \mu^* \\ \pi^* \end{pmatrix} + [J_y(0)]^{-1}\left[-J_\xi^*(0)\right]\xi \tag{2.159}$$

where J_y is the Jacobian with respect to y and J_ξ is the Jacobian with respect to ξ of the Kuhn-Tucker system

$$\nabla L(\cdot) = \nabla f(x^*, \xi) + \sum_{i=1}^{m} \mu_i^* \nabla g_i(x^*) + \sum_{j=1}^{q} v_j^* \nabla h_j(x^*) = 0 \tag{2.160}$$

$$\mu^T g(x, \xi) = 0 \tag{2.161}$$

$$h(x, \xi) = 0 \tag{2.162}$$

(3) For ξ near zero, the set of binding inequality constraints is unchanged, strict complementary slackness holds, and the gradients of binding constraints are linearly independent at $x(\xi)$.

Proof. We begin by noting that x^* is a strict local minimum of MP(0) by virtue of assumption (ii), which also requires that

$$\nabla L(x^*, \mu^*, v^*, 0) = 0$$

By virtue of Theorem 2.21, such stationarity of the Lagrangean together with assumption (iii) assures the uniqueness of $\mu^*(0)$ and $v^*(0)$. If Result 2 holds, $x(\xi)$ uniquely solves MP(ξ) for arbitrarily small ξ, and Result 1 follows immediately.

In order to prove Result 2, we first note that assumption (ii) implies the satisfaction of the first-order Kuhn-Tucker system (2.160)–(2.162); by assumption (i), that system is once continuously differentiable with respect to all its arguments. As a consequence, any Jacobian of that same system is well defined. Because the assumptions of the implicit function theorem (Theorem 2.20) relative to the first order Kuhn-Tucker system are satisfied, there exists, in a neighborhood of $y(0)$, a unique once continuously differentiable function $y(\xi)$ satisfying system (2.160)–(2.162) for ξ near zero. Thus, $x(\xi)$ is a locally unique minimum, and $\mu(\xi)$ and $v(\xi)$ are unique multipliers associated with it. Moreover, assumptions (ii), (iii), and (iv) imply that J_y has an inverse at $y(0)$; thus, the differential approximation (2.159) obtains. To complete the proof of Result 2, it remains to show that $y(\xi)$ satisfies the second-order sufficient conditions for a local minimum of MP(ξ). That demonstration is fundamentally similar to the proof of Theorem 2.21 and is not repeated here.

To prove Result 3, we begin by noting that, since $x(\xi)$ solves MP(ξ) per Result 2, $x(\xi)$ satisfies both the perturbed equality and inequality constraints. In particular

$$h_i[x(\xi), \xi] = 0 \qquad \forall i \in [1, p]$$

$$g_i[x(\xi), \xi] \leq 0 \qquad \forall i \in I^*$$

near $\xi = 0$. When $g_i[x(0), 0] = 0$ for some i, we know, by strict complementary slackness for MP(0), that $\mu_i(0) < 0$. By virtue of the continuity of $\mu(\xi)$, it must be that $g_i[x(\xi), \xi] = 0$ and $\mu_i(\xi) > 0$ near $\xi = 0$. Furthermore, if $g_i[x(0), 0] < 0$ for some i, then $g_i[x(\xi), \xi] < 0$ near $\xi_i = 0$, by virtue of continuity. Thus, we have proven that strict complementary slackness holds and the set of the binding constraints does not change at $x(\xi)$. Any subsystem of (2.160)–(2.162) corresponding to binding constraints has an invertible Jacobian near $\xi = 0$, based on our prior observations. Thereby, linear independence of binding constraints is assured. Result 3 is now established; thus, the proof of the theorem itself is complete. ■

2.9 Numerical and Graphical Examples

In this section we provide several numerical and graphical examples meant to test and refine the reader's knowledge of the material on nonlinear programming presented previously. We will need the notions of a level curve C_k and a level set S_k of the objective function $f(x)$ of a mathematical program:

$$C_k = \{x : f(x) = f_k\} \tag{2.163}$$

$$S_k = \{x : f(x) \leq f_k\} \tag{2.164}$$

where f_k signifies a numerical value of the objective function of interest. Solving any mathematical program graphically involves four steps:

(1) Draw the feasible region.

(2) Draw level curves of the objective function.

(3) Choose the optimal level curve by selecting, from the points of tangency of level curves and constraint boundaries, the feasible point or points giving the best objective function value.

(4) Identify the optimal solution as a point of tangency between the optimal level curve and the feasible region.

2.9.1 LP Graphical Solution

Consider the following linear program:

$$\max f(x, y) = x + y$$

subject to

$$3x + 2y \leq 6$$

$$\frac{1}{2}x + y \leq 2$$

For the present example the optimal solution is, by inspection of the LP graphical solution Fig. 2.2, the point

$$x^* = \begin{pmatrix} x_1^* \\ x_2^* \end{pmatrix} = \begin{pmatrix} 1 \\ \frac{3}{2} \end{pmatrix} \tag{2.165}$$

One can easily verify the Kuhn-Tucker conditions hold at this point. To do so, it is helpful to restate the problem as follows:

$$\min f(x, y) = -x - y \tag{2.166}$$

subject to

$$g_1(x, y) = 3x + 2y - 6 \leq 0 \tag{2.167}$$

$$g_2(x, y) = \frac{1}{2}x + y - 2 \leq 0 \tag{2.168}$$

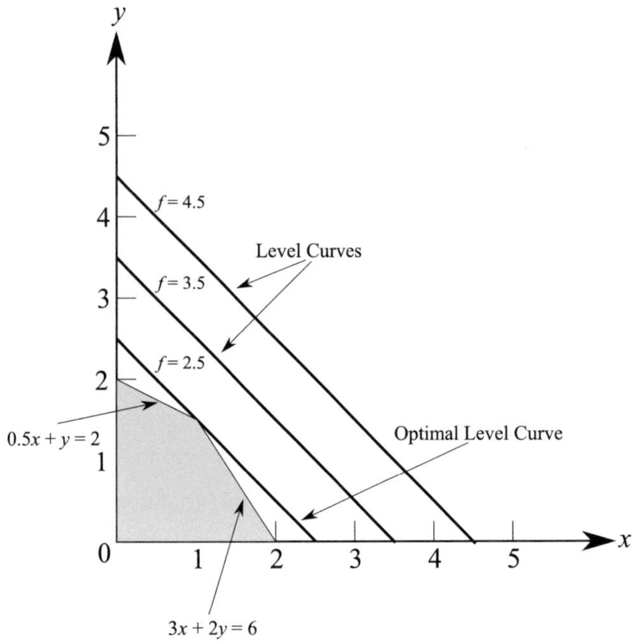

FIGURE 2.2: LP GRAPHICAL SOLUTION

We note that

$$\nabla f(x,y) = \begin{pmatrix} -1 \\ -1 \end{pmatrix} \tag{2.169}$$

$$\nabla g_1(x,y) = \begin{pmatrix} 3 \\ 2 \end{pmatrix} \tag{2.170}$$

$$\nabla g_2(x,y) = \begin{pmatrix} \frac{1}{2} \\ 1 \end{pmatrix} \tag{2.171}$$

The Kuhn-Tucker identity is

$$\nabla f(x_1,x_2) + \lambda_1 \nabla g_1(x_1,x_2) + \lambda_2 \nabla g_2(x_1,x_2) = \begin{pmatrix} 0 \\ 0 \end{pmatrix} \tag{2.172}$$

That is,

$$\begin{pmatrix} -1 \\ -1 \end{pmatrix} + \lambda_1 \begin{pmatrix} 3 \\ 2 \end{pmatrix} + \lambda_2 \begin{pmatrix} \frac{1}{2} \\ 1 \end{pmatrix} = \begin{pmatrix} 0 \\ 0 \end{pmatrix} \tag{2.173}$$

The complementary slackness conditions are

$$\lambda_1 g_1(x_1, x_2) = 0 \quad \lambda_1 \geq 0 \tag{2.174}$$

$$\lambda_2 g_2(x_1, x_2) = 0 \quad \lambda_2 \geq 0 \tag{2.175}$$

Note that the binding constraints define the set

$$I = \left\{ i : g_i\left(1, \frac{3}{2}\right) = 0 \right\} = \{1, 2\} \tag{2.176}$$

and we must find multipliers that obey

$$\lambda_1, \lambda_2 \geq 0 \tag{2.177}$$

It is easy to solve the above system and show

$$\lambda_1 = \frac{1}{4} > 0, \lambda_2 = \frac{1}{2} > 0 \tag{2.178}$$

Hence x^* satisfies the Kuhn-Tucker conditions. Because the problem is a linear program, it is a convex program. Therefore, the Kuhn-Tucker conditions are not only necessary but also sufficient, making x^* a global solution.

2.9.2 NLP Graphical Example

Consider the following nonlinear program

$$\min f(x_1, x_2) = (x_1 - 5)^2 + (x_2 - 6)^2 \tag{2.179}$$

subject to

$$g_1(x_1, x_2) = \frac{1}{2}x_1 + x_2 - 3 \leq 0 \tag{2.180}$$

$$g_2(x_1, x_2) = x_1 - 2 \leq 0 \tag{2.181}$$

The graphical solution presented in Fig. 2.3, following the procedure described above, identifies $(2, 2)$ as the globally optimal solution with a corresponding objective function value of 25. Note that

$$\nabla f(2, 2) = \begin{pmatrix} -8 \\ -6 \end{pmatrix} \tag{2.182}$$

$$\nabla g_1(2, 2) = \begin{pmatrix} \frac{1}{2} \\ 1 \end{pmatrix} \tag{2.183}$$

$$\nabla g_2(2, 2) = \begin{pmatrix} 1 \\ 0 \end{pmatrix} \tag{2.184}$$

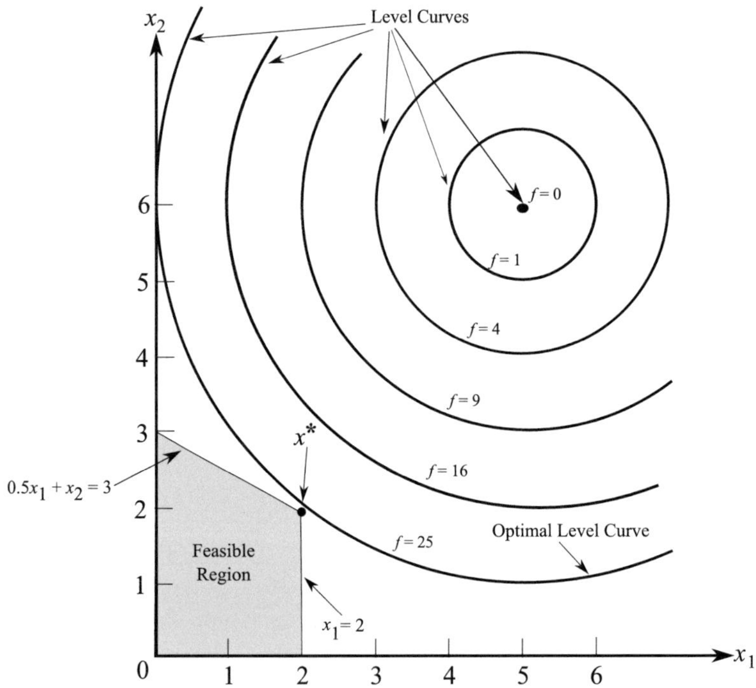

Figure 2.3: NLP Graphical Solution

The Kuhn-Tucker identity is

$$\begin{pmatrix} -8 \\ -6 \end{pmatrix} + \lambda_1 \begin{pmatrix} \frac{1}{2} \\ 1 \end{pmatrix} + \lambda_2 \begin{pmatrix} 1 \\ 0 \end{pmatrix} = \begin{pmatrix} 0 \\ 0 \end{pmatrix} \tag{2.185}$$

The complementary slackness conditions are

$$\lambda_1 g_1(x_1, x_2) = 0 \quad \lambda_1 \geq 0 \tag{2.186}$$

$$\lambda_2 g_2(x_1, x_2) = 0 \quad \lambda_2 \geq 0 \tag{2.187}$$

and

$$I = \{i : g_i(1,2) = 0\} = \{1,2\} \Longrightarrow \lambda_1, \lambda_2 \geq 0 \tag{2.188}$$

Solving the above linear system (2.185) yields multipliers of the correct sign:

$$\lambda_1 = 6 > 0 \tag{2.189}$$

$$\lambda_2 = 5 > 0 \tag{2.190}$$

Consequently, the Kuhn-Tucker conditions are satisfied. Because the program is convex with a strictly convex objective function, we know that the Kuhn-Tucker conditions are both necessary and sufficient for an unique global optimum. So, even without further analysis, we know $(2,2)$ is the unique global optimum.

2.9.3 Nonconvex, Nongraphical Example

Consider the nonlinear program

$$\min \ f(x_1, x_2) = -x_1 + 0x_2 \tag{2.191}$$

subject to

$$g_1(x_1, x_2) = (x_1)^2 + (x_2)^2 - 2 \leq 0 \tag{2.192}$$

$$g_2(x_1, x_2) = x_1 - (x_2)^2 \leq 0 \tag{2.193}$$

Note that the feasible region of this mathematical program is not convex; hence, we will have to enumerate all the combinations of binding and nonbinding constraints in order to solve it using the Kuhn-Tucker conditions alone. We begin by observing that

$$\nabla f(x_1, x_2) = \begin{pmatrix} -1 \\ 0 \end{pmatrix} \tag{2.194}$$

$$\nabla g_1(x_1, x_2) = \begin{pmatrix} 2x_1 \\ 2x_2 \end{pmatrix} \tag{2.195}$$

$$\nabla g_2(x_1, x_2) = \begin{pmatrix} 1 \\ -2x_2 \end{pmatrix} \tag{2.196}$$

The Kuhn-Tucker identity is

$$\begin{pmatrix} -1 \\ 0 \end{pmatrix} + \lambda_1 \begin{pmatrix} 2x_1 \\ 2x_2 \end{pmatrix} + \lambda_2 \begin{pmatrix} 1 \\ -2x_2 \end{pmatrix} = \begin{pmatrix} 0 \\ 0 \end{pmatrix} \tag{2.197}$$

from which we obtain the equations

$$kti1 \ : \ -1 + 2\lambda_1 x_1 + \lambda_2 = 0 \tag{2.198}$$

$$kti2 \ : \ (\lambda_1 - \lambda_2)\, x_2 = 0 \tag{2.199}$$

The complementary slackness conditions are

$$csc1 \ : \ \lambda_1 g_1(x_1, x_2) = 0 \quad \lambda_1 \geq 0 \tag{2.200}$$

$$csc2 \ : \ \lambda_2 g_2(x_1, x_2) = 0 \quad \lambda_2 \geq 0 \tag{2.201}$$

Symbol/Operator	Meaning
$\oplus$	consider two statements
$\Longrightarrow$	the implication of such a consideration
$\pitchfork$	a contradiction has occurred
dno	does not occur

Table 2.1: Some Symbols and Operators

Because there are $N = 2$ inequality constraints, there are $2^N = 2^2 = 4$ possible cases of binding and nonbinding constraints:

Case	g_1	g_2
I	< 0	< 0
II	< 0	$= 0$
III	$= 0$	< 0
IV	$= 0$	$= 0$

(2.202)

It is convenient to use the symbols and operators in Table 2.1 for analyzing each of the four cases. Remembering that we must show each case to either involve a contradiction, thereby indicating that case does not occur, or derive non-negative multipliers that satisfy the Kuhn-Tucker conditions. We present the following analysis:

Case I: $[csc1 \oplus csc2] \Longrightarrow [\lambda_1 = \lambda_2 = 0] \oplus [kti1] \Longrightarrow [-1 = 0 \pitchfork] \Longrightarrow$ dno

Case II: $csc1 \Longrightarrow [\lambda_1 = 0] \oplus [kti1, kti2] \Longrightarrow [\lambda_2 = 1 > 0, \lambda_2 x_2 = 0] \Longrightarrow$

$[x_2 = 0] \oplus \left[g_2 = x_1 - (0)^2 = 0\right] \Longrightarrow csc2$ satisfied $\Longrightarrow$

$\left[x^A = (0,0)^T \text{ is a valid Kuhn-Tucker point}\right]$

Case III: $csc2 \Longrightarrow [\lambda_2 = 0] \oplus [kti1, kti2] \Longrightarrow [-1 + 2\lambda_1 x_1 = 0, \lambda_1 x_2 = 0] \Longrightarrow$

Subcase IIIA: $[\lambda_1 = 0] \oplus [-1 + 2\lambda_1 x_1 = 0] \Longrightarrow [-1 = 0 \pitchfork] \Longrightarrow$ dno

Subcase IIIB: $[\lambda_1 > 0] \oplus [\lambda_1 x_2 = 0] \Longrightarrow$

$[x_2 = 0] \oplus \left[g_1 = (x_1)^2 + (0)^2 - 2 = 0\right] \Longrightarrow$

$\left[x_1 = \pm\sqrt{2}\right] \oplus \left[g_2 = x_1 - (0)^2 \leq 0\right] \Longrightarrow \left[x_1 = -\sqrt{2}\right] \oplus [-1 + 2\lambda_1 x_1 = 0] \Longrightarrow$

$\left[0 \leq \lambda_1 = (2x_1)^{-1} = \left(-2\sqrt{2}\right)^{-1} < 0 \pitchfork\right] \Longrightarrow$ dno

Case IV: $\left[g_1 = (x_1)^2 + (x_2)^2 - 2 = 0\right] \oplus \left[g_2 = x_1 - (x_2)^2 = 0\right] \Longrightarrow$

$[x_1 = 1, x_2 = \pm 1] \oplus [kti1, kti2] \Longrightarrow [-1 + 2\lambda_1 + \lambda_2 = 0, \lambda_1 - \lambda_2 = 0] \Longrightarrow$

$[\lambda_1 = 1/3 > 0, \lambda_2 = 1/3 > 0] \Longrightarrow csc1$ and $csc2$ satisfied $\Longrightarrow$

$\left[x^B = (1,1)^T, x^C = (1,-1)^T \text{ are valid Kuhn-Tucker points}\right].$

The global optimum is found by noting

$$\begin{gathered} f\left(x^A\right) = 0 \\ f\left(x^B\right) = f\left(x^C\right) = -1 < f\left(x^A\right) \end{gathered} \tag{2.203}$$

which means x^B, x^C are alternative global minimizers. Note also that x^A is not a local minimizer.

2.9.4 A Convex, Nongraphical Example

Let us now consider the mathematical program

$$\min \ f(x_1, x_2) = 0x_1 - x_2 \tag{2.204}$$

subject to

$$g_1(x_1, x_2) = (x_1)^2 + (x_2)^2 - 2 \leq 0 \tag{2.205}$$

$$g_2(x_1, x_2) = -x_1 + x_2 \leq 0 \tag{2.206}$$

Note that this problem is a convex mathematical program since the objective function is linear and the inequality constraint functions are convex. We know the Kuhn-Tucker conditions will be both necessary and sufficient for a nonunique global minimum. This means that we need only find one case of binding and nonbinding constraints that leads to non-negative inequality constraint multipliers in order to solve (2.204)–(2.206) to global optimality. We begin by observing that

$$\nabla f\left(x_1, x_2\right) = \begin{pmatrix} 0 \\ -1 \end{pmatrix} \tag{2.207}$$

$$\nabla g_1\left(x_1, x_2\right) = \begin{pmatrix} 2x_1 \\ 2x_2 \end{pmatrix} \tag{2.208}$$

$$\nabla g_2\left(x_1, x_2\right) = \begin{pmatrix} -1 \\ 1 \end{pmatrix} \tag{2.209}$$

The Kuhn-Tucker identity is

$$\begin{pmatrix} 0 \\ -1 \end{pmatrix} + \lambda_1 \begin{pmatrix} 2x_1 \\ 2x_2 \end{pmatrix} + \lambda_2 \begin{pmatrix} -1 \\ 1 \end{pmatrix} = \begin{pmatrix} 0 \\ 0 \end{pmatrix} \tag{2.210}$$

from which we obtain the equations

$$kti1 \ : \ 2\lambda_1 x_1 - \lambda_2 = 0 \tag{2.211}$$

$$kti2 \ : \ -1 + 2\lambda_1 x_2 + \lambda_2 = 0 \tag{2.212}$$

The complementary slackness conditions are

$$csc1 \quad : \quad \lambda_1 g_1(x_1, x_2) = 0 \quad \lambda_1 \geq 0 \tag{2.213}$$

$$csc2 \quad : \quad \lambda_2 g_2(x_1, x_2) = 0 \quad \lambda_2 \geq 0 \tag{2.214}$$

Since the present mathematical program has two constraints, the table (2.202) still applies. Let us posit that both constraints are binding, so that the following analysis applies:

Case IV: $\left[g_1 = (x_1)^2 + (x_2)^2 - 2 = 0\right] \oplus [g_2 = -x_1 + x_2 = 0] \Longrightarrow$

$[x_1^* = x_2^* = 1] \oplus [kti1, kti2] \Longrightarrow [2\lambda_1 - \lambda_2 = 0, -1 + 2\lambda_1 + \lambda_2 = 0] \Longrightarrow$

$\left[\lambda_1 = \frac{1}{4} > 0, \lambda_2 = \frac{1}{2} > 0\right] \Longrightarrow [csc1 \text{ and } csc2 \text{ are satisfied}] \Longrightarrow$

$\left[x^* = (x_1^*, x_2^*)^T = (1,1)^T \text{ is a global minimizer}\right]$

However, since the objective function is only convex and not strictly convex, we cannot ascertain without analyzing the three remaining cases whether this global minimizer is unique. The reader may verify that the other three cases lead to contradictions, and thereby determine that $x^* = (1,1)^T$ is a unique global solution.

2.10 One-Dimensional Optimization

The simplest optimization problems involve a scalar function of one variable, $\theta : \Re^1 \longrightarrow \Re^1$. As is well known, in some cases we can solve such problems by finding the zero of the derivative. Unfortunately, in practice, often one cannot find the zero analytically and must, instead, resort to numerical methods. The algorithms for solving these problems are commonly referred to as *line search* methods. Our specific concern is with problems of the form:

$$\min \theta(x) \quad \text{subject to} \quad L \leq x \leq U \tag{2.215}$$

2.10.1 Derivative-Free Methods

These methods iteratively reduce an *interval of uncertainty*, $[a, b]$, that is initially equal to $[U, L]$. They terminate when the interval of uncertainty reaches a desired length. Since it is sometimes difficult to either know or calculate the derivative of θ, these methods reduce the level of uncertainty at iteration k by evaluating θ at two points in the interval, λ_k and μ_k. The viability of this approach can be summarized as follows:

Theorem 2.23 *Let $\theta : \Re \longrightarrow \Re$ be strictly quasiconvex over $[a, b]$. Let $\lambda, \mu \in [a, b]$ with $\lambda < \mu$. (i) If $\theta(\lambda) > \theta(\mu)$ then $\theta(z) \geq \theta(\mu)$ for all $z \in [a, \lambda)$. (ii) If $\theta(\lambda) \leq \theta(\mu)$ then $\theta(z) \geq \theta(\lambda)$ for all $z \in (\mu, b]$.*

Proof. (i) Suppose $\theta(\lambda) > \theta(\mu)$ and $z \in [a, \lambda)$ and assume that $\theta(z) < \theta(\mu)$. It follows from the strict quasiconvexity of θ that $\theta(\lambda) < \max\{\theta(z), \theta(\mu)\}$ since λ is a convex combination of z and μ. Now, by assumption, $\max\{\theta(z), \theta(\mu)\} = \theta(\mu)$. So, $\theta(\lambda) < \theta(\mu)$ which is a contradiction.

(ii) This portion of the result can be demonstrated in a similar fashion.

■

Using Theorem 2.23, one can create a variety of different methods by varying the way in which λ and μ are selected.

The *golden section method* generates one new test point for each iteration and identifies another test point by either setting $\lambda_{k+1} = \mu_k$ or $\mu_{k+1} = \lambda_k$. That is:

Case 1: $\theta(\lambda_k) > \theta(\mu_k)$

$a_{k+1} = \lambda_k$

$\lambda_{k+1} = \mu_k$

μ_{k+1} is in $[\mu_k, b_k)$

$b_{k+1} = b_k$

Case 2: $\theta(\lambda_k) \leq \theta(\mu_k)$

$a_{k+1} = a_k$

λ_{k+1} is in $(a_k, \lambda_k]$

$\mu_{k+1} = \lambda_k$

$b_{k+1} = \mu_k$

The golden section method chooses the new test point in a way that ensures the length of the new interval of uncertainty does not depend on the outcome of the test at the current iteration. That is, it chooses the test point to ensure that:

$$b_k - \lambda_k = \mu_k - a_k. \tag{2.216}$$

It accomplishes this by choosing λ_k and μ_k as follows:

$$\lambda_k = a_k + (1 - \alpha)(b_k - a_k) \tag{2.217}$$

$$\mu_k = a_k + \alpha(b_k - a_k) \tag{2.218}$$

for $\alpha = 0.618$ which is the *golden ratio* minus 1. (The golden ratio, sometimes known as the divine proportion, has connections with many aspects of mathematics and can be motivated in a variety of different ways. It is the value $\frac{1}{2}(1+\sqrt{5})$.) Since, at each iteration, the interval of uncertainty is reduced by a factor of 0.618, it follows that:

$$(b_k - a_k) = (b_1 - a_1) \cdot 0.618^{k-1} \tag{2.219}$$

The *Fibonacci method* also generates one new test point each iteration, but it allows the reduction in the interval of uncertainty to be different for each iteration. In particular, letting F_k denote the kth Fibonacci number (where $F_0 = 0$, $F_1 = 1$, and $F_k = F_{k-1} + F_{k-2}$), it uses the following rules:

Case 1: $\theta(\lambda_k) > \theta(\mu_k)$

$$\begin{aligned}
a_{k+1} &= \lambda_k \\
\lambda_{k+1} &= \mu_k \\
\mu_{k+1} &= a_{k+1} + (F_{n-k-1}/F_{n-k})(b_{k+1} - a_{k+1}) \\
b_{k+1} &= b_k
\end{aligned}$$

Case 2: $\theta(\lambda_k) \leq \theta(\mu_k)$

$$\begin{aligned}
a_{k+1} &= a_k \\
\lambda_{k+1} &= a_{k+1} + (F_{n-k-2}/F_{n-k})(b_{k+1} - a_{k+1}) \\
\mu_{k+1} &= \lambda_k \\
b_{k+1} &= \mu_k
\end{aligned}$$

Since, at each iteration, the interval of uncertainty is reduced by a factor of F_{n-k}/F_{n-k+1}, it follows that:

$$(b_k - a_k) = (b_1 - a_1)/F_n. \tag{2.220}$$

2.10.2 Bolzano Search

If θ is differentiable and quasi-convex on $[L, U]$ then we can use the derivative of θ at a test point to reduce the interval of uncertainty. Letting x_k denote that (single) test point at iteration k, one can proceed as follows:

Case 1: $d\theta/dx_k < 0$

$$a_{k+1} = x_k$$

x_{k+1} is in $[x_k, b_k)$

$$b_{k+1} = b_k$$

Case 2: $d\theta/dx_k > 0$

$$a_{k+1} = a_k$$
$$x_{k+1} \text{ is in } (a_n, x_k]$$
$$b_{k+1} = x_k$$

The algorithm presented above enjoys the following convergence result:

Theorem 2.24 *Let $\{(a_k, b_k)\}$ denote the sequence generated by Bolzano search, with $b_k \geq a_k$. Then, we have*

(a)

$$(b_k - a_k) = (b_1 - a_1)/2^k$$

(b) When k becomes sufficiently large, the sequence $\{a_k - b_k\}$ converges to zero.

Proof. We separately consider the two cases identified in the theorem. To show (a), it suffices to show, in both cases, we have

$$b_{k+1} - a_{k+1} = \frac{b_k - a_k}{2}$$

Evidently, for Case 1 we have

$$a_{k+1} = \frac{a_k + b_k}{2} \tag{2.221}$$

$$b_{k+1} = b_k \tag{2.222}$$

Thus, $b_{k+1} - a_{k+1} = \frac{b_k - a_k}{2}$. Similarly, for Case 2 we have

$$b_{k+1} = \frac{a_k + b_k}{2} \tag{2.223}$$

$$a_{k+1} = a_k \tag{2.224}$$

Thus, $b_{k+1} - a_{k+1} = \frac{b_k - a_k}{2}$. Part (b) is an immediate result of Part (a). The proof is complete. ■

2.10.3 Newton's Method

Newton's method was originally developed for finding the roots of a function. However it is clear that it can also be used to solve one-dimensional optimization problems simply by finding the first real root of the derivative of the objective function. There are many ways to motivate Newton's method. We will start by considering the following second-order approximation of θ at λ_k:

$$q(\lambda) = \theta(\lambda_k) + \theta'(\lambda_k)(\lambda - \lambda_k) + \frac{1}{2}\theta''(\lambda_k)(\lambda - \lambda_k)^2 \tag{2.225}$$

Our goal at iteration k is to choose λ_{k+1} in such a way that $q'(\lambda) = 0$. Since:

$$q'(\lambda) = \theta'(\lambda_k) + \theta''(\lambda_k)(\lambda - \lambda_k) \tag{2.226}$$

we have:

$$\lambda_{k+1} = \lambda_k - \frac{\theta'(\lambda_k)}{\theta''(\lambda_k)} \tag{2.227}$$

2.10.4 Discretized Newton Methods

Based on (2.227), we may view Newton's method as taking steps along the real line by writing it as follows:

$$\lambda_{k+1} = \lambda_k - \theta''(\lambda_k)^{-1}\theta'(\lambda_k) \tag{2.228}$$

One can discretize this process as follows:

$$\lambda_{k+1} = \lambda_k - \left[\frac{\theta'(\lambda_k + h_k) - \theta'(\lambda_k)}{h_k}\right]^{-1} \theta'(\lambda_k) \tag{2.229}$$

In the *regula falsi method*, $h_k = \overline{\lambda} - \lambda_k$ for some fixed $\overline{\lambda}$, which leads to:

$$\lambda_{k+1} = \lambda_k - \left[\frac{\theta'(\overline{\lambda}) - \theta'(\lambda_k)}{(\overline{\lambda} - \lambda_k)}\right]^{-1} \theta'(\lambda_k) \tag{2.230}$$

In the *secant method*, $h_k = \lambda_{k-1} - \lambda_k$, which leads to:

$$\lambda_{k+1} = \lambda_k - \left[\frac{\theta'(\lambda_{k-1}) - \theta'(\lambda_k)}{(\lambda_{k-1} - \lambda_k)}\right]^{-1} \theta'(\lambda_k) \tag{2.231}$$

2.11 Descent Algorithms in $\Re^n$

For a convex mathematical program with a differentiable objective function and differentiable constraints, a particularly effective solution method is based on the notion of a feasible direction of descent introduced via Definitions 2.4–2.6. The algorithm may be stated as follows:

GENERIC FEASIBLE DIRECTION ALGORITHM

Step 0. *(Initialization)* Determine $x^0 \in X$. Set $k = 0$.

Step 1. *(Feasible direction of descent determination)* Determine a feasible direction of descent. Find d^k such that

$$\begin{aligned} x^k + \theta d^k &\in X \quad \forall \theta \in [0,1] \\ \nabla [Z(x^k)]^T d^k &< 0 \end{aligned}$$

Step 2. *(Step size determination)* Step size determination. Find the optimal step size θ_k where

$$\theta_k = \arg\min\{Z(x^k + \theta d^k) : 0 \leq \theta \leq 1\}$$

Set $x^{k+1} = x^k + \theta_k d^k$.

Step 3. *(Stopping test)* For $\varepsilon \in \Re^1_{++}$, a preset tolerance, if

$$\max_{(i,j)\in\mathcal{A}} |x_{ij}^{k+1} - x_{ij}^k| < \varepsilon$$

stop; otherwise set $k = k + 1$ and go to Step 1.

We will again encounter the above algorithm in Chap. 4. For now it is only necessary to note the algorithm's simplicity and comment that one of its most commonly encountered varieties determines the feasible direction of descent using the notion of a minimum norm projection. The minimum norm projection of a vector v onto the set X is denoted as $P_X(v)$ and defined by

$$P_X(v) = \arg\left\{ \min \|v - x\| \quad \text{subject to} \quad x \in X \right\} \tag{2.232}$$

where $\|.\|$ denotes the chosen norm. It is also important to recognize that the solution of

$$\min \frac{1}{2}(v - x)^2 \equiv \frac{1}{2}(v - x)^T (v - x)$$

subject to

$$x \in X$$

is equivalent to (2.232).

Of special importance to our discussion of algorithms in subsequent chapters is the minimum norm projection for the special case when

$$X = \{x \in \Re^n : L \leq x \leq U\} \tag{2.233}$$

where $L, U \in \Re^n_{++}$ are exogenous constant vectors representing lower and upper bounds. The associated minimum norm projection is a solution of this mathematical program:

$$\min \frac{1}{2}(v - x)^2$$

subject to

$$\begin{aligned} x - U &\leq 0 \quad (\alpha) \\ L - x &\leq 0 \quad (\beta) \end{aligned}$$

The problem's Kuhn-Tucker conditions are

$$\begin{aligned} x - v + \alpha - \beta &= 0 \\ \alpha^T (x - U) &= 0 \\ \beta^T (L - x) &= 0 \\ \alpha &\geq 0 \\ \beta &\geq 0 \end{aligned}$$

We may relax the original constraints and employ the Kuhn-Tucker conditions to state the solution of problem's optimality conditions as

$$x = \begin{cases} v & \text{if} \quad L < x < U \\ L & \text{if} \quad x \leq L \\ U & \text{if} \quad x \geq U \end{cases} \equiv [v]_L^U$$

where, on the right side of the above expression, x is now viewed as the unconstrained solution of the program.

If there are only nonnegativity constraints, the program of interest is

$$\min \frac{1}{2} (v - x)^2$$

subject to

$$-x \leq 0$$

Its solution may be conveniently summarized as

$$x = \begin{cases} v & \text{if} \quad x > 0 \\ 0 & \quad\quad x \leq 0 \end{cases} = \max(0, v) \equiv [v]_+$$

where x is again the unconstrained solution.

2.12 References and Additional Reading

Armacost, R., & Fiacco, A. V. (1974). Computational experience in sensitivity analysis for nonlinear programming. *Mathematical Programming, 6*, 301–326.

Armacost, R., & Fiacco, A. V. (1978). Sensitivity analysis for parametric nonlinear programming using penalty methods. *Computational and Mathematical Programming, 502*, 261–269.

Avriel, M. (1976). *Nonlinear programming: Analysis and applications.* Englewood Cliffs, NJ: PrenticeHall.

Bazarra, M. S., Sherali, H. D., & Shetty, C. M. (2006). *Nonlinear programming: Theory and algorithms.* Hoboken, NJ: John Wiley

Fiacco, A. V. (1983) *Introduction to sensitivity and stability analysis in nonlinear programming,* (367 pp.) New York: Academic.

Fiacco, A. V. (1973). Sensitivity analysis for nonlinear programming using penalty methods. *Technical Report*, Serial no. T-275, Institution for Management Science and Engineering, The George Washington University.

Fiacco, A. V., & McCormick G. P. (1968). *Nonlinear programming: Sequential unconstrained minimization techniques.* New York: John Wiley.

Hestenes, M. R. (1975). *Optimization theory: the finite dimensional case.* (464 pp.) New York: Wiley.

Mangasarian, O. (1969). *Nonlinear programming.* New York: McGraw-Hill.

3

Elements of Graph Theory

In an informal way, Chap. 1 began the process of both explaining why networks arise in the study of infrastructure and confirming that the spatial organization of infrastructure most generally takes the form of networks. We saw that these networks are conveniently described by mathematical models that have many common features, regardless of the particular technology and decision environment studied. However, a deeper look at infrastructure network models, which is our goal in the balance of this book, requires that we make more precise the definitions, concepts and notation introduced informally in Chap. 1.

As can easily be imagined, the fundamental cornerstone of any network model is the symbolic articulation of the essential properties of the network being studied. Certain notation has been evolved for this purpose by mathematicians and engineers who study networks; this notation must be thoroughly mastered before one can comprehend the mathematical models of different types of networks that are emphasized in subsequent chapters of this book. Fortunately, with a few exceptions, this notation accords closely with common sense and everyday experience. However, when misunderstandings of the fundamental notational conventions do occur, errors in implementation of an existing network model or innovation of a new network model to fit some special circumstance will occur. A little extra time spent now to master the fundamental notation will be more than repaid in later chapters that require fluency in the mathematical language of networks.

In this chapter we present some notation for studying network flow and routing problems along with a statement of the linear minimum cost flow problem. Subsequent to that discussion, we present some well-known network models that are special cases of the linear minimum cost flow problem, along with specialized algorithms for their solution. Our treatment is by no means exhaustive; neither is it balanced. Instead, we provide the minimum background in graph theory and specialized network optimization algorithms needed for the study of more advanced, infrastructure-related network optimization and equilibrium algorithms in subsequent chapters. A reading list at

T.L. Friesz, D. Bernstein, *Foundations of Network Optimization and Games*,
Complex Networks and Dynamic Systems 3,
DOI 10.1007/978-1-4899-7594-2_3

the end of this chapter provides references for further study. A particularly excellent introductory treatment of graph theory is contained in the book by Larson and Odoni (1981), while a more advanced text is that of Christofides (1975). Another excellent reference is Ahuja et al. (1993).

The following is an outline of the principal topics covered in this chapter:

Section 3.1: Terms from Graph Theory. In this section, we introduce the terminology employed in graph theory.

Section 3.2: Network Notation. In this section, we introduce notation for studying and modeling networks.

Section 3.3: Network Structure. We give a formal definition of what is meant by "network structure."

Section 3.4: Labeling Algorithms. In this section, we introduce the important class of algorithms known as "labeling algorithms." In particular, we present a labeling algorithm for the minimum path problem.

Section 3.5: Solving the Linear Minimum Cost Flow Problem. In this section, we discuss how graph-theoretic techniques may be used to solve the linear minimum cost flow problem.

Section 3.6: Hamiltonian Walks and the Traveling Salesman Problem. We present the famous traveling salesman problem (TSP), although discussion of an algorithm for the TSP is postponed until a subsequent chapter.

3.1 Terms from Graph Theory

A *simple graph*, $G(\mathcal{N}, \mathcal{A})$, is comprised of the pair $(\mathcal{N}, \mathcal{A})$ where $\mathcal{N}$ is a nonempty, finite set of distinct *vertices* (or *nodes*), and $\mathcal{A}$ is a finite set of distinct unordered pairs of elements of $\mathcal{N}$ called *arcs* (or *edges* or *links*). In general, a link (v, w) is said to *join* the vertices v and w. Note that there can never be more than one link joining any two vertices in a simple graph since $\mathcal{A}$ by definition contains distinct elements. Also note that since links can only join distinct vertices, simple graphs cannot contain *loops*, where a *loop* is understood to be a link connecting a given node with itself.[1] In a *directed graph* (or *digraph*), the link set $\mathcal{A}$ contains ordered pairs of elements of $\mathcal{N}$.

For our initial purposes, a *network* will be a directed simple graph. Shortly, we shall introduce the concept of a *multicopy network*, which will require that the underlying graph be a directed nonsimple graph without loops, for which there may be multiple arcs connecting the same pair of nodes.

Two nodes of a graph G are said to be *adjacent* if there is a link joining them, and the link is then said to be *incident* to those nodes. Similarly, two distinct links are said to be adjacent if they have at least one node in common. The *degree* (or *valency*) of a node v is the number of links incident to it and

[1] A *general graph* (or simply a *graph*) can contain multiple links between two vertices as well as loops.

is often written as $\rho(v)$. Any node of degree 0 is said to be *isolated*, and any node of degree 1 is said to be an *end-node.*

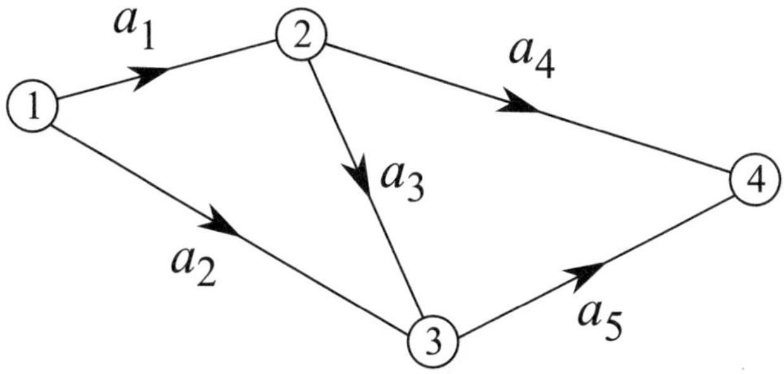

FIGURE 3.1: EXAMPLE NETWORK

If G is a network with node set $\{1, 2, \ldots, m\}$, we define its *adjacency matrix* to be the $m \times m$ matrix whose ijth entry is the number of links joining i and j. If, in addition, the link-set is $\{1, 2, \ldots, n\}$, we define its *incidence matrix* to be the $m \times n$ matrix whose ijth entry is 1 if link j is incident to and directed away from node i, -1 if link j is incident to and directed toward node i, and 0 otherwise.

A network in which the members of each pair of distinct vertices are adjacent is called a *complete network.* A network in which every vertex has the same degree is called a *regular network.* If the vertex set of network, G can be split into two disjoint sets, $\mathcal{N}_1$ and $\mathcal{N}_2$, in a such a way that every arc of G joins a node in $\mathcal{N}_1$ to a node in $\mathcal{N}_2$, then G is said to be *bipartite.*

Given a graph G, a *walk* in G is a finite sequence of connected arcs of the form (v_0, v_1), (v_1, v_2), $\cdots$,$(v_{k-1,} v_k)$ and is sometimes written as $v_1 \longrightarrow \ldots \longrightarrow v_{k-1} \longrightarrow v_k$. The vertex v_0 is referred to as the *initial vertex* and the vertex v_k is referred to as the *final vertex.* A walk in which all the edges are distinct is called a *trail*, and a trail in which all the vertices are distinct is called a *path.* A path in which $v_0 = v_k$ is called a *circuit* or *cycle.*

A general graph G is said to be *connected* if given any pair of vertices, v and w, there is a path from v to w. A graph that contains no circuits is said to be a *forest*, and a connected forest is called a *tree.* A tree that connects all of the nodes of a graph G is called a *spanning tree* of G. A *plane graph* is a graph drawn in the plane such that no two links (really the curves representing those links) intersect geometrically except at a node to which they are both incident.

We are often concerned with the concept of connectedness of networks. A network is said to be connected if the associated graph *ignoring the directionality of the links* is connected. So, when we talk about a set of links forming a spanning tree for a network, we mean that if the links were undirected they would form a spanning tree. As an example, let us consider the network of Fig. 3.1, for which the network of Fig. 3.2 is a spanning tree. This is so even though directionality of the arcs makes it impossible to actually reach node 2 from nodes 1 and 4 using only the arcs of the spanning tree.

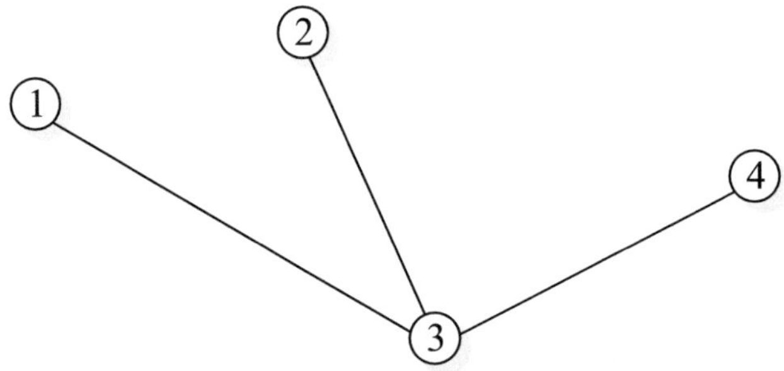

FIGURE 3.2: SPANNING TREE FOR EXAMPLE NETWORK

3.2 Network Notation

The words "network" and "graph" are sometimes used as synonyms in the technical literature, although we have emphasized above that a *network* will be a graph that has no loops. Also, in practice, most infrastructure networks are connected in the sense that, *ignoring directionality*, there is a path from any node to any other node. In this book, unless otherwise stated, any infrastructure network is a graph that has no loops and is connected in the sense just noted. Furthermore, actual infrastructure networks may be based on simple or nonsimple graphs.

3.2.1 Single Copy Networks

Let us consider for the time being only networks that accommodate the flows of a single homogeneous commodity. When we speak of flows of this single commodity, we are referring to some measure of quantity (tons, gallons, etc.) per unit time (hour, day, year, etc.). That is, when we speak of network flows, we are describing rates at which the commodity of interest moves over the arcs and across the nodes of the network. Unless otherwise stated, these flows will be continuous. The homogeneity of the commodity means that it has no attributes that require the commodity to be divided into separate classes and, hence, that we need use only a single copy of the network to model flows.

It is often convenient when working with network models to denote arcs by their tail (or "from") and head (or "to") nodes. Thus, a particular arc will be denoted as $(i,j) \in \mathcal{A}$. This notation can be confusing in that the elements of vectors will appear to have two subscripts. For example, the vector of fixed unit arc costs $c = (\ldots, c_{ij}, \ldots)^T$ is comprised of scalars c_{ij} referring to the cost on arc (i,j) and is not the ijth element of some matrix. This paired subscript notation has withstood the test of time and is generally quite useful. When the network of interest is based on a nonsimple graph, for which there may be more than one arc for each pair of nodes, the paired subscript notation cannot be used; rather we must give each arc its own unique name, such as a, which is employed as a subscript to define entities that are arc-specific. So the vector of unit arc costs becomes $c = (\ldots, c_a, \ldots)^T$ where c_a refers to the cost on arc a. It is important to note that even when this latter notation is employed every arc name a will refer to a unique ordered pair (i, j) where i is the tail node and j is the head node of arc a, although the converse is not necessarily true. That is, if for a directed nonsimple graph we are given the pair (i, j) and no other information, we have no way of associating an unique arc with it.

Next, consider an arbitrary network based on the simple graph G with node set $\mathcal{N} = \{1, \ldots, m\}$ and directed link set $\mathcal{A} = \{1, \ldots, n\}$. All links point out of exactly one node and into exactly one other node. Let us create a matrix in which the columns represent the n links; the rows represent the m nodes; and any element a_{ij} equals $+1$ if the link connecting nodes i and j is (i, j), while a_{ij} equals -1 if the connecting link is (j, i). The resulting matrix $A = (a_{ij} : i = 1, \ldots, m,\ j = 1, \ldots, n)$ has an extremely important property we explore in some depth in Chap. 4: total unimodularity. Briefly stated, a matrix is *totally unimodular* if every column has exactly one $+1$ entry and one -1 entry while all other entries are zero.

For the general case, the *node-arc incidence* matrix is a matrix with columns corresponding to each network arc (i, j); in particular, the ijth column of A is

$$[A]_{ij} = \begin{bmatrix} a_{ij}^1 \\ a_{ij}^2 \\ \vdots \\ a_{ij}^m \end{bmatrix}, \tag{3.1}$$

for which

$$a_{ij}^k = \begin{cases} +1 & \text{if } k = i \\ -1 & \text{if } k = j \\ 0 & \text{otherwise} \end{cases} \tag{3.2}$$

and the index k denotes the node whose flow conservation statement is placed in row k. Note also that the column $[A]_{ij} = \mathbf{1}_j - \mathbf{1}_i$ where $\mathbf{1}_i$ denotes a vector with a 1 in position i and zeroes elsewhere

Another entity, already referred to above, that characterizes a network is the *cost vector*:

$$c = \begin{bmatrix} \vdots \\ c_{ij} \\ \vdots \end{bmatrix} \in \Re^{|\mathcal{A}|} \tag{3.3}$$

where c_{ij} is the unit cost of flow[2] on every arc, $|\mathcal{A}|$ is the cardinality of the set

[2]By unit cost of flow, we mean the cost per unit of flow or average cost of flow:

$$c_{ij} = \frac{\text{total cost of flow on link } (i, j)}{\text{flow on link } (i, j)}.$$

$\mathcal{A}$, and $\Re^{|\mathcal{A}|}$ is $|\mathcal{A}|$-dimensional Euclidean space. A vector defined conformally with the cost vector is the *flow vector*:

$$x = \begin{bmatrix} \vdots \\ x_{ij} \\ \vdots \end{bmatrix} \in \Re^{|\mathcal{A}|} \tag{3.4}$$

where x_{ij} is the flow on arc (i, j). Consequently, the objective of minimizing the total costs of flow may be expressed as

$$\min c^T x \tag{3.5}$$

where of course $c^T x$ is the scalar product.

Finally, we denote the vector of net supplies at each node of the network by

$$b = \begin{bmatrix} \vdots \\ b_k \\ \vdots \end{bmatrix} \in \Re^{|\mathcal{N}|} \tag{3.6}$$

where b_k is the net supply at node $k \in \mathcal{N}$, $|\mathcal{N}|$ is the cardinality of the set $\mathcal{N}$ and $\Re^{|\mathcal{N}|}$ is $|\mathcal{N}|$-dimensional Euclidean space. It is immediate from the above that the flow conservation constraints take the form

$$Ax = b \tag{3.7}$$

It will frequently be the case that the arc flows are constrained from above and below; that is

$$L_{ij} \leq x_{ij} \leq U_{ij} \qquad (i, j) \in \mathcal{A} \tag{3.8}$$

where L_{ij} is a known exogenous lower bound on flow and U_{ij} is a known exogenous upper bound on flow on arc $(i, j) \in \mathcal{A}$. By defining the vectors of bounds

$$U = \begin{bmatrix} \vdots \\ U_{ij} \\ \vdots \end{bmatrix} \in \Re^{|\mathcal{A}|} \tag{3.9}$$

$$L = \begin{bmatrix} \vdots \\ L_{ij} \\ \vdots \end{bmatrix} \in \Re^{|\mathcal{A}|} \tag{3.10}$$

the constraints (3.8) are easily restated; in fact

$$L \leq x \leq U \tag{3.11}$$

is that restatement.

The preceding notation allows the problem of minimizing the total cost of flow subject to constraints on flow conservation and nonnegativity to be stated as:

$$\left.\begin{array}{ll} & \min c^T x \\ \text{subject to} & \\ & Ax = b \\ & U \geq x \geq L \end{array}\right\} \qquad (3.12)$$

This problem and several of its variants are known as the *single commodity linear minimum cost flow problem* when c is a constant vector. We will use the convention that any linear minimum cost flow problem (LMCFP) is single commodity in nature unless otherwise stated. We will have much more to say about the LMCFP shortly. For now, we merely note that the LMCFP is a fundamental problem of network analysis in the sense that many other network problems may be viewed as generalizations or simplifications of it, as we shall see.

3.2.2 Multicopy Networks

Now consider a generalization of the single copy, simple network wherein there may be more than one arc joining any given pair of nodes. Such a network is by its vary nature *nonsimple.* The need to employ such nonsimple networks arises because:

(1) multiple, physically distinct infrastructures in the form of arcs directly connect pairs of nodes of the network; or

(2) distinct classes of flows operate over the same physical arcs and nodes used to describe the infrastructure of interest.

We shall see that both of the above circumstances may be viewed as essentially mathematically the same.

In particular, when there are distinct flow classes, it is frequently desirable to employ a so-called *multicopy network formulation* created from the original network. In a multicopy network, we make fictitious class-specific copies of each real physical network arc, and sometimes copies of the real physical nodes when appropriate, to create, in effect, coupled class-specific networks. Collectively these coupled class-specific networks are called a *multicopy network.* We will see in the following discussion that, by identifying each arc with a specific class, it is possible to avoid the explicit use of indices to identify classes, resulting in much simplified notation. Furthermore, this simplified multicopy notation will be identical to that of a single class problem on a nonsimple network, provided we correctly account for the coupling of the various class-specific subnetworks.

The separate classes of flows referred to above arise when there are disparate types of commodities (a multicommodity problem) requiring that separate classes be defined to describe class-specific costs or other essential aspects of network flow. New notation is required because we cannot employ variables subscripted by i and j to denote the flow on arc $a = (i, j)$ of a multicopy network since the underlying graph is nonsimple and there will potentially be more than one arc joining real physical node i to real physical node j.

To develop this notation, suppose we have a real physical network based on the graph $G\left(\mathcal{N}^R, \mathcal{A}^R\right)$ with a set of flow classes $\mathcal{K}$. We could use the superscript k to denote a specific class $k \in \mathcal{K}$. This means that for a given physical arc $a \in \mathcal{A}^R$ we could define distinct flow variables f_a^k, one for each class $k \in \mathcal{K}$. Each flow f_a^k will of course have the units of quantity (also called volume) per unit time, but the quantity (volume) will not necessarily be expressed in the same units for each class. Consequently, it may occur that if two classes $k \in \mathcal{K}$ and $l \in \mathcal{K}$ are truly distinct, the corresponding arc flows f_a^k and f_a^l will not be commensurable: they cannot be directly added, but must be first expressed in terms of a common numeraire before addition is possible.

However, an alternative to the use of $k \in \mathcal{K}$ subscripts is to *create a multicopy network*. This process is most easily understood by first focusing on a single arc of the real network, say arc $a \in \mathcal{A}^R$, and imagining that arc to be copied $|\mathcal{K}|$ times, where $|\mathcal{K}|$ is the cardinality of the set $\mathcal{K}$. We will refer to the original arc $a \in \mathcal{A}^R$ as the *real physical arc*. We will denote the various copies by $a_1, a_2, \ldots, a_{|\mathcal{K}|}$ having the same head node and tail node as $a \in \mathcal{A}^R$, where a_k is called the kth *copy* of $a \in \mathcal{A}^R$. In making these copies, we have in effect increased the number of arcs in the network, and we denote the set of arcs in the multicopy network by $\mathcal{A}$. The cardinality of $\mathcal{A}$, that is $|\mathcal{A}|$, is consistent with having made $|\mathcal{K}|$ copies of each real physical arc; thus

$$|\mathcal{A}| = |\mathcal{K}| \cdot \left|\mathcal{A}^R\right| \tag{3.13}$$

If we make copies in this fashion for every arc, we have a network in which each arc $a \in \mathcal{A}$ carries only a single class of flow; the arcs are naturally partitioned into class-specific subsets $\mathcal{A}_k$ where

$$\begin{aligned} \mathcal{A}_k &\subset \mathcal{A} \qquad && k \in \mathcal{K} \\ \mathcal{A}_k \bigcap \mathcal{A}_l &= \emptyset && k \neq l \text{ and } k, l \in \mathcal{K} \\ \bigcup_{k \in \mathcal{K}} \mathcal{A}_k &= \mathcal{A} \end{aligned}$$

We also introduce at this time the notation $\xi \risingdotseq a \in \mathcal{A}^R$, which signifies that arc $\xi \in \mathcal{A}$ is a copy of $a \in \mathcal{A}^R$.

When a multicopy formulation is employed, something very interesting happens to the functional dependencies of associated arc unit costs. In particular, a flow-dependent unit cost function for arc $\xi \in \mathcal{A}$ when $\xi \risingdotseq a \in \mathcal{A}^R$, that is, when ξ is a copy of the real physical arc $a \in \mathcal{A}^R$, must necessarily depend on

$$\left(f_a^1, f_a^2, \ldots, f_a^{|\mathcal{K}|}\right)$$

The arc cost functions

$$c_a\left(f_a^1, f_a^2, \ldots, f_a^{|\mathcal{K}|}\right) \qquad a \in \mathcal{A}^R$$

are replaced by

$$c_\xi\left(f_\gamma : \gamma \risingdotseq a \in \mathcal{A}^R\right) \qquad \forall \xi \risingdotseq a \in \mathcal{A}^R$$

where $\left(f_\gamma : \gamma \risingdotseq a \in \mathcal{A}^R\right)$ is a vector of interacting flows on the multiple copies of arc a. That is, on the multicopy network, we may view arc unit cost functions as depending on *all* the non-own flows that are copies of the same physical arc and the superscripts $k \in \mathcal{K}$ may be suppressed.

Further reflection suggests that many network technologies involve the interaction of flows on one arc with flows on another, physically distinct arc. An elementary example is provided by automobile traffic networks, wherein traffic on real physical arc $a \in \mathcal{A}^R$ interacts with traffic on real physical arc $b \in \mathcal{A}^R$ at an intersection where the two arcs meet. As a consequence, the unit cost of flow on arc $\xi \in \mathcal{A}$ where $\xi \risingdotseq a \in \mathcal{A}^R$, again must necessarily depend on $\left(f_a^1, f_a^2, \ldots, f_a^{|\mathcal{K}|}\right)$ and now also on

$$\left(f_b^1, f_b^2, \ldots, f_b^{|\mathcal{K}|}\right),$$

the vector of class-specific flows on arc $b \in \mathcal{A}^R$. The arc cost functions

$$c_a\left(f_a^1, f_a^2, \ldots, f_a^{|\mathcal{K}|}, f_b^1, f_b^2, \ldots, f_b^{|\mathcal{K}|}\right)$$

$$c_b\left(f_a^1, f_a^2, \ldots, f_a^{|\mathcal{K}|}, f_b^1, f_b^2, \ldots, f_b^{|\mathcal{K}|}\right)$$

are replaced by

$$c_\xi\left(f_\gamma : \gamma \risingdotseq a, b \in \mathcal{A}^R\right) \qquad \forall \xi \risingdotseq a, b \in \mathcal{A}^R$$

where $\left(f_\gamma : \gamma \risingdotseq a, b \in \mathcal{A}^R\right)$ is a vector of interacting flows on the copied arcs. It is easy to see that by considering all possible inter-arc and intra-arc interactions, we are led to unit cost functions that depend on the full vector of arc flows of the multicopy network:

$$f = (f_a : a \in \mathcal{A}) \tag{3.14}$$

So, for convenience, we frequently presume from the outset that the network of interest is multicopy in nature and that its unit cost functions are of the form

$$c_a(f) \qquad a \in \mathcal{A} \tag{3.15}$$

That is, we view each arc as carrying a specific class of flow; the identity of that class is known from the arc's name (through a correspondence table). Moreover, congestion on any arc $a \in \mathcal{A}$ potentially depends on the flow activity of all arcs of the network. Sometimes beginning students question how the dependency (3.15) may be used to describe networks for which the cost on arc $a \in \mathcal{A}$ depends only on selected arcs $b \in S(a) \subset \mathcal{A}$ where $b \neq a$ and not on the full vector of network flows f. This is easily answered by including appropriate trivial flow dependencies in the arc unit cost function:

$$c_a(f) = \psi_a(f_a, f_b : b \in S(a) \subset \mathcal{A}) + \sum_{b \in [\mathcal{A} \backslash S(a)]} 0 \cdot f_b$$

where $S(a)$ is the set of arcs whose flows interact with those of arc $a \in \mathcal{A}$, while $[\mathcal{A} \backslash S(a)]$ is the set of arcs that do *not* influence flow on arc $a \in \mathcal{A}$, and $\psi_a(.)$ is the nontrivial portion of unit cost on arc $a \in \mathcal{A}$.

3.2.3 Remarks on Algorithm Complexity

It is customary to provide an assessment of complexity for finite network optimization algorithms. Complexity is generally expressed as the upper bound on the number of *elementary operations* needed to find an optimal solution under worst-case conditions. An elementary operation is any one of the arithmetic operations of addition, subtraction, multiplication and division together with the comparison of two numbers and branching instructions. The number of operations is generally articulated in terms of some characteristic parameter of the problem being studied, say n.

A distinction is made between *polynomially bounded* algorithms and *exponentially bounded* algorithms. Briefly stated, a polynomially bounded algorithm is one whose complexity is proportional to n^γ, where γ is some positive real number (frequently a positive integer) and we write $O(n^\gamma)$ to express this fact. By contrast, an exponentially bounded algorithm is one whose complexity is proportional to γ^n, where again γ is a positive real number, and we write $O(\gamma^n)$ to express this fact. Evidently, a polynomial worst case bound is vastly superior to an exponential bound when the characteristic parameter n is large.

3.3 Network Structure

In this section we extend the discussion of the formulation and qualitative properties of the single commodity minimum cost flow problem introduced in the previous section. Recall that, in its most general form, the single commodity minimum cost flow problem seeks to determine a least cost shipment of known nodal supplies of a single commodity through the network of interest in order to satisfy known nodal demands. The unit (or average) costs of flow on each arc are allowed to be functions of flow levels on own arcs in order to reflect congestion. When the unit arc costs are constant (i.e., they do not vary with flow levels), we obtain the previously introduced *linear minimum cost flow problem*. As we will discuss subsequently, several of the most important classical network flow problems are special cases of the single commodity linear minimum cost flow problem.

Every single commodity minimum cost flow problem exhibits a kind of special structure to its constraint matrix that we call *network structure*. This special structure has very important implications for computation, allowing efficient calculations and the relaxation of integrality constraints under appropriate conditions.

3.3.1 The Nonlinear Minimum Cost Flow Problem

Recall the following notation introduced previously in narrative form and reiterated here for convenience:

$\mathcal{A}$	the set of arcs with cardinality $\lvert\mathcal{A}\rvert = n$
$\mathcal{N}$	the set of nodes with cardinality $\lvert\mathcal{N}\rvert = m$
$G(\mathcal{N}, \mathcal{A})$	graph describing the relationship among nodes and arcs
$[(i,j) \in \mathcal{A}\,]$	an arbitrary arc of the network
x_{ij}	the continuous flow on arc $(i,j) \in \mathcal{A}$ of the single commodity
$c_{ij}(x_{ij})$	the unit (average) cost of flow on arc $(i,j) \in \mathcal{A}$
b_i	the net supply at node $i \in \mathcal{N}$
$\left(L_{ij} \in \Re^1_+\right)$	the lower bound on flow on $(i,j) \in \mathcal{A}$
$\left(U_{ij} \in \Re^1_{++}\right)$	the upper bound on flow on $(i,j) \in \mathcal{A}$

We are concerned with routing a single type of commodity simultaneously between multiple sources and sinks so as to minimize the total cost of flow. The *nonlinear minimum cost flow problem* (NMCFP) may be stated using the above notation as follows:

$$\min \sum_{(i,j)\in A} c_{ij}(x_{ij})\, x_{ij} \tag{3.16}$$

subject to

$$\sum_{i:(i,j)\in\mathcal{A}} x_{ij} - \sum_{i:(j,i)\in\mathcal{A}} x_{ji} = b_i \qquad \forall i \in N \tag{3.17}$$

$$L_{ij} \le x_{ij} \le U_{ij} \qquad \forall\, (i,j) \in A \tag{3.18}$$

Clearly, the linear minimum cost flow problem (3.12) is a special case of the above formulation.

Note that presently the *unit costs are separable functions*; that is to say, each unit arc cost depends only on the flow on its own arc. Note also that constraints (3.17) describe flow conservation at each node of the network, and constraints (3.18) enforce known bounds on arc flows. A compact way of writing formulation (3.16)–(3.18) is

$$\left.\begin{array}{r} \min\ [c(x)]^T x \\ \text{subject to} \quad Ax = b \\ U \geq x \geq L \\ x \in \Re^n \\ \text{matrix } A \text{ has network structure} \end{array}\right\} \text{MCFP} \tag{3.19}$$

where

$$\begin{aligned} c(x) &\equiv (c_{ij}(x_{ij}) : (i,j) \in \mathcal{A}) \in \Re^{|\mathcal{A}|} \\ b &\in \Re^{|\mathcal{N}|} = (b_i : i \in \mathcal{N})^T \\ x &\in \Re^{|\mathcal{A}|} \\ L &\in \Re^{|\mathcal{A}|} \\ U &\in \Re^{|\mathcal{A}|} \end{aligned}$$

and A is an $|\mathcal{A}| \times |\mathcal{N}|$ matrix of coefficients needed to replicate the flow conservation constraints (3.17) and having a special structure we call *network structure*. Since we assume that the cardinality of the set of arcs is $|\mathcal{A}| = n$ and the cardinality of the set of nodes is $|\mathcal{N}| = m$, the matrix A is $n \times m$. As we have previously noted, the matrix A is extremely important. So, in the next section, we take some time to become familiar with it and to give a rigorous definition of the notion of network structure.

3.3.2 Linear Example of Network Structure

To that end consider the example network given in Fig. 3.3 for which $\mathcal{N} = \{1, 2, 3, 4, 5\}$ and $\mathcal{A} = \{(1,2), (1,3), (2,4), (2,5), (3,4), (4,5)\}$. That is, the network consists of five nodes ($m = 5$) and six arcs ($n = 6$). Let us assume

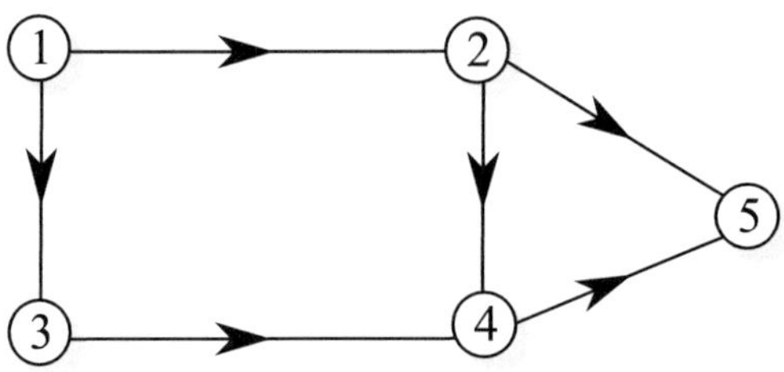

Figure 3.3: An Illustration of Network Structure

that the nodal net supplies are

$$\begin{aligned} b_1 &= 50 \text{ (supply)} \\ b_5 &= -50 \text{ (demand)} \\ b_i &= 0 \text{ for } i = 2, 3, 4 \text{ (transshipment)} \end{aligned}$$

As a consequence, the flow conservation constraints by node are:

$$\begin{array}{llll} \text{Node 1:} & x_{12} + x_{13} & = 50 & \text{(supply)} \\ \text{Node 2:} & x_{24} + x_{25} - x_{12} & = 0 & \text{(transshipment)} \\ \text{Node 3:} & x_{34} - x_{13} & = 0 & \text{(transshipment)} \\ \text{Node 4:} & x_{45} - x_{24} - x_{34} & = 0 & \text{(transshipment)} \\ \text{Node 5:} & -x_{25} - x_{45} & = -50 & \text{(demand)} \end{array}$$

The pertinent vectors describing flows, arc unit costs and nodal net supplies are

$$\begin{aligned} x &= (x_{12}, x_{13}, x_{24}, x_{25}, x_{34}, x_{45})^T \\ c &= (c_{12}, c_{13}, c_{24}, c_{25}, c_{34}, c_{45})^T \\ b &= (+50, 0, 0, 0, -50)^T \end{aligned}$$

Moreover, the A matrix corresponds to the following tableau:

	x_{12}	x_{13}	x_{24}	x_{25}	x_{34}	x_{45}	b_i
Node 1	+1	+1	0	0	0	0	50
Node 2	−1	0	+1	+1	0	0	0
Node 3	0	−1	0	0	+1	0	0
Node 4	0	0	−1	0	−1	+1	0
Node 5	0	0	0	−1	0	−1	−50

That is to say

$$A = \begin{pmatrix} 1 & 1 & 0 & 0 & 0 & 0 \\ -1 & 0 & 1 & 1 & 0 & 0 \\ 0 & -1 & 0 & 0 & 1 & 0 \\ 0 & 0 & -1 & 0 & -1 & 1 \\ 0 & 0 & 0 & -1 & 0 & -1 \end{pmatrix}$$

Note that every column of A has exactly one $+1$ and one -1; all other entries are 0. Any matrix with this property is said to have *network structure*. Flow conservation constraints always give rise to an A matrix with network structure. Any mathematical program whose constraints (other than upper and lower bounds on decision variables) cause the associated A matrix to have network structure is said to be a *mathematical program with network structure*.

3.3.3 Formal Definitions

We formalize the above observations regarding network structure for arc variable formulations of the minimum cost flow problem in the following two definitions:

Definition 3.1 (Matrix with network structure) Any matrix A with the property that every column has exactly one $+1$ and one -1 entry, with all other entries zero, is said to have network structure.

Definition 3.2 (Mathematical program with network structure) A mathematical program with the property that its constraints, excluding lower and upper variable bounds or integrality restrictions, may be stated in the linear form $Ax = b$ where A has network structure is said to be a mathematical program with network structure.

Network structure means that the column of A corresponding to the flow variable x_{ij} can be written as

$$a(i,j) = \begin{pmatrix} 0 \\ 0 \\ \vdots \\ 0 \\ +1 \\ 0 \\ \vdots \\ 0 \\ -1 \\ 0 \\ \vdots \\ 0 \end{pmatrix} \tag{3.20}$$

where the $+1$ entry is in the ith row and the -1 entry is in the jth row.

Given that we now know how to state the LMCFP, it is appropriate to ask how it may be solved. Clearly, the LMCFP is a linear program and, as such, may be solved by the unembellished simplex algorithm of linear programming. However, that approach is not likely to be very efficient since A is a very sparse matrix and b contains many zeros. The presence of zeros in the b vector means that there is the theoretical prospect of cycling due to degeneracy. In truth this is not a very big problem and can be easily dealt with in practice through established techniques. Much more significant and much more likely is the potential for the unembellished simplex to *stall* for a highly degenerate problem with a sparse constraint matrix. Stalling means that the simplex visits a long sequence of bases that leave the objective either unchanged or only very slightly improved. So, a more efficient method is needed; the *network simplex algorithm*, which we discuss in more detail in Chap. 4, is that method.

3.3.4 Implications of Network Structure

As discussed in the introduction to this chapter, many network problems are IPs or MIPs. In fact, the continuous single commodity minimum cost flow problem can be modified to stipulate that all its solutions must be integers, as might occur if discrete vehicles, individual shipments, or indivisible message units were being modeled. At first glance, the integer minimum cost flow problem appears to be quite different than the linear minimum cost flow problem and to require techniques of integer programming for solution. However, it turns out that the presence of network structure allows us to relax integrality restrictions and to obtain integer solutions from the continuous LMCFP under the right circumstances.

Problems with Natural Integer Solutions

Specifically, we are interested in m-dimensional linear systems of the form:

$$Bx = b \tag{3.21}$$

for which the inverse of the $m \times m$ matrix B is well defined and whose solutions $x = B^{-1}b$ are such that x_i is an integer for all $i = 1, \ldots, m$. To understand when this might be the case, first recall:

Lemma 3.1 *The set of integers is closed under addition, subtraction, and multiplication.*

That is, given any two integers, α and β, we know that $\alpha + \beta$, $\alpha - \beta$, and $\alpha\beta$ are all integers. Thus, it follows that if B^{-1} and b are both integer then $x = B^{-1}b$ is also integer (since matrix multiplication involves only the addition and multiplication of scalars). Hence, we have the following:

Theorem 3.1 *For any nonsingular, integer matrix B and integer vector b, if $|B|$ equals 1 or -1 then $x = B^{-1}b$ is integer.*

Proof. Recall that for any nonsingular matrix, B, the inverse of B can be written as $B^{-1} = \text{adj}(B)/|B|$. Hence, since the integers are closed under addition and multiplication it follows that if B is integer then adj(B) is integer. Finally, since $|B|$ equals 1 or -1, the result follows. ■

Hence, the following result is immediate:

Theorem 3.2 *If a_{ij} is integer for all $i = 1, \ldots, m$ and $j = 1, \ldots, n$, the determinant of all bases of A are 1 or -1, and b_i is integer for all $i = 1, \ldots, m$, then the solution to*

$$\min c^T x$$

subject to

$$Ax = b$$

$$L \leq x \leq U$$

is integer.

Note that the condition that the determinant of *all* bases of A be 1 or -1 is sufficient but not necessary. Indeed, it is not even necessary that the determinant of the optimal basis be 1 or -1. For example, Veinott (1968) considers a class of problems with integer solutions that does not have this property.

Total Unimodularity

Matrices with the property of total unimodularity have been well-studied; see, for example, Heller (1957), Hoffman and Kruskal (1958), Hoffman and Heller (1962), and Chandrasekaran (1969). In our discussion we employ the following formal definition:

Definition 3.3 (Unimodularity) A square, integer matrix, B, is said to be *unimodular* if $|B|$ equals $0, 1$, or -1. An integer matrix A is said to be *totally unimodular* if and only if every square (nonsingular) submatrix of A is unimodular.

Of course, given this definition, it is relatively difficult to determine whether a particular matrix A is totally unimodular since it requires the examination of the determinant of every square submatrix. Fortunately, we also know the following:

Theorem 3.3 *(Heller and Tompkins) An integer matrix, A, with $a_{ij} \in \{-1, 0, 1\}$ for all i, j is totally unimodular if:*

(1) No more than two nonzero elements appear in each column; and

(2) The rows can be partitioned into two subsets, I_1 and I_2 such that:

  (a) If a column contains two nonzero elements with the same sign, one element is in each of the subsets; and

  (b) If a column contains two nonzero elements with opposite signs, both elements are in the same subset.

Proof. Let A_k be any submatrix of A of rank k. We show that A_k satisfies the definition of total unimodularity given above using induction. First, suppose that A_{k-1} is totally unimodular and observe that each column of A_k has either all zeros, a single nonzero element, or two nonzero elements. Thus, there are three cases to consider. (1) If a column of A_k has all zeros then $|A_k| = 0$. (2) If every column in A_k has two nonzero elements then by property 2:

$$\sum_{i \in I_1} a_{ij} = \sum_{i \in I_2} a_{ij} \quad j = 1, \ldots, n$$

Hence, the rows of A_k are linearly independent and $|A_k| = 0$. (3) If a column contains a single nonzero element, then we can expand the determinant on that element so that:

$$|A_k| = \pm |A_{k-1}|.$$

Since $|A_{k-1}|$ equals $-1, 0$, or 1 (by assumption) this implies that $|A_k|$ equals $-1, 0$, or 1. Thus, if A_{k-1} is totally unimodular then A_k is totally unimodular. Finally, since we know the property is true for A_1, the result follows. ■

This leads immediately to the following:

Theorem 3.4 *If each column of a matrix, A, has exactly one $+1$, one -1, and all other entries are 0 (i.e., if A has network structure), then A is totally unimodular.*

The implication of this theorem is quite significant:

Corollary 3.1 *Any linear single commodity minimum cost flow problem will have integer solutions so long as the vector of right hand sides b is comprised of integers*

Proof. Any single commodity minimum cost flow problem has network structure, and thus its constraint matrix is totally unimodular. There is an optimal basic feasible solution to any linear program. The result is then immediate. ■

3.3.5 Near Network Structure

Although it seems paradoxical to say, it must be noted that many of the network models we will consider in later chapters will *not* have network structure. This is because the notion of network structure we have introduced here depends on the fact that the only constraints are *flow conservation constraints written in terms of arc flow variables* and upper and lower bounds on arc flows. In modeling actual networks, we often have to introduce additional constraints, beyond those needed to express flow conservation and arc flow bounds. Furthermore, it is also sometimes necessary to employ path rather than arc variables. Both of these generalizations, additional constraints and the use of path variables, can prevent formal network structure from being attained.

That is, networks that do not display network structure may have

(1) so-called *near network structure*,

(2) limited network structure, or

(3) no network structure of any kind.

The notion of near network structure is somewhat subjective, based as it is on the presence of a relatively small number of constraints whose removal would leave behind a problem with network structure. No precise guideline can be given for what percentage of constraints may violate total unimodularity and yet allow a model to have near network structure. However, the presence of any subset of constraints with network structure can lead, as we discuss in detail in later chapters, to important computational efficiencies.

3.4 Labeling Algorithms

In this section we are concerned with stating and then providing algorithms for certain classical problems from graph theory. These are:

(1) the path finding problem,

(2) the tree growing problem,

(3) the minimum spanning tree problem,

(4) the shortest or minimum path problem,

(5) the maximal flow problem, and

(6) The matching problem.

These problems are intellectually interesting in their own right. The models underlying them are, however, difficult to use directly, without modification, for studying real-world networks because of their high degree of abstraction. Nonetheless, these classical problems and the algorithms for their solution are the "workhorses" of network analysis, arising again and again as subproblems in both the theoretical and numerical study of large scale network systems.

There is a common perspective to all the algorithms we shall develop for the classical graph-theoretic problems listed above, namely that of *labeling*. Labeling is the notion of using specially selected designations for network elements (nodes and/or arcs) that indicate the status of those elements relative to the goal of the algorithm. Most labeling schemes use either single or dual (ordered pair) node labels.

3.4.1 Path Generation and Tree Growing Problems

In our earlier remarks concerning graphs and graph-theoretic definitions, we introduced the notion of a *path*. Not surprisingly, because the real physical routes of interest in network engineering are graph-theoretic paths connecting origins and destinations of interest, the ability to systematically determine paths is fundamental to network analysis. Indeed the ability to determine – or as we say *generate* – paths is of fundamental importance, and the availability of a path generation utility algorithm is presupposed at several points in later chapters of this book.

The determination of any path that will allow a given origin to be reached from a given destination is sometimes the goal of an analysis, although more common is the need to find a path that satisfies some specific criterion. The most fundamental of all criterion-specific path generation problems is the so-called *shortest path problem*. Also called the *minimum path problem* when a routing criterion other than distance is employed, the shortest path problem is a special case of the linear minimum cost flow problem introduced earlier. In particular, the shortest path problem is obtained from the linear minimum cost flow problem, by stipulating that all nodal net supplies are zero except for those of the origin (source) node s and destination (sink) node t.

The net supply of the origin node is $+1$ and that of the destination node is -1 to indicate that exactly one unit is to be routed from the origin to the destination. Also the upper bounds on flows are usually irrelevant as it is generally assumed that each arc can accommodate a single unit of flow and we need only know whether a given arc belongs to the shortest path or not. The lower bound on each arc flow is typically zero. To be more specific, the flow variables x_{ij} are constrained to be binary variables, taking on the values 0 or 1, with 0 indicating the arc is not part of the shortest path and 1 that it is.

As a consequence of the preceding remarks, the deterministic shortest path problem has the form

$$\min \sum_{(i,j)\in\mathcal{A}} c_{ij}x_{ij} \tag{3.22}$$

subject to

$$\sum_{i:(i,j)\in\mathcal{A}} x_{ij} - \sum_{i:(j,i)\in\mathcal{A}} x_{ji} = \begin{cases} +1 \text{ if } i = s \\ -1 \text{ if } i = t \\ 0 \text{ otherwise} \end{cases} \quad \forall i \in \mathcal{N} \tag{3.23}$$

$$x_{ij} = (0,1) \qquad \forall (i,j) \in \mathcal{A} \tag{3.24}$$

Note that the primary constraints of the shortest path problem are the flow conservation constraints (3.23). Sometimes such constraints are referred to as *flow propagation constraints*, as they ensure our single unit of flow actually arrives at its destination. We shall see below that, under appropriate circumstances, the integrality restriction on flow variables may be relaxed to simple non-negativity.

Still another criterion-specific path generation problem is the *maximal flow problem*, another classical network problem that is intimately related to the minimum cost flow problem. In the maximal flow problem, the flow between the source and sink is unknown and maximized subject to the flow conservation constraints and arc flow bounds (both upper and lower) of the linear minimum cost flow problem. That is, we wish to solve

$$\left.\begin{aligned} &\max v \\ \text{subject to}& \\ &\sum_{i:(i,j)\in\mathcal{A}} x_{ij} - \sum_{i:(j,i)\in\mathcal{A}} x_{ji} = \begin{cases} +v & \text{if } i = s \\ -v & \text{if } \ i = t \\ 0 & \text{otherwise} \end{cases} \\ &U_{ij} \geq x_{ij} \geq L_{ij} \qquad \forall (i,j) \in \mathcal{A} \end{aligned}\right\} \tag{3.25}$$

where s and t are again the source and sink nodes, respectively, and v is the desired maximal flow. Note that without the capacity constraints, the maximal flow problem is really a shortest path problem for flow v from source to sink.

A graph-theoretic problem related to path generation is that of *tree building*, wherein one endeavors to find a tree that spans a set of nodes of interest, although this set of nodes does not have to include all the nodes of the graph. In its most general form the problem of tree building is concerned with finding any tree. More specific tree building problems may also be defined, and the one we shall emphasize below is the so-called *minimum spanning tree problem* for which the least length spanning tree for a graph is sought.

The subject of specialized algorithms for classical graph-theoretic and network optimization problems enjoys an extensive literature. It is beyond our scope to provide a comprehensive review of that literature. Rather, the labeling algorithms we next present are those that have proven pedagogical value, have had a substantial historical impact on the practice of network modeling, and whose philosophies have inspired improved algorithms. In fact, in later chapters, we shall take the view that highly efficient algorithms for the classical graph-theoretic and network optimization problems listed above are available as software utilities that we exploit to solve subproblems arising in algorithms for more complicated network models. As such, it will not generally matter in subsequent chapters what specific algorithm and associated software implementation is used to solve a given classical subproblem. Instead, we will be concerned with showing whether the solution of a given model can be accomplished through sequences of solutions of classical subproblems. It follows that the reader with prior exposure to classical graph-theoretic and network optimization problems will want to skip ahead to the chapters dealing with the application domains of his/her greatest interest.

3.4.2 Path Generation and Tree Building

To solve some network problems, including the maximal flow problem, we need to be able to build trees (not necessarily spanning trees) of networks that will allow us to identify several (and potentially all) paths from a given source to a given sink. Clearly, a shortest path algorithm such as that developed subsequently could be used to do this by repeatedly assigning arbitrary arc lengths and keeping track of the results, since its output is a spanning tree. However, because our interest is not now in optimal paths but instead in the generation of alternative paths and the building of trees comprised of paths, shortest path algorithms contain unnecessary overhead.

We will see that our focus on generic path generation and tree building is well served by the notion of *fanning out*, which in its most elementary form is the process of reaching out to adjacent nodes from the current node for the purpose of assigning or updating the labels of the adjacent nodes. Fanning out is intimately related to *scanning*, a term used to describe when all the label setting and/or label correcting stipulated for the fanning out from a given node is completed. It is common to refer to a node whose role in fanning out and scanning is complete as having been *scanned.* Sometimes fully scanned nodes are referred to as *closed* to indicate that their labels are no longer subject to alteration.

In the discussion that follows we will combine the concepts of fanning-out and scanning with node labels of the form $[s, p]$ where s denotes that the node is scanned and p denotes the predecessor. Moreover, these labels will be assigned for each fanning out stage even if a label already exists for a node. In this way there will be layers of labels for each node: one layer for each iteration.

With these preliminary notions in mind, a basic algorithm for path generation and tree building can now be stated as follows:

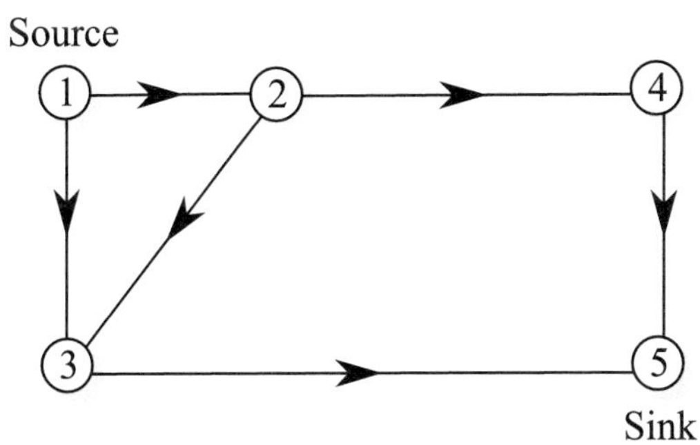

FIGURE 3.4: ORIGINAL NETWORK FOR PATH GENERATION EXAMPLE

ELEMENTARY PATH GENERATION AND TREE BUILDING ALGORITHM

Step 0. *(Initialization)* Label the source node predecessor index p as $*$, since it has no predecessor. Scan the source node by fanning out to all adjacent nodes j. Label each such node j with the source as its predecessor index. Mark the source node as scanned ($\surd$).

Step 1. *(Fanning out)* Choose any labeled, unscanned node i. Scan node i by fanning out to all adjacent nodes j. Label each such node j with i as its predecessor index. (Note that each node may have more than one predecessor.) Mark node i as scanned ($\surd$).

Step 2. *(Stopping)* If all nodes have been scanned, stop. Otherwise, return to Step 1.

Step 3. *(Predecessors and path reconstruction)* Begin at the sink. Write in reverse order from sink to source a sequence of predecessor nodes describing a path. Continue this tracing back from the sink until all paths from source to sink are listed.

Example of Path Generation/Tree Building

The above algorithm can perhaps be best understood by considering a simple example. In particular, let us find paths from the source to the sink in the network of Fig. 3.4 using the elementary fanning out algorithm. We open by scanning node 1, then fanning out to its adjacent nodes. The source node has no predecessor. Nodes 2 and 3 have node 1 as their predecessor.

Node 1 is labeled with a checkmark to indicate that it has been scanned and an asterisk "*" is employed to indicate that it has no predecessor. Nodes 2 and 3 are labeled to indicate that their predecessor is node 1. These actions constitute iteration 1 and are shown in Fig. 3.5.

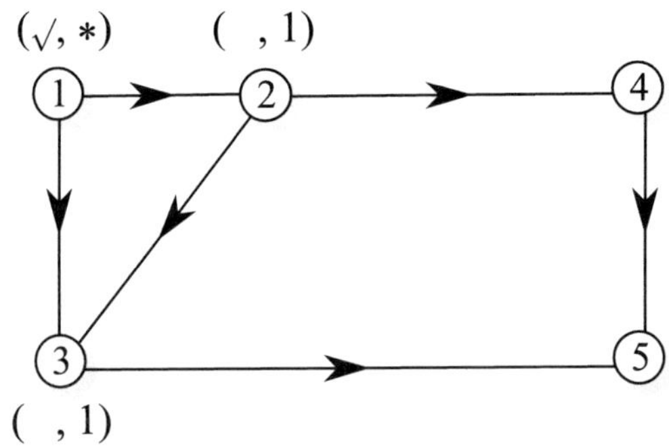

FIGURE 3.5: ITERATION 1 OF PATH GENERATION ALGORITHM

Next, for iteration 2, scan node 2 by fanning out to nodes 3 and 4. Nodes 3 and 4 are labeled to indicate that they are preceded by node 2. Node 2 is labeled to indicate that it was scanned. Note the two layers of labels for node 3 since it has two potential predecessors. Figure 3.6 depicts this step.

To start iteration 3, scan node 3 by fanning out to node 5. Note also the breakthrough to the sink node. This breakthrough shows the existence of two paths. They are: $\{(1,3),(3,5)\}$ and $\{(1,2),(2,3),(3,5)\}$. Node 3 is labeled to

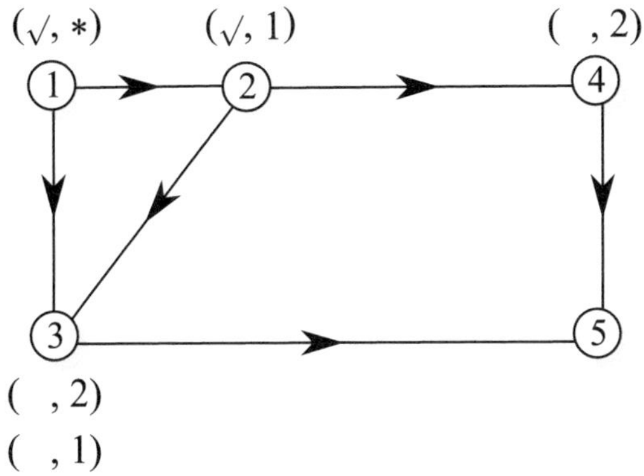

FIGURE 3.6: ITERATION 2 OF PATH GENERATION ALGORITHM

indicate that it was scanned. Node 5 is labeled to indicate that it is preceded by node 3 and was scanned. The result of iteration 3 is shown in Fig. 3.7.

To begin iteration 4, scan node 4 by fanning out to node 5. Note the second breakthrough to the sink node. This breakthrough shows the existence of a third path. This path is $\{(1,2),(2,4),(4,5)\}$. Node 4 is labeled to indicate that it was scanned. Node 5 is labeled to indicate that it is preceded by node 4 and was scanned. The result of iteration 4 is that all nodes have been scanned and three breakthroughs are made, as depicted in Fig. 3.8.

In summary, the three paths generated are the following sequences of arcs:

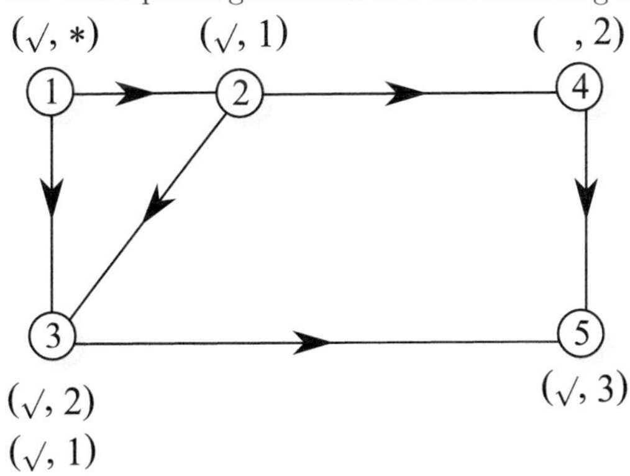

FIGURE 3.7: ITERATION 3 OF PATH GENERATION ALGORITHM

$$p_1 = \{(1,3),(3,5)\}$$

$$p_2 = \{(1,2),(2,3),(3,5)\}$$

$$p_3 = \{(1,2),(2,4),(4,5)\}$$

Note that none of these trees is a spanning tree. We next discuss how to find spanning trees.

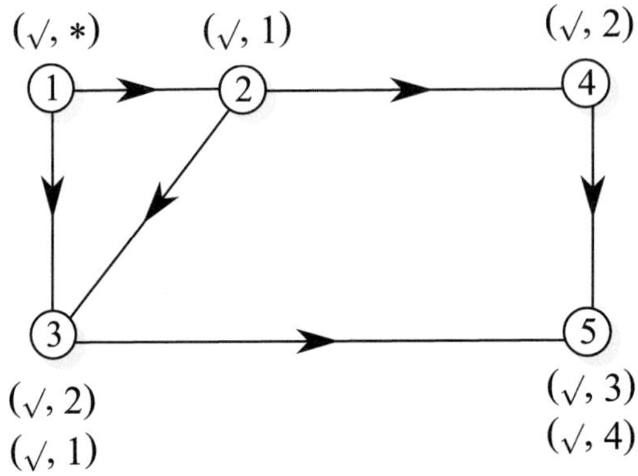

FIGURE 3.8: ITERATION 4 OF PATH GENERATION ALGORITHM

3.4.3 Spanning Trees

As made clear by the example of the last section, the elementary tree building algorithm based on fanning out is not adequate for the generation of spanning trees; we must use an alternative approach. Two main algorithmic philosophies exist for constructing spanning trees:

(1) Labeling with multiple arc introductions, and

(2) Single node/arc introduction with implicit labeling.

In the discussion that next follows we give algorithms that illustrate each of these philosophies. In particular, we present a multiple arc introduction algorithm for generating spanning trees that are not necessarily minimum spanning trees. This is followed by a single arc introduction algorithm for finding minimum spanning trees.

Labeling with Multiple Arc Introduction

In the first algorithmic philosophy, there are three label states familiar from our preceding discussion of tree building: unlabeled, labeled unscanned, and labeled scanned. As before, scanning occurs by fanning out to all eligible nodes reachable from the node being scanned, and when a node is fully scanned it is closed. A *list* of labeled unscanned nodes is kept. Nodes are dropped from the list once scanned.

The following algorithm embodies the philosophy of labeling with multiple arc introduction for constructing spanning trees:

MULTIPLE INTRODUCTION SPANNING TREE ALGORITHM

Step 0. *(Initialization)* Pick a node as the root. Label this root with an asterisk (*). Place the chosen node in a list. Set the pointer i to the root node.

Step 1. *(Main step)* Scan node i and determine all adjacent arcs (i, j) and (j, i) belonging to the nascent tree for which j is not in the list. Introduce all such j into the list and drop node i from the list. Pick a successor to node i. Repeat the step. The algorithm terminates when all nodes are scanned and the list is empty.

Example of Multiple Arc Introduction Spanning Tree Algorithm

Consider the 5-node, 5-arc example of Fig. 3.9, for which we pick node 1 as the root node in order to initialize the problem. The root is labeled with an asterisk "*" and placed in the list of nodes. The pointer i is set equal to the root node. The initial list and initial tree are:

root = 1

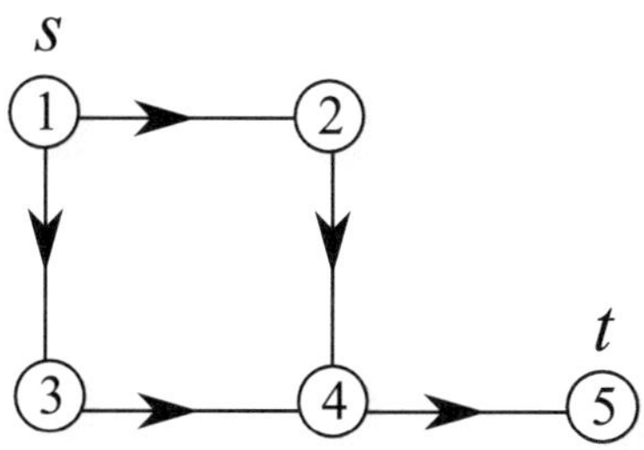

FIGURE 3.9: EXAMPLE NETWORK FOR MULTIPLE INTRODUCTION SPANNING TREE ALGORITHM

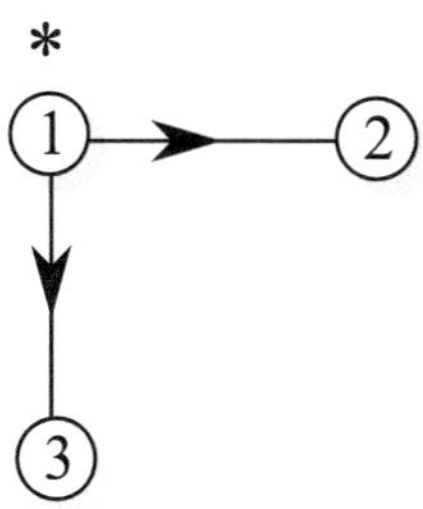

LIST AND TREE FOR $k = 0$

Node 1 is now scanned. All arcs (i, j) and (j, i) belonging to $\mathcal{A}$ for which j is not in the list are identified. The jth nodes in these arcs are introduced into the list, and the ith node is dropped. In our example, the arcs belonging to $\mathcal{A}$ for which j is not in the list are $(1, 2)$ and $(1, 3)$. Nodes 2 and 3 are introduced into the list, and node 1 is dropped. The resulting list is: 2 and 3. The pointer i is set equal to 2. The updated list and tree are

1 - dropped from list
2
3

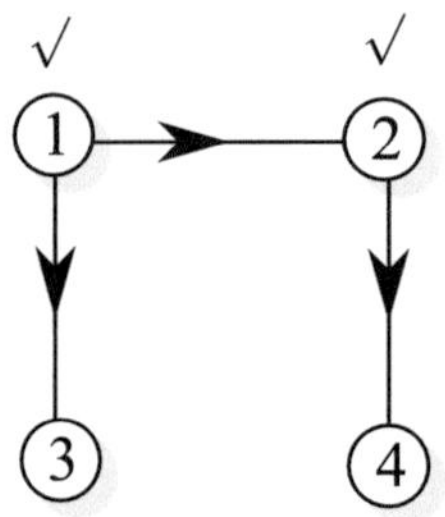

LIST AND TREE FOR $k = 1$

Node 2 is now scanned. The arc belonging to $\mathcal{A}$ for which j is not in the list is $(2, 4)$. Node 4 is introduced into the list, and node 2 is dropped. The resulting list is: 3 and 4. The pointer i is set equal to 3. The list and tree (unchanged) become

2 - dropped from list
3
4

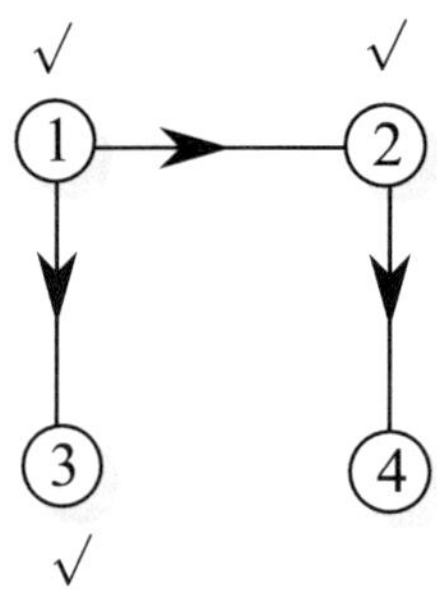

LIST AND TREE FOR $k = 2$

Node 3 is next scanned; it is seen that no node is reachable from node 3. For this reason, node 3 is dropped from the list. The resultant list contains only node 4. The pointer i is set equal to 4. The list and tree are

3 - dropped from list
4

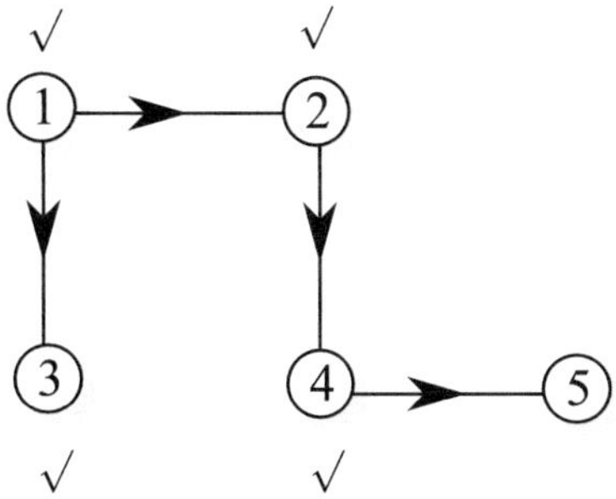

LIST AND TREE FOR $k = 3$

Node 4 is now scanned. The arc belonging to the current tree for which j is not in the list is $(4, 5)$. Node 5 is introduced into the list, and node 4 is dropped. The pointer i is set equal to 5. The list and tree (unchanged) are

4 - dropped from list
5

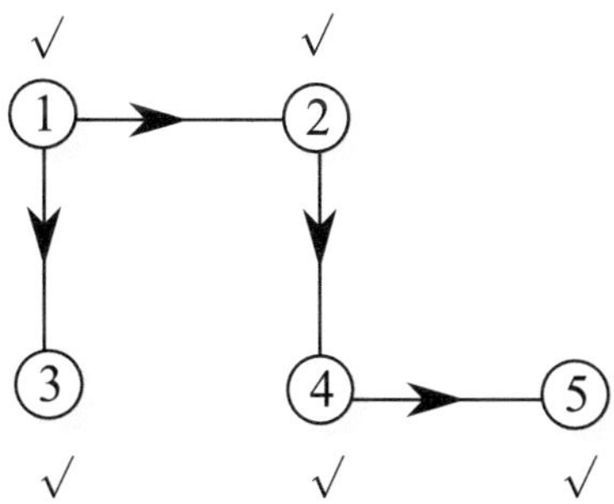

LIST AND TREE FOR $k = 4$

Node 5 is next scanned; it is seen that no node is reachable from node 5. For this reason, node 5 is dropped from the list. The list is now empty, indicating that all nodes have been scanned. Each node is reached from every other node, ignoring directionality. The algorithm may be terminated with the following final list and spanning tree:

5 - dropped from list
θ

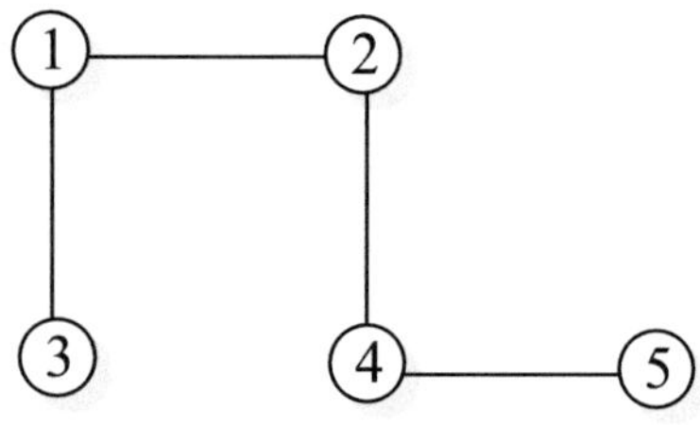

LIST AND TREE FOR $k = 5$

Single Node/Arc Introduction

Among all the spanning trees of a given graph is a *minimum spanning tree* (MST). Relative to total length, this MST may not be unique. However, no other spanning tree will be of shorter length. The algorithm we emphasize here for MSTs begins with the n isolated nodes of the original graph. To construct the minimum spanning tree linking these n nodes, an arbitrary initial node is selected. Its closest node is then identified, and these two nodes are connected, creating a tree of two nodes and a single arc. The isolated node that is closest to this created tree is then identified and connected to the tree. When all nodes have been connected, a minimum spanning tree has been found. The following algorithm formalizes this approach for constructing a minimum spanning tree using single arc introduction, where $\ell(i, j)$ is the length of arc (i, j):

SINGLE ARC INTRODUCTION MINIMUM SPANNING TREE ALGORITHM

Step 0. *(Initialization)* Set the iteration counter $k = 0$. Select an arbitrary node $r \in \mathcal{N}$ to serve as the root node. Find node c such that the arc connecting the root r to node c is the shortest arc out of node r. If ties for the shortest arc exist, break them arbitrarily. Connect node r and node c and form the initial tree, whose arc set is $\mathcal{E}_0 = \{(r, k)\}$. The initial set of connected nodes is $\mathcal{C}_0 = \{r, k\}$; the initial set of isolated (unconnected) nodes is $\mathcal{I}_0 = \mathcal{N} \backslash \mathcal{C}_0$.

Step 1. *(Stopping test)* If $\mathcal{I}_k = \emptyset$ (no isolated nodes exist), stop. The current tree $\mathcal{E}_k$ is a minimum spanning tree for the nodal set $\mathcal{N}$. If $\mathcal{I}_k \neq \emptyset$ (isolated nodes still exist), go to Step 2.

Step 2. *(Find next node and update)* Find the isolated node x that is closest to the already connected nodes, and in doing find the arc

$$(x, y) = \arg\{\min \ell(i, j) : i \in \mathcal{C}_k, j \in \mathcal{I}_k\}$$

Set $k = k + 1$ and update according to

$$\mathcal{C}_{k+1} = \mathcal{C}_k \cup \{(r, k)\}$$

$$\mathcal{I}_{k+1} = \mathcal{I}_k \backslash y$$

$$\mathcal{E}_{k+1} = \mathcal{E}_k \cup \{(r, k)\}$$

Go to Step 1.

It is important to note that, in the manual application of the MST algorithm, explicit labels are usually not employed. It is readily observed, however, that the algorithm may be thought of as updating a dual label for each connected node i of the form $[k, \ell(i, k)]$, where k is the nearest unconnected neighbor node and $\ell(i, k)$ is the distance to that neighbor; a dummy label $[-, -]$ may be used to indicate a node is not yet connected to the emerging tree.

Simple Example of MST Algorithm

We consider an example due to Larson and Odoni (1981) and based on the graph of Fig. 3.10, for which all arcs are potentially bidirectional and arc lengths are denoted in parentheses next to each arc.

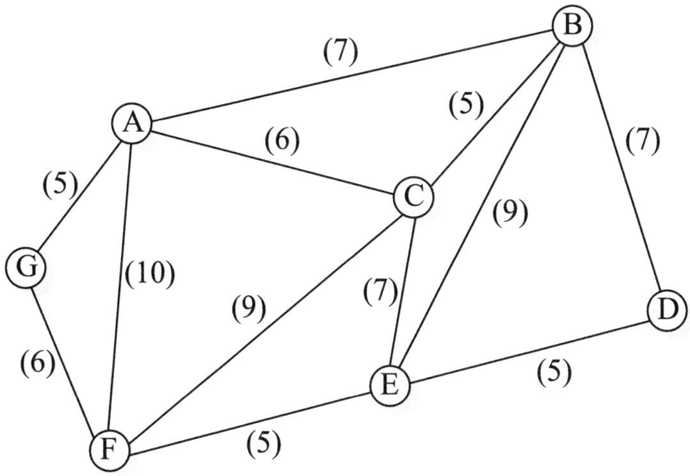

FIGURE 3.10: EXAMPLE NETWORK FOR MST ALGORITHM

The algorithm for single arc introduction works as follows: let us suppose that we choose node A to begin construction of the minimum spanning tree. We first find the isolated node that is closest to node A. Node G is this node, and so node G is connected to node A by introduction of the arc (A, G). These

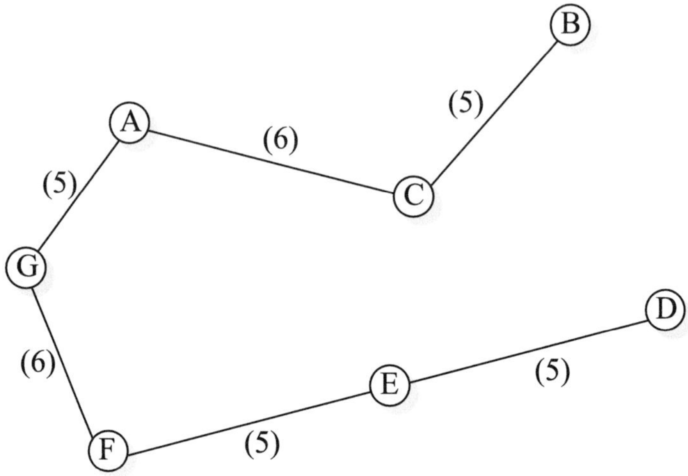

FIGURE 3.11: MINIMUM SPANNING TREE SOLUTION

nodes form a minimum spanning tree of two nodes and a single arc. Next, the still-isolated node that is closest to this tree is identified. There exists a tie between node C and node F as the closest isolated node. Node C is six units away from node A and node F is six units away from node G. The tie must be broken arbitrarily. Suppose we choose node F as the next node to be connected to the MST. Consequently, arc (G, F) is introduced and node F is connected to the tree. Continuing in this manner, nodes E, D, C, and B, in that order, are connected to the tree. The resulting MST is shown in Fig. 3.11 with a total length of 32 units.

3.4.4 The Minimum Path Problem

The most well-known of the specialized algorithms for solving the shortest path problem is *Dijkstra's labeling algorithm.* This algorithm is used to find the shortest path between a given node and all other nodes of a given graph $G(\mathcal{N}, \mathcal{A})$. In our presentation of Dijkstra's algorithm, we assume that all arc lengths $\ell\,(i, j)$ between nodes of a given graph $G(\mathcal{N}, \mathcal{A})$ are nonnegative.

The algorithm begins at the specified "source" node s and then successively finds its closest, second closest, third closest, and so on, node. This process continues until all nodes in the network have been scanned. A two-entry label for each node j is employed for bookkeeping purposes. For any given iteration and any step within that iteration, each node can be in one of two *states*:

(1) the *open state*, for which the node label is tentative; or

(2) the *closed state*, for which the node label is permanent.

In particular the label entries for node j are of the form $[d(j), p(j)]$ where

$d(j)$ is the length of the shortest path from s to j
$p(j)$ is the predecessor node of j in the shortest path from s to j

These labels are determined with respect to the paths and path segments established as of iteration j of the algorithm. We use the symbol $+$ to indicate node closure and the dummy symbol $*$ to indicate the predecessor of the source node s. As a consequence of these conventions, Larson and Odoni (1981) give a statement of Dijkstra's algorithm nearly identical to the following:

Dijkstra's Minimum Path Algorithm

Step 0. *(Initialization)* Set $d(s) = 0$, $p(s) = *$. Set $d(j) = \infty$, $p(j) = -$ for all other nodes $j \neq s$. Label node s as $+$ (closed). Label all other nodes as $-$ (open). Set $k = s$ (i.e., s is the last closed node).

Step 1. *(Updating of distance labels)* Examine all arcs (k, j) out of the last closed node. If node j is closed, go to the next arc. If node j is an open node, set the first portion of its label to

$$d(j) = \min\{d(j), d(k) + \ell(k, j)\} \tag{3.26}$$

Step 2. *(Choose node to close)* Compare the $d(j)$ entries for all nodes that are open. Choose the node with the smallest $d(j)$ as the next node to be closed. If ties exist, break them arbitrarily. Call the next node to be closed node i.

Step 3. *(Identify predecessor node)* Consider all arcs (j, i) leading from closed nodes to i. Identify the node j for which

$$d(i) - \ell(j, i) = d(j)$$

If ties exist, break them arbitrarily. The identified node is the predecessor node to node i. Set $p(i)$ equal to this node. Label node i as closed.

Step 4. *(Stopping)* If all nodes are closed, stop. The shortest path solution has been found. If open nodes still exist, set $k = i$ and return to Step 1.

Clearly, the output of this algorithm is a tree of shortest paths, for which the $d(j)$ entry of the label for node j indicates the length of the shortest path from s to j. The $p(i)$ entry of the label for node j indicates the predecessor node to j on this shortest path. This tree is used to determine the shortest path from the sink node s to any other node in the graph $G(\mathcal{N}, \mathcal{A})$ by starting at the terminal node of interest and tracing backward until the source node is reached.

A few remarks are necessary regarding the use of this algorithm:

(1) Ties among two or more nodes having equal $d(j)$ in Step 3 are broken arbitrarily. The same applies for predecessor node ties in Step 4.

(2) The algorithm is easy to carry out in tableau format and to translate into software for computer implementation.

(3) This algorithm can be used with directed, undirected, or mixed graphs, as long as the condition $\ell(i,j) \geq 0$ holds for all $(i,j) \in \mathcal{A}$.

(4) A variation of this algorithm is attributed to Dijkstra, but many similar algorithms have been presented over the years; so one may encounter in the technical literature different names and attributions for algorithms that are essentially the same as the one we have described.

(5) The algorithm is provably finite.

Although Dijkstra's algorithm is intuitively appealing, we must establish that it in fact uncovers the desired shortest path(s) in a finite number of steps. We also need to establish a measure of its worst-case performance; in particular, we are interested in whether the complexity of Dijkstra's algorithm is polynomial or exponential in nature. These matters are considered in the next section.

Finiteness and Complexity of Dijkstra's Algorithm

We wish to prove the following result pertaining to the finiteness and worst-case performance of Dijkstra's labeling algorithm for the minimum path problem:

Theorem 3.5 *For a connected graph $G(\mathcal{N},\mathcal{A})$ whose edges all have nonnegative lengths $\ell(i,j) \geq 0$, Dijkstra's labeling algorithm for the shortest path problem is finite with regard to finding the tree of shortest paths from the source to all other nodes and has computational complexity $O(n^2)$, where $n = |\mathcal{N}|$.*

Proof. We use a nontraditional method of proof. In particular, we note that the algorithm is wholly equivalent to a dynamic program since expression (3.26) is the basic recursive relationship of dynamic programming. It, therefore, follows from Bellman's Principle of Optimality that the algorithm will compute the desired optimal paths when all nodes are scanned and closed. Hence, because the number of nodes is finite, the algorithm is finite. Furthermore, we observe that the worst-case performance of Dijkstra's algorithm will surely occur for a completely connected graph wherein it is possible to reach every node directly from every other node. In this extreme case, Step 2 necessitates $n(n-1)/2$ additions and comparisons, while Step 3 requires another $n(n-1)/2$ comparisons for a single origin-destination pair. Additionally, for the same origin-destination pair, Steps 2 and 3 compel an extra $n(n-1)/2$ comparisons to assign temporary labels. The worst-case computational burden is therefore found by adding up these operations:

$$\frac{3}{2}n(n-1) = \frac{3}{2}\left(n^2 - n\right)$$

which is $O\left(n^2\right)$. ■

Example of Dijkstra's Algorithm

We now consider an instructive numerical example of Dijkstra′s labeling algorithm posed and solved by Larson and Odoni (1981) and based on the mixed graph shown in Fig. 3.12. Suppose that the source node is a. Directed arcs are denoted by arrows. Numbers indicate the "lengths" of arcs. Our problem is: find the shortest paths from source (origin) a to all the other nodes.

Figure 3.13 shows the labels that exist on the nodes of this graph after completion of the first iteration of the labeling algorithm. Node b is identified as the next node to be closed after the source. The two closed nodes up to this point, a and b, are labeled with a "+" to indicate that they are closed. Their labels are permanent.

Figure 3.14 shows the status of the network's nodes after completion of the second iteration of the algorithm. Node d is identified as the next node to be closed and node a is identified as the predecessor to node d.

Figure 3.15 shows the status of the network's nodes after completion of the third iteration of the labeling algorithm. At the start of this iteration of the algorithm, the arcs out of d to open nodes are (d, c) and (d, g). In Step 1 of the algorithm, the length of the shortest path from c to a is evaluated as

$$d(c) = \min\{d(c), d(d) + \ell(d, c)\} = \min\{8, 5 + 2\} = 7$$

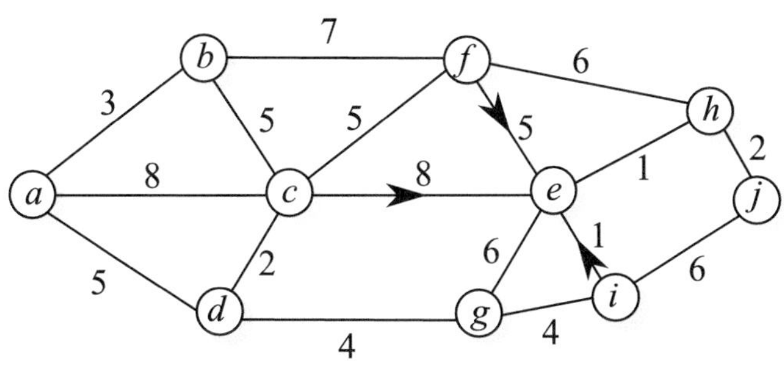

FIGURE 3.12: LARSON AND ODONI (1981) EXAMPLE NETWORK

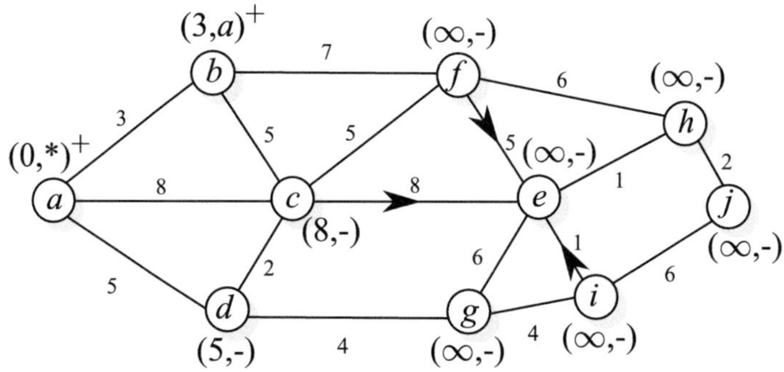

FIGURE 3.13: ITERATION 1 OF DIJKSTRA'S ALGORITHM

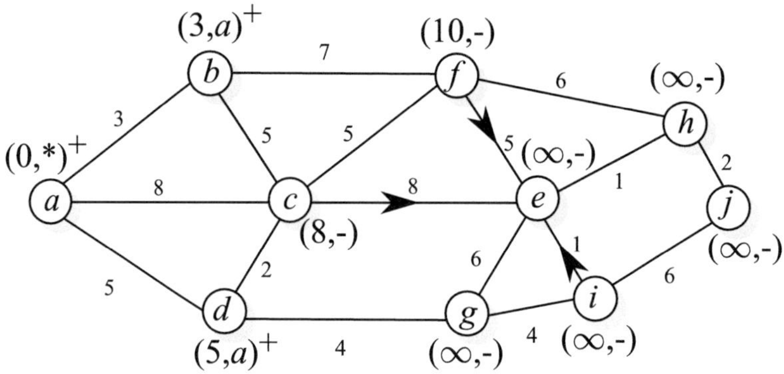

FIGURE 3.14: ITERATION 2 OF DIJKSTRA'S ALGORITHM

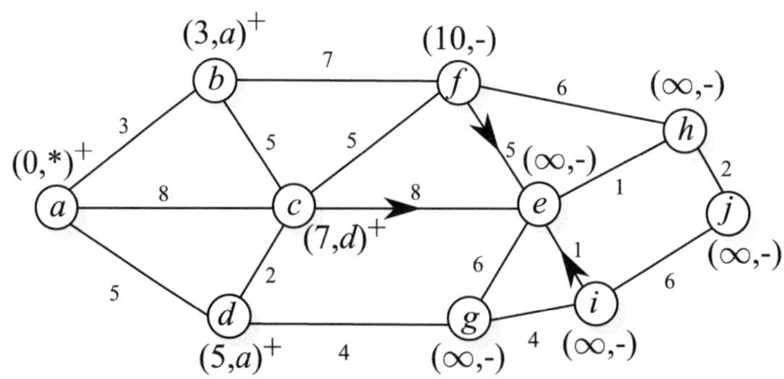

FIGURE 3.15: ITERATION 3 OF DIJKSTRA'S ALGORITHM

Thus the label, $d(c)$, is changed from 8 to 7. Likewise, $d(g)$ is changed from ∞ to 9. In Step 2 of the algorithm, we find that

$$\begin{aligned}\min\{d(c), d(e), d(f), d(g), d(h), d(i), d(j)\} &= \min\{7, \infty, 10, 9, \infty, \infty, \infty\} \\ &= 7\end{aligned}$$

Therefore, node c will be closed next. The arcs to c from closed nodes are (b, c), (a, c), and (d, c). We find that $d(c) - \ell(d, c) = 7 - 2 = 5 = d(d)$. Therefore, node d is the predecessor of node c, so we set $p(c) = d$.

After six additional iterations of the algorithm, we obtain on the ninth iteration the circumstance shown in Fig. 3.16. All nodes are closed, all labels are permanent, and the shortest path solution is obtained. From this labeled graph we may extract a tree containing the shortest paths from the source node a to all other nodes on the graph. For example, the shortest path from node a to node h is of length 15. This is readily apparent by looking at the first part of the label for node h. Tracing backward through the tree from $p(h)$ to $p(e)$ to $p(i)$ and so forth, we see that the shortest path is the arc sequence $\{(a, d), (d, g), (g, i), (i, e), (e, h)\}$.

Figure 3.17 shows the tree of shortest paths referred to above and which constitutes the answer to the problem originally posed. Note that this tree is a spanning tree. An interesting question for the reader to consider is whether this spanning tree is a minimum spanning tree.

3.4.5 Maximal Flow

Recall that the maximal flow problem (MFP) aims to find the largest flow and corresponding path from a specified source to a specified sink in a capacitated network. As shown previously in (3.25) the MFP can be stated as a continuous linear program. It is quite evident that, because of the prevalence of zeros as right hand sides of the flow conservation constraints for this model, the linear program is highly degenerate. Although there are reliable means of ensuring

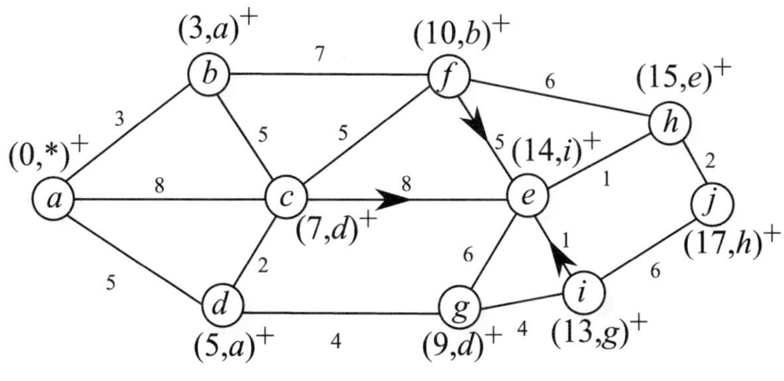

FIGURE 3.16: ITERATION 9 OF DIJKSTRA'S ALGORITHM

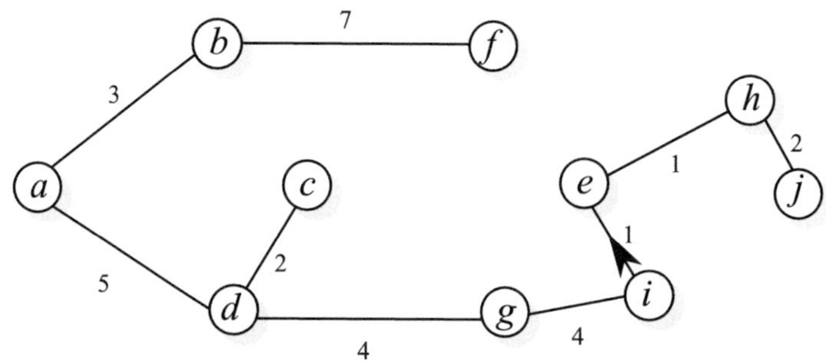

FIGURE 3.17: TREE OF SHORTEST PATHS FROM DIJKSTRA'S ALGORITHM

convergence in the face of degeneracy, it comes as no surprise that use of simplex-type algorithms for the MFP *may* lead to *stalling*: long sequences of pivots wherein very minor progress toward optimality is made. It is for this reason that we include below a discussion of one type of labeling algorithm for the MFP.

Associated with the maximal flow problem is a theorem known as the *minimum-cut/maximal-flow theorem* in which the result depends on the notion of a cut, which we define as follows: $Q(S_1, S_2)$ is called a *cut for the directed simple graph* $G(\mathcal{N}, \mathcal{A})$ if its node set $\mathcal{N}$ may be partitioned into two nonempty sets S_1 and S_2 such that S_2 is the complement of S_1; that is, $S_2 = \mathcal{N} \backslash S_1$. It is also helpful to introduce the following notation relative to $Q(S_1, S_2)$:

$$Q^+ \equiv \{(i,j) \in \mathcal{A} : i \in S_1, j \in S_2\}$$

$$Q^- \equiv \{(i,j) \in \mathcal{A} : i \in S_2, j \in S_1\}$$

for which Q^+ is said to be the *set of arcs forward in the cut* and Q^- the *set of arcs reverse in the cut*. The cut is also said to separate node $s \in \mathcal{N}$ from node $t \in \mathcal{N}$ if $s \in S_1$ and $t \in S_2$ since by construction $S_1 \cap S_2 = \emptyset$. A cut is nonempty if $Q^+ \cup Q^- \neq \emptyset$. We use the notation Ψ_{st} to denote the set of all cuts separating the specified source s from the specified node t.

Assuming finite upper and lower bounds for each arc given by our previous notation, we may define the *capacity of a cut* as

$$C(Q) = \sum_{(i,j) \in Q^+} U_{ij} - \sum_{(i,j) \in Q^-} L_{ij} \tag{3.27}$$

We define the minimal cut set for source-sink pair (s,t) as

$$Q_{st} = \arg\min \left[C(Q) \quad \text{subject to} \quad Q \in \Psi_{st}\right] \tag{3.28}$$

In light of the preceding definitions we state and prove the following:

Theorem 3.6 *(Minimum-cut/maximal-flow) In $G(\mathcal{N}, \mathcal{A})$ the value of the maximal flow is equal to the minimal cut capacity for each source-sink pair.*

Proof. Without loss of generality we take the lower bound on flow to be zero (0) on every arc, and postulate the existence of an upper bound on maximal flow so that the linear program (3.25) becomes

$$\left.\begin{aligned} &\max v \\ &\text{subject to} \\ &\sum_{i:(i,j)\in\mathcal{A}} x_{ij} - \sum_{i:(j,i)\in\mathcal{A}} x_{ji} = \begin{cases} +v & \text{if } i = s \\ -v & \text{if } i = t \\ 0 & \text{if } i \in \mathcal{N} - \{s,t\} \end{cases} \\ &0 \leq v \leq v_{\max} \\ &U_{ij} \geq x_{ij} \geq 0 \qquad \forall (i,j) \in \mathcal{A} \end{aligned}\right\} \tag{3.29}$$

Our proof depends on noting that the dual of this maximal flow linear program is

$$\left.\begin{aligned} &\min \sum_{(i,j)\in\mathcal{A}} U_{ij} w_{ij} + v_{\max} z \\ &\text{subject to} \\ &\pi_i - \pi_j + w_{ij} \geq 0 \quad \forall (i,j) \in \mathcal{A} \\ &\pi_t - \pi_s + z \geq 1 \quad \forall (i,j) \in \mathcal{A} \\ &\pi_i \text{ unrestricted} \quad \forall i \in \mathcal{N} \\ &z \geq 0 \\ &w_{ij} \geq 0 \quad \forall (i,j) \in \mathcal{A} \end{aligned}\right\} \tag{3.30}$$

The dual variables w_{ij} indicate the impact on the primal objective of a unit change in flow on arc (i,j), while the dual variable z measures the impact on the primal objective of a unit change in throughput from s to t. Consequently, the dual objective measures the capacity of alternative cuts:

$$Q_{st} = \sum_{(i,j)\in\mathcal{A}} U_{ij} w_{ij}^* + v_{\max} z^*$$

where the asterisk superscript "*" denotes an optimal solution of the dual. By linear programming strong duality, we know that the optimal primal and dual objective functions must be equal. This establishes the desired result. ■

A Path Augmentation Algorithm for the MFP

The solution of the maximal flow problem and other network models depends on the availability of a path finding utility. Such a utility algorithm based on the concept of fanning out was presented previously. Assuming this or a similar utility is available, a rather simple method known as *path augmentation* can be developed for the maximal flow problem. A concept central to development of such an algorithm for the maximal flow problem is that of a *flow augmenting path* (FAP). An FAP is a path (sequence of consecutive arcs) connecting source s and sink t, such that

$$\begin{aligned} U_{ij} - x_{ij} &> 0 \qquad \forall (i,j) \text{ forward in } p \\ x_{ij} - L_{ij} &> 0 \qquad \forall (i,j) \text{ reverse in } p \end{aligned}$$

where U_{ij} and L_{ij} are recognized as our notation for the upper and lower bounds on the flow on arc (i,j), respectively. Note that reverse flow need not physically occur, but is used purely for the purposes of implementing the algorithm we next describe.

Given a feasible path flow vector $x^k = \left(x_{ij}^k : (i,j) \in \mathcal{A}\right)^T$ for iteration k, namely an x^k for which flow conservation at every node is satisfied, and an associated path p with positive residual capacity opened from source to sink, we can use the notion of an FAP to articulate a simple procedure for increasing flow between s and t. To that end, let P^+ denote the set of arcs that are forward and P^- the set of arcs that are reverse for the path in question. Also define

$$\delta = \min \left\{ \left(U_{ij} - x_{ij}^k : (i,j) \in P^+\right), \left(x_{ij}^k - L_{ij} : (i,j) \in P^-\right) \right\}$$

The new iterate x^{k+1} that increases flow from s to t obeys

$$x_{ij}^{k+1} = \begin{cases} x_{ij}^k + \delta & \text{if } (i,j) \in P^+ \\ x_{ij}^k - \delta & \text{if } (i,j) \in P^- \\ x_{ij}^k & \text{otherwise} \end{cases} \tag{3.31}$$

We call (3.31) the flow augmenting step. The following is the maximal flow algorithm based on the notion of flow augmentation:

PATH AUGMENTATION ALGORITHM FOR MFP

Step 1. Find a flow augmenting path from source to sink with strictly positive flow capacity. Stop if no flow augmenting path can be found.

Step 2. Find the minimal residual capacity on the new flow augmenting path and assign that amount of flow to the path by carrying out the flow augmentation step (3.31).

Step 3. Update the residual arc capacities. Return to Step 1.

Termination and optimality occur when no augmenting path from source to sink with strictly positive flow capacity can be found. The augmenting paths themselves are found from a fanning out search, which simply stated, is: start at one node, employ a path finding utility until no additional FAPs are found, go to the next node, and repeat the process systematically. This algorithm may be thought of as updating a two-entry label of the form [residual capacity, flow] at each iteration. The flow augmenting algorithm for the MFP is classified as a labeling algorithm because it relies on a path finding utility; we saw previously that such a utility is readily expressed as a labeling algorithm.

History, Finiteness and Complexity of Flow Augmentation Algorithm for the MFP

We state, but do not prove, that the unembellished flow augmenting path algorithm for the MFP that we have presented converges when arc flow bounds are integer and the initial flow pattern used to start the algorithm is also integer. Flow augmentation as we have described it here may actually fail to solve the MFP when there arc *noninteger arc capacities.* To ensure convergence in the presence of noninteger capacities, we must employ a search method that can deal with nonintegrality.

The concept of flow augmentation and its use to solve network problems may be traced to Fulkerson and Dantzig (1955), Ford and Fulkerson (1957), and Ford and Fulkerson (1962). Indeed, the algorithm we have presented is often called the Ford-Fulkerson algorithm. For integer arc capacities, the Ford-Fulkerson algorithm terminates in a finite number of iterations with the measure of complexity $O(nmU)$, where $n = |\mathcal{N}|$ is the number of nodes, $m = |\mathcal{A}|$ is the number of arcs and $U = \max\{U_{ij} : (i,j) \in \mathcal{A}\}$ is the upper bound on arc capacities for the directed network whose graph is $G(\mathcal{N}, \mathcal{A})$.

Dinc (1970) introduced the concept of *layered networks* into the path augmentation algorithmic structure we have emphasized here and used these layers to save labeling information from the construction of each augmenting path, obtaining thereby complexity $O(n^2 m)$. Better worst case computational bounds have been obtained using the concept of *preflow-push* on layered networks, wherein flows are pushed along arcs in such a way that flow conservation need not be preserved prior to optimality; see Ahuja et al. (1993) for a discussion of these alternative algorithms.

Example of Flow Augmentation Algorithm for the MFP

We consider an especially informative example due to Hillier and Lieberman (1955) based on the network of Fig. 3.18, for which we wish to find the maximum flow from node O to node T. The arc capacities and lengths for this network appear as ordered pairs of the form (capacity, length) next to each arc. Arcs are potentially bidirectional. The lower flow bound on all arcs is presumed to be 0. The network's minimum cut is 14.

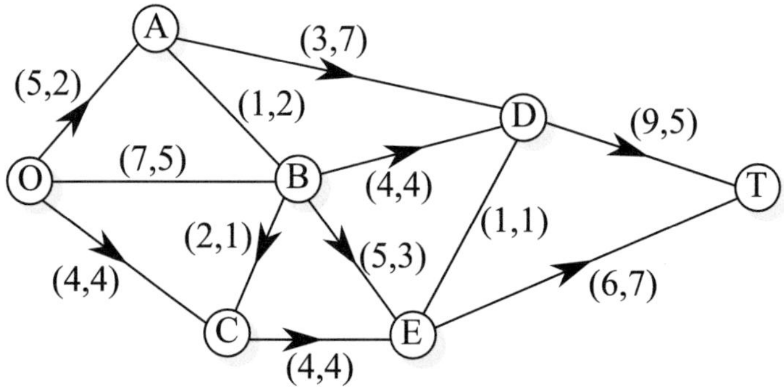

FIGURE 3.18: NETWORK FOR MAXIMAL FLOW EXAMPLE

In iteration 1, path O-B-E-T is identified as an augmenting path from source to sink with strictly positive flow. The maximum capacities on each arc of this FAP are:

$$\text{O to B capacity} = 7$$
$$\text{B to E capacity} = 5$$
$$\text{E to T capacity} = 6$$

The minimum residual capacity on the augmenting path O-B-E-T is the minimum of these capacities or 5, which is the assigned path flow. The residual arc capacities are then calculated as follows

$$\text{O to B residual capacity} = 7 - 5 = 2$$
$$\text{B to E residual capacity} = 5 - 5 = 0$$
$$\text{E to T residual capacity} = 6 - 5 = 1$$

The arcs of the network are relabeled in Fig. 3.19 with ordered pairs of the form (residual capacity, flow) in preparation for the next iteration.

In iteration 2, O-A-D-T is identified as an augmenting path from source to sink with strictly positive flow. The minimum residual capacity on this augmenting path is 3, which is the assigned path flow. The residual arc capacities are then recalculated and labeled as in Fig. 3.20. This process is repeated until, in iteration 8, one obtains the fully labeled graph of Fig. 3.21. It is clear from Fig. 3.21 that no paths with strictly positive flow remain. Note that the maximal flow (14) is identical to the minimal cut capacity (14), in accord with Theorem 3.6.

3.5 Solving the Linear Minimum Cost Flow Problem Using Graph-Theoretic Methods

It is instructive to now discuss how one may employ graph-theoretic methods to solve the linear minimum cost flow problem (LMCFP). The approach we employ depends on the successive use of a minimum path algorithm and is similar

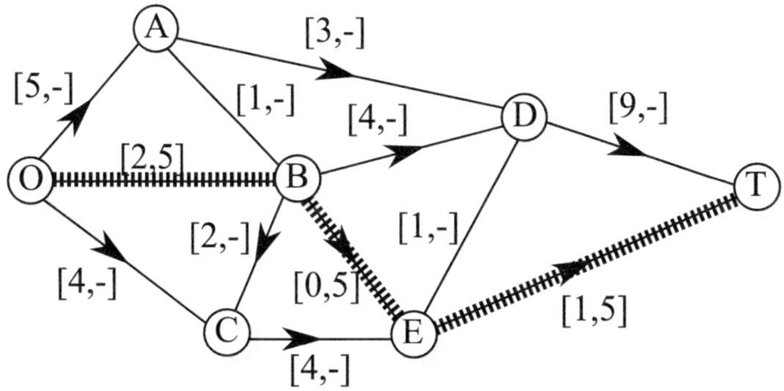

FIGURE 3.19: ITERATION 1 OF FLOW AUGMENTATION ALGORITHM

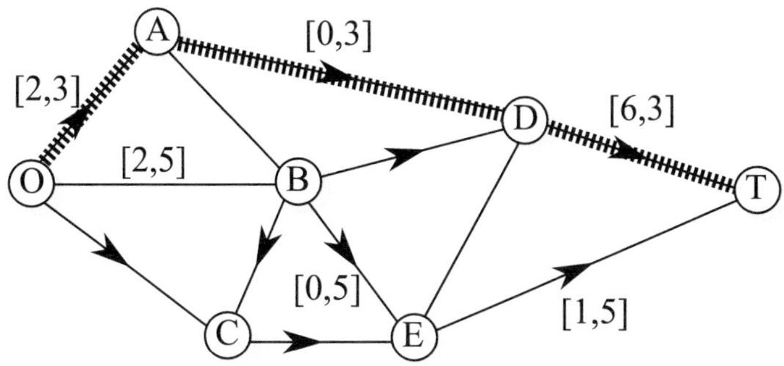

FIGURE 3.20: ITERATION 2 OF FLOW AUGMENTATION ALGORITHM

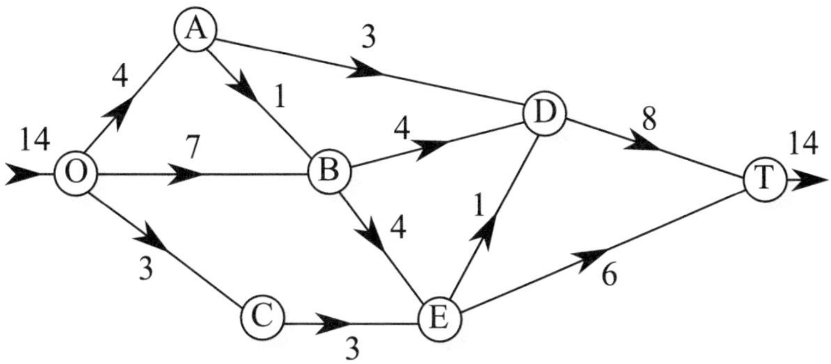

FIGURE 3.21: MAXIMAL FLOW SOLUTION

in some respects to the flow augmentation calculations introduced previously for finding maximal flows. In fact the main differences between the *successive minimum path algorithm* (SMPA) for solving the minimum cost flow problem and the flow augmentation algorithm for solving the maximal flow problem are:

(1) for the SMPA, we are concerned with flows between all origin-destination pairs, not just the flow between a given source and sink;

(2) for the SMPA, we limit the flow between nodal pairs to that which is needed to satisfy flow conservation as well as upper and lower bound constraints; maximal flows are not computed; and

(3) for the SMPA, the paths employed at each iteration are always minimum paths for the current residual network.

In Chap. 4 we introduce the network simplex algorithm as a preferred method for solving the LMCFP, so in practice one is not likely to employ the SMPA.

For convenience, we restate the LMCFP as

$$\left.\begin{aligned} \min c^T x \\ \text{subject to} \quad b - Ax = 0 \\ L - x \leq 0 \\ x - U \leq 0 \end{aligned}\right\} \tag{3.32}$$

for a network based on the simple directed graph $G(\mathcal{N}, \mathcal{A})$. We will define the excess supply at any node $j \in \mathcal{N}$ during iteration k as

$$E_j^k \equiv b_j - \left[\sum_{i:(i,j)\in\mathcal{A}} x_{ij}^k - \sum_{i:(j,i)\in\mathcal{A}} x_{ji}^k \right] \quad \forall j \in \mathcal{N} \tag{3.33}$$

where b_j is of course the net supply of node $j \in \mathcal{N}$. It is clear that the excess supply of every node must ultimately vanish so that feasibility will be achieved. In fact, it is the vanishing of excess supply that we shall use as a stopping criterion.

The origin-destination pair (r, s) of interest and its minimum path are found for iteration k by solving

$$\min \left\{ c_p : (i,j) \in \mathcal{W}, p \in \mathcal{P}_{ij}, E_i^k \neq 0, E_j^k \neq 0 \right\} \tag{3.34}$$

where $\mathcal{W}$ is the set of origin-destination pairs and $\mathcal{P}_{ij}$ is the set of paths connecting $(i,j) \in \mathcal{W}$. Note that this minimization is carried out for each origin-destination pair corresponding to nontrivial supply and demand. For the minimum path p^* found by solving (3.34), we carry out the updating

$$x_{ij}^{k+1} = \begin{cases} x_{ij}^k + \delta & \text{if arc } (i,j) \in p^* \\ x_{ij}^k & \text{otherwise} \end{cases} \tag{3.35}$$

The flow increment δ is defined as

$$\delta = \min \left\{ E_i^k - E_j^k, U_{ij} - x_{ij}^k \right\} \tag{3.36}$$

As a consequence of these observations, the algorithm may be stated as follows:

Successive Minimum Path Algorithm for the LMCFP

Step 0. *(Initialization)* Pick

$$x^0 = L \tag{3.37}$$

and set

$$S^0 = \emptyset \tag{3.38}$$

$$k = 0 \tag{3.39}$$

Step 1. *(Find minimum paths)* Identify all paths that solve (3.34) and their associated origin-destination pairs.

Step 2. *(Flow updating)* For each of the paths identified in Step 1, calculate the increment δ according to (3.36). Select the path and associated origin-destination pair corresponding to the largest value of δ, breaking ties arbitrarily. Find, per the flow updating rules (3.35), the corresponding x^{k+1}.

Step 3. *(Stopping test and determination of residual network)* If

$$E_i^{k+1} = 0 \quad \forall i \in \mathcal{N}, \tag{3.40}$$

then stop: $x^* = x^{k+1}$. Otherwise update the set of arcs whose residual capacities vanish, according to

$$S^{k+1} = S^k \cup \{(i,j) \in \mathcal{A} : U_{ij} - x_{ij}^{k+1} = 0\} \tag{3.41}$$

and form the residual network

$$G(\mathcal{N}, \mathcal{A}^{k+1}) \tag{3.42}$$

where

$$\mathcal{A}^{k+1} = \mathcal{A} \backslash S^{k+1} \tag{3.43}$$

is the set of arcs with nontrivial residual capacity. (Note that it is equivalent to stipulate

$$c_{ij} = M \quad \forall\, (i,j) \in S_{k+1} \tag{3.44}$$

where $M \gg 1$ is a very large number.) Set $k = k + 1$ and go to Step 1.

Furthermore, the finite nature of the SMPA is the subject of the following theorem:

Theorem 3.7 *On the simple directed graph $G(\mathcal{N}, \mathcal{A})$, the sequential minimum path algorithm (SMPA) will solve the linear minimum cost flow problem (LMCFP) with integer b, U, and L in at most $n \cdot \mathcal{B}$ iterations, where $n = |\mathcal{N}|$ and $\mathcal{B} = \max[b_i : i \in \mathcal{N}]$.*

Proof. The proof is trivial and left as an exercise for the reader. ■

We comment that the main work performed in iterations of the SMPA is the solution of the minimum path problem. Since polynomial bounded minimum path algorithms exist, it is clear that the SMPA is polynomially bounded.

3.6 Hamiltonian Walks and the Traveling Salesman Problem

The routing problems we have discussed up to this point are, for the most part, based on the minimum cost flow problem. Models derived from the minimum cost flow problem have optimal solutions that visit some but not all arcs and some but not all nodes. In this section we want to focus on a more restrictive class of models that require that all nodes be visited in the route from the source to the sink. Such models are aptly called node covering problems and are concerned with determining walks and tours that traverse designated vertices (nodes) of the relevant graph and are in some sense optimal. Unquestionably, the most well-known node covering problem is the so-called *traveling salesman problem* (TSP), which may be articulated for directed, nondirected and mixed graphs. The TSP is deceptively easy to state but immensely difficult to solve: a salesman wishes to find the minimum distance route that begins at a given node (depot), visits all nodes of a specified subset of nodes of a graph at least once, and returns ultimately to the starting node (depot).

Preliminary Assumptions, Definitions and NP-Completeness

Note that, if we require that all nodes (rather than a subset of nodes) of the graph be visited by a solution of the TSP, we may find there is no feasible solution. Consequently, it is usually assumed that the graph is fully connected and nondirected so that the TSP may be stated in a form that requires visiting all nodes of the graph. We shall also assume that the graph has a travel metric that obeys the *triangle inequality*; that is, we stipulate that

$$d(i,j) \leq d(i,k) + d(k,j) \quad \forall i,j,k \in \mathcal{N} \tag{3.45}$$

where $d(i,j)$ denotes the shortest distance from node $i \in \mathcal{N}$ to node $j \in \mathcal{N}$. We further assume that the distance matrix $d = [d(i,j)]$ is symmetric. The full connectivity and the triangle inequality assumptions we have made mean that there is a TSP route of shortest length that visits every node only once.

Algorithms

We do not present any graph-theoretic methods for solving the TSP since none is particularly powerful. Instead, we discuss the TSP from the point of view of Lagrangean relaxation and near network structure in Chap. 5.

3.7 Summary

In this chapter, we have demonstrated that certain classical network problems are special cases of the linear minimum cost flow problem. These include the minimum path problem and the maximal flow problem. We noted that the network simplex algorithm studied in Chap. 4 may be applied to the minimum path and maximal flow problems. However, specialized algorithms for solving these two types of problems are more efficient. The most well known of the specialized algorithms for solving the minimum path problem is Dijkstra's labeling algorithm. A specialized algorithm for solving the maximal flow problem based on the idea of flow augmenting paths is another labeling method. As such, the flow augmentation algorithm depends on the availability of a path finding utility. Such a utility algorithm was presented and allows the building of trees (not necessarily spanning trees) that identify paths from a given source to a given sink.

For constructing spanning trees, two algorithmic philosophies were reviewed. These are: (i) labeling with multiple arc introduction, and (ii) single arc introduction. We will see in Chap. 4 that the notion of a spanning tree and algorithms for finding spanning trees are fundamental to developing a generalization of the simplex algorithm of linear programming applicable to LPs with network structure.

3.8 References and Additional Reading

Ahuja, R. K., Magnanti, T. L., & Orlin, J. B. (1993). *Network flows: Theory, algorithms and applications*. Englewoord Cliffs, NJ: Prentice-Hall.

Berge, C. (1962). *The theory of graphs and its applications*. London: Methuen.

Chandrasekaran, R. (1969). Total unimodularity of matrices. *SIAM Journal on Applied Mathematics, 11*, 1032–1034.

Christofides, N. (1975). *Graph theory: An algorithmic approach*. New York: Academic.

Dinc, E. A. (1970). Algorithm for solution of a problem of maximum flow in networks with power estimation. *Soviet Mathematics Doklady, 11*, 1277–1280.

Edmonds, J., & Johnson, E. (1973). Matching, Euler tours and the Chinese postman problem. *Mathematical Programming, 5*, 88–124.

Ford, L. R., & Fulkerson, D. R. (1957). A simple algorithm for finding maximal network flows and an application to the Hitchcock problem. *Canadian Journal of Mathematics, 9*, 210–218.

Ford, L. R., & Fulkerson, D. R. (1962). *Flows in networks.* Princeton, NJ: Princeton University Press.

Fulkerson, D. R., & Dantzig, G. B. (1955). Computation of maximal flows in networks. *Naval Research Logistics Quarterly, 2*, 277–283.

Gondran, M., & Minoux, M. (1984). *Graphs and algorithms.* New York: John Wiley.

Heller, I. (1957). On linear systems with integral valued solutions. *Pacific Journal of Mathematics, 7*, 1351–1364.

Hillier, F. S., & Lieberman, G. J. (1955). *Introduction to operations research.* New York: McGraw Hill.

Heller, I., & Tompkins, C. B. (1956). An extension of a theorem of Dantzig. In H. W. Kuhn, & A. W. Tucker (Eds.), *Linear inequalities and related systems* (pp. 247–254). Princeton, NJ: Princeton University Press.

Hoffman, A. J., & Heller, I. (1962). On unimodular matrices. *Pacific Journal of Mathematics, 12*, 1321–1327.

Hoffman, A. J., & Kruskal, J. B. (1958). Integer boundary points of convex polyhedra. In H. W. Kuhn, & A. W. Tucker (Eds.), *Linear inequalities and related systems* (pp. 223–246). Princeton, NJ: Princeton University Press.

Larson, R. C., & Odoni, A. R. (1981). *Urban operations research.* Englewood Cliffs, NJ: Prentice-Hall.

Mei-Ko, K. (1952). Graphic programming using odd or even points. *Chinese Mathematics, 1*(3), 237–277.

Veinott, A. F. (1968). Extreme points of Leontief substitution systems. *Linear Algebra Applications, 1*, 181–194.

4

Programs with Network Structure

IN THIS CHAPTER WE present an algorithm for solving the most fundamental of all network flow problems, the single commodity linear minimum cost flow problem. The algorithm we emphasize is the *network simplex algorithm*. Our point of view relies heavily on the so-called *revised form of the simplex algorithm* of linear programming.

The following is an outline of the principal topics covered in this chapter:

Section 4.1: Revised Form of the Simplex. We present the most commonly encountered form of the simplex algorithm for numerical solution of large linear programs. Knowledge of its structure will facilitate our explanation of the network simplex algorithm in this chapter.

Section 4.2: The Network Simplex. We explain both informally and formally how the simplex algorithm may be implemented for LPs with totally unimodular constraint matrices in a way that obviates explicit matrix inversion and requires only addition and subtraction.

Section 4.3: Degeneracy. We briefly discuss the problem of revisiting a basis.

Section 4.4: Explicit Upper and Lower Bounds. We introduce explicit upper and lower bounds for arc variables and describe how the reduced cost optimality test must be modified to account for them.

Section 4.5: Detailed Example of the Network Simplex. We present a numerical example due to Bradley et al. (1977) that illustrates in some detail how to apply the network simplex to actual problems.

Section 4.6: Nonlinear Programs with Network Structure. We discuss the role of congestion in motivating nonlinear minimum cost flow models and introduce the notion of a feasible direction algorithm.

Section 4.7: The Frank-Wolfe Algorithm. We discuss a popular feasible direction algorithm that has been widely employed to solve nonlinear programs arising in the study of network flows.

T.L. Friesz, D. Bernstein, *Foundations of Network Optimization and Games*,
Complex Networks and Dynamic Systems 3,
DOI 10.1007/978-1-4899-7594-2_4

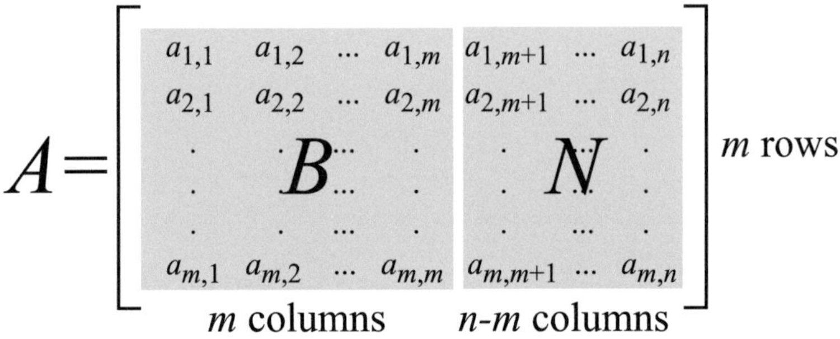

FIGURE 4.1: PARTITION OF THE CONSTRAINT MATRIX

Section 4.9: Primal Affine Scaling. We introduce one variety of interior point algorithm known as affine scaling and show how it arises from a careful analysis of the optimality conditions for linearly constrained nonlinear programs when barrier functions are employed to assure interiority.

Section 4.10: Nonlinear Network Example of the Frank-Wolfe Algorithm. In this section we present the numerical solution of a nonlinear minimum cost flow problem.

Section 4.11: Network Example of Primal Affine Scaling. In this section we use primal affine scaling to solve a problem with network structure.

Section 4.12: Linear Minimum Cost Flow Example of Affine Scaling. In the final section, we present an example that uses affine scaling to solve a linear minimum cost flow problem.

4.1 The Revised Form of the Simplex

Consider the following abstract linear program

$$\left.\begin{array}{c} \min\ Z = c^T x \\ \\ Ax = b \\ \\ x \geq 0 \end{array}\right\} \text{LP} \tag{4.1}$$

subject to

where there is now neither the presumption that A has network structure nor the presumption that the decision variables correspond to arc flows.

We assume that $c \in \Re^n$, $x \in \Re^n$ and $b \in \Re^m$ are column vectors, and construct a conformal partition of linear program (4.1) into basic and nonbasic components. The essential aspects of this partition are summarized by Fig. 4.1, identifying basic and nonbasic submatrices of A for which the number of columns (also the number of decision variables) n is strictly greater than the number of rows (constraint equations) m. That is, $n > m$. The A matrix is evidently rectangular, the B matrix is square, and the number of partitions $A = (B\ N)$ may be large but is definitely finite. We now make a conformal partition of the x and c vectors:

$$x = \begin{pmatrix} x_B \\ x_N \end{pmatrix}$$

$$c = \begin{pmatrix} c_B \\ c_N \end{pmatrix}$$

where the subscript B refers to columns of A in the basis matrix B and the subscript N refers to columns of A in nonbasis matrix N.

We take A to be of full row rank; so the squareness of B means that B^{-1} exists and is well defined. It follows immediately that

$$Ax = b \Longrightarrow \begin{pmatrix} B & N \end{pmatrix} \begin{pmatrix} x_B \\ x_N \end{pmatrix} = b \tag{4.2}$$

$$\Longrightarrow Bx_B + Nx_N = b \tag{4.3}$$

$$\Longrightarrow x_B = B^{-1}b - B^{-1}Nx_N \tag{4.4}$$

We are now free to define a *basic solution* as one for which

$$\left.\begin{array}{r} x_B = B^{-1}b \\ \\ x_N = 0 \end{array}\right\} \tag{4.5}$$

If in addition $x_B = B^{-1}b \geq 0$, (4.5) is said to be a *basic feasible solution.*

A consequence of (4.4) is that

$$\begin{aligned} c^T x &= c_B^T x_B + c_N^T x_N \\ &= c_B^T (B^{-1}b - B^{-1}Nx_N) \\ &= c_B^T B^{-1}b + [c_N^T - c_B^T B^{-1}N]x_N \\ &= Z_0 + \bar{c}_N^T x_N \end{aligned} \tag{4.6}$$

where $Z_0 = c_B^T B^{-1}b$ is the "original" objective function value prior to a basis change and

$$\bar{c}_N^T \equiv c_N^T - c_B^T B^{-1}N \tag{4.7}$$

is the reduced cost vector for non-basic variables. Expression (4.6) makes clear that there will be no potential to improve the objective function if $\bar{c}_N \geq 0$. This optimality test is easily carried out by performing the multiplications intrinsic to the definition $\bar{c}_N \equiv c_N - c_B B^{-1}N$. It is also apparent from (4.6) that if any component of $\bar{c}_N$, say $\bar{c}_{N_j}$, is negative there is a potential to improve the objective function by *pivoting*. That is, the variable x_{N_j} is said to wish to enter the basis. Our job in this event is to ascertain which basic variable x_{B_i} leaves the basis so that exactly m variables are basic. This is done by using the ratio test familiar from the tableau form of the simplex algorithm. The ratio test, as its name implies, involves division.

The following is a succinct statement of the revised simplex algorithm:

THE REVISED SIMPLEX ALGORITHM

Step 0. *(Initialization)* Determine an initial basic feasible solution (BFS) and associated conformal partition

$$\begin{aligned} A &= \begin{pmatrix} B & N \end{pmatrix} \\ x &= \begin{pmatrix} x_B \\ x_N \end{pmatrix} = \begin{pmatrix} B^{-1}b \\ 0 \end{pmatrix} \\ c &= \begin{pmatrix} c_B \\ c_N \end{pmatrix} \end{aligned}$$

Step 1. *(Optimality test)* If

$$\bar{c}_N^T \equiv c_N^T - c_B^T B^{-1} N \geq 0$$

then stop, since the current bfs is optimal. Otherwise choose a nonbasic variable x_s for which $(\bar{c}_N)_s < 0$ to enter the basis.

Step 2. *(Unboundedness test and selection of leaving variable)* If

$$\bar{a}_{is} \leq 0 \quad i = 1, \ldots, m$$

where

$$B^{-1}N \equiv (\bar{a}_{ij})$$

then stop, since the linear program is unbounded. Otherwise select the basic variable x_r, where

$$\begin{aligned} r &= \arg\min_{i \in [1,m]} \left\{ \frac{\bar{b}_i}{\bar{a}_{is}} : \bar{a}_{is} > 0 \right\} \\ \bar{b} &= B^{-1}b, \end{aligned}$$

to leave the basis.

Step 3. *(Pivoting)* Where a_k is the kth column of the $A = (a_1, \ldots, a_n)$ matrix, that is

$$a_k \equiv \begin{pmatrix} a_{1k} \\ \vdots \\ a_{mk} \end{pmatrix},$$

perform a pivot creating a new conformal partition with

$$B \longleftarrow (a_1, \ldots, a_{r-1}, a_s, a_{r+1}, \ldots, a_m)$$

$$N \longleftarrow (a_{m+1}, \ldots, a_{s-1}, a_r, a_{s+1}, \ldots, a_n)$$

Go to Step 1.

We will find that both the determination of entering and leaving variables may be replaced, *for problems with network structure*, by a pivoting mechanism that avoids all multiplication and division, making the simplex into an algorithm that requires only addition and subtraction for problems with network structure. This important and computationally attractive feature depends on the concept of a spanning tree and the relationship of spanning trees to bases for problems with network structure.

4.2 The Network Simplex

Let us consider the network LP or linear minimum cost flow problem (LMCFP)

subject to

$$\left.\begin{array}{r} \min c^T x \\ Ax = b \\ x \geq 0 \end{array}\right\} \text{LMCFP} \tag{4.8}$$

where the associated graph is $G(\mathcal{N}, \mathcal{A})$; the cardinality of the node set is $|\mathcal{N}| = m$; the cardinality of the arc set is $|\mathcal{A}| = n$; A is an $m \times n$ matrix that has network structure; $x \in \Re^n$; $b \in \Re^m$; $c \in \Re^n$; $b \in \Re^n$; and we have no capacity constraints (although we will reintroduce them, in due course). We assume that the network is in equilibrium; that is, the sum of net supplies is zero. A direct consequence of this assumption is that it is not immediately obvious how to form a basis from A. This is because the sum of the rows of A is zero and, hence, the rows are not linearly independent; so A is *not* of rank m. However, it turns out that A has rank $m - 1$, and we can add a dummy column to submatrices of A to obtain a basis.

Perhaps the easiest way to understand the above point regarding the rank of A is with an example. Specifically, let us consider the example network of Fig. 4.2. Let us define the arc flow vector by

$$x = \begin{bmatrix} x_{12} & x_{13} & x_{23} & x_{24} & x_{34} \end{bmatrix}^T$$

and conformally define the cost vector

$$c = \begin{bmatrix} c_{12} & c_{13} & c_{23} & c_{24} & c_{34} \end{bmatrix}^T = \begin{bmatrix} 1 & 4 & 3 & 2 & 5 \end{bmatrix}^T \tag{4.9}$$

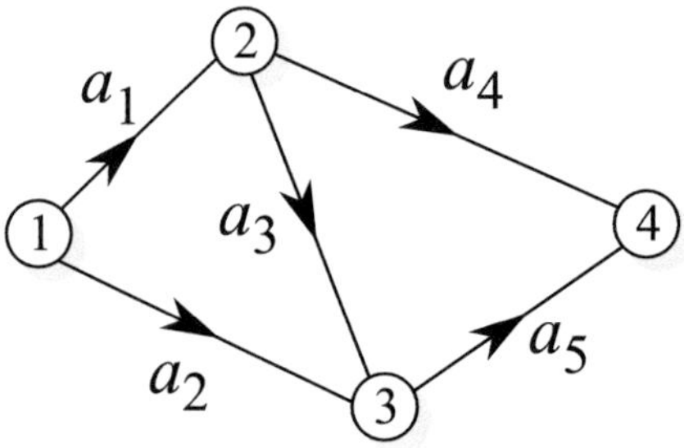

FIGURE 4.2: EXAMPLE NETWORK

The corresponding A matrix for this network is given by:

$$A = \begin{bmatrix} +1 & +1 & 0 & 0 & 0 \\ -1 & 0 & +1 & +1 & 0 \\ 0 & -1 & -1 & 0 & +1 \\ 0 & 0 & 0 & -1 & -1 \end{bmatrix}. \tag{4.10}$$

This matrix is clearly not of rank 4 since

$$\text{Row } 4 = (-1)\,(\text{row } 1 + \text{row } 2 + \text{row } 3)$$

To show that A has rank 3 we need only find a 3×3 submatrix of A that is nonsingular. To do so, first consider the following matrix constructed by taking the first, second, and fifth columns of A

$$A_S = \begin{bmatrix} +1 & +1 & 0 \\ -1 & 0 & 0 \\ 0 & -1 & +1 \\ 0 & 0 & -1 \end{bmatrix} \tag{4.11}$$

Note that A_S corresponds to a spanning tree of the original network. By dropping the last row of A_S and rearranging the remaining rows, create the following square submatrix of A:

$$M_{A_S} = \begin{bmatrix} -1 & 0 & 0 \\ +1 & +1 & 0 \\ 0 & -1 & +1 \end{bmatrix} \tag{4.12}$$

Since this matrix is lower triangular, it clearly has an inverse. Hence the rank of M_{A_S} is 3 and, consequently, the rank of A is 3. Therefore, in order to create a basis, we need only select three columns from A. However, the basis must be square and have rank equal to the number of variables. The way out of this quandary is to designate a so-called *root arc* which is a *headless* arc outbound from the designated *root node*; without loss of generality we may take the root node to be node m. The root arc has zero cost. Because the root arc has no head node, its corresponding row of the basis carries a single +1 entry. Introduction of the root arc leads to the $m \times m$ basis matrix

$$B = \begin{pmatrix} A_S & \begin{matrix} 0_{(m-1)\times 1} \\ +1 \end{matrix} \end{pmatrix} \tag{4.13}$$

which for our specific example becomes

$$B = \begin{bmatrix} +1 & +1 & 0 & 0 \\ -1 & 0 & 0 & 0 \\ 0 & -1 & +1 & 0 \\ 0 & 0 & -1 & +1 \end{bmatrix} \tag{4.14}$$

Since the root arc is artificial, there are only three "real" basic variables corresponding to the first, second, and fifth columns of A selected to form the basis. That is, the conformal partition we have selected consists of (4.14) together with

$$\begin{aligned} N &= \begin{bmatrix} 0 & 0 \\ +1 & +1 \\ -1 & 0 \\ 0 & -1 \end{bmatrix} \\ x_B &= \begin{bmatrix} x_{12} & x_{13} & x_{34} \end{bmatrix}^T \\ x_N &= \begin{bmatrix} x_{23} & x_{24} \end{bmatrix}^T \\ c_B &= \begin{bmatrix} c_{12} & c_{13} & c_{34} \end{bmatrix}^T = \begin{bmatrix} 1 & 4 & 5 \end{bmatrix}^T \\ c_N &= \begin{bmatrix} c_{23} & c_{24} \end{bmatrix}^T = \begin{bmatrix} 3 & 2 \end{bmatrix}^T \end{aligned}$$

where the cost coefficients of the objective function are introduced immediately above for the first time in this discussion. The basis (4.14) can be restated in the lower triangular form

$$B' = \begin{bmatrix} -1 & 0 & 0 & 0 \\ 1 & +1 & 0 & 0 \\ 0 & -1 & +1 & 0 \\ 0 & 0 & -1 & +1 \end{bmatrix} \tag{4.15}$$

by reordering rows, so that we see immediately that the inverse basis matrix B exists and is well-defined.

The matrix B' in (4.15) indicates that the only flow outbound from node 4 is over the root arc, since there is only a single +1 entry in the fourth column. Note that the graph of A_S is a spanning tree of the original network. The graph of B is called a *rooted spanning tree* of the original network, where by "rooted spanning tree" we mean a spanning tree with a root arc connected to it. We naturally suspect that there is a correspondence between bases and spanning trees.

4.2.1 Bases for Network Programs

To explore the relationship between bases and spanning trees, we begin with the following result pertaining to equivalent characterizations of trees:

Theorem 4.1 *(Equivalence of trees) Let S be a network with m nodes. Then, the following statements are equivalent:*

(1) S is a tree; that is, S is connected and does not possess any loops (circuits);

(2) S contains no circuits and has $m-1$ arcs;

(3) S is connected and has $m-1$ arcs;

(4) Any two nodes of S are connected by exactly one path;

(5) S contains no circuits, but the addition of any new arc creates exactly one circuit; and

(6) S is connected but loses this property if any arc is deleted.

Proof. See Berge (1962). ■

Next we develop the lower triangular property of certain submatrices of the arc-node incidence matrix:

Lemma 4.1 *(Lower triangular arc-node incidence matrix) Let $\mathbf{M}_{A_S}$ be an $(m-1) \times (m-1)$ submatrix of A, the arc-node incidence matrix. Then, $\mathbf{M}_{A_S}$ is lower triangular (or can be made lower triangular).*

Proof. Our proof follows Bazaraa et al. (2011). Start with an $m \times n$ incidence matrix, A, and identify a spanning tree, T, and associated submatrix, A_S, consisting of the m nodes together with $m-1$ arcs that do not form a loop. Now, drop one node (row) to obtain the $(m-1) \times (m-1)$ matrix $\mathbf{M}_{A_S}$. The network associated with $\mathbf{M}_{A_S}$ will have at least one end (i.e., one node with only one arc incident to it) since the network is a tree. By conducting a permutation of rows and columns of $\mathbf{M}_{A_S}$, this single non-zero entry can be moved to the first row; that is

$$M_{A_S} = \begin{bmatrix} \pm 1 & 0^T \\ p & M'_{A_S} \end{bmatrix} \tag{4.16}$$

where p is the matrix dictated by the manipulations required to assure M'_{A_S} is now an $(m-1) \times (m-2)$ matrix. Again, there exists a node which has exactly one arc incident to it corresponding to a single non-zero entry in the $(m-1)$th row of M'_{A_S}. By permuting rows and columns, this non-zero entry can be brought to the $(2, 2)$ position as below:

$$A_S = \begin{bmatrix} \pm 1 & 0 & 0^T \\ p_1 & \pm 1 & 0^T \\ p_2 & q & M''_{A_S} \end{bmatrix} \tag{4.17}$$

where p_1, p_2, and q are matrices dictated by the operations that produce the indicated structure. If we conduct the same procedure $m-1$ times, all $m-1$ columns will become fixed. We are left with a $(m-1) \times (m-1)$ matrix which is lower triangular. ■

Another result important to our development is

Lemma 4.2 *(Lower triangular pre-basis) From A, the arc-node incidence matrix, select $m-1$ columns to form the $m \times (m-1)$ submatrix A_S. Next, form the $m \times m$ matrix B from A_S according to*

$$B = \begin{pmatrix} A_S & \begin{matrix} 0_{(m-1)\times 1} \\ 1 \end{matrix} \end{pmatrix}$$

Then B is lower triangular (or can be made so) and corresponds to a rooted spanning tree of the network giving rise to A.

Proof. Lower triangularity of B is immediate from the lower triangularity of M_{A_S} ensured by Lemma 4.1, since B can be formed by adding a final row and a root column to M_{A_S}. We seek a contradiction to establish the correspondence. Specifically, assume an $(m-1) \times (m-1)$ triangular submatrix does not give rise to a tree, since this is the only way B can fail to be a rooted spanning tree. To this end, note that it follows from Theorem 4.1 that there must be a circuit in the network, which implies the $m-1$ rows are not independent. But this contradicts the fact that we have an $(m-1) \times (m-1)$ triangular matrix. So an $(m-1) \times (m-1)$ triangular matrix must give rise to a tree. The fact that it is a spanning tree is immediate from the dimensionality. The rooted nature of the spanning tree is immediate by virtue of the way B is constructed. ■

We can now state and prove the following:

Theorem 4.2 *(Basic solution to a spanning tree) A rooted spanning tree corresponds to a basis. That is, a feasible solution is basic if and only if the associated subnetwork is a rooted spanning tree.*

Proof. The proof is divided into two parts.

(i) [rooted spanning tree $\Longrightarrow$ basis] Let B be a matrix corresponding to a rooted spanning tree of A. If we take $x_N = 0$ then all we must show is that $x_B = B^{-1}b$ uniquely determines the basic variables. It follows from Lemma 4.2 that $Bx_B = b$ can be written in the following form:

$$\begin{aligned}
\beta_{11}x_1 &= b_1 \\
\beta_{21}x_1 + \beta_{22}x_2 &= b_2 \qquad (4.18) \\
&\vdots \\
\beta_{t1}x_{11} + \beta_{t2}x_2 + \cdots + \beta_{tt}x_t &= b_t, \qquad (4.19)
\end{aligned}$$

where $t = m - 1$ and

$$x_B = \begin{pmatrix} x_1 & x_2 & \ldots & x_t \end{pmatrix}^T$$

is the vector of basic variables. That is, for $k \in [1, t]$, each x_k is some particular basic arc flow x_{ij}. Clearly the solution of this system is unique and given by

$$\begin{aligned}
x_1 &= b_1/\beta_{11} \\
x_k &= (1/\beta_{kk})[b_k - \sum_{j=1}^{k-1} \beta_{kj}x_j] \quad k > 1
\end{aligned}$$

(ii) [Basis $\Longrightarrow$ spanning tree] The only way this can fail to be true is if the subnetwork associated with the basis (and having $m - 1$ arcs) contains a circuit. But if a circuit exists, some of the columns of the basis are not linearly independent. This is a contradiction. Hence, an acyclic subnetwork with $m - 1$ arcs is a spanning tree. ■

4.2.2 Determining the Entering Column

In the usual implementation of the simplex algorithm, to determine the entering column, we need to determine the reduced costs of the nonbasic variables x_N given by

$$\bar{c}_N = c_N - w^T N \qquad (4.20)$$

where $w^T = c_B B^{-1}$ is the vector of dual variables for the flow conservation constraints and is the solution of the system $w^T B = c_B$. Recall that, in simplex calculations, the reduced costs of basic variables are always zero by construction:

$$\begin{aligned}
\bar{c}_B &= c_B - w^T B \\
&= c_B - \left(c_B B^{-1}\right) B = c_B - c_B = 0 \qquad (4.21)
\end{aligned}$$

Further recall, unless otherwise stated, the network flow pattern is an equilibrium (vanishing net supply, $\sum_{i \in \mathcal{N}} b_i = 0$).

Consequently, since the root arc has zero cost, we have

$$w^T A = (w_1, w_2, \ldots, w_{m-1}, w_m) \begin{pmatrix} A_S & 0_{(m-1)\times 1} \\ 0_{1\times(m-1)} & 1 \end{pmatrix} = \begin{pmatrix} c_B \\ 0 \end{pmatrix} \quad (4.22)$$

A consequence of this identity is that the value of the last dual variable (w_m) is set to zero. That is, as can be seen by carrying out the relevant matrix multiplication, (4.22) is equivalent to

$$(w_1, w_2, \ldots, w_{m-1})\, A_S = c_B \quad (4.23)$$

$$w_m = 0 \quad (4.24)$$

Note that node m chosen for fixing the dual variable is the root node. We may designate any node to serve as the root node and assign any numerical value to the dual variable associated with that root node, although the value zero simplifies the associated arithmetic. The act of arbitrarily fixing the value of one of the dual variables means that we have precisely the number of equations, given by (4.23), needed to solve for the remaining $m-1$ dual variables. Given the lower triangular nature of B, it is very easy to calculate w, provided one of the dual variables is set arbitrarily, by use of the reduced cost formula for basic variables:

$$(\bar{c}_B)_{ij} = (c_B)_{ij} - w_{B_i} + w_{B_j} = 0 \quad (4.25)$$

obtained from (4.23) and the totally unimodular structure of A and, hence, of B. Knowledge of the dual variables gained in this way allows us to determine the reduced costs for each nonbasic variable:

$$\bar{c}_N = c_N - w^T N \quad (4.26)$$

Again since A is totally unimodular so is N. Therefore, $[N]_{ij}$ is a column vector with $+1$ in row i, -1 in row j, and 0 in all other positions; it follows immediately that

$$(\bar{c}_N)_{ij} = (c_N)_{ij} - w_i + w_j \quad (4.27)$$

So, it is very easy to calculate the reduced costs $\bar{c}_N$ needed to determine entering variables and check for optimality.

We reiterate that there are exactly as many equations of the type (4.25) as there are basic variables, namely $m-1$ when there are m nodes (flow conservation equations). Yet we need to find m dual variables w_i since there are m nodes. That is to say, we have one too few equations to determine the dual variables uniquely; this difficulty is overcome by arbitrarily assigning a convenient value to one of the dual variables and determining the remaining dual variables in light of this assigned value.

For an illustration of the mechanics of determining dual variables and reduced costs, again consider the network of Fig. 4.2. A spanning tree (and hence a basis) for this network is given in Fig. 4.3, where it is evident that arcs a_1,

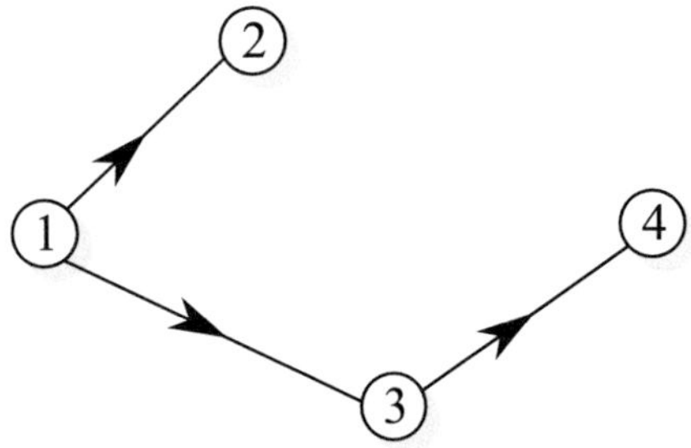

FIGURE 4.3: SPANNING TREE (IGNORING ARC DIRECTION) FOR EXAMPLE NETWORK

a_2, and a_5 of the network of Fig. 4.2 are included in the spanning tree. That is, (4.27) becomes

$$\begin{bmatrix} w_1 & w_2 & w_3 & w_4 \end{bmatrix} \cdot \begin{bmatrix} +1 & +1 & 0 & 0 \\ -1 & 0 & 0 & 0 \\ 0 & -1 & +1 & 0 \\ 0 & 0 & -1 & +1 \end{bmatrix} = \begin{bmatrix} c_{12} \\ c_{13} \\ c_{34} \\ 0 \end{bmatrix}^T = \begin{bmatrix} 1 \\ 4 \\ 5 \\ 0 \end{bmatrix} \tag{4.28}$$

since we have previously chosen the first, second, and fifth columns of A to enter the basis, and also recognized that a last column is required to account for the root node. Starting with the last column of B in (4.28), we get:

$$w_4 = 0 \tag{4.29}$$

Working backward we find:

$$w_3 - w_4 = c_{34} \Longrightarrow w_3 = c_{34} + w_4 = 5 + 0 = 5 \tag{4.30}$$

$$w_1 - w_3 = c_{13} \Longrightarrow w_1 = c_{13} + w_3 = 4 + 5 = 9 \tag{4.31}$$

$$w_1 - w_2 = c_{12} \Longrightarrow w_2 = w_1 - c_{12} = 9 - 1 = 8 \tag{4.32}$$

These dual variables allow the unambiguous determination of reduced costs and, thereby, optimality. In particular, we find that the reduced costs of the nonbasic variables are

$$\bar{c}_{23} = c_{23} - w_2 + w_3 = 3 - 8 + 5 = 0$$

$$\bar{c}_{24} = c_{24} - w_2 + w_4 = 2 - 8 + 0 = -6$$

from which we see that

$$\bar{c}_N = \begin{bmatrix} \bar{c}_{23} & \bar{c}_{24} \end{bmatrix}^T = [0 \ -6]^T \ngeq 0$$

so that the current basis is not optimal. We say that nonbasic variable x_{24} wishes to enter the basis since its reduced cost is negative.

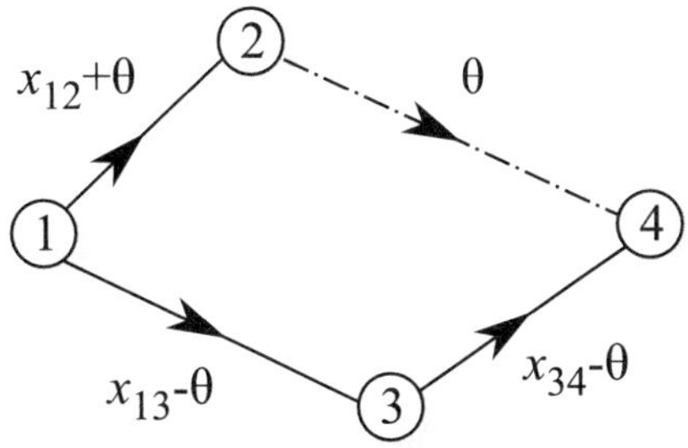

FIGURE 4.4: CYCLE CREATED BY ENTERING VARIABLE

4.2.3 Determining the Exiting Column

Observe that the addition of any nonbasic arc (i, j) to a basis creates a loop (ignoring the orientation of the arcs) since each basis is a tree. As a result, to complete a simplex pivot, some previously basic arc must be removed from the newly formed loop to maintain the tree structure of the basis. Determination of which variable leaves the basis is greatly facilitated by the network structure of the minimum cost flow problem. In particular, observe that if flow conservation is to be maintained at the nodes, then flows will be updated according to:

$$x_{ij} \longleftarrow \begin{cases} x_{ij} + \theta & \text{if } (i,j) \text{ is forward in the newly created loop} \\ x_{ij} - \theta & \text{if } (i,j) \text{ is reverse in the newly created loop} \\ x_{ij} & \text{if } (i,j) \text{ is not in the newly created loop,} \end{cases} \tag{4.33}$$

where θ is the flow on the entering arc. Consequently, for the example network of Fig. 4.2 and the example spanning tree of Fig. 4.3, introduction of the entering variable x_{24} means that

$$\left.\begin{aligned} x_{24} &\longleftarrow \theta \\ x_{12} &\longleftarrow x_{12} + \theta \\ x_{13} &\longleftarrow x_{13} - \theta \\ x_{34} &\longleftarrow x_{34} - \theta \end{aligned}\right\} \tag{4.34}$$

That is, the loop of Fig. 4.4 is created. Let us suppose $x_{13} > x_{34}$; thus, because we have imposed no upper bound restrictions, θ is set to the current value of x_{34}, x_{24} becomes basic, and x_{34} is driven from the basis as indicated in (4.34). For networks whose flows are non-negative but not explicitly bounded from above, this example makes clear that the variable that leaves the basis is the one made zero. Since only reverse arcs are decreasing, this means that the arc that leaves the basis is the reverse arc with the smallest flow.

4.2.4 The Network Simplex Algorithm and Initial Solutions

The following is a succinct statement of the network simplex algorithm:

The Network Simplex Algorithm

Step 0. *(Initialization)* Determine an initial basic feasible solution (bfs) that is a rooted spanning tree for the network of interest.

Step 1. *(Update dual variables)* Calculate one dual variable w_i for each flow conservation constraint (node $i \in \mathcal{N}$) of the network.

Step 2. *(Optimality and selection of entering variable)* Find the reduced costs of all nonbasic flow variables. If

$$(\bar{c}_N)_{ij} = (c_N)_{ij} - w_i + w_j \geq 0 \tag{4.35}$$

stop; the current bfs is optimal. Otherwise select any nonbasic arc with negative reduced cost to enter the basis.

Step 3. *(Pivoting)* Identify the loop created by the introduction of the new basic arc identified in Step 2. Within this loop, distinguish between forward and reverse arcs and update flows to create a new basic feasible solution. Go to Step 1.

A detailed numerical example of the network simplex algorithm is presented in Sect. 4.5.

Finding feasible tree solutions with which to begin the network simplex is not at all trivial, although initial solutions are typically automatically generated by commercial software package. One approach is to choose the initial solution according to the following:

$$\begin{aligned} x_{kj} &= b_j && \text{if } b_j \geq 0, j \neq k \\ x_{ik} &= -b_i && \text{if } b_i < 0, i \neq k \\ x_{ij} &= 0 && \text{if } (i,j) \notin T_k \end{aligned} \tag{4.36}$$

where $k \in \mathcal{N}$ is the node to which we may associate a tree T_k having an arc from k to each sink or intermediate node and an arc to k from each source. Of course, an actual network may fail to have such a node $k \in \mathcal{N}$ and associated tree T_k of the type we have just described. In particular, we may find that construction of T_k will require the introduction of *artificial arcs* that are not part of the network of interest. In this case, we attach to such artificial arcs very high costs so that they will be driven out of the solution, leaving behind a feasible solution as in the traditional Phase I approach of linear programming.

4.3 Degeneracy

As in ordinary linear programming, the network simplex may encounter degeneracy, by which we mean $B^{-1}b$ has one or more components which are zero. An iteration, or pivot, during which this occurs is said to be a degenerate pivot, and degenerate pivots are of importance because they may lead to *cycling* (revisiting a previous basic feasible solution) and, hence, nonconvergence. The following result from Chvatal (1983) gives one situation in which cycling does not occur even in the presence of degeneracy:

Theorem 4.3 *If in each degenerate pivot leading from S (the spanning tree of the current basis) to $S+e-f$ (the spanning tree formed by adding arc e and dropping arc f), the entering arc is directed away from the root in $S+e-f$, then the network simplex does not cycle.*

Degeneracy is rarely encountered in practice. When it is encountered, cycling is prevented by a procedure due to Cunningham (1979) that may be viewed as relying on Theorem 4.3. In particular, one exploits the notion of a *strongly feasible tree*, which is a tree such that every arc $(i,j) \in \mathcal{A}$ with flow $x_{ij} = 0$ is directed away from the root node. If all the trees that are constructed by the network simplex are strongly feasible, then the hypothesis of Theorem 4.3 is met at each iteration and cycling cannot occur. As explained in Chvatal (1983), selecting an initial basis that has a strongly feasible tree is not difficult; furthermore, each subsequent basic feasible solution will have an associated strongly feasible tree if the leaving arc is appropriately selected.

4.4 Explicit Upper and Lower Bound Constraints

As is known from the theory of the simplex method of linear programming, the presence of upper bound constraints on decision variables requires that the reduced cost optimality criterion be modified. Specifically, if upper and lower bound constraints of the form

$$L = \begin{pmatrix} \vdots \\ L_{ij} \\ \vdots \end{pmatrix} \leq x = \begin{pmatrix} \vdots \\ x_{ij} \\ \vdots \end{pmatrix} \leq U = \begin{pmatrix} \vdots \\ U_{ij} \\ \vdots \end{pmatrix} \tag{4.37}$$

are appended to the linear program (4.1), where

$$\begin{aligned} L &\in \Re_+^{|\mathcal{A}|} \\ U &\in \Re_+^{|\mathcal{A}|} \\ L_{ij} &\leq U_{ij} \quad \forall\, (i,j) \in \mathcal{A}, \end{aligned}$$

we have the following Kuhn-Tucker necessary and sufficient conditions for (4.1) with (4.37):

$$\left.\begin{array}{lcl}\bar{c}-\rho+\eta & = & 0 \\ \rho^T\,(L-x) & = & 0 \\ \eta^T(x-\;U) & = & 0 \\ \rho & \geq & 0 \\ \eta & \geq & 0\end{array}\right\} \quad (4.38)$$

where

$$\begin{array}{lcl}\bar{c} & \in & \Re^{|\mathcal{A}|} \\ \rho & \in & \Re^{|\mathcal{A}|} \\ \eta & \in & \Re^{|\mathcal{A}|}\end{array}$$

The conditions (4.38) tell us that

$$\bar{c}=\rho-\eta$$

which in turn tells us that for optimality

$$\left.\begin{array}{lll}(\bar{c}_N)_{ij}=0 & \text{if} & U_{ij}>(x_N)_{ij}>L_{ij} \\ (\bar{c}_N)_{ij}=\rho_{ij}\geq 0 & \text{if} & (x_N)_{ij}=L_{ij} \\ (\bar{c}_N)_{ij}=-\eta_{ij}\leq 0 & \text{if} & (x_N)_{ij}=U_{ij}\end{array}\right\} \quad (4.39)$$

That is, for optimality, the reduced costs of nonbasic variables not at their bounds must be zero. Furthermore, the reduced costs of nonbasic variables at their lower bounds must be nonnegative, as expected from our knowledge of problems with nonnegativity restrictions but no upper bounds on variables. However, for optimality, the reduced costs of nonbasic variables at their upper bounds must be nonpositive.

4.5 Detailed Example of the Network Simplex

Consider the network of Fig. 4.5 which corresponds to a numerical example originally proposed and solved by Bradley et al. (1977). The network in question clearly has five nodes ($m=|\mathcal{N}|=5$) and nine arcs ($n=|\mathcal{A}|=9$). In Fig. 4.5 the double arc labels describe the maximal flow capacity and unit flow cost for each arc; that is to say, each double label is of the form

$$(\text{arc capacity},\ \text{unit arc cost})$$

To initiate the network simplex algorithm, we need an initial basic feasible solution (bfs). One initial bfs is provided in Fig. 4.6 where the single arc labels describe arc flows; arcs not indicated carry zero flow. Note that in this initial

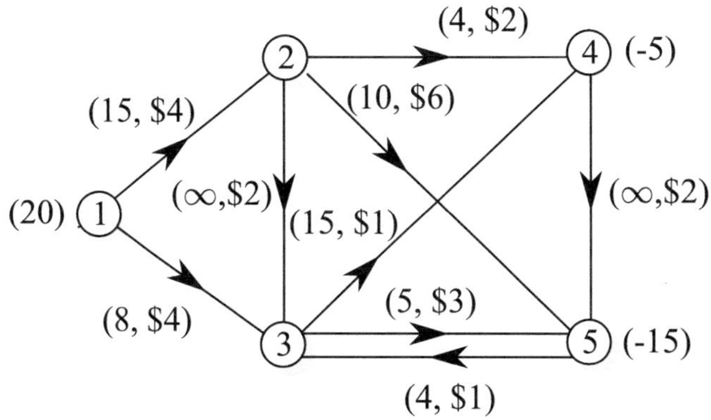

FIGURE 4.5: EXAMPLE CAPACITATED NETWORK

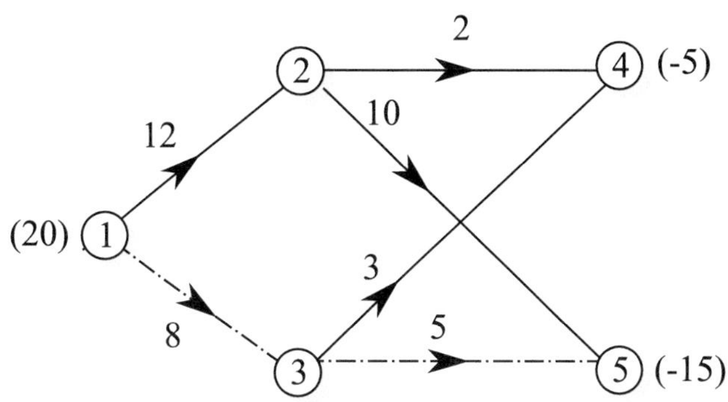

FIGURE 4.6: INITIAL BASIC FEASIBLE SOLUTION

bfs the flows x_{13} and x_{35} are at their upper bounds and declared nonbasic to assure that the number of non-root basic arcs is $m-1=5-1=4$. In Fig. 4.6, as well as all subsequent figures related to this example, such nonbasic arcs with flows at their upper bounds are indicated by "dash-dot" lines.

In Step 1, where the iteration counter k is 1, we must determine the dual variables corresponding to Fig. 4.6 so that reduced costs can be calculated and the test for optimality conducted. By arbitrarily setting $y_2=0$ and exploiting the fact that $\bar{c}_{ij}=c_{ij}-y_i+y_j=0$ for all basic variables, it is straightforward to determine that

$$\begin{aligned} y_1 &= -4 \\ y_2 &= 0 \\ y_3 &= -1 \\ y_4 &= -2 \\ y_5 &= -6 \end{aligned}$$

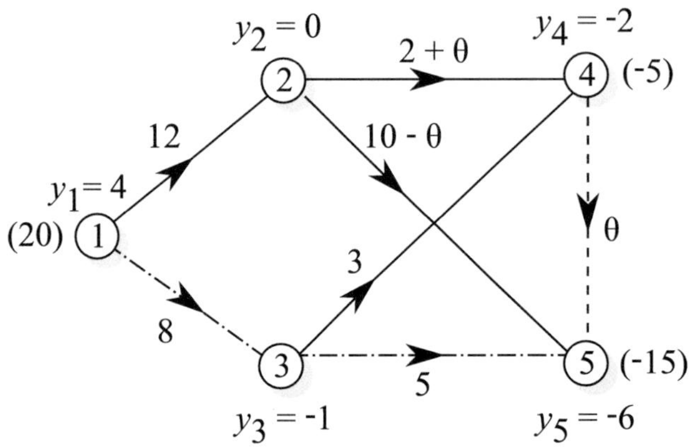

FIGURE 4.7: ITERATION 1: INTRODUCING A NEW BASIC ARC

Moreover, the values

$$
\begin{aligned}
\bar{c}_{13} &= 4 - 4 + (-1) = -1 \\
\bar{c}_{23} &= 2 - 0 + (-1) = 1 \\
\bar{c}_{35} &= 3 - (-1) + (-6) = -2 \\
\bar{c}_{45} &= 2 - (-2) + (-6) = -2 \\
\bar{c}_{53} &= 1 - (-6) + (-1) = 6
\end{aligned}
$$

follow at once.

We now select an arc whose reduced has the greatest magnitude and appropriate sign indicating nonoptimality; ties can be broken arbitrarily. In this case, we select x_{45} to enter the basis. The associated pivot operation (Step 2, $k = 1$) is summarized in Fig. 4.7 where a dashed line is used to indicate the entering arc whose flow θ is yet to be determined. The value of θ is found by incrementing and decrementing arc flows of the loop formed by the introduction of arc $(4, 5)$. We see that the least upper bound on θ is the capacity of arc $(2, 4)$, which forces us to set $\theta = 2$ and declare arc $(2, 4)$ nonbasic at its upper bound, since arc $(4, 5)$ clearly becomes basic.

The new spanning tree basis is depicted in Fig. 4.8, where we have also indicated the new values of dual variables. The dual variable values were obtained by arbitrarily setting $y_2 = 0$ and again exploiting the identity $\bar{c}_{ij} = c_{ij} - y_i + y_j = 0$ for basic variables. Knowledge of the dual variables of course allows calculation of the new reduced costs:

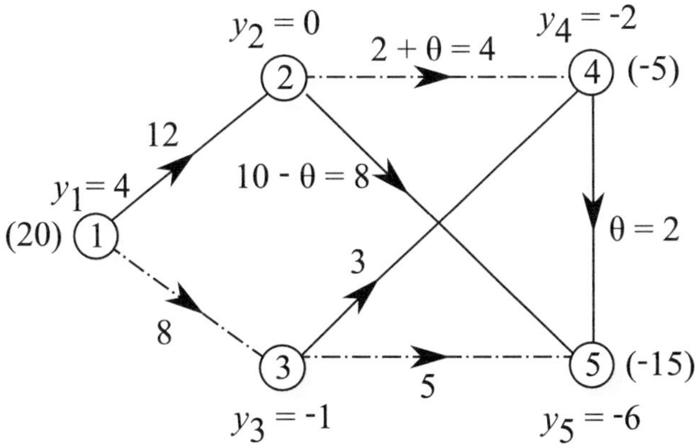

FIGURE 4.8: ITERATION 1: DETERMINING LEAVING ARC

$$\begin{aligned}
\bar{c}_{13} &= 4 - 4 + (-3) = -3 \\
\bar{c}_{23} &= 2 - 0 + (-3) = -1 \\
\bar{c}_{24} &= 2 - 0(+ - 4) = -2 \\
\bar{c}_{35} &= 3 - (-3) + (-6) = 0 \\
\bar{c}_{53} &= 1 - (-6) + (-3) = 4
\end{aligned}$$

Of the reduced costs with signs indicating nonoptimality, $\bar{c}_{23}$ has the greatest magnitude and so we select (Step 1, $k = 1$) x_{23} to enter the basis. The associated pivot operation (Step 2, $k = 1$) is also summarized in Fig. 4.8 where a dashed line is used to indicate the entering arc whose flow θ is yet to be determined. The value of θ is found by incrementing and decrementing arc flows of the loop formed by the introduction of arc $(2, 3)$. We see that the least upper bound on θ is the current flow on arc $(2, 5)$, which forces us to set $\theta = 8$ and declare arc $(2, 5)$ nonbasic.

The new spanning tree basis is depicted in Fig. 4.9, where we have also indicated the new values of dual variables. The dual variable values were obtained by again arbitrarily setting $y_2 = 0$ and exploiting the identity $\bar{c}_{ij} = c_{ij} - y_i + y_j = 0$ for basic variables. Knowledge of the dual variables of course allows calculation of the new reduced costs:

$$\begin{aligned}
\bar{c}_{13} &= 4 - 4 + (-2) = -2 \\
\bar{c}_{24} &= 2 - 0 + (-3) = -1 \\
\bar{c}_{25} &= 6 - 0 + (-5) = 1 \\
\bar{c}_{35} &= 3 - (-2) + (-5) = 0 \\
\bar{c}_{53} &= 1 - (-5) + (-2) = 4
\end{aligned}$$

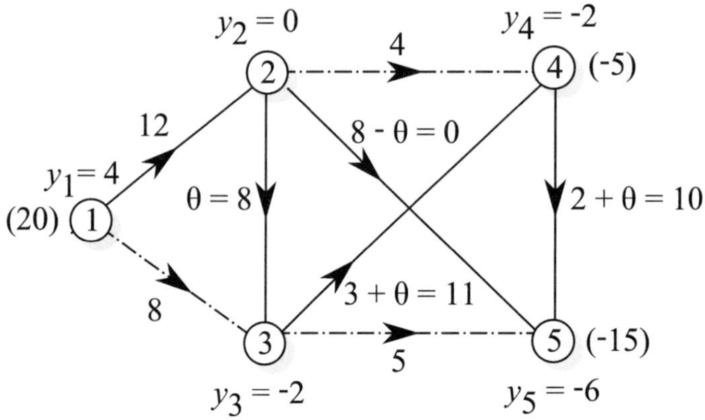

FIGURE 4.9: ITERATION 2: ADJUSTMENT FOR LOOP 2-3-4-5-2

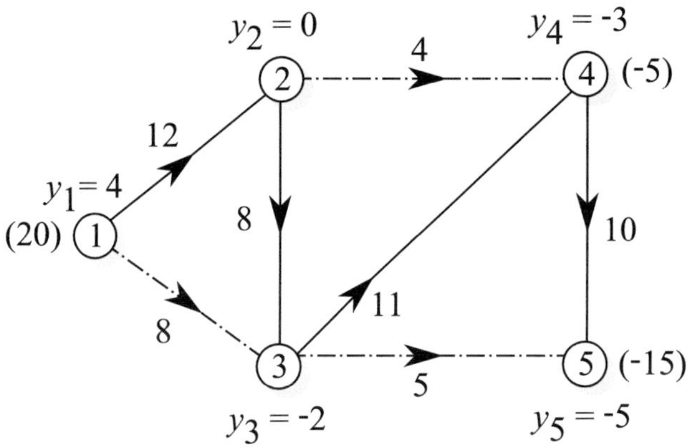

FIGURE 4.10: OPTIMAL SOLUTION

These reduced costs, when compared to (4.39), indicate clearly that an optimal solution has been achieved. That solution is presented in Fig. 4.10, for which there are six arcs with nonzero flows. However, two of these, arcs $(1,3)$ and $(2,4)$, are nonbasic and carry flows at their respective upper bounds; that is, there are $m-1=4$ non-root basic arcs, as required. As determined above, the reduced cost $\bar{c}_{35}=0$, indicating that an alternative solution may exist. In fact, it is easily verified that an alternative optimal solution is the one described by Fig. 4.11.

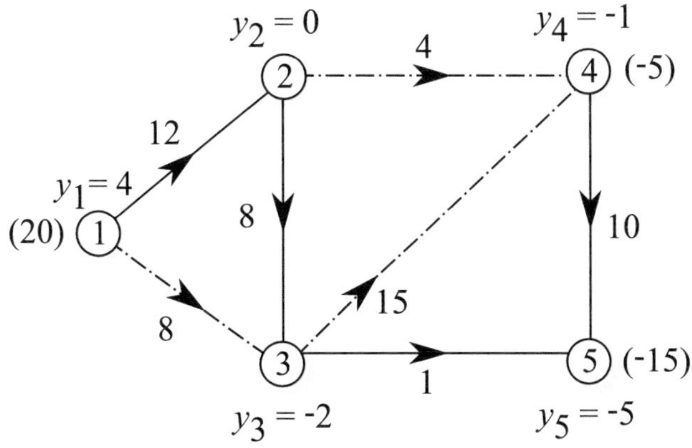

FIGURE 4.11: ALTERNATIVE OPTIMAL SOLUTION

4.6 Nonlinear Programs with Network Structure

In this section we are concerned with the nonlinear minimum cost flow problem. That is, we allow arc unit costs to explicitly reflect nonlinearities that describe congestion externalities while constraining flows to obey the same flow conservation constraints that we considered previously and that give rise to total unimodularity of the A matrix; nonnegativity of arc flows and sometimes upper bounds on arc flows are also enforced. Variants of this basic nonlinear model arise routinely in transportation, logistics, telecommunications, and spatial economics (as we shall see in later chapters). We will find that, when congestion is introduced into the minimum cost flow problem, the resulting model is still quite computationally tractable, so long as congestion makes the network-wide total cost convex.

4.6.1 Congestion

We will assume that for every arc $(i,j) \in \mathcal{A}$ of the graph $G(\mathcal{N}, \mathcal{A})$ associated with the network of interest there are arc-specific congestion cost functions of either the form

$$c_{ij}(x_{ij}) : \Re^1 \longrightarrow \Re^1_+ \tag{4.40}$$

or the form

$$c_{ij}(x) : \Re^{|\mathcal{A}|} \longrightarrow \Re^1_+ \tag{4.41}$$

where

$$x = (x_{ij} : (i,j) \in \mathcal{A})^T \in \Re^{|\mathcal{A}|} \tag{4.42}$$

and x_{ij} is of course the flow on arc $(i,j) \in \mathcal{A}$. Furthermore, we continue to assume that

$$|\mathcal{N}| = m$$

$$|\mathcal{A}| = n$$

are, respectively, the number of nodes and the number of arcs for the graph under consideration.

The type of flow dependence (4.40), where the cost function's subscripts are identical to those of its flow argument, is called *own flow dependence* and the functions (4.40) themselves are called *separable* cost functions. It is also possible because of turning phenomena and class interactions that *nonseparable* unit cost functions that include *non-own flow dependence* like (4.41) describe the network of interest.[1] So, in general, the vector unit delay (generalized cost) function is $c(x) : \Re^{|\mathcal{A}|} \longrightarrow \Re_+^{|\mathcal{A}|}$; that is,

$$c(x) = (c_{ij}(x) : (i,j) \in \mathcal{A})^T \in \Re_+^{|\mathcal{A}|} \tag{4.43}$$

Whether separable or nonseparable in nature, if $c : \Re^{|\mathcal{A}|} \longrightarrow \Re_+^{|\mathcal{A}|}$ causes the total delay (generalized cost) function

$$Z(x) = \sum_{(i,j)\in\mathcal{A}} c_{ij}(x)\, x_{ij} \tag{4.44}$$

to be convex and twice differentiable for all feasible flow patterns

$$x \in X \equiv \{x : Ax = b,\ \ U \geq x \geq L\} \subset \Re^{|\mathcal{A}|} \tag{4.45}$$

we say the cost function is *regular with regard to its depiction of congestion phenomena*, where A is the totally unimodular $|\mathcal{N}| \times |\mathcal{A}|$ matrix associated with the flow conservation equations, $b \in \Re^m$ is the vector of net nodal supplies, and $U \in \Re^{|\mathcal{A}|}$ and $L \in \Re^{|\mathcal{A}|}$ are respectively vectors of upper and lower bounds on arc flows. For the sake of brevity, we will generally simply say that such a cost function $c(x)$ is *regular*. Evidently regular separable cost functions are a special case of regular nonseparable cost functions, and so results obtained for regular nonseparable functions must apply to the separable case.

The single commodity nonlinear (congested) minimum cost flow problem is of course

$$\min Z(x) = \sum_{(i,j)\in\mathcal{A}} c_{ij}(x)\, x_{ij} = [c(x)]^T x \tag{4.46}$$

subject to

$$Ax = b \tag{4.47}$$

$$U \geq x \geq L \tag{4.48}$$

Note that the single commodity congested minimum cost flow problem is a convex mathematical program when the vector cost function $c(x)$ is regular in the sense defined above. On occasion, we will write this problem in the more terse but equivalent form

$$\min Z(x) = [c(x)]^T x \quad \text{subject to} \quad x \in X \tag{4.49}$$

[1]The reader is referred to the discussion in Chap. 3 of multicopy networks for an explanation of why nonseparable functions allow a single-commodity, single-class model to describe multi-commodity, multi-class networks.

4.6.2 Feasible Direction Algorithms for Linearly Constrained NLPs

For the linearly constrained nonlinear program

$$\min Z(x) = [c(x)]^T x \quad \text{subject to} \quad x \in X = \{x : Ax = b, U \geq x \geq L\}$$

where $c(x)$ is regular, so that $Z(x)$ is convex and twice differentiable for all $x \in X$, we make the following definition:

Definition 4.1 The vector $d^k \in X$ is a feasible direction of descent if and only if

$$x^k + \theta d^k \in X, \quad \forall\, \theta \in [0,1] \tag{4.50}$$

$$\left[\nabla Z(x^k)\right]^T d^k < 0 \tag{4.51}$$

Note that, since X is a convex set, condition (4.50) assures that every point encountered along the direction vector d^k in moving away from x^k lies in the feasible region X. Furthermore, condition (4.51) assures that d^k is a direction of descent, for it requires that the vector d^k be resolvable in a way that causes one of its components to point in the direction $-\nabla Z(x^k)$. Since $-\nabla Z(x^k)$ is, definitionally, the direction of maximal decrease of $Z(\cdot)$ pointing away from x^k, we are assured that following d^k causes $Z(\cdot)$ to decrease.

The basic structure of descent algorithms based on feasible directions for linearly constrained nonlinear programs is the following:

Generic Feasible Direction Algorithm

Step 0. *(Initialization)* Determine $x^0 \in X$. Set $k = 0$.

Step 1. *(Feasible direction of descent determination)* Determine a feasible direction of descent. Find d^k such that

$$x^k + \theta d^k \in X \quad \forall \theta \in [0,1]$$

$$\nabla [Z(x^k)]^T d^k < 0$$

Step 2. *(Step size determination)* Step size determination. Find the optimal step size θ_k where

$$\theta_k = \arg\{\min \; Z(x^k + \theta d^k) : 0 \leq \theta \leq 1\}$$

Set $x^{k+1} = x^k + \theta_k d^k$.

Step 3. *(Stopping test)* For $\varepsilon \in \Re^1_{++}$, a preset tolerance, if

$$\max_{(i,j)\in\mathcal{A}} |x_{ij}^{k+1} - x_{ij}^k| < \varepsilon$$

stop; otherwise set $k = k + 1$ and go to Step 1.

When implementing feasible descent direction methods, it is generally necessary to bound the direction vector. Also, in the presentation of specific descent algorithms that follows, we do not formally prove convergence but instead are content to demonstrate that the direction vectors of specific algorithms are in fact feasible directions of descent. It is intuitive that, if such a direction is followed at each iteration of the solution of a continuous, smooth convex mathematical program, a global solution will be reached in the limit $k \longrightarrow \infty$. Formal proofs of convergence may be found in any of several texts on mathematical programming; see in particular Minoux (1986).

4.7 The Frank-Wolfe Algorithm

The Frank-Wolfe algorithm is a particularly easy to explain feasible direction algorithm. Although this algorithm is known to have a linear rate of convergence at best and may exhibit oscillation (alternately overshooting and undershooting the optimum) as it converges, it is especially easy to implement and to employ for problems with path variables. The Frank-Wolfe algorithm is based on observing that the original problem may be approximated by what we shall call the *approximating linear program* at iteration k (ALP^k):

$$\min Z(x^k) + \left[\nabla Z(x^k)\right]^T (x - x^k) \tag{4.52}$$

subject to

$$Ax = b \tag{4.53}$$

$$U \geq x \geq L \tag{4.54}$$

Clearly, the program immediately above is equivalent to

$$\text{ALP}^k : \min \left[\nabla Z(x^k)\right]^T x \quad \text{subject to} \quad Ax = b \quad U \geq x \geq L \tag{4.55}$$

The solution of ALP^k will be called y^k; we will show that the vector

$$d^k = y^k - x^k$$

is a feasible direction of improvement for our original linearly constrained NLP (4.49) when the cost function $c(x)$ giving rise to $Z(x)$ is regular. In fact, we will prove the following theorem:

Theorem 4.4 *(Frank-Wolfe descent directions) For the linearly constrained nonlinear program*

$$\min Z(x) \quad \textit{subject to} \quad x \in X = \{x : Ax = b, U \geq x \geq L\},$$

$d^k = y^k - x^k$ *is a feasible direction of descent at* $x^k \in X$ *where*

$$y^k = \arg\min_{x \in X} \left\{ \left[\nabla Z(x^k)\right]^T x \right\}$$

provided $Z(x)$ is a convex and differentiable function of $x \in X$. Moreover, if $\left[\nabla Z(x^k)\right]^T d^k = 0$, then x^k is a global minimizer.

Proof. We first show that the direction d^k is feasible. To see this, observe that the feasible region $X = \{x : Ax = b, U \geq x \geq L\}$ for our problem is a convex set. Since $y^k \in X$ by construction, $x^k \in X$ and d^k is a vector joining x^k and y^k, it follows immediately that every point on d^k is in X. Hence, d^k is a feasible direction pointing away from x^k.

To show that d^k is a direction of descent is somewhat more complicated. Because $Z(x)$ is convex on X, we know it is underestimated by any tangent line. That is

$$Z(v) + [\nabla Z(v)]^T (w - v) \leq Z(w) \tag{4.56}$$

for any $v, w \in X$. Using the fact that y^k solves ALP^k, we obtain

$$Z(x^k) + \left[\nabla Z(x^k)\right]^T (x^* - x^k) \geq Z(x^k) + \left[\nabla Z(x^k)\right]^T (y^k - x^k) \tag{4.57}$$

Using the inequalities (4.56) and (4.57) gives

$$\begin{aligned} Z(x^*) &\geq Z(x^k) + \left[\nabla Z(x^k)\right]^T (x^* - x^k) \\ &\geq Z(x^k) + \left[\nabla Z(x^k)\right]^T (y^k - x^k) \\ &\implies 0 \geq Z(x^*) - Z(x^k) \geq \left[\nabla Z(x^k)\right]^T (y^k - x^k) \\ &\implies 0 \geq \left[\nabla Z(x^k)\right]^T d^k \end{aligned} \tag{4.58}$$

From (4.58) it is clear that d^k is a direction of descent except when $\left[\nabla Z(x^k)\right]^T d^k = 0$.

As is intuitive, the case $\left[\nabla Z(x^k)\right]^T d^k = 0$ corresponds to optimality in the original NLP. We show this rigorously by noting that the Kuhn-Tucker conditions for (4.49), which because of convexity are also sufficient, are

$$\nabla Z(x^k) + A^T u + (-I)v = 0, \quad v \geq 0 \tag{4.59}$$

The original problem constraints $Ax = b$ and $x \geq 0$ can be recast in terms of the direction vector d^k pointing away from x^k. For simplicity we assume the coordinate axis has been shifted so that x^k is the origin. Then $x \geq 0$ clearly implies $d \geq 0$. Moreover,

$$\begin{aligned} A(x^k + \beta d^k) &= Ax^k + \beta A d^k = b \\ \implies A d^k &= (\tfrac{1}{\beta})(b - Ax^k) = 0 \end{aligned} \tag{4.60}$$

Thus, we may characterize feasible directions of improvement at $x^k (= 0)$ by the system

$$\left[\nabla Z(x^k)\right]^T d^k < 0, \quad Ad^k = 0, \quad d^k \geq 0$$

Using a corollary to Farka's lemma from classical linear analysis, we know that exactly one of the following systems has a solution:

$$\text{System 1:} \qquad Md \leq 0 \quad Nd = 0 \quad c^T d > 0$$

$$\text{System 2:} \qquad M^T \rho + N^T \mu = c \quad \rho \geq 0$$

where

$$\begin{aligned} M &= -I \\ N &= A \\ c &= -\left[\nabla Z\left(x^k\right)\right]^T \end{aligned}$$

where I is now the identity matrix, while ρ is a conformally defined vector of dual variables for inequality constraints and μ a conformally defined vector of dual variables for equality constraints. Note that System 2 constitutes the Kuhn-Tucker identity and nonnegativity of the dual variables corresponding to the upper and lower bound constraints. Thus, when System 1 has a solution, we know $\left[\nabla Z\left(x^k\right)\right]^T d < 0$ and that x^k is not a Kuhn-Tucker point. However, System 1 does not have a solution when $\left[\nabla Z\left(x^k\right)\right]^T d = 0$. Thus, $\left[\nabla Z\left(x^k\right)\right]^T d = 0$ corresponds to a Kuhn-Tucker point. ■

The above results mean that Step 1 of the generic descent algorithm is modified to obtain the Frank-Wolfe algorithm:

FRANK-WOLFE ALGORITHM

Step 0. *(Initialization)* Determine an initial feasible solution

$$x^0 \in X = \{x : Ax = b, U \geq x \geq L\}$$

and set $k = 0$.

Step 1. *(Feasible direction of descent determination)* Solve ALP^k and call that solution y^k. Compute

$$d^k = y^k - x^k$$

Step 2. *(Step size determination and updating)* Find the optimal step size θ_k where

$$\theta_k = \arg\min \left\{ Z(x^k + \theta d^k) : 0 \leq \theta \leq 1 \right\}$$

Set

$$x^{k+1} = x^k + \theta_k d^k$$

Step 3. *(Stopping test)* For $\varepsilon \in \Re^1_{++}$, a preset tolerance, if

$$\max_{(i,j)\in\mathcal{A}} |x_{ij}^{k+1} - x_{ij}^k| < \varepsilon,$$

then stop; otherwise set $k = k + 1$ and go to Step 1.

Some important observations are in order here. The Frank-Wolfe algorithm involves the solution at each iteration of an approximating linear program as part of the direction finding step. As such, this method is primarily useful in cases where this linear program can be solved relatively easily. Furthermore, the statement and proof of this Theorem in no way requires that the A matrix be totally unimodular. Yet it is clear that property results in linear programming subproblems within the Frank-Wolfe algorithm which are linear minimum cost flow problems, readily solved by the network simplex algorithm. Note also that the assumption of convexity can be relaxed if one modifies the step size determination procedure of the general descent algorithm and is content with determining only local minima. For a discussion of step size rules for nonconvex problems see Avriel (1976) or Bertsekas (1997).

4.8 Steepest Descent Algorithm

Recall that $\|\cdot\|$ denotes the Euclidean norm, unless otherwise stated. The problem of interest is the unconstrained nonlinear program

$$\min f(x) \tag{4.61}$$

$$s.t. \quad x \in \Re^n \tag{4.62}$$

where $f(\cdot) : \Re^n \to \Re^1$ is a convex function. Additionally, we assume that f is continuously differentiable. The gradient of f is denoted by $\nabla f : \Re^n \to \Re^n$ and satisfies Lipschitz continuity:

$$\|\nabla f(x) - \nabla f(y)\| \leq L\|x - y\| \quad \forall x, y \in \Re^n \tag{4.63}$$

Also, we shall assume that the gradient satisfies a generalization of strong pseudomonotonicity known as the Dunn property[2]; that property is

$$\langle \nabla f(x) - \nabla f(y),\ x - y \rangle \geq \frac{1}{L} \|\nabla f(x) - \nabla f(y)\|^2,\ \forall x, y \tag{4.64}$$

where $L > 0$. Theorem 2.1.5 of Nesterov (2004) establishes that

$$f(x) - f(y) \leq \langle \nabla f(y),\ x - y \rangle + \frac{L}{2} \|x - y\|^2,\ \forall x, y \in \Re^n \tag{4.65}$$

Expressions (4.64) and (4.65) will be useful in our subsequent analysis. The steepest descent algorithm itself is the following:

STEEPEST DESCENT ALGORITHM IN $\Re^n$

Step 0. *(Initialization)* Determine $x^0 \in \Re^n$ and set $k = 0$.

Step 1. *(Descent direction determination)* Evaluate the gradient $\nabla f(x^k)$ of the objective function and let $d^k = \nabla f(x^k)$

Step 2. *(Step size determination)* Find the optimal step size θ_k where

$$\theta_k = \arg\min\{f(x^k - \theta d^k) : \ \theta \geq 0\}.$$

Set $x^{k+1} = x^k + \theta_k d^k$.

Step 3. *(Stopping test)* For $\epsilon \in \Re^1_{++}$, a preset tolerance, if

$$\max_i |x_i^{k+1} - x_j^k| \leq \epsilon$$

stop. Otherwise, set $k = k + 1$ and go to Step 1.

In order to establish convergence of the algorithm, the following lemmas are useful.

Lemma 4.3 *The gradient $\nabla f(x^{k+1})$ at x^{k+1} is orthogonal to $\nabla f(x^k)$ at x^k. That is $\langle \nabla f(x^{k+1}),\ \nabla f(x^k) \rangle = 0$.*

Proof. Notice that the step size is determined by solving the following one dimensional minimization problem

$$\min f(x^k - \theta \nabla f(x^k))$$

[2] See El Farouq (2001) for definitions and comparisons among various types of generalized monotonicity.

subject to $0 \le \theta \le 1$, whose first-order optimality condition is

$$\langle \nabla f(x^k - \theta \nabla f(x^k)),\ \nabla f(x^k)\rangle = \langle \nabla f(x^{k+1}),\ \nabla f(x^k)\rangle = 0$$

which immediately yields the desired result. ■

Lemma 4.4 *For all $k \ge 0$, we have $\theta_k \ge \frac{1}{L}$ unless $\|\nabla f(x^k)\| = 0$.*

Proof. Notice, per the Dunn property of the gradient ∇f, we have that

$$\langle \nabla f(x^{k+1}) - \nabla f(x^k),\ x^{k+1} - x^k\rangle \ge \frac{1}{L}\|\nabla f(x^{k+1}) - \nabla f(x^k)\|^2$$

Also notice that $x^{k+1} = x^k - \theta_k \nabla f(x^k)$; thus, we have immediately

$$\langle \nabla f(x^{k+1}) - \nabla f(x^k),\ -\theta_k \nabla f(x^k)\rangle \tag{4.66}$$

$$= \langle \nabla f(x^{k+1}),\ -\theta_k \nabla f(x^k)\rangle + \theta_k \|\nabla f(x^k)\|^2 \tag{4.67}$$

$$\ge \frac{1}{L}\|\nabla f(x^{k+1}) - \nabla f(x^k)\|^2 \tag{4.68}$$

$$= \frac{1}{L}\|\nabla f(x^{k+1})\|^2 + \|\nabla f(x^k)\|^2 - 2\langle \nabla f(x^{k+1}),\ \nabla f(x^k)\rangle \tag{4.69}$$

Invoking Lemma 4.3, we have that

$$\theta_k \|\nabla f(x^k)\|^2 \ge \frac{1}{L}\|\nabla f(x^{k+1})\|^2 + \|\nabla f(x^k)\|^2$$

Unless $\|\nabla f(x^k)\| = 0$, we have

$$\theta_k \ge \frac{1}{L}\left(1 + \frac{\|\nabla f(x^{k+1})\|^2}{\|\nabla f(x^k)\|^2}\right)$$

which immediately leads to the desired result. ■

Theorem 4.5 *(Consider problem (4.61)–(4.62)) Assume that there exists a minimizer of f denoted as x^*, whose objective value is denoted as $f^* > -\infty$. Further assume (4.63) is satisfied. Then*

(1) The sequence of the objective function values $\{f(x^k)\}$ is non-increasing.

(2) If $\|\nabla f(x^k)\| > 0$ for all $k \ge 0$, then

$$f(x^k) - f^* \le \frac{L\|x_0 - x^*\|^2}{2k}$$

(3) The sequence $\{f(x^k)\}$ of the objective function value converges to f^* when k is sufficiently large.

Proof. Per (4.65), if we let $x^{k+1} := x^k - \theta_k \nabla f(x^k)$, we obtain

$$f(x^{k+1}) \leq f(x^k) - \left(1 - \frac{L\theta_k}{2}\right) \theta_k \|\nabla f(x^k)\|^2$$

Invoking convexity of f we have $f(x^k) \geq f^* + \langle \nabla f(x^*), x^k - x^* \rangle$. Furthermore, notice that unless $\nabla f(x^k) = 0$, there always exists $\theta_k \geq 0$ such that $f(x^{k+1}) < f(x^k)$. Per Lemma 4.4, we have that $\theta_k \geq \frac{1}{L}$.

Notice that per continuous differentiability, we have

$$f(x^{k+1}) \leq f^* + \langle \nabla f(x^*), x^k - x^* \rangle - \frac{\theta_k}{2} \|\nabla f(x^k)\|^2 \tag{4.70}$$

$$= f^* + \frac{1}{2\theta_k} (\|x^k - x^*\|^2 - \|y_{k+1} - x^*\|^2). \tag{4.71}$$

Applying the above inequality recursively, we obtain

$$\sum_{i=1}^{k} (f(x_i) - f^*) \leq \frac{1}{2 \min_{1 \leq i \leq k} \theta_i} (\|x_0 - x^*\|^2 - \|x^k - x^*\|^2) \tag{4.72}$$

$$\leq \frac{L}{2} \|x_0 - x^*\|^2 \tag{4.73}$$

which immediately leads to the desired result in Part 2 of the theorem by noticing that $\{f(x_i)\}$ is non-increasing.

To show Part 3, we notice that per Part 2, if $\|\nabla f(x^k)\| > 0$ for all $k \geq 0$, then the sequence $\{f(x^k)\}$ converges to f^*. Otherwise, if $\|\nabla f(x^k)\| = 0$, per convexity of f, $f^* = f(x^k) \geq f(x^i) \geq f^*$ for all $i \geq k$. This immediately leads to the desired result, and the proof is complete. ■

4.9 A Primal Affine Scaling Algorithm

Consider the following program

$$\min \; Z(x) \quad \text{subject to} \quad x \in X \tag{4.74}$$

where now

$$X = \{x : Ax = b, \, x \geq 0\} \tag{4.75}$$

When Newton's method for solving an unconstrained program is combined with the notion of re-scaling and a requirement that iterates stay away from positivity boundaries, one type of interior point algorithm known as *primal affine scaling* results. The fundamental notion employed in such an algorithm is that of rescaling to place the current iterate at or near the center of the feasible region; when this occurs, a feasible direction that is nearly parallel to the gradient may be found, with the consequence that relatively long steps can be taken without, according to the numerical precision of one's computer, prematurely touching a constraint boundary. Such an interior point algorithm holds the potential for very efficient computation because of its ability to take a "shortcut" through the feasible set to the global optimum.

The manner of expressing the interior point solution philosophy stressed in this section relies on restating (4.74) as follows:

$$\left.\begin{array}{lc} & \min F(x,\mu) = Z(x) - \mu \sum_{(i,j)\in\mathcal{A}} \ln x_{ij} \\ \text{subject to} & Ax = b \\ & x > 0 \end{array}\right\} \qquad (4.76)$$

where we abuse our own stipulations concerning the matrix A for network problems, and now consider the matrix to be comprised only of linearly independent rows; this means, of course, that during implementation we will have to take care to select an appropriate submatrix of the flow-conservation constraint matrix in order to implement the numerical procedures that follow. In (4.76) the interiority constraint $x > 0$ is assured by the sum of logarithmic barrier functions $-\mu \sum_{(i,j)\in\mathcal{A}} \ln x_{ij}$ when we begin with an initial solution $x^0 > 0$ and require $\mu > 0$; so we may drop $x > 0$ from further explicit consideration. Because of our use of logarithmic barrier functions, the method we now develop is properly named *primal affine scaling with logarithmic barriers.*

Clearly, the Lagrangian for (4.76) is

$$L(x,\mu) = F(x,\mu) + (b - Ax)^T \lambda$$

Assuming that $F(x,\mu)$ is convex and twice continuously differentiable in x, the unconstrained problem

$$\min L(x,\mu)$$

has a necessary and sufficient optimality condition that may be approximated by

$$0 = \nabla_x L\left(x^{k+1},\mu_k\right) \approx \nabla_x L\left(x^k,\mu_k\right) + \left[\nabla_x^2 L\left(x^k,\mu_k\right)\right]^T \left(x^{k+1} - x^k\right) \quad (4.77)$$

From (4.77) we are led to

$$\nabla Z(x^k) - \mu D_k^{-1} e - A^T\lambda + \left[\nabla^2 Z(x^k) + \mu_k D_k^{-2}\right] d^k = 0 \qquad (4.78)$$

where x^k is the kth iterate of a descent algorithm based on step sizes $\theta_k > 0$ and d^k is a Newton descent direction based on a full step, while

$$\begin{aligned} D &= \operatorname{diag}\left(x^k\right) \\ e &= \begin{pmatrix} 1 & 1 & \cdots & 1 \end{pmatrix}^T \end{aligned}$$

It follows that we may restate (4.78) as

$$d^k = H_k \left(-g_k + A^T \lambda^k\right) \tag{4.79}$$

where

$$H_k = \left[\nabla^2 Z(x^k) + \mu_k D_k^{-2}\right]^{-1} \tag{4.80}$$

$$g^k = \left[\nabla Z(x^k) - \mu_k D_k^{-1} e\right] \tag{4.81}$$

Furthermore, we know that the direction vector must belong to the null space of A; hence, we have

$$Ad^k = AH_k \left(-g^k + A^T \lambda^k\right) = 0 \tag{4.82}$$

From (4.82) it is immediate that

$$\lambda^k = \left(AH_k A^T\right)^{-1} AH_k g^k \tag{4.83}$$

To summarize, we collect and present the critical expressions from the above analysis:

$$\left.\begin{array}{lll} H_k & = & \left[\nabla^2 Z(x^k) + \mu_k D_k^{-2}\right]^{-1} \\ g^k & = & \nabla Z(x^k) - \mu_k D_k^{-1} e \\ \lambda^k & = & \left(AH_k A^T\right)^{-1} AH_k g^k \\ d^k & = & H_k \left(-g^k + A^T \lambda^k\right) \end{array}\right\} \tag{4.84}$$

In (4.84) we have assigned the superscript k to the dual variable vector for equality constraints to recognize it is updated during each iteration. Observe that, based on (4.84), we may write the direction vector as

$$\begin{aligned} d^k &= H_k \left[-g_k + A^T \left(AH_k A^T\right)^{-1} AH_k g^k\right] \\ &= (-1) \left[I - H_k A^T \left(AH_k A^T\right)^{-1} A\right] H_k g^k \end{aligned} \tag{4.85}$$

since $I - H_k A^T \left(AH_k A^T\right)^{-1} A$ is idempotent while H_k is symmetric. We also note that the logarithmic barriers become unbounded at the positivity boundaries; thus, to maintain finiteness as the relevant computations are carried out, we must steadily decrease the value of the barrier multipliers $\mu_k \in \Re^1_{++}$. That is

$$\lim_{k \longrightarrow \infty} \mu_k = 0$$

The affine scaling algorithm has the following structure:

Primal Affine Scaling Algorithm with Logarithmic Barriers

Step 0. *(Initialization)* Determine a strictly interior feasible solution $x^0 > 0$ such that $Ax^0 = b$. Pick $\eta \in (0,1)$ and $\mu_0 > 0$; set $k = 0$.

Step 1. *(Feasible direction of descent determination)* Calculate

$$\begin{aligned} H_k &= \left[\nabla^2 Z(x^k) + \mu_k D_k^{-2}\right]^{-1} \\ g^k &= \nabla Z(x^k) - \mu_k D_k^{-1} s \\ d^k &= (-1)\left[I - H_k A^T \left(A H_k A^T\right)^{-1} A\right] H_k g^k \end{aligned}$$

Step 2. *(Step size determination)* Determine the step size θ_k according to

$$\theta_k = \eta \cdot \xi$$

where

$$\xi \equiv \min_{(i,j)\in\mathcal{A}} \left(\frac{x_{ij}^k}{\left|d_{ij}^k\right|} \; : \; d_{ij}^k < 0 \right) \tag{4.86}$$

Step 3. *(Updating and stopping)* Set

$$x^{k+1} = x^k + \theta_k d^k \tag{4.87}$$

For ε, a preset tolerance, if

$$\max_i \left|x_i^{k+1} - x_i^k\right| < \varepsilon,$$

stop. Otherwise pick $\mu_{k+1} < \mu_k$, set $k = k + 1$, and go to Step 1.

A key simplification of the affine scaling algorithm over the standard gradient projection algorithm is that we no longer look for an optimal step size, but instead take the largest step that maintains interiority. We do this because the rescaling that occurs from the introduction of the matrices H_k and D_k in every iteration k moves the current iterate to the approximate geometrical center of the feasible region expressed in the variables $z = D_k^{-1} x$ so that we have a better "aim" at the optimal solution. Note carefully that, in order to ensure the interiority of each x^k, the full step to the boundary is *never* taken.

For the primal affine scaling algorithm introduced above, we follow Vanderbei and Shanno (1999) in providing a proof of convergence. In particular it is our intent to prove the following theorem:

Theorem 4.6 *(convergence of the affine scaling algorithm) For a proper choice of $\{\mu^k\}$ and $\{\theta^k\}$, the sequence produced by the primal affine scaling algorithm converges to a solution of the system of equations (4.78) and (4.82). For the case of convex $Z(x)$, primal affine scaling with logarithmic barriers algorithm leads to a globally optimal solution x^* for the linearly constrained nonlinear program (4.74) when $F(x,\mu)$ is twice continuously differentiable in x. That is,*

$$\lim_{k \longrightarrow \infty} x^k = x^* \tag{4.88}$$

Proof. Following Vanderbei and Shanno (1999) we introduce the following merit function for the relevant Kuhn-Tucker system:

$$\Psi_0(x^k, \lambda^k) = \left\|\nabla Z(x_k) - A^T\lambda^k\right\|^2 + \left\|Ax^k - b\right\|^2 \tag{4.89}$$

It is necessary to show the above function converges to zero as $k \longrightarrow 0$. The second term on the right-hand side of (4.89) is zero due to the simple fact that each x^k in primal affine scaling is a feasible solution to the original problem. Then we calculate the first term on the right-hand side of (4.89) to find the following:

$$A^T\lambda^k = A^T(AH_kA^T)^{-1}AH_kg^k \tag{4.90}$$

$$= A^T(A^T)^{-1}(AH_k)^{-1}AH_kg^k \tag{4.91}$$

$$= g^k \tag{4.92}$$

Thus

$$\left\|\nabla Z(x^k) - A^T\lambda^k\right\|^2 = \left\|\nabla Z(x^k) - g^k\right\|^2 \tag{4.93}$$

$$= \left\|\nabla Z(x^k) - \nabla Z(x^k) + \mu^k D_k^{-1}e\right\|^2 \tag{4.94}$$

$$= \left\|\mu^k D_k^{-1}e\right\|^2 \tag{4.95}$$

which, as a proper sequence of μ^k, goes to zero. Therefore, the merit function (4.89) decreases monotonically given the proper choice of $\{\theta^k\}$ and $\{\mu^k\}$. Consequently, the algorithm itself converges to a solution of the relevant system of equations. ■

4.10 Nonlinear Network Example of the Frank-Wolfe Algorithm

Consider a minimum cost flow problem with unit arc costs

$$[c(x)]^T = (A_{ij} + B_{ij}x_{ij} : (i,j) \in \mathcal{A})^T$$

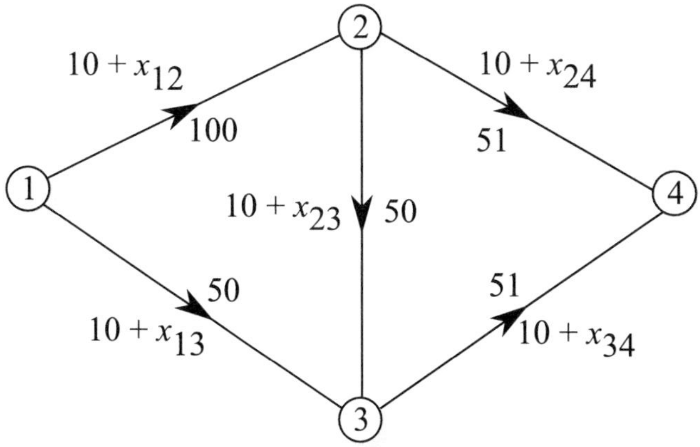

FIGURE 4.12: A NETWORK WITH FOUR NODES AND FIVE ARCS

and the extended forward star array

From (i)	To (j)	A_{ij}	B_{ij}	Capacity
1	2	10	1	100
1	3	10	1	50
2	3	10	1	50
2	4	10	1	51
3	4	10	1	51

together with the nodal net supplies

Node	Net Supply
1	+100
2	0
3	0
4	−100

This network is depicted in Fig. 4.12. Evidently

$$\mathcal{A} = \{(1,2), (1,3)\,(2,3), (2,4), (3,4)\}$$

$$\mathcal{N} = \{1,2,3,4\}$$

while

$$A = \begin{pmatrix} 1 & 1 & 0 & 0 & 0 \\ -1 & 0 & 1 & 1 & 0 \\ 0 & -1 & -1 & 0 & 1 \\ 0 & 0 & 0 & -1 & -1 \end{pmatrix}$$

$$b = \begin{pmatrix} 100 \\ 0 \\ 0 \\ -100 \end{pmatrix}$$

and

$$x^T = (x_{12}, x_{13}, x_{23}, x_{24}, x_{34})^T$$

$$L^T = (0, 0, 0, 0, 0)^T$$

$$U^T = (100, 50, 50, 50, 50)^T$$

Thus, the problem of interest may be expressed as

$$\left.\begin{array}{l} \min \displaystyle\sum_{(i,j)\in\mathcal{A}} (A_{ij} + B_{ij}x_{ij})\, x_{ij} \\ \text{subject to} \\ Ax = b \;\; L \leq x \leq U \end{array}\right\} \quad (4.96)$$

Note that the approximating linear program ALP^k at each iteration k is

$$\left.\begin{array}{l} \min \displaystyle\sum_{(i,j)\in\mathcal{A}} \left(10 + 2x_{ij}^k\right) x_{ij} \\ \text{subject to} \\ Ax = b, \quad L \leq x \leq U \end{array}\right\} \quad (4.97)$$

Furthermore, the optimal step size θ at iteration k is the solution of

$$\begin{aligned} \min Z(\theta) &= \sum_{(i,j)\in\mathcal{A}} \left[A_{ij} + B_{ij}\left(x_{ij}^k + \theta d_{ij}^k\right)\right]\left(x_{ij}^k + \theta d_{ij}^k\right) \\ &= \left[A_{ij}\left(x_{ij}^k + \theta d_{ij}^k\right) + B_{ij}\left(x_{ij}^k + \theta d_{ij}^k\right)^2\right] \end{aligned}$$

or

$$\min Z(\theta) = \sum_{(i,j)\in\mathcal{A}} \Big[A_{ij}x_{ij}^k + A_{ij}\theta d_{ij}^k + B_{ij}\left(x_{ij}^k\right)^2 + \\ 2B_{ij}x_{ij}^k\theta d_{ij}^k + B_{ij}\theta^2\left(d_{ij}^k\right)^2\Big]$$

so that without binding constraints

$$\begin{aligned}\frac{dZ(\theta)}{d\theta} &= \sum_{(i,j)\in\mathcal{A}} \left[A_{ij}d_{ij}^k + 2B_{ij}x_{ij}^k d_{ij}^k + 2B_{ij}\left(d_{ij}^k\right)^2\theta\right] \\ &= \sum_{(i,j)\in\mathcal{A}} \left[A_{ij}d_{ij}^k + 2B_{ij}x_{ij}^k d_{ij}^k\right] + 2\theta \sum_{(i,j)\in\mathcal{A}} B_{ij}\left(d_{ij}^k\right)^2 = 0\end{aligned}$$

Therefore letting $[a]_0^1$ be defined as:

$$[a]_0^1 = \begin{cases} 0 & \text{if } a < 0 \\ a & \text{if } 0 \le a \le 1 \\ 1 & \text{if } a > 0 \end{cases}$$

(i.e., the projection of a onto the interval $[0, 1]$), it follows that

$$\begin{aligned}\theta_k &= \left[\frac{-\sum_{(i,j)\in\mathcal{A}}\left[A_{ij}d_{ij}^k + 2B_{ij}x_{ij}^k d_{ij}^k\right]}{2\sum_{(i,j)\in\mathcal{A}} B_{ij}\left(d_{ij}^k\right)^2}\right]_0^1 \\ &= \left[\frac{-\sum_{(i,j)\in\mathcal{A}}\left[10d_{ij}^k + 2x_{ij}^k d_{ij}^k\right]}{2\sum_{(i,j)\in\mathcal{A}}\left(d_{ij}^k\right)^2}\right]_0^1\end{aligned}$$

We execute the following steps:

Step 0. *(Initialization)* We select the initial solution $x^0 = (100\ \ 0\ \ 50\ \ 50\ \ 50)^T$.

Step 1. *(Feasible direction of descent determination, $k = 0$)* Note that

$$\sum_{(i,j)\in\mathcal{A}} \left(10 + 2x_{ij}^k\right) y_{ij} = 210y_{12} + 10y_{13} + 110y_{23} + 110y_{24} + 110y_{34}$$

so ALP^0 is

$$\min 210y_{12} + 10y_{13} + 110y_{23} + 110y_{24} + 110y_{34}$$

subject to

$$
\begin{aligned}
y_{12} + y_{13} &= 100 \\
-y_{12} + y_{23} + y_{24} &= 0 \\
-y_{13} - y_{23} + y_{34} &= 0 \\
-y_{24} - y_{34} &= -100 \\
y_{12}, y_{13}, y_{23}, y_{24}, y_{34} &\geq 0 \\
y_{12} &\leq 100 \\
y_{13}, y_{23} &\leq 50 \\
y_{24}, y_{34} &\leq 51
\end{aligned}
$$

Note that the above linear program has network structure; thus, it may be solved using the network simplex. Its solution is:

$$y_{12} = 50, y_{13} = 50, y_{23} = 0, y_{24} = 50, y_{34} = 50$$

Therefore

$$
\begin{aligned}
d^0 &= y^0 - x^0 \\
&= (50, 50, 0, 50, 50)^T - (100, 0, 50, 50, 50)^T \\
&= (-50, 50, -50, 0, 0)^T \qquad (4.98)
\end{aligned}
$$

Step 2. *(Step size determination and updating, $k = 0$)* The optimal step size is

$$\theta_0 = \left[\frac{-\sum_{(i,j)\in\mathcal{A}} \left[10 d_{ij}^0 + 2 x_{ij}^0 d_{ij}^0\right]}{2 \sum_{(i,j)\in\mathcal{A}} \left(d_{ij}^0\right)^2} \right]_0^1$$

Some tedious but straightforward arithmetic leads to

$$\theta_0 = \left[\frac{15500}{15000} \right]_0^1 = 1.0$$

and it follows that

$$
\begin{aligned}
x^1 &= x^0 + 1.0 d^0 \\
&= (100, 0, 50, 50, 50)^T + 1.0 \, (-50, 50, -50, 0, 0)^T \\
&= (50, 50, 0, 50, 50)^T \qquad (4.99)
\end{aligned}
$$

which is known to be the optimal solution by symmetry arguments. The next iteration will produce a direction vector

$$d^1 = (0,0,0,0,0)^T \tag{4.100}$$

affirming optimality.

4.11 Nonlinear Network Example of Primal Affine Scaling

We consider the same example studied in Sect. 4.10. Since only three of the four flow conservation constraints are linearly independent, we arbitrarily select the third row of the A matrix for removal and carry out manipulations using the following reduced matrix:

$$M = \begin{pmatrix} 1 & 1 & 0 & 0 & 0 \\ -1 & 0 & 1 & 1 & 0 \\ 0 & 0 & 0 & -1 & -1 \end{pmatrix}$$

We execute the following steps:

Step 0. *(Pick the interior solution, $k = 0$)* Let $x^0 = (51, 49, 1, 50, 50)^T$. Set the initial parameter values as follows:

$$\begin{aligned} k &= 0 \\ \mu_0 &= 2 \\ \eta &= 0.95 \end{aligned}$$

Step 1. *(Feasible direction of descent determination, $k = 0$)*

$$\nabla^2 Z(x^0) = \begin{pmatrix} 2 & 0 & 0 & 0 & 0 \\ 0 & 2 & 0 & 0 & 0 \\ 0 & 0 & 2 & 0 & 0 \\ 0 & 0 & 0 & 2 & 0 \\ 0 & 0 & 0 & 0 & 2 \end{pmatrix}$$

$$D_0 = \begin{pmatrix} 51 & 0 & 0 & 0 & 0 \\ 0 & 49 & 0 & 0 & 0 \\ 0 & 0 & 1 & 0 & 0 \\ 0 & 0 & 0 & 50 & 0 \\ 0 & 0 & 0 & 0 & 50 \end{pmatrix}$$

$$D_0^{-1} = \begin{pmatrix} 0.0196 & 0 & 0 & 0 & 0 \\ 0 & 0.0204 & 0 & 0 & 0 \\ 0 & 0 & 1 & 0 & 0 \\ 0 & 0 & 0 & 0.02 & 0 \\ 0 & 0 & 0 & 0 & 0.02 \end{pmatrix}$$

$$D_0^{-2} = \begin{pmatrix} 51 & 0 & 0 & 0 & 0 \\ 0 & 49 & 0 & 0 & 0 \\ 0 & 0 & 1 & 0 & 0 \\ 0 & 0 & 0 & 50 & 0 \\ 0 & 0 & 0 & 0 & 50 \end{pmatrix}$$

$$H_0 = \left[\nabla^2 Z(x^0) + \mu_0 D_0^{-2}\right]^{-1}$$

Solving for H_0 yields

$$\begin{aligned} H_0 &= \left[\begin{pmatrix} 2 & 0 & 0 & 0 & 0 \\ 0 & 2 & 0 & 0 & 0 \\ 0 & 0 & 2 & 0 & 0 \\ 0 & 0 & 0 & 2 & 0 \\ 0 & 0 & 0 & 0 & 2 \end{pmatrix} + 2\begin{pmatrix} 51 & 0 & 0 & 0 & 0 \\ 0 & 49 & 0 & 0 & 0 \\ 0 & 0 & 1 & 0 & 0 \\ 0 & 0 & 0 & 50 & 0 \\ 0 & 0 & 0 & 0 & 50 \end{pmatrix}\right]^{-1} \\ &= \begin{pmatrix} 0.0096 & 0 & 0 & 0 & 0 \\ 0 & 0.01 & 0 & 0 & 0 \\ 0 & 0 & 0.25 & 0 & 0 \\ 0 & 0 & 0 & 0.0098 & 0 \\ 0 & 0 & 0 & 0 & 0.0098 \end{pmatrix} \end{aligned}$$

Similar calculations for g^0 result in

$$\nabla Z(x^0) = \begin{pmatrix} 10 + 2x_{12}^0 \\ 10 + 2x_{13}^0 \\ 10 + 2x_{23}^0 \\ 10 + 2x_{24}^0 \\ 10 + 2x_{34}^0 \end{pmatrix}$$

$$\nabla Z(x^0) = \begin{pmatrix} 112 \\ 108 \\ 12 \\ 110 \\ 110 \end{pmatrix}$$

$$g^0 = \left[\nabla Z(x^0) - \mu_0 D_0^{-1} e\right]$$

$$\begin{aligned} g^0 &= \begin{pmatrix} 112 \\ 108 \\ 12 \\ 110 \\ 110 \end{pmatrix} - 2 \begin{pmatrix} 0.0196 & 0 & 0 & 0 & 0 \\ 0 & 0.0204 & 0 & 0 & 0 \\ 0 & 0 & 1 & 0 & 0 \\ 0 & 0 & 0 & 0.02 & 0 \\ 0 & 0 & 0 & 0 & 0.02 \end{pmatrix} \begin{pmatrix} 1 \\ 1 \\ 1 \\ 1 \\ 1 \end{pmatrix} \\ &= \begin{pmatrix} 111.9608 \\ 107.5510 \\ 10 \\ 109.96 \\ 109.96 \end{pmatrix} \end{aligned}$$

Finally, d^0 can be calculated using the results from above

$$d^0 = (-1)\left[I - H_0 M^T (M H_0 M^T)^{-1} M\right] H_0 g^0$$

$$d^0 = \begin{pmatrix} -0.0684 \\ 0.0684 \\ -0.1151 \\ 0.0468 \\ -0.0468 \end{pmatrix}$$

Step 2. *(Step size determination)* Recall that

$$\theta_0 = \eta \cdot \xi$$

where

$$\xi \equiv \min_{(i,j)\in A} \left(\frac{x_{ij}^0}{\left|d_{ij}^0\right|} : d_{ij}^0 < 0 \right)$$

Solving for ξ and θ_0 results in

$$\begin{aligned} \xi &= \min\left(\frac{51}{0.0684}, \frac{1}{0.1151}, \frac{50}{0.0468} \right) \\ &= 8.6881 \\ \theta_0 &= 0.95(8.6881) = 8.2536 \end{aligned}$$

Step 3. *(Updating and stopping, $k = 0$)*

$$\begin{aligned} x^1 &= x^0 + \theta_0 d^0 \\ &= \begin{pmatrix} 50 \\ 49 \\ 1 \\ 50 \\ 50 \end{pmatrix} + 8.2536 \begin{pmatrix} -0.0684 \\ 0.0684 \\ -0.1151 \\ 0.0468 \\ -0.0468 \end{pmatrix} \\ &= (50.4356, 49.5644, 0.0497, 50.386, 49.614)^T \end{aligned}$$

Similar calculations for $k = 1$ yield

$$d^1 = \begin{pmatrix} -1.4397 \\ 1.4397 \\ -2.2216 \\ 0.782 \\ -0.782 \end{pmatrix}$$

$$\begin{aligned} \xi &= \min\left(\frac{50.4356}{1.4397}, \frac{0.0497}{2.2216}, \frac{49.619}{0.782}\right) \\ &= 0.0223 \\ \theta_1 &= 0.95(0.0223) = 0.0212 \\ x^2 &= x^1 + \theta_1 d^1 \\ &= (50.405, 49.595, 0.0025, 50.4026, 49.5974)^T \end{aligned}$$

Subsequent iterations confirm that

$$\lim_{k \longrightarrow \infty} x^k = (50, 50, 0, 50, 50)^T$$

4.12 Linear Network Example of Affine Scaling

It is instructive to note that the primal affine scaling algorithm may also be applied to linear programs. In fact, it generally performs well when used to solve the linear minimum cost flow problem.

As an example, let us apply the primal affine scaling algorithm to the example above, but after setting all B_{ij}, where $(i, j) \in \mathcal{W}$, to zero. We also assume that arc flows retain their lower bounds of zero, and that there are no upper bounds on arc flows. That is, the relevant extended forward-star array is

From (i)	To (j)	A_{ij}	B_{ij}	Capacity
1	2	10	0	$+\infty$
1	3	10	0	$+\infty$
2	3	10	0	$+\infty$
2	4	10	0	$+\infty$
3	4	10	0	$+\infty$

We select the third row for removal and carry out manipulations using the reduced matrix

$$M = \begin{pmatrix} 1 & 1 & 0 & 0 & 0 \\ -1 & 0 & 1 & 1 & 0 \\ 0 & 0 & 0 & -1 & -1 \end{pmatrix}$$

We execute the following specific steps:

Step 0. *(Pick the interior solution, $k = 0$)* Set $x^0 = (85, 15, 36, 49, 51)^T$ and set initial parameters to:

$$\begin{aligned} k &= 0 \\ \mu_0 &= 0.1 \\ \eta &= 0.75 \end{aligned}$$

Step 1. *(Feasible direction of descent determination, $k = 0$)*

$$\nabla^2 Z(x^0) = 0$$

$$D_0 = \begin{pmatrix} 85 & 0 & 0 & 0 & 0 \\ 0 & 15 & 0 & 0 & 0 \\ 0 & 0 & 36 & 0 & 0 \\ 0 & 0 & 0 & 49 & 0 \\ 0 & 0 & 0 & 0 & 51 \end{pmatrix}$$

$$D_0^{-1} = \begin{pmatrix} 0.0118 & 0 & 0 & 0 & 0 \\ 0 & 0.0667 & 0 & 0 & 0 \\ 0 & 0 & 0.0278 & 0 & 0 \\ 0 & 0 & 0 & 0.0204 & 0 \\ 0 & 0 & 0 & 0 & 0.0196 \end{pmatrix}$$

$$D_0^{-2} = \begin{pmatrix} 85 & 0 & 0 & 0 & 0 \\ 0 & 15 & 0 & 0 & 0 \\ 0 & 0 & 36 & 0 & 0 \\ 0 & 0 & 0 & 49 & 0 \\ 0 & 0 & 0 & 0 & 51 \end{pmatrix}$$

$$H_0 = \left[\nabla^2 Z(x^0) + \mu_0 D_0^{-2}\right]^{-1}$$

Computation of H_0 proceeds as follows:

$$\begin{aligned} H_0 &= \left[0 + 0.1 \begin{pmatrix} 85 & 0 & 0 & 0 & 0 \\ 0 & 15 & 0 & 0 & 0 \\ 0 & 0 & 36 & 0 & 0 \\ 0 & 0 & 0 & 49 & 0 \\ 0 & 0 & 0 & 0 & 51 \end{pmatrix} \right]^{-1} \\ &= \begin{pmatrix} 0.1176 & 0 & 0 & 0 & 0 \\ 0 & 0.6667 & 0 & 0 & 0 \\ 0 & 0 & 0.2778 & 0 & 0 \\ 0 & 0 & 0 & 0.2041 & 0 \\ 0 & 0 & 0 & 0 & 0.1961 \end{pmatrix} \end{aligned}$$

Similar calculations for g^0 result in

$$\nabla Z(x^0) = \begin{pmatrix} 10 \\ 10 \\ 10 \\ 10 \\ 10 \end{pmatrix}$$

$$\begin{aligned} g^0 &= \left[\nabla Z(x^0) - \mu_0 D_0^{-1} e\right] \\ &= \begin{pmatrix} 10 \\ 10 \\ 10 \\ 10 \\ 10 \end{pmatrix} - 0.1 \begin{pmatrix} 0.0118 & 0 & 0 & 0 & 0 \\ 0 & 0.0667 & 0 & 0 & 0 \\ 0 & 0 & 0.0278 & 0 & 0 \\ 0 & 0 & 0 & 0.0204 & 0 \\ 0 & 0 & 0 & 0 & 0.0196 \end{pmatrix} \begin{pmatrix} 1 \\ 1 \\ 1 \\ 1 \\ 1 \end{pmatrix} \\ &= \begin{pmatrix} 9.9988 \\ 9.9933 \\ 9.9972 \\ 9.9980 \\ 9.9980 \end{pmatrix} \end{aligned}$$

Finally d^0 can be calculated using the above results to obtain

$$d^0 = \begin{pmatrix} -0.5817 \\ 0.5817 \\ -1.1628 \\ 0.5811 \\ -0.5811 \end{pmatrix}$$

Step 2. *(Step size determination, $k = 0$)* Note that

$$\theta_0 = \eta \cdot \xi$$

where

$$\xi \equiv \min_{(i,j)\in A} \left(\frac{x_{ij}^0}{\left|d_{ij}^0\right|} : d_{ij}^0 < 0 \right)$$

Consequently

$$\begin{aligned} \xi &= \min\left(\frac{85}{0.5817}, \frac{36}{1.1628}, \frac{51}{0.5811}\right) \\ &= 30.9600 \\ \theta_0 &= 0.75(30.9600) = 23.2200 \end{aligned}$$

Step 3. *(Updating, $k = 0$)* We update according to

$$x^1 = x^0 + \theta_0 d^0$$

$$x^1 = \begin{pmatrix} 85 \\ 15 \\ 36 \\ 49 \\ 51 \end{pmatrix} + 23.22 \begin{pmatrix} -0.5817 \\ 0.5817 \\ -1.1628 \\ 0.5811 \\ -0.5811 \end{pmatrix}$$

$$= (71.4937, 28.5063, 9.0000, 62.4937, 37.5063)^T$$

Calculations similar to those above yield the following:

$$\mu_1 = 0.01$$

$$H_1 = \begin{pmatrix} 1.3987 & 0 & 0 & 0 & 0 \\ 0 & 3.5080 & 0 & 0 & 0 \\ 0 & 0 & 11.1111 & 0 & 0 \\ 0 & 0 & 0 & 1.6002 & 0 \\ 0 & 0 & 0 & 0 & 2.6662 \end{pmatrix}$$

$$g^1 = \begin{pmatrix} 9.9999 \\ 9.9996 \\ 9.9989 \\ 9.9998 \\ 9.9997 \end{pmatrix}$$

$$d^1 = \begin{pmatrix} -8.4738 \\ 8.4738 \\ -16.9474 \\ 8.4735 \\ -8.4735 \end{pmatrix}$$

$$\xi = \min\left(\frac{71.4937}{8.4738}, \frac{9.0000}{16.9474}, \frac{37.5063}{8.4735}\right)$$

$$= 0.5311$$

$$\theta_1 = 0.75(0.5311) = 0.3983$$

$$x^2 = x^1 + \theta_1 d^1$$

$$= (68.1187, 31.8813, 2.2500, 65.8687, 34.1313)^T$$

A summary of several subsequent iterations is provided by

Iterations (K)	x^k
0	$(85.0000, 15.0000, 36.000, 49.0000, 51.0000)^T$
1	$(71.4937, 28.5063, 9.0000, 62.4937, 37.5063)^T$
2	$(68.1187, 31.8813, 2.2500, 65.8687, 34.1313)^T$
3	$(67.2749, 32.7251, 0.5625, 66.7124, 33.2876)^T$
4	$(67.0640, 32.9360, 0.1406, 66.9233, 33.0767)^T$
5	$(67.0112, 32.9888, 0.0352, 66.9761, 33.0239)^T$
6	$(66.9980, 33.0020, 0.0088, 66.9893, 33.0107)^T$
7	$(66.9948, 33.0052, 0.0022, 66.9926, 33.0074)^T$
8	$(66.9939, 33.0061, 0.0005, 66.9934, 33.0066)^T$
9	$(66.9937, 33.0063, 0.0001, 66.9936, 33.0064)^T$

Subsequent iterations confirm that

$$\lim_{k \longrightarrow \infty} x^k = (67, 33, 0, 67, 33)^T$$

4.13 References and Additional Reading

Avriel, M. (1976). *Nonlinear programming.* Englewood Cliffs, NJ: Prentice-Hall.

Bazaraa, M. S., Jarvis, J. J., & Sherali, H. D. (2011). *Linear programming and network flows.* Hoboken, NJ: John Wiley.

Berge, C. (1962). *The theory of graphs and its applications.* London: Methuen.

Bertsekas, D. P. (1997). Nonlinear programming. *Journal of the Operational Research Society, 48*(3), 334–334.

Bradley, S., Hax, A., & Magnanti, T. (1977). *Applied mathematical programming.* Boston, MA: Addison-Wesley.

Chandrasekaran, R. (1969). Total unimodularity of matrices. *SIAM Journal on Applied Mathematics, 11*, 1032–1034.

Christofides, N. (1975). *Graph theory: An algorithmic approach.* New York: Academic.

Chvatal V. (1983). *Linear programming.* New York: W.H. Freeman.

Cunningham, W. H. (1979). Theoretical properties of the network simplex method. *Mathematics of Operations Research, 4*, 196–208.

El Farouq, N. (2001). Pseudomonotone variational inequalities: Convergence of proximal methods. *Journal of Optimization Theory and Applications, 109*(2), 311–326.

Fang, S.-C., & Puthenpura, S. (1993). *Linear optimization and extensions: Theory and algorithms.* Englewood Cliffs, NJ: Prentice-Hall.

Heller, I. (1957). On linear systems with integral valued solutions. *Pacific Journal of Mathematics, 7*, 1351–1364.

Heller, I., & Tomkins, C. B. (1958). An extension of a theorem of Dantzig. In H. W. Kuhn & A. W. Tucker (Eds.), *Linear inequalities and related systems* (pp. 247–254). Princeton, NJ: Princeton University Press.

Hoffman, A. J., & Heller, I. (1962). On unimodular matrices. *Pacific Journal of Mathematics, 12*, 1321–1327.

Hoffman, A. J., & Kruskal, J. B. (1958). Integer boundary points of convex polyhedra. In H. W. Kuhn & A. W. Tucker (Eds.), *Linear inequalities and related systems* (pp. 223–246). Princeton, NJ: Princeton University Press.

Larson, R. C., & Odoni, A. R. (1981). *Urban operations research.* Englewood Cliffs, NJ: Prentice-Hall.

Minoux, M. (1986). *Mathematical programming: Theory and algorithms.* New York: Wiley.

Nesterov, Y. (2004). *Introductory lectures on convex programming, volume I: Basic course.* Boston: Kluwer Academic.

Nesterov, Y., & Nemirovskii, A. (1994a). *Interior point polynomial algorithms in convex programming.* Philadelphia: SIAM.

Nesterov, Y. E., & Nemirovskii, A. S. (1994b). *Interior-point polynomial algorithms in convex programming.* Philadelphia: SIAM.

Rockafeller, R. T. (1970). *Convex analysis.* Princeton, NJ: Princeton University Press.

Rosen, J. B. (1960). The gradient projection method for nonlinear programming: Part I, linear constraints. *SIAM Journal on Applied Mathematics, 8*, 181–217.

Rosen, J. B. (1961). The gradient projection method for nonlinear programming: Part II, nonlinear constraints. *SIAM Journal on Applied Mathematics, 9*, 514–553.

Vanderbei, R. J., & Shanno, D. F. (1999). An interior-point algorithm for nonconvex nonlinear programming. *Computational Optimization and Applications, 13*, 231–252.

Veinott, A. F. (1968). Extreme points of leontief substitution systems. *Linear Algebra Applications, 1*, 181–194.

5

Near-Network and Large-Scale Programs

In this chapter we are interested in studying two types of mathematical programs. The first type consists of programs that have so-called *near-network structure*. The second type consists of large-scale mathematical programs that may be derived from network considerations, but whose constraints may **not** be characterized as nearly totally modular. This chapter is organized as follows.

Section 5.1: Programs with Near-Network Structure. This section considers programs that have a constraint matrix that is "almost" totally unimodular. That is, with small changes to the constraints, these programs have network structure.

Section 5.2: Near-Network Examples. This section considers some examples of problems that arise as natural extensions of the foundation models studied previously and have near network structure.

Section 5.3: Nonlinear Programming Duality Theory. This section develops a duality theory for nonlinear mathematical programming that will be useful in subsequent sections.

Section 5.4: A Non-Network Example of Subgradient Optimization. This section considers a specific example of the use of subgradient optimization. Although it is not a network example, it is instructive nonetheless.

Section 5.5: Large-Scale Programs. Actual network models are often quite large. In such situations, the classical algorithms presented in the previous chapters may not be appropriate. This section considers how to solve such large problems.

Section 5.6: The Representation Theorem. The representation theorem tells us that any feasible solution of constraints forming a convex polyhedral set may be expressed as a linear combination of extreme points and extreme rays. This result is the basis for a variety of algorithms.

T.L. Friesz, D. Bernstein, *Foundations of Network Optimization and Games*, Complex Networks and Dynamic Systems 3,
DOI 10.1007/978-1-4899-7594-2_5

Section 5.7: Dantzig-Wolfe Decomposition and Column Generation. This section considers Dantzig-Wolfe decomposition and column generation, and how they relate to near network and large network programs.

Section 5.8: Benders Decomposition. Dantzig-Wolfe decomposition is based on the ability to discriminate among constraints (e.g., totally unimodular vs complicating). This section also considers Benders decomposition, which discriminates among types of variables.

Section 5.9: Simplicial Decomposition. This section considers the direct operationalization of the representation theorem of convex analysis. That is, it considers an extreme point generation/constraint accumulation method distinct from Dantzig-Wolfe decomposition.

5.1 Programs with Near-Network Structure

Let us first consider programs of the form

$$\min f(x) \tag{5.1}$$

subject to

$$x \in \Omega = \{x : Ax = b,\ L \leq x \leq U\} \tag{5.2}$$

$$\Gamma x \leq q \tag{5.3}$$

for which flow is over the graph $\mathcal{G}(\mathcal{N}, \mathcal{A})$, where A is the totally unimodular $|\mathcal{N}| \times |\mathcal{A}|$ matrix associated with the flow conservation equations, $b \in \Re^{|\mathcal{N}|}$ is the vector of net nodal supplies, and $U \in \Re^{|\mathcal{A}|}$ and $L \in \Re^{|\mathcal{A}|}$ are respectively vectors of upper and lower bounds on arc flows, while Γ is an $\eta \times |\mathcal{A}|$ matrix without special structure and $q \in \Re^{\eta}$. This information is conveniently summarized in the following list:

$$\begin{aligned}
x &\in \Re^{|\mathcal{A}|} \\
f(x) &: \Re^{|\mathcal{A}|} \longrightarrow \Re^1 \\
A &\equiv \text{totally unimodular } |\mathcal{N}| \times |\mathcal{A}| \text{ matrix} \\
b &\in \Re^{|\mathcal{N}|} \\
U &\in \Re^{|\mathcal{A}|} \\
L &\in \Re^{|\mathcal{A}|} \\
\Gamma &\equiv \eta \times |\mathcal{A}| \text{ matrix} \\
q &\in \Re^{\eta}
\end{aligned}$$

The linearly constrained nonlinear program (5.1)–(5.3) is said to have *near network structure* when the matrix A is totally unimodular, the matrix Γ is such that the matrix

$$\begin{bmatrix} A \\ \Gamma \end{bmatrix}$$

is **not** totally unimodular, and the number of rows of Γ is few relative to the number of rows of A. Such problems arise in a number of contexts, including shortest path problems with time window constraints and minimum cost flow problems with bundle constraints, examples of which we discuss in this chapter.

Actually, the methods we study in this chapter also allow the constraints that destroy total unimodularity to be nonlinear. That is, the linear constraints (5.3) may be replaced with nonlinear constraints of the form

$$g(x) \leq 0 \tag{5.4}$$

where

$$g(x) : \Re^{|\mathcal{A}|} \longrightarrow \Re^{\eta}$$

In fact, in our abstract development of Lagrangean duality theory we will assume that the non-totally unimodular constraints are of the more general form (5.4), although the numerical network example we study in this chapter will have constraints like (5.3).

There are two broad categories of methods used for problems with near network structure: *decomposition methods* and *relaxation methods*. Both categories seek to break down the original problem into smaller subproblems which are more manageable and to which known, efficient algorithms may be applied. It is the manner in which these smaller subproblems are created and interact with one another that distinguishes relaxation and decomposition methods from one another. In *relaxation*, we literally remove constraints from the problem. In *Lagrangean relaxation*, we append the relaxed constraints to the objective function using appropriate dual variables. This terminology can be confusing because some authors have referred to Lagrangean relaxation as a type of *price directive decomposition* since the subproblems created are concerned with exploiting shadow prices (dual variables). Two other broad categories of decomposition are formally known as (1) *resource directive decomposition* and (2) *simplicial decomposition.*

As already noted, to motivate Lagrangean relaxation it will be necessary to present some results from nonlinear programming duality theory. However, prior to embarking on that discussion, we take time in the next section to describe some relatively simple extensions of the classical models introduced in previous chapters that involve near network structure.

5.2 Near-Network Examples

In this section we briefly describe some problems that arise as natural extensions of the foundation models studied previously and which have near network structure. The problems we consider are:

(1) the time constrained shortest path problem;

(2) the linear minimum cost flow problem with bundle constraints;

(3) the linear multicommodity flow problem;

(4) the congested multicommodity flow problem; and

(5) the fuel constrained congested multicommodity flow problem.

Although each of these models is an extension of a classical network model, each nonetheless involves a relatively high degree of abstraction and is of limited use without further embellishments. As such, the near network structure examples we now describe should be thought of as points of departure for more detailed modeling efforts.

5.2.1 Time Constrained Shortest Paths

Consider a graph $\mathcal{G}(\mathcal{N},\mathcal{A})$ for which two non-commensurable attributes are known for each arc $(i,j)\in\mathcal{A}$: distance c_{ij} and travel time τ_{ij}. The primary routing criterion is the minimization of total distance traveled from the source to the sink. The constraints are the usual flow conservation and integrality of flows (we are routing a single unit of flow) augmented by the requirement that total travel time be bounded from above by the exogenous parameter $\beta\in\Re^1_{++}$. We, of course, denote the flow on arc $(i,j)\in\mathcal{A}$ by x_{ij}. That is, we wish to solve

$$\min \sum_{(i,j)\in\mathcal{A}} c_{ij}x_{ij} \tag{5.5}$$

subject to

$$\sum_{j:(i,j)\in\mathcal{A}} x_{ij} - \sum_{j:(j,i)\in\mathcal{A}} x_{ji} = \begin{cases} +1 & \text{if } i=s \\ -1 & \text{if } i=t \\ 0 & \text{otherwise} \end{cases} \qquad \forall i\in\mathcal{N} \tag{5.6}$$

$$\sum_{(i,j)\in\mathcal{A}} \tau_{ij}x_{ij} \leq \beta \tag{5.7}$$

$$x_{ij}=(0,1) \qquad \forall (i,j)\in\mathcal{A} \tag{5.8}$$

where each unit arc cost $c_{ij}\in\Re^1_+$ is a known constant, s is the source node and t is the terminal or sink node. Evidently it is the single time budget constraint (5.7) that destroys the total unimodularity of this program, and so it is appropriate to refer to (5.5)–(5.8) as a linear program with near network structure. Note that a similar problem can be used to find alternatives to the optimal path; that problem is described by Scott et al. (1997).

5.2.2 Minimum Cost Flow with Bundle Constraints

Sometimes we have arcs whose flow activities are technologically tied to the flows of other arcs. A simple example is that of a freight terminus with two incoming traffic arcs but only one forklift to offload shipments. Both arcs are therefore interdependent and constrained by the limited capacity of the terminus to process incoming traffic, a restriction that can be expressed as an upper bound on the sum of traffic on the two arcs. In fact, we employ the name *bundle constraint* to refer to any such constraint requiring multiple network activities to obey a joint capacity restriction. Let us use the notation q_k to denote the capacity of the kth bundle and B_k to denote the set of arcs corresponding to the kth bundle. Then, the linear minimum cost flow problem with bundle constraints is stated as

$$\min \sum_{(i,j)\in\mathcal{A}} c_{ij}x_{ij} \tag{5.9}$$

subject to

$$\sum_{j:(i,j)\in\mathcal{A}} x_{ij} - \sum_{j:(j,i)\in\mathcal{A}} x_{ji} = b_i \qquad \forall i \in \mathcal{N} \tag{5.10}$$

$$\sum_{(i,j)\in B_k} x_{ij} \leq q_k \qquad \forall k \in \mathcal{K} \tag{5.11}$$

$$L_{ij} \leq x_{ij} \leq U_{ij} \qquad \forall (i,j) \in \mathcal{A} \tag{5.12}$$

where each unit arc cost $c_{ij} \in \Re^1_+$ is a known constant, each b_i is the net supply of node i, k is an index denoting the kth bundle, $\mathcal{K}$ is the set of bundles, and $L_{ij} \in \Re^1_+$ and $U_{ij} \in \Re^1_+$ are the respective lower and upper bounds on the flow over arc $(i,j) \in \mathcal{A}$. Clearly, it is the bundle constraints (5.11) that prevent this model from having network structure.

5.2.3 Multicommodity Flow

A model that is mathematically similar to the linear minimum cost flow model with bundle constraints is the linear multicommodity flow problem. It too is a minimum cost flow problem, but differs from the single commodity case in that multiple commodities flow over the same physical arc. This essential feature is modeled using flow variables

$$x^k_{ij} = \text{flow of commodity } k \text{ over arc } (i,j)$$

where the superscript $k \in \mathcal{K}$ now denotes the commodity of interest and $\mathcal{K}$ is the set of all commodities. It is presumed that each physical arc $(i,j) \in \mathcal{A}$ has a capacity expressed in terms of some common numeraire. This restriction on total arc capacity is a form of bundle constraint expressed as

$$\sum_{k\in\mathcal{K}} \alpha_k x^k_{ij} \leq q_{ij} \qquad \forall (i,j) \in \mathcal{A}$$

where α_k is a factor that converts flows of commodity k into flows of the numeraire and q_{ij} is the total capacity of arc (i,j). It is then immediate that the linear multicommodity flow problem is stated as

$$\min \sum_{(i,j)\in\mathcal{A}} \sum_{k\in\mathcal{K}} c_{ij}^k x_{ij}^k \tag{5.13}$$

subject to

$$\sum_{j:(i,j)\in\mathcal{A}} x_{ij}^k - \sum_{j:(j,i)\in\mathcal{A}} x_{ji}^k = b_i^k \qquad \forall i \in \mathcal{N}, k \in \mathcal{K} \tag{5.14}$$

$$\sum_{k\in\mathcal{K}} \alpha_k x_{ij}^k \leq q_{ij} \qquad \forall (i,j) \in \mathcal{A} \tag{5.15}$$

$$L_{ij}^k \leq x_{ij}^k \leq U_{ij}^k \qquad \forall (i,j) \in \mathcal{A}, k \in \mathcal{K} \tag{5.16}$$

where c_{ij}^k is the constant unit cost of flow of commodity k over arc (i,j), b_i^k is the net supply of commodity k at node i, and $L_{ij}^k \in \Re_+^1$ and $U_{ij}^k \in \Re_+^1$ are the respective lower and upper bounds on the flow of commodity k over arc $(i,j) \in \mathcal{A}$. We see immediately that (5.15) are the constraints that destroy network structure. It is also instructive to note that, for appropriately defined vectors c, x, b, L and U and matrices A and Γ, the linear programs with near network structure described above have the form (5.1)–(5.3).

5.2.4 Congested Multicommodity Flow

If congestion occurs, then each arc $(i,j) \in \mathcal{A}$ and commodity $k \in \mathcal{K}$ has a unit cost function $c_{ij}^k(x)$ and the multicommodity flow problem becomes

$$\min \sum_{(i,j)\in\mathcal{A}} \sum_{k\in\mathcal{K}} c_{ij}^k(x) x_{ij}^k \tag{5.17}$$

subject to

$$\sum_{j:(i,j)\in\mathcal{A}} x_{ij}^k - \sum_{j:(j,i)\in\mathcal{A}} x_{ji}^k = b_i^k \qquad \forall i \in \mathcal{N}, k \in \mathcal{K} \tag{5.18}$$

$$\sum_{k\in\mathcal{K}} \alpha_k x_{ij}^k \leq q_{ij} \qquad \forall (i,j) \in \mathcal{A} \tag{5.19}$$

$$L_{ij}^k \leq x_{ij}^k \leq U_{ij}^k \qquad \forall (i,j) \in \mathcal{A}, k \in \mathcal{K} \tag{5.20}$$

where $x = (x_{ij} : (i,j) \in \mathcal{A})^T \in \Re^{|\mathcal{A}|}$ is the vector of arc flows. Note that each arc cost $c_{ij}(.)$ is assumed to depend on the full vector of arc flows in order to represent the interdependence of arc costs that arise from flows interacting at locations (nodes) where arcs meet. In subsequent chapters on applications, we will gain a more complete understanding of the various uses of such *nonseparable arc costs* to represent multiple modes and multiple commodities.

5.2.5 Fuel Constrained Congested Flow

It is well known that, in some types of physical transportation networks, fuel consumption may vary with the square of speed. Since speed will generally be flow dependent when congestion is present, it is immediate that one can associate with each arc $(i,j) \in \mathcal{A}$ the nonlinear function $v_{ij}(x_{ij})$ to describe fuel consumption. These nonlinear fuel consumption functions together with a fuel budget F (i.e., an upper bound on fuel consumption) result in the fuel constrained congested flow problem:

$$\min \sum_{(i,j)\in\mathcal{A}} \sum_{k\in\mathcal{K}} c_{ij}^k(x) x_{ij}^k \tag{5.21}$$

subject to

$$\sum_{j:(i,j)\in\mathcal{A}} x_{ij}^k - \sum_{j:(j,i)\in\mathcal{A}} x_{ji}^k = b_i^k \qquad \forall i \in \mathcal{N}, k \in \mathcal{K} \tag{5.22}$$

$$\sum_{k\in\mathcal{K}} \alpha_k x_{ij}^k \leq q_{ij} \qquad \forall (i,j) \in \mathcal{A} \tag{5.23}$$

$$\sum_{(i,j)\in\mathcal{A}} v_{ij}(x_{ij}) \leq F \tag{5.24}$$

$$L_{ij}^k \leq x_{ij}^k \leq U_{ij}^k \qquad \forall (i,j) \in \mathcal{A}, k \in \mathcal{K} \tag{5.25}$$

where previously introduced notation is employed without any change in meaning. Note that there are now nonlinearities in both the objective function and the constraints of this model. Models of this type – because fuel consumption can be a surrogate for atmospheric pollution – are particularly relevant to analyses of the environmental impacts of transportation.

5.2.6 Common Structure

The formulations given above for the constrained shortest path problem, the linear minimum cost flow problem with bundle constraints, the linear multicommodity flow problem, the congested minimum cost flow problem, and the congested minimum cost flow problem with fuel constraints can be put in the form (5.1)–(5.3), with (5.3) replaced by (5.4) as is meaningful. That is, each of these models has *near network structure*.

5.3 Nonlinear Programming Duality Theory

We need to develop a duality theory for nonlinear mathematical programming problems. This theory will allow us to estimate program solutions when simultaneously perturbing multiple objective and constraint function parameters.

5.3.1 Definition of the Primal and Dual Programs

Let $f : \Re^n \longrightarrow \Re^1$, $g : \Re^m \longrightarrow \Re^n$, $x \in \Re^n$, $u \in \Re^m$ and $\Omega \subseteq \Re^n$. Now consider the following nonlinear programs:

$$\text{Primal } (P) : v = \min f(x) \quad \text{subject to} \quad g(x) \leq 0, \;\; x \in \Omega \tag{5.26}$$

$$\text{Dual } (D) : d = \max L(u) \text{ subject to } u \leq 0 \tag{5.27}$$

where the dual objective function $L(u)$ is defined as follows:

$$L(u) \equiv \min_{x \in \Omega} f(x) + u^T g(x), \tag{5.28}$$

or

$$L(u) \equiv \min_{x \in \Omega} L(x, u) \tag{5.29}$$

with

$$L(x, u) \equiv f(x) + u^T g(x) \tag{5.30}$$

Note that $L(x, u)$ is generally referred to as the *Lagrangean* or as the *primal objective function with priced out constraints* $g(x) \leq 0$. By assumption, Ω is convex and compact in this discussion unless otherwise stated. Moreover, $f(x)$ and $g(x)$ are continuous on Ω.

5.3.2 Global Optimality Conditions

We employ the following definition of optimality suggested by Shapiro (1979):

Definition 5.1 (Global optimality conditions) A pair (x^*, u^*) with $x^* \in \Omega$ and $u^* \geq 0$ satisfies the global optimality conditions for the primal problem (P) if

$$\begin{array}{ll} (1) & f(x^*) + (u^*)^T g(x^*) = \min{}_{x \in \Omega}[f(x) + (u^*)^T g(x)] \\ (2) & (u^*)^T g(x^*) = 0 \\ (3) & g(x^*) \leq 0 \end{array} \tag{5.31}$$

Note that these global optimality conditions do not require differentiability. Based on Definition 5.1 and again following Shapiro (1979), we state and prove the following theorem:

Theorem 5.1 *(Global optimality and the Lagrangean) If (x^*, u^*) satisfies the global optimality conditions, then x^* is optimal in the primal problem (P).*

Proof. For x^* to satisfy the global optimality conditions, x^* must satisfy primal feasibility ($x^* \in \Omega$, $g(x^*) \leq 0$). Let x be any other feasible solution of (P). Note that, because $(u^*)^T g(x^*) = 0$ from the global optimality conditions, we may write

$$f(x^*) = f(x^*) + (u^*)^T g(x^*) = L(u^*) \tag{5.32}$$

But because x^* minimizes $f(x) + (u^*)^T g(x)$, we may state that

$$f(x^*) = f(x^*) + (u^*)^T g(x^*) = L(u^*) \leq f(x) + (u^*)^T g(x) \tag{5.33}$$

By the global optimality conditions, we also know $u^* \geq 0$ (dual feasibility). This together with $g(x) \leq 0$, tells us that $(u^*)^T g(x) \leq 0$. Thus, we have

$$f(x^*) \leq f(x) + (u^*)^T g(x) \leq f(x) \tag{5.34}$$

Since x is any feasible solution, the desired result holds. ■

5.3.3 Properties of the Dual Program

The dual program D introduced in Sect. 5.3.1 has several intellectually interesting as well as practically important properties. In the presentation that follows, we assume $f(\cdot)$ and $g(\cdot)$ are continuous and that Ω is nonempty and compact. The following are fundamental results of nonlinear duality theory:

Theorem 5.2 *(Weak duality) For any $u \geq 0$, we have that*

$$L(u) \leq v, \tag{5.35}$$

where v is the minimum value of the primal (P) objective function.

Proof. If the primal has no solution, then by convention we take $v = +\infty$ and there is nothing to prove. Otherwise, take x to be an optimal feasible solution to the primal. Consequently, $g(x) \leq 0$. Because we are given $u \geq 0$, we may write

$$L(u) \leq f(x) + (u)^T g(x) \leq f(x) = v \tag{5.36}$$

■

Corollary 5.1 *(Implication of weak duality) If $x^* \in X = \{x : x \in \Omega,\ g(x) \leq 0\}$ and $u^* \in U = \{u : u \geq 0\}$ satisfy $f(x^*) = L(u^*)$, then x^* is optimal in (P) and u^* is optimal in (D).*

Proof. Note that

$$f(x^*) = L(u^*) \leq f(x) \text{ for all } x \in X$$

and

$$L(u^*) = f(x^*) \geq L(u) \text{ for all } u \in U$$

■

Theorem 5.3 *(Strong duality) If (x, u^*) satisfy the global optimality conditions, then x^* is optimal to the primal and u^* is optimal to the dual. Moreover, the optimal primal and dual objective functions are equal: $v = d$.*

Proof. In Theorem 5.1 on global optimality, we have established optimality for the primal. By the definition of the dual

$$d \geq L(u^*) \tag{5.37}$$

By global optimality

$$L(u^*) = f(x^*) + (u^*)^T g(x^*) \tag{5.38}$$

But global optimality also ensures $(u^*)^T g(x^*) = 0$, so

$$L(u^*) = f(x^*) \leq d \tag{5.39}$$

The assumed global optimality conditions also guarantee $x^* \in \Omega$ is feasible to the primal, so by weak duality

$$v = f(x^*) \geq d \tag{5.40}$$

Thus

$$L(u^*) = f(x^*) = d, \tag{5.41}$$

proving u^* is optimal to the dual since $u^* \geq 0$ by the global optimality conditions. Moreover, since $v = f(x^*)$ we have $v = d$. ■

Theorem 5.4 *(Finiteness and concavity of the dual objective function) The dual function is finite and concave.*

Proof. Because we have assumed Ω is compact (closed and bounded) and $f(x)$ and $g(x)$ are continuous, the dual objective function $L(u)$ must be finite on $\Re^n$. To show concavity, we apply the definition of a concave function. Let u^1 and u^2 be any two points feasible to the dual while x^0 is feasible to the primal, and consider $\alpha \in [0, 1]$ so that

$$L[\alpha u^1 + (1-\alpha)u^2] = f(x^0) + [\alpha u^1 + (1-\alpha)u^2]g(x^0) \tag{5.42}$$

By the definition of L

$$L(u^1) \leq f(x^0) + u^1 g(x^0) \tag{5.43}$$

$$L(u^2) \leq f(x^0) + u^2 g(x^0) \tag{5.44}$$

Multiply the first inequality by α and the second by $(1-\alpha)$ and add the results to obtain

$$\begin{aligned} \alpha L(u^1) + (1-\alpha)L(u^2) &\leq f(x^0) + [\alpha u^1 + (1-\alpha)u^2]g(x^0) \\ &= L[\alpha u^1 + (1-\alpha)u^2] \end{aligned} \tag{5.45}$$

which is the defining property of a concave function. ■

The implications of the last theorem are profound: *every* dual program is a concave maximization problem with only nonnegativity constraints. Intuitively, we expect to be able to find the global solution of the dual problem relatively easily. However, there is one main difficulty: the dual objective function is generally not differentiable everywhere.

To see both the allure of and the difficulty posed by the dual program, consider the following primal linear programming problem with *near network structure*:

subject to

$$\left.\begin{aligned} v = \min c^T x \\ \Gamma x - q \leq 0 \\ x \in \Omega = \{x : Ax = b, \quad x \geq 0\} \end{aligned}\right\} \tag{5.46}$$

where A is the node-arc incidence matrix of the network, Γ is some matrix without special structure, q is a vector and $\Gamma x - q \leq 0$ are the complicating constraints that destroy the network structure. The associated dual program is

$$d = \max L(u) \quad \text{subject to} \quad u \geq 0 \tag{5.47}$$

where

$$\begin{aligned} L(u) &= \min_x [cx + u^T(\Gamma x - q)] \quad \text{subject to} \quad x \in \Omega \\ &= -u^T q + \min_x (c + u^T \Gamma)x \quad \text{subject to} \quad x \in \Omega \end{aligned}$$

By strong duality, we know, of course, that $v = d$ since we are dealing with a linear program. Thus, we can solve the original primal by solving the dual. Note that the primal problem is a linear program with near network structure. Since the matrix A is totally unimodular by assumption. Also the dual problem is seemingly rather simple in that $L(\cdot)$ is linear in u and there are only nonnegativity constraints. Consequently, the approach of *pricing out* the complicating constraints, $\Gamma x - q \leq 0$, which destroy network structure, is very intriguing. However, because the Lagrangean is, as such, the solution of a linear programming problem defined over a network, we may expect it to have alternative optima for a given vector of dual variables; that is, we could have distinct $x^1, x^2 \in \Omega$ such that

$$L(u) = cx^1 + u^T(\Gamma x^1 - q) = cx^2 + u^T(\Gamma x^2 - q) \tag{5.48}$$

Taking the gradient of $L(\cdot)$ with respect to the dual variables u leads us to conclude that its derivatives *do not* exist, since in general

$$\Gamma x^1 - q \neq \Gamma x^2 - q \tag{5.49}$$

Thus, if we are to use duality to deal with near network structure, we must develop methods for dealing with the nondifferentiability of $L(\cdot)$. In fact, the problem of differentiability is pervasive in duality theory, making it imperative that we develop algorithmic philosophies for nondifferentiable, concave maximization problems. In a subsequent section, we give a concrete numerical example of nondifferentiability of $L(u)$.

5.3.4 Comment on the Duality Gap

Unless the primal is a convex mathematical program, the optimal primal objective function $v = f(x^*)$ and optimal dual objective function $d = L(u^*)$ will generally not be equal. When equality does occur, we say there is a nontrivial duality gap and refer to

$$v - d = f(x^*) - L(u^*) \tag{5.50}$$

as the *duality gap*.

5.3.5 A Non-network Closed Form Example of Lagrangean Duality

To gain some experience with the mechanics of forming and solving the dual problem, consider the following convex example due to Shapiro (1979):

$$\left.\begin{aligned} v = \min 4\left(x_1\right)^2 + 2x_1x_2 + \left(x_2\right)^2 \\ \text{subject to} \qquad 3x_1 + x_2 \geq 6 \\ x_1 \geq 0 \\ x_2 \geq 0 \end{aligned}\right\} \tag{5.51}$$

The Lagrangean for this problem is

$$\begin{aligned} L(x,u) &= 4\left(x_1\right)^2 + 2x_1x_2 + \left(x_2\right)^2 + u(6 - 3x_1 - x_2) \\ &= 6u + 4\left(x_1\right)^2 + 2x_1x_2 + \left(x_2\right)^2 - 3ux_1 - ux_2 \end{aligned}$$

where $u \in \Re^1_+$, so that

$$L(u) = 6u + \min_{x \in \Omega} \left(4 (x_1)^2 + 2x_1 x_2 + (x_2)^2 \right) - 3ux_1 - ux_2$$

where $x = (x_1, x_2)^T$ and $\Omega = \Re^2_+$. Note $L(x, u)$ is convex in x since its Hessian with respect to x is positive definite. Therefore, the minimum obeys $\nabla_x L(x, u) = 0$ for $x_1 > 0$ and $x_2 > 0$. This condition gives the linear system

$$\begin{array}{ccccc} 8x_1 & + & 2x_2 & = & 3u \\ 2x_1 & + & 2x_2 & = & u \end{array}$$

which may be solved to yield

$$x_1 = \frac{4u}{12} \qquad x_2 = \frac{2u}{12}$$

Substituting these results into the expression for $L(u)$ gives the concave Lagrangean

$$L(u) = 6u - \frac{7u^2}{12}$$

Note that for this simple example, the dual objective function is in fact differentiable. Assuming $u^* > 0$, we maximize the dual objective function by setting

$$\frac{dL}{du} = 0$$

to obtain

$$6 - \frac{7}{6} u^* = 0 \longrightarrow u^* = \frac{36}{7}$$

and

$$x_1^* = \left[\left(\frac{4}{12} \right) \left(\frac{36}{7} \right) \right]_+ = \frac{12}{7}$$

$$x_2^* = \left[\left(\frac{2}{12} \right) \left(\frac{36}{7} \right) \right]_+ = \frac{6}{7}$$

The global optimality conditions may be checked and shown to be satisfied along with the condition $v^* = d^*$ for this example.

5.3.6 Lagrangean Relaxation

Often in mathematical programming we choose to temporarily ignore selected constraints. Such a decision is referred to as the *relaxation* of the selected constraints. When a relaxation is accompanied by the act of appending the impacted constraints to the objective function using dual variables, we call it *Lagrangean relaxation.*

5.3.7 Nondifferentiable and Subgradient Optimization

To solve the dual, a concave maximization problem, we will need to determine directions of improvement. As we have noted previously for the case of mathematical programs with near network structure, this determination is complicated by the potential nondifferentiability of the Lagrangean. To clarify this point, consider the example

$$\min -2x_1 + x_2 \tag{5.52}$$

subject to

$$x_1 + x_2 - 3 \leq 0$$

$$(x_1, x_2) \in \Omega$$

where

$$\Omega = \{x : U_1 \geq x_1 \geq 0, x_2 \geq 0\}$$

Then, for $u \in \Re^1_+$, we have

$$\begin{aligned} L(u) &= \min_{x \in \Omega} -2x_1 + x_2 + u(x_1 + x_2 - 3) \\ &= -3u + \min_{x \in \Omega} (u-2)x_1 + (u+1)x_2 \end{aligned}$$

Clearly

$$\min_{x \in \Omega} (u-2)x_1 + (u+1)x_2$$

is solved by

$$\begin{aligned} x_1 &= \begin{cases} 0 & \text{if } u - 2 \geq 0 \\ U_1 & \text{if } u - 2 < 0 \end{cases} \\ x_2 &= 0 \text{ if } u \geq 0 \end{aligned}$$

Because $L(u)$ is piecewise linear in u, with a kink at $u = 2$, it has no well defined derivative at $u = 2$. In fact, at $u = 2$, the "derivative from the left" is $U_1 - 3$ and the "derivative from the right" is -3. Although a continuous function need not always have a gradient everywhere, it may have a generalization of the gradient called the *subgradient*, which we define in the next section.

Having established the need to be able to solve nondifferentiable concave maximization problems, we next develop tools for such problems. In particular, consider the following problem:

$$w = \max L(u) \quad \text{subject to} \quad u \in \Re^{|\mathcal{N}|}_+ \tag{5.53}$$

where $L(u)$ is a concave real-valued function defined for all $u \in \Re^{|\mathcal{N}|}_+$. We assume w is finite. Additionally, the function $L(u)$ is continuous but not necessarily differentiable everywhere. Note that (5.53) does not involve any constraints, and so (5.53) is not equivalent to the Lagrangean dual problem in all cases. However, the development of a theory for nondifferentiable optimization is somewhat easier for this special case. We state subsequently how the main results for the unconstrained case may be extended to constrained problems.

Subgradients and Their Properties

Although the derivatives of $L(u)$ in (5.53) may not be defined everywhere, $L(u)$ does have a generalization of the gradient everywhere, known as the subgradient:

Definition 5.2 A vector γ is called a *subgradient* of the concave function $L(u)$ at $\overline{u}$ if

$$L(u) \leq L(\overline{u}) + \gamma^T(u - \overline{u}) \quad \forall u \tag{5.54}$$

and the set of all subgradients at $\overline{u}$ is denoted by

$$\partial L(\overline{u}) = \{\gamma : L(u) \leq L(\overline{u}) + \gamma^T(u - \overline{u})\ \} \tag{5.55}$$

Note that, if the subgradient is unique at a point, it is the gradient at that point.

The following properties of subgradients may now be stated and proven:

Lemma 5.1 *Let $\overline{x} \in \Omega$ denote an optimal solution at $\overline{u}$ of the problem*

$$\min f(x) \qquad \textit{subject to} \qquad g(x) \leq 0, \;\; x \in \Omega \tag{5.56}$$

used to define the Lagrangean function. That is,

$$L(\overline{u}) = \min_{x \in \Omega}\{f(x) + (\overline{u})^T g(x)\} = f(\overline{x}) + (\overline{u})^T g(\overline{x}) \tag{5.57}$$

Then $\gamma = g(\overline{x})$ is a subgradient of $L(u)$ at $\overline{u}$.

Proof. We begin by forming the following difference using the definition of the Lagrangean dual objective function:

$$L(\overline{u}) - L(u) = \min_{x \in \Omega}\{f(x) + (\overline{u})^T g(x)\} - \min_{x \in \Omega}\{f(x) + (u)^T g(x)\}$$

which can be simplified to

$$\begin{aligned} L(\overline{u}) - L(u) &= f(\overline{x}) + (\overline{u})^T g(\overline{x}) - \min_{x \in \Omega}\{f(x) + (u)^T g(x)\} \\ &\geq f(\overline{x}) + (\overline{u})^T g(\overline{x}) - \left[f(\overline{x}) + u^T g(\overline{x})\right] \\ &= (\overline{u} - u)^T g(\overline{x}) \end{aligned}$$

since $\min_{x \in \Omega}\{f(x) + (u)^T g(x) \leq f(\overline{x}) + ug(\overline{x})$. It follows at once that

$$L(\overline{u}) + (u - \overline{u})^T g(\overline{x}) \geq L(u)$$

which clearly indicates that $\gamma = g(\overline{x})$ is a subgradient. ■

Lemma 5.2 *Let γ denote any subgradient of the concave function $L(u)$ at $\overline{u}$. Then all optimal solutions to the concave maximization problem*

$$\max L(u) \quad \textit{subject to} \quad u \in \Re_+^{|\mathcal{N}|} \tag{5.58}$$

are contained in the set

$$\{u \in \Re_+^{|\mathcal{N}|} \ : \ (u - \overline{u})^T \gamma \geq 0\} \tag{5.59}$$

Proof. Because γ is a subgradient, we have for all u that

$$(u - \overline{u})^T \gamma \geq L(u) - L(\overline{u}) \tag{5.60}$$

Suppose u is optimal; then $L(u) - L(\overline{u}) \geq 0$. Hence, $(u - \overline{u})\gamma \geq 0$. ∎

Furthermore, all concave functions $G(u)$ which are differentiable satisfy the tangent line property: the tangent to a concave function generally overestimates that function. We state this as

$$G(\overline{u}) + [\nabla G(\overline{u})]^T (u - \overline{u}) \geq G(u) \tag{5.61}$$

for all pertinent u and $\overline{u}$. The similarity of expression (5.61) to the definition of a subgradient is hard to overlook and suggests that subgradients may well have properties similar to those of gradients and directional derivatives. In fact it may be shown that subgradients may be used as directions of ascent when maximizing concave functions.

Ascent Algorithms for Nondifferentiable Problems

We are now ready to explore the use of *ascent algorithms* for maximization problems whose objective functions are not differentiable. Note that the preceding section provides a way of testing for optimality in a nondifferentiable programming problem. In particular, if we consider the problem

$$v = \max \ \ L(u) \quad \text{subject to} \quad u \in \Re_+^{|\mathcal{N}|} \tag{5.62}$$

and we assume that a *direction of ascent* exists at all points $u \in \Re_+^{|\mathcal{N}|}$ which are not optimal, then we are ready to represent the basic concept of an ascent algorithm for nondifferentiable programs. Specifically, an ascent algorithm generates a sequence (generally, but not always, infinite) of solutions, which we shall denote by $\{u^l\}$, such that

$$\begin{aligned} &u^l \in \Re_+^{|\mathcal{N}|} \\ &u^{l+1} = u^l + \theta_l d^l \in \Re_+^{|\mathcal{N}|}, \end{aligned} \tag{5.63}$$

where $d^l \in \Re_+^{|\mathcal{N}|}$ $(d^l \neq 0)$ is a feasible direction of ascent from u^l and θ_l is a scalar step length. Thus, we must pick d^l such that

$$L(u^{l+1}) > L(u^l), \tag{5.64}$$

which is assured if the directional derivative at u^l in the direction d^l is positive; that is, if

$$\nabla L(u^l\ ;\ d^l) > 0 \tag{5.65}$$

This is merely a statement that moving in the direction d^l from the point u^l increases the objective function.

Subgradient Optimization Algorithm

What we want to do in this section is study a relatively simple and effective ascent algorithm for use in solving dual programs. There are two key assumptions we make:

(1) the norms of subgradients encountered by the proposed algorithm are uniformly bounded; and

(2) the value w of the maximal objective function is known and may be used in determining step lengths at each iteration.

It is intuitive that the second of these assumptions is rarely satisfied, making subgradient optimization a heuristic algorithm in practice.

The subgradient optimization algorithm generates solutions to the problem

$$\max\ L(u) \quad \text{subject to} \quad u \in \Re_+^{|\mathcal{N}|} \tag{5.66}$$

according to the rule

$$u^{k+1} = u^k + \theta_k \gamma^k,$$

where γ^k is any subgradient of $L(u)$ at u^k and

$$\theta_k = \frac{\beta_k [w - f(u^k)]}{\parallel \gamma^k \parallel^2} \tag{5.67}$$

with

$$0 < \epsilon_1 < \beta_k < 2 - \epsilon_2 \tag{5.68}$$

$$\epsilon_2 > 0 \tag{5.69}$$

$$u_i^k + \theta_k \gamma_i^k \geq 0 \quad \forall i \in \mathcal{N} \tag{5.70}$$

Note that w is the objective function "target value." Thus, a generic subgradient optimization algorithm for (5.66) can be stated as:

SUBGRADIENT OPTIMIZATION ALGORITHM

Step 0. *(Initialization)* Determine an initial feasible solution $u^0 \in \Re_+^{|\mathcal{N}|}$, and set $k = 0$.

Step 1. *(Find subgradient)* Determine any subgradient of L at u^k and call the subgradient γ^k.

Step 2. *(Step size determination)* Determine the step size θ_k according to (5.67), (5.68), (5.69) and (5.70).

Step 3. *(Updating and stopping test)* Calculate

$$u^{k+1} = u^k + \theta_k \gamma^k$$

For $\varepsilon \in \Re_{++}^1$, a preset tolerance, if

$$\max_{(i,j)\in\mathcal{A}} |x_{ij}^{k+1} - x_{ij}^k| < \varepsilon$$

stop; otherwise set $k = k + 1$ and go to Step 1.

Note that, in practice, direction finding (Step 2) identifies any subgradient, and no effort is spent to determine if $L(u)$ actually increases in the subgradient direction. The following theorem specifying conditions that ensure convergence of subgradient optimization and its proof are adapted from Shapiro (1979):

Theorem 5.5 *(Convergence of the subgradient optimization algorithm) Consider the concave maximization problem*

$$\max w = L(u) \quad \textit{subject to} \quad u \in \Re_+^{|\mathcal{N}|}$$

and suppose an optimal solution u^* exists. Further suppose that we apply the subgradient optimization algorithm with the additional assumption that there exists $M > 0$ such that $\| \gamma \|^2 \leq M$ for all $\gamma \in \partial L(u)$ and any u in the set $\{u : \| u - u^* \| \leq \| u^0 - u^* \|\}$. Then

$$\lim_{k \longrightarrow \infty} L(u^k) = w$$

and any limit point of the sequence $\{u^k\}$ is an optimal solution.

Proof. First note that feasibility of every iterate $u^k \geq 0$ is assured by the step size condition (5.70). Next, observe that:

$$\begin{aligned} \| u^{k+1} - u^* \|^2 &= \| u^k + \theta_k^k \gamma^k - u^* \|^2 \\ &= \| u^k - u^* \|^2 + \theta_k^2 \| \gamma^k \|^2 + 2\theta_k (u^k - u^*)\gamma^k \\ &\leq \| u^k - u^* \|^2 + \theta_k^2 \| \gamma^k \|^2 - 2\theta_k [L(u^*) - L(u^k)] \\ &= \| u^k - u^* \|^2 + \frac{(\beta_k^2 - 2\beta_k)[L(u^*) - L(u^k)]^2}{\| \gamma^k \|^2} \end{aligned} \quad (5.71)$$

where the inequality follows because γ^k is a subgradient, and the final equality is obtained from (5.67). Now let

$$Z = \frac{[L(u^*) - L(u)]^2}{\| \gamma^k \|^2} \geq 0 \quad (5.72)$$

so that

$$(\beta_k^2 - 2\beta_k)Z = \beta_k(\beta_k - 2)Z \leq -\epsilon_1\epsilon_2 Z \quad (5.73)$$

since $\beta_k \geq \epsilon_1$ and $\beta_k \leq 2 - \epsilon_2$ from (5.68) and (5.69). Combining Eqs. (5.71) and (5.73), one easily obtains

$$\| u^{k+1} - u^* \| \leq \| u^k - u^* \|^2 + (-1)\frac{\epsilon_1\epsilon_2[L(u^*) - L(u^k)]^2}{\| \gamma^k \|^2} \quad (5.74)$$

The immediate implication of this inequality is that the sequence of nonnegative numbers $\{\| u^k - u^* \|^2\}$ is monotonically decreasing. Consequently, we know that

$$\lim_{k \longrightarrow \infty} \| u^k - u^* \|^2 \quad (5.75)$$

exists. Given the sign of

$$-\frac{[L(u^*) - L(u^k)]^2}{\| \gamma^k \|^2} \quad (5.76)$$

and the existence of (5.75), inequality (5.74) requires that

$$\lim_{k \longrightarrow \infty} \frac{[L(u^*) - L(u^k)]^2}{\| \gamma^k \|^2} = 0, \quad (5.77)$$

Further, because $\| \gamma^k \|^2 \leq M$ for all k, we know that

$$\lim_{k \longrightarrow \infty} L(u^k) = L(u^*) = w \quad (5.78)$$

Lastly, the sequence $\{u^k\}$ must have at least one converging subsequence. This is because the u^k are restricted to the bounded set $\{u : \left\|u^k - u^*\right\| \leq \left\|u^0 - u^*\right\|\}$. When $\{u^{k_i}\}$ is some subsequence converging to u^{**}, it follows since L is continuous that

$$\lim_{k \longrightarrow \infty} L(u^{k_i}) = L(\lim_{k \longrightarrow \infty} u^{k_i}) = L(u^{**}) = L(u^*) = w, \quad (5.79)$$

and thus u^{**} is optimal in (5.66). ■

5.4 A Non-network Example of Subgradient Optimization

Let us return to problem (5.51), which we were able to solve in closed form using duality theory. That is, we again consider

$$v = \min 4\left(x_1\right)^2 + 2x_1x_2 + \left(x_2\right)^2 \tag{5.80}$$

subject to

$$g(x) = 6 - 3x_1 - x_2 \leq 0$$

$$x_1 \geq 0$$

$$x_2 \geq 0$$

where $x = (x_1, x_2)^T$ with Lagrangean

$$L(x,u) = 6u + 4\left(x_1\right)^2 + 2x_1x_2 + \left(x_2\right)^2 - 3ux_1 - ux_2 \tag{5.81}$$

The steps of the subgradient optimization algorithm applied to this problem are:

Step 0. *(Initialization)* Pick $u^0 = 0$ and set $k = 0$.

Step 1. *(Find subgradient, $k = 0$)* Solve

$$\min L(x, u^0) = 4\left(x_1\right)^2 + 2x_1x_2 + \left(x_2\right)^2 \quad \text{subject to} \quad x_1 \geq 0, x_2 \geq 0$$

If $x_1^0 > 0$ and $x_2^0 > 0$, the we have

$$\frac{\partial L(x, u^0)}{\partial x_1} = 8x_1 + 2x_2 = 0$$

$$\frac{\partial L(x, u^0)}{\partial x_2} = 2x_1 + 2x_2 = 0$$

which has the following solution:

$$x_1(u^0) = x_2(u^0) = [0]_+ = 0$$

where the projection onto the nonnegative real line is used to ensure primal feasibility. Compute the subgradient

$$\gamma^0 = g\left(x(u^0)\right) = 6 - 3x_1(u^0) - x_2(u^0) = 6$$

Step 2 and 3. *(Select step and update, $k = 0$)* Take a step $\theta_0 = 1$ according to

$$u^1 = u^0 + \theta_0\gamma^0 = 0 + 1(6) = 6$$

Step 1. *(Find subgradient, $k=1$)* Solve

$$\begin{aligned}\min L(x,u^1) &= 6u^1 + 4\left(x_1\right)^2 + 2x_1x_2 + \left(x_2\right)^2 - 3u^1x_1 - u^1x_2 \\ &= 36 + 4(x_1)^2 + 2x_1x_2 + (x_2)^2 - 3(6)x_1 - (6)x_2 \\ \text{subject to} \quad & x_1 \geq 0, x_2 \geq 0\end{aligned}$$

If $x_1(u^1) > 0$ and $x_2(u^1) > 0$, then we have

$$\begin{aligned}\frac{\partial L(x,u^1)}{\partial x_1} &= 8x_1 + 2x_2 - 18 = 0 \\ \frac{\partial L(x,u^1)}{\partial x_2} &= 2x_1 + 2x_2 - 6 = 0\end{aligned}$$

whose solution is

$$\begin{aligned}x_1(u^1) &= [2]_+ = 2 \\ x_2(u^1) &= [1]_+ = 1\end{aligned}$$

Compute the subgradient

$$\begin{aligned}\gamma^1 &= g\left(x(u^1)\right) = 6 - 3x_1(u^1) - x_2(u^1) \\ &= 6 - 3(2) - 1(1) = -1\end{aligned}$$

Step 2 and 3. *(Select step and update, $k=1$)* Take a step $\theta_1 = \frac{6}{7}$ according to

$$u^2 = u^1 + \theta_1\gamma^1 = 6 + \frac{6}{7}(-1) = \frac{36}{7}$$

Step 1. *(Find subgradient, $k=2$)* Solve

$$\begin{aligned}\min L(x,u^2) &= 6u^2 + 4\left(x_1\right)^2 + 2x_1x_2 + \left(x_2\right)^2 - 3u^2x_1 - u^2x_2 \\ &= 6\left(\frac{36}{7}\right) + 4\left(x_1\right)^2 + 2x_1x_2 + \left(x_2\right)^2 - 3\left(\frac{36}{7}\right)x_1 - \left(\frac{36}{7}\right)x_2 \\ \text{subject to} \quad & x_1 \geq 0, x_2 \geq 0\end{aligned}$$

If $x_1(u^2) > 0$ and $x_2(u^2) > 0$

$$\begin{aligned}\frac{\partial L(x,u^2)}{\partial x_1} &= 8x_1 + 2x_2 - 3\left(\frac{36}{7}\right) = 0 \\ \frac{\partial L(x,u^2)}{\partial x_2} &= 2x_1 + 2x_2 - \frac{36}{7} = 0\end{aligned}$$

leading to the solution

$$\begin{aligned} x_1(u^2) &= \left[\frac{12}{7}\right]_+ = \frac{12}{7} \\ x_2(u^2) &= \left[\frac{6}{7}\right]_+ = \frac{6}{7} \end{aligned}$$

Compute the subgradient

$$\begin{aligned} \gamma^2 &= g\left(x(u^2)\right) = 6 - 3x_1(u^2) - x_2(u^2) \\ &= 6 - 3\left(\frac{12}{7}\right) - 1\left(\frac{6}{7}\right) = 0 \end{aligned}$$

confirming that a solution has been reached. Thus, we conclude that

$$\begin{aligned} u^* &= u^2 = \frac{36}{7} \\ x_1^* &= x_1(u^2) = \frac{12}{7} \\ x_2^* &= x_2(u^2) = \frac{6}{7} \end{aligned}$$

5.5 Large-Scale Programs

Actual network models are often quite large. Such network models, although it may seem paradoxical to say, sometimes lack discernible network structure or that structure is not dominant in terms of the number of constraints. When this occurs the classical algorithms presented in the previous chapters either cannot be used or require some modification. In this section we discuss how to solve large problems in network analysis, which may or may not involve integer variables, without the presumption of network or near network structure. Lagrangean relaxation remains a viable tool under these circumstances provided "bad" constraints can be identified and priced out. However, other methods known collectively as *decomposition algorithms* have historically also played a major role in the solution of large-scale and integer network models. We will see that when near network structure does occur increased computational efficiency can be realized from decomposition algorithms.

5.5.1 Price Directive Versus Resource Directive Decomposition

Each of the algorithms emphasized in this section is based on one of three concepts: *decomposition*, *constraint accumulation*, and *column generation*. Loosely put, decomposition refers to a *divide-and-conquer* strategy for problem solving whereby the original problem is broken down into smaller, more numerically tractable problems. That is, we will first decompose the problem to be solved into easier subproblems, and then either generate constraints or columns of the relevant constraint matrix *only as they are needed.* Although this will require us to solve many simplified problems, it obviates the need for us to ever solve the complete problem with all of the constraints. Sometimes, but not always, the decomposition strategy will be designed around complicating constraints which prevent a pure network structure from being realized. However, regardless of the decomposition strategy employed, efficacy of a particular approach depends on the ease of solution of the individual mathematical programs created by the decomposition.

By itself, the above definition of decomposition can be confusing. After all, the Lagrangean relaxation scheme satisfies the superficial definition of decomposition just given, since in that method a near-network program with complicating constraints is broken down into a sequence of programs with totally unimodular constraint matrices that may be solved by the network simplex. Consequently, additional nomenclature is required. In particular, we acknowledge two types of decomposition: price directive decomposition and resource directive decomposition. This dichotomy depends on viewing the optimization problem of interest as the depiction of an "organization" comprised of a headquarters managing resources shared or allocated to a number of (sub)divisions, each with its own specific constraints. This story is consistent with the following problem structure:

$$\min \quad (c^1)^T x^1 + \cdots + (c^R)^T x^R \tag{5.82}$$

subject to

$$Q^1 x^1 + \cdots + Q^R x^R \leq q \tag{5.83}$$

$$A^1 x^1 = b^1 \tag{5.84}$$

$$A^2 x^2 = b^2 \tag{5.85}$$

$$\vdots$$

$$A^{R-1} x^{R-1} = b^{R-1} \tag{5.86}$$

$$A^R x^R = b^R \tag{5.87}$$

$$x^1 \geq 0,\ x^2 \geq 0,\ \ldots,\ x^{R-1} \geq 0,\ x^R \geq 0 \tag{5.88}$$

where $r \in [1, R]$, $R \in \Re^1_{++}$, $c^r \in \Re^{n_r}$, $x^r \in \Re^{n_r}$, $q \in \Re^{\rho}$, Q^r is a $\rho \times n_r$ matrix, $b^r \in \Re^{m_r}$, A^r is an $m_r \times n_r$ matrix, $\rho \in \Re^1_{++}$, $m_r \in \Re^1_{++}$, and $n_r \in \Re^1_{++}$, with the obvious restriction that

$$n_r > m_r \quad \forall r \in [1, R] \tag{5.89}$$

Also note that we have assumed linearity of the objective function and all constraints, since linearly constrained nonlinear programs can be solved as sequences of appropriately defined linear programs. Note that the constraints (5.84)–(5.87) are rather aptly described as *block diagonal* in nature. Because we make no assumption about the number of resource constraints (5.83) relative to the number of block diagonal constraints, it is not appropriate to say that this program has near network structure when each matrix A^r is totally unimodular.

For the dichotomy of decomposition methods we have described, Lagrangean relaxation is classified as a *price directive decomposition* approach since it sets prices (dual variables) $u \geq 0$ on the shared resource q so that each of the R divisions can autonomously optimize its own operations. By contrast, in *resource directive decomposition*, the coordinator wishes to select resource vectors

$$q^1, q^2, \ldots, q^R \in \Re^\rho \tag{5.90}$$

satisfying

$$\sum_{r=1}^{R} q^r \leq q \tag{5.91}$$

so that the global problem (5.82)–(5.88) is solved when each division solves its own linear programming problem:

$$\min c^r x^r \tag{5.92}$$

subject to

$$Q^r x^r \leq q^r \tag{5.93}$$

$$A^r x^r = b^r \tag{5.94}$$

$$x^r \geq 0 \tag{5.95}$$

where $r = 1, 2, \ldots, R$.

The balance of this section is organized as separate sections describing the following algorithmic philosophies for solving problems such as (5.82)–(5.88) and illustrative numerical examples of each:

Lagrangean Relaxation. Lagrangean relaxation is a price directive decomposition algorithm wherein we price out complicating constraints and solve the dual program to bound the original primal problem.

Dantzig-Wolfe Decomposition. Dantzig-Wolfe decomposition is a price directive decomposition technique that employs a master problem and subproblems created by use of the representation theorem of convex analysis and the generation of extreme points of the feasible region. The master problem determines shadow prices (dual variables) that allow the coordinated but sequential solution of smaller subproblems. Each subproblem may be viewed as generating new columns for the master problem constraint matrix. The master problem and subproblems are usually selected by distinguishing between constraints with network structure and complicating constraints which destroy that structure.

Simplicial Decomposition. Simplicial decomposition may be thought of as a kind of general philosophy for extreme point generation/column generation methods without reference to the specific master problems and subproblems that define Dantzig-Wolfe decomposition. It is a price directive algorithmic philosophy.

Benders Decomposition. Benders decomposition is a resource directive decomposition technique that defines a master problem and subproblems by partitioning and fixing variables and by application of linear programming duality theory. The master problem evolves as the algorithm progresses by a process known as *constraint accumulation*. This method has many advantages for mixed-integer models.

5.5.2 Lagrangean Relaxation

Lagrangean relaxation is one of the most widely used solution methods in all of mathematical programming. Moreover, it would be hard to overstate the impact of Lagrangean relaxation on the actual practice and application of network modeling. Accordingly, we stress that the utility of the method is in no way limited to problems with near network structure. In fact, Lagrangean relaxation can be quite effective for solving mathematical programs that do not involve total unimodularity in any subset of their constraints.

We take it to be self evident that the technique of Lagrangean relaxation in conjunction with subgradient optimization may be applied to the linear program (5.82)–(5.88) as well as to an extension of it resulting from making the objective function nonlinear through the use of flow dependent unit arc costs. The obvious constraints to price out are the resource constraints (5.83), for then the relaxed subproblems encountered in subgradient optimization may be placed in the form

$$\min\left(c^1x^1+\ldots+c^Rx^R\right)+u^T\left(Q^1x^1+\ldots+Q^Rx^R-q\right) \tag{5.96}$$

subject to

$$A^rx^r=b^r \quad \forall r\in[1,R] \tag{5.97}$$

$$x^r\geq 0 \quad \forall r\in[1,R], \tag{5.98}$$

where $u\in\Re^\rho$, which can be further decomposed into

$$\min c^rx^r+u^T\left[Q^rx^r-q\right] \tag{5.99}$$

subject to

$$A^r x^r = b^r \tag{5.100}$$

$$x^r \geq 0 \tag{5.101}$$

for each $r \in [1, R]$, allowing any special structure of the matrices A^r to be exploited; even if no such special structure exists, the subproblems are substantially smaller in terms of both the number of constraints and the number of variables that each involves.

5.6 The Representation Theorem

One of the key results of linear analysis is the so-called *representation theorem* which tells us, in essence, that any feasible solution of constraints forming a convex polyhedral set may be expressed as a linear combination of extreme points and extreme rays. The formal statement of the theorem is:

Theorem 5.6 *(Representation theorem) Let S be a nonempty polyhedral set in $\Re^n$ of the form $\{x : Ax = b, x \geq 0\}$ where A is an $m \times n$ matrix with rank m. Let $v^1, \ldots, v^t$ be the extreme points of S and $d^1, \ldots, d^s$ be the extreme rays of S. Then, $x \in S$ if and only if x can be written as*

$$\begin{aligned}
x &= \sum_{j=1}^{t} \theta_j v^j + \sum_{j=1}^{s} \mu_j d^j \\
\sum_{j=1}^{t} \theta_j &= 1 \\
\theta_j &\geq 0 \quad i = 1, \cdots, t \\
\mu_j &\geq 0 \quad j = 1, \cdots, s
\end{aligned}$$

Proof. See Bazarra et al. (2011). ■

Theorem 5.6 is the foundation for a family of price directive decomposition methods that constitute an alternative to Lagrangean relaxation. In that capacity, the theorem is employed to effect approximations of the feasible region of large-scale linearly constrained programs in terms of a subset of the full set of extreme points. The prototypical price directive decomposition method based on such a philosophy is Dantzig-Wolfe decomposition, which is the subject of the next section.

5.7 Dantzig-Wolfe Decomposition and Column Generation

Let us consider the following linear program:

$$\left.\begin{array}{ll} & \min c^T x \\ \text{subject to} & \\ & \Gamma x \leq q \\ & x \in S = \{x : x \geq 0,\ Ax = b\} \end{array}\right\} \tag{5.102}$$

where $x \in \Re^n$, $c \in \Re^n$, $q \in \Re^\gamma$, $b \in \Re^m$, Γ is a $\gamma \times n$ matrix, and A is an $m \times n$ matrix. Evidently (5.102) is a version of the general large-scale LP (5.82)–(5.88). Clearly in this notation S is the region defined by the nonnegativity constraints taken together with the constraints $Ax = b$.

We assume that S is bounded. Obviously S is closed. Thus, S is compact (closed and bounded). Consequently, the representation theorem tells us that any point in S may be represented as a convex combination of the extreme points of S, since there will be no extreme rays. That is, if $v^1, v^2, \ldots, v^t$ are the extreme points of S, then

$$x \in S \Longrightarrow x = \sum_{j=1}^{t} v^j \theta_j,$$

where

$$\sum_{j=1}^{t} \theta_j = 1 \tag{5.103}$$

$$\theta_j \geq 0 \qquad j = 1, 2, \ldots, t \tag{5.104}$$

and t presently denotes the number of extreme points. Substituting for x from this representation in terms of extreme vectors allows us to restate the original problem (5.102) as the following so-called *master problem* (MP):

$$\left.\begin{array}{ll} & \min \sum_{j=1}^{t} \left(c^T v^j\right) \theta_j \\ \text{subject to} & \\ & \sum_{j=1}^{t} (\Gamma v^j)\theta_j \leq q \\ & \sum_{j=1}^{t} \theta_j = 1 \\ & \theta_j \geq 0 \quad j = 1, 2, \ldots, t \end{array}\right\} \text{MP} \tag{5.105}$$

which is itself restated as

$$\left.\begin{aligned} &\min\ Z_{\text{MP}} = \sum_{j=1}^{t} (c^T v^j)\theta_j \\ &\text{subject to} \\ &\sum_{j=1}^{t} (\Gamma v^j)\theta_j - q \leq 0 && (y) \\ &1 - \sum_{j=1}^{t} \theta_j = 0 && (\alpha) \\ &\theta_j \geq 0 \quad j = 1, 2, \ldots, t \end{aligned}\right\} \text{MP} \tag{5.106}$$

where $s \in \Re^{\gamma}$ is a vector of slack variables, $0 \in \Re^{\gamma}$ is the null vector, $y \in \Re^{\gamma}$ is a vector of dual variables for the "bad" constraints $q - \sum_{j=1}^{t} (\Gamma v^j)\theta_j \leq 0$, and α is the single dual variable for the normalization constraint $1 - \sum_{j=1}^{t} \theta_j = 0$. Then

$$u = \begin{pmatrix} y \\ \alpha \end{pmatrix}$$

is the complete vector of dual variables.

Problem (5.106), as we have already observed, is known as the *master problem* (MP). It must also be noted that, since t, the number of extreme points of S, is typically very large, attempting to enumerate all the points $v^1, v^2, \ldots, v^t$ is in general impractical, if not impossible. The main issue in Dantzig-Wolfe decomposition is the efficient generation of extreme points. In fact, we shall find that it is possible to generate extreme points only as needed, thereby avoiding complete enumeration. This algorithmic philosophy is known as *column generation* because it has the effect of adding additional columns to the constraint matrix of MP only as needed.

If the simplex algorithm is applied to MP, we are of course interested in the the jth component of reduced cost corresponding to variable θ_j, which is

$$\bar{c}_j = c^T v^j - y^T (\Gamma v^j) - \alpha \tag{5.107}$$

We select a variable θ_k to enter the basis, if any, corresponding to

$$k = \arg\left\{ \min_{1 \leq j \leq t} c^T v^j - y^T (\Gamma v^j) - \alpha \right\} \tag{5.108}$$

Determining the index k satisfying relationship (5.108) is computationally infeasible in general, since t is generally very large and the extreme points v^j are not all known at any given iteration of the algorithm. However, because S is compact, the minimum of any linear objective function over S must be achieved by one of its extreme points. Therefore,

$$\min_{1 \leq j \leq t} \ c^T v^j - y^T \Gamma v^j - \alpha = \min_{x \in S} (c^T - y^T \Gamma) x - \alpha \tag{5.109}$$

Thus, we have illustrated the fundamental importance of the following *subproblem* (SP):

$$\left.\begin{aligned} \min\ Z_{SP} &= \left(c^T - y^T\Gamma\right)x - \alpha \\ \text{subject to} \quad x \in S &= \{x : x \geq 0,\ Ax = b\} \end{aligned}\right\} \text{SP} \tag{5.110}$$

In the event that A is totally unimodular, the subproblem SP is especially attractive. However, even if A is not totally unimodular, SP still has considerable appeal since it involves fewer constraints than the original program. The following key result concerning SP guides the termination of Dantzig-Wolfe decomposition:

Theorem 5.7 *(Optimality in Dantzig-Wolfe decomposition) Optimality for the original problem (5.102) is equivalent to nonnegativity of the subproblem objective function (5.109).*

Proof. Trivial. ■

An important consequence of the results developed in this section is that, in order to solve the MP, one may generate one extreme point at each iteration by solving an appropriate subproblem. That is, one may add columns to MP only as needed.

The aforementioned algorithmic philosophy, as had already been noted, is known as *column generation* and is reflected in the following formal statement of the Dantzig-Wolfe (DW) decomposition algorithm:

DANTZIG-WOLFE DECOMPOSITION ALGORITHM

Step 0. *(Initialization)* Determine an initial set

$$V^1 = \left\{x^1, x^2, \ldots, x^t\right\} \tag{5.111}$$

of extreme points for

$$S = \{x : x \geq 0 \text{ and } Ax = b\} \tag{5.112}$$

where $t \geq 1$. Set $k = 1$.

Step 1. *(Form and solve master problem)* Using the extreme points V^k and the representation

$$x = \sum_{j=1}^{t} \theta_j v^j \tag{5.113}$$

form the kth master problem

$$\left.\begin{array}{ll}
\min \sum_{j=1}^{t}(cv^j)\theta_j & \\
\sum_{j=1}^{t}(\Gamma v^j)\theta_j - q \leq 0 & (y) \\
1 - \sum_{j=1}^{t}\theta_j = 0 & (\alpha) \\
\theta_j \geq 0 \ \ j = 1, 2, \cdots, t &
\end{array}\right\} \mathrm{MP}^k \qquad (5.114)$$

Solve MP^k to obtain the weights and dual variables

$$\begin{aligned}
\theta^k &= (\theta_1^k, \theta_2^k, \ldots, \theta_t^k)^T \\
y^k &= (y_1^k, y_2^k, \ldots, y_m^k)^T \\
& \alpha_k
\end{aligned}$$

where m is the number of rows of A.

Step 2. *(Form and solve subproblem)* Form the subproblem

$$\left.\begin{array}{l}
Z_{SP}^k = \min\left[c^T - (y^k)^T\Gamma\right]x - \alpha_k \\
\text{subject to} \quad x \in S = \{x : x \geq 0, \ Ax = b\}
\end{array}\right\} SP^k \qquad (5.115)$$

Solve SP^k to obtain the new extreme point

$$v^{t+1} \qquad (5.116)$$

Step 3. *(Updating and stopping)* If $Z_{SP}^k \geq 0$ stop; the current weights are optimal with associated optimal solution

$$x^* = \sum_{j=1}^{t}\theta_j v^j \qquad (5.117)$$

Otherwise, set

$$\begin{aligned}
V^{k+1} &= V^k \cup v^{t+1} \\
k &= k+1 \\
t &= t+1
\end{aligned}$$

and go to Step 1.

Some comments are in order regarding this algorithm. For DW decomposition to be attractive, the subproblems SP^k must be manageable. Moreover, MP^k has only $\gamma + 1$ constraints rather than $m + \gamma$, where γ is the number of rows of the Γ matrix used to define the constraints $\Gamma x - q \leq 0$ and m is the number of rows of A. As stressed previously, if A is totally unimodular additional efficiency can be realized.

5.8 Benders Decomposition

Dantzig-Wolfe decomposition is based on the ability to discriminate among constraints (e.g., totally unimodular vs complicating). By contrast, *Benders decomposition* discriminates between types of variables (e.g., continuous vs integer or linear vs nonlinear). Specifically, we study the following so-called *Benders problem* (BP):

$$\left.\begin{aligned} &\min c^T x + f(y) \\ \text{subject to}\quad &Ax + By = b \\ &x \geq 0 \\ &y \in Y \end{aligned}\right\} \text{BP} \tag{5.118}$$

In applications, x is typically a flow vector and y is a vector of binary decision variables. Note that we may think of this problem as having near network structure if the x variables are significantly more plentiful than the y variables and A is totally unimodular. However, near network structure is not required.

In our presentation, we will make use of the following lemma whose statement[1] and proof follow Lasdon (1970):

Lemma 5.3 *$Z \geq f(y) + w^T(b - By)$ for each w such that $w^T A \leq c$ if and only if $Z \geq f(y) + (w^j)^T(b - By)$ and $(d^j)^T(c - By) \leq 0$ for every extreme point w^j and extreme direction d^j of the cone $K(c) = \{w : w^T A \leq c\}$.*

Proof. We need to recall the following form of Farkas's lemma: there exists a vector $x \geq 0$ satisfying $Ax = b$ if and only if $w^T b \geq 0$ for all w satisfying $w^T A \geq 0$.[2] Our interest in applying Farkas's lemma is motivated by the intuitive strategy of solving BP by fixing y so that one has only to deal with a continuous LP in x. Only those values of y for which there exist x satisfying the constraints resulting from this perspective may be employed. That is, y must belong to the set

[1] We will use the notation w^j for extreme points rather than v^j since the extreme pints of interest in Benders method are those of the cone $K(c)$, not those of the primal formulation (5.118).

[2] Farkas's lemma and other theorems of the alternative are well discussed in Mangasarian (1993) and Bazarra et al. (2011).

$$R(y) = \{y : x \geq 0, \quad Ax = b - By, \, y \in Y\}$$

Applying Farkas's lemma to the following linear system for y fixed:

$$Ax = b - By \quad x \geq 0, \tag{5.119}$$

tells us that y is feasible if and only if

$$w^T(b - By) \leq 0 \tag{5.120}$$

for all w satisfying $w^T A \leq 0$. Since the cone $K(0) = \{w : w^T A \leq 0\}$ is polyhedral, it has a finite number of generators. That is, any $w \in K(0)$ can be written as

$$w = \sum_{j=1}^{s} \theta_j d^j, \quad \theta_j \geq 0 \tag{5.121}$$

Moreover, the d^j, $j = 1, 2, \ldots, s$, also generate the translated cone $K(c) = \{w : wA \leq c\}$. Substituting (5.121) into the expression $w(b - By) \leq 0$ gives

$$\sum_{j=1}^{s} \theta_j (d^j)^T (b - By) \leq 0, \tag{5.122}$$

which holds for all $\theta_j \geq 0$ if and only if $d^j(b - By) \leq 0, \quad j = 1, \ldots, s$. This, with the fact that only extreme points w^j can be solutions of

$$\max[f(y) + w^T(b - By)] : w \in K(c) = \{w : w^T A \leq c\} \tag{5.123}$$

proves Lemma 5.3. ■

Lemma 5.3 will be critical to the implementation of Bender's method.

To continue, we will need the following knowledge:

(1) if a set is bounded, it has no extreme directions;

(2) extreme points are vertices of the polyhedral set forming the constraints;

(3) extreme directions generate all points in a cone defined by these directions; and

(4) the representation theorem in summary form, once again. That is, if S is a polyhedral set (the intersection of a finite number of half spaces), then any point in S can be represented as a convex combination of its extreme points plus a nonnegative linear combination of its extreme directions.

Armed with this information, we note that the original problem BP can be rewritten as

$$\left.\min_{y \in Y} \left\{ f(y) + \min \left[c^T x : \; Ax = b - By, \, x \geq 0 \right] \right\} \right\} \text{BP}' \tag{5.124}$$

The dual of the inner problem in (5.124) is clearly

$$\max[w^T(b - By) : w^T A \leq c]$$

Thus, by strong duality, we know

$$\min\ \left[c^T x : Ax = b - By,\, x \geq 0\right] = \max\left[w^T(b - By) : w^T A \leq c\right] \quad (5.125)$$

Consequently, we are led to

$$\min_{y \in Y}\ \max_{wA \leq c}\ \left[f(y) + w^T(b - By)\right] \quad (5.126)$$

which may be conveniently rewritten as

$$\left.\begin{array}{l} \min Z \\ \text{subject to} \\ Z \geq f(y) + w^T(b - By) \\ w^T A \leq c \\ y \in Y \\ w \ \text{unrestricted} \end{array}\right\} \text{BP}' \quad (5.127)$$

Finally, we observe that BP$'$ together with Lemma 5.3 above leads to Benders master problem (MP):

$$\left.\begin{array}{l} \min Z \\ \text{subject to} \\ Z \geq f(y) + (w^j)^T(b - By) \qquad j = 1, \ldots, t \\ (d^j)^T(b - By) \leq 0 \qquad j = 1, \ldots, s \\ y \in Y \end{array}\right\} \text{MP} \quad (5.128)$$

where t is the number of extreme points and s the number of extreme directions of the cone $K(c) = \{w : w^T A \leq c\}$.

Clearly, we will need some sort of column generation to avoid enumeration of all extreme points and rays in (5.128). That is, we need a way to generate extreme points and rays only as they are required, rather than exhaustively in advance. To this end, we employ as a subproblem (SP) our dual of the inner problem, restated here for convenience:

$$\left.\begin{array}{l} \max w^T(b - By^k) \\ \text{subject to} \\ w^T A \leq 0 \\ w \ \text{unrestricted} \end{array}\right\} \text{SP}^k \quad (5.129)$$

where k is an iteration index.

How then do we implement Benders partitioning?
The basic algorithm involves "constraint accumulation" and has the following structure:

Benders Decomposition Algorithm

Step 0. *(Initialization)* Find an initial feasible solution $y^0 \in Y$. Set $k = 0$.

Step 1. *(Form and solve subproblem)* Solve SP^k (5.129) for each new $y^k \in Y^k$ to generate a new set W^k of active extreme points of $\{w : wA \leq c\}$ and a set D^k of associated extreme directions.

Step 2. *(Form and solve master problem)* Solve MP^k stated as

$$\left.\begin{array}{lll} & \min Z & \\ \text{subject to} & & \\ & Z \geq f(y) + (w^j)^T(b - By) & j = 1, \ldots, t^k \\ & (d^j)^T(b - By) \leq 0 & j = 1, \ldots, s^k \end{array}\right\} \tag{5.130}$$

where $t^k \equiv$ current number of extreme points in W^k and $s^k \equiv$ current number of extreme directions in D^k, and in so doing generate y^{k+1}.

Step 3. *(Stopping and updating)* Test (x^k, y^k) for optimality in BP, where (x^k, w^k) are a primal dual pair for (5.125) when $y = y^k$. If not optimal, set $k = k + 1$ and go to Step 1.

5.9 Simplicial Decomposition

The ideas presented for finding extreme points needed in DW decomposition may be applied to problems without using the particular master problems and subproblems introduced above. Such other extreme point generation/constraint accumulation methods we collectively refer to as *simplicial decomposition*. That is to say, all column generation techniques may be thought of as related to a method often referred to as simplicial decomposition. This simple but powerful idea may be applied to any mathematical programming problem whose constraints form a polyhedral set. In that linearly constrained problems with near network structure fall into this category, simplicial decomposition is of particular interest when dealing with large-scale models with such structure.

In effect, simplicial decomposition is the operationalization of the representation theorem of convex analysis. That is to say, using the representation theorem, one can *always* proceed to solve the program

$$\min f(x) \quad \text{subject to} \quad x \in S$$

where S is a closed convex set, formed by generating some extreme points and extreme directions to form an approximation of S. In the next iteration some more extreme points and extreme directions are generated, and perhaps some are dropped, to form an improved approximation of S.

The aforementioned approach of adding/dropping extreme points or columns of the constraint matrix is based on the following argument: suppose, for simplicity of exposition, that the feasible region S of some linear program of interest is also compact (as well as convex) and that $f(x)$ is convex and differentiable. Then, we know that the optimal solution is a linear combination of extreme points. Of course, enumeration of extreme points is impractical. Instead, we generate the extreme points as needed, and *approximate S as the convex hull of the extreme points generated to date.* Since S is compact and convex, we will eventually represent S exactly if we generate the entire set of extreme points and do not need to concern ourselves with extreme rays. We may also get "lucky" and find the extreme points whose linear combination exactly represents the optimal solution before completely enumerating the set of extreme points. These ideas are easily extended to nonlinear linearly constrained mathematical programs if we minimize an appropriately constructed *gap function* that monitors progress toward the optimal solution.

In fact, the algorithmic approach we call simplicial decomposition has the following structure when $f(x)$ is convex and differentiable for all $x \in S$ and S is convex and compact (closed and bounded):

Simplicial Decomposition Algorithm

Step 0. *(Initialization)* Let $v^1, v^2, \ldots, v^t$ be some initial extreme points of the closed, convex set S for $t \geq 2$. Set

$$V^1 = \{v^1, v^2, \ldots, v^t\} \tag{5.131}$$

$$g_1 = +\infty \tag{5.132}$$

and let $k = 1$.

Step 1. *(Solve program constrained by convex hull)* Find x^k which solves

$$\min f(x) \quad \text{subject to} \quad x \in H(V^k)$$

where $H(V^k)$ is the convex hull of V^k. Let $D^k \equiv$ set comprised of elements of V^k with zero weights when x^k is expressed as a linear combination of the extreme points contained in V^k.

Step 2. *(Generation of new extreme point and stopping test)* Solve

$$\min_{y \in S} \nabla f(x^k)(y - x^k) \Longrightarrow \min_{y \in S} \nabla f(x^k) y \tag{5.133}$$

which will clearly generate an extreme point of S. Call it y^k. If

$$\nabla f(x^k)(y^k - x^k) = 0 \tag{5.134}$$

stop; optimality has been reached.

Step 3. *(Add/delete extreme points)* If $\nabla f(x^k)(y^k - x^k) \neq 0$, we must add and drop columns from V^k as is appropriate. For example, we may employ a gap measure g_k for this purpose:

(1) if $\left|\nabla f(x^k)(y^k - x^k)\right| \leq g_k$ (direction vector improving), then $V^{k+1} = (V^k \backslash D^k) \cup y^k$

(2) if $\left|\nabla f(x^k)(y^k - x^k)\right| > g_k$ (direction vector worsening), then $V^{k+1} = (V^k \backslash D^k)$

Step 4. *(Updating)* Update the gap measure according to

$$g_{k+1} = \min\left[g_k, \nabla f(x^k)(y^k - x^k)\right] \tag{5.135}$$

Set $k = k + 1$ and go to Step 1.

The optimality condition (5.134) is familiar from our study of nonlinear programming algorithms in Chap. 2. Although we do not formally demonstrate that this algorithm converges, it is intuitive that the method must ultimately find some set of extreme points that will represent the optimal solution and satisfy the optimality condition when the feasible region is closed, bounded, and convex. In fact, Lawphongpanich and Hearn (1984) establish that, under rather mild regularity conditions, the gap measure employed above leads to a convergent algorithm. Although not necessary for convergence, dropping unnecessary columns lessens storage overhead in digital computation.

5.10 References and Additional Reading

Bazaraa, M. S., Jarvis, J. J., & Sherali, H. D. (2011). *Linear programming and network flows*. John Wiley & Sons

Bertsekas, D. B. (1998). *Network optimization: Continuous and discrete models*. Cambridge, MA: Athena Publishing.

Bradley, S. P., Hax, A. C., & Magnanti, T. L. (1977). *Applied mathematical programming*. Reading, MA: Addison-Wesley.

Gabriel, S. A., & Bernstein, D. (2000). Nonadditive shortest paths: Subproblems in multi-agent competitive network models. *Computational and Mathematical Organization Theory, 6*, 29–45.

Guignard, M., & Kim, S. (1987). Lagrangean decomposition: A model yielding stronger lagrangean bounds. *Mathematical Programming, 39*(2), 215–230.

Lasdon, L. (1970). *Optimization theory for large systems.* New York: Macmillan.

Lawphongpanich, S., & Hearn, D. W. (1984). Simplicial decomposition of the assymmetric traffic assignment problem. *Transportation Research, 18B*, 123–133.

Mangasarian, O. L. (1993). *Nonlinear programming*, Philadelphia: SIAM

Rockafeller, R. T. (1970). *Convex analysis.* Princeton, NJ: Princeton University Press.

Scott, K., Pabon-Jimenez, G., & Bernstein, D. (1997). Finding alternatives to the best path. In *Presented at the 76th transportation research board annual meeting*, Washington, DC.

Shapiro, J. (1979). *Mathematical programming: Structure and algorithms.* New York: Wiley.

6

Normative Network Models and Their Solution

MODELERS COMMONLY DISTINGUISH BETWEEN positive and normative models. Loosely, a *positive model* is descriptive (i.e., involves "what is") and a *normative model* is prescriptive (i.e., involves "what should be"). Optimization models can be either positive or normative, depending on whether they are descriptions of actual behaviors/circumstances or are prescriptions for desired behaviors/circumstances. In this chapter we focus on a variety of network and near network models that are most commonly used in a prescriptive fashion.

Section 6.1: The Classical Linear Network Design Problem. This problem is concerned with the optimal way to introduce arcs into a network within a specified budget.

Section 6.2: Variants of the Transportation Problem. This section considers the transportation problem with multiple commodities.

Section 6.3: Variants of the Minimum Cost Flow Problem. There are many variants of the minimum cost flow problem. This section considers both bundle constraints and nonlinear objectives.

Section 6.4: The Traveling Salesman Problem. The objective of the traveling salesman problem is to find a least cost tour. The constraints ensure that the tour begins at a given node of the network of interest, visits all members of a set of specified nodes at least once, and returns to the starting node.

Section 6.5: The Vehicle Routing Problem. The vehicle routing problem is a variant of the traveling salesman problem wherein there are multiple vehicles (salesmen), each covering only a portion of the nodes of a given network.

Section 6.7: Irrigation Networks. The reader should note that the model of irrigation network capacity expansion presented in Sect. 1.5.1 will, in actual deployment, be a large-scale nonlinear mathematical program to which some of the algorithms presented in Chap. 5 are applicable. This section explores such models and algorithms.

T.L. Friesz, D. Bernstein, *Foundations of Network Optimization and Games*, Complex Networks and Dynamic Systems 3,
DOI 10.1007/978-1-4899-7594-2_6

Section 6.8: Telecommunications Flow Routing and System Optimal Traffic Assignment. Furthermore, as will be seen in Chap. 8, the system optimal traffic assignment model and the telecommunication flow routing model introduced in Sect. 1.3 are isomorphic to one another. Consequently, in actual deployment, both are large-scale nonlinear programs, and algorithms from Chap. 5 may be helpful in obtaining numerical solutions. This section explores such models and algorithms.

6.1 The Classical Linear Network Design Problem

The *classical linear network design problem* is concerned with the optimal introduction of additional arcs within a specified budget. To articulate this model, we use the notation F_{ij} for the fixed design (construction) cost for arc $(i,j) \in \mathcal{A}$ of a graph $G(\mathcal{N}, \mathcal{A})$, where $\mathcal{N}$ is the set of nodes and $\mathcal{A}$ the set of arcs. We let $\mathcal{K}$ denote the set of commodities of interest and x_{ij}^k the fraction of the flow of commodity $k \in \mathcal{K}$ that is routed from a prespecified source (origin) node $s_k \in \mathcal{N}$ to a prespecified sink (destination) node $t_k \in \mathcal{N}$ over arc $(i,j) \in \mathcal{A}$. We also define the improvement variables

$$y_{ij} = \begin{cases} 1 & \text{if arc } (i,j) \text{ is constructed} \\ 0 & \text{if arc } (i,j) \text{ is not constructed} \end{cases} \tag{6.1}$$

for every arc $(i,j) \in \mathcal{A}$. We presume a budget $B \in \Re^1_{++}$ for the construction of arcs, so that

$$\sum_{(i,j)\in\mathcal{A}} F_{ij} y_{ij} \leq B \tag{6.2}$$

is the relevant budget constraint when the cost of constructing arc $(i,j) \in \mathcal{A}$ is F_{ij}. We also need to assure that the source and sink are connected; this will be achieved by enforcing an appropriate form of the flow conservation constraints. Also x_{ij}^k will denote the fraction of total flow of commodity $k \in \mathcal{K}$ between source $s_k \in \mathcal{N}$ and sink $t_k \in \mathcal{N}$. Finally, we use c_{ij}^k to denote the total cost of transporting commodity $k \in \mathcal{K}$ over arc $(i,j) \in \mathcal{A}$ if all flow from the source $s_k \in \mathcal{N}$ to the sink $t_k \in \mathcal{N}$ were routed over this arc.

In light of the notation introduced above, the following network design model is immediate:

$$\min \sum_{(i,j)\in\mathcal{A}} \sum_{k\in\mathcal{K}} c_{ij}^k x_{ij}^k \tag{6.3}$$

subject to

$$\sum_{j:(i,j)\in\mathcal{A}} x_{ij}^k - \sum_{j:(j,i)\mathcal{A}} x_{ji}^k = \begin{cases} +1 & \text{if } i = s_k \\ -1 & \text{if } i = t_k \\ 0 & \text{otherwise} \end{cases} \qquad \forall i \in \mathcal{N}, k \in \mathcal{K} \tag{6.4}$$

$$\sum_{(i,j)\in\mathcal{A}} F_{ij} y_{ij} \leq B \tag{6.5}$$

$$x_{ij}^k \leq y_{ij} \qquad \forall (i,j) \in \mathcal{A}, k \in \mathcal{K} \tag{6.6}$$

$$0 \leq x_{ij}^k \leq 1 \qquad \forall (i,j) \in \mathcal{A}, k \in \mathcal{K} \tag{6.7}$$

$$y_{ij} = (0,1) \qquad \forall (i,j) \in \mathcal{A} \tag{6.8}$$

Note that in this model it is possible to drop the budget constraint if we are merely trying to find a cheapest design when there is no notion of strategic choice that will impact expenditure.

6.2 The Transportation Problem

Let us recall the linear minimum cost flow problem with bundle constraints introduced in Chap. 5, where we offered the following formulation:

$$\min \sum_{(i,j)\in\mathcal{A}} \sum_{k\in\mathcal{K}} c_{ij}^k x_{ij}^k \tag{6.9}$$

subject to

$$\sum_{j:(i,j)\in\mathcal{A}} x_{ij}^k - \sum_{j:(j,i)\in\mathcal{A}} x_{ji}^k = b_i^k \qquad \forall i \in \mathcal{N}, k \in \mathcal{K} \tag{6.10}$$

$$\sum_{k\in\mathcal{K}} x_{ij}^k \leq q_{ij} \qquad \forall (i,j) \in \mathcal{A} \tag{6.11}$$

$$L_{ij}^k \leq x_{ij}^k \leq U_{ij}^k \qquad \forall (i,j) \in \mathcal{A}, k \in \mathcal{K} \tag{6.12}$$

where c_{ij}^k is the constant unit cost of flow of commodity k over arc (i,j), b_i^k is the net supply of commodity k at node i, and $L_{ij}^k \in \Re_+^1$ and U_{ij}^k are the respective upper and lower bounds on the flow of commodity k over arc $(i,j) \in \mathcal{A}$.

We now wish to consider a specialization of the above model known as the multicommodity transportation problem, where in all nodes are either origins or destinations, but never both. Flows occur over arcs that directly connect an origin to a destination, but there is no requirement that every origin-destination pair is connected. The graph on which such a network model is based is called a *bipartite graph*.

It is convenient to refer to the flow on each arc $(i,j) \in \mathcal{A}$ of the bipartite graph as x_{ij} and to refer to the origin nodes by the set $\{1,\ldots,m\}$ and the destination nodes by the set $\{1,\ldots,n\}$. Accordingly the multicommodity transportation problem is

$$\min \sum_{i\in[1,m]} \sum_{j\in[1,n]} \sum_{k\in\mathcal{K}} c_{ij}^k x_{ij}^k \tag{6.13}$$

subject to

$$\sum_{j:(i,j)\in\mathcal{A}} x_{ij}^k = O_i \qquad i\in[1,m], k\in\mathcal{K} \tag{6.14}$$

$$\sum_{i:(i,j)\in\mathcal{A}} x_{ji}^k = D_j \qquad j\in[1,n], k\in\mathcal{K} \tag{6.15}$$

$$L_{ij}^k \leq x_{ij}^k \leq U_{ij}^k \qquad i\in[1,m], j\in[1,n], k\in\mathcal{K} \tag{6.16}$$

where O_i is the flow originated at origin $i\in[1,m]$ and D_j is the flow destined for node $j\in[1,n]$.

Note that bundle-type capacity constraints may be imposed on the above model. When that is done we have the following formulation

$$\min \sum_{i\in[1,m]} \sum_{j\in[1,n]} \sum_{k\in\mathcal{K}} c_{ij}^k x_{ij}^k \tag{6.17}$$

subject to

$$\sum_{j:(i,j)\in\mathcal{A}} x_{ij}^k = O_i \qquad i\in[1,m] \tag{6.18}$$

$$\sum_{i:(i,j)\in\mathcal{A}} x_{ji}^k = D_j \qquad j\in[1,n] \tag{6.19}$$

$$\sum_{k\in\mathcal{K}} x_{ij}^k \leq q_{ij} \qquad i\in[1,m], j\in[1,n] \tag{6.20}$$

$$L_{ij}^k \leq x_{ij}^k \leq U_{ij}^k \qquad i\in[1,m], j\in[1,n], k\in\mathcal{K} \tag{6.21}$$

We now consider a numerical example based on a specific instance of model (6.17)–(6.21).

Specifically, we consider a multicommodity transportation problem on a bipartite graph with bundle constraints adapted from Bradley et al. (1977). In particular the extended forward-star array for the bipartite graph of this problem is

Commodity	From	To	Unit Profit
1	1	1	100
1	1	2	120
1	1	3	90
1	2	1	80
1	2	2	70
1	2	3	140
2	1	1	40
2	1	2	20
2	1	3	30
2	2	1	20
2	2	2	40
2	2	3	10

for which the set of origin nodes $\{1,2\}$ is distinct from the set of destination nodes $\{1,2,3\}$. As previously, we employ decision variables x_{ij}^k to denote the flow of commodity k on arc (i,j). Consequently, the objective is

$$\max 100x_{11}^1 + 120x_{12}^1 + 90x_{13}^1 + 80x_{21}^1 + 70x_{22}^1 + 140x_{23}^1$$

$$+40x_{11}^2 + 20x_{12}^2 + 30x_{13}^2 + 20x_{21}^2 + 40x_{22}^2 + 10x_{23}^2 \quad (6.22)$$

where it should be noted that this problem is a *maximization problem*, since we take the objective to be the maximization of profits, and each coefficient in the objective function is the profit earned from the associated activity. The bundle or resource constraints

$$x_{11}^1 + x_{11}^2 \leq 30 \quad (6.23)$$

$$x_{13}^1 + x_{13}^2 \leq 30 \quad (6.24)$$

prevent this problem from having pure network structure.

Because of the bipartite graph, instead of a two-commodity minimum cost flow problem, we have a two-commodity transportation problem whose flow conservation and nonnegativity constraints are

$$\left.\begin{aligned}
x_{11}^1 + x_{12}^1 + x_{13}^1 &= 25 \\
x_{21}^1 + x_{22}^1 + x_{23}^1 &= 15 \\
x_{11}^2 + x_{12}^2 + x_{13}^2 &= 50 \\
x_{21}^2 + x_{22}^2 + x_{23}^2 &= 30 \\
x_{11}^1 + x_{21}^1 &= 20 \\
x_{12}^1 + x_{22}^1 &= 10 \\
x_{13}^1 + x_{23}^1 &= 10 \\
x_{11}^2 + x_{21}^2 &= 20 \\
x_{12}^2 + x_{12}^2 &= 40 \\
x_{13}^2 + x_{23}^2 &= 20
\end{aligned}\right\} \tag{6.25}$$

$$\left.\begin{aligned}
x_{11}^1, x_{12}^1, x_{13}^1, x_{21}^1, x_{22}^1, x_{23}^1 \geq 0 \\
x_{11}^2, x_{12}^2, x_{13}^2, x_{11}^2, x_{12}^2, x_{13}^2 \geq 0
\end{aligned}\right\} \tag{6.26}$$

We note that in the absence of the bundle constraints (6.23) and (6.24) this LP has block-diagonal constraints and decomposes into two commodity-specific transportation problems:

$$\left.\begin{aligned}
&\max 100x_{11}^1 + 120x_{12}^1 + 90x_{13}^1 + 80x_{21}^1 + 70x_{22}^1 + 140x_{23}^1 \\
&\text{subject to} \\
&\qquad x_{11}^1 + x_{12}^1 + x_{13}^1 = 25 \\
&\qquad x_{21}^1 + x_{22}^1 + x_{23}^1 = 15 \\
&\qquad x_{11}^1 + x_{21}^1 = 20 \\
&\qquad x_{12}^1 + x_{22}^1 = 10 \\
&\qquad x_{13}^1 + x_{23}^1 = 10 \\
&\qquad x^1 = (x_{11}^1, x_{12}^1, x_{13}^1, x_{21}^1, x_{22}^1, x_{23}^1)^T \geq 0
\end{aligned}\right\} \tag{6.27}$$

$$\left.\begin{array}{l} \min 40x_{11}^2+20x_{12}^2+30x_{13}^2+20x_{21}^2+40x_{22}^2+10x_{23}^2 \\ \text{subject to} \\ \qquad x_{11}^2+x_{12}^2+x_{13}^2=50 \\ \qquad x_{21}^2+x_{22}^2+x_{23}^2=30 \\ \qquad x_{11}^2+x_{21}^2=20 \\ \qquad x_{12}^2+x_{22}^2=40 \\ \qquad x_{13}^2+x_{23}^2=20 \\ \qquad x^1=(x_{11}^2,x_{12}^2,x_{13}^2,x_{11}^2,x_{12}^2,x_{13}^2)^T \geq 0 \end{array}\right\} \tag{6.28}$$

This natural decomposition by commodity suggests we employ two transportation subproblems at each iteration and DW decomposition in which the bundle constraints are used to form the master problem. We will represent the jth extreme point using the notation

$$v(j)=\begin{pmatrix} v^1(j) \\ v^2(j) \end{pmatrix}$$

where

$$\begin{aligned} v^1(j) &= \left(v_{11}^1(j), v_{12}^1(j), v_{13}^1(j), v_{21}^1(j), v_{22}^1(j), v_{23}^1(j)\right)^T \\ v^2(j) &= \left(v_{11}^2(j), v_{12}^2(j), v_{13}^2(j), v_{21}^2(j), v_{22}^2(j), v_{23}^2(j)\right)^T \end{aligned}$$

are the respective extreme points for each of the commodity-specific transportation problems (6.27) and (6.28).

With this preamble we are ready to implement DW decomposition:

Step 0. *(Initialization)* Set $k=1$. The optimal solutions of (6.27) and (6.28) are readily determined using the network simplex and lead us directly to the extreme points

$$v^1(1)=(15,10,0,5,0,10)^T \qquad v^2(1)=(0,0,0,0,0,0)^T \tag{6.29}$$

$$v^1(2)=(0,0,0,0,0,0)^T \qquad v^2(2)=(20,10,20,0,30,0)^T \tag{6.30}$$

which are obvious choices for constructing initial extreme points of the original problem. We also consider a third initial extreme point of the original problem with the bundle constraints relaxed to initiate the algorithm, namely:

$$v^1(3)=(5,10,10,15,0,0) \quad v^2(3)=(0,0,0,0,0,0) \tag{6.31}$$

So our initial set of extreme points is

$$V^1 = \{v(1), v(2), v(3)\}$$

We employ in the first iteration ($k = 1$) the following representations:

$$\begin{aligned} x^1 &= \lambda_1 v^1(1) + \lambda_2 v^1(2) + \lambda_3 v^1(3) \\ &= (15\lambda_1 + 5\lambda_3, 10\lambda_1 + 10\lambda_3, 10\lambda_3, 5\lambda_1 + 15\lambda_3, 0, 10\lambda_1)^T \end{aligned} \quad (6.32)$$

$$\begin{aligned} x^2 &= \mu_1 v^2(1) + \mu_2 v^2(2) + \mu_3 v^2(3) \\ &= (20\mu_2, 10\mu_2, 20\mu_2, 0, 30\mu_2, 0)^T \end{aligned} \quad (6.33)$$

Step 1. *(Form and solve master problem, $k = 1$)* The current representations (6.32) and (6.33) lead to the master problem MP^1 objective

$$\max 100(15\lambda_1 + 5\lambda_3) + 120(10\lambda_1 + 10\lambda_3) + 90(10\lambda_3)$$
$$+ 80(5\lambda_1 + 15\lambda_3) + 70(0) + 140(10\lambda_1)$$
$$+ 40(20\mu_2) + 20(10\mu_2) + 30(20\mu_2) + 20(0) + 40(30\mu_2) + 10(0)$$

or

$$\max \quad 4500\lambda_1 + 3800\lambda_3 + 2800\mu_2 \quad (6.34)$$

subject to

$$15\lambda_1 + 5\lambda_3 + 20\mu_2 + s_1 = 30 \quad (y_1) \quad (6.35)$$

$$0\lambda_1 + 10\lambda_3 + 20\mu_2 + s_2 = 30 \quad (y_2) \quad (6.36)$$

$$\lambda_1 + \lambda_3 = 1 \quad (\alpha_1) \quad (6.37)$$

$$\mu_2 = 1 \quad (\alpha_2) \quad (6.38)$$

$$\lambda_1, \lambda_3, \mu_2 \geq 0 \quad (6.39)$$

where s_1 and s_2 are slack variables associated with the bundle constraints and the entities in parentheses next to the constraints are corresponding dual variables. The master problem MP^1 given by (6.34)–(6.39) is readily solved to yield:

$$\lambda_1 = \lambda_3 = \frac{1}{2}, \quad \mu_2 = 1, \quad s_1 = 0, \quad s_2 = 5$$

$$y_1 = 70, \quad y_2 = 0, \quad \alpha_1 = 3450, \quad \alpha_2 = 1400$$

Step 2. *(Form and solve subproblems, $k = 1$)* We now specify and solve two subproblems, one for each commodity. Referring to (5.110) and noting that

$$y^T\Gamma = (y_1, y_2)\begin{pmatrix} 1 & 0 & 0 & 0 & 0 & 0 & 1 & 0 & 0 & 0 & 0 & 0 \\ 0 & 0 & 1 & 0 & 0 & 0 & 0 & 0 & 1 & 0 & 0 & 0 \end{pmatrix} \quad (6.40)$$

$$= (y_1, 0, y_2, 0, 0, 0, y_1, 0, y_2, 0, 0, 0) \quad (6.41)$$

$$= (-70, 0, 0, 0, 0, 0, -70, 0, 0, 0, 0, 0) \quad (6.42)$$

we see that the subproblem for commodity ℓ (where $\ell = 1$ or 2) has the objective

$$Z_l = (c - y^T\Gamma)x - \alpha_\ell$$

These subproblem objective functions will be the same as the original objective except for the coefficients of the variables x_{11}^1 and x_{11}^2. That is, we update the objectives of (6.27) and (6.28) according to

$$c_{11}^1 x_{11}^1 \implies (100 - 70)\, x_{11}^1 - 3,450$$

$$c_{11}^2 x_{11}^2 \implies (40 - 70)\, x_{11}^2 - 1,400$$

so that the subproblems at $k = 1$ are

$$\max_{x^1 \in \mathcal{F}_1} Z_1 = 30x_{11}^1 + 120x_{12}^1 + 90x_{13}^1 + 80x_{21}^1 + 70x_{22}^1 + 140x_{23}^1 - 3,450 \quad (6.43)$$

$$\max_{x^2 \in \mathcal{F}_2} Z_2 = -30x_{11}^2 + 20x_{12}^2 + 30x_{13}^2 + 20x_{21}^2 + 40x_{22}^2 + 10x_{23}^2 - 1,400 \quad (6.44)$$

where $\mathcal{F}_1$ and $\mathcal{F}_2$ are a shorthand for the feasible regions for (6.27) and (6.28) respectively. The solutions are:

$$\text{solution of (6.43)} \; : \; x_{SP}^1 = (15, 10, 0, 5, 0, 10)^T \quad (6.45)$$

$$\text{solution of (6.44)} \; : \; x_{SP}^2 = (0, 30, 20, 20, 10, 0)^T \quad (6.46)$$

Note that (6.45) is identical to the previously generated solution $x^1(1)$ that is already used in the representation, and so it need not be considered. Thus, the single new extreme point is

$$v^1(4) = (0, 0, 0, 0, 0, 0)^T \quad v^2(4) = (0, 30, 20, 20, 10, 0)^T$$

Step 3. *(Updating, $k = 1$)* The new set of extreme points is

$$V^2 = V^1 \cup \{v(4)\} = \{v(1), v(2), v(3), v(4)\}$$

and the new representation is

$$\begin{aligned} x^1 &= \lambda_1 v^1(1) + \lambda_2 v^1(2) + \lambda_3 v^1(3) + \lambda_4 v^1(4) \\ &= (15\lambda_1 + 5\lambda_3, 10\lambda_1 + 10\lambda_3, 10\lambda_3, 5\lambda_1 + 15\lambda_3, 0, 10\lambda_1)^T \quad (6.47) \end{aligned}$$

$$\begin{aligned} x^2 &= \mu_1 v^2(1) + \mu_2 v^2(2) + \mu_3 v^2(3) + \mu_4 v^2(4) \\ &= (20\mu_2, 10\mu_2 + 30\mu_4, 20\mu_2 + 20\mu_4, 20\mu_4, 30\mu_2 + 10\mu_4, 0)^T \quad (6.48) \end{aligned}$$

Step 1. *(Form and solve master problem, $k = 2$)* The representations (6.47) and (6.48) lead to the master problem MP^2:

$$\max 4500\lambda_1 + 3800\lambda_3 + 2800\mu_2 + 2000\mu_4$$

subject to

$$\begin{aligned} 15\lambda_1 + 5\lambda_3 + 20\mu_2 + 0\mu_4 + s_1 = 30 \qquad & (y_1) \\ \lambda_1 + 10\lambda_3 + 20\mu_2 + 20\mu_4 + s_2 = 30 \qquad & (y_2) \\ \lambda_1 + \lambda_3 = 1 \qquad & (\alpha_1) \\ \mu_2 + \mu_4 = 1 \qquad & (\alpha_2) \\ \lambda_1, \lambda_3, \mu_2, \mu_4 \geq 0 \end{aligned}$$

Solution of MP^2 gives

$$\lambda_1 = 1, \quad \lambda_3 = 0, \quad \mu_2 = \frac{3}{4}, \quad \mu_4 = \frac{1}{4}, \quad s_1 = 0, \quad s_2 = 10$$

$$y_1 = 40, \quad y_2 = 0, \quad \alpha_1 = 3900, \quad \alpha_2 = 2000$$

Step 2. *(Form and solve subproblem, $k = 2$)* By the same reasoning used in the previous iteration we determine that the subproblems have objective functions that differ from (6.27) and (6.28) according to

$$\begin{aligned} c_{11}^1 x_{11}^1 &\implies (100 - 40)\, x_{11}^1 - 3900 \\ c_{11}^2 x_{11}^2 &\implies (40 - 0)\, x_{11}^2 - 2000 \end{aligned}$$

giving rise to the specific subproblems

$$\max_{x^1 \in F_1} Z_1 = 60x_{11}^1 + 120x_{12}^1 + 90x_{13}^1 + 80x_{21}^1 + 70x_{22}^1 + 140x_{23}^1 - 3900$$

$$\max_{x^2 \in F_2} Z_2 = 40x_{11}^2 + 20x_{12}^2 + 30x_{13}^2 + 20x_{21}^2 + 40x_{22}^2 + 10x_{23}^2 - 2000$$

for $k = 2$. These subproblems have the respective solutions

$$\begin{aligned} x_{SP}^1 &= (15, 10, 0, 5, 0, 10)^T \quad Z_1 = 0 \\ x_{SP}^2 &= (20, 10, 20, 0, 30, 0)^T \quad Z_2 = 0 \end{aligned}$$

These solutions correspond to previously used extreme points, so there is no new extreme point.

Step 3.(*Updating and stopping test, $k = 2$*) The list of current extreme points is

$$V^3 = V^1 \cup \emptyset = \{x(1), x(2), x(3), x(4)\}$$

This circumstance suggests we have reached optimality. Formally, we note that the potential for the current extreme points to alter the solution of the original model is measured by the subproblem objective functions; since these vanish, we accept the linear combination of extreme points found during iteration $k = 2$ as the optimal solution. That is

$$\begin{aligned} x^1 &= (15\lambda_1 + 5\lambda_3, 10\lambda_1 + 10\lambda_3, 10\lambda_3, 5\lambda_1 + 15\lambda_3, 0, 10\lambda_1)^T \\ &= (15 \cdot 1 + 5 \cdot 0, 10 \cdot 1 + 10 \cdot 0, 10 \cdot 0, 5 \cdot 1 + 15 \cdot 0, 0, 10 \cdot 1)^T \\ &= (15, 10, 0, 5, 0, 10)^T \end{aligned}$$

$$\begin{aligned} x^2 &= (20\mu_2, 10\mu_2 + 30\mu_4, 20\mu_2 + 20\mu_4, 20\mu_4, 30\mu_2 + 10\mu_4, 0)^T \\ &= \left(20 \cdot \frac{3}{4}, 10 \cdot \frac{3}{4} + 30 \cdot \frac{1}{4}, 20 \cdot \frac{3}{4} + 20 \cdot \frac{1}{4}, 20 \cdot \frac{1}{4}, 30 \cdot \frac{3}{4} + 10 \cdot \frac{1}{4}, 0\right)^T \\ &= (15, 15, 20, 5, 25, 0)^T \end{aligned}$$

Therefore, the optimal solution is

$$x^* = \begin{pmatrix} x^1 \\ x^2 \end{pmatrix} = (15, 10, 0, 5, 0, 10, 15, 15, 20, 5, 25, 0)^T$$

6.3 Variants of the Minimum Cost Flow Problem

In this section we consider two interesting variants of the minimum cost flow problem, recapped as expressions (6.9)–(6.12).

6.3.1 Bundle Constraints and Lagrangean Relaxation

Consider the multi-commodity flow problem on a general graph described by the following forward-star array and supporting data:

From	To	Commodity	Unit Cost
1	2	1	1
1	3	1	10
2	3	1	1
1	2	2	2
1	3	2	10
2	3	2	2

with a single joint capacity restriction, or bundle constraint, on arc $(2,3)$:

$$g(x) = x_{23}^1 + x_{23}^2 - 19 \leq 0 \tag{6.49}$$

The vector of net nodal supplies is

$$b = \left(b_1^1, b_2^1, b_3^1, b_1^2, b_2^2, b_3^2\right)^T = (10, 0, -10, 10, 0, -10)^T$$

The vector of primal variables is

$$x = \left(x_{12}^1, x_{13}^1, x_{23}^1, x_{12}^2, x_{13}^2, x_{23}^2\right)^T$$

All other arcs have no capacity restrictions. That is, we seek to solve

$$\min Z = 1x_{12}^1 + 10x_{13}^1 + 1x_{23}^1 + 2x_{12}^2 + 10x_{13}^2 + 2x_{23}^2$$

subject to

$$Ax = b \tag{6.50}$$

$$x \geq 0 \tag{6.51}$$

$$g(x) \leq 0 \tag{6.52}$$

where

$$A = \begin{pmatrix} 1 & 1 & 0 & 1 & 1 & 0 \\ -1 & 0 & 1 & -1 & 0 & 1 \\ 0 & -1 & -1 & 0 & -1 & -1 \end{pmatrix}$$

The Lagrangean is

$$L(x,u) = Z + u\left(x_{23}^1 + x_{23}^2 - 19\right) \tag{6.53}$$

$$= \left[x_{12}^1 + (1+u)\, x_{23}^1\right] + 10x_{13}^1$$

$$+ \left[2x_{12}^1 + (2+u)\, x_{23}^2\right] + 10x_{13}^2 - 19u \tag{6.54}$$

We seek the minimum of (6.54) subject to

$$Ax = b \tag{6.55}$$

$$x \geq 0 \tag{6.56}$$

$$g(x) \leq 0 \tag{6.57}$$

The steps of the subgradient algorithm are the following:

Step 0. *(Initialization, $k = 0$)* Pick $u^0 = 10$ and set $k = 0$.

Step 1. *(Find subgradient, $k = 0$)* Solve

$$\min L\left(x, u^0\right) = \left(x_{12}^1 + 11x_{23}^1\right) + 10x_{13}^1 + \left(2x_{12}^2 + 12x_{23}^2\right) + 10x_{13}^2 - 190$$

subject to flow conservation and nonnegativity constraints. The solution is

$$x_{13}^1\left(u^0\right) = x_{13}^2\left(u^0\right) \quad = \quad 10 \tag{6.58}$$

$$\text{all other variables} \quad = \quad 0 \tag{6.59}$$

Step 2 and 3. *(Select step and update, $k = 0$)* Compute the subgradient

$$\begin{aligned} \gamma^0 &= g\left[x\left(u^0\right)\right] \\ &= x_{23}^1\left(u^0\right) + x_{23}^2\left(u^0\right) - 19 = -19 \end{aligned}$$

Pick $\theta_0 = \frac{4}{19}$ so that

$$u^1 = u^0 + \theta_0 \gamma^0 = 10 + \frac{4}{19}(-19) = 6$$

Step 1. *(Find subgradient, $k = 1$)* Solve

$$\min L\left(x, u^1\right) = x_{12}^1 + 7x_{23}^1 + 10x_{13}^1 + 2x_{12}^2 + 8x_{23}^2 + 10x_{13}^2 - 19 \cdot 6$$

subject to flow conservation and nonnegativity constraints. Note that this linear program has alternative optima. We select the nonunique global solution

$$x_{12}^1\left(u^1\right) \quad = \quad x_{23}^1\left(u^1\right) = 10, \quad x_{13}^1 = 0 \tag{6.60}$$

$$x_{12}^2\left(u^1\right) \quad = \quad x_{23}^2\left(u^1\right) = 9, \quad x_{13}^2 = 1 \tag{6.61}$$

Step 2 and 3. *(Stop for any step, $k = 1$)* Compute the subgradient

$$\begin{aligned} \gamma^1 &= g\left[x\left(u^1\right)\right] \\ &= x_{23}^1\left(u^0\right) + x_{23}^2\left(u^0\right) - 19 \\ &= 10 + 9 - 19 = 0 \end{aligned}$$

Had a different optimum been selected in Step 1 for $k = 1$, the subgradient γ^1 would not vanish and the algorithm will oscillate. The vanishing of the subgradient in the previous step indicates optimality and we conclude:

$$\begin{aligned} u^* &= u^1 = 6 \\ x_{12}^{1*} &= x_{23}^{1*} = 10 \\ x_{12}^{2*} &= x_{23}^{2*} = 9 \\ x_{13}^{1*} &= 0 \\ x_{13}^{2*} &= 1 \end{aligned}$$

That this solution is optimal is easily verified by visual inspection of the network.

6.3.2 Bundle Constraints and Dantzig-Wolfe Decomposition

We next address how to employ Dantzig-Wolfe decomposition to solve the linear minimum cost flow problem when bundle constraints are present. For that purpose, let us consider a slightly different example based on the the following extended forward-star array that describes the network of interest:

From	To	c_{ij}
1	2	2
1	3	1
2	3	2
3	1	5

The relevant conformal cost and flow vectors are

$$\begin{aligned} c &= (c_{12}, c_{13}, c_{23}, c_{31})^T = (2, 1, 2, 5)^T \\ x &= (x_{12}, x_{13}, x_{23}, x_{31})^T \end{aligned}$$

Note that we have not used commodity superscripts, yet we will address a problem with bundle constraints. The bundle constraints we will consider set upper bounds on the combined flow of certain arcs without referring to commodities. The reader should reflect on the meaning of such constraints. One possible story motivating such a model formulation is that the flow on arcs of a given bundle must be inspected by a single individual who has an upper bound on his rate of inspection. We further assume that there is a single source at node 1 with net supply $+100$ and a single sink at node 3 with net supply -100. There is also a joint capacity constraint involving arcs $(1, 3)$ and

(3, 1) that stipulates an upper limit on combined flow of 99. Therefore, the following constraints obtain:

$$\begin{aligned} x_{12} + x_{13} &= 100 \\ x_{23} - x_{12} &= 0 \\ x_{31} - x_{13} - x_{23} &= -100 \\ x_{13} + x_{31} &\leq 99 \end{aligned}$$

In terms of the notation we have employed to explain Dantzig-Wolfe decomposition in Chap. 5, our problem is

$$\min \quad c^T x \tag{6.62}$$

$$\text{subject to} \quad x \in S \tag{6.63}$$

$$\Gamma x \leq q \tag{6.64}$$

where

$$A = \begin{pmatrix} 1 & 1 & 0 & -1 \\ -1 & 0 & 1 & 0 \\ 0 & -1 & -1 & 1 \end{pmatrix}$$

$$b = \begin{pmatrix} 100 \\ 0 \\ -100 \end{pmatrix}$$

$$\Gamma = \begin{pmatrix} 0 & 1 & 0 & 1 \end{pmatrix}$$

$$q = 99 \in \Re^1_+$$

$$S = \left\{ x \in \Re^4 : Ax = b,\ x \geq 0 \right\} \tag{6.65}$$

$$x = (x_{12},\, x_{12},\, x_{23},\, x_{31})^T \tag{6.66}$$

It is easy to verify that

$$x_{12} = 1,\ x_{13} = 99,\ x_{23} = 1,\ x_{31} = 0$$

is a solution of the linear program (6.62)–(6.64). We wish to illustrate that Dantzig-Wolfe decomposition yields the same result.

The DW algorithm proceeds as follows:

Step 0. *(Initialization)* Let us employ

$$\begin{aligned} v^1 &= (100, 0, 100, 0)^T \\ v^2 &= (0, 100, 0, 0)^T \end{aligned}$$

as our initial extreme points for the relaxed feasible region S. Set $k = 1$.

Step 1. *(Solve the master problem, $k = 1$)* The current representation of x is

$$\begin{aligned} x^1 &= \lambda_1 v^1 + \lambda_2 v^2 \\ &= \lambda_1 (100, 0, 100, 0)^T + \lambda_2 (0, 100, 0, 0)^T \\ &= (100\lambda_1, 100\lambda_2, 100\lambda_1, 0)^T \end{aligned}$$

As a consequence

$$\begin{aligned} x_{13} + x_{31} &= 100\lambda_2 + 0 \leq 99 \\ \lambda_2 &\leq \frac{99}{100} \end{aligned}$$

and

$$\begin{aligned} c^T x^1 &= \begin{pmatrix} 2 & 1 & 2 & 5 \end{pmatrix} \begin{pmatrix} 100\lambda_1 \\ 100\lambda_2 \\ 100\lambda_1 \\ 0 \end{pmatrix} \\ &= 400\lambda_1 + 100\lambda_2 \end{aligned}$$

The master problem is therefore

$$\left.\begin{array}{ll} \min \ (400\lambda_1 + 100\lambda_2) & \\ \text{subject to} \quad \lambda_1 + \lambda_2 = 1 & (y) \\ \lambda_2 \leq \dfrac{99}{100} & (\alpha) \\ \lambda_1 \geq 0 & \\ \lambda_2 \geq 0 & \end{array}\right\} MP^1 \tag{6.67}$$

where α and y are dual variables. The solution is

$$\left.\begin{array}{l} \lambda_1 = \frac{1}{100} \\ \lambda_2 = \frac{99}{100} \\ y = -300 \\ \alpha = 400 \end{array}\right\} \text{optimal solution of } MP^1 \tag{6.68}$$

Step 2. *(Solve the subproblem, $k = 1$)* The subproblem SP^1 is

$$\min Z_{\text{SP}}^1 \left[c^T - y\Gamma\right] x - \alpha \tag{6.69}$$

subject to the "good" constraints so that

$$\begin{aligned}
Z_{SP}^1 &= \left[c^T - y^T\Gamma\right] x - \alpha \\
&= \left[\begin{pmatrix} 2 & 1 & 2 & 5 \end{pmatrix} - (-300)\begin{pmatrix} 0 & 1 & 0 & 1 \end{pmatrix}\right] \begin{pmatrix} x_{12} \\ x_{13} \\ x_{23} \\ x_{31} \end{pmatrix} - 400 \\
&= \begin{pmatrix} 2 & 301 & 2 & 305 \end{pmatrix} \begin{pmatrix} x_{12} \\ x_{13} \\ x_{23} \\ x_{31} \end{pmatrix} - 400 \\
&= 2x_{12} + 301x_{13} + 2x_{23} + 305x_{31} - 400
\end{aligned} \tag{6.70}$$

Consequently, the subproblem takes the form

$$\left.\begin{aligned}
\min Z_{SP}^1 = 2x_{12} + 301x_{13} + 2x_{23} + 305x_{31} - 400 \\
\text{subject to} \quad x_{12} + x_{13} - x_{31} = 100 \\
x_{23} - x_{12} = 0 \\
x_{31} - x_{13} - x_{23} = -100 \\
x_{12} \geq 0 \\
x_{13} \geq 0 \\
x_{23} \geq 0 \\
x_{31} \geq 0
\end{aligned}\right\} SP^1 \tag{6.71}$$

with solution

$$x_{12} = 100, \quad x_{13} = 0, \quad x_{23} = 100, \quad x_{31} = 0$$

Thereby we have generated the "new" extreme point

$$v^3 = (100, 0, 100, 0)^T$$

which is identical to x^1. The objective value

$$Z_{SP}^1 = 2\,(100) + 301\,(0) + 2\,(100) + 305\,(0) - 400 = 0$$

indicates we have found the optimal solution and no further iterations are required. Values of the optimal variables are found by using the current weights and extreme points. That is,

$$\lambda_1^* = \frac{1}{100}$$

$$\lambda_2^* = \frac{99}{100}$$

so that for this problem

$$\begin{aligned} x^* &= \left(100\lambda_1^*, 100\lambda_2^*, 100\lambda_1^*, 0\right)^T \\ &= \left(100\left(\frac{1}{100}\right), 100\left(\frac{99}{100}\right), 100\left(\frac{1}{100}\right), 0\right)^T \\ &= \left(1, 99, 1, 0\right)^T \end{aligned} \quad (6.72)$$

which agrees with the known solution.

6.3.3 Nonlinear Unit Arc Costs

We now consider a small nonlinear minimum cost flow problem described by the following extended forward-star array:

From	To	A_{ij}	B_{ij}	$c_{ij}(x_{ij}) = A_{ij} + B_{ij}x_{ij}$
1	2	2	1	$c_{12}(x_{12}) = 2 + x_{12}$
1	3	10	10	$c_{13}(x_{13}) = 10 + 10x_{13}$
2	3	2	1	$c_{23}(x_{23}) = 2 + x_{23}$
2	4	2	1	$c_{24}(x_{24}) = 2 + x_{24}$
3	4	2	1	$c_{34}(x_{34}) = 2 + x_{34}$

The relevant conformal cost and flow vectors are

$$c(x) = \left[c_{12}(x_{12}), c_{13}(x_{13}), c_{23}(x_{23}), c_{24}(x_{24}), c_{34}(x_{34})\right]^T$$

$$x = \left(x_{12}, x_{13}, x_{23}, x_{24}, x_{34}\right)^T$$

We assume that there is a single source at node 1 with net supply +200 and two sink nodes: one at node 3 with net supply -100 and the other at node 4 also with net supply -100. Furthermore, there is a joint capacity constraint involving arcs $(2,4)$ and $(3,4)$ that stipulates an upper limit on combined flow of 99. Therefore, our problems

$$\begin{aligned}\min \quad Z = c^T x &= c_{12}(x_{12})\, x_{12} + c_{13}(x_{13})\, x_{13} + c_{23}(x_{23})\, x_{23} \\ &\quad + c_{24}(x_{24})\, x_{24} + c_{34}(x_{34})\, x_{34} \\ &= (2 + x_{12})\, x_{12} + (10 + 10x_{13})\, x_{13} + (2 + x_{23})\, x_{23} \\ &\quad + (2 + x_{24})\, x_{24} + (2 + x_{34})\, x_{34} \end{aligned} \tag{6.73}$$

subject to

$$x_{12} + x_{13} = 200 \tag{6.74}$$

$$x_{23} + x_{24} - x_{12} = 0 \tag{6.75}$$

$$x_{34} - x_{13} - x_{23} = -100 \tag{6.76}$$

$$-x_{24} - x_{34} = -100 \tag{6.77}$$

$$x_{23} + x_{24} \leq 99 \tag{6.78}$$

$$x_{12}, x_{13}, x_{23}, x_{24}, x_{34} \geq 0 \tag{6.79}$$

We now illustrate how simplicial decomposition may be employed to solve the linearly constrained nonlinear program (6.73)–(6.79).

Step 0. *(Initialization)* Let us initially employ the following extreme points of the polytope formed by (6.74)–(6.77):

$$v^1 = (100, 100, 0, 100, 0)^T \tag{6.80}$$

$$v^2 = (0, 200, 0, 0, 100)^T \tag{6.81}$$

Define

$$\Lambda^1 = \{v^1, v^2\} \tag{6.82}$$

$$g^1 = +\infty \tag{6.83}$$

and set $k = 1$.

Step 1. *(Solve program constrained by convex hull, $k = 1$)* We note

$$\begin{aligned} x^1 &= \lambda_1 v^1 + \lambda_2 v^2 \\ &= \lambda_1 (100, 100, 0, 100, 0) + \lambda_2 (0, 200, 0, 0, 100) \\ &= (100\lambda_1, 100\lambda_1 + 200\lambda_2, 0, 100\lambda_1, 100\lambda_2)^T \end{aligned}$$

Substituting x^1 for x in (6.73) we obtain:

$$\begin{aligned} Z &= (2+100\lambda_1)\,100\lambda_1 + (10+10\,(100\lambda_1+200\lambda_2))\,(100\lambda_1+200\lambda_2) \\ &\quad + (2+0)\,0 + (2+100\lambda_1)\,100\lambda_1 + (2+100\lambda_2)\,100\lambda_2 \\ &= 1400\lambda_1 + 120000\,(\lambda_1)^2 + 2200\lambda_2 + 400000\lambda_1\lambda_2 + 410000\,(\lambda_2)^2 \end{aligned}$$

so that the relevant mathematical program on the unit simplex is

$$\left.\begin{aligned} &\min\ 14\lambda_1+1200\,(\lambda_1)^2+22\lambda_2+4000\lambda_1\lambda_2+4100\,(\lambda_2)^2 \\ &\text{subject to} \quad \lambda_1+\lambda_2=1 \\ &\qquad\qquad \lambda_1,\lambda_2 \geq 0 \end{aligned}\right\} \tag{6.84}$$

which is readily restated as

$$\begin{aligned} \min\ F(\lambda_1) = 14\lambda_1 + 1200\,(\lambda_1)^2 + 22\,(1-\lambda_1) \\ + 4000\lambda_1\,(1-\lambda_1) + 4100\,(1-\lambda_1)^2 \end{aligned} \tag{6.85}$$

subject to

$$\lambda_1 \geq 0$$

The first-order condition is

$$\lambda_1 = \left[\arg\left\{\frac{dF}{d\lambda_1} = -4208 + 2600\lambda_1 = 0\right\}\right]_0^1 \tag{6.86}$$

where

$$[v]_0^1 = \begin{cases} 1 & \text{if } v>1 \\ 0 & \text{if } v<0 \\ v & \text{if } 0\leq v\leq 1 \end{cases} \tag{6.87}$$

for $v \in \Re^1$. It follows that

$$\lambda_1 = \left[\frac{4208}{2600} > 1\right]_0^1 = 1 \tag{6.88}$$

$$\lambda_2 = 1-\lambda_1 = 0 \tag{6.89}$$

Therefore, the current approximation is

$$x^1 = v^1 = (100, 100, 0, 100, 0)^T \tag{6.90}$$

Step 2. *(Generate new extreme point and apply stopping test, $k = 1$)* Note that

$$\begin{aligned}\nabla f(x^1) &= \left(2 + 2x_{12}^1, 10 + 20x_{13}^1, 2 + 2x_{23}^1, 2 + 2x_{24}^1, 2 + 2x_{34}^1\right)^T \\ &= (2 + 2(100), 10 + 20(100), 2 + 2(0), 2 + 2(100), 2 + 2(0))^T \\ &= (202, 2010, 2, 202, 2)^T \end{aligned} \tag{6.91}$$

Solve subproblem

$$\begin{aligned}\min_{y \in S} \left[\nabla f(x^k)\right]^T y &= (202, 2010, 2, 202, 2) \begin{pmatrix} y_{12} \\ y_{13} \\ y_{23} \\ y_{24} \\ y_{34} \end{pmatrix} \\ &= 202y_{12} + 2010y_{13} + 2y_{23} + 202y_{24} + 2y_{34} \end{aligned} \tag{6.92}$$

That is, solve

$$\left.\begin{array}{c} \min 202y_{12} + 2010y_{13} + 2y_{23} + 202y_{24} + 2y_{34} \\ \text{subject to} \quad y_{12} + y_{13} = 200 \\ y_{23} + y_{24} - y_{12} = 0 \\ y_{34} - y_{13} - y_{23} = -100 \\ -y_{24} - y_{34} = -100 \\ y_{23} + y_{24} \leq 199 \\ y_{12} \geq 0 \\ y_{13} \geq 0 \\ y_{23} \geq 0 \\ y_{24} \geq 0 \\ y_{34} \geq 0 \end{array}\right\} \tag{6.93}$$

to obtain the extreme point

$$\begin{aligned} v^3 &= y^1 = (y_{12}, y_{13}, y_{23}, y_{24}, y_{34})^T \\ &= (199, 1, 199, 0, 100)^T \end{aligned} \tag{6.94}$$

and the direction vector

$$\begin{aligned} y^1 - x^1 &= (199, 1, 199, 0, 100)^T - (100, 100, 0, 100, 0)^T \\ &= (99, -99, 199, -100, 100)^T \end{aligned} \tag{6.95}$$

Note that, although (6.93) has as many constraints as the original nonlinear program, it is a linear minimum cost flow problem, which can be solved with the network simplex. Observe that

$$\left[\nabla f(x^1)\right]^T (y^1 - x^1) = \begin{pmatrix} 202 & 2010 & 2 & 202 & 2 \end{pmatrix} \begin{pmatrix} 99 \\ -99 \\ 199 \\ -100 \\ 100 \end{pmatrix} \tag{6.96}$$

$$= -1.9859 \times 10^5 < 0 \tag{6.97}$$

so optimality has not been reached.

Step 3. *(Add/delete extreme points, $k = 1$)* Since we found $\lambda_2 = 0$ we must drop v^2; furthermore since

$$\left| \left[\nabla f(x^1)\right]^T (y^1 - x^1) \right| = 1.9859 \times 10^5 < g_1 = +\infty \tag{6.98}$$

we must add v^3, so that

$$\Lambda^2 = \{v^1, v^3\} \tag{6.99}$$

Step 4. *(Updating, $k = 1$)* Update the gap measure according to

$$\begin{aligned} g_2 &= \min \left\{ g_1, \left[\nabla f(x^1)\right]^T (y^1 - x^1) \right\} \\ &= \min \left[+\infty, 1.9859 \times 10^5 \right] = 1.9859 \times 10^5 \end{aligned} \tag{6.100}$$

Set $k = 2$ and go to Step 1.

Step 1. *(Solve program constrained by convex hull, $k = 2$)* We now use the representation

$$\begin{aligned} x^2 &= \lambda_1 v^1 + \lambda_3 v^3 \\ &= \lambda_1 (100, 100, 0, 100, 0)^T + \lambda_3 (199, 1, 199, 0, 100)^T \\ &= (100\lambda_1 + 199\lambda_3, 100\lambda_1 + \lambda_3, 199\lambda_3, 100\lambda_1, 100\lambda_3)^T \end{aligned}$$

Substituting x^2 for x in (6.73), upon eliminating redundant constraints and trivial identities, we obtain:

$$\begin{aligned} Z\left(x^2\right) &= \left(2+x_{12}^2\right)x_{12}^2+\left(10+10x_{13}^2\right)x_{13}^2+\left(2+x_{23}\right)x_{23}^2 \\ &\quad +\left(2+x_{24}^2\right)x_{24}^2+\left(2+x_{34}^2\right)x_{34}^2 \end{aligned}$$

Therefore, the relevant mathematical program on the unit simplex is

$$\min\ 1400\lambda_1+1006\lambda_3+41800\lambda_1\lambda_3+120000\lambda_1^2+89212\lambda_3^2$$

subject to

$$\lambda_1+\lambda_3=1$$

$$\lambda_1,\lambda_2\geq 0$$

which is readily restated as

$$\min\ F\left(\lambda_1\right)=1400\lambda_1+1006\left(1-\lambda_1\right)+41\,800\lambda_1\left(1-\lambda_1\right)$$
$$+120\,000\lambda_1^2+89\,212\left(1-\lambda_1\right)^2$$

subject to

$$\lambda_1\geq 0$$

It follows that

$$\begin{aligned} \lambda_1 &= \left[\frac{136230}{334824}\right]_+\approx 0.407>0 \\ \lambda_3 &= 1-\lambda_1=1-0.407=0.593 \end{aligned}$$

Therefore, the current approximation is

$$\begin{aligned} x^2 &= \lambda_1 v^1+\lambda_3 v^3 \\ &= \left(100\lambda_1+199\lambda_3,100\lambda_1+\lambda_3,199\lambda_3,100\lambda_1,100\lambda_3\right)^T \\ &= \left(158.72,41.28,118.03,40.69,59.31\right)^T \end{aligned}$$

Step 2. *(Generate new extreme point and apply stopping test, $k=2$)* Note that

$$\begin{aligned} \nabla f(x^2) &= \left(2+2x_{12}^1,10+20x_{13}^1,2+2x_{23}^1,2+2x_{24}^1,2+2x_{34}^1\right)^T \\ &= \left(319.44,835.6,238.06,83.374,120.63\right)^T \end{aligned}$$

We need to solve

$$\min_{y \in S} \left[\nabla f(x^2)\right]^T y = (319.44, 835.6, 238.06, 83.374, 120.63) \begin{pmatrix} y_{12} \\ y_{13} \\ y_{23} \\ y_{24} \\ y_{34} \end{pmatrix}$$

That is, we solve

$$\min\ 319.44y_{12} + 835.6y_{13} + 238.06y_{23} + 83.374y_{24} + 120.63y_{34}$$

subject to

$$\begin{aligned}
y_{12} + y_{13} &= 200 \\
y_{23} + y_{24} - y_{12} &= 0 \\
y_{34} - y_{13} - y_{23} &= -100 \\
-y_{24} - y_{34} &= -100 \\
y_{23} + y_{24} &\leq 199 \\
y_{12} &\geq 0 \\
y_{13} &\geq 0 \\
y_{23} &\geq 0 \\
y_{24} &\geq 0 \\
y_{34} &\geq 0
\end{aligned}$$

to obtain the new extreme point

$$\begin{aligned}
y^2 &= \left(y_{12}^2, y_{13}^2, y_{23}^2, y_{24}^2, y_{34}^2\right)^T \\
&= (199, 1, 99, 100, 0)^T
\end{aligned}$$

and direction

$$\begin{aligned}
(y^2 - x^2) &= (199, 1, 99, 100, 0) - (158.72, 41.28, 118.03, 40.69, 59.31)^T \\
&= (40.28, -40.28, -19.03, 59.13, 59.13)^T
\end{aligned}$$

It follows that

$$\left[\nabla f(x^1)\right]^T (y^2 - x^2) = (319.44, 835.6, 238.06, 83.374, 120.63)\begin{pmatrix} 40.28 \\ -40.28 \\ -19.03 \\ 59.313 \\ -59.313 \end{pmatrix}$$

$$= -27,531 < 0$$

so optimality has not been reached.

Step 3. *(Add/delete extreme points, $k = 2$)* Since

$$\left|\left[\nabla f(x^2)\right]^T (y^2 - x^2)\right| = 27,531 < g_2 = 1.9859 \times 10^5$$

we add a column

$$v^4 = y^2 = (199, 1, 199, 0, 100)^T$$

so that

$$\mathbf{\Lambda}^2 = \{v^1, v^3, v^4\}$$

Step 4. *(Updating, $k = 2$)* Update the gap measure according to

$$\begin{aligned} g_3 &= \min\left\{g_2, \left|\left[\nabla f(x^2)\right]^T (y^2 - x^2)\right|\right\} \\ &= \min\left[1.9859 \times 10^5, 27541\right] = 27541 \end{aligned}$$

Set $k = 3$ and go to Step 1.

Step 1. *(Solve program constrained by convex hull, $k = 3$)* We now use the representation

$$\begin{aligned} x^3 &= \lambda_1 v^1 + \lambda_3 v^3 + \lambda_4 v^4 \\ &= \lambda_1 (100, 100, 0, 100, 0) + \lambda_3 (199, 1, 199, 0, 100) \\ &\quad + \lambda_4 (199, 1, 199, 0, 100) \\ &= (100\lambda_1 + 199\lambda_3 + 199\lambda_4, 100\lambda_1 + \lambda_3 + \lambda_4, 199\lambda_3 \\ &\quad + 99\lambda_4, 100\lambda_1 + 100\lambda_4, 100\lambda_3) \end{aligned}$$

Substituting x^3 for x in (6.73), upon eliminating redundant constraints and trivial identities, we obtain:

$$\begin{aligned} Z\left(x^3\right) &= (2+100\lambda_1+199\lambda_3+199\lambda_4)(100\lambda_1+199\lambda_3+199\lambda_4) \\ &\quad +(10+10(100\lambda_1+\lambda_3+\lambda_4))(100\lambda_1+\lambda_3+\lambda_4) \\ &\quad +(2+199\lambda_3+99\lambda_4)(199\lambda_3+99\lambda_4) \\ &\quad +(2+100\lambda_1+100\lambda_4)(100\lambda_1+100\lambda_4) \\ &\quad +(2+100\lambda_3)(100\lambda_3) \\ &= 20000\lambda_1^2+41800\lambda_1\lambda_3+61800\lambda_1\lambda_4+89212\lambda_3^2 \\ &\quad +118624\lambda_3\lambda_4+59412\lambda_4^2+1400\lambda_1+1006\lambda_3+806\lambda_4 \end{aligned}$$

so that the relevant mathematical program on the unit simplex is

$$\begin{aligned} \min\, & 20000\lambda_1^2+41800\lambda_1\lambda_3+61800\lambda_1\lambda_4+89212\lambda_3^2+118624\lambda_3\lambda_4 \\ & +59412\lambda_4^2+1400\lambda_1+1006\lambda_3+806\lambda_4 \end{aligned}$$

subject to

$$\lambda_1+\lambda_3+\lambda_4=1$$

$$\lambda_1,\lambda_3,\lambda_4\geq 0$$

It follows that

$$\begin{aligned} \lambda_1 &\approx 0.24675 \\ \lambda_3 &\approx 0.08143 \\ \lambda_4 &\approx 0.67182 \end{aligned}$$

Therefore, the current approximation is

$$\begin{aligned} x^3 &= \lambda_1 v^1+\lambda_3 v^3+\lambda_4 v^4 \\ &= (100\lambda_1+199\lambda_3+199\lambda_4, 100\lambda_1+\lambda_3+\lambda_4, 199\lambda_3 \\ &\quad +99\lambda_4, 100\lambda_1+100\lambda_4, 100\lambda_3)^T \\ &= (174.57143, 25.42857, 82.71429, 91.85714, 8.14286)^T \end{aligned}$$

Step 2. *(Generation of new extreme point and stopping test, $k = 3$)* Note that

$$\begin{aligned}\nabla f(x^3) &= \left(2 + 2x_{12}^3, 10 + 20x_{13}^3, 2 + 2x_{23}^3, 2 + 2x_{24}^3, 2 + 2x_{34}^3\right) \\ &= (351.14286, 518.57143, 167.42857, 185.71429, 18.28571)^T\end{aligned}$$

We need to solve

$$\min_{y \in S} \left[\nabla f(x^2)\right]^T y = (351.14286, 518.57143, 167.42857, 185.71429, 18.28571) \begin{pmatrix} y_{12} \\ y_{13} \\ y_{23} \\ y_{24} \\ y_{34} \end{pmatrix}$$

That is, we solve

$$\min\ 351.14286 y_{12} + 518.57143 y_{13} + 167.42857 y_{23} + 185.71429 y_{24} + 18.28571 y_{34}$$

subject to

$$\begin{aligned} y_{12} + y_{13} &= 200 \\ y_{23} + y_{24} - y_{12} &= 0 \\ y_{34} - y_{13} - y_{23} &= -100 \\ -y_{24} - y_{34} &= -100 \\ y_{23} + y_{24} &\leq 199 \\ y_{12} &\geq 0 \\ y_{13} &\geq 0 \\ y_{23} &\geq 0 \\ y_{24} &\geq 0 \\ y_{34} &\geq 0 \end{aligned}$$

to obtain the new extreme point

$$\begin{aligned} v^5 = y^3 &= \left(y_{12}^2, y_{13}^2, y_{23}^2, y_{24}^2, y_{34}^2\right)^T \\ &= (0, 200, 0, 0, 100)^T \end{aligned}$$

and direction

$$\begin{aligned}(y^3 - x^3)^T &= (0, 200, 0, 0, 100)^T \\ &\quad -(174.57143, 25.42857, 82.71429, 91.85714, 8.14286)^T \\ &= (-174.57143, 174.57143, 82.71429, -91.85714, 91.85714)^T\end{aligned}$$

It follows that

$$\left[\nabla f(x^3)\right]^T (y^3 - x^3)$$

$$= (351.14286, 518.57143, 167.42857, 185.71429, 18.28571) \begin{pmatrix} -174.57143 \\ 174.57143 \\ 82.71429 \\ -91.85714 \\ 91.85714 \end{pmatrix}$$

$$= 0.000010 \approx 0$$

So the gap function is effectively zero and the optimal solution is approximately

$$\begin{aligned} x^* &\approx x^3 = \lambda_1 a_1 + \lambda_3 a_3 + \lambda_4 a_4 \\ &= 0.24675\,(100, 100, 0, 100, 0)^T + 0.08143(199, 1, 199, 0, 100)^T \\ &\quad +0.67182(199, 1, 199, 0, 100)^T \\ &= (175, 25, 83, 92, 8)^T \end{aligned}$$

6.4 The Traveling Salesman Problem

The *traveling salesman problem* (TSP) is perhaps the most famous of all problems from classical graph theory; it is the foundation model for all routing and scheduling models. The TSP seeks as a solution the least cost path that begins at a given node of the network of interest, visits all members of a set of specified nodes at least once, and returns to the starting node. As such, the TSP is the prototypical *node covering problem.* Traditionally, feasible solutions of the TSP are referred to as *tours.* Formally, a tour is a simple forward cycle that contains all the nodes of the relevant graph.

When all nodes of the graph $\mathcal{G}(\mathcal{N}, \mathcal{A})$ on which the network is based are to be visited at least once, the expression of the TSP as a mathematical program is

$$\min \sum_{(i,j)\in\mathcal{A}} c_{ij}x_{ij} \tag{6.101}$$

subject to

$$\sum_{j\in(\mathcal{N}\backslash i)} x_{ij} = 1 \quad \forall i \in \mathcal{N} \tag{6.102}$$

$$\sum_{i\in(\mathcal{N}\backslash j)} x_{ij} = 1 \quad \forall j \in \mathcal{N} \tag{6.103}$$

$$x_{ij} = \begin{cases} 1 & \text{if } (i,j) \text{ belongs to the tour} \\ 0 & \text{if } (i,j) \text{ does not belong to the tour} \end{cases} \tag{6.104}$$

$$\sum_{j\notin S}\sum_{i\in S} (x_{ij} + x_{ji}) \geq 2 \quad \forall S \subset \mathcal{N} \tag{6.105}$$

where x_{ij} and c_{ij} are, respectively, the flow and the unit cost of flow on arc $(i, j) \in \mathcal{A}$, S is a nonempty proper subset of nodes of $\mathcal{G}(\mathcal{N}, \mathcal{A})$, and it is presumed that the subgraph $\mathcal{G}(\mathcal{N}, \mathcal{A}^*)$ formed from the optimal solution x^* where

$$\mathcal{A}^* = \left\{(i,j) \in \mathcal{A} : x^*_{ij} = 1\right\} \tag{6.106}$$

is connected. This last stipulation is merely a requirement that there be a feasible solution of the TSP. Less intuitive are the *subtour constraints* (6.105). It is these constraints that prevent the TSP from being a special case of a version of the minimum cost flow problem known as the assignment problem.

The subtour constraints prevent the optimal solution from having multiple, disconnected cycles. Because the number of subtour constraints is potentially very large, we do not consider the TSP to have near network structure. Consequently, it is not at all obvious that performing a Lagrangean relaxation of the subtour constraints will be helpful, since there are potentially so many such constraints. So we follow a suggestion of Bertsekas (1998) and instead price out the constraints (6.102) and (6.103), mandating that each node be visited once. This means that the subproblems for iteration k are

$$\min \quad L\left(x,\mu^k,\nu^k\right) = \sum_{(i,j)\in\mathcal{A}} c_{ij}x_{ij} + \sum_{i\in\mathcal{N}} \mu_i^k \left(\sum_{j\in(\mathcal{N}\backslash i)} x_{ij} - 1\right)$$
$$+ \sum_{j\in\mathcal{N}} \nu_j^k \left(\sum_{i\in(\mathcal{N}\backslash j)} x_{ij} - 1\right) \tag{6.107}$$
$$= \sum_{(i,j)\in\mathcal{A}, i\neq j} \left(c_{ij} + \mu_i^k + \nu_j^k\right) x_{ij} - \sum_{i\in\mathcal{N}} \mu_i^k$$
$$- \sum_{j\in\mathcal{N}} \nu_j^k \tag{6.108}$$

subject to

$$\sum_{j\notin S}\sum_{i\in S} (x_{ij} + x_{ji}) \geq 2 \qquad \forall S \subset \mathcal{N} \tag{6.109}$$

$$x_{ij} = (0,1) \qquad \forall (i,j) \in \mathcal{A} \tag{6.110}$$

where

$$x \in (0,1)^{|\mathcal{A}|}$$
$$\mu^k \in \Re^{|\mathcal{N}|}$$
$$\nu^k \in \Re^{|\mathcal{N}|}$$

are the vectors of arc flows and Lagrange multipliers. Note that the remaining constraints (6.109) and (6.110) require that a connected subtour be selected.

The subproblem (6.107), (6.109), and (6.110) can be solved with relative ease if we restrict the tours we examine to so-called *one-trees*. We define a *one-tree* to be a tree that spans nodes $2, 3, \ldots, |N|$ *plus* two access/egress arcs that are incident on node 1, where node 1 is the source and sink of the TSP, in a way that ensures the one-tree is a tour. We further define a *one-set* to be the set of arcs with nontrivial flow that correspond to a given one-tree. It is intuitive, and can be shown formally that, when constraints (6.102) and (6.103) bind, a one-tree will be equivalent to a tour that satisfies the subtour constraints. Consequently, the subproblems are of the form

$$\min_x L\left(x,\mu^k,\nu^k\right) = \sum_{(i,j)\in\mathcal{A}, i\neq j} \left(c_{ij} + \mu_i^k + \nu_j^k\right) x_{ij} - \sum_{i\in\mathcal{N}} \mu_i^k - \sum_{j\in\mathcal{N}} \nu_j^k$$

subject to

$$Q = \{(i,j) : x_{ij} \neq 0\} \text{ being a one-set}$$

$$x_{ij} = (0,1) \quad \forall (i,j) \in \mathcal{A}$$

As subgradient optimization works its way toward a solution where the constraints mandating that each node be visited once hold as equalities, it is also working toward a solution of the TSP. Since we are not considering all conceivable tours that satisfy the subtour constraints (but rather one-trees only), the resulting algorithm is not exact, although it will definitely yield a feasible tour.

To clarify the notions we have just introduced, let us consider a simple example based on the following extended forward star array:

From	To	c_{ij}
1	2	1
2	3	1
2	4	1
3	1	1
4	3	1

(6.111)

Consequently

$$
\begin{aligned}
x &= (x_{12}, x_{23}, x_{24}, x_{31}, x_{43})^T \\
c &= (c_{12}, c_{23}, c_{24}, c_{31}, c_{43})^T \\
\mu &= (\mu_1, \mu_2, \mu_3, \mu_4)^T \\
\nu &= (\nu_1, \nu_2, \nu_3, \nu_4)^T \\
\mathcal{N} &= \{1, 2, 3, 4\}
\end{aligned}
$$

It will also be useful to employ the following notation for the priced-out constraints:

$$g_{1i} = \sum_{j \neq i} x_{ij} - 1 \quad \forall i \in \mathcal{N} \tag{6.112}$$

$$g_{2j} = \sum_{i \neq j} x_{ij} - 1 \quad \forall j \in \mathcal{N} \tag{6.113}$$

$$g_1 = (g_{1i} : i \in \mathcal{N}) \tag{6.114}$$

$$g_2 = (g_{2j} : j \in \mathcal{N}) \tag{6.115}$$

The subproblems are of the form

$$
\begin{aligned}
\min L\left(x, \mu^k, \nu^k\right) &= c^T x + \mu^T g_1(x) + \nu^T g_2(x) \\
&= \left(1 + \mu_1^k + \nu_2^k\right) x_{12} + \left(1 + \mu_2^k + \nu_3^k\right) x_{23} \\
&\quad + \left(1 + \mu_2^k + \nu_4^k\right) x_{24} + \left(1 + \mu_3^k + \nu_1^k\right) x_{31} \\
&\quad + \left(1 + \mu_4^k + \nu_3^k\right) x_{43}
\end{aligned} \tag{6.116}
$$

for flows that correspond to one-trees. Note that in (6.116) we have ignored additive constants stemming from the fixed dual vectors μ^k and ν^k that will be employed in the kth iteration. Because we are requiring that subproblem solutions be one-trees, the value of the integer flow variables for arcs $(1,2)$ and $(3,1)$ must always be unity since these two arcs are the only access/egress arcs for the depot at node 1. This fortunate state of affairs of course will not be observed in more complicated networks; that is to say, general networks will involve multiple choices for the access/egress arcs. In short, the network of this example requires that

$$x_{12}^k = x_{31}^k = 1$$

in the optimal solution of each kth subproblem.

The one-tree Lagrangean relaxation algorithm then proceeds as follows:

Step 0. *(Initialization)* Pick $u^0 = \nu^0 = (0,0,0,0)^T$ and set $k = 0$.

Step 1. *(Lagrangean relaxation, $k = 0$)* Solve

$$\min L\left(x, \mu^0, \nu^0\right) = x_{12} + x_{23} + x_{24} + x_{31} + x_{43}$$

for unit flows corresponding to a one-tree. There are three possible one trees for this simple network; they are

$$\left.\begin{array}{r} x_{12}^0 = x_{31}^0 = 1 \\ x_{24}^0 = x_{43}^0 = 1 \\ x_{23}^0 = 0 \end{array}\right\} T_1^0 \tag{6.117}$$

$$\left.\begin{array}{r} x_{12}^0 = x_{31}^0 = 1 \\ x_{23}^0 = x_{24}^0 = 1 \\ x_{43}^0 = 0 \end{array}\right\} T_2^0 \tag{6.118}$$

$$\left.\begin{array}{r} x_{12}^0 = x_{31}^0 = 1 \\ x_{23}^0 = x_{43}^0 = 1 \\ x_{24}^0 = 0 \end{array}\right\} T_3^0$$

Note that $x_{12}^0 = x_{31}^0 = 1$, as stressed previously, is dictated by the need for access/egress arcs to define a tour, while the remaining choices of zero or unit flows are dictated by the fact that we must have a spanning tree for nodes 2, 3 and 4 with exactly two arcs. Each one-tree T_1^0, T_2^0, and T_3^0 has the identical tour length (cost):

$$\begin{aligned} L\left(x\left(T_0^1\right), \mu^0, \nu^0\right) &= L\left(x\left(T_0^2\right), \mu^0, \nu^0\right) = L\left(x\left(T_0^3\right), \mu^0, \nu^0\right) \\ &= 1 + 1 + 1 + 1 = 4 \end{aligned}$$

We arbitrarily pick T_0^2.

Step 2. *(Computation of subgradient, $k = 0$)* Note that for T_2^0 the following statements hold

$$g_{11}^0 = \sum_{j \neq 1} x_{1j}^0 - 1 = x_{12}^0 - 1 = 0 \tag{6.119}$$

$$g_{12}^0 = \sum_{j \neq 2} x_{2j}^0 - 1 = x_{23}^0 + x_{24}^0 - 1 = 1 \tag{6.120}$$

$$g_{13}^0 = \sum_{j \neq 3} x_{3j}^0 - 1 = x_{31}^0 - 1 = 0 \tag{6.121}$$

$$g_{14}^0 = \sum_{j \neq 4} x_{4j}^0 - 1 = x_{43}^0 - 1 = -1 \tag{6.122}$$

$$g_{21}^0 = \sum_{i \neq 1} x_{i1}^0 - 1 = x_{31}^0 - 1 = 0 \tag{6.123}$$

$$g_{22}^0 = \sum_{i \neq 2} x_{i2}^0 - 1 = x_{12}^0 - 1 = 0 \tag{6.124}$$

$$g_{23}^0 = \sum_{i \neq 3} x_{i3}^0 - 1 = x_{23}^0 + x_{43}^0 - 1 = 0 \tag{6.125}$$

$$g_{24}^0 = \sum_{i \neq 4} x_{i4}^0 - 1 = x_{24}^0 - 1 = 0 \tag{6.126}$$

Consequently

$$\begin{aligned}
\gamma^0 &= \begin{pmatrix} g_1\left(x^0\right) \\ g_2\left(x^0\right) \end{pmatrix} \\
&= \Big(g_{11}\left(x^0\right), g_{12}\left(x^0\right), g_{13}\left(x^0\right), g_{14}\left(x^0\right), g_{21}\left(x^0\right), g_{22}\left(x^0\right), \\
&\qquad g_{23}\left(x^0\right), g_{24}\left(x^0\right)\Big)^T \\
&= (0, +1, 0, -1, 0, 0, 0, 0)^T
\end{aligned} \tag{6.127}$$

Step 3 and 4. *(Step determination and updating, $k = 0$)* Pick $\theta_0 = 1$ so that

$$\begin{aligned}
\begin{pmatrix} \mu^1 \\ \nu^1 \end{pmatrix} &= \begin{pmatrix} \mu^0 \\ \nu^0 \end{pmatrix} + \theta_0 \gamma^0 \\
&= \begin{pmatrix} 0 \\ 0 \\ 0 \\ 0 \\ 0 \\ 0 \\ 0 \\ 0 \end{pmatrix} + (1) \begin{pmatrix} 0 \\ +1 \\ 0 \\ -1 \\ 0 \\ 0 \\ 0 \\ 0 \end{pmatrix} = \begin{pmatrix} 0 \\ +1 \\ 0 \\ -1 \\ 0 \\ 0 \\ 0 \\ 0 \end{pmatrix} \equiv \begin{pmatrix} \mu_1^1 \\ \mu_2^1 \\ \mu_3^1 \\ \mu_4^1 \\ \nu_1^1 \\ \nu_2^1 \\ \nu_3^1 \\ \nu_4^1 \end{pmatrix}
\end{aligned}$$

Note that since we are pricing out equality constraints there is no requirement that the dual variables be nonnegative.

Step 1. *(Lagrangean relaxation, $k = 1$)* Solve

$$\min L\left(x, \mu^1, \nu^1\right) = 1x_{12} + 2x_{23} + 2x_{24} + 1x_{31} + 0x_{43}$$

for unit flows corresponding to a one-tree. The solution must be chosen from the three feasible one-trees

$$\left.\begin{array}{c} x_{12}^1 = x_{31}^1 = 1 \\ x_{24}^1 = x_{43}^1 = 1 \\ x_{23}^1 = 0 \end{array}\right\} T_1^1$$

$$\left.\begin{array}{c} x_{12}^1 = x_{31}^1 = 1 \\ x_{23}^1 = x_{24}^1 = 1 \\ x_{43}^1 = 0 \end{array}\right\} T_2^1$$

$$\left.\begin{array}{c} x_{12}^1 = x_{31}^1 = 1 \\ x_{23}^1 = x_{43}^1 = 1 \\ x_{24}^1 = 0 \end{array}\right\} T_3^1$$

The tour lengths (costs) for these one-trees obey

$$\begin{aligned}
L\left(x^1\left(T_1^1\right), \mu^1, \nu^1\right) &= 1(1) + 2(0) + 2(1) + 1(1) + 0(1) = 4 \\
L\left(x^1\left(T_2^1\right), \mu^1, \nu^1\right) &= 1(1) + 2(1) + 2(1) + 1(1) + 0(0) = 6 \\
L\left(x^1\left(T_3^1\right), \mu^1, \nu^1\right) &= 1(1) + 2(1) + 2(0) + 1(1) + 0(1) = 4
\end{aligned}$$

So we must pick either the one-tree T_1^1 or the one-tree T_3^1 as the solution to this subproblem; we arbitrarily select T_1^1.

Step 2.(*Computation of subgradient, $k = 1$*) Note that for T_1^1 the following statements hold:

$$g_{11}^1 = \sum_{j \neq 1} x_{1j}^1 - 1 = x_{12}^1 - 1 = 0 \tag{6.128}$$

$$g_{12}^1 = \sum_{j \neq 2} x_{2j}^1 - 1 = x_{23}^1 + x_{24}^1 - 1 = 0 \tag{6.129}$$

$$g_{13}^1 = \sum_{j \neq 3} x_{3j}^1 - 1 = x_{31}^1 - 1 = 0 \tag{6.130}$$

$$g_{14}^1 = \sum_{j \neq 4} x_{4j}^1 - 1 = x_{43}^1 - 1 = 0 \tag{6.131}$$

$$g_{21}^1 = \sum_{i \neq 1} x_{i1}^1 - 1 = x_{31}^1 - 1 = 0 \tag{6.132}$$

$$g_{22}^1 = \sum_{i \neq 2} x_{i2}^1 - 1 = x_{12}^1 - 1 = 0 \tag{6.133}$$

$$g_{23}^1 = \sum_{i \neq 3} x_{i3}^1 - 1 = x_{23}^1 + x_{43}^1 - 1 = 0 \tag{6.134}$$

$$g_{24}^1 = \sum_{i \neq 4} x_{i4}^1 - 1 = x_{24}^1 - 1 = 0 \tag{6.135}$$

so that

$$\gamma^1 = \begin{pmatrix} g_1\left(x^1\right) \\ g_2\left(x^1\right) \end{pmatrix} = (0,0,0,0,0,0,0,0)^T = 0 \tag{6.136}$$

Step 3 and 4.(*Updating and stopping, $k = 1$*) Since $\gamma^1 = 0$, the optimal flow pattern is

$$x\left(T_1^1\right) = x^* = (1,0,1,1,1)^T \tag{6.137}$$

the optimality of which may be verified by inspection of the graph associated with the forward-star array (6.111).

6.5 The Vehicle Routing Problem

The *vehicle routing problem* (VRP) is a variant of the traveling salesman problem wherein there are multiple vehicles (salesmen), each covering only a portion of the nodes of a given network with auxiliary constraints pertaining to the number of vehicles, vehicle capacity, energy consumption, time windows, or any of a myriad of considerations that arise in actual applications. Consequently, there are many variants of the vehicle routing problem and it is difficult to provide a canonical form. Even so, the version we now offer represents the core features common to all vehicle routing models.

Referring again to the graph $\mathcal{G}(\mathcal{N},\mathcal{A})$, we take x_{ij}^k to be the flow on arc $(i,j)\in\mathcal{A}$ of vehicle k and restrict its values to be binary so that

$$x_{ij}^k = \begin{cases} 1 & \text{if vehicle } k \text{ traverses arc } (i,j) \\ 0 & \text{if vehicle } k \text{ does not traverse arc } (i,j) \end{cases} \tag{6.138}$$

and it is understood that $k\in\mathcal{K}$, the set of all vehicles considered for dispatch. Of course, c_{ij}^k is the cost incurred by vehicle $k\in\mathcal{K}$ when traversing arc $(i,j)\in\mathcal{A}$. We also make use of the binary variable y_{ij} to indicate whether any vehicle traverses arc (i,j); that is,

$$y_{ij} = \begin{cases} 1 & \text{if some vehicle traverses arc } (i,j) \\ 0 & \text{if no vehicle traverses arc } (i,j) \end{cases} \tag{6.139}$$

for all $(i,j)\in\mathcal{A}$. We also use the notation s to denote the source (depot) from which all vehicles depart and to which all return, while D_j denotes the demand for carriage at node $j\in\mathcal{N}$ and $B\in\Re_{++}^1$ is the fixed carrying capacity common to each vehicle.

The VRP takes the form:

$$\min \sum_{k\in\mathcal{K}}\sum_{(i,j)\in\mathcal{A}} c_{ij}^k x_{ij}^k \tag{6.140}$$

subject to

$$\sum_{k\in\mathcal{K}} x_{ij}^k = y_{ij} \qquad \forall\,(i,j)\subset\mathcal{A} \tag{6.141}$$

$$\sum_{i:(i,j)\in\mathcal{A}} y_{ij} = 1 \qquad \forall i\in\mathcal{N}\backslash s \tag{6.142}$$

$$\sum_{j:(i,j)} y_{ij} = 1 \qquad \forall i\in\mathcal{N}\backslash s \tag{6.143}$$

$$\sum_{j\in\mathcal{N}} y_{sj} = |\mathcal{K}| \tag{6.144}$$

$$\sum_{i\in\mathcal{N}} y_{is} = |\mathcal{K}| \tag{6.145}$$

$$\sum_{(i,j)\in\mathcal{A}:i\neq s} D_i x_{ij}^k \leq B \qquad \forall k \in \mathcal{K} \tag{6.146}$$

$$\sum_{(i,j)\in Q} y_{ij} \leq |Q| - 1 \qquad \forall Q \subset [\mathcal{N}\backslash s] \tag{6.147}$$

$$y_{ij} = (0,1) \qquad \forall\, (i,j) \in \mathcal{A} \tag{6.148}$$

$$x_{ij} = (0,1) \qquad \forall\, (i,j) \in \mathcal{A} \tag{6.149}$$

Constraint (6.141) assures that vehicles are only assigned to arcs comprising their own subtour. Constraints (6.142) and (6.143) assure that there is an arc of some subtour entering and leaving every node except for the depot, as is appropriate. Constraints (6.144) and (6.145) assure that all vehicles depart from and return to the depot. Constraint (6.146) assures that no vehicle's capacity is exceeded. Constraints (6.148) and (6.149) are of course integrality restrictions. The constraints (6.147) are called *subtour breaking constraints*, and they prevent each vehicle-specific subtour from containing a cycle involving the nodes $\mathcal{N}\backslash s$. Note that the subtour breaking constraints are articulated for all subsets Q of the graph's nodes, excluding the depot node.

6.6 The Capacitated Plant Location Problem

The *classical capacitated plant location problem* depends on the following notation:

- N_O the set of all candidate plant locations (origins)
- N_D the set of all demand sites (destinations)
- D_j the demand at $j \in N_D$ for a single homogeneous commodity
- f_i the known, fixed cost of locating a facility at $i \in N_O$
- x_{ij} the fraction of the jth node's demand satisfied by a facility at node i
- c_{ij} the known fixed transport cost of supplying *all* of the jth node's demand from node i
- e_i the known fixed unit production cost of a facility at $i \in N_O$

and the following definition:

$$y_i = \begin{cases} 1 & \text{if a facility (plant or warehouse) is located at } i \in N_O \\ 0 & \text{otherwise} \end{cases}$$

With this notation we may state the following model for minimizing total cost subject to relevant constraints:

$$\min \sum_{i\in N_O} \sum_{j\in N_D} c_{ij} x_{ij} + \sum_{i\in N_O} e_i \sum_{j\in N_D} D_j x_{ij} + \sum_{i\in N_O} f_i y_i \tag{6.150}$$

subject to

$$\sum_{i \in N_O} x_{ij} \geq 1 \qquad (v_j) \qquad \forall j \in N_D \tag{6.151}$$

$$y_i \geq x_{ij} \qquad (u_{ij}) \qquad \forall i \in N_O, j \in N_D \tag{6.152}$$

$$y_i = (0, 1) \qquad \forall i \in N_O \tag{6.153}$$

$$x_{ij} \geq 0 \qquad \forall i \in N_O, j \in N_D \tag{6.154}$$

In the above formulation the objective (6.150) expresses the desire to minimize total cost written as the sum of transport, production, and location costs. The constraints (6.151) assure that all demands are satisfied. The constraints (6.152) are logical conditions that prevent flow from a nonexisting facility, while (6.153) and (6.154) are, respectively, integrality and nonnegativity constraints on the decision variables. Note that (6.150)–(6.154) may be thought of as "a network model without an explicit network," by which we mean the candidate locations are nodes of a transport network and the costs c_{ij} are found by application of a minimum path algorithm to that network.

A special case of the capacitated plant location problem is the *warehouse location problem*, for which there is no production but only warehousing of the homogeneous commodity at some or all of the nodes of N_O. This is tantamount to stipulating that $e_i = 0$ for all $i \in N_O$ and changes the objective (6.150) to

$$\min \sum_{i \in N_O} \sum_{j \in N_D} c_{ij} x_{ij} + \sum_{i \in N_O} f_i y_i \tag{6.155}$$

but leaves the constraints unaltered.

The dual of the warehouse location problem ignoring (relaxing) the integrality restrictions is the subproblem of a Benders decomposition and takes the form

$$\left.\begin{array}{ll} & \max \sum_{j \in N_D} v_j - \sum_{i \in N_O} \sum_{j \in N_D} y_i^k u_{ij} \\ \text{subject to} & \\ & v_j - u_{ij} \leq c_{ij} \quad \forall i \in N_O, j \in N_D \\ & v_j \geq 0 \quad \forall j \in N_D \\ & u_{ij} \geq 0 \quad \forall i \in N_O, j \in N_D \end{array}\right\} SP^k \tag{6.156}$$

where the y_i^k are current values of the integer variables at iteration k of the decomposition. The master problem of Benders decomposition may be constructed from (5.130) by making the following identifications:

portion of original objective function involving y: $f(y) \longrightarrow \sum_{i \in N_O} f_i y_i$

$$\text{dual objective function: } w^T(b - By) \longrightarrow \sum_{j \in N_D} v_j - \sum_{i \in N_O} \sum_{j \in N_D} y_i u_{ij}$$

We will assume that the feasible region is bounded and there are no extreme rays. Then the master problem (MP) becomes

$$\left.\begin{array}{l} \min Z^k \\ \text{subject to} \\ Z^k \geq \sum_{i \in N_O} f_i y_i + \sum_{j \in N_D} v_j^p - \sum_{i \in N_O} \sum_{j \in N_D} u_{ij}^p y_i \quad p = 1, \ldots, t^k \\ y_i = (0, 1) \quad \forall i \in N_O \end{array}\right\} MP^k \quad (6.157)$$

where the index p refers to an extreme point and the index k to the current iteration of the decomposition algorithm.

To illustrate the method we employ the following data from an example by Lasdon (1970):

$$N_O = \{1, 2, 3, 4\}$$

$$N_D = \{1, 2, 3, 4\}$$

$$(c_{ij}) = \begin{pmatrix} 0 & 12 & 20 & 18 \\ 12 & 0 & 8 & 6 \\ 20 & 8 & 0 & 6 \\ 18 & 6 & 6 & 0 \end{pmatrix}$$

$$f_i = 7 \qquad i = 1, 2, 3, 4$$

The calculations relevant to employing Benders method for the example problem described above are the following:

Step 0. *(Initialization, $k = 0$)* Set $k = 0$. Pick $y^0 = (0, 1, 0, 0)$.

Step 1. *(Form and solve the subproblem, $k = 0$)* The relevant primal (P) and dual (D) programs are:

$$\left.\begin{array}{l} \min \sum_{i \in N_O} \sum_{j \in N_D} c_{ij} x_{ij} + \sum_{i \in N_O} f_i y_i^0 \\ \text{subject to} \\ \sum_{i \in N_O} x_{ij} \geq 1 \quad \forall j \in N_D \\ y_i^0 \geq x_{ij} \quad \forall i \in N_O, j \in N_D \\ x_{ij} \geq 0 \quad \forall i \in N_O, j \in N_D \end{array}\right\} \text{P} \qquad (6.158)$$

$$\left.\begin{array}{c} \max \sum_{j \in N_D} v_j - \sum_{i \in N_O} \sum_{j \in N_D} y_i^0 u_{ij} \\ \text{subject to} \\ v_j - u_{ij} \leq c_{ij} \quad \forall i \in N_O, j \in N_D \\ v_j \geq 0 \quad \forall j \in N_D \\ u_{ij} \geq 0 \quad \forall i \in N_O, j \in N_D \end{array}\right\} \text{D} \tag{6.159}$$

where the dual is of course the Benders subproblem. The solutions are

$$\begin{aligned} v_1^0 &= 12 \quad v_2^0 = 0 \quad v_3^0 = 8 \quad v_4^0 = 6 \\ u_{11}^0 &= 12 \quad u_{33}^0 = 8 \quad u_{44}^0 = 8 \quad \text{all other } u_{ij}^0 = 0 \end{aligned}$$

Step 2. *(Form and solve the master problem, $k = 0$)* This means that the master problem

$$\min\ Z^0$$

subject to

$$Z^0 \geq \sum_{i \in N_O} f_i y_i + \sum_{j \in N_D} v_j^0 - \sum_{i \in N_O} \sum_{j \in N_D} u_{ij}^0 y_i$$

$$y_i = (0, 1) \quad \forall i \in N_O$$

becomes

$$\min\ Z^0$$

subject to

$$Z^0 \geq 26 - 5y_1 + 7y_2 - y_3 - y_4$$

$$y_i = (0, 1) \quad i = 1, 2, 3, 4$$

Note that this first master problem may be solved by inspection:

$$y^1 = (1, 0, 1, 1)^T \Longrightarrow Z^0 = 19$$

This completes the first ($k = 0$) iteration.

Step 1. *(Form and solve the subproblem, $k = 1$)* Again solve for the primal-dual pair using the current values of the integer variables given by y^1:

$$\min \sum_{i \in N_O} \sum_{j \in N_D} c_{ij} x_{ij} + \sum_{i \in N_O} f_i y_i^1$$

subject to

$$\sum_{i \in N_O} x_{ij} \geq 1 \quad \forall j \in N_D$$

$$y_i^1 \geq x_{ij} \quad \forall i \in N_O, j \in N_D$$

$$x_{ij} \geq 0 \quad \forall i \in N_O, j \in N_D$$

The results are

$$v_1^1 = 0, \quad v_2^1 = 6, \quad v_3^1 = v_4^1 = 0$$

$$u_{22}^1 = 6, \quad \text{all other } u_{ij}^1 = 0$$

Step 2. *(Form and solve the master problem, $k = 1$)* This means that

$$Z^1 \geq 6 + 7y_1 + y_2 + 7y_3 + 7y_4$$

so that the master problem becomes

$$\min Z^1$$

subject to

$$Z^1 \geq 26 - 5y_1 + 7y_2 - y_3 - y_4$$

$$Z^1 \geq 6 + 7y_1 + y_2 + 7y_3 + 7y_4$$

$$y_i = (0, 1) \quad i = 1, 2, 3, 4$$

Note carefully that the inequalities associated with the extreme points *accumulate* in the formation of the master problem. The solution is readily found by enumeration to be

$$y^2 = (1, 0, 0, 1) \text{ or } (1, 0, 1, 0) \Longrightarrow Z^1 = 20$$

Continuing in the fashion indicated above, one obtains the results in Table 6.1, where $(\cdot)y_i$ refers to the coefficient of y_i in the constraint added to the master problem in each iteration k. We, of course, terminate when the lower bound on the primal objective, that is Z^k, equals the primal objective (PO) value given by $\sum_{ij} c_{ij} x_{ij}^k + \sum_i f_i y_i^k$.

k	y_1^k	y_2^k	y_3^k	y_4^k	PO	Z^k	$\geq$	$(\cdot)$	$+(\cdot)\,y_1$	$+(\cdot)\,y_2$	$(\cdot)\,y_3$	$(\cdot)\,y_4$	Z^k
0	0	1	0	0	33	Z^0	$\geq$	26	−5	7	−1	−1	19
1	1	0	1	1	27	Z^1	$\geq$	6	7	1	7	7	20
2	1	0	0	1	26	Z^2	$\geq$	12	7	1	1	7	20
3	1	0	1	0	28	Z^3	$\geq$	14	7	-1	7	−1	21
4	1	0	0	0	57	Z^4	$\geq$	50	7	−29	−29	−31	24
5	0	0	1	1	38	Z^5	$\geq$	24	−11	−5	7	7	26
6	1	0	0	1	26								

Table 6.1: Solving the Capacitated Plant Location Problem

6.7 Irrigation Networks

We consider now a water supply system comprised of streams feeding reservoirs which are sources of water supplied to an urban area. Our focus is on the operation of interdependent reservoirs so we do not consider the detailed water delivery network after water is diverted from the reservoirs for urban use. Instead we will be concerned with how much yield can be taken from a network of reservoirs in order to obtain the upper bound on water yield from the system, which information can in turn be used to forecast when new sources of water supply or water conservation will be needed to accommodate growing demands for water.

6.7.1 Irrigation Network Capacity Expansion Planning

It has become traditional to refer to specific segments of streams which comprise a river basin as *reaches*. A *reach* is defined when it is necessary to identify specific hydrological properties of a portion of some waterway or when there are head and tail nodes, like reservoirs and conjunctions with other streams, which naturally define the reach. We consider each reach to be an arc (i, j) of the water supply system; the tail and head nodes of the reaches are taken to be nodes of the network. Of course reservoirs and the drainage areas from which the streams originate are nodes associated with appropriately defined reaches. Because our focus is reservoir yield, we are able to treat the reservoirs as the locations of final urban water demands. In this way the water supply system is viewed as a graph $\mathcal{G}(\mathcal{N}, \mathcal{A})$ where $\mathcal{A}$ is the set of arcs corresponding to reaches and $\mathcal{N}$ is the set of nodes associated with the reaches.

We begin formally by stating inter-temporal flow conservation equations for water at individual nodes of the irrigation network in the form

$$I_j^t + \sum_{i:(i,j)\in\mathcal{A}} f_{ij}(1 - a_{ij}) - \sum_{i:(j,i)\in\mathcal{A}} f_{ji}^t - d_j^t = 0 \qquad \forall j \in \mathcal{N},\ t \in [1, N] \quad (6.160)$$

where the following definitions obtain:

i, j	subscripts referring to nodes of the irrigation network
t	superscript referring to season
N	the total number of discrete seasons
I_j^t	water inflow to the irrigation system at node j in season t
f_{ij}^t	water flow in season t from node i to node j
a_{ij}	water evaporation and seepage loss coefficient
d_j^t	water demand at node j in season t

For simplicity we have assumed in (6.160) that water intakes exist at every node; this assumption is easily relaxed. We must also impose constraints which assure that a priori levels of drainage reclamation are met, ground water potentials are never exceeded, intake flows are never negative, link carrying capacities are not violated, flows are bounded from above and below, and the total budget is not violated. That is

$$d_j^t - \sum_{i:(j,i)\in\mathcal{A}} f_{ji}^t = 0 \qquad \forall j \in \mathcal{N},\, t \in [1,N] \tag{6.161}$$

$$0 \le I_j^t \le P_j^t \qquad \forall j \in \mathcal{N},\, t \in [1,N] \tag{6.162}$$

$$0 \le f_{ij}^t \le g_{ij} + g_{ij}^e \qquad \forall (i,j) \in \mathcal{A},\, t \in [1,N] \tag{6.163}$$

$$\sum_{(i,j)\in\mathcal{A}} \Psi_{ij}(g_{ij}) \le B \tag{6.164}$$

where

P_j^t	maximum available inflow of water at node j in season t
g_{ij}	increment to flow capacity of arc (i,j)
g_{ij}^e	existing flow capacity of arc (i,j)
B	the total budget for irrigation capacity expansion
$\Psi_{ij}(g_{ij})$	the cost of irrigation capacity expansion g_{ij} of arc (i,j)

It is also convenient to define the following decision vectors

$$f = \left(f_{ij}^t : (i,j) \in \mathcal{A},\, t \in [1,N]\right) \tag{6.165}$$

$$I = \left(I_j^t : j \in \mathcal{N},\, t \in [1,N]\right) \tag{6.166}$$

$$g = \left(g_{ij} : (i,j) \in \mathcal{A}\right) \tag{6.167}$$

so that

$$\Omega = \{(f,I,g) : \text{ constraints (6.160)–(6.164) are satisfied}\}$$

is the set of all feasible capacity expansion plans for a single year comprised of N seasons. It should be noted that the cost functions $\Psi_{ij}(g_{ij})$ reflect the capital costs of new and improved infrastructure (new pumping stations, improved pumping stations, new canals and pipelines, improved canals and pipelines, and the like). These capacity expansion costs are known to be nonlinear in many circumstances. In fact one possible arc cost model for capacity expansion is

$$\Psi_{ij}(g_{ij}) = K_{ij}^1 + K_{ij}^2 \left(g_{ij} - g_{ij}^e\right)^{n_{ij}} \tag{6.168}$$

where g_{ij}^e is the existing flow capacity, K_{ij}^1 is a parameter reflecting initial costs, K_{ij}^2 is a parameter reflecting scale costs, and n_{ij} is an exponent describing the degree of nonlinearity of arc (i,j). Generally speaking, the capacity expansion functions will exhibit economies and diseconomies of scale for different levels of added capacity g_{ij}, as occurs when n_{ij} equals 3 in (6.168).

If we assume, demand for irrigation is price inelastic, then it is appropriate to take the objective of capacity expansion to be the minimization of costs associated with irrigation. In this case, the short run irrigation network planning problem may be stated as

$$\left.\begin{array}{l} \min \displaystyle\sum_{t=1}^{T} \sum_{(i,j)\in\mathcal{A}} C_{ij}^{t}(f_{ij}^{t}) f_{ij} \\ \text{subject to} \\ (f,g,I) \in \Omega \end{array}\right\} \quad (6.169)$$

where $C_{ij}^{t}(f_{ij}^{t})$ is the unit cost of irrigation flow over arc (i,j) in season t. A fundamental component of the cost function C_{ij}^{t} is the cost of energy needed to effect water delivery and reclamation on arc (i,j). Evidently (6.169) is a nonlinear mathematical program, which is potentially nonconvex owing to the budget constraint (6.164) and the possibly nonconvex objective function in (6.169).

6.7.2 Municipal Water Supply

Municipal water supply networks can be modeled in much the same fashion as the irrigation network of the preceding example. However, for the purpose of this example, our focus will be on operation of the reservoirs connected to the water supply network in a fashion which meets prespecified, known demands without capacity expansion considerations. It is convenient to use much of the same notation of the previous example with the appropriate re-interpretation of key variables and parameters to fit the new setting; we shall also need some new definitions. We begin by distinguishing the nodes which are reservoirs from the other nodes of the network; specifically we define $\mathcal{N}_R$ to be the set of reservoir nodes so that $\mathcal{M} = \mathcal{N}\backslash\mathcal{N}_R$ is the set of all other nodes. We also employ a different time scale: instead of seasons, we speak of a sequence of days spanning a season or a even a year. Consequently, in general, we have two varieties of flow conservation equations. The first variety is comprised of the following flow conservation equations:

$$I_j^t + \sum_{i:(i,j)\in\mathcal{A}} f_{ij}^t - \sum_{i:(j,i)\in\mathcal{A}} f_{ji}^t - d_j^t = 0 \quad \forall j \in \mathcal{N}_R,\, t \in [1,N] \quad (6.170)$$

$$\sum_{i:(i,j)\in\mathcal{A}} f_{ij}^t - \sum_{i:(j,i)\in\mathcal{A}} f_{ji}^t - d_j^t = 0 \quad \forall j \in \mathcal{M},\, t \in [1,N] \quad (6.171)$$

where now the following definitions obtain

i, j	subscripts referring to nodes of the municipal water supply network
t	superscript referring to a given period
N	the total number of periods considered
I_j^t	water inflow to the network from reservoir at node j in period t
f_{ij}^t	water flow in period t along arc (i, j)
d_j^t	water demand at node j in period t

We have also to write flow conservation equations for the reservoirs; ensure that intakes by the municipal water network are never negative and do not exceed reservoir storage less a predetermined reserve; and express reservoir capacities that cannot be exceeded. These considerations take the following form:

$$S_j^{t+1} = S_j^t + W_j^t - w_j^t - I_j^t \qquad \forall j \in \mathcal{N}_R,\ t \in [1, N] \qquad (6.172)$$

$$0 \leq I_j^t \leq S_j^t - R_j \qquad \forall j \in \mathcal{N}_R,\ t \in [1, N] \qquad (6.173)$$

$$S_j^t \leq K_j \qquad \forall j \in \mathcal{N}_R,\ t \in [1, N] \qquad (6.174)$$

where the following additional definitions also obtain:

S_j^t	storage of the node j reservoir at the end of period t
W_j^t	naturally occurring stream intake charging the node j reservoir during period t
w_j^t	release by the node j reservoir during period t to stream flow
R_j	pre-specified reserve storage for the node j reservoir
K_j	known capacity of the node j reservoir

We refer to constraints (6.172) as intertemporal storage dynamics.

In (6.172) I_j^t describes the release during period t from the node j reservoir to assist in servicing municipal water demand, and the position of I_j^t in this equation recognizes that release to be identical to the intake defined previously. Note that each reservoir has the option to release water not only to satisfy municipal demand but also to directly release to stream flow to prevent its capacity from being exceeded. It remains to stipulate that municipal water demands are satisfied and that flows on arcs of the supply network are nonnegative and do not exceed arc capacities; these considerations are stated as

$$d_j^t - \sum_{i:(j,i)\in\mathcal{A}} f_{ji}^t = 0 \qquad \forall j \in \mathcal{M},\ t \in [1, N] \qquad (6.175)$$

$$0 \leq f_{ij}^t \leq g_{ij}^e \qquad \forall (i, j) \in \mathcal{A},\ t \in [1, N] \qquad (6.176)$$

where g_{ij}^e is of course the existing capacity of arc (i, j).

Defining f and I as in (6.165) and (6.166), we have the feasible set

$$\Lambda = \{(f, I, w) : \text{constraints (6.170)–(6.176) are satisfied}\}$$

Our model for the coordination of reservoirs releases and municipal water supply activities is

$$\left.\begin{array}{l} \min \displaystyle\sum_{t=1}^{N} \sum_{(i,j)\in\mathcal{A}} C^t_{a,ij} \cdot (f^t_{ij})^2 + C_{b,ij} \cdot f^t_{ij} \\ \text{subject to} \\ (f, I, w) \in \Lambda \end{array}\right\} \tag{6.177}$$

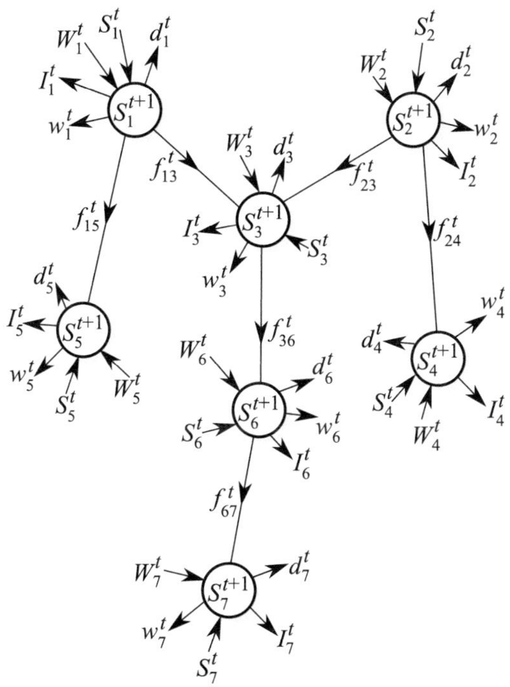

FIGURE 6.1: MUNICIPAL WATER SUPPLY NETWORK

where the cost coefficients $C^t_{a,ij}$ and $C^t_{b,ij}$ describe the marginal cost and fixed cost of providing water service on each arc (i, j) during period t. We have also assumed that the demands d^t_j are inelastic at every node $j \in \mathcal{M}$. Note that (6.177) is a quadratic program with linear constraints.

6.7.3 Numerical Example

We now consider a municipal water supply problem corresponding to the network of Fig. 6.1, where the nodes correspond to reservoirs of a given municipality. Arcs over which flows are shared between reservoirs carry labels of the f^t_{ij}

type. The arcs incident on each node but without a predecessor or a successor node carry flows that remain within the municipality. Note that there are no nodes without reservoirs and there is no stream inflow for either reservoir 6 or reservoir 7. The fundamental flow conservation constraints are

$$I_1^t - f_{13}^t - f_{15}^t = d_1^t \tag{6.178}$$

$$I_2^t - f_{23}^t - f_{24}^t = d_2^t \tag{6.179}$$

$$I_3^t + f_{13}^t + f_{23}^t - f_{36}^t = d_3^t \tag{6.180}$$

$$I_4^t + f_{24}^t = d_4^t \tag{6.181}$$

$$I_5^t + f_{15}^t = d_5^t \tag{6.182}$$

$$I_6^t + f_{36}^t - f_{67}^t = d_6^t \tag{6.183}$$

$$I_7^t + f_{67}^t = d_7^t \tag{6.184}$$

The inter-temporal storage constraints are

$$S_1^{t+1} = S_1^t + W_1^t - w_1^t - I_1^t \tag{6.185}$$

$$S_2^{t+1} = S_2^t + W_2^t - w_2^t - I_2^t \tag{6.186}$$

$$S_3^{t+1} = S_3^t + W_3^t - w_3^t - I_3^t \tag{6.187}$$

$$S_4^{t+1} = S_4^t + W_4^t - w_4^t - I_4^t \tag{6.188}$$

$$S_5^{t+1} = S_5^t + W_5^t - w_5^t - I_5^t \tag{6.189}$$

$$S_6^{t+1} = S_6^t - w_6^t - I_6^t \tag{6.190}$$

$$S_7^{t+1} = S_7^t - w_7^t - I_7^t \tag{6.191}$$

We also assume that every flow is bounded from above and from below (by zero). We use the parameter values given in Table 6.2. We also assume that there is an upper bound of 1,200 on each reservoir's capacity; we additionally assume each arc of the water distribution network has the same upper bound of 200.

We elect to solve the above example using simplicial decomposition as presented Chap. 5. Figure 6.2 gives the convergence plot of the simplicial decomposition. As we can tell from the plot, the algorithm terminates in a small number of iterations. Per each iteration, the simplicial decomposition solves a linear program and a set of quadratic programs with only linear constraints as the subproblems. Therefore, simplicial decomposition involves low computational overhead in solving our numerical example. Figure 6.3 plots the solutions.

		t_1	t_2	t_3	t_4	t_5
Unit Cost	$C^t_{a,13}$	200.00	200.00	200.00	200.00	200.00
	$C^t_{a,15}$	200.00	200.00	200.00	200.00	200.00
	$C^t_{a,23}$	200.00	200.00	200.00	200.00	200.00
	$C^t_{a,24}$	200.00	200.00	200.00	200.00	200.00
	$C^t_{a,36}$	400.00	400.00	400.00	400.00	400.00
	$C^t_{a,67}$	200.00	200.00	200.00	200.00	200.00
Fixed Cost	$C^t_{b,13}$	100.00	100.00	100.00	100.00	100.00
	$C^t_{b,15}$	100.00	100.00	100.00	100.00	100.00
	$C^t_{b,23}$	100.00	100.00	100.00	100.00	100.00
	$C^t_{b,24}$	100.00	100.00	100.00	100.00	100.00
	$C^t_{b,36}$	250.00	250.00	250.00	250.00	250.00
	$C^t_{b,67}$	10.00	10.00	10.00	10.00	10.00
Natural stream intake	W^t_1	400.00	400.00	400.00	300.00	300.00
	W^t_2	400.00	400.00	400.00	300.00	300.00
	W^t_3	400.00	400.00	400.00	300.00	300.00
	W^t_4	200.00	200.00	200.00	250.00	250.00
	W^t_5	200.00	200.00	200.00	250.00	250.00
	W^t_6	200.00	200.00	200.00	250.00	250.00
	W^t_7	200.00	200.00	200.00	250.00	250.00
Reservoir storage	w^t_1	50.00	50.00	50.00	50.00	50.00
	w^t_2	50.00	50.00	50.00	50.00	50.00
	w^t_3	50.00	50.00	50.00	50.00	50.00
	w^t_4	50.00	50.00	50.00	50.00	50.00
	w^t_5	50.00	50.00	50.00	50.00	50.00
	w^t_6	50.00	50.00	50.00	50.00	50.00
	w^t_7	50.00	50.00	50.00	50.00	50.00
Demand	d^t_1	100.00	150.00	80.00	150.00	100.00
	d^t_2	100.00	80.00	130.00	110.00	110.00
	d^t_3	200.00	100.00	100.00	150.00	105.00
	d^t_4	200.00	250.00	200.00	190.00	250.00
	d^t_5	200.00	200.00	200.00	230.00	200.00
	d^t_6	150.00	260.00	580.00	100.00	250.00
	d^t_7	200.00	130.00	170.00	350.00	250.00

		t_1	t_2	t_3	t_4	t_5
	R_1^t	25.00	25.00	25.00	25.00	25.00
	R_2^t	25.00	25.00	25.00	25.00	25.00
	R_3^t	25.00	25.00	25.00	25.00	25.00
Pre-specified reserves	R_4^t	25.00	25.00	25.00	25.00	25.00
	R_5^t	25.00	25.00	25.00	25.00	25.00
	R_6^t	25.00	25.00	25.00	25.00	25.00
	R_7^t	25.00	25.00	25.00	25.00	25.00

Table 6.2: Parameter Values of the Model

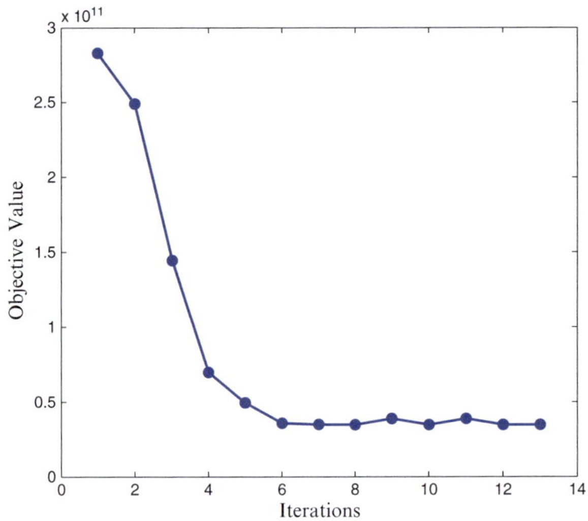

Figure 6.2: Convergence Plot of the Simplicial Decomposition

Figure 6.2 shows the relatively fast convergence of simplicial decomposition, which can be traced to the fact that, at each iteration, the method requires a linear program and a set of quadratic programs with linear constraints to be solved. The same figure also shows reservoir storage at different nodes and different times, and allows comparison of arc flows to both storage and water demands. Note that, despite demand fluctuations, arc flows do not vary much. This has occurred despite the demand surge experienced by node 6 in period 3. The detailed numerical solution of this example is presented in Table 6.3.

We now compare the affine scaling method with variant step size (ASM-VS) with that with constant step size (ASM-CS) in solving the same problem. The former is the affine scaling method presented earlier. The latter is a simple variant that uses a constant step size θ. Table 6.4 gives the solution and the corresponding objective value generated during the first 28 iterations of the algorithm. Figure 6.4 compares the objective values for 100 iterations. We observe that ASM-CS converged in 10 iterations, while ASM-VS zig-zagged and did not converge in 20 iterations (though it does converge in 100 iterations).

6.8 Telecommunications Flow Routing and System Optimal Traffic Assignment

We now consider the management of message demand in telecommunications networks. Demand management of the type we now consider is frequently referred to as *flow control*. It depends on the articulation of a penalty function

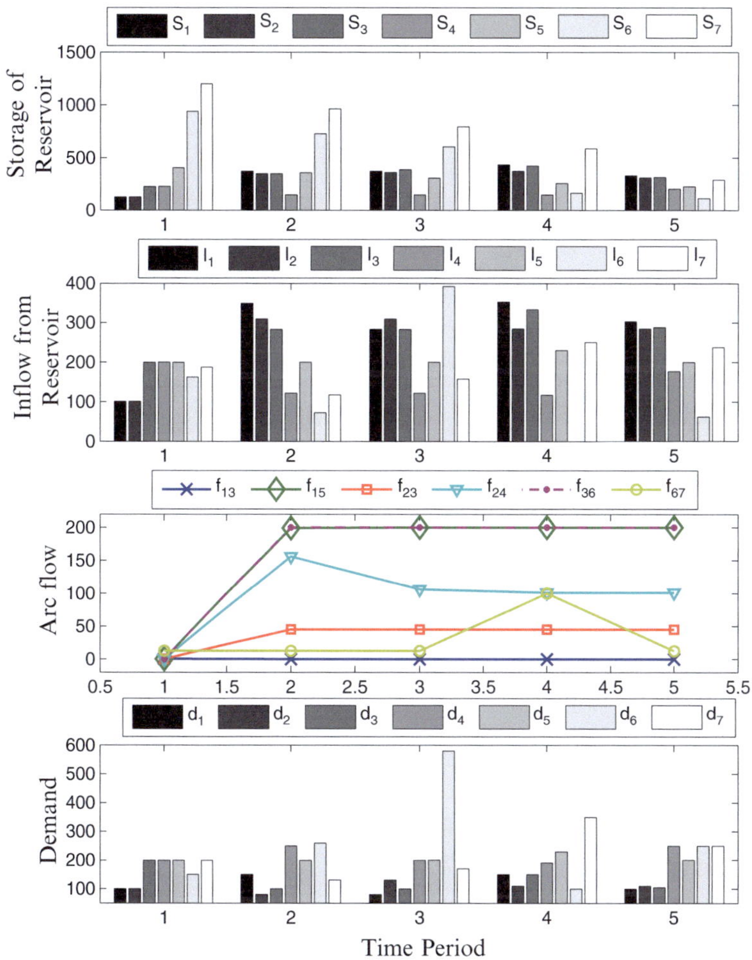

FIGURE 6.3: SOLUTION PLOTS OF THE WATER SUPPLY MODEL

		t_1	t_2	t_3	t_4	t_5
	I_1^t	100.60	349.60	283.33	353.33	303.33
	I_2^t	100.60	309.11	309.31	284.33	284.33
	I_3^t	199.44	283.11	283.11	333.11	288.11
Inflow from Reservoir	I_4^t	199.72	122.08	121.98	116.97	176.97
	I_5^t	199.59	200.00	200.00	230.00	200.02
	I_6^t	162.31	72.48	392.48	0.00	62.48
	I_7^t	187.49	117.49	157.49	250.15	237.49
	S_1^t	125.60	374.60	371.67	435.00	328.33
	S_2^t	125.60	346.77	359.43	371.89	309.33
	S_3^t	224.44	346.86	385.61	424.36	313.11
Reservoir Storage	S_4^t	224.72	147.08	146.98	146.97	201.97
	S_5^t	404.62	355.04	305.04	255.04	225.02
	S_6^t	939.76	727.44	604.96	162.48	112.48
	S_7^t	1,200.00	962.53	795.06	587.59	287.47
	f_{13}^t	0.41	0.00	0.00	0.00	0.00
	f_{15}^t	0.19	199.20	200.00	200.00	200.00
Arc Flow	f_{23}^t	0.31	45.03	45.03	45.03	45.03
	f_{24}^t	0.28	155.84	106.04	101.06	101.06
	f_{36}^t	0.17	200.00	200.00	200.00	200.00
	f_{67}^t	12.48	12.48	12.48	99.83	12.48

TABLE 6.3: SOLUTION OF THE WATER SUPPLY PROBLEM

for each origin-destination pair $(i, j) \in \mathcal{W}$ which we denote as

$$\theta_{ij}\left(Q_{ij}\right) \tag{6.192}$$

where

$$u_{ij} = \min_{p \in \mathcal{P}_{ij}} c_p\left(h\right) \quad \forall \left(i, j\right) \in \mathcal{W}$$

The penalty function (6.192) is a strictly monotonically decreasing function of demand Q_{ij} and is meant to be appended to the routing objective function of (1.17) to create the following model:

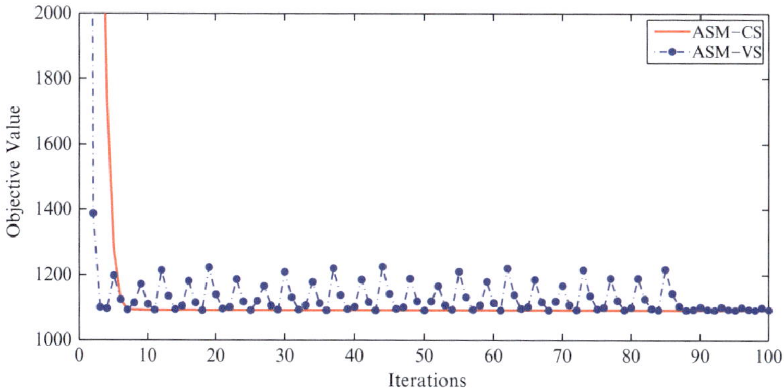

Figure 6.4: Comparison of ASM-CS with ASM-VS

$$
\left.\begin{aligned}
&\min \sum_{a\in\mathcal{A}} c_a(f)\,f_a + \sum_{(i,j)\in\mathcal{W}} \theta_{ij}(Q_{ij}) \\
\text{subject to}\quad & \\
&Q_{ij} - \sum_{p\in\mathcal{P}_{ij}} h_p = 0 \quad \forall\,(i,j)\in\mathcal{W} \\
&h_p > 0 \quad \forall p\in\mathcal{P} \\
&0 \le Q_{ij} \le Q_{ij}^{\max} \\
&f_a - \sum_{p\in\mathcal{P}} \delta_{ap} h_p = 0 \quad \forall a\in\mathcal{A}
\end{aligned}\right\} \qquad (6.193)
$$

where $Q_{ij}^{\max}$ is the upper bound on demand for every $(i,j) \in \mathcal{W}$. By penalizing demand, this model controls flow entering the network as well as determines the optimal routing of demands. As such (6.193) is actually a *combined flow routing and flow control model.* Note that (6.193) is not a telecommunications analog of the equilibrium network design model used in transportation since message packets do not have the autonomy of automobile drivers in selecting their own routes; as a consequence flow control does not have the bilevel structure of equilibrium network design and is, as a consequence, computationally much more tractable.

In Chap. 8 we discuss the numerical solution of a traffic assignment problem that is essentially identical to the quasi-static flow routing problem (1.17). For that reason let us restrict our attention to a numerical example of the flow control problem (6.193). Let us consider a network with the following extended forward-star array:

	ASM-CS ($\theta = 1$)			ASM-VS		
Iter.	Flow 1,2	Q_{13}	Obj.	Flow 1,2	Q_{13}	Obj.
1	10.00	20.00	10,314.00	10.00	20.00	10,314.00
2	11.98	23.97	5,228.31	19.00	38.00	1,387.88
3	14.33	28.66	2,829.31	27.10	54.20	1,101.22
4	17.05	34.10	1,735.63	24.39	48.78	1,097.57
5	20.03	40.06	1,278.47	31.95	63.90	1,197.41
6	22.87	45.75	1,124.77	28.76	57.51	1,124.69
7	24.83	49.66	1,094.29	25.88	51.76	1,093.09
8	25.49	50.98	1,092.54	23.29	46.58	1,114.47
9	25.55	51.09	1,092.55	30.96	61.93	1,171.91
10	25.55	51.09	1,092.55	27.87	55.73	1,110.55
11	25.55	51.09	1,092.55	25.08	50.16	1,093.21
12	25.55	51.09	1,092.55	32.57	65.14	1,214.54
13	25.55	51.09	1,092.55	29.31	58.63	1,135.17
14	25.55	51.09	1,092.55	26.38	52.77	1,095.34
15	25.55	51.09	1,092.55	23.75	47.49	1,105.85
16	25.55	51.09	1,092.55	31.37	62.74	1,182.15
17	25.55	51.09	1,092.55	28.23	56.47	1,115.98
18	25.55	51.09	1,092.55	25.41	50.82	1,092.57
19	25.55	51.09	1,092.55	32.87	65.74	1,223.00
20	25.55	51.09	1,092.55	29.58	59.16	1,140.56
21	25.55	51.09	1,092.55	26.62	53.25	1,096.98
22	25.55	51.09	1,092.55	23.96	47.92	1,102.58
23	25.55	51.09	1,092.55	31.57	63.13	1,187.18
24	25.55	51.09	1,092.55	28.41	56.82	1,118.78
25	25.55	51.09	1,092.55	25.57	51.14	1,092.56
26	25.55	51.09	1,092.55	23.01	46.02	1,121.12
27	25.55	51.09	1,092.55	30.71	61.42	1,165.77
28	25.55	51.09	1,092.55	27.64	55.28	1,107.48

TABLE 6.4: COMPARISON OF ASM-CS WITH ASM-VS

Arc Index (i)	From Node k	To Node l	Arc Name (a_i)	A_i	B_i
1	1	2	a_1	10	0.01
2	2	3	a_2	5	0.05
3	2	3	a_3	5	0.05

which clearly describes a network of three nodes and three arcs, two of which are connecting node 2 to node 3. The unit cost functions associated with this network are of the form

$$c_{a_i}(f_{a_i}) = A_i + B_i f_{a_i} \qquad i = 1, 2, 3 \tag{6.194}$$

The single origin-destination pair to be considered is $(1, 3)$ so that

$$\begin{aligned} \mathcal{W} &= \{(1,3)\} \\ p_1 &= \{a_1, a_2\} \\ p_2 &= \{a_1, a_3\} \\ \mathcal{P} &= \mathcal{P}_{13} = \{p_1, p_2\} \end{aligned}$$

Since we are considering flow control, the demand Q_{13} is a decision variable. The relevant origin-destination travel demand constraint is

$$Q_{13} - h_{p_1} - h_{p_2} = 0 \tag{6.195}$$

where h_{p_1} and h_{p_2} are the path flows. We also note that

$$\begin{aligned} f_{a_1} &= h_{p_1} + h_{p_2} \\ f_{a_2} &= h_{p_1} \\ f_{a_3} &= h_{p_2} \\ c_{p_1} &= c_{a_1} + c_{a_2} \\ c_{p_2} &= c_{a_1} + c_{a_3} \end{aligned}$$

and select the demand penalty

$$\theta_{ij}(Q_{13}) = \left(\frac{200}{Q_{13}}\right)^4$$

We elect to solve this problem using primal affine scaling.

Table 6.5 presents the numerical solution of the example problem described immediately above, calculated using affine scaling. Figure 6.5 illustrates how the objective function changes from iteration to iteration, as demand evolves.

Path Flow (h_p)		Arc Flow (f_a)					
Path 1 (p_1)	Path 2 (p_2)	Arc 1 (a_1)	Arc 2 (a_2)	Arc 3 (a_3)	Q_{13}	Obj.	Time (s)
25.55	25.55	51.10	25.55	25.55	51.09	1,092.54	0.02

Table 6.5: Numerical Result for the Telecommunications Network

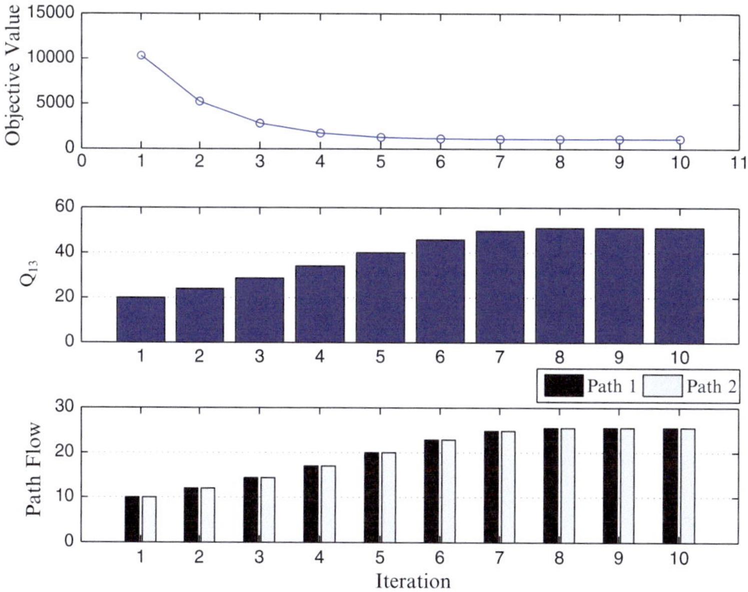

FIGURE 6.5: CONVERGENCE PLOT AND EVOLUTION OF SOLUTIONS OVER ITERATIONS

6.9 References and Additional Reading

Bazaraa, M. S., Jarvis, J. J., & Sherali, H. D. (2011). *Linear programming and network flows.* John Wiley & Sons

Bertsekas, D. B. (1998). *Network optimization: Continuous and discrete models.* Cambridge, MA: Athena Publishing.

Bradley, S., Hax, A., & Magnanti, T. (1977). *Applied mathematical programming.* Reading, MA: Addison-Wesley.

Fang, S. C., & Puthenpura, S. (1993). *Linear optimization and extensions: Theory and algorithms.* Englewood Cliffs, NJ: Prentice-Hall.

Lasdon, L. (1970). *Optimization theory for large systems.* New York: Macmillan.

Minoux, M. (1986). *Mathematical programming: Theory and algorithms,* New York: John Wiley.

Ramos, F. (1981). *Capacity expansion of regional urban water supply networks.* Ph.D. Dissertation, Cambridge, MA: M.I.T.

Ramos, F., & Marks, D. H. (1978). Irrigation distribution planning in the nile river delta. *ASCE specialty conference on water resource systems*, Houston, TX.

Shapiro, J. (1979). *Mathematical programming: Structure and algorithms*. New York: John Wiley.

7

Nash Games

UP TO THIS POINT, we have only considered optimization problems. However, many important network models do not involve optimization. For example, consider the problem of trying to determine what prices and shipment patterns over global commodity and freight networks will make the world market for wheat clear.[1] In other words, the hypothetical problem we have proposed is to determine equilibrium prices on a network, not optimal prices. The extremal techniques we have discussed thus far for finding minima and maxima are, therefore, not entirely appropriate.

Fortunately, there are nonextremal network models that are appropriate to the study of suitably defined equilibria. The nonextremal models discussed in this chapter are a type of static noncooperative mathematical game known as a *Nash game*. We present key mathematical results about variational inequalities needed for the analysis and computation of solutions to such games. Because Nash games arise in many fields of application, the presentation in this initial chapter about games is purposely abstract, referring only to the general notions of decision-making agents, decision variables, and constraints. In later chapters we apply these abstract notions to important network engineering and network economic problems.[2]

We also hasten to add that there is a rich and extensive literature on the subject of noncooperative games and variational inequalities, and we make no pretense of providing a comprehensive treatment of those topics. Rather, we provide an introduction that is adequate to begin the study of noncooperative games on networks. The references and suggested reading at the end of this chapter include an assortment of sources wherein the interested reader can find more mathematical detail and additional algorithms.

Section 7.1: Some Basic Notions. This section presents some basic ideas needed for our consideration of mathematical games.

[1] That is, the total world demand of wheat will be made exactly equal to the total world supply of that commodity, after transportation over the global freight network.

[2] This chapter is highly similar to a chapter of Friesz (2010) that reviews the foundations of finite-dimensional Nash games.

T.L. Friesz, D. Bernstein, *Foundations of Network Optimization and Games*,
Complex Networks and Dynamic Systems 3,
DOI 10.1007/978-1-4899-7594-2_7

Section 7.2: Nash Equilibria and Normal Form Games. This section introduces the notion of a noncooperative mathematical game and the definition of Nash equilibria.

Section 7.3: Variational Inequalities and Related Nonextremal Problems. This section considers some non-extremal problems that are related to mathematical games. These problems will be used to develop existence and uniqueness results, as well as algorithms for solving mathematical games.

Section 7.4: Relationship of Variational Inequalities and Mathematical Programs. This section contains a key result that relates variational inequalities to mathematical programs.

Section 7.5: Kuhn-Tucker Conditions for Variational Inequalities. This section develops Kuhn-Tucker type conditions for variational inequalities.

Section 7.6: Quasivariational Inequalities. This section contains one generalization of variational inequality problems.

Section 7.7: Relationships Among Nonextremal Problems. There are several relationships among the various nonextremal problems that are important in discussions of network games. This section considers those relationships.

Section 7.8: Variational Inequality Representation of Nash Equilibrium. This section demonstrates how variational inequalities can be used to formulate both network and nonnetwork game-theoretic equilibrium models.

Section 7.9: User Equilibrium. This section considers non-extremal formulations of a Nash-like model that is used to model vehicular traffic.

Section 7.10: Variational Inequality Existence and Uniqueness. This section considers conditions that ensure the existence and uniqueness of solutions to variational inequalities.

Section 7.11: Sensitivity Analysis of Variational Inequalities. This section considers perturbed problems and how sensitivity analysis can be used in the study of mathematical games.

Section 7.12: Diagonalization Algorithms. This section focuses on diagonalization algorithms for solving variational inequalities and how they can be used to find solutions to mathematical games.

Section 7.13: Gap Function Methods for $VI(F, \Lambda)$. There is a special class of functions associated with variational inequality problems, so-called gap functions, which forms the foundation of a family of algorithms useful for solving mathematical games.

Section 7.14: Other Algorithms for $VI(F, \Lambda)$. This section discusses several other methods for solving finite-dimensional variational inequalities, including methods based on differential equations, fixed-point methods, generalized linear methods, and successive linearization.

Section 7.15: Computing Network User Equilibria This section demonstrates how a fixed point algorithm and a successive linearization algorithm can be used to solve the network user equilibrium problem.

7.1 Some Basic Notions

A mathematical game is a mathematical representation of some form of competition among agents or "players" of the game. Most mathematical games have rules of play, agent-specific utilities or payoffs, and a notion of solution. These may be expressed in two fundamental ways: the so-called extensive form and the normal form. A *game in extensive form* is a presentation, usually via a table or a decision tree, of all possible sequences of decisions that can be made by the game's players. This presentation is, by its very nature, exhaustive and potentially tedious or even impossible for large games involving multiple players and numerous decisions. By contrast, a *game in normal form* is expressed via mappings, equations, inequalities, and extremal principles. As such, large normal form games are potentially much more computationally tractable than large extensive form games, since in solving normal form games we may draw upon the computational methods of mathematical programming, as well as variational methods.

7.2 Nash Equilibria and Normal Form Games

The best understood and most widely used mathematical games are noncooperative games wherein game players pursue their own selfish interests and do not collude. As we have already mentioned, a noncooperative mathematical game in normal form uses mappings, inequalities, and extremal principles to describe competition among agents – who are intrinsically in conflict and do not collude – informed by some notion of utility and acting according to rules known by the agents of the game. We are especially interested in a notion of solution of noncooperative games known as a *Nash equilibrium* (named after John Forbes Nash, who proposed it). A set of actions undertaken by the noncooperative agents of interest is a Nash equilibrium if each agent knows the equilibrium strategies of the other agents, and no agent has anything to gain by unilaterally changing his/her own strategy. In particular, if no agent can benefit by changing his/her strategy while the other agents keep theirs unchanged, then the current set of strategy choices and the corresponding payoffs constitute a Nash equilibrium. As such, finding the Nash equilibrium of a noncooperative game in normal form is not generally equivalent to a single optimization problem; however, it is naturally articulated as a family of coupled optimization problems. We will learn how, for certain assumptions, those coupled optimization problems may be expressed as so-called *nonextremal problems*. Certain nonextremal problems have a structure that makes them quite amenable to analysis and solution. For our purposes in this chapter, the nonextremal problems known as fixed-point problems, variational inequality problems, and nonlinear complementarity problems are the most important; below, we define each in turn.

The following definition will apply:

Definition 7.1 (Nash equilibrium) Suppose there are N agents, each of which chooses a feasible strategy vector x^i from his/her strategy set Ω_i, where Ω_i is independent of the other players' strategies. Furthermore, every agent $i \in [1, N] \subseteq \Re^1_{++}$ has a cost (disutility) function $\Theta_i(x) : \Omega \longrightarrow \Re^1$ that depends on all agents' strategies where

$$\Omega = \prod_{i=1}^{N} \Omega_i$$

$$x = \left(x^i : i = 1, \ldots, N\right)$$

Every agent $i \in [1, N]$ seeks to solve the problem

$$\min \Theta_i(x^i, x^{-i}) \quad \text{subject to} \quad x^i \in \Omega_i \tag{7.1}$$

for each fixed yet arbitrary non-own tuple

$$x^{-i} = \left(x^j : j \neq i\right)$$

A Nash equilibrium is a tuple of strategies $x = \left(x^i : i = 1, \ldots, N\right)$ such that each x^i solves the mathematical program (7.1). A Nash equilibrium is denoted as $NE(\Theta, \Omega)$.

In other words, in a Nash equilibrium no agent may lower his/her cost (disutility) by unilaterally altering his/her strategy.

When the strategy set of any agent $i \in [1, N]$ depends on non-own strategies x^j, where $j \neq i$, the natural extension of the definition of a Nash equilibrium is called a *generalized Nash equilibrium.* That is, we have the following definition:

Definition 7.2 (Generalized Nash equilibrium) Suppose there are N agents, each of which chooses a feasible strategy vector x^i from the strategy set $\Omega_i(x)$ that depends on all agents' strategies where

$$x = \left(x^i : i = 1, \ldots, N\right)$$

Furthermore, every agent $i \in [1, N] \subseteq \Re^1_{++}$ has a cost (disutility) function $\Theta_i(x) : \Omega(x) \longrightarrow \Re^1$ that depends on all agents' strategies where

$$\Omega(x) = \prod_{i=1}^{N} \Omega_i(x)$$

Every agent $i \in [1, N]$ seeks to solve the problem

$$\min \Theta_i(x^i, x^{-i}) \quad \text{subject to} \quad x^i \in \Omega_i(x) \tag{7.2}$$

for each fixed yet arbitrary non-own tuple

$$x^{-i} = \left(x^j : j \neq i\right)$$

A generalized Nash equilibrium is a tuple of strategies x such that each x^i solves the mathematical program (7.2) and is denoted by $GNE(\Theta, \Omega)$.

7.3 Variational Inequalities and Related Nonextremal Problems

We now define some abstract problems that may not appear to be related to the notions of a Nash equilibrium or a generalized Nash equilibrium but which, as we shall ultimately demonstrate, constitute alternative ways of expressing such equilibria. We begin by defining the fixed-point problem:

Definition 7.3 (Fixed-point problem) Given a nonempty set, $\Lambda \subseteq \Re^n$, and a function, $F : \Lambda \longrightarrow \Lambda$, the fixed-point problem $FPP\,(F, \Lambda)$ is to find a vector y such that

$$\left.\begin{array}{c} y \in \Lambda \\ \\ y = F(y) \end{array}\right\} \quad FPP\,(F, \Lambda) \tag{7.3}$$

If $\Lambda \subseteq \Re^1$, then $FPP\,(G, \Lambda)$ seeks to find a point where the graph of F crosses the 45-degree line.

It will also be useful to define an extension of $FPP\,(F, \Lambda)$ which employs the notion of a minimum norm projection. The reader will recall from Chap. 2 that the minimum norm projection of the vector $v \in \Re^n$ onto the set Λ is denoted as $P_\Lambda\,[v]$ and has the following definition:

Definition 7.4 (Minimum norm projection) $P_\Lambda\,[v]$, the minimum norm projection of the vector $v \in \Re^n$ onto the set $\Lambda \subseteq \Re^n$, is the vector

$$y = \arg\left\{\min_x \|v - x\| : x \in \Lambda\right\}$$

The fixed-point problem with projection is:

Definition 7.5 (Fixed-point problem based on projection) Given a nonempty set, $\Lambda \subseteq \Re^n$, and a function, $F : \Lambda \longrightarrow \Lambda$, the fixed-point problem based on the minimum norm projection $FPP_{\min}(F,\Lambda)$ is to find a vector y such that

$$\left.\begin{array}{r} y \in \Lambda \\ \\ y = P_{\Lambda}\left[y - F(y)\right] \end{array}\right\} \quad FPP_{\min}(F,\Lambda) \tag{7.4}$$

That is, the solution of $FPP_{\min}(F,\Lambda)$ obeys

$$y = \arg\left\{\min_{x} \|y - F(y) - x\| : x \in \Lambda\right\} \tag{7.5}$$

by virtue of the definition of the minimum norm operator.

Next, we define the variational inequality problem:

Definition 7.6 (Variational inequality) Given a nonempty set, $\Lambda \subseteq \Re^n$, and a function, $F : \Lambda \longrightarrow \Re^n$, the variational inequality problem $VI(F,\Lambda)$ is to find a vector y such that

$$\left.\begin{array}{c} y \in \Lambda \\ \left[F(y)\right]^T (x - y) \geq 0 \quad \forall\, x \in \Lambda \end{array}\right\} \; VI(F,\Lambda) \tag{7.6}$$

Geometrically, a vector y is a solution of $VI(F,\Lambda)$ if and only if $F(y)$ forms an acute or right angle with all feasible vectors emanating from y.

Finally, we define the nonlinear complementarity problem:

Definition 7.7 (Nonlinear complementarity problem) Given a (nonlinear) function, $F : \Re^n \longrightarrow \Re^n$, the nonlinear complementarity problem $NCP(F)$ is to find a vector $y \in \Re^n$ such that

$$\left.\begin{array}{r} \left[F(y)\right]^T y = 0 \\ \\ F(y) \geq 0 \\ \\ y \geq 0 \end{array}\right\} \quad NCP(F) \tag{7.7}$$

Geometrically, a vector y is a solution of $NCP(F)$ if and only if y is nonnegative, $F(y)$ is nonnegative, and $F(y)$ is orthogonal to y. Alternatively, a vector y is a solution of $NCP(F)$ if and only if all elements of y are nonnegative, all elements of $F(y)$ are nonnegative, and for each positive element of y, denoted by y_i, $F_i(y)$ is zero (and vice versa).

7.4 Relationship of Variational Inequalities and Mathematical Programs

Let us begin our analysis of nonextremal problems by stating and proving a key result that relates variational inequalities to mathematical programs.

That result, known as the *minimum principle* of nonlinear programming, has the following statement:

Theorem 7.1 *(Minimum principle) The mathematical program*

$$\left.\begin{array}{ll}\min & Z(x) \\ \text{subjectto} & x \in \Lambda\end{array}\right\} NLP(F, \Lambda) \tag{7.8}$$

when Λ is nonempty, closed and convex as a set and $Z(x)$ is convex and differentiable as a function for all $x \in \Lambda$, has the following variational inequality as a necessary and sufficient condition for $y \in \Lambda \subseteq \Re^n$ to be a global optimum:

$$[\nabla Z(y)]^T (x - y) \geq 0 \quad \forall x \in \Lambda \tag{7.9}$$

Proof. The proof is in two parts:

(i) [(7.8)$\Longrightarrow$ (7.9)] The well-known property that any tangent to a differentiable convex function underestimates that function is expressed for the present case as

$$Z(x) \geq Z(y) + [\nabla Z(y)]^T (x - y) \quad \forall x \in \Lambda \tag{7.10}$$

It is immediate from (7.10) that

$$Z(x) - Z(y) \geq [\nabla Z(y)]^T (x - y) \geq 0 \quad \forall x \in \Lambda \tag{7.11}$$

in light of the given (7.8), thereby establishing sufficiency.

(ii) [(7.9) $\Longrightarrow$ (7.8)] Necessity is established by observing that following any direction vector $(x-y)$ rooted at the global optimum y must lead to another feasible solution that increases the objective function of (7.9). That is, every $(x-y)$ must have a component in the direction of $\nabla Z(y)$, a circumstance ensured by (7.8). ■

Note further that variational inequalities are more "general" than nonlinear programs. To see this, consider the nonlinear program

$$\left.\begin{array}{ll} & \min \oint_0^x F(z)dz \\ \text{subject to} & \\ & x \in \Lambda\end{array}\right\} \quad NLP\left[\oint F(z)dz, \Lambda\right] \tag{7.12}$$

where $\oint$ denotes a line integral which must be well defined and yield a single-valued function on Λ for (7.12) to be meaningful. For this program, we have the following result:

Lemma 7.1 *(Nonlinear program and variational inequality equivalence) Let Λ be convex. Then, any local minimum of the nonlinear program*

$NLP\left[\oint F(z)dz, \Lambda\right]$ is a solution of the variational inequality $VI(F,\Lambda)$. Moreover, if

$$Z(x) = \oint_0^x F(z)dz$$

is single-valued and convex on Λ, the variational inequality $VI(F,\Lambda)$ is equivalent to the nonlinear program $NLP\left[\oint F(z)dz, \Lambda\right]$.

Proof. By Theorem 7.1 we know that, for the given, a necessary and sufficient condition for optimality of $NLP\left[\oint F(z)dz, \Lambda\right]$ is

$$\begin{aligned} \left[\nabla Z(x)\right]^T (x-y) &= \left[\nabla_x \oint_0^x F(z)dz\right]^T_{x=y} (x-y) \\ &= \left[F(y)\right]^T (x-y) \geq 0, \quad \forall\, x \in \Lambda \end{aligned}$$

which is $VI(F,\Lambda)$. ■

7.5 Kuhn-Tucker Conditions for Variational Inequalities

The so-called Kuhn-Tucker necessary conditions for finite-dimensional mathematical programs were presented in Chap. 2. Kuhn-Tucker type necessary conditions may also be developed for variational inequalities; these conditions are needed for a variety of applications in subsequent chapters, as well as for the sensitivity analysis of variational inequalities discussed in the next section. Our development of Kuhn-Tucker conditions for variational inequalities parallels that in Tobin (1986) and depends on observing that $VI(F,\Lambda)$ requires

$$\left[F\left(x^*\right)\right]^T x \geq \left[F\left(x^*\right)\right]^T x^* \quad \forall x \in \Lambda \tag{7.13}$$

which is recognized as the definition of a constrained global minimum for the objective function $\left[F\left(x^*\right)\right]^T x$. That is, $VI(F,\Lambda)$ can be restated as the following mathematical program:

$$\min \left[F\left(x^*\right)\right]^T x \quad \text{subject to} \quad x \in \Lambda \subseteq \Re^n \tag{7.14}$$

where

$$F(x) : \Re^n \longrightarrow \Re^n$$

Note carefully that (7.14) is of no real use for computation as it presumes knowledge of the solution $x^* \in \Lambda$.

In our development of Kuhn-Tucker conditions for variational inequalities, we will consider the feasible region Λ to be determined by equality and inequality constraints; that is

$$\Lambda = \left\{x \in \Re^n : h(x) = 0,\, g(x) \leq 0\right\} \tag{7.15}$$

where

$$h(x) : \Re^n \longrightarrow \Re^q$$

$$g(x) : \Re^n \longrightarrow \Re^m$$

We will further assume that the functions $F(x)$ and $g(x)$ are both continuous, $g(x)$ is differentiable on Λ, and $h(x)$ is linear affine on Λ. The key result is:

Theorem 7.2 *(Kuhn-Tucker necessary conditions for $VI(F,\Lambda)$) Let*

$$x^* \in \Lambda = \left\{ x \in X_0 : h(x) = 0,\ g(x) \leq 0 \right\}$$

be a solution of $VI(F,\Lambda)$, where X_0 is an open set in $\Re^n$. Further assume that $F(x)$ and $g(x)$ are continuous on Λ, $g(x)$ is differentiable on Λ, and $h(x)$ is linear affine on Λ. Then, if the gradients $\nabla g_i(x^*)$ for i such that $g_i(x^*) = 0$ together with the gradients $\nabla h_i(x^*)$ for $i \in [1,q]$, are linearly independent, there exist multipliers $\pi \in \Re^m$ and $\mu \in \Re^q$ such that

$$F(x) + [\nabla g(x^*)]^T \pi + [\nabla h(x^*)]^T \mu = 0 \tag{7.16}$$

$$\pi^T g(x^*) = 0 \tag{7.17}$$

$$\pi \geq 0 \tag{7.18}$$

Proof. Observe that x^* also solves the nonlinear program

$$\min Z(x^*) \equiv [F(x^*)]^T x \quad \text{subject to} \quad x \in \Lambda \subseteq \Re^n \tag{7.19}$$

The assumption of linear independence of the gradients of binding constraints provides a constraint qualification, and we may be certain the Kuhn-Tucker conditions hold at x^*; therefore, the Kuhn-Tucker conditions for this mathematical program are

$$\nabla Z(x^*) + [\nabla g(x^*)]^T \pi + [\nabla h(x^*)]^T \mu = 0 \tag{7.20}$$

$$\pi^T g(x^*) = 0 \tag{7.21}$$

$$\pi \geq 0 \tag{7.22}$$

However

$$\nabla Z(x^*) = F(x^*) \tag{7.23}$$

so (7.20)–(7.22) are equivalent to (7.16)–(7.18). ■

Note that Theorem 7.2 can be strengthened by employing a weaker (less restrictive) constraint qualification.

We further comment that the variational inequality necessary conditions become sufficient if we stipulate that the inequality constraint functions $g_i(x)$ are convex. This observation is formalized in the next theorem:

Theorem 7.3 *(Sufficient conditions for $VI(F,\Lambda)$) Suppose the assumptions of Theorem (7.2) hold; the $g_i(x)$ for $i \in [1,m]$ are convex on Λ; and $x^* \in \Lambda$, $\pi \in \Re^m$, $\mu \in \Re^q$ satisfy (7.16)–(7.18). Then x^* is a solution to $VI(F,\Lambda)$.*

Proof. By the given of this theorem, the nonlinear program (7.19) is a convex mathematical program. Thus, (7.16)–(7.18) are sufficient to conclude that x^* solves (7.19). Consequently

$$[F(x^*)]^T x \geq [F(x^*)]^T x^* \quad \forall x \in \Lambda \tag{7.24}$$

demonstrating that x^* solves $VI(F,\Lambda)$. ■

7.6 Quasivariational Inequalities

It is possible to generalize $VI(F,\Lambda)$ in a variety of ways. One generalization of importance is the following:

Definition 7.8 (Quasivariational inequality problem) Given a nonempty set $\Lambda \subseteq \Re^n$ and a function $F : \Re^n \longrightarrow \Re^n$, let Λ be a point-to-set mapping from $\Re^n$ to subsets of $\Re^n$. The *quasivariational inequality problem* $QVI(F,\Lambda)$ is to find a vector $y \in \Lambda(y)$ such that

$$\left.\begin{array}{c} y \in \Lambda(y) \\ [F(y)]^T (x-y) \geq 0 \qquad \forall x \in \Lambda(y) \end{array}\right\} QVI(F,\Lambda)$$

Under certain conditions, one may create a variational inequality $VI(F,\Lambda_0)$ whose solutions are also solutions of the quasivariational inequality $QVI(F,\Lambda)$ for appropriately defined sets Λ_0 and Λ. To formally establish such a result, let us partition the decision variables of $QVI(F,\Lambda)$ by defining the tuples

$$F^v = (F_i : i \in \Lambda_v) \tag{7.25}$$

$$x^v = (x_i : i \in \Lambda_v) \tag{7.26}$$

$$x^{-v} = (x_i : i \notin \Lambda_v) \tag{7.27}$$

Furthermore, we employ the following notational conventions:

$$(x^v, x^{-v}) \equiv (x_1, x_2, \ldots, x_n)^T = x \in \Re^n$$

$$(F^v, F^{-v}) \equiv (F_1, F_2, \ldots, F_n)^T = F \in \Re^n$$

Next define

$$\Lambda_0 \subset \Re^n \tag{7.28}$$

$$\Lambda_v(x^{-v}) \equiv \left\{x^v : (x^v, x^{-v}) \in \Lambda_0\right\} \tag{7.29}$$

$$\Lambda_v(x^v) \equiv \left\{x^{-v} : (x^v, x^{-v}) \in \Lambda_0\right\} \tag{7.30}$$

$$\Lambda(x) \equiv \Lambda_v(x^{-v}) \times \Lambda_v(x^v) \tag{7.31}$$

We are now ready to state and prove the following result due to Facchinei et al. (2007):

Theorem 7.4 *(Variational inequality and quasivariational inequality relationship) Suppose that Λ_0 is closed and convex. Then any solution of $VI(F, \Lambda_0)$ is a solution of $QVI(F, \Lambda_0)$ under the definitions (7.25)–(7.31).*

Proof. Let $x^v \in \Lambda_v(y^{-v})$ and observe that $x^0 = (x^v, y^{-v}) \in \Lambda_0$. Take y to be a solution of $VI(F, \Lambda_0)$; thus

$$[F^v(y)]^T (x^v - y^v) + \left[F^{-v}(y)\right]^T \left(x^{-v} - y^{-v}\right) \geq 0 \tag{7.32}$$

for all $x = (x^v, x^{-v}) \in \Lambda_0$. If we consider $x = x^0$, it follows at once from (7.6) that

$$[F^v(y)]^T (x^v - y^v) \geq 0 \quad \forall x^v \in \Lambda_v(y^{-v}) \tag{7.33}$$

Without loss of generality, we may exchange the roles of v and $-v$ and write

$$\left[F^{-v}(y)\right]^T \left(x^{-v} - y^{-v}\right) \geq 0 \quad \forall x^{-v} \in \Lambda_v(y^v)$$

Therefore

$$\begin{bmatrix} F^v(y) \\ F^{-v}(y) \end{bmatrix}^T \begin{pmatrix} x^v - y^v \\ x^{-v} - y^{-v} \end{pmatrix} \geq 0$$

for all $x = (x^v, x^{-v}) \in \Lambda_v(x^{-v}) \times \Lambda_v(x^v)$, which is recognized as $QVI(F, \Lambda)$. ■

7.7 Relationships Among Nonextremal Problems

There are several relationships among the various nonextremal problems we have defined that will be important in our subsequent discussion of network games. The first of these is formalized in the following lemma:

Lemma 7.2 *(Nonlinear complementarity and variational inequality equivalence) If $\Lambda = \Re^n_+$ then the variational inequality problem $VI(F, \Lambda)$ is equivalent to the nonlinear complementarity problem $NCP(F)$.*

Proof. The proof is in two parts:

(i) $[NCP\,(F) \Longrightarrow VI\,(F,\Lambda)]$ First we show that if y is a solution of $NCP\,(F)$ then it is also a solution to $VI\,(F,\Lambda)$. To do so, note that, if y is a solution to $NCP\,(F)$, then $F(y) \geq 0$. Therefore, $[F(y)]^T x \geq 0$ for all $x \in \Lambda$. Thus, since $[F(y)]^T y = 0$ for all $y \geq 0$, it follows that

$$[F(y)]^T x - [F(y)]^T y \geq 0 \tag{7.34}$$

$$\Longrightarrow \quad [F(y)]^T (x - y) \geq 0 \quad x, y \in \Lambda. \tag{7.35}$$

(ii) $[VI\,(F,\Lambda) \Longrightarrow NCP\,(F)]$ Next we show that if y is a solution of $VI\,(F,\Lambda)$ then it is also a solution of $NCP\,(F)$. To do so, note that if y is a solution to $VI\,(F,\Lambda)$ then

$$[F(y)]^T (x - y) \quad \geq \quad 0 \quad \forall\, x \in \Lambda \tag{7.36}$$

$$\Longrightarrow \quad [F(y)]^T (-y) \geq 0, \text{ since } x = 0 \in \Lambda \tag{7.37}$$

$$\Longrightarrow \quad [F(y)]^T y \leq 0 \tag{7.38}$$

Also note that $x = 2y \in \Lambda$ since $y \in \Lambda$. Thus,

$$[F(y)]^T (2y - y) \geq 0 \Longrightarrow [F(y)]^T y \geq 0. \tag{7.39}$$

However

$$[F(y)]^T y \geq 0 \text{ and } [F(y)]^T y \leq 0 \Longrightarrow [F(y)]^T y = 0 \tag{7.40}$$

By assumption

$$[F(y)]^T (x - y) = \sum_{i=1}^{n} F_i(y)(x_i - y_i) \geq 0 \quad \forall\, x \in \Lambda \tag{7.41}$$

Now, suppose $F(y) \neq 0$ and $F(y) \not> 0$. Then, there exists a $j \in [1, n]$ such that $F_j(y) < 0$. So, pick $x_j \gg 0$, a feasible value. Then, it is immediate that

$$\sum_{i=1}^{n} F_i(y)(x_i - y_i) < 0 \tag{7.42}$$

which is a contradiction of our supposition; hence $F(y) \geq 0$. Also, since $y \in \Lambda$, it is immediate that $y \geq 0$. Thus,

$$[F(y)]^T y = 0, \quad F(y) \geq 0, \qquad y \geq 0. \tag{7.43}$$

■

Lemma 7.3 *(Fixed-point and variational inequality equivalence) The fixed-point problem $FPP_{\min}(F,\Lambda)$ is equivalent to the variational inequality problem $VI(F,\Lambda)$ when $\Lambda \subseteq \Re^n$ is compact and convex.*

Proof. By the definition of $FPP_{\min}(F,\Lambda)$, $y = x^*$ where

$$x^* = \arg\min_x \|y - F(y) - x\| \quad \text{subject to} \quad x \in \Lambda \tag{7.44}$$

The mathematical program of (7.44) is equivalent to

$$\min_x \frac{1}{2}(y - F(y) - x)^T (y - F(y) - x) \equiv Z(x,y) \quad \text{subject to} \quad x \in \Lambda \tag{7.45}$$

since the objective function of (7.45) is a monotonic transformation of the objective function of (7.44). By Theorem 7.1 a necessary and sufficient condition for $x^* \in \Lambda$ to be an optimal solution of (7.45) is

$$[\nabla_x Z(x^*,y)]^T (x - x^*) \geq 0 \quad \forall x \in \Lambda \tag{7.46}$$

or

$$(-1)(y - F(y) - x^*)^T (x - x^*) \geq 0 \quad \forall x \in \Lambda \tag{7.47}$$

Because $y = x^*$, it is immediate from (7.47) that

$$[F(x^*)]^T (x - x^*) \geq 0 \quad \forall x \in \Lambda$$

as required. ■

Observe that if the vector function $F(y)$ of the fixed point problem $FPP_{\min}(F,\Lambda)$ is replaced by $\eta F(y)$ where $\eta \in \Re^1_{++}$ the result is unchanged.

It is interesting to note that the following result also holds:

Theorem 7.5 *(Nonlinear complementarity and variational inequality equivalence) There is a nonlinear complementarity problem that is equivalent to $VI(F,\Lambda_0)$ provided $VI(F,\Lambda_0)$ obeys a constraint qualification and*

$$\Lambda_0 = \{x \geq 0 : g(x) \leq 0,\, h(x) = 0\} \subseteq \Re^n_+$$

is convex.

Proof. Take

$$F(x) : \Re^n \longrightarrow \Re^n$$

$$g(x) : \Re^n \longrightarrow \Re^m$$

$$h(x) : \Re^n \longrightarrow \Re^q$$

Define the nonlinear complementarity problem $NCP(\Psi)$ for which

$$[\Psi(y)]^T y = 0$$
$$\Psi(y) \geq 0$$
$$y \geq 0$$

where

$$\Psi(y) = \begin{pmatrix} F(x^*) + [\nabla g(x^*)]^T \lambda + [\nabla h(x^*)]^T \mu \\ -g(x^*) \\ h(x^*) \\ -h(x^*) \end{pmatrix} \in \Re^{n+m+2q} \tag{7.48}$$

$$y = \begin{pmatrix} x \\ \lambda \\ \gamma \\ \eta \end{pmatrix} \in \Re^{n+m+2q} \tag{7.49}$$

Note that if $x \in \Lambda_0$ then $x \geq 0$. Thus, complementary slackness for $VI(F, \Lambda_0)$ requires

$$\rho^T x^* = 0 \tag{7.50}$$

$$x^* \geq 0 \tag{7.51}$$

$$\rho \geq 0 \tag{7.52}$$

$$h(x^*) = 0 \tag{7.53}$$

The Kuhn-Tucker conditions for $VI(F, \Lambda)$ are

$$F(x^*) + [\nabla g(x^*)]^T \lambda + [\nabla h(x^*)]^T \mu = \rho \tag{7.54}$$

$$\lambda^T g(x^*) = 0 \tag{7.55}$$

$$-g(x^*) \geq 0 \tag{7.56}$$

$$\lambda \geq 0 \tag{7.57}$$

$$\rho^T x^* = 0 \tag{7.58}$$

$$x^* \geq 0 \tag{7.59}$$

$$\rho \geq 0 \tag{7.60}$$

$$\gamma^T h(x^*) = 0 \tag{7.61}$$

$$h(x^*) \geq 0 \tag{7.62}$$

$$\gamma \geq 0 \tag{7.63}$$

$$\eta^T [-h(x^*)] = 0 \tag{7.64}$$

$$-h(x^*) \geq 0 \tag{7.65}$$

$$\eta \geq 0 \tag{7.66}$$

It is immediate from complementary slackness that (7.54)–(7.66) may be restated as

$$\left\{F(x^*) + [\nabla g(x^*)]^T \lambda + [\nabla h(x^*)]^T \mu\right\}^T x^* = 0 \tag{7.67}$$

$$F(x^*) + [\nabla g(x^*)]^T \lambda + [\nabla h(x^*)]^T \mu \geq 0 \tag{7.68}$$

$$x \geq 0 \tag{7.69}$$

$$[g(x^*)]^T \lambda = 0 \tag{7.70}$$

$$-g(x^*) \geq 0 \tag{7.71}$$

$$\lambda \geq 0 \tag{7.72}$$

$$[h(x^*)]^T \gamma = 0 \tag{7.73}$$

$$h(x^*) \geq 0 \tag{7.74}$$

$$\gamma \geq 0 \tag{7.75}$$

$$[-h(x^*)]^T \eta = 0 \tag{7.76}$$

$$-h(x^*) \geq 0 \tag{7.77}$$

$$\eta \geq 0 \tag{7.78}$$

Thus, if we employ definitions (7.48) and (7.49), we obtain $NCP(\Psi)$. Because of convexity the Kuhn-Tucker conditions are also sufficient. Hence, the two problems are equivalent. ■

7.8 Variational Inequality Representation of Nash Equilibrium

Although the kinds of nonextremal problems introduced above are interesting in their own right, their greatest value lies in the assistance they provide in the formulation of both network and non-network game-theoretic equilibrium models. Loosely speaking, a system is in equilibrium when it has stopped changing. Thus, if we think of the function $G(y)$ as embodying the signals that guide how the system of interest evolves, an equilibrium exists when the fixed-point problem $G(y) = y$ obtains. It is, therefore, no surprise that most equilibrium models may be formulated as fixed-point problems. So we fully expect that a Nash equilibrium in the sense of Definition 7.1 will be equivalent to a variational inequality under appropriate regularity conditions. In fact, the following result may be stated and proved:

Theorem 7.6 *(Nash equilibrium equivalent to a variational inequality) The Nash equilibrium $NE(\Theta, \Omega)$ of Definition 7.1 is equivalent to the variational inequality $VI(\nabla\Theta, \Omega)$ provided that, for all $i \in [1, N]$, the following regularity conditions hold: (1) each $\Theta_i(x) : \Omega_i \longrightarrow \Re^1$ is convex and continuously differentiable in x^i; and (2) each Ω_i is closed and convex.*

Proof. Each agent $i \in [1, N]$ seeks to solve

$$\min \Theta_i(x^i, x^{-i}) \quad \text{subject to} \quad x^i \in \Omega_i \tag{7.79}$$

Because of convexity and differentiability, the minimum principle provides a necessary and sufficient condition for $y^i \in \Omega_i$ to be an equilibrium, namely

$$\nabla_i\Theta_i(y^i, y^{-i})\left(x^i - y^i\right) \geq 0 \quad \forall x^i \in \Omega_i \tag{7.80}$$

where ∇_i denotes the gradient operator relative to x^i for $i \in [1, N]$. Concatenating based on (7.80) gives

$$\left[\nabla\Theta(y)\right]^T (x - y) \geq 0 \; \forall x \in \Omega \tag{7.81}$$

where

$$\Omega = \prod_{i=1}^{N} \Omega_i$$

$$x = \left(x^i : i = 1, \ldots, N\right)$$

which is recognized as $VI(\nabla\Theta, \Omega)$. Now suppose we are given (7.81); we may, for any arbitrary $i \in [1, N]$, select the tuple x to have y^j as its jth subvector for every $j \neq i$. As a consequence of such choices, (7.81) yields (7.80). Thereby, the desired equivalency has been demonstrated. ■

7.9 User Equilibrium

In vehicular traffic science much effort has been devoted to modeling and computing a Nash-like equilibrium known as *user equilibrium.* This type of equilibrium is a steady-state flow pattern that is sometimes also called a *user-optimized flow.* Traffic is said to achieve a user equilibrium when no traveler can change his/her route without experiencing greater travel delay or increased generalized cost (that includes consideration of the value of time).

To construct a model of user equilibrium we begin with a general graph $G(\mathcal{N}, \mathcal{A})$, where $\mathcal{N}$ is a set of nodes and $\mathcal{A}$ is a set of arcs. We use $(i, j) \in \mathcal{W}$ to denote an origin-destination (OD) pair for which the origin is node i and the destination is node j while the set of all OD pairs is $\mathcal{W}$. There is a fixed travel demand Q_{ij}, expressed in flow units, for each OD pair $(i, j) \in \mathcal{W}$. Furthermore, the minimum travel cost for OD pair $(i, j) \in \mathcal{W}$ is u_{ij}. The set of paths from node i to node j is denoted by $\mathcal{P}_{ij}$, while the unit cost of travel over path $p \in \mathcal{P}_{ij}$ is denoted by c_p. In addition, we denote the flow on path p by h_p. Letting $\mathcal{P}$ denote the set of all paths in the network, we are able to say the vector $h = (h_p : p \in \mathcal{P}) \geq 0$ is a user equilibrium when it obeys the following:

$$h_p > 0, \;\; p \in \mathcal{P}_{ij} \Longrightarrow c_p = u_{ij} \tag{7.82}$$

where

$$u_{ij} = \min_{p \in \mathcal{P}_{ij}} c_p$$

and flow conservation constraints are also enforced. The condition

$$c_p > u_{ij}, \;\; p \in \mathcal{P}_{ij} \Longrightarrow h_p = 0 \tag{7.83}$$

is automatically enforced and need not be separately articulated, as may be easily established by assuming $h_p > 0$ when $c_p > u_{ij}$ for $p \in \mathcal{P}_{ij}$. Using (7.82), a contradiction immediately results, verifying (7.83).

Usually path costs are taken to be additive in unit arc costs; that is

$$c_p = \sum_{a \in \mathcal{A}} \delta_{ap} c_a(f) \quad \forall p \in \mathcal{P} \tag{7.84}$$

where c_a is a unit cost function that reflects congestion by depending on the vector of arc flows $f = (f_a : a \in \mathcal{A})$ while f_a is the flow on each arc $a \in \mathcal{A}$. We will use the vectors

$$c = (c_a : a \in \mathcal{A})$$

$$C = (c_p : p \in \mathcal{P})$$

to denote the vector of unit arc costs and the vector of unit path costs, respectively. Also

$$\delta_{ap} = \begin{cases} 1 & \text{if arc } a \text{ belongs to path } p \\ 0 & \text{if arc } a \text{ does not belong to path } p \end{cases} \tag{7.85}$$

for each arc $a \in \mathcal{A}$ and path $p \in \mathcal{P}$. Arc flows are related to path flows according to

$$f_a = \sum_{p \in \mathcal{P}} \delta_{ap} h_p \quad \forall a \in \mathcal{A} \tag{7.86}$$

The relationships

$$Q_{ij} - \sum_{p \in \mathcal{P}_{ij}} h_p = 0 \qquad \forall (i,j) \in \mathcal{W} \tag{7.87}$$

are the conservation of flow constraints. Clearly, then, the set

$$\Upsilon = \left\{ h \geq 0 : Q_{ij} - \sum_{p \in \mathcal{P}_{ij}} h_p = 0 \quad \forall (i,j) \in \mathcal{W} \right\}$$

is the set of feasible flows from which the user equilibrium must be selected.

The user equilibrium problem we have described above may be restated in a number of ways. One version is the following:

Definition 7.9 (User equilibrium with fixed demand) A user equilibrium $UE(C, \Upsilon)$ with fixed demand $T = (Q_{ij} : (i,j) \in \mathcal{W})$ is a flow pattern $h \equiv (h_p : p \in \mathcal{P})$ such that

$$(c_p - u_{ij})\, h_p = 0 \qquad \forall (i,j) \in \mathcal{W}, p \in \mathcal{P}_{ij} \tag{7.88}$$

$$c_p - u_{ij} \geq 0 \qquad \forall (i,j) \in \mathcal{W}, p \in \mathcal{P}_{ij} \tag{7.89}$$

$$\sum_{p \in \mathcal{P}_{ij}} h_p - Q_{ij} = 0 \qquad \forall (i,j) \in \mathcal{W} \tag{7.90}$$

$$h_p \geq 0 \qquad \forall p \in \mathcal{P} \tag{7.91}$$

where

$$u_{ij} = \min_{p \in \mathcal{P}_{ij}} c_p \qquad \forall (i,j) \in \mathcal{W}$$

The system (7.88)–(7.91) looks quite similar to a nonlinear complementarity problem, but is not. However, under the assumption of cost positivity, it is equivalent to a nonlinear complementarity problem:

Theorem 7.7 *(User equilibrium as a nonlinear complementarity problem) Assume each arc cost $c_a(f)$ is strictly positive for all feasible flows and all $a \in \mathcal{A}$. Any pair (h, u), where $h = (h_p : p \in \mathcal{P})$ and $u = (u_{ij} : (i,j) \in \mathcal{W})$, is a user* *equilibrium $UE(C,\Upsilon)$ if it satisfies the following nonlinear complementarity problem:*

$$(c_p - u_{ij})\, h_p = 0 \qquad \forall\, (i,j) \in \mathcal{W}, p \in \mathcal{P}_{ij} \tag{7.92}$$

$$c_p - u_{ij} \geq 0 \qquad \forall\, (i,j) \in \mathcal{W}, p \in \mathcal{P}_{ij} \tag{7.93}$$

$$\left(\sum_{q \in \mathcal{P}_{ij}} h_q - Q_{ij} \right) u_{ij} = 0 \qquad \forall\, (i,j) \in \mathcal{W} \tag{7.94}$$

$$\left(\sum_{p \in \mathcal{P}_{ij}} h_p - Q_{ij} \right) \geq 0 \qquad \forall\, (i,j) \in \mathcal{W} \tag{7.95}$$

$$h_p \geq 0 \qquad \forall p \in \mathcal{P} \tag{7.96}$$

Proof. That any solution of system (7.92)–(7.96) is a solution of system (7.88)–(7.91) is seen by noting that if

$$\sum_{q \in \mathcal{P}_{ij}} h_q - Q_{ij} > 0 \tag{7.97}$$

then there exists $r \in \mathcal{P}_{ij}$ such that $h_r > 0$, which in turn requires that

$$c_r = u_{ij} = 0 \tag{7.98}$$

Clearly, (7.98) contradicts the assumption of cost positivity. Thus, we have established that any solution of (7.92)–(7.96) is a user equilibrium. ■

It is an easy matter to show that a flow pattern is a user equilibrium if and only if it satisfies an appropriate variational inequality:

Theorem 7.8 *(User equilibrium as a variational inequality) The flow pattern $h^* = \left(h_p^* : p \in \mathcal{P}\right)$ is a user equilibrium $UE(C,\Upsilon)$ if and only if*

$$\left.\begin{array}{c} h^* \in \Upsilon \\ \sum_{p \in \mathcal{P}} c_p\,(h^*)\left(h_p - h_p^*\right) \geq 0 \qquad \forall h \in \Omega \end{array}\right\} VI(c,\Omega) \tag{7.99}$$

where

$$\Upsilon = \left\{ h \geq 0 : Q_{ij} - \sum_{p \in \mathcal{P}_{ij}} h_p = 0 \quad \forall (i,j) \in \mathcal{W} \right\} \tag{7.100}$$

Proof. The proof is in two parts:

(i) $[UE(C, \Upsilon) \Longrightarrow VI(C, \Upsilon)]$ Note that

$$c_p(h^*) \geq u_{ij}$$

for any $p \in \mathcal{P}_{ij}$. Thus

$$c_p(h^*)\left(h_p - h_p^*\right) \geq u_{ij}\left(h_p - h_p^*\right), \tag{7.101}$$

including the case of $\left(h_p - h_p^*\right) < 0$, for then

$$h_p^* > h_p \geq 0 \Longrightarrow c_p(h^*) = u_{ij}$$

Therefore, from (7.101), upon summing over paths, and exploiting the flow conservation constraints, we have at once the variational inequality (7.99).

(ii) $[VI(C, \Upsilon) \Longrightarrow UE(C, \Upsilon)]$ The Kuhn-Tucker conditions for (7.99) are

$$c_p(h^*) - u_{ij} - \rho_p = 0 \qquad \forall (i,j) \in \mathcal{W}, p \in \mathcal{P}_{ij}$$

$$\rho_p h_p = 0 \qquad \forall (i,j) \in \mathcal{W}, p \in \mathcal{P}_{ij}$$

$$\rho_p \geq 0 \qquad \forall (i,j) \in \mathcal{W}, p \in \mathcal{P}_{ij}$$

which are easily seen to yield the conditions that define $UE(C, \Upsilon)$. ■

7.10 Variational Inequality Existence and Uniqueness

There is an existence and uniqueness theory for finite-dimensional games and variational inequalities. The relevant starting point for studying existence is the following version of Brouwer's existence theorem for fixed-point problems in $\Re^n$:

Theorem 7.9 *(Brouwer's fixed-point theorem) If Λ is a convex, compact set, and $F(x)$ is continuous on Λ, then the fixed-point problem $FPP(F, \Lambda)$ has a solution.*

Proof. See Todd (1976). ■

In particular, we have the following result:

Theorem 7.10 *(Stampacchia existence theorem) If Λ is a convex, compact set and $F(x)$ is continuous on Λ, then $VI(F, \Lambda)$ has a solution.*

Proof. By the given, $FPP_{\min}(F,\Lambda)$ satisfies the regularity conditions of Brouwer's fixed-point theorem and must, therefore, have a solution. It is immediate that $VI(F,\Lambda)$ also has a solution, since by Lemma 7.3 we know that any solution of $FPP_{\min}(F,\Lambda)$ is a solution of $VI(F,\Lambda)$. ■

This last theorem has an important implication for equilibria of Nash and Nash-like noncooperative games. In particular, we have:

Corollary 7.1 *(Existence of $NE(\Theta,\Omega)$) For all $i \in [1,N]$, assume Ω_i is a convex, compact set and $\Theta_i(x)$ is continuously differentiable. Then a Nash equilibrium $NE(\Theta,\Omega)$ exists.*

Proof. The result is immediate from Theorems 7.6 and 7.10. ■

We now discuss the uniqueness of solutions to variational inequality problems. To this end, we introduce the notion of monotonicity of a vector function:

Definition 7.10 (Monotonically increasing function) A function $F(y) : \Re^n \longrightarrow \Re^n$ is monotonically increasing on Λ if

$$[F(y^1) - F(y^2)]^T (y^1 - y^2) \geq 0 \tag{7.102}$$

for all $y^1, y^2 \in \Lambda$.

We also introduce at this time the notion of strict monotonicity:

Definition 7.11 (Strictly monotonically increasing function) A function $F(y) : \Re^n \longrightarrow \Re^n$ is strictly monotonically increasing on Λ if

$$[F(y^1) - F(y^2)]^T (y^1 - y^2) > 0 \tag{7.103}$$

for all $y^1, y^2 \in \Lambda$ such that $y^1 \neq y^2$.

Of course, monotone decreasing versions of the above definitions are obtained by reversing the inequalities. The notion of strict monotonicity allows us to establish the following uniqueness result:

Theorem 7.11 *($VI(F,\Lambda)$ uniqueness) If $y \in \Lambda \subseteq \Re^n$ is a solution of $VI(F,\Lambda)$ and $F(x)$ is strictly monotonically increasing then y is unique.*

Proof. Suppose there are two solutions $y^1 \in \Lambda$ and $y^2 \in \Lambda$, where $y^1 \neq y^2$; as such the following variational inequalities obtain:

$$\left[F(y^1)\right]^T (y^2 - y^1) \geq 0 \text{ and } \left[F(y^2)\right]^T (y^1 - y^2) \geq 0 \tag{7.104}$$

Adding these inequalities leads to

$$[F(y^1) - F(y^2)]^T (y^1 - y^2) \leq 0, \tag{7.105}$$

which contradicts strict monotonicity (7.103). Hence $y^1 = y^2$, and any solution is unique. ■

There is an intimate relationship between differentiable convex functions and monotonically increasing functions. That result is:

Theorem 7.12 *(Relationship of convexity and monotonicity) If the differentiable function $E(x) : \Lambda \subseteq \Re^n \longrightarrow \Re^n$ is (strictly) convex for all $x \in \Lambda$, then its gradient $\nabla E(x)$ is (strictly) monotonically increasing for all $x \in \Lambda$.*

Proof. Convexity and differentiability of $E(x)$ ensure that

$$E\left(y^1\right) \geq E\left(y^2\right) + \left[\nabla E\left(y^2\right)\right]^T \left(y^1 - y^2\right) \tag{7.106}$$

$$E\left(y^2\right) \geq E\left(y^1\right) + \left[\nabla E\left(y^1\right)\right]^T \left(y^2 - y^1\right) \tag{7.107}$$

for all $y^1, y^2 \in \Lambda$. Adding these two inequalities leads directly to

$$0 \geq \left[\nabla E\left(y_2\right)\right]^T \left(y^1 - y^2\right) + \left[\nabla E\left(y^1\right)\right]^T \left(y^2 - y^1\right) \tag{7.108}$$

which is easily manipulated to obtain

$$-\left[\nabla E\left(y_2\right)\right]^T \left(y^1 - y^2\right) + \left[\nabla E\left(y^1\right)\right]^T \left(y^1 - y^2\right) \geq 0 \tag{7.109}$$

or

$$\left\{\left[\nabla E\left(y^1\right)\right]^T - \left[\nabla E\left(y_2\right)\right]^T\right\} \left(y^1 - y^2\right) \geq 0 \tag{7.110}$$

The last expression is recognized as a condition defining the monotonically increasing nature of $\nabla E(.)$. The strictly convex, strictly monotone case is a trivial specialization of the above arguments. ■

Existence and uniqueness results may also be developed using the notions of strong monotonicity and coerciveness. To that end, we need the following definitions:

Definition 7.12 (Strong monotonicity) The function $F(x) : \Re^n \longrightarrow \Re^n$ is strongly monotonically increasing on Λ with constant $K \in \Re^1_{++}$ if

$$\langle F(x) - F(y), x - y \rangle \geq \frac{K}{2} \|x - y\|^2$$

for all $x, y \in \Lambda$.

Definition 7.13 (Coerciveness) The function $F(x) : \Re^n \longrightarrow \Re^n$ is coercive on Λ if

$$\frac{\langle F(x) - F\left(x^0\right), x - x^0 \rangle}{\|x - x^0\|} \longrightarrow +\infty$$

as $\|x\| \longrightarrow 0$ for all $x \in \Lambda$ and some $x^0 \in \Lambda$.

We will also need the following theorem:

Theorem 7.13 *(Existence for a closed ball) Let $N_R(0)$ denote a closed ball of radius R centered at $0 \in \Re^n$ and define*

$$\Lambda_0 = N_R(0) \cap \Lambda$$

where Λ is convex. A necessary and sufficient condition for the variational inequality $VI(F, \Lambda)$ to have a solution $x^* \in \Lambda$ is that there exist $x^R \in \Lambda_0$ solving $VI(F, \Lambda_0)$ and a nontrivial radius $R \in \Re^1_{++}$ such that

$$\left\|x^R\right\| < R$$

Proof. The proof is in two parts:

(i) $[VI(F, \Lambda) \Longrightarrow VI(F, \Lambda_0)]$ Take $x^R \in \Lambda$ to be a solution of $VI(F, \Lambda)$ and select $R \in \Re^1_{++}$ such that $\left\|x^R\right\| < R$. It follows immediately that x^R is a solution of $VI(F, \Lambda_0)$.

(ii) $[VI(F, \Lambda_0) \Longrightarrow VI(F, \Lambda)]$ Now suppose $x^R \in \Lambda_0$ solves $VI(F, \Lambda_0)$ and $\left\|x^R\right\| < R$. Then, for sufficiently small $\varepsilon \geq 0$, we may construct $w = x^R + \varepsilon\left(y - x^R\right) \in \Lambda_0$, for $y \in \Lambda$, such that

$$0 \leq \left[F\left(x^R\right)\right]^T\left(w - x^R\right) = \varepsilon\left[F\left(x^R\right)\right]^T\left(y - x^R\right) \qquad y \in \Lambda \tag{7.111}$$

from which we know that x^R solves $VI(F, \Lambda)$. ■

The preceding theorem leads to the following result:

Theorem 7.14 *(Coerciveness and existence for $VI(F, \Lambda)$) Suppose $F(x) : \Re^n \longrightarrow \Re^n$ is coercive for some point $x^0 \in \Lambda$. Then $VI(F, \Lambda)$ has a solution.*

Proof. Pick $K > \left\|F\left(x^0\right)\right\|$ and $R > \left\|x^0\right\|$ such that

$$\left[F(x) - F\left(x^0\right)\right]^T\left(x - x^0\right) \geq K\left\|x - x^0\right\|$$

for $\|x\| \geq K$, $x \in \Lambda$. If follows that

$$\begin{aligned}
[F(x)]^T\left(x - x^0\right) &\geq K\left\|x - x^0\right\| - \left[F\left(x^0\right)\right]^T\left(x - x^0\right) \\
&\geq K\left\|x - x^0\right\| - \left\|F\left(x^0\right)\right\|\left\|x - x^0\right\| \\
&= \left(K - \left\|F\left(x^0\right)\right\|\right)\left\|x - x^0\right\| \\
&\geq \left(K - \left\|F\left(x^0\right)\right\|\right)\left(\|x\| - \left\|x^0\right\|\right) > 0 \quad (7.112)
\end{aligned}$$

if we take $\|x\| = R$. Using the notation introduced previously in Theorem 7.13, let $x^R \in \Lambda_0$ solve $VI(F, \Lambda_0)$; consequently $\|x^R\| \leq R$. That is, we have

$$\left[F\left(x^R\right)\right]^T \left(x - x^R\right) \geq 0 \quad \forall x \in \Lambda_0 \tag{7.113}$$

For $x^0 \in \Lambda_0$, the last result yields

$$\left[F\left(x^R\right)\right]^T \left(x^0 - x^R\right) \geq 0 \tag{7.114}$$

which may be restated as

$$\left[F\left(x^R\right)\right]^T \left(x^R - x^0\right) \leq 0 \tag{7.115}$$

If in (7.112), one sets $x = x^R \in \Lambda_0$, then

$$\left[F\left(x^R\right)\right]^T \left(x^R - x^0\right) > 0 \quad \text{for} \quad \left\|x^R\right\| = R \tag{7.116}$$

By virtue of the fact $x^R \in \Lambda_0$, we know $x^R \in N_R(0)$ and $\|x^R\| \leq R$. However, (7.115) and (7.116) are mutually contradictory; hence $\|x^R\| \neq R$. Therefore $\|x^R\| < R$, and by Theorem 7.13 we are assured that $VI(F, \Lambda)$ has a solution. ■

Lemma 7.4 *(Implications of strong monotonicity) A strongly monotonically increasing operator is coercive as well as strictly monotonically increasing.*

Proof. We leave the proof of this result as an exercise for the reader. ■

Theorem 7.15 *(Variational inequality existence for strongly monotone operators) The variational inequality $VI(F, \Lambda)$ has exactly one solution if $F(x)$ is strongly monotonically increasing on Λ.*

Proof. The given strong monotonicity of $F(x)$ assures, by Lemma 7.4, that $F(x)$ is both strictly monotone and coercive. Hence, by Theorem 7.10 a solution of $VI(F, \Lambda)$ exists; by Theorem 7.11 that solution is unique. ■

7.11 Sensitivity Analysis of Variational Inequalities

In this section we are interested in sensitivity analysis of perturbed variational inequalities obeying the following definition:

Definition 7.14 (Perturbed variational inequality) Given a vector of exogenous parameter perturbations $\xi \in \Re^s$, a function $h(x^*; \xi) : \Re^n \longrightarrow \Re^q$, a function $g(x^*; \xi) : \Re^n \longrightarrow \Re^m$, a function $F(x; \xi) : \Lambda \longrightarrow \Re^n$ and the feasible set

$$\Lambda(\xi) = \{x \in \Re^n : h(x^*, \xi) = 0, g(x^*, \xi) \leq 0\}, \tag{7.117}$$

the perturbed variational inequality problem $VI(F, \Lambda;\xi)$ is to find a vector y such that

$$\left.\begin{array}{r} y \in \Lambda(\xi) \\ \left[F(y;\xi)\right]^T (x-y) \geq 0 \quad \forall\, x \in \Lambda \end{array}\right\} VI(F,\Lambda;\xi) \tag{7.118}$$

It is a simple matter to generalize the theory of sensitivity analysis of nonlinear programs presented in Chap. 2 to address $VI(F, \Lambda; \xi)$ by noting that (7.118) is equivalent to

$$\left.\begin{array}{r} \min\, [F(y;\xi)]^T x \\ \text{subject to} \quad x \in \Lambda(\xi) \end{array}\right\} MP\left([F(y;\xi)]^T x, \Lambda; \xi\right) \tag{7.119}$$

where y solves $VI(F, \Lambda; \xi)$. Note that when $\xi = 0$ the Lagrangian for (7.119) is

$$L_1(x^*, \mu^*, v^*, 0) = \sum_{i=1}^{n} F_i(y;0)x_i + \sum_{i=1}^{m} \pi_i^* g_i(x^*, 0) + \sum_{j=1}^{q} \mu_j^* h_j(x^*, 0)$$

Therefore, the second-order sufficient conditions for $MP\left([F(y;\xi)]^T x, \Lambda; \xi\right)$ are

$$y^T \left[\nabla^2 L_1(x^*, \mu^*, v^*, 0)\right] y > 0 \tag{7.120}$$

for all $z \neq 0$ such that

$$[\nabla g_i(x^*, 0)]^T z \leq 0 \quad \text{for all } i \in I^* \tag{7.121}$$

$$[\nabla g_i(x^*, 0)]^T z = 0 \quad \text{for all } i \in J^* \tag{7.122}$$

$$[\nabla h_i(x^*, 0)]^T z = 0 \quad \text{for all } i \in [1, q] \tag{7.123}$$

where

$$I^* = \{i : g_i(x^*, 0) = 0\}$$

$$J^* = \{i : \mu_i^* > 0\}$$

We are now able to state the following result:

Theorem 7.16 *(Sensitivity analysis of the perturbed variational inequality $VI(F, \Lambda; \xi)$) Suppose that in a neighborhood of $(x^*, \xi = 0)$: (i) The functions F, g and h defining $VI(F, \Lambda; \xi)$ are such that F is once continuously differentiable with respect to x, while g and h are twice continuously differentiable with respect to x; F as well as the gradients of g and h with respect to x are once continuously differentiable with respect to ξ; and the constraint functions g and h are themselves once continuously differentiable with respect to ξ. (ii) The* *second-order sufficient conditions (7.120) for a local solution of* $VI(F, \Lambda; 0)$ *hold at* (x^*, μ^*, v^*). *(iii) The gradients* $\nabla g_i(x^*, 0)$ *for all* $i \in I^* = \{i : g_i(x^*, 0) = 0\}$ *are linearly independent, while the gradients* $\nabla h_i(x^*, 0)$ *for all* $i \in [1, q]$ *are also linearly independent. And (iv) the strict complementary slackness condition*

$$\mu_i^* > 0 \text{ when } g_i(x^*, 0) = 0 \tag{7.124}$$

is satisfied. Then the following results obtain:

(1) The point x^* *is a local isolated solution of* $VI(F, \Lambda; 0)$ *and the associated multipliers* $\mu^*(0) \in \Re_+^m$ *and* $v^*(0) \in \Re^q$ *are unique.*

(2) For ξ *near zero, there exists a unique once continuously differentiable function*

$$y(\xi) = \begin{pmatrix} x(\xi) \\ \pi(\xi) \\ \mu(\xi) \end{pmatrix} \tag{7.125}$$

satisfying the second-order sufficient conditions (7.120) such that $x(\xi)$ *is a locally unique solution of* $VI(F, \Lambda; \xi)$ *for which* $\pi(\xi)$ *and* $\mu(\xi)$ *are unique multipliers associated with it. Moreover*

$$y(0) = \begin{pmatrix} x^* \\ \pi^* \\ \mu^* \end{pmatrix}$$

Furthermore, a first-order differential approximation of $y(\xi)$ *is given by*

$$y(\xi) = \begin{pmatrix} x^* \\ \pi^* \\ \mu^* \end{pmatrix} + [J_y(0)]^{-1}\left[-J_\xi^*(0)\right]\xi \tag{7.126}$$

where J_y *is the Jacobian with respect to* y *and* J_ξ *is the Jacobian with respect to* ξ *of the Kuhn-Tucker system*

$$F(x^*, \xi) + \sum_{i=1}^{m} \pi_i^* \nabla g_i(x^*) + \sum_{j=1}^{q} \mu_j^* \nabla h_j(x^*) = 0 \tag{7.127}$$

$$\pi^{*T} g(x^*, \xi) = 0 \tag{7.128}$$

$$h(x^*, \xi) = 0 \tag{7.129}$$

(3) For ξ *near zero, the set of binding inequality constraints is unchanged, strict complementary slackness holds, and the gradients of binding constraints are linearly independent at* $x(\xi)$.

Proof. This result is a trivial extension of the sensitivity analysis results presented in Chap. 2. ■

7.12 Diagonalization Algorithms

Since Nash and many Nash-like equilibria may be articulated as variational inequalities, we focus in this section on algorithms for variational inequalities. On the surface, it would appear that variational inequalities can be solved by reformulating them as mathematical programs using Lemma 7.1. However, that result depends on the introduction of an objective function that involves a line integral. Line integrals are not generally single-valued; in fact, their value typically depends on the path of integration one employs. As this is a somewhat subtle point, an example is warranted. Consider the line integral

$$I = \oint_{(a_1,a_2)}^{(b_1,b_2)} [F(x)]^T dx \tag{7.130}$$

for which $x \in \Re^2$ and $F : \Re^2 \longrightarrow \Re^2$. In summation notation we write

$$I = \sum_{i=1}^{2} \int_{a_i}^{b_i} F_i(x_1, x_2)\, dx_i \tag{7.131}$$

Let

$$F_1(x_1, x_2) = x_1 + 2x_2$$

$$F_2(x_1, x_2) = x_1 + x_2$$

$$a_1 = a_2 = 0$$

$$b_1 = b_2 = 1$$

and consider two distinct paths of integration:

Path	1st segment	2nd segment
1	$x_1 = 0, x_2 \in [0,1]$	$x_1 \in [0,1], x_2 = 1$
2	$x_1 \in [0,1], x_2 = 0$	$x_1 = 1, x_2 \in [0,1]$

For path 1 we have

$$\begin{aligned} I &= \int_0^1 F_2(0, x_2)\, dx_2 + \int_0^1 F_1(x_1, 1)\, dx_1 \\ &= \int_0^1 x_2 dx_2 + \int_0^1 (x_1 + 2)\, dx_1 = 3 \end{aligned} \tag{7.132}$$

For path 2 we have

$$I = \int_0^1 F_1(x_1, 0)\, dx_1 + \int_0^1 F_2(1, x_2)\, dx_2$$
$$= \int_0^1 x_1 dx_1 + \int_0^1 (1 + x_2)\, dx_2 = 2 \tag{7.133}$$

Evidently the value of this line integral depends on the path of integration. In fact, it is well known that a line integral

$$I = \oint_a^b F(x)dx = \sum_{i=1}^{n} \int_{a_i}^{b_i} F_i(x_1, x_2)\, dx_i \tag{7.134}$$

where $a, b, x \in \Re^n$ and $F(x) : \Re^n \longrightarrow \Re^n$ has a value independent of the path of integration if and only if

$$\frac{\partial F_i}{\partial x_j} = \frac{\partial F_j}{\partial x_i} \quad \forall i, j \in [1, n] \tag{7.135}$$

The restrictions (7.135) are known as symmetry conditions since they make the Jacobian matrix

$$J(F) \equiv \begin{pmatrix} \frac{\partial F_1}{\partial x_1} & \cdots & \frac{\partial F_1}{\partial x_n} \\ \vdots & \ddots & \vdots \\ \frac{\partial F_n}{\partial x_1} & \cdots & \frac{\partial F_n}{\partial x_n} \end{pmatrix} \tag{7.136}$$

symmetric. It is significant that one class of functions $F(x) : \Re^n \longrightarrow \Re^n$ always leads to a symmetric $J(F)$ and thereby satisfaction of (7.135); that is, the class of functions known as *separable functions* for which each scalar component has only an own-variable dependence, which we express symbolically as

$$F_i = F_i(x_i) \quad \forall i \in [1, n] \tag{7.137}$$

By inspection we see that the Jacobian matrix for the vector function $F(x)$ whose scalar components obey (7.137) is a diagonal and therefore symmetric matrix.

7.12.1 The Diagonalization Algorithm

The algorithm we emphasize in this section is called the *diagonalization algorithm*, or *diagonalization* for short; it is a specific realization of an algorithmic philosophy referred to in the numerical analysis literature as the block Jacobi method.[3] Diagonalization is appealing for solving finite-dimensional variational

[3] See Ortega and Rheinboldt (1970) for a typology of iterative algorithms in numerical analysis.

inequalities because the resulting subproblems are all nonlinear programs that can be solved with well-understood nonlinear programming algorithms, which are often available in the form of commercial software. This fact not withstanding, diagonalization may fail to converge and its use on large-scale problems can be frustrating.

The diagonalization algorithm rests on the creation of separable functions at each iteration k of the form

$$F_i^k(x_i) \equiv F_i\left(x_i, x_j = x_j^k \ \ \forall\, j \neq i\right) \tag{7.138}$$

Evidently the functions $F_i^k(x_i)$ are separable by construction, so that the Jacobian of $F^k = (\ldots, F_i^k, \ldots)$ is diagonal; hence, the name of the method. The diagonalization algorithm may be stated as follows:

Diagonalization Algorithm for $VI(F,\Lambda)$

Step 0. *(Initialization)* Determine an initial feasible solution $x^0 \in \Lambda$ and set $k = 0$.

Step 1. *(Solve diagonalized variational inequality)* Form the separable functions $F_i^k(x_i)$ for all $i \in [1,n]$ and solve the associated diagonalized variational inequality problem. That is, find $x^{k+1} \in \Lambda$ such that

$$\sum_{i=1}^{n} F_i^k(x_i^{k+1})(x_i - x_i^{k+1}) \geq 0 \quad \forall x \in \Lambda \tag{7.139}$$

Step 2. *(Stopping test and updating)* For $\eta \in \Re^1_{++}$, a preset tolerance, if

$$\max_{i\in[1,n]} |x_i^{k+1} - x_i^k| < \eta$$

stop; otherwise set $k = k+1$ and go to Step 1.

Note that the variational inequalities of Step 1 of the above algorithm may be solved using the nonlinear program

$$\min Z_k\left(x\right) = \sum_i \int_0^{x_i} F_i^k(z_i)dz_i \quad \text{subject to} \quad x \in \Lambda\ , \tag{7.140}$$

where the z_i are dummy variables of integration, provided Λ is a convex set, and each $Z_k(x)$ is a convex function. Under such circumstances, we may invoke Lemma 7.1 since the integral in (7.140) is an ordinary integral, not a line integral. That is, no symmetry restrictions need be imposed because the functions $F_i^k(\cdot)$ are separable. Thus, the diagonalization algorithm may be implemented by solving well-defined mathematical programs.

7.12.2 Convergence of Diagonalization

Global convergence of the diagonalization method may be proven if one invokes relatively strong regularity conditions. In fact, Pang and Chan (1982), Dafermos (1983), and Hammond (1984) give such global proofs of convergence. The principal requirement for global convergence is that of diagonal dominance for the Jacobian $\nabla F(x^*)$. Although the diagonalization method may converge when the available global convergence criteria are violated, examples of nonconvergence are also known and the method must be used with great caution. Pang and Chan (1982) also offer a proof of local convergence, applicable when the starting solution is not too far from x^*, a solution of $VI\,(F,\Gamma)$. That result is the following:

Theorem 7.17 *(Convergence of diagonalization) Let D and B denote, respectively, the diagonal and off-diagonal portions of $\nabla F(x^*)$. If x^* is a solution of $VI\,(F,\Gamma)$ and*

(1) *Γ is convex*

(2) *$F\,(x)$ is differentiable $\forall x \in \Gamma$*

(3) *$F\,(x)$ is continuously differentiable in a neighborhood of x^**

(4) $\dfrac{\partial F_i\,(x)}{\partial x_i} \geq 0 \;\; \forall\, i \in [1,n]\,,\; x \in \Gamma$

(5) $\dfrac{\partial F_i(x^*)}{\partial x_i} > 0 \;\; \forall\, i \in [1,n]$

(6) $\| D^{-1/2} B D^{-1/2} \| < 1,$

then, provided that the initial vector x^0 is chosen in a suitable neighborhood of x^*, the diagonalization algorithm will converge to x^*.

Proof. The proof is tedious; see Pang and Chan (1982) for the details. ∎

7.12.3 A Nonnetwork Example of Diagonalization

In this section we consider an example given originally by Tobin (1986). In particular, we study the following variational inequality: find $(x_1^*, x_2^*)^T \in \Gamma$ such that

$$F_1\,(x_1^*, x_2^*)\,(x_1 - x_1^*) + F_2\,(x_2^*, x_2^*)\,(x_2 - x_2^*) \geq 0 \quad \forall\,(x_1, x_2)^T \in \Gamma \qquad (7.141)$$

where

$$\Gamma = \left\{ (x_1, x_2)^T : g_1\,(x_1, x_2) \leq 0, g_2\,(x_1, x_2) \leq 0, g_3\,(x_1, x_2) \leq 0 \right\}$$

and

$$F_1(x_1,x_2) = x_1 - 5$$

$$F_2(x_1,x_2) = 0.1x_1x_2 + x_2 - 5$$

$$g_1(x_1,x_2) = -x_1 \leq 0 \quad (\lambda_1)$$

$$g_2(x_1,x_2) = -x_2 \leq 0 \quad (\lambda_2)$$

$$g_3(x_1,x_2) = x_1 + x_2 - 1 \leq 0 \quad (\lambda_3)$$

By inspection, the Jacobian

$$[\nabla F(x_1,x_2)]^T = \begin{pmatrix} \dfrac{\partial F_1}{\partial x_1} & \dfrac{\partial F_2}{\partial x_1} \\ \\ \dfrac{\partial F_1}{\partial x_2} & \dfrac{\partial F_2}{\partial x_2} \end{pmatrix}^T = \begin{pmatrix} 1 & 0.1x_2 \\ 0 & 0.1x_1 + 1 \end{pmatrix} \tag{7.142}$$

is asymmetric and, consequently, we cannot construct an equivalent optimization problem with a single-valued objective function. In particular, we note that an equivalent optimization problem must have as an objective the line integral

$$Z = \oint_{(0,0)}^{(x_1,x_2)} [F(z)]^T dz \tag{7.143}$$

We diagonalize by constructing

$$F_1^k(x_1) \equiv F_1\left(x_1, x_2^k\right) = x_1 - 5 \tag{7.144}$$

$$F_2^k(x_2) \equiv F_2\left(x_1^k, x_2\right) = \left(0.1x_1^k + 1\right) x_2 - 5 \tag{7.145}$$

where $\left(x_1^k, x_2^k\right)^T \in \Gamma$ is the current approximate solution. Thus, the mathematical program solved at iteration $(k+1)$ has the objective

$$\left.\begin{aligned} \min Z^k &= \int_0^{x_1} F_1^k(z_1)\, dz_1 + \int_0^{x_2} F_2^k(z_2)\, dz_2 \\ &= \int_0^{x_1} (z_1 - 5)\, dz_1 + \int_0^{x_2} \left[\left(0.1x_1^k + 1\right) z_2 - 5\right] dz_2 \\ &= \frac{1}{2}(x_1)^2 - 5x_1 + \frac{1}{2}\left(0.1x_1^k + 1\right)(x_2)^2 - 5x_2 \\ \text{subject to} \quad & \\ (x_1,x_2)^T &\in \Gamma \end{aligned}\right\} \tag{7.146}$$

We denote the solution of the diagonalized subproblem (7.146) by $\left(x_1^{k+1}, x_2^{k+1}\right)^T$, which of course satisfies the Kuhn-Tucker conditions:

$$\frac{\partial Z^k}{\partial x_1} + \lambda_1 \frac{\partial g_1}{\partial x_1} + \lambda_2 \frac{\partial g_2}{\partial x_1} + \lambda_3 \frac{\partial g_3}{\partial x_1} = x_1 - 5 - \lambda_1 + \lambda_3 = 0 \tag{7.147}$$

$$\frac{\partial Z^k}{\partial x_2} + \lambda_1 \frac{\partial g_1}{\partial x_2} + \lambda_2 \frac{\partial g_2}{\partial x_2} + \lambda_3 \frac{\partial g_3}{\partial x_2} = \left(0.1 x_1^k + 1\right) x_2 - 5 - \lambda_2 + \lambda_3 = 0 \tag{7.148}$$

$$\lambda_1 x_1 = 0 \tag{7.149}$$

$$\lambda_2 x_2 = 0 \tag{7.150}$$

$$\lambda_3 \left(x_1 + x_2 - 1\right) = 0 \tag{7.151}$$

$$\lambda_1, \lambda_2, \lambda_3 \geq 0 \tag{7.152}$$

Assuming a primal solution is in the first quadrant and that $g_3\left(x_1, x_2\right)$ binds at optimality, as is easily verified by graphical solution of (7.146), these conditions reduce to

$$x_1 + \lambda_3 = 5$$

$$\left(0.1 x_1^k + 1\right) x_2 + \lambda_3 = 5$$

$$x_1 + x_2 = 1$$

$$\lambda_1 = \lambda_2 = 0$$

which yield the convenient formulae

$$x_1 = \frac{x_1^k + 10}{x_1^k + 20} \tag{7.153}$$

$$x_2 = \frac{10}{x_1^k + 20} \tag{7.154}$$

$$\lambda_1 = \lambda_2 = 0 \tag{7.155}$$

$$\lambda_3 = 2 \frac{2 x_1^k + 45}{x_1^k + 20} \tag{7.156}$$

It must be noted that generally the mathematical programming subproblems resulting from diagonalization are not this simple and one must select an appropriate numerical algorithm for their solution.

With the results developed above, we can describe the iterations of the diagonalization algorithm:

Step 0. *Initialization* Pick $\left(x_1^0, x_2^0\right)^T = (1, 0)^T$ and set $k = 0$.

Step 1. *Solve diagonalized variational inequality* $(k = 0)$ Solve the diagonalized variational inequality using (7.153) and (7.154) to find:

$$\begin{pmatrix} x_1^1 \\ x_2^1 \end{pmatrix} = \begin{pmatrix} \frac{x_1^0+10}{x_1^0+20} \\ \frac{10}{x_1^0+20} \end{pmatrix} = \begin{pmatrix} \frac{11}{21} \\ \frac{10}{21} \end{pmatrix} = \begin{matrix} 0.52381 \\ 0.47619 \end{matrix}$$

Step 2. *Updating* $(k = 0)$ Set $k = 0 + 1 = 1$.

Step 1. *Solve diagonalized variational inequality* $(k = 1)$ Solve the diagonalized variational inequality using (7.153) and (7.154) to find:

$$\begin{pmatrix} x_1^2 \\ x_2^2 \end{pmatrix} = \begin{pmatrix} \frac{x_1^1+10}{x_1^1+20} \\ \frac{10}{x_1^1+20} \end{pmatrix} = \begin{pmatrix} \frac{0.52381+10}{0.52381+20} \\ \frac{10}{0.52381+20} \end{pmatrix} = \begin{pmatrix} 0.51276 \\ 0.48724 \end{pmatrix}$$

Step 2. *Stopping test and updating* $(k = 1)$ Set $k = 1 + 1 = 2$.

Step 1. *Solve diagonalized variational inequality* $(k = 2)$ Solve the diagonalized variational inequality using (7.153) to find:

$$\begin{pmatrix} x_1^3 \\ x_2^3 \end{pmatrix} = \begin{pmatrix} \frac{x_1^2+10}{x_1^2+20} \\ \frac{10}{x_1^2+20} \end{pmatrix} = \begin{pmatrix} \frac{0.51276+10}{0.51276+20} \\ \frac{10}{0.51276+20} \end{pmatrix} = \begin{pmatrix} 0.5125 \\ 0.4875 \end{pmatrix}$$

Step 2. *Stopping test and updating* $(k = 2)$ Assuming a stopping tolerance $\eta = 0.001$, we see that

$$\max_{i \in [1,2]} \left| x_i^3 - x_i^2 \right| = \max \left\{ |0.51276 - 0.5125| , |0.48724 - 0.4875| \right\}$$

$$= 0.000\,26 < 0.001 \tag{7.157}$$

$$\Longrightarrow \begin{pmatrix} x_1^* \\ x_2^* \end{pmatrix} \approx \begin{pmatrix} x_1^3 \\ x_2^3 \end{pmatrix} = \begin{pmatrix} 0.5125 \\ 0.4875 \end{pmatrix} \tag{7.158}$$

Note also that the dual variables associated with solution (7.158) are

$$\lambda_1^* = \lambda_2^* = 0 \tag{7.159}$$

$$\lambda_3^* = 2\frac{2x_1^* + 45}{x_1^* + 20} = 2\frac{2\,(0.5125) + 45}{(0.5125) + 20} = 4.\,4875 \tag{7.160}$$

By inspection, the inequality constraint functions are linearly independent and convex. Consequently, the Kuhn-Tucker conditions for this variational inequality are necessary and sufficient, so that any solution to

$$F_j\left(x_1^*, x_2^*\right) + \sum_{i=1}^{3} \lambda_i \frac{\partial g_i\left(x_1^*, x_2^*\right)}{\partial x_i} = 0 \quad j = 1, 2 \tag{7.161}$$

$$\lambda_i g_i\left(x_1^*, x_2^*\right) = 0 \quad i = 1, 2, 3 \tag{7.162}$$

$$\lambda_i \geq 0 \quad i = 1, 2, 3 \tag{7.163}$$

is the desired global solution. These conditions yield

$$x_1^* - 5 - \lambda_1^* + \lambda_3^* = 0 \tag{7.164}$$

$$0.1x_1^* x_2^* + x_2^* - 5 - \lambda_2^* + \lambda_3^* = 0 \tag{7.165}$$

$$\lambda_1^* x_1^* = 0 \tag{7.166}$$

$$\lambda_2^* x_2^* = 0 \tag{7.167}$$

$$\lambda_3^* \left(x_1^* + x_2^* - 1\right) = 0 \tag{7.168}$$

$$\lambda_1^*, \lambda_2^*, \lambda_3^* \geq 0 \tag{7.169}$$

which are subtly different than conditions (7.147)–(7.152). In fact, (7.166)–(7.169) are seen by inspection to be satisfied and (7.164) and (7.165) give

$$x_1^* - 5 - \lambda_1^* + \lambda_3^* = 0.5125 - 5 - 0 + 4.4875 = 0.0000$$

$$0.1x_1^* x_2^* + x_2^* - 5 - \lambda_2^* + \lambda_3^* = 0.1\left(0.5125\right)\left(0.4875\right) + 0.4875 - 5 - 0 + 4.4875$$

$$= -1.5625 \times 10^{-5}$$

That is, the variational inequality Kuhn-Tucker conditions are approximately satisfied by our solution obtained from the diagonalization algorithm.

Next imagine that the function $F_2\left(x_1, x_2\right) = 0.1x_1x_2 + x_2 - 5$ is perturbed according to

$$F_2\left(x_1, x_2; \xi\right) = \left(0.1 + \xi\right) x_1 x_2 + x_2 - 5 \tag{7.170}$$

where now $\xi \in \Re^1$. To apply the sensitivity analysis results derived in Sect. 7.11, we employ the Kuhn-Tucker system for the perturbed problem:

$$x_1 - 5 - \lambda_1 + \lambda_3 = 0 \tag{7.171}$$

$$\left(0.1 + \xi\right) x_1 x_2 + x_2 - 5 - \lambda_2 + \lambda_3 = 0 \tag{7.172}$$

$$\lambda_1 x_1 = 0 \tag{7.173}$$

$$\lambda_2 x_2 = 0 \tag{7.174}$$

$$\lambda_3 \left(x_1 + x_2 - 1\right) = 0 \tag{7.175}$$

where, of course, $\lambda_1, \lambda_2, \lambda_3 \geq 0$. The relevant Jacobians of this system are

$$J_y(\xi) = \begin{pmatrix} 1 & 0 & -1 & 0 & 1 \\ (0.1+\xi)\,x_2 & (0.1+\xi)\,x_1 & 0 & -1 & 1 \\ \lambda_1 & 0 & x_1 & 0 & 0 \\ 0 & \lambda_2 & 0 & x_2 & 0 \\ \lambda_3 & \lambda_3 & 0 & 0 & x_1+x_2-1 \end{pmatrix}$$

$$J_\xi^*(\xi) = \begin{pmatrix} 0 \\ x_1 x_2 \\ 0 \\ 0 \\ 0 \end{pmatrix}$$

where

$$y = \begin{pmatrix} x_1 & x_2 & \lambda_1 & \lambda_2 & \lambda_3 \end{pmatrix}^T$$

Consequently

$$\begin{bmatrix} x_1(\xi) \\ x_2(\xi) \\ \lambda_1(\xi) \\ \lambda_2(\xi) \\ \lambda_3(\xi) \end{bmatrix} = \begin{bmatrix} x_1(0) \\ x_2(0) \\ \lambda_1(0) \\ \lambda_2(0) \\ \lambda_3(0) \end{bmatrix} + \left[J_y(0)\right]^{-1}\left[-J_\xi^*(0)\right]\xi$$

$$= \begin{pmatrix} x_1^* \\ x_2^* \\ \lambda_1^* \\ \lambda_2^* \\ \lambda_3^* \end{pmatrix} - \begin{pmatrix} 1 & 0 & -1 & 0 & 1 \\ (0.1+\xi)\,x_2^* & (0.1+\xi)\,x_1^* & 0 & -1 & 1 \\ \lambda_1^* & 0 & x_1^* & 0 & 0 \\ 0 & \lambda_2^* & 0 & x_2^* & 0 \\ \lambda_3^* & \lambda_3^* & 0 & 0 & x_1^*+x_2^*-1 \end{pmatrix}^{-1} \begin{pmatrix} 0 \\ x_1^* x_2^* \\ 0 \\ 0 \\ 0 \end{pmatrix} \xi$$

$$= \begin{pmatrix} 0.5125 + 1.4006 \times 10^9 \frac{\xi}{5.6199\times10^9+1.4015\times10^8\xi} \\ 0.4875 - 1.4006 \times 10^9 \frac{\xi}{5.6199\times10^9+1.4015\times10^8\xi} \\ 0 \\ 0 \\ 4.4875 - 1.4006 \times 10^9 \frac{\xi}{5.6199\times10^9+1.4015\times10^8\xi} \end{pmatrix} \tag{7.176}$$

Use of (7.176) leads to the following table of results:

Perturb. ξ	Exact $x_1^*(\xi)$	1st order $x_1(\xi)$	Exact $x_2^*(\xi)$	1st order $x_2(\xi)$	Exact $\lambda_3^*(\xi)$	1st order $\lambda_3(\xi)$
0.00	0.5125	0.5125	0.4875	0.4875	4.4875	4.4875
0.01	0.5137	0.5150	0.4863	0.4850	4.4863	4.4850
0.05	0.5187	0.5250	0.4813	0.4751	4.4813	4.4751
0.10	0.5249	0.5374	0.4751	0.4626	4.4751	4.4626
0.15	0.5311	0.5497	0.4689	0.4503	4.4689	4.4503

Note that in the table we have used the notation $x_1^*(\xi)$, $x_2^*(\xi)$, and $\lambda_3^*(\xi)$ to denote the so-called exact solutions of the perturbed problem, and the notation $x_1(\xi)$, $x_2(\xi)$, and $\lambda_3(\xi)$ to denote the first-order approximate solutions found using sensitivity analysis. The exact solutions were found using separate software and are included for comparison. Even for rather large perturbations, the first-order approximations stemming from the sensitivity analysis are quite good. This accuracy for large perturbations, although not guaranteed, is not uncommon for the sensitivity analysis theory we have presented.

7.13 Gap Function Methods for $VI(F,\Lambda)$

There is a special class of functions associated with variational inequality problems, so-called gap functions, which forms the foundation of a family of algorithms that are sometimes very effective for solving $VI(F,\Lambda)$. A gap function has two important and advantageous properties: (1) it is always nonnegative and (2) it has zero value if and only if a solution of the corresponding variational inequality has been achieved.

7.13.1 Gap Function Defined

Formally, we define a gap function for $VI(F,\Lambda)$ as follows:

Definition 7.15 (Gap function) A function $\zeta : \Lambda \subseteq \Re^n \longrightarrow \Re_+^1$ is called a gap function for $VI(F,\Lambda)$ when the following statements hold:

(1) $\zeta(y) \geq 0$ for all $y \in \Lambda$

(2) $\zeta(y) = 0$ if and only if y is a solution of $VI(F,\Lambda)$

Clearly, a gap function with the properties of Definition 7.15 allows us to re-formulate $VI(F,\Lambda)$ as an optimization problem, namely as

$$\min_{y\in\Lambda} \zeta(y) \tag{7.177}$$

An optimal solution of (7.177) solves $VI(F,\Lambda)$ provided $\zeta(y)$ may be driven to zero.

7.13.2 The Auslender Gap Function

In considering the gap function due to Auslender (1976), it is convenient to define

$$\Phi(y) \equiv \left\{ \arg\min_{x\in\Lambda} \left[F(y)\right]^T x \right\} \subseteq \Lambda \tag{7.178}$$

In terms of (7.178), the Auslender gap function associated with $VI(F,\Lambda)$ is

$$\zeta(y) = \max_{x\in\Lambda} \left[F(y)\right]^T (y-x) \tag{7.179}$$

$$= \left[F(y)\right]^T (y-x) \quad \text{for any } x \in \Phi(y) \tag{7.180}$$

Furthermore, $y^* \in \Lambda$ is a solution of $VI(F,\Lambda)$ if and only if $\zeta(y^*) = 0$. It is also true that $\zeta(y)$ is nonnegative on the feasible set Λ, as we shall shortly demonstrate. Hence, $VI(F,\Lambda)$ is solved by solving the convex program

$$\min \zeta(y) \quad \text{subject to} \quad y \in \Lambda \tag{7.181}$$

In fact the Auslender gap function is the subject of the following result:

Theorem 7.18 *(Auslender's gap function) The function*

$$\zeta(y) = \max_{x\in\Lambda} \langle F(y), y-x \rangle \tag{7.182}$$

is a gap function for $VI(F,\Lambda)$, where Λ is convex.

Proof. The proof is in two parts:

(i) $[\zeta(y) \geq 0]$ To establish Property 1 of Definition 7.15, we observe that, when Λ is convex, a necessary and sufficient condition for $x \in \Lambda$ to solve (7.182) is

$$\left[F(z)\right]^T (z-x) \geq 0 \qquad \forall z \in \Lambda \tag{7.183}$$

Picking $z = y$, it is immediate that $\zeta(y)$ is a nonnegative function of y.

(ii) $[\zeta(y) = 0 \Longleftrightarrow VI(F,\Lambda)]$ If $y \in \Lambda$ solves $VI(F,\Lambda)$ then

$$\left[F(y)\right]^T (x-y) \geq 0 \qquad \forall x \in \Lambda$$

or

$$\left[F(y)\right]^T (y-x) \leq 0 \qquad \forall x \in \Lambda \tag{7.184}$$

Comparing (7.184) to (7.182) assures $\zeta(y) = 0$, which is one of the requirements of Property 2. To show $\zeta(y) = 0$ assures y solves $VI(F,\Lambda)$, let us assume it does not; that is, we assume there exists $x \in \Lambda$ such that

$$\left[F(y)\right]^T (y-x) > 0 \tag{7.185}$$

However, (7.185) means that $\zeta(y) = 0$ cannot be the result of solving (7.182), which is a contradiction; therefore $\zeta(y) = 0$ assures y solves $VI(F,\Lambda)$, and Property 2 is demonstrated. ∎

For the Auslender gap function, we may rewrite (7.177) as

$$\min_{y\in\Lambda} \zeta(y) = \min_{y\in\Lambda} \max_{x\in\Lambda} \langle F(y), y-x\rangle$$
$$= \min_{y\in\Lambda} \left\{ \langle F(y), y\rangle + \max_{x\in\Lambda} \langle F(y), -x\rangle \right\} \tag{7.186}$$

a format that reveals the underlying min-max nature of the gap function perspective for solving variational inequalities. Note further that the Auslender gap function $\zeta(y)$ is not in general differentiable, even if F is differentiable.

7.13.3 Fukushima-Auchmuty Gap Functions

Auchmuty (1989) and Fukushima (1992) independently suggested a class of differentiable gap functions of the form

$$\zeta_\alpha(y) = \max_{x\in\Lambda} \left\{ \langle F(y), y-x\rangle - \frac{\alpha}{2}\|y-x\|^2 \right\} \tag{7.187}$$

for $\alpha \in \Re^1_{++}$. Function (7.187) is differentiable whenever F is differentiable. In particular, because

$$\|y-x\|^2 = (y-x)^T (y-x) \equiv (y-x)^2,$$

the gradient of (7.187) with respect to y is given by

$$\nabla\zeta_\alpha(y) = F(y) + \langle \nabla F(y), y-x_\alpha\rangle - \alpha(y-x_\alpha)$$

where x_α denotes the unique maximizer of (7.187). The differentiability of (7.187) is due to the uniqueness and realized finiteness of x_α, which occurs because the objective function on the right-hand side of (7.187) is strongly convex in x.

Wu et al. (1993) proposed the following generalization of the Fukushima-Auchmuty gap function(7.187) :

$$\zeta_\alpha(y) = \max_{x\in\Lambda} \{\langle F(y), y-x\rangle - \alpha\phi(y,x)\} \tag{7.188}$$

In (7.188) ϕ is a function that satisfies the following conditions:

(1) ϕ is continuously differentiable on $\Re^{2n}$;

(2) ϕ is nonnegative on $\Re^{2n}$;

(3) $\phi(y,\cdot)$ is strongly convex for any $y \in \Re^n$; and

(4) $\phi(y,x) = 0$ if and only if $y = x$.

If (7.188) is a gap function, it gives rise to the following constrained mathematical program

$$\min_{y \in \Lambda} \zeta_\alpha(y)$$

which is equivalent to $VI(F, \Lambda)$ provided $\zeta_\alpha(y)$ may be driven to zero. That is, we are now ready to state and prove the following result:

Theorem 7.19 *(Fukushima-Auchmuty gap function) The function (7.188) is a gap function for $VI(F, \Lambda)$ where Λ is convex.*

Proof. The proof is in two parts:

(i) $[\zeta_\alpha(y) \geq 0]$ To establish Property 1 of Definition 7.15, we observe that (7.188) is equivalent to

$$\min_{x \in \Lambda} [F(y)]^T x + \alpha\phi(y, x) \tag{7.189}$$

Strong convexity of $\phi(y, \cdot)$ assures that the maximum in (7.188) and the minimum in (7.189) are bounded away from zero and may actually be attained. Furthermore, (7.189) has the necessary and sufficient condition

$$[F(y) + \alpha\nabla_x\phi(y, x)]^T (z - x) \geq 0 \qquad \forall z \in \Lambda$$

which upon picking $z = y$ becomes

$$[F(y)]^T (y - x) + \alpha [\nabla_x\phi(y, x)]^T (y - x) \geq 0 \qquad \forall z \in \Lambda \tag{7.190}$$

Because $\phi(y, \cdot)$ is strongly convex it is also convex so that

$$\phi(y, z) \geq \phi(y, x) + [\nabla_x\phi(y, x)]^T (y - x) \; \forall z \in \Lambda$$

Taking $z = y$ in the last expression and noting that by the given $\phi(y, y) = 0$, we have

$$-\phi(y, x) \geq [\nabla_x\phi(y, x)]^T (y - x) \tag{7.191}$$

It is immediate from (7.190) and (7.191) that

$$\zeta_\alpha(y) = [F(y)]^T (y - x) - \alpha\phi(y, x) \geq 0 \qquad \forall z \in \Lambda \tag{7.192}$$

(ii) $[\zeta_\alpha(y) = 0 \iff VI(F, \Lambda)]$ If $y \in \Lambda$ solves $VI(F, \Lambda)$ then

$$[F(y)]^T (x - y) \geq 0 \qquad \forall x \in \Lambda$$

or

$$[F(y)]^T (y - x) \leq 0 \qquad \forall x \in \Lambda \tag{7.193}$$

So because $\phi(y, x) \geq 0$ we have

$$[F(y)]^T (y - x) - \alpha\phi(y, x) \leq 0 \qquad \forall x \in \Lambda \tag{7.194}$$

Comparing (7.194) and (7.192) assures $\zeta_\alpha(y) = 0$. On the other hand if $\zeta_\alpha(y) = 0$, then

$$[F(y)]^T (y - x) \geq [F(y)]^T (y - x) - \alpha\phi(y, x) = 0$$

which assures y solves $VI(F, \Lambda)$. ■

7.13.4 The D-Gap Function

The gap functions introduced above all lead to equivalent constrained mathematical programs. It is reasonable to ask whether there is a gap function that leads to an equivalent unconstrained mathematical program. In fact, the so-called *D-gap function* proposed by Peng (1997) and generalized by Yamashita et al. (1997) is such a function. A D-gap function is the difference between two gap functions. The D-gap function we will consider is

$$\begin{aligned}\psi_{\alpha\beta}(y) &= \zeta_{\alpha}(y) - \zeta_{\beta}(y) \\ &= \max_{x\in\Lambda}\{\langle F(y), y-x\rangle - \alpha\phi(y,x)\} \\ &\quad - \max_{x\in\Lambda}\{\langle F(y), y-x\rangle - \beta\phi(y,x)\}\end{aligned} \tag{7.195}$$

where $0 < \alpha < \beta$ and the conditions imposed on the function $\phi(y,x)$ are the same as those given in the discussion of the Fukushima-Auchmuty gap function. The corresponding unconstrained mathematical program equivalent to $VI(F,\Lambda)$ is

$$\min_{y} \psi_{\alpha\beta}(y) \tag{7.196}$$

Moreover, the gradient of $\psi_{\alpha\beta}(y)$ is well defined. To express the gradient let us define $x_{\alpha}(y)$ and $x_{\beta}(y)$ such that

$$\max_{x\in\Lambda}\{\langle F(y), y-x\rangle - \alpha\phi(y,x)\} = \langle F(y), y-x_{\alpha}(y)\rangle - \alpha\phi(y, x_{\alpha}(y))$$

$$\max_{x\in\Lambda}\{\langle F(y), y-x\rangle - \beta\phi(y,x)\} = \langle F(y), y-x_{\beta}(y)\rangle - \beta\phi(y, x_{\beta}(y))$$

That is

$$x_{\alpha}(y) = \arg\max_{x\in\Lambda}\{\langle F(y), y-x\rangle - \alpha\phi(y,x)\}$$

$$x_{\beta}(y) = \arg\max_{x\in\Lambda}\{\langle F(y), y-x\rangle - \beta\phi(y,x)\}$$

As a consequence we may rewrite (7.195) as

$$\begin{aligned}\psi_{\alpha\beta}(y) &= \langle F(y), y-x_{\alpha}(y)\rangle - \alpha\phi(y,x_{\alpha}(y)) \\ &\quad - \langle F(y), y-x_{\beta}(y)\rangle + \beta\phi(y,x_{\beta}(y)) \\ &= \langle F(y), x_{\beta}(y)-x_{\alpha}(y)\rangle + \beta\phi(y,x_{\beta}(y)) - \alpha\phi(y,x_{\alpha}(y))\end{aligned} \tag{7.197}$$

Since $\phi(y,\cdot)$ is strongly convex in y and Λ is convex and compact, $x_{\alpha}(y)$ and $x_{\beta}(y)$ are unique and realized as vectors whose components are finite. From (7.197) the gradient of $\psi_{\alpha\beta}(y)$ is readily seen to be

$$\nabla\psi_{\alpha\beta}(y) = \nabla F(y)(x_{\beta}(y)-x_{\alpha}(y)) + \beta\nabla_{y}\phi(y,x_{\beta}(y)) - \alpha\nabla_{y}\phi(y,x_{\alpha}(y))$$

For detailed proofs of the assertions we have made concerning $\psi_{\alpha\beta}(y)$ see Yamashita et al. (1997).

7.13.5 The D-Gap Function Algorithm

Once a differentiable gap function has been formed for $VI(F, \Lambda)$, it is used to create a corresponding nonlinear program that may be solved by conventional nonlinear programming methods. This is now illustrated for the D-gap function:

D-GAP ALGORITHM FOR $VI(F, \Lambda)$

Step 0. *(Initialization)* Determine an initial feasible solution $y^0 \in \Re^n$ and set $k = 0$.

Step 1. *(Finding the steepest descent direction)* Find the gradient of the D-gap function:

$$\begin{aligned}\nabla\psi_{\alpha\beta}\left(y^k\right) = {} & \nabla F\left(y^k\right)\left(x_\beta\left(y^k\right) - x_\alpha\left(y^k\right)\right) \\ & + \beta\nabla_y\phi\left(y^k, x_\beta\left(y^k\right)\right) \\ & - \alpha\nabla_y\phi\left(y^k, x_\alpha\left(y^k\right)\right)\end{aligned}$$

where

$$x_\alpha\left(y^k\right) = \arg\max_{x\in\Lambda}\left\{\left\langle F\left(y^k\right), y^k - x\right\rangle - \alpha\phi\left(y^k, x\right)\right\}$$

$$x_\beta\left(y^k\right) = \arg\max_{x\in\Lambda}\left\{\left\langle F\left(y^k\right), y^k - x\right\rangle - \beta\phi\left(y^k, x\right)\right\}$$

Then find

$$d^k = \arg\min\left\{\left[-\nabla\psi_{\alpha\beta}\left(y^k\right)\right]^T y \quad \text{subject to} \quad \|y\| \leq 1\right\}$$

Note that the negative gradient itself may be used as a steepest descent direction so long as it has a bounded norm.

Step 2. *(Step size determination)* Find

$$\theta_k = \arg\min\left\{\psi_{\alpha\beta}\left(y^k + \theta d^k\right) \quad \text{subject to} \quad 0 \leq \theta \leq 1\right\} \tag{7.198}$$

or employ a suitably small constant step size.

Step 3. *(Stopping test and updating)* For $\varepsilon \in \Re^1_{++}$, a preset tolerance, if

$$\left\|\nabla\psi_{\alpha\beta}\left(y^k\right)\right\| < \varepsilon,$$

stop; otherwise set

$$y^{k+1} = y^k - \theta_k d^k\left(y^k\right)$$

and go to Step 1 with k replaced by $k + 1$.

7.13.6 Convergence and Numerical Example of the D-Gap Algorithm

For a numerical example of the gap function method, let us consider $VI(F,\Lambda)$ where

$$x = \begin{pmatrix} x_1 \\ x_2 \end{pmatrix}, \quad y = \begin{pmatrix} y_1 \\ y_2 \end{pmatrix}$$

$$F(x) = \begin{pmatrix} F_1(x_1,x_2) \\ F_2(x_1,x_2) \end{pmatrix} = \begin{pmatrix} x_1 - 5 \\ 0.1x_1x_2 + x_2 - 5 \end{pmatrix}$$

$$\Lambda = \{(x_1,x_2) : x_1 \geq 0, x_2 \geq 0, x_1 + x_2 - 1 \leq 0\}$$

In this example, we employ a D-gap function of the form

$$\psi_{\alpha\beta}(y) = \zeta_\alpha(y) - \zeta_\beta(y)$$

where

$$\zeta_\alpha(y) = \max_{x\in\Lambda}\left\{\langle F(y), y - x\rangle - \frac{\alpha}{2}\|y - x\|^2\right\}$$

$$\zeta_\beta(y) = \max_{x\in\Lambda}\left\{\langle F(y), y - x\rangle - \frac{\beta}{2}\|y - x\|^2\right\}$$

and $0 < \alpha < \beta$. Thereby, we have defined ϕ to be

$$\phi \equiv \frac{1}{2}\|y - x\|^2$$

Then the gradient information we need is

$$\begin{aligned}\nabla\psi_{\alpha\beta}(y) &= \nabla F(y)(x_\beta(y) - x_\alpha(y)) + \beta\nabla_y\phi(y, x_\beta(y)) - \alpha\nabla_y\phi(y, x_\alpha(y)) \\ &= \begin{pmatrix} 1 & 0 \\ 0.1y_2 & 0.1y_1 + 1 \end{pmatrix}\begin{pmatrix} x_{\beta1}(y) - x_{\alpha1}(y) \\ x_{\beta2}(y) - x_{\alpha2}(y) \end{pmatrix} + \beta\begin{pmatrix} y_1 - x_{\beta1}(y) \\ y_2 - x_{\beta2}(y) \end{pmatrix} \\ &\quad - \alpha\begin{pmatrix} y_1 - x_{\alpha1}(y) \\ y_2 - x_{\alpha2}(y) \end{pmatrix}\end{aligned}$$

which leads to

$$\nabla\psi_{\alpha\beta}(y) = \begin{pmatrix} x_{\beta1}(y) - x_{\alpha1}(y) + \beta(y_1 - x_{\beta1}(y)) - \alpha(y_1 - x_{\alpha1}(y)) \\ 0.1y_2(x_{\beta1}(y) - x_{\alpha1}(y)) + (0.1y_1 + 1)(x_{\beta2}(y) - x_{\alpha2}(y)) + K \end{pmatrix}$$

where

$$K = \beta(y_2 - x_{\beta2}(y)) - \alpha(y_2 - x_{\alpha2}(y))$$

Also

$$x_{\alpha}(y) = \arg\max_{x\in\Lambda} \{\langle F(y), y-x\rangle - \alpha\phi(y,x)\}$$

$$= \arg\max_{x\in\Lambda} \left\{ \begin{pmatrix} y_1 - 5 \\ 0.1y_1y_2 + y_2 - 5 \end{pmatrix}^T \begin{pmatrix} y_1 - x_1 \\ y_2 - x_2 \end{pmatrix} - \frac{\alpha}{2} \left\| \begin{pmatrix} y_1 - x_1 \\ y_2 - x_2 \end{pmatrix} \right\|^2 \right\}$$

$$= \arg\max_{x\in\Lambda} \{(y_1 - 5)(y_1 - x_1) + (0.1y_1y_2 + y_2 - 5)(y_2 - x_2) - A\}$$

$$x_{\beta}(y) = \arg\max_{x\in\Lambda} \{(y_1 - 5)(y_1 - x_1) + (0.1y_1y_2 + y_2 - 5)(y_2 - x_2) - B\}$$

where

$$A = \frac{1}{2}\alpha\left((x_1 - y_1)^2 + (x_2 - y_2)^2\right)$$

$$B = \frac{1}{2}\beta\left((x_1 - y_1)^2 + (x_2 - y_2)^2\right)$$

If we employ the constant step size $\theta_k = 0.5$, the following table of results is generated:

k	Gap $\psi_{\alpha\beta}(y^k)$	y^k	$x_{\alpha}(y^k)$	$x_{\beta}(y^k)$
0	0.375	$(0,0)$	$(0.5000, 0.5000)$	$(0.5000, 0.5000)$
1	2.3512×10^{-2}	$(0.3750, 0.3750)$	$(0.5141, 0.4859)$	$(0.5035, 0.4965)$
2	1.0139×10^{-4}	$(0.4750, 0.4635)$	$(0.5167, 0.4833)$	$(0.5081, 0.4919)$
3	7.005×10^{-6}	$(0.5017, 0.4826)$	$(0.5147, 0.4853)$	$(0.5108, 0.4892)$
4	4.9345×10^{-7}	$(0.5095, 0.4866)$	$(0.5133, 0.4867)$	$(0.5119, 0.4881)$
5	3.5878×10^{-8}	$(0.5117, 0.4873)$	$(0.5123, 0.4872)$	$(0.5123, 0.4877)$
6	2.7672×10^{-9}	$(0.5123, 0.4875)$	$(0.5126, 0.4874)$	$(0.5124, 0.4876)$
7	1.1008×10^{-10}	$(0.5124, 0.4875)$	$(0.5125, 0.4875)$	$(0.5125, 0.4875)$

Evidently, the algorithm terminates with a gap less than 10^{-9} and approximate solution $y = (0.5125, 0.4875)$.

7.14 Other Algorithms for $VI(F,\Lambda)$

In addition to gap function methods, there are four main classes of other methods for solving finite-dimensional variational inequalities:

(1) methods based on differential equations

(2) fixed-point methods

(3) generalized linear methods

(4) successive linearization and Lemke's algorithm.

Methods based on differential equations express the variational inequality's decision variables as functions of an independent variable t, conveniently called "time",[4] to create differential equations for trajectories that may be continuously deformed to approximate the solution of an equivalent fixed-point problem; the stationary states of these differential equations for $t \longrightarrow \infty$ generate a sequence that converges to the solution of the original variational inequality problem. Fixed-point methods exploit the relationship between variational inequalities and fixed-point problems, which enjoy an obvious iterative algorithm of the form

$$x^{k+1} = G(x^k)$$

We have already discussed some aspects of generalized linear methods in Sect. 7.12. Differential equation and fixed-point methods are discussed by Scarf (1967), Smith et al. (1997), and Zangwill and Garcia (1981). Generalized linear methods for variational inequalities are reviewed by Pang and Chan (1982), Hammond (1984), and Harker and Pang (1990).

Extensive computational experience during the last decade has produced convincing empirical evidence that a particular method is especially attractive for solving many finite-dimensional variational inequalities. This approach is based on linearization of the nonlinear complementarity formulation of a variational inequality in conjunction with an efficient linear complementarity algorithm – specifically, Lemke's method. See Cottle et al. (1992) for a discussion of algorithms for linear complementarity problems and Facchinei and Pang (2003a,b) for additional detail regarding algorithms that exploit the nonlinear complementarity formulation of variational inequalities and Nash equilibria.

7.14.1 Methods Based on Differential Equations

Although there are a variety of differential equations describing solution trajectories of variational inequalities, a particularly straightforward approach studied by Smith et al. (1997) is to equate the rates of change of decision variables to the degree to which the fixed-point equivalent of $VI(F, \Lambda)$ fails to be satisfied, denoted by

$$\Delta \equiv P_\Lambda \{x(t) - \eta F[x(t)]\} - x(t)$$

That is, we write

$$\frac{dx(t)}{dt} = \mu \Delta$$

$$= \mu [P_\Lambda \{x(t) - \eta F[x(t)]\} - x(t)] \tag{7.199}$$

$$x(0) = x^0 \tag{7.200}$$

[4] The independent variable t need not refer to physical time; rather it may be a surrogate for the progress of an algorithm toward the solution of the underlying variational inequality.

where

$$\mu, \eta \in \Re^1_{++}$$

are parameters adjusted to control stability and assure convergence. It should be apparent that any steady state for which

$$\frac{dx(t)}{dt} = 0 \tag{7.201}$$

must correspond to

$$x = P_\Lambda [x - \eta F(x)] \tag{7.202}$$

which is recognized, per Lemma 7.3, as the fixed-point equivalent of $VI(F, \Lambda)$. Thus, if the dynamics (7.199) and (7.200) lead to (7.201) as $t \longrightarrow \infty$, the desired variational inequality solution is obtained.

7.14.2 Fixed Point Methods

As we have commented before, there is a natural and obvious algorithm associated with any fixed-point problem

$$y = G(y),$$

namely

$$y^{k+1} = G\left(y^k\right) \tag{7.203}$$

where k is of course the iteration counter. Again we make use of the fact that, for convex feasible regions, $VI(F, \Lambda)$ is equivalent to the fixed-point problem $FPP_{\min}(F, \Lambda)$; that is

$$G(y) = P_\Lambda [y - \eta F(y)] \tag{7.204}$$

where $P_\Lambda [.]$ is the minimum norm projection operator. It is, therefore, quite reasonable to consider an algorithm for $VI(F, \Lambda)$ wherein the iterations follow

$$y^{k+1} = P_\Lambda \left[y - \eta F\left(y^k\right)\right] \tag{7.205}$$

and

$$\eta \in \Re^1_{++}$$

can be considered a step size that may be adjusted to aid convergence. Of course, the righthand side of (7.205) may be expressed as a mathematical program owing to the presence of the minimum norm projection operator. That is, the new iterate y^{k+1} must be the solution of

$$\min_{y \in \mathbf{\Lambda}} Z^k(y) = \frac{1}{2}\left[y^k - \eta F\left(y^k\right) - y\right]^T \left[y^k - \eta F\left(y^k\right) - y\right]$$

$$= \frac{1}{2}\left[\left(y^k - y\right) - \eta F\left(y^k\right)\right]^T \left[\left(y^k - y\right) - \eta F\left(y^k\right)\right]$$

$$= \frac{1}{2}\left\{\left(y^k - y\right)^T \left(y^k - y\right) - 2\eta \left(y^k - y\right)^T F\left(y^k\right) + \eta^2 \left[F\left(y^k\right)\right]^T F\left(y^k\right)\right\}$$

Upon eliminating the additive constant and multiplying by $(2\eta)^{-1}$, this last expression gives the following form for the subproblems arising in a fixed-point algorithm when the minimum norm projection is involved:

$$\min_{y \in \mathbf{\Lambda}} \left(y - y^k\right)^T F\left(y^k\right) + \frac{1}{2\eta}\left(y - y^k\right)^T \left(y - y^k\right) \tag{7.206}$$

which is meant to be solved by an appropriate nonlinear programming algorithm. Browder (1966), Bakusinskii and Poljak (1974), Dafermos (1980), and Bertsekas and Gafni (1982) have used these notions with subtle embellishments to develop algorithms that have linear rates of convergence and perform quite similarly in practice.

The unembellished fixed-point algorithm enjoys a simple proof of convergence when the principal operator is strongly monotonically increasing. To present that proof, we need to first introduce the notion of a nonexpansive operator:

Definition 7.16 (Nonexpansive operator) The operator $G : D \subset \Re^n \longrightarrow \Re^n$ is said to be nonexpansive on a set $D_0 \subset D$ if

$$\|G(x) - G(y)\| \leq \alpha \|x - y\| \tag{7.207}$$

for all $x, y \in D_0$.

We also need the following result pertinent to iterative algorithms that are based on contraction mappings:

Theorem 7.20 *(Contraction mapping theorem) Suppose that $G : D \subset \Re^n \longrightarrow \Re^n$ is nonexpansive on a closed set $D_0 \subset D$ and that $G(D_0) \subset D_0$. Then $x = G(x)$ has a unique solution in D_0.*

Proof. We follow closely the arguments of Ortega and Rheinboldt (1970) for a similar theorem. Let x^0 be an arbitrary point in D_0 and form the sequence $\{x^k\}$, with the property that

$$x^k = G(x^{k-1}) \qquad k = 1, 2, \ldots \tag{7.208}$$

Because $G(D_0) \subset D_0$ by assumption, we know $\{x^k\}$ lies in D_0. Consequently, we can write

$$\|x^{k+1} - x^k\| = \|G(x^k) - G(x^{k-1})\| \leq \alpha \|x^k - x^{k-1}\| \tag{7.209}$$

by virtue of the fact $G(\cdot)$ is nonexpansive. It follows that

$$\left.\begin{aligned} \|x^{k+p} - x^k\| &\leq \sum_{i=1}^{p} \|x^{k+i} - x^{k+i-1}\| \\ &\leq \left(\alpha^{p-1} + \cdots + 1\right) \|x^{k+1} - x^k\| \\ &\leq \left[\frac{\alpha^k}{1-\alpha}\right] \|x^1 - x^0\| \end{aligned}\right\} \tag{7.210}$$

Result (7.210) is obtained from the geometric series

$$\sum_{i=1}^{p} \alpha^{i-1} = \frac{1-\alpha^p}{1-\alpha} \leq \frac{1}{1-\alpha}, \tag{7.211}$$

since $1-\alpha^p \leq 1$ for all integer $p \geq 0$ because $\alpha < 1$. Taking the limit as $k \longrightarrow +\infty$ in (7.210) clearly yields

$$\lim_{k \longrightarrow +\infty} \left\| x^{k+p} - x^k \right\| = 0 \tag{7.212}$$

That is, $\{x^k\} \longrightarrow x^*$, the limit point. Thus, $x = G(x)$ has a unique fixed point since $G(\cdot)$ is continuous by virtue of being contractive. ■

We also need the following definition:

Definition 7.17 (Lipschitz continuity) The function $F(x): \Re^n \longrightarrow \Re^n$ obeys a Lipschitz condition on Λ if

$$\left\| F^{k+1} - F^k \right\| \leq \sqrt{K_0} \left\| x^{k+1} - x^k \right\|$$

for all $x^k, x^{k+1} \in \Lambda$ and some $K_0 \in \Re^1_{++}$, where

$$F^k \equiv F\left(x^k\right)$$

Now we are ready to present and prove the following result about convergence of the fixed-point algorithm:

Theorem 7.21 *(Convergence of the fixed point algorithm) Let Λ be a closed set. The algorithm*

$$x^{k+1} = P_\Lambda\left[x - \eta F\left(x^k\right)\right]$$

converges to $x^* \in \Lambda$ if $F(x): \Re^n \longrightarrow \Re^n$ satisfies a Lipschitz condition and is strongly monotonically increasing on Λ while $\eta \in \Re_{++}$ is sufficiently small.

Proof. To apply Theorem 7.20, we need to establish that the operator

$$x^{k+1} = M\left(x^k\right) = P_\Lambda\left[x^k - \eta F(x^k)\right]$$

is nonexpansive. It is well known that the minimum norm projection is itself nonexpansive; therefore we have

$$\left\| M\left(x^{k+1}\right) - M\left(x^k\right) \right\| \leq \left\| \left[x^{k+1} - \eta F\left(x^{k+1}\right)\right] - \left[x^k - \eta F\left(x^k\right)\right] \right\|$$

or

$$\left\| M\left(x^{k+1}\right) - M\left(x^k\right) \right\| \leq \left\| \left(x^{k+1} - x^k\right) - \eta\left(F^{k+1} - F^k\right) \right\|$$

where the obvious notation

$$F^k \equiv F(x^k)$$

is employed. Thus

$$\left\|M\left(x^{k+1}\right)-M\left(x^k\right)\right\|^2 \leq \left\|\left(x^{k+1}-x^k\right)-\eta\left(F^{k+1}-F^k\right)\right\|^2 \equiv \Phi^{\tau,k}$$

so that

$$\Phi^{\tau,k} = \left\|x^{k+1}-x^k\right\|^2 - 2\eta\langle F^{k+1}-F^k, x^{k+1}-x^k\rangle + \eta^2\left\|F^{k+1}-F^k\right\|^2$$

From the given, we know that $F(x)$ obeys a Lipschitz condition with constant $\sqrt{K_0}$ and is strongly monotonically increasing with constant K_1; therefore

$$\begin{aligned}
\Phi^{\tau,k} &\leq \left\|x^{k+1}-x^k\right\|^2 - 2\eta\langle F^{k+1}-F^k, x^{k+1}-x^k\rangle + \eta^2 K_0\left\|x^{k+1}-x^k\right\|^2 \\
&\leq \left(1-2\eta\frac{K_1}{2}+\eta^2 K_0\right)\left\|x^{k+1}-x^k\right\|^2
\end{aligned}$$

If

$$1-2\eta\frac{K_1}{2}+\eta^2 K_0 \leq 1 \tag{7.213}$$

then the nonexpansiveness criterion

$$\left\|M\left(x^{k+1}\right)-M\left(x^k\right)\right\| \leq \left\|x^{k+1}-x^k\right\|$$

is satisfied. Expression (7.213) yields

$$\eta\left(-K_1+\eta K_0\right) \leq 0 \Longrightarrow \eta \leq \frac{K_1}{K_0}$$

This completes the proof. ■

7.14.3 Generalized Linear Methods

Pang and Chan (1982) offer a very useful and succinct typology of generalized linear methods. In particular, they describe the fundamental subproblem of a generalized linear algorithm to be the following variational inequality

$$F^k(y^{k+1})(x-y^{k+1}) \geq 0 \quad \forall x \in \Lambda$$

which approximates $VI(F,\Lambda)$. Each specific approximation results in a different algorithm. For example, if

$$F^k(y) = F(y^k) + \left[\nabla F(y^k)\right]^T (y-y^k) \tag{7.214}$$

then the result is Newton's method. If, on the other hand, we use

$$F^k(y) = F(y^k) + \text{diag}\left[\nabla F(y^k)\right]^T (y - y^k) \tag{7.215}$$

then the result is the linearized Jacobi method. Moreover, the diagonalization method introduced in Sect. 7.12 may be considered a generalized linear method.

Generalized linear algorithms for variational inequalities are described in some detail by Harker (1988) and Harker and Pang (1990). As we have described above, algorithms belonging to this class proceed by creating a linear approximation of the function $F(x)$ of the variational inequality. The resulting quadratic program can be approached in a variety of ways, including decomposition methods that exploit special structure. Details and applications of generalized linear methods are described by Pang and Chan (1982), Dafermos (1983), Harker (1983), Hammond (1984), Friesz et al. (1985), Nagurney (1987), and Goldsman and Harker (1990).

7.14.4 Successive Linearization and Lemke's Algorithm

We have shown that for certain regularity conditions a variational inequality may be expressed as a nonlinear complementarity problem. Assume that we have a test solution x^k for the equivalent $NCP(F)$ and the function $F(\cdot)$ is continuously differentiable. We approximate F by the first two terms of a Taylor series expansion:

$$F(x) \approx F^k(x) \equiv F\left(x^k\right) + \nabla\left[F(y^k)\right]^T\left(x - x^k\right)$$

which yields the following linear complementarity problem, denoted by $LCP\left(F^k\right)$:

$$\left[F^k(x)\right]^T x = 0$$

$$F^k(x) \geq 0$$

$$x \geq 0$$

The following algorithm is based on successive linear approximations of $NCP(F)$ of the type presented above:

Successive Linearization Algorithm for $NCP(F)$

Step 0. *(Initialization)* Determine an initial feasible solution $x^0 \in \Re^n_+$ and set $k = 0$.

Step 1. *(Solve the LCP)* Approximate the function F about the current solution x^k and solve

$$\left[F^k(x)\right]^T x = 0$$

$$F^k(x) \geq 0$$

$$x \geq 0$$

where

$$F^k(x) \equiv F\left(x^k\right) + \left[\nabla F(x^k)\right]^T \left(x - x^k\right)$$

Call the solution x^{k+1}.

Step 2. *(Stopping test and updating)* For $\varepsilon \in \Re^1_{++}$, a preset tolerance, if

$$\left\|x^{k+1} - x^k\right\| < \varepsilon,$$

stop; otherwise set $k = k + 1$ and go to Step 1.

Convergence of the successive linearization algorithm for nonlinear complementarity problems is proven by Pang and Chan (1982).

7.14.5 The Linear Complementarity Problem

In the successive linearization scheme presented above, one faces a linear complementarity problem (LCP) in each major iteration. The LCP is a special case of the nonlinear complementarity problem $NCP(F)$ for which

$$F(x) = q + Mx$$

where $F : \Re^n \longrightarrow \Re^n$, $q \in \Re^n$ and M is an $n \times n$ matrix. The problem

$$[F(x)]^T x = 0$$

$$F(x) \geq 0$$

$$x \geq 0$$

may therefore be expressed as

$$(q + Mx)^T x = 0 \tag{7.216}$$

$$q + Mx \geq 0 \tag{7.217}$$

$$x \geq 0 \tag{7.218}$$

However, by defining

$$w = F(x)$$

it is possible to restate (7.216)–(7.218) as

$$w - Mx = q \tag{7.219}$$

$$w^T x = 0 \tag{7.220}$$

$$x \geq 0 \tag{7.221}$$

$$w \geq 0 \tag{7.222}$$

We refer to the problem defined by (7.219)–(7.222) as $LCP(M, q)$.

Finding an Initial Feasible Solution for $LCP(M, q)$

To facilitate finding an initial feasible solution for $LCP(M, q)$ we use an approach analogous to the Phase I method of linear programming and introduce the artificial variable $x^0 \in \Re^1_+$:

$$w - Mx - 1_n x_0 = q \tag{7.223}$$

$$w^T x = 0 \tag{7.224}$$

$$x \geq 0 \tag{7.225}$$

$$w \geq 0 \tag{7.226}$$

$$x_0 \geq 0 \tag{7.227}$$

where

$$1_n = \begin{pmatrix} 1 \\ 1 \\ \vdots \\ 1 \\ 1 \end{pmatrix} \in \Re^n$$

We will refer to the problem defined by (7.223)–(7.227) as $LCP_0(M, q)$. By setting

$$x_0 = \max\{-q_i : i \in [1, n]\}$$

$$x = 0 \in \Re^n$$

$$w = q + 1_n x_0$$

we obtain an initial feasible solution to $LCP_0(M, q)$, as may be easily verified by the reader. If we are able to subsequently drive x_0 to zero while satisfying the original problem, then we will have a basic feasible solution to the complementarity problem of interest, namely $LCP(M, q)$. We say such a solution is a *complementary basic feasible solution*.

We will use a notion of pivoting reminiscent of the simplex algorithm to move from one feasible solution to another. As in the simplex, when the problem of interest is nondegenerate, a variable is called nonbasic if it vanishes, and basic if it is strictly greater than zero. We shall consider a pivot to have occurred if w^s or z^s is made strictly positive and, thereby, basic while some positive w^k or z^k, where $k \neq s$, is set to zero and thereby made nonbasic.

Details of Lemke's Method

Note that $LCP_0(M, q)$ may be restated as

$$Ay = q \tag{7.228}$$

where

$$A = \begin{pmatrix} I & -M & -1_n \end{pmatrix} \quad \text{and} \quad y = \begin{pmatrix} w \\ x \\ x_0 \end{pmatrix} \tag{7.229}$$

so that our notions of bases and basic solutions from linear programming may be applied. Naturally the matrix A and the vector y may be conformally partitioned according to

$$A = \begin{pmatrix} B & N \end{pmatrix}$$

$$y = \begin{pmatrix} y_B \\ y_N \end{pmatrix}$$

where B is $n \times n$ and N is $n \times (n+1)$. Moreover, the following familiar identity obtains

$$y_B = B^{-1}q - B^{-1}Ny_N \tag{7.230}$$

for each partition.

We are now ready to give an annotated statement of the pivoting algorithm due to Lemke (1968):

LEMKE'S METHOD FOR $LCP(M, q)$

Step 0. *(Initialization)* If $q \geq 0$, stop. A solution of $LCP(M, q)$ is

$$w = q \text{ and } x = 0$$

Otherwise form the problem $LCP_0(M, q)$ by introducing the artificial variable $x_0 \in \Re^1_+$ and obtain an initial solution y for it by setting

$$y_i = w_i = q_i + x_0 \qquad i = 1, \ldots, n \tag{7.231}$$

$$y_{n+i} = x_i = 0 \qquad i = 1, \ldots, n \tag{7.232}$$

$$y_{2n+1} = x_0 = -q_s \tag{7.233}$$

where

$$s = \arg\max \{-q_i : i \in [1, n]\}$$

Note that

$$w_s = q_s + x_0 = q_s - q_s = 0$$

is nonbasic, so we have exactly n basic variables, as required. Select $y_s = x_s$ to be the most recent nonbasic variable selected to be made basic.

Step 1. *(Finding the leaving variable)* Let a_s be the column of A corresponding to y_s. If $a_s \leq 0 \in \Re^n$, go to Step 4. Otherwise determine the index r of the current basic variable to be made nonbasic according to

$$r = \arg\min \left\{ \frac{\bar{q}_i}{\bar{a}_{is}} : \bar{a}_{is} > 0, \ i \in [1, n+1] \right\} \tag{7.234}$$

where

$$\bar{q} = B^{-1}b$$

$$(\bar{a}_{ij}) = B^{-1}N$$

Update the basic and nonbasic variables according to the current basis partition. If r corresponds to x_0 go to Step 3; otherwise continue.

Step 2. *(Completing the pivot)* The basic variable that was removed in Step 1 with current index r is either w_ℓ or x_ℓ for some $\ell \neq s$. If r corresponds to w_ℓ, the new nonbasic variable to enter the basis is $y_s = x_\ell$. If r corresponds to x_ℓ, the new nonbasic variable to enter the basis is $y_s = w_\ell$. Go to Step 1.

Step 3. *(Stopping with complementarity)* At this step y_s enters the basis and x_0 leaves the basis. Stop, a complementary basic feasible solution has been attained.

Step 4. *(Stopping without complementarity)* At this step the algorithm stops without driving x_0 from the basis and we say an *almost complementary basic feasible solution* has been found.

Finiteness of Lemke's Method

The similarity of Lemke's algorithm for solving linear complementarity problems to the simplex algorithm for linear programs is apparent. A key question is whether or not the algorithm is finite. Bazaraa et al. (2006) show that Lemke's method for $LCP(M, q)$ is finite or terminates with an extreme ray when no degeneracy is encountered.

7.15 Computing Network User Equilibria

In Section 7.9 we discussed the Nash-like equilibrium known as user equilibrium and saw that such problems may be formulated as nonlinear complementarity problems or as variational inequalities. In this section we employ a numerical example of user equilibrium to illustrate a fixed-point algorithm as well as successive linearization via Lemke's method.

For our example of a user equilibrium let us consider the network of Fig. 7.1, consisting of 5 arcs and 4 nodes. For this example, the set of origin-destination (OD) pairs is a singleton: $\mathcal{W} = \{(1,4)\}$; as a consequence there are three paths belonging to the set $\mathcal{P} = \mathcal{P}_{14} = \{p_1, p_2, p_3\}$, namely

$$p_1 = \{1,4\}, p_2 = \{2,3,4\}, p_3 = \{2,5\}$$

In addition we assume the unit travel cost for each arc is of the form

$$c_a = A_a + B_a (f_a)^2 \qquad a = 1,2,3,4,5$$

where f_a denotes the total flow on arc a. Moreover, the arc flows and the path flows obey the following relationships:

$$f_1 = h_{p_1}$$

$$f_2 = h_{p_2} + h_{p_3}$$

$$f_3 = h_{p_2}$$

$$f_4 = h_{p_1} + h_{p_2}$$

$$f_5 = h_{p_3}$$

The numerical values for the coefficients A_a and B_a are given in Table 7.1. Furthermore, assuming path costs are additive in arc costs, we may write

$$c_{p_1} = c_1 + c_4$$

$$c_{p_2} = c_2 + c_3 + c_4$$

$$c_{p_3} = c_2 + c_5$$

Finally, we stipulate the fixed travel demand

$$Q_{14} = 100$$

so that the relevant variational inequality formulation of this particular user equilibrium $UE(C, \Upsilon)$ is: find the traffic pattern $h^* \in \Upsilon$ such that

$$[C(h)]^T (h - h^*) \geq 0 \quad \forall h \in \Upsilon \tag{7.235}$$

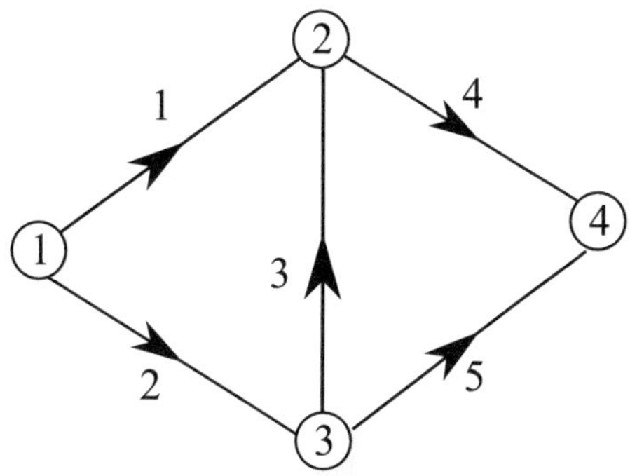

FIGURE 7.1: A SIMPLE TRAVEL NETWORK WITH 5 ARCS AND 4 NODES

a	A_a	B_a
1	25.0	0.010
2	25.0	0.010
3	75.0	0.001
4	25.0	0.010
5	25.0	0.010

TABLE 7.1: PARAMETERS

where

$$C(h) = \begin{bmatrix} A_1 + B_1 (h_{p_1})^2 + A_4 + B_4 (h_{p_1} + h_{p_2})^2 \\ A_2 + B_2 (h_{p_2} + h_{p_3})^2 + A_3 + B_3 (h_{p_2})^2 + A_4 + B_4 (h_{p_1} + h_{p_2})^2 \\ A_2 + B_2 (h_{p_2} + h_{p_3})^2 + A_5 + B_5 (h_{p_3})^2 \end{bmatrix}$$

$$h = \begin{pmatrix} h_{p_1} \\ h_{p_2} \\ h_{p_3} \end{pmatrix}$$

$$\Upsilon = \left\{ (h_{p_1}, h_{p_2}, h_{p_3})^T : h_{p_1} + h_{p_2} + h_{p_3} = Q_{14} \text{ and } h_{p_1}, h_{p_2}, h_{p_3} \geq 0 \right\}$$

Evidently, the feasible region Υ is convex.

For the problem at hand, $UE(C, \Upsilon)$ given by (7.235) takes the following form:

$$C_{p_1}(h^*)\left(h_{p_1} - h^*_{p_1}\right) + C_{p_2}(h^*)\left(h_{p_2} - h^*_{p_2}\right) + C_{p_3}(h^*)\left(h_{p_3} - h^*_{p_3}\right) \geq 0$$

Since $h^*, h \in \Upsilon$, we consider the substitutions

$$h^*_{p_1} = Q_{14} - \left(h^*_{p_2} + h^*_{p_3}\right)$$

$$h_{p_1} = Q_{14} - (h_{p_2} + h_{p_3})$$

Therefore

$$C(h^*)(h-h^*) = C_{p_1}(h^*)\left(-\left(h_{p_2}+h_{p_3}\right)+\left(h^*_{p_2}+h^*_{p_3}\right)\right)$$
$$+C_{p_2}(h^*)\left(h_{p_2}-h^*_{p_2}\right)+C_{p_3}(h^*)\left(h_{p_3}-h^*_{p_3}\right)$$
$$= -C_{p_1}(h^*)\left(h_{p_2}-h^*_{p_2}\right)-C_{p_1}(h^*)\left(h_{p_3}-h^*_{p_3}\right)$$
$$+C_{p_2}(h^*)\left(h_{p_2}-h^*_{p_2}\right)+C_{p_3}(h^*)\left(h_{p_3}-h^*_{p_3}\right)$$
$$= \left(-C_{p_1}(h^*)+C_{p_2}(h^*)\right)\left(h_{p_2}-h^*_{p_2}\right)$$
$$+\left(-C_{p_1}(h^*)+C_{p_3}(h^*)\right)\left(h_{p_3}-h^*_{p_3}\right)$$

The above variational inequality may now be written as follows: find

$$h^* = \begin{pmatrix} h^*_{p_2} & h^*_{p_3} \end{pmatrix}^T \geq 0$$

such that

$$\begin{bmatrix} -C_{p_1}(h^*)+C_{p_2}(h^*) \\ -C_{p_1}(h^*)+C_{p_3}(h^*) \end{bmatrix}^T \begin{bmatrix} h_{p_2}-h^*_{p_2} \\ h_{p_3}-h^*_{p_3} \end{bmatrix} \geq 0$$

for all

$$h = \begin{pmatrix} h_{p_2} & h_{p_3} \end{pmatrix}^T \geq 0$$

The corresponding fixed-point iterative scheme is

$$\begin{bmatrix} h^{k+1}_{p_2} \\ h^{k+1}_{p_3} \end{bmatrix} = \begin{bmatrix} h^k_{p_2}-\alpha\left\{-C_{p_1}\left(h^k\right)+C_{p_2}\left(h^k\right)\right\} \\ h^k_{p_3}-\alpha\left\{-C_{p_1}\left(h^k\right)+C_{p_3}\left(h^k\right)\right\} \end{bmatrix}_+$$

where

$$[v]_+ = \max(0, v)$$

for any $\alpha > 0$.

Table 7.2 contains a record of iterations corresponding to this fixed-point computational scheme with starting solution

$$h^0_{p_1} = 30, \; h^0_{p_2} = 50, \; h^0_{p_3} = 20$$

We see that the solution is

$$h^*_{p_1} = 50, \; h^*_{p_2} = 0, \; h^*_{p_3} = 50$$

The corresponding path costs are

$$c^*_{p_1} = 100, \; c^*_{p_2} = 175, \; c^*_{p_3} = 100 \; ,$$

indicating a user equilibrium has been obtained.

Iteration	h_{p_1}	h_{p_2}	h_{p_3}	Error
0	30	50	20	
1	43	16	41	42.0238
2	50.2	0	49.8	19.6286
3	50.04	0	49.96	0.2263
4	50.008	0	49.992	0.0453
5	50.0016	0	49.9984	0.0091
6	50.0003	0	49.9997	0.0018
7	50.0000	0	50.0000	0.0002

TABLE 7.2: ITERATIONS OF THE FIXED-POINT ALGORITHM

7.16 References and Additional Reading

Auchmuty, G. (1989). Variational principles for variational inequalities. *Numerical Functional Analysis and Optimization, 10*, 863–874.

Auslender, A. (1976). *Optimisation: Methodes numeriques.* Paris: Masson.

Avriel, M. (1976). *Nonlinear programming: Analysis and methods.* Engelwood Cliffs, NJ: Prentice-Hall.

Bazaraa, M. S., Sherali, H. D., & Shetty, C. M. (2006). *Nonlinear programming: theory and algorithms.* Hoboken, NJ: Wiley-Interscience.

Bakusinskii, A. B., & Poljak, B. T. (1974). On the solution of variational inequalities. *Soviet Mathematics Doklady, 17*, 1705–1710.

Bertsekas, D. P., & Gafni, E. M. (1982). Projection methods for variational inequalities with application to the traffic assignment problem. *Mathematical Programming Studies, 17*, 139–159.

Browder, P. E. (1966). Existence and approximation of solutions to variational inequalities. *Proceedings of the National Academy of Sciences, 56*, 1080–1086.

Cottle, R. W., Pang, J.-S., & Stone, R. E. (1992). *The linear complementarity problem.* Boston, MA: Academic.

Dafermos, S. C. (1980). Traffic equilibrium and variational inequalities. *Transportation Science, 14*, 43–54.

Dafermos, S. C. (1983). An iterative scheme for variational inequalities. *Mathematical Programming, 26*(1), 40–47.

Facchinei, F., & Pang, J. S. (2003a). *Finite-dimensional variational inequalities and complementarity problems* (Vol. 1). New York: Springer.

Facchinei, F., & Pang, J. S. (2003b). *Finite-dimensional variational inequalities and complementarity problems* (Vol. 2). New York: Springer.

Facchinei, F., Fischer, A., & Piccialli, V. (2007). On generalized Nash games and variational inequalities. *Operations Research Letters, 35*, 159–164.

Fiacco, A. V. (1983). *Introduction to sensitivity and stability analysis in nonlinear programming.* Boston, MA: Academic.

Friesz, T. L., Viton, P. A., & Tobin, R. L. (1985). Economic and computational aspects of freight network equilibrium: A synthesis. *Journal of Regional Science, 25*, 29–49.

Friesz, T. L. (2010). *Dynamic optimization and differential games* (Vol. 135). New York: Springer.

Fukushima, M. (1992). Equivalent differentiable optimization problems and descent methods for asymmetric variational inequality problems. *Mathematical Programming, 53*, 99–110.

Garcia, C. B., & Zangwill, W. I. (1981). *Pathways to solutions, fixed points and equilibria.* Englewood Cliffs, NJ: Prentice-Hall.

Goldsman, L., & Harker, P. T. (1990). A note on solving general equilibrium problems with variational inequality techniques. *Operations Research Letters, 9*(5), 335–339.

Hammond, J. H. (1984). *Solving asymmetric variational inequality problems and systems of equations with generalized nonlinear programming algorithms.* Ph.D. Dissertation, M.I.T.

Harker, P. T. (1983). *Prediction of intercity freight flows: Theory and application of a generalized spatial price equilibrium model.* Ph.D. Dissertation, University of Pennsylvania.

Harker, P. T. (1988). Accelerating the convergence of the diagonalization and projection algorithms for finite-dimensional variational inequalities. *Mathematical Programming, 41*, 29–59.

Harker, P. T., & Pang, J.-S. (1990). Finite-dimensional variational inequality and nonlinear complementarity problems: A survey of theory, algorithms, and applications. *Mathematical Programming, 48B*(2), 161–220.

Lemke, C. E. (1968). On complementary pivot theory, In G. B. Dantzig & A. F. Veinott Jr. (Eds.), *Mathematics of decision sciences* (pp. 95–113). Providence: American Mathematical Society.

Luthi, H.-J., Jr. (1985). On the solution of variational inequalities by the ellipsoid method. *Mathematics of Operations Research, 10*(3), 515–522.

Nagurney, A. (1987). Competitive equilibrium problems, variational inequalities and regional science. *Journal of Regional Science, 27*, 55–76.

Ortega, J. M., & Rheinboldt, W. C. (1970). *Iterative solution of nonlinear equations in several variables.* Boston, MA: Academic.

Pang, J.-S., & Chan, D. (1982). Iterative methods for variational and complementarity problems. *Mathematical Programming, 24*(3), 284–313.

Peng, J.-M. (1997). Equivalence of variational inequality problems to unconstrained minimization. *Mathematical Programming, 78*, 347–355.

Rudin, W. (1986). *Real and complex analysis.* New York: McGraw-Hill.

Scarf, H. E. (1967). The approximation of fixed points of a continuous mapping. *SIAM Journal on Applied Mathematics, 15*, 1328–1342.

Scarf, H. E. (1973). *Computation of economic equilibria.* New Haven, CT: Yale University Press.

Scarf, H. E. (1984). The computation of equilibrium prices. In H. E. Scarf & J. B. Shoven (Eds.), *Applied general equilibrium analysis* (chapter 1, pp. 1–49). Cambridge: Cambridge University Press.

Smith, T. E., Friesz, T. L., Bernstein, D., & Suo, Z. (1997). A comparison of two minimum norm projective dynamic systems and their relationship to variational inequalities. In M. Ferris & J.-S. Pang (Eds.), *Complementarity and variational problems* (pp. 405–424). Philadelphia: SIAM.

Todd, M. J. (1976). *The computation of fixed points and applications.* New York: Springer.

Todd, M. J. (1984). Efficient methods of computing economic equilibria. In H. E. Scarf & J. B. Shoven (Eds.), *Applied general equilibrium analysis* (chapter 2, pp. 51–68). New York: Cambridge University Press.

Tobin, R.L. (1986). Sensitivity analysis for variational inequalities. *Journal of Optimization Theory and Applications, 48*(1), 191–204.

Wu, J. H., Florian, M., & Marcotte, P. (1993). A general descent framework for the monotone variational inequality problem. *Mathematical Programming, 61*, 281–300.

Yamashita, N., Taji, K., & Fukushima, M. (1997). Unconstrained optimization reformulations of variational inequality problems. *Journal of Optimization Theory and Applications, 92*(3), 439–456.

8

Network Traffic Assignment

In this chapter we are concerned with two schemes for allocating traffic to the arcs of congested road networks: system optimal traffic assignment and user equilibrium traffic assignment. We begin with some cautionary remarks concerning terminology. Techniques for determining Nash equilibria of road networks are frequently collectively referred to by transportation engineers as *traffic assignment.* In some ways this choice of terminology is unfortunate since other branches of engineering tend to reserve the word "assignment" for normative, value-laden judgments informed by some measure of performance or social welfare. However, to transportation engineers, traffic assignment is the behavior-based allocation of origin-destination specific, forecasted travel demands to the arcs of a real physical road network. As such, traffic assignment involves foresight and is intrinsically a descriptive or positive modeling exercise. Furthermore, because traffic assignment allocates origin-destination specific travel demands to paths of the network of interest in order to determine arc flows, traffic assignment is fundamentally a problem of *route selection.*

In fact, the British traffic engineer Wardrop (1952) proposed two principles for route choice in networks that are the foundation of all static traffic assignment models for road networks. These are:

- **Wardrop's First Principle**. Each user noncooperatively seeks to minimize his/her cost of transportation. A network flow pattern consistent with this principle is said to be *user-optimized* or a *user equilibrium.* Specifically, a user equilibrium is reached when no user may lower his/her transportation cost through unilateral action.

- **Wardrop's Second Principle**. The total cost of transportation in the system is minimized. A network flow pattern consistent with this principle is said to be *system optimized* and requires that users cooperate fully or that a central authority controls the transportation system. Specifically, a system-optimized solution is reached when the marginal total costs of transportation alternatives are equal.

T.L. Friesz, D. Bernstein, *Foundations of Network Optimization and Games*, Complex Networks and Dynamic Systems 3,
DOI 10.1007/978-1-4899-7594-2_8

Wardrop's main interest was in road traffic. Today Wardrop's Second Principle (WSP) is thought to have little relevance to road passenger traffic that is not centrally controlled. Rather, WSP is more frequently applied to freight transportation problems. Wardrop's First Principle (WFP) is used almost universally today in the construction of static network models to predict passenger transportation flows.

An example of a system optimal flow pattern is a futuristic vehicular traffic network with centralized control. Other system optimal examples are data flow routing and data flow control for centrally controlled telecommunications networks. On the other hand, user equilibrium flow patterns are computed on a routine basis by metropolitan planning organizations (MPOs) as part of the widely practiced four-step transportation planning process for road networks: trip generation, trip distribution, modal split, and traffic assignment.

In this chapter, we will find that, unlike the classical minimum cost flow problem, network flow models of vehicular traffic on road networks, whether system or user optimal in nature, necessitate the introduction of path variables. Unfortunately, the introduction of path variables destroys the totally unimodular nature of flow conservation constraints, although totally unimodular subproblems may emerge when feasible direction algorithms are applied and properly interpreted.

The following is a summary of the topics discussed in this chapter:

Section 8.1: A Comment on Notation. We begin this chapter with a comment on notation that will facilitate the discussion that follows.

Section 8.2: System Optimal Traffic Assignment. This section considers models in which the total cost of transportation in the system is minimized. Such models conform to Wardrop's Second Principle.

Section 8.3: User Optimal Traffic Assignment with Separable Functions. This section considers an equilibrium model of travel behavior conforming to Wardrop's First Principle. In particular, this section considers a model in which the arc cost functions are separable and travel demands are fixed.

Section 8.4: Beckmann-Type Programs for Nonseparable User Equilibrium. This section expands the results from the previous section to include nonseparable elastic demand and arc cost functions.

Section 8.5: Frank-Wolfe Algorithm for Beckmann's Program. This section considers the Frank-Wolfe algorithm and how it may be used to solve Beckmann's equivalent mathematical program.

Section 8.6: Nonextremal Formulations of Wardropian Equilibrium. This section emphasizes variational inequality problems in the study of user equilibrium without invoking symmetry conditions.

Section 8.7: Diagonalization Algorithms for Nonextremal User Equilibrium Models. This section considers how diagonalization algorithms discussed in Chap. 7 may be used to solve nonextremal user equilibrium models.

Section 8.8: Nonlinear Complementarity Formulation of User Equilibrium. This section emphasizes nonlinear complementarity formulations for the study of user equilibrium, without invoking symmetry conditions.

Section 8.9: Numerical Examples of Computing User Equilibrium. This section presents specific numerical examples of diagonalization and sequential linearization algorithms.

Section 8.10: Sensitivity Analysis of User Equilibrium. This section presents one approach to conducting sensitivity analysis for user equilibrium flows.

8.1 A Comment on Notation

We will be emphasizing model formulations based on the concepts of an arc, a path, and an origin-destination pair. Although, a totally unimodular constraint matrix will not be in the forefront of our discussions, the networks considered will continue to be created from a graph $\mathcal{G}(\mathcal{N}, \mathcal{A})$, where $\mathcal{N}$ is the set of nodes and $\mathcal{A}$ is the set of directed arcs.

8.2 System Optimal Traffic Assignment

As we have already commented, there is a class of network models that employ path flows rather than arc flows as decision variables. The need for path variables arises when there is requirement to know the precise path taken by a given unit of flow from its origin to its destination as opposed to merely knowing flows on arcs of the network. Path variables also arise when the demand for flow over the network is naturally expressed at the origin-destination level and not as nodal net supplies. Both of these factors arise in the so-called *telecommunications flow routing problem* for which the network controller seeks to route known origin-destination message demands in a way that minimizes total routing delay and recognizes that messages are not fungible. An essentially mathematically identical model arises when a freight transportation company controls its own network infrastructure and seeks to route transportation demands in a way that minimizes network-wide congestion, although few frieght transportation systems are so simple. In the transportation context, such a network optimization problem is called the *system optimal traffic assignment problem*. The systems optimal traffic assignment problem may, in theory, also arise in the study of passenger-vehicle flows when there is a central controller, although centrally controlled passenger networks do not presently exist. For simplicity we will refer to data, freight, and passenger traffic assignment based on the presumption of centralized control by the single appellation *system optimal traffic assignment*.

8.2.1 Notation and Formulation

We begin the symbolic articulation of the system optimal traffic assignment problem by introducing the following sets and set-related notation:

$\mathcal{A}$	set of all arcs
a	index denoting an arc of $\mathcal{A}$
$\mathcal{N}$	set of all nodes
i, j	indices referring to nodes
$\mathcal{W}$	set of all origin-destination (OD) pairs
$\mathcal{P}_{ij}$	set of paths connecting OD pair $(i, j) \in \mathcal{W}$
$\mathcal{P}$	the set of all paths
p	index referring to a path of $\mathcal{P}$

Note that $\mathcal{P} = \cup_{(i,j)\in\mathcal{W}}\mathcal{P}_{ij}$. We will also employ the following notation for arc flows, path flows, demands, and latencies (delays and costs):

h_p	flow on path p
h	$= (h_p : p \in \mathcal{P}) \in \Re^{\lvert\mathcal{P}\rvert}$
f_a	flow on arc a
f	$= (f_a : a \in \mathcal{A}) \in \Re^{\lvert\mathcal{A}\rvert}$
u_{ij}	the minimum latency for travel between OD pair $(i, j) \in \mathcal{W}$
u	$= (u_{ij} : (i, j) \in \mathcal{W}) \in \Re^{\lvert\mathcal{W}\rvert}$
Q_{ij}	the demand for flow between OD pair $(i, j) \in \mathcal{W}$
Q	$= (Q_{ij} : (i, j) \in \mathcal{W}) \in \Re^{\lvert\mathcal{W}\rvert}$
c_a	unit latency (delay or cost) function for arc $a \in \mathcal{A}$
c_p	unit latency (delay or cost) function for arc $p \in \mathcal{P}$
MC_a	marginal latency (delay or cost) of arc $a \in \mathcal{A}$
MC_p	marginal latency (delay or cost) for path $p \in \mathcal{P}$

We also define

$$\delta_{ap} = \begin{cases} 1 & \text{if link } a \text{ is on path } p \\ 0 & \text{otherwise} \end{cases} \tag{8.1}$$

to be an element of the arc path incidence matrix

$$\Delta = (\delta_{ap})$$

We further note that marginal arc latencies are defined as

$$MC_a = \frac{\partial}{\partial f_a}\left[c_a \cdot f_a\right] \tag{8.2}$$

for each arc $a \in \mathcal{A}$.

The preceding definitions lead to some key identities. The first of these is

$$c_p = \sum_{a\in\mathcal{A}} \delta_{ap} c_a \tag{8.3}$$

for each path $p \in \mathcal{P}$, which merely states that unit path latencies are the sum of unit arc latencies for the arcs traversed by each path. A very similar additive relationship exists between marginal path latencies and marginal arc latencies, namely

$$MC_p = \sum_{a \in \mathcal{A}} \delta_{ap} MC_a \tag{8.4}$$

for path $p \in \mathcal{P}$. To express the relationship of arc flows and path flows we write

$$f_a = \sum_{p \in \mathcal{P}} \delta_{ap} h_p \tag{8.5}$$

for each arc $a \in \mathcal{A}$, which may be equivalently expressed as

$$f = \Delta h$$

Note that Δ will generally **not** be square since the number of paths typically exceeds the number of arcs. As a consequence, we cannot uniquely determine path flows from known arc flows. Note also that we will use $c(f) : \Re^{|\mathcal{A}|} \longrightarrow \Re^{|\mathcal{A}|}$ to denote the vector of arc latency (delay or cost) functions and $C(h) : \Re^{|\mathcal{P}|} \longrightarrow \Re^{|\mathcal{P}|}$ to denote the vector of path latency (delay or cost) functions.

In the above notation, arcs are now identified by a single subscript a and arc flows by the new symbol f_a, partly to conform to conventions employed in the telecommunications and transportation literature, and also to signal that we are developing a formulation that is mathematically distinct from the classical minimum cost flow problem and its special cases. Furthermore, for the time being, transportation (or data) demand is taken to be fixed and articulated at the origin-destination level. Finally, we observe that the notation we have introduced leads to flow conservation constraints of the form

$$Q_{ij} = \sum_{p \in \mathcal{P}_{ij}} h_p \tag{8.6}$$

for every $(i, j) \in \mathcal{W}$.

8.2.2 The Notion of Path-Based Network Structure

Sometimes we will find it convenient to collectively restate all flow conservation equations (8.6) using the origin-destination-path incidence matrix

$$\Gamma = \left(\gamma_{ij}^p\right) \tag{8.7}$$

$$\gamma_{ij}^p = \begin{cases} 1 & \text{if } p \in \mathcal{P}_{ij},\ (i,j) \in \mathcal{W}_{ij} \\ 0 & \text{if } p \in \mathcal{P}_{ij},\ (i,j) \notin \mathcal{W}_{ij} \end{cases} \tag{8.8}$$

In particular, (8.6) is equivalent to

$$Q = \Gamma h \tag{8.9}$$

Our notation also leads to the following definition of the feasible region for system optimal and user equilibrium flows, when demand is not fixed:

$$\Omega_0 = \left\{ \begin{pmatrix} f \\ Q \end{pmatrix} : f = \Delta h,\ Q = \Gamma h,\ h \geq 0 \right\} \tag{8.10}$$

where in a slight abuse of notation we agree to consider (f, Q) a column vector unless otherwise stated. When demand is fixed, the set of feasible arc flows is

$$\Omega_1 = \{ f : f = \Delta h,\ Q = \Gamma h,\ h \geq 0 \} \tag{8.11}$$

It should be noted that arc variables are the fundamental decision variables and path variables are in a sense intermediate variables. An alternative feasible region that views path variables as the fundamental decision variables when demand is fixed is

$$\Omega_2 = \{ h : Q = \Gamma h,\ h \geq 0 \} \tag{8.12}$$

Our choice of feasible region representation will depend on the decision environment and the particular observation being made. When the network flow problem of interest has only constraints of the form

$$h \in \Omega_2 \tag{8.13}$$

we say it is *merely path-based.*

8.2.3 Arc Unit Latency Functions

It is common to assume that telecommunications arc unit latency functions are rectangular hyperbolas obeying

$$c_a\left(f_a\right) = A_a + \frac{B_a}{K_a - f_a} \qquad \forall a \in \mathcal{A} \tag{8.14}$$

where A_a is free flow latency (the latency experienced if there is little or no competing use of the network), B_a is a coefficient expressing sensitivity of latency to changes in flow, and K_a is the capacity of arc $a \in \mathcal{A}$. It can be shown that (8.14) roughly corresponds to the first two terms of a queueing approximation for which nodes of the network are relatively far apart. In road network traffic assignment of automobiles, somewhat different unit latency functions are employed, namely

$$c_a\left(f_a\right) = A_a + B_a \left(\frac{f_a}{K_a}\right)^q \qquad \forall a \in \mathcal{A} \tag{8.15}$$

where the fixed exponent obeys $q > 1$. Moreover, K_a is now interpreted as the effective capacity of arc $a \in \mathcal{A}$ and can be exceeded, but only at the price of rapidly accelerating congestion. Richer models of arc congestion make it necessary to use unit arc latency functions which are nonseparable, by which we mean that arc latency may depend on non-own as well as own flow. We denote such a circumstance by writing

$$c_a = c_a(f) \tag{8.16}$$

where f is of course the full vector of arc flows.

A dependence such as (8.16) can arise for several reasons. Perhaps the most fundamental reason for nonseparable latencies is the presence of nodal junctions comprised of message switching and signal-enhancing equipment upon which the flows of multiple arcs are incident; the congestion at such junctions is determined by the interaction of incident flows. Another reason for nonseparability is the existence of multiple message classes, and hence of multiple classes of flow, on a given arc. Multiple flow classes can occur because of distinct message priorities arising from differential pricing in telecommunications networks. In the event that there are multiple flow classes, their interaction would require that

$$c_b = c_b\left(f_b^1, f_b^2, \ldots, f_b^{|\mathcal{K}|}\right) \qquad \forall b \in \mathcal{A} \tag{8.17}$$

where $\mathcal{K}$ is the set of classes and f_b^k is the flow of class $k \in \mathcal{K}$ on arc $b \in \mathcal{A}$. By making $|\mathcal{K}|$ copies of arc $b \in \mathcal{A}$ and creating an expanded arc set $\mathcal{A}'$ that includes those copies, the functional dependence (8.17) can be restated in single-class form as

$$c_a = c_a(f) \qquad \forall a \in \mathcal{A}' \tag{8.18}$$

where $f = (f_a : a \in \mathcal{A}')$ and each arc now carries only a single class of flow. A network model expressed in such a way is said to be a multicopy formulation.

An example may help to clarify the proceeding observations concerning multicopy formulations. Suppose we are given a simple network consisting only of the real physical arc $a \in \mathcal{A}$. We further suppose that there are two flow classes: $k = 1, 2$. The latency function of the real physical arc a is

$$c_a(f) = 15.3 + \frac{25.7}{f_a^1 + f_a^2} + 0.031 \cdot f_a^1 \cdot f_a^2$$

and

$$0.031 \cdot f_a^1 \cdot f_a^2$$

is the congestion due to class interactions. Making two copies, named a_1 and a_2, of the arc real physical arc a, we call the class $k = 1$ flow f_{a_1} and the class $k = 2$ flow f_{a_2}. We are now able to articulate the unit latency functions of each copy as

$$\begin{aligned} c_a^1(f) &= 15.3 + \frac{25.7}{f_{a_1} + f_{a_2}} + 0.031 \cdot f_{a1} \cdot f_{a2} \\ c_a^2(f) &= 15.3 + \frac{25.7}{f_{a_1} + f_{a_2}} + 0.031 \cdot f_{a1} \cdot f_{a2} \end{aligned}$$

It is evident that the multicopy notation allows us to capture interactions of physically distinct arcs as well as the interactions of distinct classes of flow on the same physical arc.

It follows that the most general form of the system optimal traffic assignment problem is

$$\min \qquad Z(f) = \sum_{a \in \mathcal{A}} c_a(f) f_a \tag{8.19}$$

subject to

$$\left.\begin{array}{lll} f_a - \sum\limits_{p \in \mathcal{P}} \delta_{ap} h_p = 0 & \forall a \in \mathcal{A} & \\ G_{ij} = Q_{ij} - \sum\limits_{p \in \mathcal{P}_{ij}} h_p = 0 & \forall (i,j) \in \mathcal{W} & (u) \\ h_p \geq 0 & \forall\, p \in \mathcal{P} & (\rho) \end{array}\right\} \tag{8.20}$$

where $u \in \Re^{|\mathcal{W}|}$ and $\rho \in \Re^{|\mathcal{P}|}$ are vectors of dual variables. Furthermore, we will subsequently employ the notation $G = (G_{ij} : (i,j) \in \mathcal{W})$.

8.2.4 Analysis of Necessary Conditions and Their Economic Interpretation

The Kuhn-Tucker necessary conditions for (8.19)–(8.20) are

$$\nabla_h Z + [\nabla_h G]^T u - \rho = 0 \qquad \rho h = 0 \qquad \rho \geq 0$$

where

$$\nabla_h Z = \left(\frac{\partial Z}{\partial h_p} : p \in \mathcal{P} \right) \tag{8.21}$$

$$\nabla_h G = \left(\frac{\partial G}{\partial h_p} : p \in \mathcal{P} \right) \tag{8.22}$$

$$\frac{\partial Z}{\partial h_p} = \sum_{a \in \mathcal{A}} \frac{\partial f_a}{\partial h_p} \frac{\partial Z}{\partial f_a} \tag{8.23}$$

$$= \sum_{a \in \mathcal{A}} \delta_{ap} \frac{\partial [c_a(f) f_a]}{\partial f_a} \tag{8.24}$$

$$= \sum_{a \in \mathcal{A}} \delta_{ap} MC_a \tag{8.25}$$

$$\equiv MC_p \tag{8.26}$$

$$\frac{\partial G_{ij}}{\partial h_p} = \begin{cases} -1 & \text{if } p \in \mathcal{P}_{ij} \\ 0 & \text{if } p \notin \mathcal{P}_{ij} \end{cases} \tag{8.27}$$

In the above, we have employed the following definitions of marginal arc latency and marginal path latency:

$$MC_a \equiv \frac{\partial [c_a(f) f_a]}{\partial f_a}$$

$$MC_p \equiv \sum_a \delta_{ap} MC_a$$

Therefore

$$MC_p - u_{ij} - \rho_p = 0, \quad p \in \mathcal{P}_{ij} \tag{8.28}$$

$$h_p > 0 \Longrightarrow \rho_p = 0 \tag{8.29}$$

$$MC_p > u_{ij} \Longrightarrow \rho_p > 0 \Longrightarrow h_p = 0 \tag{8.30}$$

Consequently

$$h_p > 0,\ p \in \mathcal{P}_{ij} \Longrightarrow \quad MC_p = u_{ij} \quad \forall\,(i,j) \in \mathcal{W},\ p \in \mathcal{P}_{ij} \tag{8.31}$$

$$MC_p > u_{ij},\ p \in \mathcal{P}_{ij} \Longrightarrow \quad h_p = 0 \quad \forall\,(i,j) \in \mathcal{W},\ p \in \mathcal{P}_{ij} \tag{8.32}$$

Note that (8.32) is derivable from (8.31) and need not be separately articulated. Expression (8.31) is the mathematical representation of Wardrop's Second Principle. The economic interpretation of (8.31)–(8.32) is immediate: all utilized paths for a given origin-destination (OD) pair must have equal marginal latencies. If this did not occur, it would be possible to lower total (system-wide) latency by shifting flows among paths. The preceding development suggests the following result:

Theorem 8.1 *(System optimality in terms of marginal path latencies, delays or costs) A flow pattern $h^* \in \Omega_2$ is a systems optimal flow pattern when individual arc latency functions are differentiable and the total latency function (8.19) is convex for all $f \in \Omega_1$ if and only if*

$$\left.\begin{aligned} &[MC_p(h^*) - u_{ij}]\, h_p^* = 0 \quad \forall\,(i,j) \in \mathcal{W}, p \in \mathcal{P}_{ij} \\ &u_{ij} = \arg\min_{p \in \mathcal{P}_{ij}} [MC_p(h^*)] \quad \forall\,(i,j) \in \mathcal{W} \end{aligned}\right\} \tag{8.33}$$

Proof. The Kuhn-Tucker conditions are necessary and sufficient since the program (8.19) is convex. The result follows immediately from (8.31) and (8.32). ■

8.2.5 The Frank-Wolfe Algorithm for System Optimal Traffic Assignment

A seemingly major problem associated with model (8.19) is that it employs explicit path variables, and there can literally be millions of paths in a network containing several hundred arcs and several dozen nodes. It is possible, however, to avoid complete enumeration of paths by carefully employing the Frank-Wolfe algorithm, introduced in a Chap. 7 without consideration of path variables. To see how this is done, we construct a linear approximation of the objective function of (8.19) at the current path flow vector h^k:

$$Z(h) \approx Z_L(h) = Z(h^k) + \left[\nabla_h Z(h^k)\right]^T (h - h^k) \tag{8.34}$$

where

$$Z(h) = [Z(f)]_{f=\Delta h} \tag{8.35}$$

denotes the substitution of the definitional constraints, relating arc flows to path flows, into the objective function. Also recall from (8.26) that

$$\nabla_h Z = (MC_p : p \in \mathcal{P})$$

Hence

$$Z_L = \sum_{p \in \mathcal{P}} MC_p(h^k)(h_p - h_p^k) \tag{8.36}$$

Because we may ignore additive constants, $\min Z_L \Longleftrightarrow \min Z'_L$, where

$$Z'_L = \sum_{p \in \mathcal{P}} MC_p(h^k) h_p$$

Furthermore, note that $\min Z'_L \Longleftrightarrow \min Z''_L$, where

$$Z''_L = \sum_{(i,j) \in \mathcal{W}} MC_{ij}^{k*} \sum_{p \in \mathcal{P}_{ij}} h_p$$

and

$$\begin{aligned}
MC_{ij}^{k*} &\equiv \min\{MC_p(h^k) : p \in \mathcal{P}_{ij}\} && (8.37)\\
&= \min\left\{\sum_{a \in \mathcal{A}} \delta_{ap} MC_a\left(f^k\right) : p \in \mathcal{P}_{ij}\right\} && (8.38)\\
&= \min\left\{\sum_{a \in \mathcal{A}} \delta_{ap} \frac{\partial}{\partial f_a}\left[c_a\left(f^k\right) f_a^k\right] : p \in \mathcal{P}_{ij}\right\} && (8.39)
\end{aligned}$$

That is, MC_{ij}^{k*} is the minimum marginal path latency between origin i and destination j under flow conditions h^k and can be determined from arc level flow and latency information according to (8.39). For reasons discussed previously, we have indicated in (8.39) that arc latencies may potentially be nonseparable. The above observations indicate that Step 1 (ALP^k) of the Frank-Wolfe algorithm is most easily solved by assigning all of a given origin-destination demand to the minimum path connecting that OD pair when arc impedances are taken to be marginal arc latencies evaluated for the current arc flow vector. This procedure is called all-or-nothing assignment and is explained in detail through numerical examples introduced below.

For the moment, it is enough to say that the Frank-Wolfe algorithm for system optimal traffic assignment is the following:

Frank Wolfe Algorithm for the System Optimal Traffic Assignment

Step 0. *(Initialization)* Set $k = 0$. Determine an initial feasible solution $h^0 \in \Omega_2$. Compute $f^0 = \Delta h^0$.

Step 1A. *(All-or-nothing assignment)* Based on the fixed arc impedances $\{MC_a(f^k)\}$, perform an all-or-nothing assignment to determine the arc flow pattern $\bar{h}^k$. That is, if $q \in \mathcal{P}_{ij}$ is the current minimum path between OD pair (i, j), then

$$\bar{h}_q^k = Q_{ij} \quad \text{and} \quad \bar{h}_p^k = 0 \quad \forall p \in (\mathcal{P}_{ij} \backslash q)$$

for all $(i, j) \in \mathcal{W}$.

Step 1B. *(Determine the direction vector)* Calculate the direction vector

$$d^k = \bar{h}^k - h^k$$

Step 2. *(Determine step size)* Calculate the optimal step size

$$\theta_k = \arg \min_{0 \leq \theta \leq 1} \{Z(h^k + \theta d^k)\}$$

Step 3. *(Updating and stopping test)* Calculate the new flows according to

$$h^{k+1} = h^k + \theta^k d^k \tag{8.40}$$

$$f^{k+1} = \Delta h^{k+1} \tag{8.41}$$

If

$$\max_a \mid h_p^{k+1} - h_p^k \mid < \epsilon_1 \tag{8.42}$$

where ϵ_1 is a preset tolerance, stop. Otherwise set $k = k + 1$ and go to Step 1A.

The careful reader will note that the Frank-Wolfe algorithm may be implemented in terms of arc flows in a way that determines arc flows from the current minimum paths found with a minimum-path algorithm; thereupon one may discard all path information. In doing so there is no need to enumerate paths a priori. It is instructive for the reader to re-state the Frank-Wolfe algorithm in its arc-flow form.

8.2.6 Variational Inequality Formulation of System Optimal Traffic Assignment

We note in this section that it is possible to state the system optimal traffic assignment problem as a variational inequality and that this form is completely equivalent to the optimization form (8.19). The relevant result is:

Theorem 8.2 *(Variational inequality for system optimal flow) Assume the arc latency functions are differentiable. The system optimal traffic assignment problem (8.19) is equivalent to the following variational inequality problem: find $f^* \in \Omega_1$ such that*

$$\sum_{a\in\mathcal{A}} MC_a(f^*)(f_a - f_a^*) \geq 0 \qquad \forall f \in \Omega_1 \tag{8.43}$$

Proof. The proof is in two parts: (i) show that conditions (8.33) for a system optimal flow pattern imply variational inequality (8.43) and (ii) show that (8.43) implies (8.33).

(i) [system optimal$\Longrightarrow$(8.43)] Note that (8.33) requires

$$\begin{aligned} MC_p(h^*) &\geq u_{ij} \qquad \forall p \in \mathcal{P}_{ij} \\ &\Longrightarrow MC_p(h^*)\left(h_p - h_p^*\right) \geq u_{ij}\left(h_p - h_p^*\right) \end{aligned} \tag{8.44}$$

where $h, h^* \in \Omega_2$ since

$$\left(h_p - h_p^*\right) < 0 \Longrightarrow h_p^* > h_p \geq 0 \Longrightarrow MC_p(h^*) = u_{ij}$$

Summing both sides of (8.44) over all paths gives

$$\begin{aligned} \sum_{p\in\mathcal{P}} MC_p(h^*)\left(h_p - h_p^*\right) &\geq \sum_{(i,j)\in\mathcal{W}} u_{ij} \sum_{p\in\mathcal{P}_{ij}} \left(h_p - h_p^*\right) \\ &= \sum_{(i,j)\in\mathcal{W}} u_{ij}\left(Q_{ij} - Q_{ij}\right) = 0 \end{aligned} \tag{8.45}$$

Note that

$$\begin{aligned} \sum_{p\in\mathcal{P}} MC_p(h^*)\left(h_p - h_p^*\right) &= \sum_{p\in\mathcal{P}} \sum_{a\in\mathcal{A}} \delta_{ap} MC_a(f^*)\left(h_p - h_p^*\right) \\ &= \sum_{p\in\mathcal{P}} MC_a(f^*)\left(\sum_{a\in\mathcal{A}} \delta_{ap} h_p - \sum_{a\in\mathcal{A}} \delta_{ap} h_p^*\right) \\ &= \sum_{p\in\mathcal{P}} MC_a(f^*)(f_a - f_a^*) \end{aligned} \tag{8.46}$$

Results (8.45) and (8.46) yield (8.43). This completes part (i).

(ii) [(8.43)$\Longrightarrow$system optimal] We note that (8.43) implies that h^* solves the primal linear program

$$\min \left[MC(h^*)\right]^T h$$

subject to

$$\Gamma h = Q$$

$$h \geq 0$$

whose dual is

$$\max u^T Q \quad \text{subject to} \quad u^T \Gamma \leq MC(h^*)$$

Dual feasibility requires

$$u^T \Gamma \leq MC(h^*) \Longrightarrow u_{ij} \leq MC_p(h^*) \qquad \forall (i,j) \in \mathcal{W},\, p \in \mathcal{P}_{ij} \tag{8.47}$$

Complementary slackness means

$$\left[MC(h^*) - u^T \Gamma\right] h^* = 0 \Longrightarrow$$

$$\left[MC_p(h^*) - u_{ij}\right] h_p = 0 \qquad \forall (i,j) \in \mathcal{W},\, p \in \mathcal{P}_{ij} \tag{8.48}$$

Primal feasibility, dual feasibility and complementary slackness give (8.33). ■

8.2.7 Existence of System Optimal Solutions and Sensitivity Analysis

We know from Chap. 7 that existence of a solution to a mathematical program or a variational inequality problem is assured if the feasible set is convex and compact while the relevant vector function is continuous. The formal statement of this result for the system optimal traffic assignment problem is:

Theorem 8.3 *(Existence of a system optimal flow pattern) If demands are bounded while the arc latency functions $c_a(f) : \Re^{|\mathcal{A}|} \longrightarrow \Re^{|\mathcal{A}|}$ for all $a \in \mathcal{A}$ are continuously differentiable, then a solution of the system optimal traffic assignment problem (8.19) exists.*

Proof. The proof is immediate if the Stampacchia existence theorem of Chap. 7 is applied to the variational inequality representation. ■

It is also possible to apply our previous results on sensitivity analysis to study how an optimal solution of the system optimal traffic assignment problem changes as a result of parameter perturbations, but only if great care is exercised in dealing with path variables. Path variables pose a problem since generally speaking flow patterns that are unique in arc variables are not unique in path variables. Since the issue of sensitivity analysis of problems with path variables arises again in our study of user equilibrium traffic assignment for road networks, we postpone a discussion of such matters for the time being.

8.2.8 Telecommunications Combined Routing and Flow Control Problem

It is sometimes necessary in telecommunications networks to reject demand. Questions of equity, market share, regulation and law abound when demand requests are refused. When demands are endogenously modeled as continuous variables, we refer to demand rejection as *flow control*. For our purposes, we distinguish between two types of flow control:

(1) Arc-by-arc flow control, and

(2) End-to-end flow control

In this section we present a particularly simple model of end-to-end flow control that is due to Gafni and Bertsekas (1984) and Bertsekas and Gallager (1992).

Consider a type of end-to-end flow control, in a quasi-static environment, that restricts flow through the manipulation of both routes and the fraction of demand admitted to the network. This is accomplished by the relaxation of the demand constraints and their replacement by penalty functions $\mathcal{F}_{ij}(Q)$ for every origin-destination pair $(i,j) \in \mathcal{W}$. These penalty functions must assure that a substantial penalty is imposed on the rejection of all demand. If the penalty functions are separable and of the form

$$\mathcal{F}_{ij}(Q_{ij}) = \left(\frac{\alpha_{ij}}{Q_{ij}}\right)^z \quad \forall\, (i,j) \in \mathcal{W} \tag{8.49}$$

for scalar $z \geq 1$ and $\alpha_{ij} \in \Re^1_{++}$ for all origin-destination pairs $(i,j) \in \mathcal{W}$, we are assured of the correct behavior since then

$$\frac{d\mathcal{F}_{ij}(Q_{ij})}{dQ_{ij}} < 0 \tag{8.50}$$

as Gafni and Bertsekas (1984) point out.

As a consequence of the above development, the mathematical program stating the simultaneous flow control and routing problem is

$$\min \qquad Z(f,Q) = \sum_{a\in\mathcal{A}} c_a(f) f_a + \sum_{(i,j)\in\mathcal{W}} \mathcal{F}_{ij}(Q_{ij}) \tag{8.51}$$

subject to

$$f_a - \sum_{p \in \mathcal{P}} \delta_{ap} h_p = 0 \quad \forall a \in \mathcal{A} \tag{8.52}$$

$$Q_{ij} - \sum_{p \in \mathcal{P}_{ij}} h_p = 0 \quad \forall (i,j) \in \mathcal{W} \tag{8.53}$$

$$h_p \geq 0 \quad \forall p \in \mathcal{P} \tag{8.54}$$

The above formulation is very similar but not identical to the fixed demand system optimal traffic assignment problem. The key aspect of (8.51)–(8.54) that distinguishes it from the system optimal traffic assignment problem is the presence of demand variables. When we turn to the study of user equilibrium, we shall develop an algorithm capable of solving (8.51)–(8.54).

8.2.9 Numerical Example: F-W Algorithm and System Optimal Traffic Assignment

Let us now consider a simple transportation example and speak of all impedances as costs per unit of flow. The Frank-Wolfe algorithm presented in Sect. 8.2.5 may be implemented in such a way that path variables are not saved but rather only arc flows are saved from iteration to iteration. This means that only one path is generated per origin-destination pair per iteration of the algorithm. Furthermore, the optimal step θ_k at iteration k must solve the following mathematical program:

$$\left.\begin{array}{l} \min Z(f^k + \theta d^k) = \sum_{a \in \mathcal{A}} c_a(f^k + \theta d^k) \cdot \left(f_a^k + \theta d_a^k\right) \\ \text{subject to} \\ \theta \in [0,1] \end{array}\right\} \tag{8.55}$$

Since

$$\frac{d}{d\theta} = \sum_{b \in \mathcal{A}} \frac{\partial \left(f_b^k + \theta d_b^k\right)}{\partial \theta} \frac{\partial}{\partial \left(f_b^k + \theta d_b^k\right)} = \sum_{b \in \mathcal{A}} d_b^k \frac{\partial}{\partial \left(f_b^k + \theta d_b^k\right)}$$

we have

$$\begin{aligned} \frac{dZ\left(f^k + \theta d^k\right)}{d\theta} &= \sum_{b \in \mathcal{A}} d_b^k \frac{\partial}{\partial \left(f_b^k + \theta d_b^k\right)} \sum_{a \in \mathcal{A}} c_a(f^k + \theta d^k) \cdot \left(f_a^k + \theta d_a^k\right) \\ &= \sum_{a \in \mathcal{A}} d_a^k \cdot c_a(f^k + \theta d^k) + \sum_{a \in \mathcal{A}} \sum_{b \in \mathcal{A}} d_b^k \frac{\partial c_a(f^k + \theta d^k)}{\partial \left(f_b^k + \theta d_b^k\right)} \equiv F_k(\theta) \end{aligned}$$

so that

$$\theta_k = \left[\arg\left\{F^k(\theta) = 0\right\}\right]_0^1 \tag{8.56}$$

where

$$[v]_0^1 \equiv \begin{cases} 1 & \text{if } v > 1 \\ v & \text{if } 0 \leq v \leq 1 \\ 0 & \text{if } v < 0 \end{cases}$$

Note that generally one would employ a one-dimensional line search algorithm to find θ_k, for the method employed above depends on $F^k(\theta)$ being convex and $F^k(\theta) = 0$ having real roots. Note also that when the arc cost functions are separable

$$F_k(\theta) = \sum_{a \in \mathcal{A}} d_a^k \cdot \left[c_a(f^k + \theta d^k) + \frac{\partial c_a(f_a^k + \theta d_a^k)}{\partial (f_a^k + \theta d_a^k)} \right],$$

a particularly simple form.

For a numerical example, consider the network defined by the forward star array

From i	To j	(i,j)	Arc name
1	2	$(1,2)$	a_1
2	3	$(2,3)$	a_2
2	4	$(2,4)$	a_3
4	3	$(4,3)$	a_4

so that the arc set is

$$\mathcal{A} = \{a_1, a_2, a_3, a_4\}$$

The single origin node is node 1, and the demand nodes are 3 and 4. That is, $\mathcal{W} = \{(1,3), (1,4)\}$. The fixed origin-destination demands themselves are

$$Q_{13} = 60$$

$$Q_{14} = 40$$

The arc unit latency functions are

$$c_{a_i} = A_i + \frac{B_i}{K_i - f_{a_i}} \qquad i = 1, 2, 3, 4$$

These are rectangular hyperbolas whose parameters are given by the following table:

Arc index (i)	A_i	B_i	K_i
1	10	0	∞
2	10	50	50
3	100	50	100
4	100	50	100

For this network we need to articulate path definitions and path marginal costs. In particular, note that there are three paths:

$$\begin{aligned} p_1 &= \{a_1, a_2\} \\ p_2 &= \{a_1, a_3, a_4\} \\ p_3 &= \{a_1, a_3\} \end{aligned}$$

It follows that the arc flows and path flows are related according to

$$\begin{aligned} f_{a_1} &= h_{p_1} + h_{p_2} + h_{p_3} \\ f_{a_2} &= h_{p_1} \\ f_{a_3} &= h_{p_2} + h_{p_3} \\ f_{a_4} &= h_{p_2} \end{aligned}$$

It is also immediate that arc marginal costs and path marginal costs obey

$$\begin{aligned} MCp_1 &= MC_{a_1} + MC_{a_2} \\ MCp_2 &= MC_{a_1} + MC_{a_3} + MC_{a_4} \\ MCp_3 &= MC_{a_1} + MC_{a_3} \end{aligned}$$

The marginal cost function for each arc a_i has the form

$$\begin{aligned} MC_{a_i} &= \frac{\partial}{\partial f_{a_i}} \left[\left(A_i + \frac{B_i}{K_i - f_{a_i}} \right) f_{a_i} \right] \\ &= A_i + \frac{B_i}{K_i - f_{a_i}} + \frac{B_i f_{a_i}}{(K_i - f_{a_i})^2} \end{aligned}$$

The flow conservation constraints are of course

$$\begin{aligned} h_{p_1} + h_{p_2} &= 60 \\ h_{p_3} &= 40 \end{aligned}$$

We are now ready to begin the formal application of the Frank-Wolfe algorithm to our problem:

Step 0. *(Initialization)* Set $k = 0$ and pick the initial solution

$$h^0 = (0, 60, 40)^T \Longrightarrow f^0 = (100, 0, 100, 60)^T$$

Step 1._(All-or-Nothing Assignment, $k = 0$)_ The relevant arc marginal costs are readily calculated to be

$$\begin{aligned}
MC_{a_1}^0 &= 10 + 0 = 10 \\
MC_{a_2}^0 &= 10 + \frac{50}{50 - f_{a_2}^0} + 50\frac{f_{a_2}^0}{(50 - f_{a_2}^0)^2} = 11 \\
MC_{a_3}^0 &= 100 + \frac{50}{100 - f_{a_3}^0} + 50\frac{f_{a_3}}{(100 - f_{a_3}^0)^2} = +\infty \\
MC_{a_4}^0 &= 100 + \frac{50}{100 - f_{a_4}^0} + 50\frac{f_{a_4}}{(100 - f_{a_4}^0)^2} \\
&= 100 + \frac{50}{100 - 60} + 50\frac{60}{(100 - 60)^2} \\
&= 100 + 1.125 + 0.1875 = 101.31
\end{aligned}$$

Therefore, the associated path marginal costs are

$$MC_{p_1} = 10 + 11 = 21,\ MC_{p_2} = +\infty,\ MC_{p_3} = 10 + \ \infty = \infty$$

Hence, the "shortest" path for OD pair $(1, 3)$ is p_1 and for OD pair $(1, 4)$ is p_3. It follows that the all-or-nothing assignment is

$$\bar{h}^0 = (60, 0, 40)^T \Longrightarrow \bar{f}^{\,0} = (100, 60, 40, 0)^T$$

The direction vector may be based on either the arc flows or the path flows. In order to obtain an answer expressed in terms of path flows, as would be appropriate when considering a freight network, we elect the following representation of the direction vector

$$\begin{aligned}
d^0 &= \bar{h}^0 - h^0 \\
&= (60, 0, 40)^T - (0, 60, 40)^T \\
&= (60, -60, 0)^T
\end{aligned}$$

Step 2._(Select step, $k = 0$)_ We may calculate the optimal step size

$$\theta_0 = \arg\left\{\min_{0 \leq \theta \leq 1} \left(h^0 + \theta d^0\right)\right\}$$

using a line search algorithm, or instead elect to use a sequence of slowly decreasing step sizes and avoid the step-size computational overhead. We choose the latter approach and set

$$\theta_0 = \frac{5}{6}$$

Step 3. *(Updating, $k = 0$)* The new iterate is

$$\begin{aligned} h^1 &= h^0 + \theta_0 d^0 = (0, 60, 40)^T + \frac{5}{6}(60, -60, 0)^T = (50, 10, 40)^T \\ &\Longrightarrow f^{\,1} = (100, 50, 50, 10)^T \end{aligned}$$

Set $k = 0 + 1 = 1$.

Step 1. *(All-or-nothing assignment, $k = 1$)* The relevant marginal costs are

$$\begin{aligned} MC_1^1 &= 10 \\ MC_2^1 &= 10 + \frac{50}{50-50} + \frac{50(50)}{(50-50)^2} = \infty \\ MC_3^1 &= 100 + \frac{50}{100-50} + \frac{50(50)}{(100-50)^2} = 102 \\ MC_4^1 &= 100 + \frac{50}{100-10} + \frac{50(10)}{(100-10)^2} = 100.62 \\ MC_{p_1}^1 &= 10 + \infty = \infty \\ MC_{p_2}^1 &= 10 + 102 + 100.62 = 212.62 \Longrightarrow p_2 \text{ shortest for OD } (1,3) \\ MC_{p_3}^1 &= 10 + 102 = 112 \Longrightarrow p_3 \text{ shortest for OD } (1,4) \end{aligned}$$

The all-or-nothing assignments is

$$\bar{h}^1 = (0, 60, 40)^T$$

The direction vector is

$$\begin{aligned} d^1 &= \bar{h}^1 - h^1 \\ &= (0, 60, 40)^T - (50, 10, 40)^T \\ &= (-50, 50, 0)^T \end{aligned}$$

Step 2. *(Select step, $k = 1$)* We choose

$$\theta_1 = .41$$

Step 3. *(Updating, $k = 1$)* The new iterate is

$$h^2 = h^1 + \theta_0 d^1 = (50, 10, 40)^T + 0.42(-50, 50, 0)^T = (29, 31, 40)^T$$

$$\Longrightarrow f^{\,2} = (100, 29, 71, 31)^T$$

Set $k = 1 + 1 = 2$.

If we continue in the fashion indicated above, the following iteration log is created:

k	Iteration h^k	$MC^k_{p_1}$	$MC^k_{p_2}$	Ddirection d^k	Step θ_k
0	$(0, 60, 40)^T$	21	∞	$(60, -60, 0)^T$	0.83
1	$(50, 10, 40)^T$	∞	212.62	$(-50, 50, 0)^T$	0.41
2	$(29, 31, 40)^T$	25.669	217.45	$(31, -31, 0)^T$	0.21
3	$(35.5, 24.5, 40)^T$	31.891	214.84	$(24.5, -24.5, 0)^T$	0.20
4	$(40.4, 19.6, 40)^T$	47.127	213.84	$(19.6, -19.6, 0)^T$	0.20
5	$(44.3, 15.7, 40)^T$	96.947	213.25	$(15.7, -15.7, 0)^T$	0.14
6	$(46.5, 13.5, 40)^T$	224.09	212.98		

Based on our knowledge that, for system optimal flows, marginal costs are equal for utilized paths connecting the same origin-destination pair, we may calculate the accuracy of the approximation achieved for $k = 6$:

$$\frac{\left| MC^6_{p_2} - MC^6_{p_1} \right|}{MC^6_{p_2}} 100 = \left(\frac{224.09 - 212.98}{224.09} \right) 100 \approx 4.96\,\%$$

So, if the stated stopping criterion is "within 5 % of equilibrium", we stop after six iterations. Note that for this problem the chosen step size sequence was highly inefficient since the qualitative nature of the direction vector did not change between iterations 2 and 6. This means that a bolder step size could have taken us directly from the approximation h^2 to the approximation h^6.

8.3 User Optimal Traffic Assignment with Separable Functions

We now turn our attention to modeling and computing network user equilibria. We consider user optimal flows to be appropriate for vehicular networks. Hence, for this example, we do not speak of latencies and message demands but rather of unit latencies and transportation demands. We first note that transportation demand need not be fixed; instead it may be determined endogenously in a fashion that is consistent with known models of transportation demand. For our present purposes, we employ transportation demand functions of the form

$$Q_{ij}(u_{ij}) \quad (i, j) \in \mathcal{W}$$

where

$$u_{ij} = \min\left(c_p : p \in \mathcal{P}_{ij}\right) \quad \forall (i,j) \in \mathcal{W}$$

The vector of these demand functions is denoted by $Q(u) : \Re^{|\mathcal{W}|} \longrightarrow \Re^{|\mathcal{W}|}$. We shall denote the inverse demand functions by

$$u_{ij} = \theta_{ij}(Q_{ij}) \quad (i,j) \in \mathcal{W}$$

and the vector of such functions as $\theta(Q) : \Re^{|\mathcal{W}|} \longrightarrow \Re^{|\mathcal{W}|}$. Let us also assume that arc latency functions are separable; that is, we use the following representation for unit arc latency:

$$c_a(f_a) \quad \forall a \in \mathcal{A}$$

from which it follows that

$$c_p(h) = \sum_{a \in \mathcal{A}} \delta_{ap} c_a(f_a)$$

In light of the above and using the notation introduced for system optimal traffic assignment, Wardrop's First Principle may be expressed symbolically as

$$(c_p - u_{ij})h_p = 0 \quad \forall\ (i,j) \in \mathcal{W},\ p \in \mathcal{P}_{ij} \tag{8.57}$$

$$c_p - u_{ij} \geq 0 \quad \forall\ (i,j) \in \mathcal{W},\ p \in \mathcal{P}_{ij} \tag{8.58}$$

$$h_p \geq 0 \quad \forall\ (i,j) \in \mathcal{W},\ p \in \mathcal{P}_{ij} \tag{8.59}$$

$$Q_{ij}(u_{ij}) - \sum_{p \in \mathcal{P}_{ij}} h_p = 0 \quad \forall\ (i,j) \in \mathcal{W} \tag{8.60}$$

Note, in particular, that (8.57) requires travel latency to equal minimum travel latency when path flow is positive

Beckmann et al. (1956) presented a mathematical program equivalent to user equilibrium for the case of separable latency and separable, invertible demand. That program is the following:

$$\min \quad Z(f,Q) = \sum_{a \in \mathcal{A}} \int_0^{f_a} c_a(x_a)dx_a - \sum_{(i,j) \in \mathcal{W}} \int_0^{T_{ij}} \theta_{ij}(y_{ij})dy_{ij} \tag{8.61}$$

subject to

$$f_a - \sum_{p \in \mathcal{P}} \delta_{ap} h_p = 0 \qquad \forall\, a \in \mathcal{A} \tag{8.62}$$

$$G_{ij} = Q_{ij} - \sum_{p \in \mathcal{P}_{ij}} h_p = 0 \qquad \forall\ (i,j) \in \mathcal{W} \qquad (u) \tag{8.63}$$

$$-h_p \leq 0 \qquad \forall\, p \in \mathcal{P} \qquad (\rho) \tag{8.64}$$

$$-Q_{ij} \leq 0 \qquad \forall\ (i,j) \in \mathcal{W} \qquad (\eta) \tag{8.65}$$

where, we reiterate, notation similar to that introduced in the discussion of system optimal traffic assignment is employed and $\eta \in \Re^{|\mathcal{W}|}$ is a vector of dual variables for the constraints $-Q \leq 0$; likewise u and ρ are vectors of dual variables for flow conservation and nonnegativity of path flows. It is not immediately apparent that a solution of Beckmann's program will satisfy the user equilibrium conditions (8.57)–(8.60). To establish this, we must examine the necessary conditions for (8.61)–(8.65).

The Kuhn-Tucker conditions for (8.61)–(8.65) are

$$\nabla_h Z + (\nabla_h G)^T u - \rho = 0 \quad \rho^T h = 0 \quad \rho \geq 0 \tag{8.66}$$

$$\nabla_Q Z + (\nabla_Q G)^T u - \eta = 0 \quad \eta^T Q = 0 \quad \eta \geq 0 \tag{8.67}$$

Furthermore, it is easy to show that

$$\frac{\partial Z}{\partial h_p} = c_p \tag{8.68}$$

$$\frac{\partial G_{ij}}{\partial h_p} = -1 \tag{8.69}$$

Now observe that

$$\frac{\partial Z}{\partial Q_{ij}} = -\theta_{ij}(Q_{ij}) \tag{8.70}$$

$$\frac{\partial G_{ij}}{\partial Q_{ij}} = 1 \tag{8.71}$$

Hence,

$$c_p - u_{ij} - \rho_p = 0 \qquad \rho_p h_p = 0 \quad \rho_p \geq 0 \quad \forall\, (i,j) \in \mathcal{W},\, p \in \mathcal{P}_{ij} \tag{8.72}$$

$$-\theta_{ij}(Q_{ij}) + u_{ij} - \eta_{ij} = 0 \quad \eta_{ij} Q_{ij} = 0 \quad Q_{ij} \geq 0 \quad \forall\, (i,j) \in \mathcal{W} \tag{8.73}$$

From (8.72) we clearly get

$$(c_p - u_{ij}) h_p = 0 \quad c_p - u_{ij} \geq 0 \quad \forall\, (i,j) \in \mathcal{W},\, p \in \mathcal{P}_{ij} \tag{8.74}$$

Note that (8.72) and (8.73) lead to

$$Q_{ij} > 0 \Longrightarrow \quad \eta_{ij} = 0 \tag{8.75}$$

$$\theta_{ij}(Q_{ij}) < u_{ij} \Longrightarrow \quad \eta_{ij} > 0 \Longrightarrow \quad Q_{ij} = 0 \tag{8.76}$$

Hence

$$Q_{ij} > 0 \quad \Longrightarrow \quad \theta_{ij}(Q_{ij}) = u_{ij} \tag{8.77}$$

$$\theta_{ij}(Q_{ij}) < u_{ij} \quad \Longrightarrow \quad Q_{ij} = 0 \tag{8.78}$$

That is, travel demand follows the demand schedule unless, for a given origin-destination (OD) pair, the desired travel latency $\theta_{ij}(Q_{ij})$ is less than the minimum achievable travel latency u_{ij}, in which case travel demand vanishes. The interested reader is referred to Gartner (1980a) for more discussion of the intuitive motivation for Beckmann's mathematical program.

8.3.1 Uniqueness of User Equilibrium with Separable Functions

For the mathematical program introduced in the preceding section to be fully equivalent to Wardrop's first principle (WFP), we must establish that the Kuhn-Tucker conditions (8.66) and (8.67) are not only necessary but sufficient for optimality. To do this, first recall that a minimum of the mathematical program

$$\min f(x)$$

subject to

$$g(x) = 0$$

$$h(x) \leq 0$$

will be unique when

(1) $f(x)$ is strictly convex;

(2) The $h_i(x)$ are linear; and

(3) The $q_i(x)$ are convex.

When F is a twice differentiable abstract function and $x = (x_1, x_2, \ldots, x_n)^T$, we may define the Hessian of $F(x)$ as

$$H[F(x)] \equiv \begin{pmatrix} \frac{\partial^2 F}{\partial x_1^2} & \frac{\partial^2 F}{\partial x_1 \partial x_2} & \cdots & \frac{\partial^2 F}{\partial x_1 \partial x_n} \\ \frac{\partial^2 F}{\partial x_2 \partial x_1} & \frac{\partial^2 F}{\partial x_2^2} & \cdots & \frac{\partial^2 F}{\partial x_2 \partial x_n} \\ \vdots & \vdots & \ddots & \vdots \\ \frac{\partial^2 F}{\partial x_n \partial x_1} & \frac{\partial^2 F}{\partial x_n \partial x_2} & \cdots & \frac{\partial^2 F}{\partial x_n^2} \end{pmatrix} \tag{8.79}$$

Furthermore, we know that

$$H[F(x)] \text{ positive definite} \Longrightarrow F(x) \text{ strictly convex},$$

although the converse is not necessarily true. Moreover, the $n \times n$ matrix M is said to be positive definite if its quadratic form, for any $x \neq 0$, obeys

$$xMx^T > 0, \tag{8.80}$$

Clearly, the constraints (8.62)–(8.65) are linear, so the feasible set

$$\Omega_0 = \left\{ \begin{pmatrix} f \\ Q \end{pmatrix} : f = \Delta h, \quad Q = \Gamma h, \quad h \geq 0 \right\} \tag{8.81}$$

is convex. Thus, if the Hessian of $Z(f, Q)$ in (8.61) is positive definite, Beckmann's program is a convex program with strictly convex objective function. As a consequence, any arc and origin-destination flow pattern computed from it will be unique. Let us break $Z(f, Q)$ into two pieces:

$$\Phi(f) = \sum_{a \in \mathcal{A}} \int_0^{f_a} c_a(x_a) dx_a \tag{8.82}$$

$$\Psi(Q) = \sum_{(i,j) \in \mathcal{W}} \int_0^{Q_{ij}} \theta_{ij}(y_{ij}) dy_{ij}, \tag{8.83}$$

so that $Z(f,Q) = \Phi(f) + \Psi(Q)$. If $H[\Phi(f)]$ is positive definite and $H[-\Psi(Q)]$ is positive definite, clearly $Z(f, Q)$ is strictly convex because the sum of (strictly) convex functions is itself (strictly) convex. Note that

$$H[\Phi(f)] = \begin{pmatrix} \frac{\partial c_1}{\partial f_1} & 0 & 0 & \cdots \\ 0 & \frac{\partial c_2}{\partial f_2} & 0 & \cdots \\ 0 & 0 & \ddots & \cdots \\ 0 & 0 & \cdots & \ddots \end{pmatrix} \tag{8.84}$$

$$H[-\Psi(Q)] = \begin{pmatrix} \frac{-\partial \theta_{11}}{\partial Q_{11}} & 0 & 0 & \cdots \\ 0 & \frac{-\partial \theta_{12}}{\partial Q_{12}} & 0 & \cdots \\ 0 & 0 & \ddots & \cdots \\ 0 & 0 & \cdots & \ddots \end{pmatrix} \tag{8.85}$$

Let us assume:

(1) Arc latencies are strictly monotonically increasing:

$$\frac{\partial c_a}{\partial f_a} > 0 \qquad \forall\, a$$

(2) Origin-destination inverse demands are strictly monotonically decreasing:

$$\frac{\partial \theta_{ij}}{\partial Q_{ij}} < 0 \qquad \forall\, i, j$$

Under these assumptions, both $H[\Phi(f)]$ and $H[-\Psi(Q)]$ are diagonal matrices with only positive elements on their diagonals. Such matrices are always positive definite.

We also recall that the Jacobian matrix of an abstract vector function $F(x) = [F_1(x), \ldots, F_n(x)]^T$ where $x = (x_1, \ldots, x_n)^T$ is

$$J(F) \equiv \begin{pmatrix} \frac{\partial F_1}{\partial x_1} & \frac{\partial F_1}{\partial x_2} & \cdots & \frac{\partial F_1}{\partial x_n} \\ \frac{\partial F_2}{\partial x_1} & \frac{\partial F_2}{\partial x_2} & \cdots & \frac{\partial F_2}{\partial x_n} \\ \vdots & \vdots & \ddots & \vdots \\ \frac{\partial F_n}{\partial x_1} & \frac{\partial F_n}{\partial x_2} & \cdots & \frac{\partial F_n}{\partial x_n} \end{pmatrix} \tag{8.86}$$

Thus, we see by virtue of the nature of $Z(f, Q)$ in (8.61) that

$$H[\Phi(f)] = J(c) \quad (8.87)$$

$$H[-\Psi(Q)] = J(-\theta) \quad (8.88)$$

The following result is immediate:

Theorem 8.4 *(Unique solution of Beckmann's program with separable functions) If Beckmann's program (8.61)–(8.65) with separable functions and invertible demands has a solution*

$$\begin{pmatrix} f^* \\ Q^* \end{pmatrix} \in \Omega_0$$

when $J(c)$ and $J(-\theta)$ are positive definite, that solution is unique in arc flows and origin-destination demands. Moreover, $J(c)$ and $J(-\theta)$ are respectively positive definite if arc latencies are strictly monotonically increasing and inverse demands are strictly monotonically decreasing.

Proof. Immediate from the constructive arguments leading to (8.87) and (8.88). ■

An immediate corollary to Theorem 8.4 is that (8.61)–(8.65) is a bona fide equivalent optimization problem:

Corollary 8.1 *(Equivalence of Beckmann's program and user equilibrium with separable functions) Beckmann's problem (8.61)–(8.65) with separable functions is fully equivalent to the user equilibrium conditions (8.57)–(8.60) when a constraint qualification holds and arc latencies are differentiable as well as strictly monotonically increasing while inverse demands are differentiable and strictly monotonically decreasing.*

8.3.2 The Problem of Symmetry in Equivalent Optimization Problems

The preceding discussion has been concerned entirely with transportation network equilibrium in the presence of separable latency and demand functions. In many equilibrium applications the latency and demand functions are *nonseparable*, language that means

$$c_a(f) : \Re^{|\mathcal{A}|} \longrightarrow \Re^1 \quad \forall a \in \mathcal{A} \quad (8.89)$$

$$Q_{ij}(u) : \Re^{|\mathcal{W}|} \longrightarrow \Re^1 \quad \forall (i,j) \in \mathcal{W} \quad (8.90)$$

Assuming for the moment that each $Q_{ij}(\cdot)$, although nonseparable, is still invertible (which is not generally the case), we may state the following generalization of Beckmann's equivalent program:

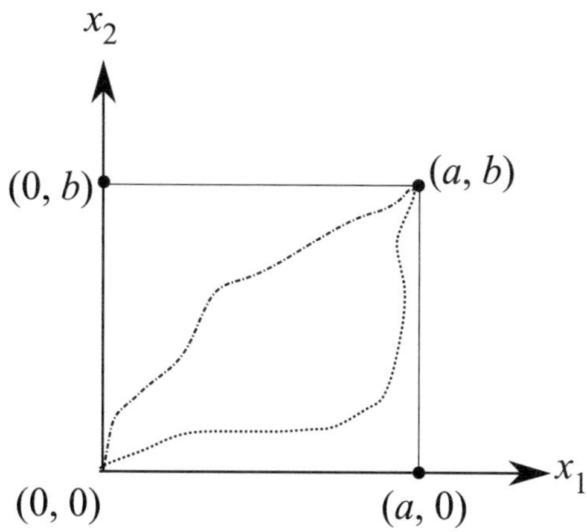

FIGURE 8.1: PATHS OF INTEGRATION

$$\left.\begin{array}{c} \min Z(f,Q) = \sum_{a\in\mathcal{A}} \oint_0^f c_a(x)dx_a - \sum_{(i,j)\in\mathcal{W}} \oint_0^Q \theta_{ij}(y)dy_{ij} \\ \text{subject to} \\ f_a - \sum_{p\in\mathcal{P}} \delta_{ap}h_p = 0 \quad \forall p\in\mathcal{P} \\ G_{ij} = Q_{ij} - \sum_{p\in\mathcal{P}_{ij}} h_p = 0 \quad \forall (i,j)\in\mathcal{W} \\ h_p \geq 0 \quad \forall p\in\mathcal{P} \end{array}\right\} \tag{8.91}$$

where "$\oint$" denotes a line integral. The Kuhn-Tucker conditions for this problem, as can be readily verified, also yield the Wardropian user equilibrium and market clearing we seek. One very critical caveat must be stated, however: the objective function $Z(f,Q)$ in (8.91) must be well-defined in the sense of being independent of the path of integration. To understand what is meant by this requirement, consider a simple line integral

$$I = \sum_{i=1}^{2} \int_{(0,0)}^{(a,b)} F_i(x_1,x_2)dx_i \tag{8.92}$$

Two right angle, *seriatim* paths of integration for (8.92) are depicted in Fig. 8.1, along with two other, arbitrary paths of integration.

For integration from $(0,0)$ to (a,b) along the first *seriatim* path (north, then east), we have

$$I_1 = \int_0^b F_2(0,x_2)dx_2 + \int_0^a F_1(x_1,b)dx_1 \tag{8.93}$$

Along the second seriatim path (east, then north), we have

$$I_2 = \int_0^a F_1(x_1, 0)dx_1 + \int_0^b F_2(a, x_2)dx_2 \tag{8.94}$$

Note that without further assumptions there is no a priori reason for the integrals I_1 and I_2 above to yield the same value. In fact, a well-known theorem related to the path independence of line integrals (Green's theorem in a plane) tells us that the general line integral

$$I = \sum_{i=0}^{n} \int_{(0,0,\ldots,0)}^{(k_1,k_2,\ldots,k_n)} F_i(x_1, x_2, \ldots)dx_i \tag{8.95}$$

is path independent (yields the same value for every path of integration) if and only if, for $x = (x_1, x_2, \ldots, x_n)^T$, we have

$$\frac{\partial F_i(x)}{\partial x_j} = \frac{\partial F_j(x)}{\partial x_i} \qquad \forall\, i, j \in [1, n]\,,\; i \neq j \tag{8.96}$$

The above conditions are a statement that the Jacobian matrix $J(F)$, where $F = (F_1, F_2, \ldots, F_n)^T$, is *symmetric*. Hence these conditions are frequently called *symmetry conditions*. They are also called *integrability conditions*.

Note that for Beckmann's equivalent program (8.91), the aforementioned symmetry conditions are

$$\frac{\partial c_a(f)}{\partial f_b} = \frac{\partial c_b(f)}{\partial f_a} \qquad \forall a, b \in \mathcal{A},\, a \neq b \tag{8.97}$$

$$\frac{\partial \theta_{ij}(Q)}{\partial Q_{kl}} = \frac{\partial \theta_{kl}(Q)}{\partial Q_{ij}} \qquad \forall\, (i,j)\,, (k,l) \in \mathcal{W},\; (i,j) \neq (k,l) \tag{8.98}$$

As a historical observation, we remark that a special case of (8.91) arises when demand is fixed:

$$\min Z(f) = \sum_{a(i,j)\in\mathcal{W}} \oint_0^f c_a(x)dx_a \tag{8.99}$$

subject to

$$\left.\begin{array}{ll} f_a - \sum_{p\in\mathcal{P}} \delta_{ap} h_p = 0 & \forall a \in \mathcal{A} \\ \sum_{p\in\mathcal{P}_{ij}} h_p = Q_{ij} & \forall\, (i,j) \in \mathcal{W} \\ h \geq 0 & \end{array}\right\} \tag{8.100}$$

Problem (8.99)–(8.100) was first studied by Dafermos (1982a,b).

It is also interesting to note that the well-known formula for integration by parts, namely

$$\int udv = u \cdot v - \int vdu, \tag{8.101}$$

allows (8.91) to be rewritten to create a further extension of Beckmann's equivalent program to nonseparable functions, namely the following:

$$\min \sum_{a \in \mathcal{A}} \oint_0^f c_a(f)df_a - \sum_{(i,j) \in \mathcal{W}} u_{ij} Q_{ij}(u) + \sum_{(i,j) \in \mathcal{W}} \oint_0^u Q_{ij}(y)dy_{ij} \tag{8.102}$$

subject to

$$\left.\begin{array}{r} f_a - \sum_{p \in \mathcal{P}} \delta_{ap} h_p = 0 \quad \forall a \in \mathcal{A} \\ \\ G_{ij} = Q_{ij}(u) - \sum_{p \in \mathcal{P}_{ij}} h_p = 0 \quad \forall (i,j) \in \mathcal{W} \\ \\ h \geq 0 \end{array}\right\} \tag{8.103}$$

Formulation (8.102)–(8.103) was first proposed by Aashtiani (1979) and is most appropriate when demand is not invertible and, of course, symmetry conditions for demand $Q(u)$ and latency $c(f)$ apply.

8.4 More About Nonseparable User Equilibrium

When demand is elastic and nonseparable and arc latency functions are nonseparable, user equilibrium may be expressed as follows:

$$(c_p - u_{ij})h_p = 0 \quad \forall\ (i,j) \in \mathcal{W},\ p \in \mathcal{P}_{ij} \tag{8.104}$$

$$c_p - u_{ij} \geq 0 \quad \forall\ (i,j) \in \mathcal{W},\ p \in \mathcal{P}_{ij} \tag{8.105}$$

$$h_p \geq 0 \quad \forall\ (i,j) \in \mathcal{W},\ p \in \mathcal{P}_{ij} \tag{8.106}$$

$$Q_{ij}(u) - \sum_{p \in \mathcal{P}_{ij}} h_p = 0 \quad \forall\ (i,j) \in \mathcal{W} \tag{8.107}$$

where

$$c_p(h) = \sum_{a \in \mathcal{A}} \delta_{ap} c_a(f) \quad \forall a \in \mathcal{A}$$

and of course $Q_{ij}(u)$ denotes nonseparable travel demand for origin-destination pair $(i,j) \in \mathcal{W}$. The defining relationships, given above, for a general, nonseparable user equilibrium differ from (8.57)–(8.60) only in their assumption of nonseparable demands and nonseparable latencies.

We may develop conditions ensuring the uniqueness of equilibrium flow patterns when either separable or nonseparable functions are employed, by defining the concept of monotonicity. To this end, consider the vector function

$$F(x) : \Re^n \longrightarrow \Re^n$$

We say that $F(x)$ is *monotonically increasing* if

$$[F(x) - F(y)]^T (x - y) \geq 0 \quad \forall x, y \tag{8.108}$$

We say $F(x)$ is *monotonically decreasing* if

$$[F(x) - F(y)]^T (y - x) \leq 0 \quad \forall x, y \tag{8.109}$$

We say $F(x)$ is *strictly monotonically increasing* if

$$[F(x) - F(y)]^T (x - y) > 0 \quad \forall x, y, \;\; x \neq y, \tag{8.110}$$

The definition of *strictly monotonically decreasing* merely requires that the direction of inequality in (8.110) be reversed. It is also true that $F(x)$ is strictly monotonically increasing if and only if $\nabla_x F(x)$ is positive definite; that is, for $\Omega \subseteq \Re^n$:

$$\left\{[F(x) - F(y)]^T (x - y) > 0 \quad \forall x, y \in \Omega, \, x \neq y\right\} \Longleftrightarrow$$

$$\{\nabla_x F(x) \text{ positive definite } \forall \; x \in \Omega\} \tag{8.111}$$

where $[\nabla_x F(x)]^T$ is the Jacobian matrix $J(F)$.

Now consider

$$Z(x) = \oint_0^x E(y)dy = \sum_{i=1}^{n} \oint_0^x E_i(y)dy_i, \tag{8.112}$$

where $E(y) \in \Re^n$, $0 \in \Re^n$, and $x, y \in \Re^n$. The program

$$\min Z(x) \quad \text{ subject to } \quad x \in X \subseteq \Re^n \tag{8.113}$$

will have a unique solution if X is convex and $Z(x)$ is strictly convex over X. If $H[Z(x)]$ is positive definite, $Z(x)$ in (8.113) will be strictly convex. However, because of the nature of $Z(x)$ in (8.112)

$$H[Z(x)] = J(E) \equiv [\nabla_x E(x)]^T \tag{8.114}$$

Hence, if we require that $\nabla_x E(x)$ be positive definite, any solution to the mathematical program (8.113) is unique. By the aforementioned equivalence between strict monotonicity and positive definiteness, we may achieve this same end by requiring that $E(x)$ be strictly monotonically increasing.

Consequently, we expect that a unique solution of (8.102)–(8.103) (if a solution exists) will be guaranteed by requiring $c(f)$ to be strictly. Monotone increasing and that

$$S(u) \equiv -\sum_{(i,j)\in\mathcal{W}} u_{ij}Q_{ij}(u) + \sum_{(i,j)\in\mathcal{W}} \oint_0^u Q_{ij}(y)dy_{ij} \tag{8.115}$$

be such that $H[S(u)]$ is positive definite. If instead we use formulation (8.91), a solution will be unique when

(1) $c(f)$ is strictly monotone increasing

(2) $-\theta(Q)$ is strictly monotone increasing,

where

$$\begin{aligned} c(f) &: \Re^{|\mathcal{A}|} \longrightarrow \Re^{|\mathcal{A}|} \\ \theta(Q) &: \Re^{|\mathcal{W}|} \longrightarrow \Re^{|\mathcal{W}|} \end{aligned}$$

Note that strict monotonicity of a function implies its inevitability, so that there is no question of the existence of inverse demands in such a situation.

We note that the above remarks allow Theorem 8.4 to be easily extended to the case of nonseparable functions if we also require that $J(c)$ and $J(-\theta)$ be symmetric. That is, the following result holds:

Theorem 8.5 *(Unique solution of Beckmann's program) Assuming demand is invertible, if program (8.91) for nonseparable functions has a solution* $\begin{pmatrix} f \\ Q \end{pmatrix} \in \Omega_0$, *as defined by (8.10), that solution is unique when*

(1) $J(c)$ *is symmetric;*

(2) $J(c)$ *is positive definite (*$c(f)$ *is strictly monotonically increasing);*

(3) $J(-\theta)$ *is symmetric; and*

(4) $J(-\theta)$ *is positive definite (*$-\theta(Q)$ *is strictly monotonically increasing).*

Proof. The symmetry conditions (1) and (3) make the objective function of (8.91) well-defined. The positive definiteness conditions (2) and (4) make $Z(f,Q)$ defined by (8.91) strictly convex. Uniqueness follows immediately. ■

We close this section with the following result:

Theorem 8.6 *(Equivalence of user equilibrium and Beckmann's program) Assume demand is invertible. Any solution of the mathematical program*

$$\min Z(f,Q) = \oint_0^f c(x)dx - \oint_0^Q \theta(y)dy \quad \text{subject to} \quad \begin{pmatrix} f \\ Q \end{pmatrix} \in \Omega_0, \quad (8.116)$$

where Ω_0 is given by (8.10), $Z(f,Q)$ is well defined, and a constraint qualification holds, is a user equilibrium. Furthermore, if the latency function $c(f)$ and negative inverse demand function $-\theta(Q)$ have symmetric, positive definite Jacobian matrices, the user equilibrium conditions (8.104)–(8.107) and the mathematical program (8.116) are equivalent.

Proof. Upon noting that the Kuhn-Tucker conditions will be both necessary and sufficient for the given assumptions, one manipulates those conditions into the form of relationships defining a user equilibrium. ■

The formulations introduced above are further characterized in Friesz (1985).

8.5 Frank-Wolfe Algorithm for Beckmann's Program

The Frank-Wolfe algorithm introduced in Chap. 4 has become the most widely used technique of nonlinear programming in applications of network equilibrium models. This popularity derives primarily from the need to generate only one shortest path per OD pair per iteration of the algorithm, obviating the requirement to enumerate all paths. Although this feature, which is essentially a form of column generation, may also be introduced into other algorithms for network equilibrium, it is especially easy to do so within the Frank-Wolfe algorithm, thereby allowing practical software to be quickly created.

We have already discussed application of the Frank-Wolfe algorithm to system optimal traffic assignment in Sect. 8.2.5. However, its use involves some subtleties that make it desirable to review the basic reasoning behind the Frank-Wolfe method before applying it to the user equilibrium problem. To that end, consider the linearly constrained nonlinear program

$$\min f(x) \quad \text{subject to} \quad Ax = b,\ x \geq 0 \tag{8.117}$$

As we established in Chap. 4, the Frank-Wolfe algorithm is especially useful for solving network equilibrium problems that posses the general structure (8.117), as is the case when Beckmann's equivalent program is applicable. Recall that in the Frank-Wolfe algorithm the direction vector d^k is determined by making the following linear approximation based on the first two terms of a Taylor series, under the assumption $f(x)$ is differentiable for all $x \in X = \{x : Ax = B, x \geq 0\}$:

$$f(x) \approx f(x^k) + \left[\nabla f(x^k)\right]^T (x - x^k) \tag{8.118}$$

Thus, the nonlinear program (8.117) may be approached through iterative solution of the following approximating linear program (ALP):

$$\left.\begin{array}{ll} & \min f(x^k) + \left[\nabla f(x^k)\right]^T (x - x^k) \\ \text{subject to} & Ax = b \\ & x \geq 0 \end{array}\right\} \text{ALP}^k \tag{8.119}$$

The solution of ALP^k is called y^k; the vector

$$d^k = y^k - x^k \tag{8.120}$$

was shown in Chap. 4 to be a feasible direction of descent when $f(x)$ is convex for all $x \in X$.

Unfortunately, the Frank-Wolfe algorithm is not the type of super-linear or quadratically convergent algorithm one would like to have, yet for Wardropian equilibrium problems it allows us to avoid complete path enumeration, as will be seen below. Although we omitted in Chap. 4 a formal proof of convergence for feasible direction algorithms in general and the Frank-Wolfe algorithm in particular, it is intuitive that, if, at each iteration of a descent algorithm, we utilize a feasible direction of descent, such algorithms will converge to a global minimum when $f(\cdot)$ is convex. Moreover, when $f(\cdot)$ is not convex, the Frank-Wolfe algorithm, as well as any other feasible direction algorithms, is capable of finding local minima for (8.117), provided step sizes are selected appropriately.

Now, consider Beckmann's program for user equilibrium with separable functions, presented in Sect. 8.3, stated in the following form:

$$\min \; Z(f,Q) = \sum_{a \in \mathcal{A}} \int_0^{f_a} c_a(x_a) dx_a - \sum_{(i,j) \in \mathcal{W}} \int_0^{Q_{ij}} \theta_{ij}(y_{ij}) dy_{ij}$$

subject to

$$f_a - \sum_{p \in \mathcal{P}} \delta_{ap} h_p = 0 \qquad \forall \, a \in \mathcal{A}$$

$$Q_{ij} - \sum_{p \in \mathcal{P}_{ij}} h_p = 0 \quad (u_{ij}) \quad \forall \, (i,j) \in \mathcal{W}$$

$$-h_p \leq 0 \quad (\rho_p) \quad \forall \, p \in \mathcal{P}$$

Note that a linear approximation of $Z(h,Q)$ at (h^k, Q^k) is

$$\begin{aligned} Z(h,Q) \approx Z_L(h,Q) \quad &= \quad \nabla_h Z(h^k, Q^k)(h - h^k) + \\ & \quad \nabla_Q Z(h^k, Q^k)(Q - Q^k) + Z(h^k, Q^k), \end{aligned} \tag{8.121}$$

where $Z(h,Q)$ denotes the substitution of the definitional constraints (8.5) into the objective function (8.61) to make it dependent only on path flows and origin-destination demands. Furthermore

$$\begin{aligned} \nabla_h Z &= (\ldots, c_p, \ldots)^T \\ \nabla_Q Z &= (\ldots, -\theta_{ij}, \ldots)^T \end{aligned}$$

Hence

$$Z_L = \sum_{p\in\mathcal{P}} c_p(h^k)(h_p - h_p^k) - \sum_{(i,j)\in\mathcal{W}} \theta_{ij}(Q_{ij}^k)(Q_{ij} - Q_{ij}^k) + Z(h^k, Q^k) \quad (8.122)$$

Because we may ignore additive constants, $\min Z_L \Longleftrightarrow \min Z'_L$, where

$$Z'_L = \sum_{p\in\mathcal{P}} c_p(h^k)h_p - \sum_{(i,j)\in\mathcal{W}} \theta_{ij}(Q_{ij}^k)Q_{ij}$$

Moreover, we note that $\min Z'_L \Longleftrightarrow \min Z''_L$, where

$$\begin{aligned} Z''_L &= \sum_{(i,j)\in\mathcal{W}} c_{ij}^{k*} \sum_{p\in\mathcal{P}_{ij}} h_p - \sum_{(i,j)\in\mathcal{W}} \theta_{ij}(Q_{ij}^k)Q_{ij} \\ &= \sum_{(i,j)\in\mathcal{W}} (c_{ij}^{k*} - \theta_{ij}^k)Q_{ij} \end{aligned}$$

and

$$c_{ij}^{k*} \equiv \min\{c_p(h^k) : p \in \mathcal{P}_{ij}\} \quad (8.123)$$

$$\theta_{ij}^k \equiv \theta_{ij}(Q_{ij}^k) \quad (8.124)$$

for every $(i,j) \in \mathcal{W}$. That is, c_{ij}^{k*} is the minimum path latency between $(i,j) \in \mathcal{W}$ under flow conditions h^k.

Recall that

$$\mathcal{N}_D = \{j : (i,j) \in \mathcal{W}, i \in \mathcal{N}\}$$

is the set of nodes that are destinations and

$$\mathcal{N}_O = \{i : (i,j) \in \mathcal{W}, j \in \mathcal{N}\}$$

Then the preceding observations lead to the linear program

$$\min \sum_{(i,j)\in\mathcal{W}} A_{ij}^k Q_{ij}$$

subject to

$$Q_{ij} \geq 0 \quad \forall (i,j) \in \mathcal{W}$$

with the following additional constraints: either

$$Q_{ij} \leq B_{ij} \quad \forall (i,j) \in \mathcal{W}$$

or

$$\sum_{j:(i,j)\in\mathcal{W}} Q_{ij} = O_i \quad \forall i \in \mathcal{N}_O$$

$$\sum_{i:(i,j)\in\mathcal{W}} Q_{ij} = D_j \quad \forall j \in \mathcal{N}_D$$

where

$$A_{ij}^k \equiv c_{ij}^{k*} - \theta_{ij}^k \tag{8.125}$$

and O_i is the flow generated at origin node $i \in \mathcal{N}_O$ and D_j is the flow attracted to destination node $j \in \mathcal{N}_D$. That is, the linear programming phase of Frank-Wolfe algorithm applied to Beckmann's program leads to one of the following problems:

(1)

$$\min \sum_i \sum_j A_{ij}^k Q_{ij} \quad \text{subject to} \quad 0 \leq Q_{ij} \leq B_{ij} \quad \forall (i,j) \in \mathcal{W} \tag{8.126}$$

which is solved trivially by observing that

$$Q_{ij}{}^k = \begin{cases} 0 & \text{if } A_{ij}^k \geq 0 \\ B_{ij} & \text{if } A_{ij}^k < 0; \end{cases}$$

(2)

$$\left.\begin{array}{ll} \min Z_L^k = \sum_{(i,j)\in\mathcal{W}} A_{ij}^k Q_{ij} & \\ \text{subject to} & \\ \sum_{j:(i,j)\in\mathcal{W}} Q_{ij} = O_i & \forall i \in \mathcal{N}_O \\ \sum_{i:(i,j)\in\mathcal{W}} Q_{ij} = D_j & \forall j \in \mathcal{N}_D \\ Q_{ij} \geq 0 & \forall (i,j) \in \mathcal{W} \end{array}\right\} \tag{8.127}$$

which is an instance of the so-called transportation problem and may be efficiently solved by the network simplex algorithm.

Of course, the linear programming phase **also** involves an all-or-nothing assignment to find the arc flow pattern, as explained below.

We now give a complete statement of the Frank-Wolfe algorithm applied to Beckmann's program with separable functions and elastic demand (assuming there are trip production and attraction constraints):

FRANK-WOLFE ALGORITHM FOR ELASTIC DEMAND TRAFFIC ASSIGNMENT

Step 0. *(Initialization)* Determine an initial feasible solution (f^0, Q^0) and set the counter $k = 0$.

Step 1A. *(Minimum path latencies)* Compute the arc impedances $\{c_a(f_a^k) : a \in \mathcal{A}\}$, then find minimum paths p_{ij}^k and minimum path latencies

$$c_{ij}^{k^*} = \min \left\{ c_p^k = \sum_{a \in \mathcal{A}} \delta_{ap} c_a \left(f_a^k \right) : p \in \mathcal{P}_{ij} \right\}$$

between each origin-destination pair $(i, j) \in \mathcal{W}$.

Step 1B. *(Solve the transportation problem)* Calculate the inverse demands $\{\theta_{ij}(Q_{ij}^k) : (i,j) \in \mathcal{W}\}$, then determine the coefficients $\{A_{ij}^k : (i,j) \in \mathcal{W}\}$ according to

$$A_{ij}^k = c_{ij}^{k^*} - \theta_{ij}^k \quad \forall (i,j) \in \mathcal{W}$$

where

$$\theta_{ij}^k = \theta_{ij}(Q_{ij}^k)$$

for each $(i, j) \in \mathcal{W}$. Form and solve the Hitchcock problem

$$\min \sum_{(i,j) \in \mathcal{W}} A_{ij}^k Q_{ij} \tag{8.128}$$

subject to

$$\sum_{j:(i,j) \in \mathcal{W}} Q_{ij} = O_i \quad \forall i \in \mathcal{N}_O$$

$$\sum_{i:(i,j) \in \mathcal{W}} Q_{ij} = D_j \quad \forall j \in \mathcal{N}_D$$

$$Q_{ij} \geq 0 \quad \forall (i,j) \in \mathcal{W}$$

where $A_{ij}^k \equiv c_{ij}^k - \theta_{ij}^k$. Call the solution of this problem $\hat{Q}^k$.

Step 1C. *(All-or-nothing assignment)* Based on the minimum latencies $\{c_{ij}^{k^*} : (i,j) \in \mathcal{W}\}$ perform an all-or-nothing assignment to determine the arc flow pattern $\hat{f}^k$ corresponding to $\hat{Q}^k$. That is, if p_{ij}^k denotes the minimum path between $(i,j) \in \mathcal{W}$ for impedances $\{c_a(f_a^k) : a \in \mathcal{A}\}$ and

$$\mathcal{W}^k(a) \equiv \{(i,j) \in \mathcal{W} : a \in p_{ij}^k\}, \tag{8.129}$$

is the set of origin-destination pairs connected by shortest paths that traverse arc $a \in \mathcal{A}$, then calculate

$$\hat{f}_a^k = \sum_{(i,j) \in \mathcal{W}^k(a)} \hat{Q}_{ij}^k \quad \forall a \in \mathcal{A} \tag{8.130}$$

Step 2. *(Determine direction vector)* Calculate

$$d^k = \begin{pmatrix} \hat{f}^k \\ \hat{Q}^k \end{pmatrix} - \begin{pmatrix} f^k \\ Q^k \end{pmatrix}$$

Step 3. *(Determine step size)* Calculate

$$\lambda_k = \arg\left\{\min Z[(f^k, Q^k) + \lambda d^k] : 0 \leq \lambda \leq 1\right\} \tag{8.131}$$

Step 4. *(Update and stopping test)* Calculate the new flows and demands according to

$$\begin{pmatrix} f^{k+1} \\ Q^{k+1} \end{pmatrix} = \begin{pmatrix} f^k \\ Q^k \end{pmatrix} + \lambda_k d^k \tag{8.132}$$

If

$$\max_{a \in \mathcal{A}} \mid f_a^{k+1} - f_a^k \mid < \epsilon_1 \tag{8.133}$$

$$\max_{(i,j) \in \mathcal{W}} \mid Q_{ij}^{k+1} - Q_{ij}^k \mid < \epsilon_2 \ , \tag{8.134}$$

where $\epsilon_1 \in \Re^1_{++}$ and $\epsilon_2 \in \Re^1_{++}$ are preset tolerances, stop. Otherwise set $k = k + 1$ and go to Step 1A.

The nature of the objective function in Beckmann's program makes the line search (step size determination) phase of the Frank-Wolfe algorithm especially easy to carry out with a Bolzano-type search method employing derivative information. This is because

$$\begin{aligned} Z_k(\lambda) &\equiv Z\left[\begin{pmatrix} f^k \\ Q^k \end{pmatrix} + \lambda d^k\right] \\ &= \sum_{a \in \mathcal{A}} \int_0^{f_a^k + \lambda d_a^k} c_a(x_a) dx_a - \sum_{(i,j) \in \mathcal{W}} \int_0^{Q_{ij}^k + \lambda d_{ij}^k} \theta_{ij}(y_{ij}) dy_{ij} \end{aligned}$$

Hence, by the chain rule

$$\begin{aligned} \frac{\partial Z(\lambda)}{\partial \lambda} &= \sum_{a \in \mathcal{A}} \frac{\partial Z_k}{\partial (f_a^k + \lambda d_a^k)} \frac{\partial (f_a^k + \lambda d_a^k)}{\partial \lambda} + \sum_{(i,j) \in \mathcal{W}} \frac{\partial Z_k}{\partial (Q_{ij}^k + \lambda d_{ij}^k)} \frac{\partial (Q_{ij}^k + \lambda d_{ij}^k)}{\partial \lambda} \\ &= \sum_{a \in \mathcal{A}} c_a(f_a^k + \lambda d_a^k)(d_a^k) - \sum_{(i,j) \in \mathcal{W}} \theta_{ij}(Q_{ij}^k + \lambda d_{ij}^k)(d_{ij}^k) \end{aligned}$$

which may be readily evaluated for any specified value of λ, since all other entities are known at iteration k of the algorithm. The interested reader is referred to Gartner (1977, 1980b) and Nagurney (1984) for more details regarding the application of the Frank-Wolfe algorithm to Beckmann's mathematical program.

The careful reader will note that the Frank-Wolfe algorithm determines arc flows from the current minimum paths found with a minimum-path algorithm; thereupon one may discard all path information. In doing so there is no need to enumerate paths a priori.

8.6 Nonextremal Formulations of Wardropian Equilibrium

Because of the symmetry conditions that must be enforced in order for equivalent optimization problems involving nonseparable functions to be well-defined, nonextremal formulations of Wardropian equilibrium have been developed. We shall emphasize variational inequality problems in the study of user equilibrium without invoking symmetry conditions. See Aashtiani and Magnanti (1981) for a discussion of a nonlinear complementarity formulation of the Wardropian user equilibrium problem to obviate the need for symmetry conditions.

8.6.1 Asymmetric User Equilibrium with Fixed Demand

Consider a road network with fixed travel demand. We have previously posited that drivers choose routes according to Wardrop's First Principle, one form of which is the following:

Definition 8.1 (Wardrop's first principle) In user equilibrium it is impossible for any driver to unilaterally change his/her route without experiencing a congestion increase.

Note that Definition 8.1 is equivalent to the one given in the opening remarks for this chapter, namely (8.57)–(8.60), which for fixed demand yields the following conditions:

$$h_p > 0, p \in \mathcal{P}_{ij} \Longrightarrow c_p = u_{ij} \quad \forall (i,j) \in \mathcal{W} \tag{8.135}$$

$$c_p > u_{ij}, p \in \mathcal{P}_{ij} \Longrightarrow h_p = 0 \quad \forall (i,j) \in \mathcal{W} \tag{8.136}$$

$$\sum_p h_p = Q_{ij} \quad \forall (i,j) \in \mathcal{W} \tag{8.137}$$

$$h_p \geq 0 \quad \forall p \in \mathcal{P} \tag{8.138}$$

We are interested in manipulating formulation (8.135)–(8.138) into a form known as a variational inequality.

In fact, we next prove the following:

Theorem 8.7 *(Variational inequality equivalent to user equilibrium for fixed demand) A flow pattern $f^* \in \Omega_1$ is a user equilibrium (satisfies Wardrop's First Principle) as defined by conditions (8.135)–(8.138) if and only if*

$$\sum_{a\in\mathcal{A}} c_a(f^*)(f_a - f_a^*) \geq 0 \quad \forall f \in \Omega_1 \tag{8.139}$$

where Ω_1 is defined by (8.11).

Proof. The proof is completely analogous to that given for Theorem 8.2.

(i) [WFP $\Longrightarrow$ (8.139)]: In particular we note that

$$c_p(h^*) \geq u_{ij} \quad \forall (i,j) \in \mathcal{W} \tag{8.140}$$

from which we have

$$c_p(h^*)(h_p - h_p^*) \geq u_{ij}(h_p - h_p^*) \; \forall (i,j) \in \mathcal{W} \tag{8.141}$$

since (8.140) holds as an equality when $(h_p - h_p^*) < 0$, for then $h_p^* > h_p \geq 0$. Summing (8.141), we have

$$\sum_{p\in\mathcal{P}} \sum_{a\in\mathcal{A}} \delta_{ap} c_a(f^*)(h_p - h_p^*) \geq \sum_{(i,j)\in\mathcal{W}} \sum_{p\in\mathcal{P}_{ij}} u_{ij}(h_p - h_p^*)$$

$$\sum_{a\in\mathcal{A}} c_a(f^*)\left(\sum_{p\in\mathcal{P}} \delta_{ap} h_p - \sum_{p\in\mathcal{P}} \delta_{ap} h_p^*\right) \geq \sum_{(i,j)\in\mathcal{W}} u_{ij}\left(\sum_{p\in\mathcal{P}_{ij}} h_p - \sum_{p\in\mathcal{P}_{ij}} h_p^*\right)$$

$$\sum_{a\in\mathcal{A}} c_a(f^*)(f_a - f_a^*) \geq 0 \tag{8.142}$$

which is the variational inequality we seek.

(ii) [(8.139)$\Longrightarrow$ WFP]: We note that (8.139) requires that $f^* \in \Omega_1$ solves the linear program

$$\min \sum_{a\in\mathcal{A}} c_a(f^*) f_a = \sum_{p\in\mathcal{P}} c_p(h^*) h_p \quad \text{subject to} \quad f \in \Omega_1 \tag{8.143}$$

whose dual is

$$\max u^T Q \quad \text{subject to} \quad u^T \Gamma \leq c(h^*)$$

Dual feasibility requires

$$u^T \Gamma \leq c(h^*) \Longrightarrow u_{ij} \leq c_p(h^*) \quad \forall (i,j) \in \mathcal{W},\, p \in \mathcal{P}_{ij}$$

Complementary slackness requires

$$\left[c\left(h^*\right) - u^T\Gamma\right] h^* = 0 \Longrightarrow \left[c_p\left(h^*\right) - u_{ij}\right] h_p = 0 \quad \forall\left(i,j\right) \in \mathcal{W},\, p \in \mathcal{P}_{ij}$$

Primal feasibility, dual feasibility and complementary slackness give (8.135)–(8.138). ■

We know from Sect. 8.4 that user equilibria may be calculated by solving the mathematical program

$$\min \sum_{a\in\mathcal{A}} \oint_0^f c_a\left(x\right) dx_a \qquad \forall f \in \Omega_1 \tag{8.144}$$

We also know that the objective function of (8.144) is a line integral and, as such, is well defined if and only if the Jacobian matrix formed from its integrand is symmetric. That symmetry condition takes the form

$$\frac{\partial c_a}{\partial f_b} = \frac{\partial c_b}{\partial f_a} \qquad \forall a, b \in \mathcal{A} \tag{8.145}$$

This result from vector calculus, known as Green's theorem in a plane, means that arbitrary latency functions cannot be employed if the user equilibrium problem is to be solved by direct application of observation (8.144). However, the special case of separable latency functions of the form $c_a\left(f_a\right)$ can be viewed as a mathematical program, namely

$$\min \sum_{a\in\mathcal{A}} \int_0^{f_a} c_a\left(x_a\right) dx_a \qquad \forall f \in \Omega_1 \tag{8.146}$$

since (8.145) is trivially satisfied and the integral in question is an ordinary integral.

Fortunately, there is a way to treat nonseparable latencies which exploits the above development, although at the expense of having to solve a *sequence* of mathematical programs rather than a single program. This method, called *diagonalization*, is most easily presented as a heuristic, although it does enjoy a proof of convergence when certain regularity conditions related to strict monotonicity and diagonal dominance of the Jacobian are invoked. Since these regularity conditions are difficult to check in practice, there is little lost in viewing diagonalization as a heuristic. We begin the explanation of the method by defining what is meant by diagonalized latency functions:

Definition 8.2 (Diagonalized latencies) The nonseparable vector latency function $c\left(f\right) = \left(c_a\left(f\right) : \left(i,j\right) \in \mathcal{A}\right)$ is diagonalized at the current flow pattern $f^k \in \Omega_1$ if each constituent arc latency function is replaced according to the scheme

$$c_a\left(f\right) \Longrightarrow c_a\left(f_a; f_b = f_b^k \;\forall b \in \left(\mathcal{A}\backslash a\right)\right) \equiv c_a^k\left(f_a\right) \tag{8.147}$$

Note that the Jacobian matrix

$$J^k\left(c^k\right) = \left(\frac{\partial c_a^k\left(f_a\right)}{\partial f_b} : a, b \in \mathcal{A}\right)$$
$$= \operatorname{diag}\left(\frac{\partial c_a^k\left(f_a\right)}{\partial f_a} : a \in \mathcal{A}\right) \tag{8.148}$$

is diagonal by construction and, thereby, satisfies the symmetry restrictions, making the line integral representation independent of the path of integration.

The diagonalization algorithm itself has the following statement:

User Equilibrium Diagonalization Algorithm for Fixed Demand

Step 0. *(Initialization)* Set $k = 1$. Find an initial feasible solution $f^{\,0} \in \Omega_1$.

Step 1. *(Diagonalization)* Construct the diagonalized unit arc latency functions (8.147).

Step 2. *(Solve the diagonalized subproblem)* Find $f^{k+1} \in \Omega_1$ such that

$$\sum_{a \in \mathcal{A}} c_a^k\left(f_a^{k+1}\right)\left(f_a - f_a^{k+1}\right) \geq 0 \quad \forall f \in \Omega_1$$

by solving the mathematical program

$$\min \sum_{a \in \mathcal{A}} \int_0^{f_a} c_a^k\left(x_a\right) dx_a \quad \text{subject to} \quad f \in \Omega_1$$

Step 3. *(Stopping test)* For $\epsilon_2 \in \Re_{++}$, a present tolerance, if

$$\max_{a \in A} \left|f_a^{k+1} - f_a^k\right| < \epsilon_2$$

stop: $f^* \approx f^{k+1}$. Otherwise set $k = k + 1$ and go to Step 1.

For this algorithm there is an interesting result that allows us to know we have found an approximate user equilibrium if convergence is achieved. That result is the following:

Theorem 8.8 (User equilibrium found by diagonalization) *If the diagonalization algorithm described above for the fixed demand user equilibrium problem with nonseparable unit arc latency functions converges, a user equilibrium has in fact been found.*

Proof. Since f_a^{k+1} is a solution of the kth diagonalized subproblem

$$\sum_{a\in\mathcal{A}} c_a^k\left(f_a^{k+1}\right)\left(f_a - f_a^{k+1}\right) \geq 0 \quad \forall f \in \Omega_1 \tag{8.149}$$

convergence means

$$f^{k+1} \approx f^k \in \Omega_1$$

so

$$c_a^k\left(f_a^{k+1}\right) \approx c_a^k(f_a^k) \tag{8.150}$$

By the mechanics of the diagonalization process

$$c_a\left(f^k\right) = c_a\left(f_a^k; f_b = f_b^k\ \forall b \in \mathcal{A}\backslash a\right) = c_a^k(f_a^k) \tag{8.151}$$

Observations (8.149)–(8.151) require

$$\sum_{a\in\mathcal{A}} c_a\left(f^k\right)\left(f_a - f_a^k\right) \geq 0 \quad \forall f \in \Omega_1 \tag{8.152}$$

Hence $f^k = f^*$. ■

8.6.2 Asymmetric User Equilibrium with Elastic Demand

Recall that user equilibrium with elastic demand may be stated as follows:

$$(c_p - u_{ij})h_p = 0 \quad \forall\ (i,j) \in \mathcal{W},\ p \in \mathcal{P}_{ij} \tag{8.153}$$

$$c_p - u_{ij} \geq 0 \quad \forall\ (i,j) \in \mathcal{W},\ p \in \mathcal{P}_{ij} \tag{8.154}$$

$$h_p \geq 0 \quad \forall\ (i,j) \in \mathcal{W},\ p \in \mathcal{P}_{ij} \tag{8.155}$$

$$Q_{ij}(u) - \sum_{p\in\mathcal{P}_{ij}} h_p = 0 \quad \forall\ (i,j) \in \mathcal{W} \tag{8.156}$$

It is quite significant that, when demand is invertible, user equilibrium with neither latency nor demand symmetry may be expressed as a variational inequality; the pertinent result is:

Theorem 8.9 *(Variational inequality equivalent to user equilibrium) When demand is invertible, a flow-demand pattern*

$$\begin{pmatrix} f^* \\ Q^* \end{pmatrix} \in \Omega_0 = \left\{ \begin{pmatrix} f \\ Q \end{pmatrix} : f_a - \sum_p \delta_{ap} h_p = 0 \ \forall a \in \mathcal{A}, \right.$$

$$\left. Q_{ij} - \sum_{p \in \mathcal{P}_{ij}} h_p = 0 \ \forall \ (i,j) \in \mathcal{W}, \ h \geq 0, Q \geq 0 \right\} \tag{8.157}$$

is a user equilibrium (satisfies Wardrop's first principle) if and only if

$$\sum_{a \in \mathcal{A}} c_a(f^*)(f_a - f_a^*) - \sum_{(i,j) \in \mathcal{W}} \theta_{ij}(Q^*)(Q_{ij} - Q_{ij}^*) \geq 0 \tag{8.158}$$

for all

$$\begin{pmatrix} f \\ Q \end{pmatrix} \in \Omega_0.$$

Proof. This proof is in two parts.

(i) [WFP $\Longrightarrow$ (8.158)]: Note that WFP ensures

$$c_p(h^*) \geq u_{ij}^* \quad \forall \ (i,j) \in \mathcal{W}, p \in \mathcal{P}_{ij}$$

It follows that if $h^* = (h_p^* : p \in \cup_{i,j} \mathcal{P}_{ij})$ is the equilibrium flow pattern and $\begin{pmatrix} f \\ Q \end{pmatrix} \in \Omega_0$, then

$$c_p(h^*)(h_p - h_p^*) \geq u_{ij}^*(h_p - h_p^*) \tag{8.159}$$

This result is obviously true when $h_p - h_p^* \geq 0$. When $h_p - h_p^* < 0$, we have that $0 \leq h_p < h_p^*$ or $h_p^* > 0$. By (8.153) $c_p(h^*) = u_{ij}^*$ when $h_p^* > 0$, and (8.159) follows at once. Summing (8.159) over all p yields

$$\sum_{p \in \mathcal{P}} c_p(h^*)(h_p - h_p^*) \geq \sum_{(i,j) \in \mathcal{W}} \sum_{p \in \mathcal{P}_{ij}} u_{ij}^*(h_p - h_p^*)$$

From this last result, we get

$$\sum_{p \in \mathcal{P}} \left[\sum_{a \in \mathcal{A}} \delta_{ap} c_a(f^*) \right] (h_p - h_p^*) \quad \geq \quad \sum_{(i,j) \in \mathcal{W}} u_{ij}^* \Big(\sum_{p \in \mathcal{P}_{ij}} h_p - \sum_{p \in \mathcal{P}_{ij}} h_p^* \Big)$$

$$\sum_{a \in \mathcal{A}} c_a(f^*) \left(\sum_{p \in \mathcal{P}} \delta_{ap} h_p - \sum_{p \in \mathcal{P}} \delta_{ap} h_p^* \right) \quad \geq \quad \sum_{(i,j) \in \mathcal{W}} u_{ij}^*(Q_{ij} - Q_{ij}^*)$$

$$\sum_{a \in \mathcal{A}} c_a(f^*)(f_a - f_a^*) \quad \geq \quad \sum_{(i,j) \in \mathcal{W}} \theta_{ij}(Q^*)(Q_{ij} - Q_{ij}^*)$$

or

$$\sum_{a\in\mathcal{A}} c_a(f^*)(f_a - f_a^*) - \sum_{(i,j)\in\mathcal{W}} \theta_{ij}(Q^*)(Q_{ij} - Q_{ij}^*) \geq 0$$

which completes Part (i).

(ii) [(8.158)$\Longrightarrow$ WFP]: From the above manipulations, it is clear that when demand is invertible (8.158) may be restated as

$$\sum_{p\in\mathcal{P}} \left[c_p(h^*) - u_{ij}^*\right] h_p \geq \sum_{p\in\mathcal{P}} (c_p(h^*) - u_{ij}^*) h_p^*$$

As we have noted before, (8.158) is a statement that h^* is a solution of the linear program

$$\min \sum_{p\in\mathcal{P}} \left[c_p(h^*) - u_{ij}^*\right] h_p$$

subject to

$$\sum_{p\in\mathcal{P}_{ij}} h_p = Q_{ij}(u^*) \quad \forall\, (i,j) \in \mathcal{W},\, p \in \mathcal{P}_{ij}$$

$$h \geq 0$$

The dual program is

$$\max u^T Q(u^*) \quad \text{subject to} \quad u^T \Gamma \leq c\,(h^*) \tag{8.160}$$

Dual feasibility requires

$$u^T \Gamma \leq c\,(h^*) \Longrightarrow u_{ij} \leq c_p\,(h^*) \quad \forall\, (i,j) \in \mathcal{W},\, p \in \mathcal{P}_{ij}$$

Complementary slackness requires

$$\left[c\,(h^*) - u^T \Gamma\right] h^* = 0 \Longrightarrow \left[c_p\,(h^*) - u_{ij}\right] h_p = 0 \qquad \forall\, (i,j) \in \mathcal{W},\, p \in \mathcal{P}_{ij}$$

Primal feasibility, dual feasibility and complementary slackness assure (8.153)–(8.156) hold. ∎

Note that the above theorem provides us with a variational inequality statement of the general (asymmetric) Wardropian user equilibrium problem. As such we have immediately from Theorem 8.9 the following result:

Theorem 8.10 *(Existence of user equilibrium) If the set*

$$\Omega_0 = \left\{ \begin{pmatrix} f \\ Q \end{pmatrix} : f_a - \sum_{p\in\mathcal{P}} \delta_{ap} h_p = 0 \;\; \forall\, a \in \mathcal{A},\, Q_{ij} - \sum_{p\in\mathcal{P}_{ij}} h_p = 0 \;\; \forall\; (i,j) \in \mathcal{W}, \right.$$

$$\left. h \geq 0,\; Q \geq 0 \right\} \tag{8.161}$$

is nonempty; each travel demand function $Q(u) : \Re^{|\mathcal{W}|} \longrightarrow \Re^{|\mathcal{W}|}$ *is invertible and bounded from above; and each of the functions* $c_a(f)$*, for all* $a \in \mathcal{A}$*, and* $\theta_{ij}(Q)$*, for all* $(i,j) \in \mathcal{W}$*, are continuous, then a user equilibrium*

$$\begin{pmatrix} f^* \\ Q^* \end{pmatrix} \in \Omega_0$$

exists.

Proof. For the given of the theorem, clearly Ω_0 is closed and convex. The boundedness of demand functions implies the boundedness of Ω_0. This, with the variational inequality representation of Theorem 8.9 and the assumptions of continuity and nonemptiness, fulfills the requirements of the Stampacchia existence theorem of Chap. 7. ■

The variational inequality representation (8.158) for user equilibrium, without symmetry or separability, allows us to establish the following uniqueness result:

Theorem 8.11 *(Uniqueness of user equilibrium) If* $(f^*, Q^*) \in \Omega_0$ *is a user equilibrium, it is unique when demand is invertible while* $c(f)$ *and* $-\theta(Q)$ *are strictly monotonically increasing.*

Proof. Trivial. ■

Recalling that, where $\mathcal{A}$ is the set of network arcs and $\mathcal{W}$ is the set of origin-destination pairs, we employ the following definitions:

$$c(f) \equiv (\ldots, c_a(f), \ldots)^T \in \Re^{|\mathcal{A}|} \tag{8.162}$$

$$\theta(y) \equiv (\ldots, \theta_{ij}(y), \ldots)^T \in \Re^{|\mathcal{W}|} \tag{8.163}$$

As a consequence, we may express the variational inequality (8.158) as

$$\left[c\left(f^*\right)\right]^T (f - f^*) - \left[\theta\left(Q^*\right)\right]^T (Q - Q^*) \geq 0, \begin{pmatrix} f \\ Q \end{pmatrix}, \begin{pmatrix} f^* \\ Q^* \end{pmatrix} \in \Omega_0, \tag{8.164}$$

Furthermore, from (8.164), we may immediately obtain Beckmann's equivalent program, as is formally stated below:

Theorem 8.12 *(Equivalence of variational inequality and Beckmann's program) Assume demand is invertible. Any solution of the mathematical program*

$$\min Z(f, Q) = \oint_0^f c(x)dx - \oint_0^Q \theta(y)dy \quad \textit{subject to} \quad \begin{pmatrix} f \\ Q \end{pmatrix} \in \Omega_0, \tag{8.165}$$

where Ω_0 is given by (8.161) and $Z(f, Q)$ is well defined, is a user equilibrium. Furthermore, if the latency function $c(f)$ and negative inverse demand function $-\theta(Q)$ have symmetric, positive definite Jacobian matrices, the user equilibrium expressed as variational inequality (8.164) and the mathematical program (8.165) are equivalent.

Proof. The proof is immediate from Theorem 8.9 upon observing that the stated assumptions make $Z(f, Q)$ well-defined and strictly convex. ■

The reader should note that Theorem 8.12 is essentially identical to Theorem 8.6, illustrating that all results obtained using Beckmann's program with symmetry assumptions are trivially reproduced using a variational inequality perspective. The variational inequality perspective, however, goes beyond the Beckmann perspective by directly considering asymmetric user equilibrium problems.

8.7 Diagonalization Algorithms for Nonextremal User Equilibrium Models

User equilibria may be found as solutions of variational inequalities, nonlinear complementarity problems, fixed point problems, and mathematical programs under appropriate assumptions. The mathematical programming formulations are readily solved as we have discussed, but are of course limited in their application by the symmetry/separability assumptions which must be made. Nonextremal formulations do not require such assumptions. We now consider algorithms for directly solving nonextremal formulations of user equilibrium. In this section we want to consider diagonalization methods for variational inequality formulations of user equilibrium. Such methods have been studied by Abdulaal and LeBlanc (1979), Florian and Spiess (1982), Pang and Chan (1982), Dafermos (1983), Friesz et al. (1983), Nagurney (1984, 1987), and others.

The implications of the diagonalization perspective for solving variational inequality formulations of Wardrop's first principal are obvious: one needs only know how to solve the equivalent mathematical programming formulations of these problems with separable functions. While this feature is alluring, we caution that proofs of convergence for diagonalization algorithms depend typically on the diagonal dominance of the relevant Jacobian matrices, a feature that can be difficult to check or may even fail to hold in practice. Diagonalization methods may fail to converge and should be used with considerable caution.

The diagonalization algorithm for finding a user equilibrium may be stated as follows:

ELASTIC DEMAND USER EQUILIBRIUM DIAGONALIZATION ALGORITHM

Step 0. *(Initialization)* Determine an initial feasible flow pattern

$$\begin{pmatrix} f^0 \\ Q^0 \end{pmatrix} \in \Omega = \{ \begin{pmatrix} f \\ Q \end{pmatrix} : \qquad \begin{array}{l} f_a - \sum\limits_p \delta_{ap} h_p = 0 \; \forall \; a \in \mathcal{A}, \\ \\ Q_{ij} - \sum\limits_{p \in \mathcal{P}_{ij}} h_p = 0 \quad \forall \; (i,j) \in \mathcal{W}, \\ \\ h \geq 0, \;\; Q \geq 0 \} \end{array}$$

Step 1. *(Diagonalize)* Create the following separable functions:

$$c_a^k(f_a) = c_a(f_a, f_b = f_b^k \quad \forall \; b \neq a) \quad \forall \; a \in \mathcal{A}$$

$$Q_{ij}^k(u_{ij}) = Q_{ij}(u_{ij}, u_{rs} = u_{rs}^k \quad \forall \; (r,s) \neq (i,j)) \quad \forall \; (i,j) \in \mathcal{W}$$

$$\Theta_{ij}^k(Q_{ij}) = (Q_{ij}^k)^{-1} \quad \forall (i,j) \in \mathcal{W}$$

Step 2. *(Solve Beckmann's equivalent program)* Using the Frank-Wolfe or other algorithm solve the mathematical program

$$\min \sum_{a \in \mathcal{A}} \int_0^{f_a} c_a^k(x_a) dx_a - \sum_{(i,j) \in \mathcal{W}} \int_0^{Q_{ij}} \Theta_{ij}^k(y_{ij}) dy_{ij} \quad \text{subject to} \quad \begin{pmatrix} f \\ Q \end{pmatrix} \in \Omega_0$$

Call the solution $\begin{pmatrix} f^{k+1} \\ Q^{k+1} \end{pmatrix}$.

Step 3. *(Stopping test)* If

$$\left. \begin{array}{ll} \max_a & | f_a^{k+1} - f_a^k | < \epsilon_1 \\ \\ \max_{i,j} & | Q_{ij}^{k+1} - Q_{ij}^k | < \epsilon_2, \end{array} \right\} \tag{8.166}$$

where ϵ_1 and ϵ_2 are preset tolerances, stop. Otherwise set $k = k + 1$ and go to Step 1.

8.8 Nonlinear Complementarity Formulation of User Equilibrium

We have already established that one formulation of the general user equilibrium problem is the following:

$$(c_p - u_{ij})h_p = 0 \quad \forall\ (i,j) \in \mathcal{W},\ p \in \mathcal{P}_{ij} \tag{8.167}$$

$$c_p - u_{ij} \geq 0 \quad \forall\ (i,j) \in \mathcal{W},\ p \in \mathcal{P}_{ij} \tag{8.168}$$

$$h_p \geq 0 \quad \forall\ (i,j) \in \mathcal{W},\ p \in \mathcal{P}_{ij} \tag{8.169}$$

$$Q_{ij}(u) - \sum_{p \in \mathcal{P}_{ij}} h_p = 0 \quad \forall\ (i,j) \in \mathcal{W} \tag{8.170}$$

This formulation may be restated as a nonlinear complementarity problem if one additional regularity condition is imposed: latency positivity for all arcs.

To see the role played by latency positivity, consider the following problem:

$$(c_p - u_{ij})h_p = 0 \quad \forall\ (i,j) \in \mathcal{W},\ p \in \mathcal{P}_{ij} \tag{8.171}$$

$$c_p - u_{ij} \geq 0 \quad \forall\ (i,j) \in \mathcal{W},\ p \in \mathcal{P}_{ij} \tag{8.172}$$

$$h_p \geq 0 \quad \forall\ (i,j) \in \mathcal{W},\ p \in \mathcal{P}_{ij} \tag{8.173}$$

$$\left(\sum_{p \in \mathcal{P}_{ij}} h_p - Q_{ij}(u) \right) u_{ij} = 0 \quad \forall\ (i,j) \in \mathcal{W} \tag{8.174}$$

$$\sum_{p \in \mathcal{P}_{ij}} h_p - Q_{ij}(u) \geq 0 \quad \forall\ (i,j) \in \mathcal{W} \tag{8.175}$$

$$u_{ij} \geq 0 \quad \forall\ (i,j) \in \mathcal{W} \tag{8.176}$$

which is definitely a nonlinear complementarity problem. Formulation (8.167)–(8.170) and (8.171)–(8.176) will be identical if condition (8.175) can never hold as a strict inequality.

Let us suppose

$$\sum_{p \in \mathcal{P}_{k\ell}} h_p - Q_{k\ell}(u) > 0 \tag{8.177}$$

for some pair $(k,\ell) \in \mathcal{W}$. By (8.174), we know that

$$u_{k\ell} = 0$$

Because of (8.177), there must exist at least one $q \in \mathcal{P}_{k\ell}$ such that $h_q > 0$. However

$$h_q > 0 \Longrightarrow c_q = u_{k\ell} = 0$$

which directly contradicts latency positivity. Thus, we have established the following result:

Theorem 8.13 *(Equivalent nonlinear complementarity formulation of user equilibrium) If arc unit latencies $c_a(f)$ are strictly positive for all $a \in \mathcal{A}$ and all $(f, Q) \in \Omega_0$, then the nonlinear complementarity problem (8.167)–(8.170) is equivalent to the user equilibrium conditions (8.171)–(8.176).*

Theorem 8.13 is of more than passing interest. It is the basis for applying the successive linearization scheme discussed in Chap. 7 to the computation of user equilibria.

8.9 Numerical Examples of Computing User Equilibria

In this section we present two specific examples of solving user equilibrium problems.

8.9.1 Frank-Wolfe Algorithm for Fixed Demand, Separable User Equilibrium

Consider the following extended forward-star array

Arc index (i)	From node k	To node l	Arc name (a_i)	A_i	B_i
1	1	2	a_1	10	0.01
2	2	3	a_2	5	0.05
3	2	3	a_3	5	0.05

which clearly describes a network of three nodes and three arcs, two of which are connecting node 2 to node 3. The unit latency functions associated with this network are of the form

$$c_{a_i}(f_{a_i}) = A_i + B_i f_{a_i} \qquad i = 1, 2, 3 \tag{8.178}$$

The single origin-destination pair to be considered is $(1, 3)$ so

$$\begin{aligned}
\mathcal{W} &= \{(1,3)\} \\
p_1 &= \{a_1, a_2\} \\
p_2 &= \{a_1, a_3\} \\
\mathcal{P} &= \mathcal{P}_{13} = \{p_1, p_2\}
\end{aligned}$$

The fixed origin-destination travel demand is

$$Q_{13} = 100 = h_{p_1} + h_{p_2} \tag{8.179}$$

where h_{p_1} and h_{p_2} are the path flows. It is evident by inspection that the user equilibrium for this problem is

$$h_{p_1}^* = 50 \qquad h_{p_2}^* = 50 \tag{8.180}$$

We also note that

$$\begin{aligned} f_{a_1} &= h_{p_1} + h_{p_2} \\ f_{a_2} &= h_{p_1} \\ f_{a_3} &= h_{p_2} \\ c_{p_1} &= c_{a_1} + c_{a_2} \\ c_{p_2} &= c_{a_1} + c_{a_3} \end{aligned}$$

Furthermore, it is convenient at this time to develop a closed-form expression for the optimal step size at each iteration. We do this by noting that the objective function of Beckmann's problem when evaluated at the new iterate $f^{k+1} = f^k + \lambda d^k$ is

$$Z(\lambda) = \sum_{i=1}^{3} \int_0^{\left(f_{a_i}^k + \lambda d_{a_i}^k\right)} c_{a_i}(x_{a_i})\, dx_{a_i}$$

This expression can be differentiated with respect to λ by employing the chain rule to obtain

$$\begin{aligned} \frac{dZ(\lambda)}{d\lambda} &= \sum_{i=1}^{3} \frac{\partial\left(f_{a_i}^k + \lambda d_{a_i}^k\right)}{\partial \lambda} \frac{\partial}{\partial\left(f_{a_i}^k + \lambda d_{a_i}^k\right)} \int_0^{\left(f_{a_i}^k + \lambda d_{a_i}^k\right)} c_{a_i}(x_{a_i})\, dx_{a_i} \\ &= \sum_{i=1}^{3} d_{a_i}^k c_{a_i}\left(f_{a_i}^k + \lambda d_{a_i}^k\right) = \sum_{i=1}^{3} d_{a_i}^k \left[A_i + B_i\left(f_{a_i}^k + \lambda d_{a_i}^k\right)\right] \end{aligned}$$

The optimal step size is obtained by setting this derivative to zero and recognizing that $0 \leq \lambda \leq 1$. That is

$$\begin{aligned} \lambda_k &= \left[(-1)\frac{c_{a_1}^k d_{a_1}^k + c_{a_2}^k d_{a_2}^k + c_{a_3}^k d_{a_3}^k}{\left(d_1^k\right)^2 + \left(d_2^k\right)^2 + \left(d_3^k\right)^2}\right]_0^1 \\ &= \left[(-1)\frac{\sum_{i=1}^{3}\left(A_i + B_i f_{a_i}^k\right) d_{a_i}^k}{\sum_{i=1}^{3} B_i\left(d_{a_i}^k\right)^2}\right]_0^1 \end{aligned} \tag{8.181}$$

where $[.]_0^1$ is the bounded projection operator obeying

$$[v]_0^1 = \begin{cases} 1 & \text{if } v \geq 1 \\ v & \text{if } 1 > v > 0 \\ 0 & \text{if } v \leq 0 \end{cases}$$

for arbitrary scalar v.

We now illustrate how Beckmann's equivalent optimization problem and the Frank-Wolfe algorithm are used to calculate the desired user equilibrium:

Step 0. *(Initialization)* Set $k = 0$ and pick $f_{a_1}^0 = 100$, $f_{a_2}^0 = 40$ and $f_{a_3}^0 = 60$, a flow pattern that is seen to be feasible by inspection.

Step 1. *(All-or-nothing assignment, $k = 0$)* Compute arc and path costs:

$$\begin{aligned}
c_{a_1}^0 &= 10 + 0.01\,(100) = 11 \\
c_{a_2}^0 &= 5 + 0.05\,(40) = 7 \\
c_{a_3}^0 &= 5 + 0.05\,(60) = 8 \\
c_{p_1}^0 &= 11 + 7 = 18 \longleftarrow \text{smallest} \\
c_{p_2}^0 &= 11 + 8 = 19
\end{aligned}$$

Therefore the all-or-nothing flow is

$$\begin{aligned}
\hat{h}^0 &= \left(\hat{h}_{p_1}^0, \hat{h}_{p_2}^0\right)^T = (100, 0)^T \\
&\Longrightarrow \hat{f}^0 = \left(\hat{f}_{a_1}^0, \hat{f}_{a_2}^0, \hat{f}_{a_3}^0\right)^T = (100, 100, 0)^T
\end{aligned}$$

and the search direction is

$$d^0 = \hat{f}^0 - f^0$$

Step 2. *(Line search, $k = 0$)* Using formula (8.181) we have

$$\begin{aligned}
\lambda_0 &= \left[(-1)\,\frac{11\,(0) + 7\,(60) + 8\,(-60)}{0.01\,(0^2) + 0.05\,(60)^2 + 0.05\,(60)^2}\right]_0^1 \\
&= \left[\frac{480 - 420}{2\,(0.05)\,3600}\right]_0^1 = \frac{1}{6}
\end{aligned}$$

so that the new iterate is

$$\begin{aligned}
f^1 &= f^0 + \lambda_0 d^0 = (100, 40, 60)^T + \frac{1}{6}\,(0, 60, -60)^T \\
&= (100, 50, 50)^T
\end{aligned}$$

Step 1. *(All-or-nothing assignment, $k = 1$)* Compute arc and path costs:

$$
\begin{aligned}
c_{a_1}^1 &= 10 + 0.01\,(100) = 11 \\
c_{a_2}^1 &= 5 + 0.05\,(50) = 7.5 \\
c_{a_3}^1 &= 5 + 0.05\,(50) = 7.5 \\
c_{p_1}^1 &= 11 + 7.5 = 18.5 \longleftarrow \text{ smallest (tie)} \\
c_{p_2}^1 &= 11 + 7.5 = 18.5 \longleftarrow \text{ smallest (tie)}
\end{aligned}
$$

The identical path costs indicate equilibrium has been reached. If, however, we continue the calculation, we note that the all-or-nothing flow is arbitrary owing to the tie, so that one all-or-nothing flow pattern is

$$
\begin{aligned}
\hat{h}^1 &= \left(\hat{h}_{p_1}^1, \hat{h}_{p_2}^1\right)^T = (50, 50)^T \\
&\Longrightarrow \hat{f}^1 = \left(\hat{f}_{a_1}^1, \hat{f}_{a_2}^1, \hat{f}_{a_3}^1\right)^T = (100, 50, 50)^T
\end{aligned}
$$

with associated search direction

$$
\begin{aligned}
d^1 &= \hat{f}^1 - f^1 = (100, 50, 50)^T - (100, 50, 50)^T \\
&= (0, 0, 0)^T
\end{aligned}
$$

which makes emphatic the fact that an equilibrium has been found.

8.9.2 Diagonalization Applied to a Nonseparable User Equilibrium Problem

We again consider the network and data introduced in the preceding example with one notable exception: the unit cost function for arc a_3 is

$$
c_{a_3}\left(f_{a_2}, f_{a_3}\right) = 5 + 0.05 f_{a_3} + 0.0001 f_{a_2} f_{a_3} \tag{8.182}
$$

This cost function represents flow interactions between arcs a_2 and a_3. Note that at an arbitrary iteration j of the diagonalization algorithm the unit cost for arc a_3 is

$$
c_{a_3}^j\left(f_{a_3}\right) = 5 + \left(0.05 + 0.0001 f_{a_2}^j\right) f_{a_3}
$$

where $f^j = \left(f_{a_1}^j, f_{a_2}^j, f_{a_3}^j\right)^T$ is the current approximate flow pattern. Note also that

$$\begin{aligned} c_{p_1} &= c_{a_1} + c_{a_2} = 10 + 0.01 f_{a_1} + 5 + 0.05 f_{a_2} \\ &= 15 + 0.01 f_{a_1} + 0.05 f_{a_2} \\ c_{p_2} &= c_{a_1} + c_{a_3} = 10 + 0.01 f_{a_1} + 5 + 0.05 f_{a_3} + 0.0001 f_{a_2} f_{a_3} \\ &= 15 + 01 f_{a_1} + 0.05 f_{a_3} + 0.0001 f_{a_2} f_{a_3} \end{aligned}$$

The diagonalization iterations are:

Step 0. *(Initialization)* Set $j = 0$. Determine an initial feasible flow pattern, say $f_{a_1}^0 = 100$, $f_{a_2}^0 = 40$ and $f_{a_3}^0 = 60$.

Step 1. *(Diagonalization, $k = 0$)* Diagonalize the cost functions and solve the associated separable user equilibrium subproblem. The only affected unit cost function is

$$\begin{aligned} c_{a_3}^0 (f_{a_3}) &= 5 + \left(0.05 + .0001 f_{a_2}^0\right) f_{a_3} \\ &= 5 + [0.05 + 0.0001\,(40)]\, f_{a_3} \\ &= 5 + 0.054 f_{a_3} \end{aligned} \tag{8.183}$$

since the other costs function are separable. Note that employing (8.183) in lieu of (8.182) leads to a separable equilibrium problem.

Step 2. *(Solve Beckmann's program, $k = 0$)* Based on (8.183) and using the Frank-Wolfe algorithm we find

$$f^1 = (100, 51.92, 48.08)^T$$

Step 1. *(Re-diagonalize, $k = 1$)* We obtain

$$\begin{aligned} c_{a_3}^1 (f_{a_3}) &= 5 + \left(0.05 + 0.0001 f_{a_2}^1\right) f_{a_3} \\ &= 5 + [0.05 + 0.0001\,(51.92)]\, f_{a_3} \\ &= 5 + 0.0052 f_{a_3} \end{aligned} \tag{8.184}$$

Step 2. *(Solve Beckmann's program, $k = 1$)* We find

$$f^1 = (100, 50.98, 49.02)' \tag{8.185}$$

Step 3. *(Stopping test, $k = 1$)* Calculation of path costs reveals

$$\begin{aligned} c_{p_1}^1 &= 18.55 \\ c_{p_2} &= 18.70 \end{aligned}$$

for an error of

$$\frac{\left|c_{p_2}^1 - c_{p_1}^1\right|}{\left(\frac{c_{p_1}^1 + c_{p_2}^1}{2}\right)} 100 = \frac{0.1500}{18.62} 100 = 0.81\,\%$$

If we employ a stopping test of 1 % deviation of equilibrated path costs from their average value, then (8.185) is our approximate solution. Note that a very small interaction effect ($0.0001 f_{a_2} f_{a_3}$) caused a change of approximately 2 % in the equilibrium arc flows.

8.10 Sensitivity Analysis of User Equilibrium

In this section we present one perspective for the sensitivity analysis of user equilibrium flow. The method employed is mainly based on ideas presented in Tobin and Friesz (1988). We will use simple extensions of the sensitivity analysis and user equilibrium notation developed earlier, with only brief explanations because of the reader's presumed familiarity with the prior notation. In particular, we consider the following perturbed, fixed-demand user equilibrium problem expressed as a variational inequality:

$$\left[c(f^*,\xi)\right]^T (f - f^*) \geq 0 \quad f, f^* \in \Omega_1(\xi) \tag{8.186}$$

where, for fixed travel demand, we have that

$$\Omega_1(\xi) \equiv \{f : f = \Delta h,\, Q(\xi) = \Gamma h,\, h \geq 0\} \tag{8.187}$$

$$c(f,\xi) : \Re_+^{|\mathcal{A}|} \times \Re_+^s \longrightarrow \Re_{++}^{|\mathcal{A}|} \tag{8.188}$$

$$Q(\xi) : \Re_+^s \longrightarrow \Re_{++}^{|\mathcal{W}|} \tag{8.189}$$

and $\xi \in E \subseteq \Re^s$ is a vector of parameter perturbations that is fixed for any given instance of formulation (8.186). Moreover, when such perturbations occur, it is implicit that the arc flow and path flow solutions are functions of ξ, and may be written as $f^*(\xi)$ and $h^*(\xi)$. Of course, when there are no perturbations, those solutions are denoted as $f^*(0)$ and $h^*(0)$.

8.10.1 Regularity and Formulae

It would seem we may invoke Theorem 2.22 provided we have a locally unique solution of the user equilibrium problem (8.186). However, solutions of user equilibrium problems, although typically unique in arc flows, are generally not unique in path flows. To get around this difficulty, Tobin and Friesz (1988) select an unperturbed path flow solution $h^*(0)$ that is a nondegenerate extreme point of $\Omega_2(0)$, if one in fact exists. If no such nondegenerate extreme point solution exists, then the version of sensitivity analysis presented below does not apply and one must employ other formulae. To invoke Theorem 2.22, the Tobin-Friesz method also employs certain other assumptions. The complete collection of assumptions is conveniently summarized in the following definition of regularity:

Definition 8.3 (Regularity with respect to perturbation) Suppose, for $\xi \in E \subseteq \Re^s$, that the following conditions are met: (i) $c(f,\xi)$ is once continuously differentiable in (f,ξ); (ii) $Q(\xi)$ is once continuously differentiable in ξ; (iii) $c(f,\xi)$ is strongly monotonically increasing in f; (iv) strong complementary slackness of the unperturbed system obtains in the sense that

$$h_p^*(0) = 0,\, p \in \mathcal{P}_{ij} \Longrightarrow c_p(h^*(0),0) > u_{ij};$$

(v) the linear independence constraint qualification for $\Omega_2^*(0)$ holds; (vi) $h^*(0)$ is a nondegenerate extreme point of $\Omega_2^*(0)$; and (vii) the Jacobian (8.203) is invertible. Then we say the user equilibrium problem (8.186) is regular with respect to perturbation $\xi \in E$.

Taking $h^*(0)$ to be a nondegenerate extreme point consistent with Definition 8.3, we observe that it must be a solution of the following Kuhn-Tucker system:

$$c\left[h^*(0),0\right] - \Gamma^T u - \rho = 0 \tag{8.190}$$

$$Q(0) - \Gamma h^*(0) = 0 \tag{8.191}$$

$$\rho^T h^*(0) = 0 \tag{8.192}$$

$$h^*(0) \geq 0 \tag{8.193}$$

$$\rho \geq 0 \tag{8.194}$$

We now consider a restricted problem involving only those paths having strictly positive flow, the vector of which is denoted by $h^{r*}(0) > 0$; for simplicity of notation, we will henceforth use h^{r*} to refer to $h^{r*}(0)$. The dual vector associated with h^{r*} will be denoted by ρ^r. Moreover, the path-OD incidence matrix for h^{r*} will be denoted by Γ^r. Also c^r will be the latency vector associated with h^{r*}. Finally, Δ^r will be the arc-path incidence matrix associated with h^{r*}.

Since we have restricted the network to one that has only paths with positive flow, the dual variables ρ^r are zero. Consequently, the restricted version of (8.190)–(8.194) is the following:

$$c(h^{r*},0) - (\Gamma^r)^T \cdot u = 0 \tag{8.195}$$

$$Q(0) - (\Gamma^r) \cdot h^{r*} = 0 \tag{8.196}$$

This system of equations may be used as the foundation for user equilibrium sensitivity analysis provided Theorem 2.22 is otherwise applicable.

Clearly, if we invoke regularity in the sense of Definition 8.3, the differentiability requirements of Theorem 2.22 are fulfilled. Linear independence of the constraints and strict complementary slackness are also satisfied, as required by regularity. Thus, it remains only to show that the sufficient conditions for a strict local solution are satisfied. To that end, consider a vector z^r such that

$$\Gamma^r z^r = 0, \tag{8.197}$$

and suppose that

$$\Delta^r z^r = 0 \tag{8.198}$$

Let

$$\begin{aligned} h' &= h^{r*} - \alpha z^r \\ h'' &= h^{r*} + \beta z^r \end{aligned}$$

for $\alpha \in \Re^1_{++}$ small enough that $h' > 0$ and $\beta \in \Re^1_{++}$ small enough that $h'' > 0$. Consequently, h', $h'' \in \Omega^{r*}(0)$ where

$$\Omega^{r*}(0) = \{h^r : f^{r*} = \Delta^r h^{r*},\, Q(0) = \Gamma^r h^{r*},\, h^{r*} \geq 0\} \tag{8.199}$$

and f^{r*} is the vector of strictly positive equilibrium arc flows corresponding to h^{r*}. Furthermore, by construction, we have

$$h^{r*} = \gamma h' + (1-\gamma)\, h'' \tag{8.200}$$

where

$$\gamma \equiv \frac{\beta}{\alpha + \beta}$$

Thus, $h^{r*} \in \Omega^{r*}(0)$ since it is a linear combination of points in $\Omega^{r*}(0)$; however, as such, its extension $h^*(0)$ cannot be an extreme point of $\Omega^{r*}(0)$. This is a contradiction because, by regularity, $h^*(0)$ is an extreme point. We are forced to conclude that

$$\Delta^r z^r \neq 0 \tag{8.201}$$

Next we observe that

$$\begin{aligned} (z^r)^T \nabla c(h^r, 0)\, z^r &= (z^r)^T (\Delta^r)^T \nabla c(f^{\,r}, 0)\, \Delta^r z^r \\ &= (\Delta^r z^r)^T \nabla c(f^{\,r}, 0)\, \Delta^r z^r > 0 \end{aligned} \tag{8.202}$$

because of (8.201) and the strong monotonicity of $c(f, \xi)$ arising from regularity. Expression (8.202) is recognized as a sufficient condition that assures local uniqueness. Thus, Theorem 2.22 is applicable to user equilibrium problems that are regular with respect to perturbation.

In fact, the sensitivity analysis formulae for variational inequalities given in Chap. 7 may be easily restated for the user equilibrium problem when regularity in the sense of Definition 8.3 occurs. To do so, we need the following Jacobian matrices:

$$J_{h^r,u} = \begin{pmatrix} \nabla c^r(h^{r*},0) & -(\Gamma^r)^T \\ \Gamma^r & 0 \end{pmatrix} \tag{8.203}$$

$$J_\xi = \begin{pmatrix} \nabla_\xi c^r(h^{r*},0) \\ -\nabla_\xi Q(0) \end{pmatrix} \tag{8.204}$$

If we introduce matrices $B_{k\ell}$, where $k, \ell \in \{1, 2\}$ and

$$[J_{h^r,u}]^{-1} = \begin{pmatrix} B_{11} & B_{12} \\ B_{21} & B_{22} \end{pmatrix}, \tag{8.205}$$

it is not hard to show

$$B_{11} = [\nabla c^r(h^{r*},0)]^{-1} \left[I - (\Gamma^r)^T M^{-1} (\Gamma^r) [\nabla c^r(h^{r*},0)]^{-1}\right] \tag{8.206}$$

$$B_{12} = [\nabla c^r(h^{r*},0)]^{-1} (\Gamma^r)^T M^{-1}$$

$$B_{21} = -M^{-1} (\Gamma^r) [\nabla c^r(h^{r*},0)]^{-1}$$

$$B_{22} = M^{-1}$$

where

$$M = (\Gamma^r) [\nabla c^r(h^{r*},0)]^{-1} (\Gamma^r)^T \tag{8.207}$$

Consequently

$$\begin{pmatrix} \nabla_\xi h^{r*} \\ \nabla_\xi u \end{pmatrix} = \begin{pmatrix} B_{11} & B_{12} \\ B_{21} & B_{22} \end{pmatrix} \begin{pmatrix} \nabla_\xi c^r(h^{r*},0) \\ -\nabla_\xi Q(0) \end{pmatrix} \tag{8.208}$$

Approximations of path flows are then made according to

$$\begin{aligned} h^{r*}(\xi) &\approx h^{r*}(0) + [\nabla_\xi h^{r*}]^T \xi \\ &= h^{r*}(0) + [B_{11}\nabla_\xi c^r(h^{r*},0) - B_{12}\nabla_\xi Q(0)]^T \xi \end{aligned}$$

so that arc flow approximation is

$$f^{r*}(\xi) \approx \Delta^r h^{r*}(0) + \Delta^r [B_{11}\nabla_\xi c^r(h^{r*},0) - B_{12}\nabla_\xi Q(0)]^T \xi \tag{8.209}$$

8.10.2 Numerical Example

We consider an example originally posed by Josefsson and Patriksson (2007). The network of interest has three nodes, four arcs, one origin-destination pair, and four paths; it is depicted in Fig. 8.2. There is a fixed demand of two units

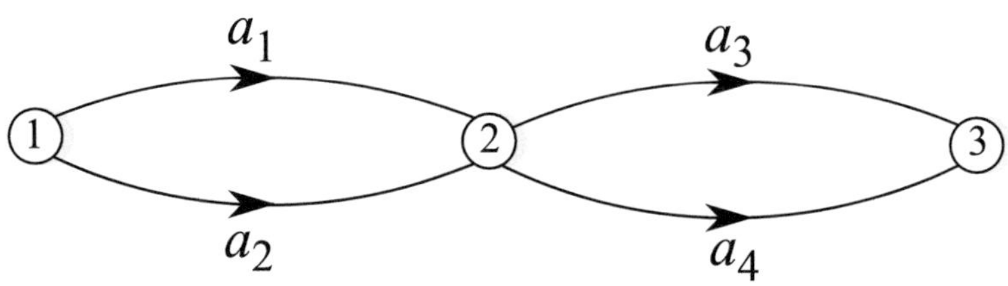

FIGURE 8.2: THE JOSEFSSON AND PATRIKSSON NETWORK

of flow for OD pair $(1, 3)$. The four paths, expressed as sequences of arcs, corresponding to the single OD pair are

$$\begin{aligned} p_1 &= \{a_1, a_3\} \\ p_2 &= \{a_1, a_4\} \\ p_3 &= \{a_2, a_3\} \\ p_4 &= \{a_2, a_4\} \end{aligned}$$

The arc cost functions are given by

$$\begin{aligned} c_{a_1}(f_{a_1}, \xi) &= f_{a_1} + \xi \\ c_{a_2}(f_{a_2}) &= f_{a_2} \\ c_{a_3}(f_{a_3}) &= f_{a_3} \\ c_{a_4}(f_{a_4}) &= f_{a_4} \end{aligned}$$

where the cost function of arc 1 has a perturbation parameter ξ. The total demand for the single OD pair considered is $Q_{13} = 2$.

When $\xi = 0$, the equilibrium arc flow solution is $f^* = (1, 1, 1, 1)^T$. Thus, the restricted arc-path and OD-path incidence matrices are

$$\Delta = \begin{pmatrix} 1 & 1 & 0 & 0 \\ 0 & 0 & 1 & 1 \\ 1 & 0 & 1 & 0 \\ 0 & 1 & 0 & 1 \end{pmatrix} \quad \text{and } \Gamma = \begin{pmatrix} 1 & 1 & 1 & 1 \end{pmatrix}$$

For h^* to be a non-degenerate extreme point of $\Omega(0)$, the number of paths with positive flow in that solution must equal the rank of

$$\begin{pmatrix} \Delta \\ \Gamma \end{pmatrix}$$

In this example, that rank is 3. As pointed out by Josefsson and Patriksson (2007), the possible number of paths having nonzero flow is either two or four.

In fact, the equilibrium solution is

$$\begin{aligned} h_{p_1}^* &= h_{p_4}^* \\ h_{p_2}^* &= 1 - h_{p_4}^* \\ h_{p_3}^* &= 1 - h_{p_4}^* \\ h_{p_4}^* &\quad \text{arbitrary} \end{aligned}$$

Therefore, it is impossible to have a vector $b \in \Re^4$ such that the linear program

$$\min \ b^T h \quad \text{subject to} \quad h \in \Omega^* (0) \tag{8.210}$$

has a solution that is a nondegenerate extreme point, where

$$\Omega^* (0) = \{h : f^*(0) = \Delta h, \ Q (0) = \Gamma h, \ h \geq 0\}$$

and $f^* (0)$ is the unperturbed equilibrium arc flow vector. That is, regularity in the sense of Definition 8.3, does not obtain, and the Tobin-Friesz perspective does not apply. This circumstance is hardly a surprise, as it amounts to saying the sensitivity apparatus presented above cannot be applied when a critical regularity condition is violated.

Brief reflection on the present numerical example, reveals it is the symmetric nature of unit latencies that has blocked the finding of a suitable nondegenerate extreme point. It is interesting, therefore, to change the unit latency of arc a_2 to the following:

$$c_{a_2} = K + f_{a_2}$$

where $K \in \Re^1_{++}$. For there to be a user equilibrium with positive flow on every path, we must have

$$\begin{aligned} c_{p_1} &= c_{p_2} = c_{p_3} = c_{p_4} \\ \sum_{i=1}^{4} h_{p_i} &= 2 \\ f_{a_1} &= h_{p_1} + h_{p_2} \\ f_{a_2} &= h_{p_3} + h_{p_4} \\ f_{a_3} &= h_{p_1} + h_{p_3} \\ f_{a_4} &= h_{p_2} + h_{p_4} \end{aligned}$$

For the present example, these considerations reduce to the system

$$\begin{aligned} f_{a_1} &= K + f_{a_2} \\ f_{a_3} &= f_{a_4} \\ f_{a_1} + f_{a_2} &= 2 \\ f_{a_3} + f_{a_4} &= 2 \end{aligned}$$

whose solution is

$$\begin{aligned} f_{a_1}^* &= 1 + \frac{K}{2} \\ f_{a_2}^* &= 1 - \frac{K}{2} \\ f_{a_3}^* &= 1 \\ f_{a_4}^* &= 1 \end{aligned}$$

with associated path flows

$$\begin{aligned} h_{p_1}^* &= \frac{1}{2}K + h_{p_4}^* \\ h_{p_2}^* &= 1 - h_{p_4}^* \\ h_{p_3}^* &= 1 - h_{p_4}^* - \frac{1}{2}K \\ & h_{p_4}^* \quad \text{arbitrary} \end{aligned}$$

We see that, for any K such that

$$1 > K > 0,$$

we may always pick a value of $h_{p_4}^*$ such that $h_{p_3}^*$ is zero and flow is conserved. Such a solution will be a nondegenerate extreme point and the sensitivity analysis formulas developed in Sect. 8.10.1 may be applied. In particular if we take $K = 1$, then the unperturbed arc flow solution is

$$f^*(0) = \left(\frac{3}{2}, \frac{1}{2}, 1, 1\right)^T$$

with which we associate the nondegenerate extreme point

$$h^*(0) = \left(1, \frac{1}{2}, 0, \frac{1}{2}\right)^T$$

Moreover, the relevant arc-path and OD-path incidence matrices are

$$\Delta = \begin{pmatrix} 1 & 1 & 0 & 0 \\ 0 & 0 & 1 & 1 \\ 1 & 0 & 1 & 0 \\ 0 & 1 & 0 & 1 \end{pmatrix} \quad \text{and} \quad \Gamma = \begin{pmatrix} 1 & 1 & 1 & 1 \end{pmatrix} \tag{8.211}$$

The reduced counterparts are

$$\Delta^r = \begin{pmatrix} 1 & 1 & 0 \\ 0 & 0 & 1 \\ 1 & 0 & 0 \\ 0 & 1 & 1 \end{pmatrix} \quad \text{and} \quad \Gamma^r = \begin{pmatrix} 1 & 1 & 1 \end{pmatrix} \tag{8.212}$$

To complete the sensitivity analysis of the modified example problem, we note that, for the functions and matrices determined above, we have

$$\begin{pmatrix} \nabla c^r(h^{r*},0) & -(\Gamma^r)^T \\ \Gamma^r & 0 \end{pmatrix} = \begin{pmatrix} 2 & 1 & 0 & -1 \\ 1 & 2 & 1 & -1 \\ 0 & 1 & 2 & -1 \\ 1 & 1 & 1 & 0 \end{pmatrix}$$

$$\begin{pmatrix} \nabla c^r(h^{r*},0) & -(\Gamma^r)^T \\ \Gamma^r & 0 \end{pmatrix}^{-1} = \begin{pmatrix} 1/2 & -1/2 & 0 & 1/2 \\ -1/2 & 1 & -1/2 & 0 \\ 0 & -1/2 & 1/2 & 1/2 \\ -1/2 & 0 & -1/2 & 1 \end{pmatrix}$$

$$\begin{pmatrix} -\nabla_\xi c^r(h^{r*},0) \\ \nabla_\xi Q(0) \end{pmatrix} = \begin{pmatrix} -1 \\ -1 \\ 0 \\ 0 \end{pmatrix}$$

For simplicity we assume that both ξ and K are positive. Based on (8.209), we compute the approximate solution and compare it to the exact solution for various values of the perturbation ξ as K is reduced. For simplicity we assume that both ξ and K are positive. These results are summarized in Tables 8.1–8.3.

8.10.3 Cautionary Remarks

The Tobin-Friesz method has been thoroughly studied, and it is both well known and unsurprising that violation of the nondegeneracy assumption can yield spurious approximations. The Tobin-Friesz method presented above is, chronologically speaking, the first sensitivity analysis method developed for user equilibrium. Therefore, it is no surprise that it invokes more restrictive regularity conditions than do the methods subsequently reported in the literature. Indeed, it is fortunate there are now other user-equilibrium sensitivity analysis perspectives, methods, and formulae that relax some of the regularity conditions introduced via Definition 8.3. Furthermore, it should be noted that the example of Sect. 8.10.2 merely shows that it is sometimes possible to alter a user equilibrium problem in a way that allows a nondegenerate extreme point to be discovered so that the Tobin-Friesz sensitivity analysis apparatus may be applied. There is no reason to expect that such alterations will be possible in general or that the altered problems will be considered relevant to the traffic study being conducted. Nonetheless, the Tobin-Friesz approach to sensitivity

Solution	$\xi = 0.05$		$\xi = 0.1$		$\xi = 0.15$		$\xi = 0.2$	
Variables	Exact	SA	Exact	SA	Exact	SA	Exact	SA
f_{a_1}	1.475	1.475	1.45	1.45	1.425	1.425	1.4	1.4
f_{a_2}	0.525	0.525	0.55	0.55	0, 575	0.575	0.6	0.6
f_{a_3}	1	1	1	1	1	1	1	1
f_{a_4}	1	1	1	1	1	1	1	1
h_{p_1}	1	1	1	1	1	1	1	1
h_{p_2}	0.475	0.475	0.45	0.45	0.425	0.425	0.4	0.4
h_{p_3}	0	0	0	0	0	0	0	0
h_{p_4}	0.525	0.525	0.55	0.55	0.575	0.575	0.6	0.6

TABLE 8.1: SENSITIVITY RESULTS FOR $K = 1$

Solution	$\xi = 0.05$		$\xi = 0.1$		$\xi = 0.15$		$\xi = 0.2$	
Variables	Exact	SA	Exact	SA	Exact	SA	Exact	SA
f_{a_1}	1.225	1.225	1.2	1.2	1.175	1.175	1.15	1.15
f_{a_1}	0.775	0.775	0.8	0.8	0, 825	0.825	0.85	0.85
f_{a_3}	1	1	1	1	1	1	1	1
f_{a_4}	1	1	1	1	1	1	1	1
h_{p_1}	1	1	1	1	1	1	1	1
h_{p_2}	0.225	0.225	0.2	0.2	0.175	0.175	0.15	0.15
h_{p_3}	0	0	0	0	0	0	0	0
h_{p_4}	0.775	0.775	0.8	0.8	0.825	0.825	0.85	0.85

TABLE 8.2: SENSITIVITY RESULTS FOR $K = 1/2$

Solution	$\xi = 0.05$		$\xi = 0.1$		$\xi = 0.15$		$\xi = 0.2$	
Variables	Exact	SA	Exact	SA	Exact	SA	Exact	SA
f_{a_1}	1.1	1.1	1.075	1.075	1.05	1.05	1.025	1.025
f_{a_2}	0.9	0.9	0.925	0.925	0.95	0.95	0.975	0.975
f_{a_3}	1	1	1	1	1	1	1	1
f_{a_4}	1	1	1	1	1	1	1	1
h_{p_1}	1	1	1	1	1	1	1	1
h_{p_2}	0.1	0.1	0.075	0.075	0.05	0.05	0.025	0.025
h_{p_3}	0	0	0	0	0	0	0	0
h_{p_4}	0.9	0.9	0.925	0.925	0.95	0.95	0.975	0.975

TABLE 8.3: SENSITIVITY RESULTS FOR $K = 1/4$

analysis is especially simple to understand and to apply when its regularity conditions are satisfied. As a consequence, it remains a popular tool.

Newer methods based on weaker (less restrictive) assumptions are not yet fully vetted from a computational point of view, and their accuracy and numerical stability are not well-documented. Broadly speaking, alternatives to the Tobin-Friesz method involve more intricate mathematical arguments. The alternative perspectives for user equilibrium sensitivity analysis include those stemming from Qui and Magnanti (1992), Cho et al. (2000), Josefsson and Patriksson (2007), Marcotte and Patriksson (2007), Yang and Bell (2005), and Yang and Huang (2005).

8.11 References and Additional Reading

Aashtiani, H. Z. (1979). *The multi-modal traffic assignment problem.* Ph.D. thesis, Sloan School of Management, M.I.T., Cambridge, MA.

Aashtiani, H. Z., & Magnanti, T. L. (1981). Equilibria on a congested transportation network. *SIAM Journal on Algebraic and Discrete Methods, 2*, 213–226.

Abdulaal, M., & LeBlanc, L. J. (1979). Methods for combining modal split and equilibrium assignment models. *Transportation Science, 13*(4), 292–314.

Avriel, M. (1976). *Nonlinear programming: Analysis and applications.* Englewood Cliffs, NJ: Prentice-Hall.

Balakrishnan, A., Magnanti, T. L., & Mirchandani, P. (1994). Modeling and worst-case performance analysis of two-level network design problem. *Management Science, 40*, 846–867.

Balakrishnan, A., Magnanti, T. L., Shulman, A., & Wong, R. T. (1991). Models for planning capacity expansion in local access telecommunications networks. *Annals of Operations Research, 33*, 239–284.

Balakrishnan, A., Magnanti, T. L., & Wong, R. T. (1989). A dual ascent procedure for large-scale uncapacitated network design. *Operations Research, 40*, 716–740.

Bazarra, M. S., Sherali, H. D., & Shetty, C. M. (2006). *Nonlinear programming: Theory and algorithms.* New York: Wiley.

Beckmann, M., McGuire, C. B., & Winsten, C. B. (1956). *Studies in the economics of transportation.* New Haven, CT: Yale University Press.

Bell, M., & Iida, Y. (1997). *Transportation network analysis.* New York: Wiley.

Bernstein, D., & Smith, T. E. (1994). Network equilibria with lower semicontinuous costs: With an application to congestion pricing. *Transportation Science, 28*, 221–235.

Bertsekas, D. P., & Gafni, E. M. (1982). Projection method for variational inequalities with application to the traffic assignment problem. *Mathematical Programming Studies, 17*, 139–159.

Bertsekas, D. P., & Gafni, E. M. (1982). Projected newton methods and optimization of multicommodity flows. *IEEE Transactions on Automatic Control, 28*, 1090–1096.

Bertsekas, D. P., & Gallager, R. G. (1992). *Data networks* (2nd ed.). Englewood Cliffs, NJ: Prentice-Hall.

Cho, H., Smith, T., & Friesz, T. (2000). A reduction method for local sensitivity analyses of network equilibrium arc flows. *Transportation Research B, 34*(1), 31–51.

Cottle, R. W., Pang, J. S., & Stone, R. E. (1992). *The linear complementarity problem.* New York: Academic.

Dafermos, S. C. (1982a). The general multi-modal network equilibrium problem with elastic demand. *Networks, 12*(1), 57–72.

Dafermos, S. C. (1982b). Relaxation algorithms for the general asymmetric traffic equilibrium problem. *Transportation Science, 16*(2), 231–240.

Dafermos, S. (1983). An iterative scheme for variational inequalities. *Mathematical Programming, 26*(1), 40–47.

Dafermos, S. C., & Mckelvey, S. C. (1986). Equilibrium analysis of competitive economic systems and variational inequalities. Report No. 82–26, Lefshetz Center for Dynamical Systems, Brown University, Providence, RI.

Fernandez, J. E., & Friesz, T. L. (1983). Travel market equilibrium: The state of the art. *Transportation Research, 17B*(2), 155–172.

Florian, M., & Spiess, H. (1982). The convergence of diagonalization algorithms for asymmetric network equilibrium problems. *Transportation Research, 16B*(6), 447–483.

Friesz, T. L. (1985). Network equilibrium design and aggregation. *Transportation Research, 19A*(5/6), 413–427.

Friesz, T. L., Weiss, J., & Gottfried, J. A. (1983). Numerical experience with diagonalization algorithms for asymmetric demand traffic assignment. *Civil Engineering Systems, 1*(2), 63–68.

Gabriel, S. A., & Bernstein, D. (1997a). The traffic equilibrium problem with nonadditive path costs. *Transportation Science, 31*, 324–336.

Gabriel, S. A., & Bernstein, D. (1997b). The traffic equilibrium problem with nonadditive path costs. *Transportation Science, 31*(4), 337–348.

Gafni, E., & Bertsekas, D. P. (1984). Dynamic control of session input rates in communication networks. *IEEE Transactions on Automatic Control, 29*, 1009–1016.

Gartner, N. H. (1977). Analysis and control of transportation networks by Frank-Wolfe decomposition. In *Proceedings of the seventh international symposium on transportation and traffic theory*, Tokyo (pp. 591–623).

Gartner, N. H. (1980a). Optimal traffic assignment with elastic demands: A review. Part I – analysis framework. *Transportation Science, 14*(2), 175–191.

Gartner, N. H. (1980b). Optimal traffic assignment with elastic demands: A review. Part II – algorithmic approaches. *Transportation Science, 14*(2), 192–208.

Gavish, B. (1991). Topological design of telecommunications network – local acces design methods. *Annals of Operations Research, 33*, 17–71.

Josefsson, M., & Patriksson, M. (2007). Sensitivity analysis of separable traffic equilibria with application to bilevel optimization in network design. *Transportation Research B, 41*(1), 4–31.

Luna, H. P., Ziviani, N., & Cabral, R. M. B. (1987). The telephonic switching center network problem: Formulation and computational experience. *Discrete Applied Mathematics, 18*, 199–210.

Maculan, N. (1987). The Steiner problem in graphs. *Annals of Discrete Mathematics, 31*, 185–212.

Magnanti, T. L., Mirchandani, P., & Vachani, R. (1993). The Convex Hull of two core capacitated network design problems. *Mathematical Programming, 60*, 223–250.

Marcotte, P., & Patriksson, M. (2007). Traffic equilibrium. In C. Barnhardt & G. Laporte (Ed.), *Transportation* (Handbooks in operations research and management science, Vol. 14, pp. 623–714). New York: North-Holland.

Mateus, G. R., Cruz, F. R. B., & Luna, H. P. L. (1994), Algorithm for hierarchical network design. *Location Science, 2*, 149–164.

Mateus, G. R., Henrique, P. L., Sirhal, L., & Sirhal, A. B. (2000). Heuristics for distribution network design in telecommunications. *Journal of Heuristics, 6*(1), 131–148.

Minoux, M. (1989). Network synthesis and optimal network design problems: Models, solution methods and applications. *Networks, 19*, 313–360.

Nagurney, A. (1984). Comparative tests of multimodal traffic equilibrium methods. *Transportation Research, 18B*, 469–485.

Nagurney, A. (1987). Computational comparisons of spatial price equilibrium methods. Journal of Regional Science, *27*(1), 55–76.

Pang, J. S., & Chan, D. (1982). Iterative methods for variational and complementarity problems. Mathematical programming, *24*(1), 284–313.

Pang, J.-S., & Yu, C.-S. (1984). Linearized simplicial decomposition methods for computing traffic equilibria on networks. *Networks, 14*(3), 427–438.

Patriksson, M. (2004). Sensitivity Analysis of Traffic Equilibria. *Transportation Science* 38 (3), 258–281.

Qui, Y., & Magnanti, T. L. (1992). Sensitivity analysis for variational inequalities. *Mathematics of Operations Research, 17*, 61–76.

Smith, T. E., & Bernstein, D. (1993). Programmable network equilibria. In T. R. Lakshmanan & P. Nijkamp (Eds.), *Structure and change in the space economy* (pp. 91–130). New York: Springer.

Tobin, R. L., & Friesz, T. L. (1983). Formulating and solving the network spatial price equilibrium problem with transshipment in terms of arc variables. *Journal of Regional Science, 23*(2), 187–198.

Tobin, R. L., & Friesz, T. L. (1988). Sensitivity analysis for equilibrium network flow. *Transportation Science, 22*, 242–250.

Wardrop, J. G. (1952). Some theoretical aspects of road traffic research. *Proceedings of the Institute of Civil Engineers, Part II, 1*, 278–325.

Wong, R. T. (1984). A dual ascent algorithm for the Steiner problem in directed graphs. *Mathematical Programming, 28*, 271–287.

Yang, H., & Bell, M. (2005). Sensitivity analysis of network traffic equilibria revisited: The corrected approach. In B. Heydecker (Ed.), Mathematics in Transport (pp. 373–411). Elsevier.

Yang, H., & Huang, H. (2005). *Mathematical and economic theory of road pricing*. Oxford: Elsevier.

9

Spatial Price Equilibrium on Networks

TRADITIONAL MICROECONOMICS CONSIDERS THE behavior of consumers and producers at isolated points in space. However, in many applications it is important to consider how markets located at different points interact. In this chapter we view markets as located at spatially distinct nodes of a transportation network that is the source of congestion externalities. We introduce and study a family of Nash games that may be expressed as variational inequalities for which commodity prices and network flows are readily computed using the algorithms introduced in previous chapters.

Section 9.1: Extensions of Samuelson-Takayama-Judge (STJ) Network Spatial Price Equilibrium. In this section, we present an updated version of the Samuelson-Takayama-Judge (STJ) model of network spatial price equilibrium that describes a perfectly competitive economy wherein the sites of production and consumption are located at the nodes of a transportation network.

Section 9.2: Algorithms for STJ Network Spatial Price Equilibrium. This section considers how the algorithms introduced in earlier chapters can be used to solve the model developed in the previous section.

Section 9.3: Sensitivity Analysis for STJ Network Spatial Price Equilibrium. This section considers the sensitivity analysis of the extended STJ spatial price equilibrium model. Sensitivity analysis can be used to determine variations of the solution in response to changes in the input data without re-solving the problem.

Section 9.4: Oligopolistic Network Competition. This section considers a small number of firms located at nodes of a transportation network and producing a homogeneous product. These firms compete in a network-wide market for their output.

T.L. Friesz, D. Bernstein, *Foundations of Network Optimization and Games*, Complex Networks and Dynamic Systems 3,
DOI 10.1007/978-1-4899-7594-2_9

Section 9.5: Inclusion of Arbitrageurs. Traditional models of oligopolistic network competition ignore the existence of arbitrageurs. This section shows how spatial price equilibrium models may be modified to directly consider arbitrage.

Section 9.6: Modeling Freight Networks. This section briefly discusses descriptive, strategic models of freight systems demonstrating how they may be created using the notions of user equilibrium and spatial price equilibrium.

9.1 Extensions of STJ Network Spatial Price Equilibrium

Models of spatially separated, perfectly competitive firms have a fairly long history, having first been formulated in the nineteenth century; see in particular Cournot (1838). In the twentieth century, Samuelson (1952) showed that for linear supply and demand functions and no transportation congestion, the problem of an equilibrium among spatially separated markets could be formulated as an extremal problem. Beckmann et al. (1956) and Takayama and Judge (1971) extended this work to treat congestion. However, both Samuelson and Takayama and Judge employed a bipartite graph and separable functions, while Beckmann considered a more general network but limited his analysis to separable functions. Friesz et al. (1981, 1983, 1984) and Tobin and Friesz (1983), further extended the Samuelson-Takayama-Judge (STJ) formulation to treat a fully general network with transshipment and nonseparable functions. Moreover, since 1952 many other researchers have contributed algorithms and enhanced formulations for the spatial price equilibrium problem; see Friesz (1985) and Nagurney (1987a) for reviews of spatial price equilibrium research up to 1987. See Florian and Hearn (1995) for a review of more recent literature.

The notation employed to describe a single commodity inter-regional flow network is slightly different than that used for our discussion of Wardropian equilibrium problems in Chap. 8. In particular, we begin with a directed graph $\mathcal{G}(\mathcal{N}, \mathcal{A})$ that is non-simple since we will allow for multiple arcs connecting the same pair of nodes in order to represent multiple transportation modes; of course, $\mathcal{A}$ is the arc set and $\mathcal{N}$ is the node set. The balance of our notation is as follows:

$i, j, \ell \in \mathcal{A}$	nodes of the network
π_ℓ	commodity price at node ℓ
S_ℓ	commodity supply at node ℓ
D_ℓ	commodity demand at node ℓ
Ψ_ℓ	inverse commodity supply at node ℓ
Θ_ℓ	inverse commodity demand at node ℓ
$\mathcal{W}$	the set of all origin-destination pairs
$\mathcal{P}$	the set of all paths defined for $\mathcal{G}(\mathcal{N}, \mathcal{A})$

$\mathcal{P}_{ij}$	the set of all paths connecting OD pair $(i,j) \in \mathcal{W}$
h_p	the flow on path $p \in \mathcal{P}$
f_a	the flow on arc $a \in \mathcal{A}$
δ_{ap}	1 if $a \in p$ and 0 otherwise
$\Delta = (\delta_{ap})$	the arc-path incidence matrix

The reader should note that the commodity supplies and demands are flows (quantities per unit time) and must necessarily have the same units as arc and path flows.

As has been our practice in previous chapters, a variable or function without a subscript will denote a vector. In particular

$$\Psi \equiv (\Psi_\ell : \ell \in \mathcal{N})^T \in \Re^{|\mathcal{N}|} \tag{9.1}$$

and

$$\Theta \equiv (\Theta_\ell : \ell \in \mathcal{N})^T \in \Re^{|\mathcal{N}|} \tag{9.2}$$

are vectors of inverse supply and demand functions, respectively. Also

$$f \equiv (f_a : a \in \mathcal{A})^T \in \Re^{|\mathcal{A}|} \tag{9.3}$$

$$h \equiv (h_p : p \in \mathcal{P})^T \in \Re^{|\mathcal{P}|} \tag{9.4}$$

$$S \equiv (S_\ell : \ell \in \mathcal{N})^T \in \Re^{|\mathcal{N}|} \tag{9.5}$$

$$D \equiv (D_\ell : \ell \in \mathcal{N})^T \in \Re^{|\mathcal{N}|} \tag{9.6}$$

are, respectively, vectors of arc flows, path flows, supplies, and demands. Note that we are employing the notation of a single homogeneous commodity problem. However, because the supply and demand functions (and their inverses) are nonseparable, we are implicitly treating multiple commodity problems as well.

A market is assumed to exist at every node (although it is quite easy to relax this assumption to treat pure demand, supply and/or transshipment nodes). Furthermore, it is useful to define the following set of feasible solutions:

$$\Lambda_0 \equiv \left\{ \begin{array}{l} (f, D, S) : f_a - \sum_{p \in \mathcal{P}} \delta_{ap} h_p = 0 \quad \forall\, a \in \mathcal{A}, \\ D_\ell - S_\ell + \sum_{j:(\ell,j) \in \mathcal{W}} \sum_{p \in \mathcal{P}_{\ell j}} h_p - \sum_{j:(j,\ell) \in \mathcal{W}} \sum_{p \in \mathcal{P}_{j\ell}} h_p = 0 \quad \forall\, \ell \in \mathcal{N}, \\ \left. h \geq 0, \quad D \geq 0, \quad S \geq 0 \right\} \subseteq \left(\Re_+^{|\mathcal{A}|} \times \Re_+^{|\mathcal{N}|} \times \Re_+^{|\mathcal{N}|} \right) \end{array} \right\} \tag{9.7}$$

It should be noted that the feasible set (9.7) recognizes that path flow variables may be used to express flow conservation. Later, in expression (9.31), we will see that flow conservation may be expressed in terms arc flows without reference to path flows.

Formally, a spatial price equilibrium (SPE) obeys the following definition:

Definition 9.1 A price-flow pair (π^*, h^*) is said to be a (perfectly competitive) network spatial price equilibrium if it obeys the following conditions:

(i) Nonnegativity of flows and prices:

$$h_p^* \geq 0 \quad \forall\, p \in \mathcal{P} \tag{9.8}$$

$$\pi_\ell^* \geq 0 \quad \forall\, \ell \in \mathcal{N} \tag{9.9}$$

(ii) Delivered prices are greater than or equal to local price

$$c_p(h^*) + \pi_i^* \geq \pi_j^* \quad \forall\, (i,j) \in \mathcal{W},\, p \in \mathcal{P}_{ij} \tag{9.10}$$

(iii) Trivial flow if delivered price exceeds local price:

$$c_p(h^*) + \pi_i^* > \pi_j^*, \;\; p \in \mathcal{P}_{ij} \Longrightarrow h_p = 0 \quad \forall\, (i,j) \in \mathcal{W} \tag{9.11}$$

(iv) Delivered price equals local price for nontrivial flows:

$$h_p^* > 0, \;\; p \in \mathcal{P}_{ij} \Longrightarrow c_p(h^*) + \pi_i = \pi_j \quad \forall\, (i,j) \in \mathcal{W} \tag{9.12}$$

(v) Market clearing (flow conservation) at every node:

$$\begin{aligned} D_\ell(\pi^*) - S_\ell(\pi^*) + &\sum_{j:(\ell,j)\in\mathcal{W}} \sum_{p\in\mathcal{P}_{\ell j}} h_p^* \\ - &\sum_{j\in(j,\ell)\in\mathcal{W}} \sum_{p\in\mathcal{P}_{j\ell}} h_p^* = 0 \quad \forall\, \ell \in \mathcal{N} \end{aligned} \tag{9.13}$$

Some comments regarding Definition 9.1 are in order:

(1) Note that (9.13) is the embodiment of the usual elementary notion of market clearing as a balance of supply and demand of the single homogeneous commodity of interest. In fact, for the trivial case of a single-node network wherein there are neither path nor arc flows, (9.13) tells us that $D_\ell(\pi^*) = S_\ell(\pi^*)$.

(2) One should also note that expression (9.10) may be motivated by assuming that

$$c_p(h^*) + \pi_i^* < \pi_j^* \tag{9.14}$$

for some $(i,j) \in \mathcal{W}$ and $p \in \mathcal{P}_{ij}$, while $h_p^* > 0$. However, such a positive path flow requires, by condition (9.12), that

$$c_p(h^*) + \pi_i^* = \pi_j^* \tag{9.15}$$

which contradicts (9.14) and thereby substantiates (9.10).

(3) Furthermore, condition (9.11) does not have to be explicit, for if we allow $h_p^* > 0$ when $c_p(h^*) + \pi_i^* > \pi_j^*$, condition (9.12) immediately requires that (9.15) holds, thereby again producing a contradiction and substantiating (9.11).

9.1.1 Variational Inequality Formulation

The key result pertaining to the formulation of network SPE in the context of perfect competition as a variational inequality is the following:

Theorem 9.1 *(Variational inequality representation of spatial price equilibrium) A flow pattern $(f^*, D^*, S^*) \in \Lambda_0$ is a spatial price equilibrium if and only if*

$$\sum_{a\in\mathcal{A}} c_a(f^*)(f_a - f_a^*) - \sum_{\ell\in\mathcal{N}} \Theta_\ell(D^*)(D_\ell - D_\ell^*)$$

$$+ \sum_{\ell\in\mathcal{N}} \Psi_\ell(S^*)(S_\ell - S_\ell^*) \geq 0 \qquad \forall\,(f,D,S) \in \Lambda_0 \tag{9.16}$$

provided there are inverse supply and inverse demand functions for each market. For convenience, the notation $VI(c, \Theta, \Psi, \Lambda_0)$ will be used to refer to variational inequality representation (9.16).

Proof. We follow Friesz et al. (1981, 1984). The proof is similar to that used to establish the variational inequality representation of Wardropian user equilibrium and is in two parts.

(i) [SPE$\Longrightarrow$(9.16)] A spatial price equilibrium obeys

$$c_p\,(h^*) \geq \pi_j - \pi_i \quad \forall (i,j) \in \mathcal{W},\, p \in \mathcal{P}_{ij}$$

Hence

$$c_p(h^*)(h_p - h_p^*) \geq (\pi_j^* - \pi_i^*)(h_p - h_p^*) \quad \forall (i,j) \in \mathcal{W},\, p \in \mathcal{P}_{ij}$$

because

$$h_p < h_p^* \Longrightarrow h_p^* > 0 \Longrightarrow c_p^* = \pi_j^* - \pi_i^* \quad \forall (i,j) \in \mathcal{W},\, p \in \mathcal{P}_{ij}$$

Thus

$$\sum_{p\in\mathcal{P}} c_p(h^*)(h_p - h_p^*) \geq \sum_{\forall (i,j)\in\mathcal{W}} \sum_{p\in\mathcal{P}_{ij}} (\pi_j^* - \pi_i^*)(h_p - h_p^*)$$

or

$$\sum_{p \in \mathcal{P}} \sum_{a \in \mathcal{A}} \delta_{ap} c_a(f^*)(h_p - h_p^*) \geq \sum_{\forall (i,j) \in \mathcal{W}} \sum_{p \in \mathcal{P}_{ij}} \pi_j^*(h_p - h_p^*) -$$

$$\sum_{\forall (i,j) \in \mathcal{W}} \sum_{p \in \mathcal{P}_{ij}} \pi_i^*(h_p - h_p^*)$$

and

$$\sum_{a \in \mathcal{A}} c_a(f^*)(f_a - f_a^*) \geq \sum_{j \in \mathcal{N}} \pi_j^* \left[\sum_{i:(i,j) \in \mathcal{W}} \sum_{p \in \mathcal{P}_{ij}} (h_p - h_p^*) - \right.$$

$$\left. \sum_{i:(j,i) \in \mathcal{W}} \sum_{p \in \mathcal{P}_{ji}} (h_p - h_p^*) \right]$$

$$= - \sum_{j \in \mathcal{N}} \pi_j^* [(S_j - S_j^*) - (D_j - D_j^*)]$$

$$= - \sum_{j \in \mathcal{N}} \Psi_j(S^*)(S_j - S_j^*) + \sum_{j \in \mathcal{N}} \Theta_j(D^*)(D_j - D_j^*)$$

This last result is easily rewritten to obtain the intended inequality:

$$\sum_{a \in \mathcal{A}} c_a(f^*)(f_a - f_a^*) - \sum_{\ell \in \mathcal{N}} \Theta_\ell(D^*)(D_\ell - D_\ell^*) + \sum_{\ell \in \mathcal{N}} \Psi_\ell(S^*)(S_\ell - S_\ell^*) \geq 0 \tag{9.17}$$

(ii) [(9.16) $\Longrightarrow$ Definition 9.1] Assume that (9.16) obtains. It follows immediately that (f^*, D^*, S^*) is an optimal solution to the following linear program:

$$\min \quad [c(f^*)]^T f - (\pi^*)^T D + (\pi^*)^T S$$

subject to

$$D_\ell - S_\ell + \sum_{j:(\ell,j) \in \mathcal{W}} \sum_{p \in \mathcal{P}_{\ell j}} h_p - \sum_{j:(j,\ell) \in \mathcal{W}} \sum_{p \in \mathcal{P}_{j\ell}} h_p = 0 \quad \forall \ell \in \mathcal{N} \;\; (u)$$

$$f_a - \sum_{p \in \mathcal{P}} \delta_{ap} h_p = 0 \quad \forall a \in \mathcal{A}$$

$$h, D, S \geq 0$$

where u is a vector of dual variables for the market clearing constraints. The dual of the above linear program is

$$\left.\begin{array}{c}\max u \cdot 0 \\ \text{subject to} \\ u_j - u_i \leq c_p(h^*) \quad \forall\,(i,j) \in \mathcal{W},\, p \in \mathcal{P}_{ij} \; (h \in \Re^{|\mathcal{P}|}) \\ u_\ell \leq \pi_\ell^* \quad \forall\, \ell \in \mathcal{N} \quad (D \in \Re^{|\mathcal{N}|}) \\ -u_\ell \leq -\pi_\ell^* \quad \forall\, \ell \in \mathcal{N} \quad (S \in \Re^{|\mathcal{N}|}) \\ u \text{ unrestricted} \end{array}\right\} \tag{9.18}$$

where h, D, and S are now vectors of dual variables associated with the constraints next to which they are written. It is, therefore, clear that a dual optimal solution is such that

$$u_\ell = \pi_\ell^* \quad \text{and} \quad \pi_i^* + c_p(h^*) \geq \pi_j^*$$

By complementary slackness, we know, for any $p \in \mathcal{P}_{ij}$, that

$$(\pi_i^* + c_p(h^*) - \pi_j^*)h_p^* = 0 \tag{9.19}$$

Hence, again for any $p \in \mathcal{P}_{ij}$, we have

$$h_p^* \;\; > \;\; 0 \implies \pi_i^* + c_p(h^*) = \pi_j^* \tag{9.20}$$

$$\pi_i^* + c_p(h^*) \;\; > \;\; \pi_j^* \implies h_p^* = 0 \tag{9.21}$$

Since $(h^*, D^*, S^*) \in \Lambda_0$, this completes the proof. ■

9.1.2 Uniqueness

To explore both uniqueness and existence, we will rely on the variational inequality formulation of spatial price equilibrium, namely $VI(f, \Theta, \Psi, \Lambda_0)$, when inverse supply and inverse demand functions are available:

$$\left.\begin{array}{c}\text{find } (f^*, D^*, S^*) \in \Lambda_0 \text{ such that} \\ \left[c(f^*)\right]^T (f - f^*) + \left[\Theta(D^*)\right]^T (D - D^*) - \left[\Psi(S^*)\right]^T (S - S^*) \geq 0 \\ \text{for all } (f, D, S) \in \Lambda_0 \end{array}\right\} \tag{9.22}$$

where Λ_0 is defined by (9.7) and

$$c(f) \;:\; \Re^{|\mathcal{A}|} \longrightarrow \Re^{|\mathcal{A}|}$$

$$\Theta(D) \;:\; \Re^{|\mathcal{N}|} \longrightarrow \Re^{|\mathcal{N}|}$$

$$\Psi(S) \;:\; \Re^{|\mathcal{N}|} \longrightarrow \Re^{|\mathcal{N}|}$$

The following result applies:

Theorem 9.2 *(Spatial price equilibrium uniqueness) If (f^*, D^*, S^*) is a spatial price equilibrium, it is unique when $c(f), -\Theta(D)$ and $\Psi(S)$ are strictly monotonically increasing.*

Proof. We begin by recalling from Chap. 7 that a variational inequality whose principal operator is strictly monotonically increasing may have at most one solution. For the spatial price equilibrium problem, we let

$$x = \begin{pmatrix} f \\ D \\ S \end{pmatrix} \in \Re^{|\mathcal{A}|\times|\mathcal{N}|\times|\mathcal{N}|} \tag{9.23}$$

$$F(x) = \begin{pmatrix} c(f) \\ -\Theta(D) \\ \Psi(S) \end{pmatrix} \in \Re^{|\mathcal{A}|\times|\mathcal{N}|\times|\mathcal{N}|} \tag{9.24}$$

By the given, we have that $c(f)$, $\Psi(S)$ and $-\Theta(D)$ are strictly monotonically increasing. Thus, $F(x)$ is strictly monotonically increasing and the desired result follows immediately. ■

Note that theorem (9.2) is a sufficient condition and presumes that an equilibrium exists.

9.1.3 Existence

We are intrinsically interested in whether a spatial price equilibrium exists for a given network and given transportation cost, commodity demand, and commodity supply functions. Existence of a spatial price equilibrium for mild regularity conditions is considerably more difficult to establish than was the case for Wardropian equilibria. This is due primarily to the fact that one cannot readily establish that the set Λ_0 is bounded, thereby preventing direct application of results based on Brouwer's fixed point theorem. However, the following theorem does obtain:

Theorem 9.3 *(Spatial price equilibrium existence) If the following regularity conditions are satisfied:*

$$\begin{array}{ll} (i) & c_a(f) > 0 \;\; \forall\, a \in \mathcal{A} \\ (ii) & c(f), D(\pi), and S(\pi) continuous \\ (iii) & D_\ell(\pi) bounded from above \forall\, \ell \in \mathcal{N} \\ (iv) & \pi_\ell = 0 \Longrightarrow D_\ell(\pi) \geq S_\ell(\pi) \;\; \forall\, \ell \\ (v) & \pi_i \geq \overline{\pi}_i >> 1 \Longrightarrow S_\ell(\pi) \geq D_\ell(\pi) \;\; \forall\, \ell \end{array}$$

a spatial price equilibrium exists.

Proof. This result is proven by converting the spatial price equilibrium problem to a fixed point problem using a projection operator and applying Brouwer's theorem together with a complicated induction argument which assures the boundedness of Λ_0. See Friesz et al. (1983). ∎

It should also be noted that Smith (1984), Smith and Friesz (1985), and Dafermos and McKelvey (1992) have reported existence results for a spatial price equilibrium without stipulating the a priori boundedness of h, D, and S. Smith (1984) accomplishes this by introducing the concept of exceptional sequences of functions, as defined below:

Definition 9.2 For any $F : \Re_+^n \longrightarrow \Re^n$, a sequence $\{x^n\}$ on $\Re_+^n$ with $\|x^n\| = n$ for all n is said to be an *exceptional sequence* for F if and only if each $x^n = (x_i^n)$ satisfies the following two conditions for some positive scalar $\omega_n > 0$:

$$x_i^n > 0 \implies F_i(x^n) = -\omega_n x_i^n \tag{9.25}$$

$$x_i^n = 0 \implies F_i(x^n) \geq 0. \tag{9.26}$$

In terms of these definitions, we now summarize the main results of Smith (1984) in the following three lemmas:

Lemma 9.1 *For any continuous function $F : \Re_+^n \longrightarrow \Re^n$, either F has a NCP-solution or there exists an exceptional sequence for F.*

Lemma 9.2 *Each continuous function $F : \Re_+^n \longrightarrow \Re^n$ for which there are no exceptional sequences has a NCP-solution.*

Lemma 9.3 *For any continuous function $F : \Re_+^n \longrightarrow \Re^n$, if every sequence $\{x^n\}$ on $\Re_+^n$ satisfies the condition that*

$$\|x^n\| \longrightarrow \infty \implies F(x^n)^T x^n \geq 0 \text{ for some } n, \tag{9.27}$$

then F has a NCP-solution.

A summary of how these results can be used to generalize STJ-type models is reported in Smith and Friesz (1985), as we do in Sect. 9.5 for the study of spatial arbitrage.

An alternative, when proving existence, to the imposition of bounds or the use of exceptional sequences is to employ the rather restrictive notion of strong monotonicity. In particular, the following result obtains:

Theorem 9.4 *(Spatial price equilibrium existence and uniqueness for strongly monotone functions) Assume $c(f)$, $-\Theta(D)$, and $\Psi(S)$ are each, respectively, strongly monotonically increasing with respect to f, D, and S. Then the spatial price equilibrium problem expressed by (9.22) has exactly one solution.*

Proof. Upon defining

$$x = \begin{pmatrix} f \\ D \\ S \end{pmatrix} \quad x^* = \begin{pmatrix} f^* \\ D^* \\ S^* \end{pmatrix} \quad F(x^*) = \begin{pmatrix} c(f^*) \\ -\Theta(D^*) \\ \Psi(S^*) \end{pmatrix} \tag{9.28}$$

the variational inequality (9.22) may be stated as

$$[F(x^*)]^T (x - x^*) \geq 0 \qquad x,x^* \in \mathbf{\Lambda_0} \tag{9.29}$$

We note that Λ_0 is convex. By the given assumptions, $F(x)$ is strongly monotonically increasing. Hence, by virtue of Lemma 7.4, $F(x)$ is both coercive and strictly monotonically increasing. As established in Theorem 7.14, coerciveness assures a solution x^* exists. Furthermore, by Theorem 7.11, strict monotonicity assures x^* is unique. ■

9.1.4 Equivalent Mathematical Program

It is also important to note that the variational inequality problem formulation of spatial price equilibrium introduced in Theorem 9.1 leads directly to an equivalent optimization problem when appropriate regularity conditions are invoked. If we assume that the relevant functions are all separable, then Tobin and Friesz (1983) demonstrate that the Kuhn-Tucker conditions of the following extremal problem are the spatial price equilibrium conditions:

$$\min \sum_{a\in\mathcal{A}} \int_0^{f_a} c_a(x_a)\,dx_a - \sum_{\ell\in\mathcal{N}} \int_0^{D_\ell} \theta_\ell(y_\ell)\,dy_\ell + \sum_{\ell\in\mathcal{N}} \int_0^{S_\ell} \Psi_\ell(z_\ell)\,dz_\ell \tag{9.30}$$

subject to

$$G_\ell = D_\ell - S_\ell + \sum_{a\in\mathcal{T}(\ell)} f_a - \sum_{a\in\mathcal{H}(\ell)} f_a = 0 \;\; \forall \ell \in \mathcal{N} \;\; (\pi) \tag{9.31}$$

$$f \geq 0 \;\; (\gamma) \tag{9.32}$$

$$D \geq 0 \;\; (\alpha) \tag{9.33}$$

$$S \geq 0 \;\; (\beta) \tag{9.34}$$

where $\mathcal{T}(\ell)$ is the set of directed arcs whose tail node is $\ell \in \mathcal{N}$, $\mathcal{H}(\ell)$ is the set of directed arcs whose head node is $\ell \in \mathcal{N}$. The entities π, γ, α, and β are vectors of dual variables associated with the constraints juxtaposed to them in (9.32)–(9.34). If each of the functions $c_a(f_a)$ and $\Psi_\ell(D_\ell)$ is increasing and each function $\Theta_\ell(D_\ell)$ is decreasing, then the above formulation is equivalent to the spatial price equilibrium conditions, and its solution yields the unique equilibrium. At optimality, each dual variable π_ℓ associated with $G_\ell(f, D_\ell, S_\ell) = 0$ is precisely the equilibrium commodity price at node $\forall \ell \in \mathcal{N}$.

In fact, the following theorem regarding an equivalent program based on line integrals holds:

Theorem 9.5 *(Spatial price equilibrium equivalent program) Any solution of the mathematical program*

$$\left.\begin{array}{l} \min Z(f,D,S)=\oint_0^f c(x)dx-\oint_0^D \Theta(y)dy+\oint_0^S \Psi(y)dy \\ \text{subject to} \\ (f,D,S)\in\Lambda_1 \end{array}\right\} \tag{9.35}$$

where

$$\Lambda_1=\{(f,D,S)\geq 0: G_\ell(f,D_\ell,S_\ell)=0 \quad \forall \ell\in\mathcal{N}\} \tag{9.36}$$

is a spatial price equilibrium provided demand and supply functions are invertible and a constraint qualification holds. Furthermore, if the cost function $c(f)$, negative inverse demand function $-\Theta(D)$ and inverse supply function $\Psi(S)$ have symmetric, positive definite Jacobian matrices, the variational inequality (9.7) and the mathematical program (9.35) are equivalent.

Proof. The proof is immediate from application of the Kuhn-Tucker conditions, upon observing that the assumptions make $Z(f,D,S)$ well-defined and strictly convex. ■

Furthermore, it may be shown that the variational inequality problem of Theorem 9.1 and the mathematical program (9.35) above remain valid characterizations of a spatial price equilibrium when the constraint set Λ_0 is replaced by Λ_1 as defined by (9.35). Note that use of the constraint set Λ_1 eliminates all considerations of path variables – a major headache in Wardropian equilibrium problems.

The above equivalences are formally demonstrated in Friesz et al. (1981, 1984) and Tobin and Friesz (1983). The mathematical program above is readily solved by the Frank-Wolfe algorithm and by other algorithms for linearly constrained nonlinear programs as discussed by Friesz et al. (1984), provided, of course, the functions c, $-\Theta$ and Ψ have symmetric, positive definite Jacobian matrices. Note, however, that the lack of path variables in reduces the Frank-Wolfe algorithm's special appeal. Other algorithms with potentially quadratic rates of convergence, such as the methods suggested by Pang (1984) and Pang and Yu (1984), consequently become much more attractive. Nagurney (1987b) also discusses the mechanics of applying a number of well known nonlinear programming and variational inequality algorithms to the calculation of spatial price equilibria, although no particular method is found to be uniformly superior.

9.2 Algorithms for STJ Network Spatial Price Equilibrium

Because the spatial price equilibrium problem introduced above for the case of perfect competition takes the form of a variational inequality, we know that it may be solved as either a linearly constrained nonlinear program or a sequence of such programs. The only potential complication is the presence of path variables. However, as we have stressed above, when it is not important to keep track of the actual routes followed by individual shipments, we may replace the path variable version of the market clearing constraints with constraints that involve only arc variables. This arc variable model is completely satisfactory for circumstances wherein it is only necessary to predict equilibrium nodal prices, equilibrium nodal consumption levels, and arc flows.

Below we discuss diagonalization and feasible direction methods for diagonalized subproblems, as these are relatively easy to program and intuitively appealing. However, we repeat our earlier warning, issued in the context of traffic equilibrium problems, that diagonalization must be employed with caution. When solving spatial price equilibrium problems, we have found it more reliable to use a nonlinear complementarity formulation with successive linearization; the linear complementarity subproblems of such an approach may be solved by Lemke's method. Also very effective are the gap function methods discussed in Chap. 7.

9.2.1 Diagonalization Algorithms

Regardless of whether we are interested in path flows or only arc flows, Samuelson-Takayama-Judge (STJ) models for perfectly competitive spatial price equilibrium take the form of variational inequalities, namely (9.16). As such, the following algorithm may be effective:

Diagonalization Algorithm for Nonseparable STJ Models

Step 0. *(Initialization)* Set $k = 1$. Find an initial feasible solution $(f^0, D^0, S^0) \in \Lambda_0$ (or Λ_1).

Step 1. *(Diagonalization)* Construct the diagonalized unit arc delay (generalized cost), nodal inverse demand, and nodal inverse supply functions:

$$c_a^k(f_a) = c_a\left(f_a; f_b = f_b^k \ \forall b \in \mathcal{A}\backslash a\right) \quad \forall a \in \mathcal{A} \tag{9.37}$$

$$\Theta_\ell^k(D_\ell) = \Theta_\ell\left(D_\ell; D_j = D_j^k \ \forall j \in \mathcal{N}\backslash \ell\right) \quad \forall \ell \in \mathcal{N} \tag{9.38}$$

$$\Psi_\ell^k(D_\ell) = \Psi_\ell\left(S_\ell; S_j = S_j^k \ \forall j \in \mathcal{N}\backslash \ell\right) \quad \forall \ell \in \mathcal{N} \tag{9.39}$$

Step 2. *(Solve the diagonalized subproblem)* Find $\left(f^{k+1}, D^{k+1}, S^{k+1}\right) \in \Lambda$ (or Λ_1) such that

$$\sum_{a\in\mathcal{A}} c_a^k\left(f_a^{k+1}\right)\left(f_a - f_a^{k+1}\right) - \sum_{\ell\in\mathcal{N}} \Theta_\ell^k\left(D_\ell^{k+1}\right)\left(D_\ell - D_\ell^{k+1}\right)$$

$$+\sum_{\ell\in\mathcal{N}} \Psi_\ell^k\left(S_\ell^{k+1}\right)\left(S_\ell - S_\ell^{k+1}\right) \geq 0$$

$$\forall \left(f, D, S\right) \in \Lambda_0 \text{ (or } \Lambda_1)$$

by solving the mathematical program

$$\min \sum_{a\in\mathcal{A}} \int_0^{f_a} c_a^k\left(x_a\right) dx_a - \sum_{\ell\in\mathcal{N}} \int_0^{D_\ell} \Theta_\ell^k\left(y_\ell\right) dy_\ell + \sum_{\ell\in\mathcal{N}} \int_0^{S_\ell} \Psi_\ell^k\left(y_\ell\right) dy_\ell \tag{9.40}$$

subject to

$$(f, D, S) \in \Lambda_0 \text{ (or } \Lambda_1) \tag{9.41}$$

Step 3. *(Stopping test)* For $\varepsilon_1, \varepsilon_2, \varepsilon_3 \in \Re^1_{++}$, pre-set tolerances, if

$$\max_{a\in\mathcal{A}} \left|f_a^{k+1} - f_a^k\right| < \varepsilon_1$$

$$\max_{a\in\mathcal{N}} \left|D_\ell^{k+1} - D_\ell^k\right| < \varepsilon_2$$

$$\max_{a\in\mathcal{N}} \left|S_\ell^{k+1} - S_\ell^k\right| < \varepsilon_3$$

stop and declare

$$\left(f^*, D^*, S^*\right) \approx \left(f^{k+1}, D^{k+1}, S^{k+1}\right)$$

Otherwise set $k = k + 1$ and go to Step 1.

Convergence results similar to those presented in Chap. 8 may be rigorously proven. See Friesz et al. (1981, 1984) for details.

9.2.2 Feasible Direction Algorithms

Clearly the Step 2 subproblems described by (9.40) and (9.41) of the diagonalization algorithm for nonseparable STJ models described immediately above are linearly constrained nonlinear mathematical programs. As such, these subproblems, as well as any STJ spatial price equilibrium problem that satisfies appropriate symmetry conditions may be solved by feasible direction algorithms like those introduced in previous chapters. Moreover, when path variables are present, the Frank-Wolfe algorithm may be employed to obviate the need to enumerate paths.

As an illustration, we now state a general feasible direction algorithm for the following version of the STJ model due to Tobin and Friesz (1983):

$$\min \sum_{a\in\mathcal{A}} \int_0^{f_a} c_a\left(x_a\right) dx_a - \sum_{\ell\in\mathcal{N}} \int_0^{D_\ell} \Theta_\ell\left(y_\ell\right) dy_\ell + \sum_{\ell\in\mathcal{N}} \int_0^{S_\ell} \Psi_\ell\left(y_\ell\right) dy_\ell \tag{9.42}$$

subject to

$$(f, D, S) \in \Lambda_1 \tag{9.43}$$

It is implicit that the above program assumes demand and supply are invertible, an arc flow representation of market clearing is employed, and the objective function in (9.42) is convex. That algorithm is as follows:

FEASIBLE DIRECTION ALGORITHM FOR SEPARABLE SPATIAL PRICE EQUILIBRIUM

Step 0. *(Initialization)* Determine an initial solution $(f^0, D^0, S^0) \in \Lambda_1$. Set $j = 0$.

Step 1. *(Find feasible direction of descent)* Find a vector $d^j \in \Lambda_1$ such that

$$\begin{pmatrix} f^j \\ D^j \\ S^j \end{pmatrix} + \theta d^j \quad \in \quad \Lambda_1 \tag{9.44}$$

$$\left(d^j\right)^T \nabla_{f,D,S} Z\left(f^j, D^j, S^j\right) \quad \leq \quad 0 \tag{9.45}$$

where $\theta \in [0, 1]$.

Step 2. *(Determine step size)* Find

$$\theta_j = \arg\left\{ \min_{\theta \in [0,1]} Z\left[(f^j, D^j, S^j) + \theta d^j\right]\right\} \tag{9.46}$$

Step 3. *(Updating and stopping)* Calculate

$$\begin{pmatrix} f^{j+1} \\ D^{j+1} \\ S^{j+1} \end{pmatrix} = \begin{pmatrix} f^j \\ D^j \\ S^j \end{pmatrix} + \theta_j d^j \tag{9.47}$$

If $\xi_1, \xi_2, \xi_3 \in \Re^1_{++}$ are pre-set tolerances and

$$\max_{a \in \mathcal{A}} \left| f_a^{j+1} - f_a^j \right| \quad < \quad \xi_1$$

$$\max_{a \in \mathcal{N}} \left| D_\ell^{j+1} - D_\ell^j \right| \quad < \quad \xi_2$$

$$\max_{a \in \mathcal{N}} \left| S_\ell^{j+1} - S_\ell^j \right| \quad < \quad \xi_3$$

stop and declare

$$\begin{pmatrix} f^* \\ D^* \\ S^* \end{pmatrix} \approx \begin{pmatrix} f^{j+1} \\ D^{j+1} \\ S^{j+1} \end{pmatrix}$$

Otherwise set $j = j + 1$ and go to Step 1.

As established in previous chapters, there are alternative methods for finding the direction vectors of Step 1. We leave as an exercise for the reader the detailed articulation of schemes for finding d^j within the algorithmic structure presented above.

9.2.3 Numerical Example

To construct a numerical example, let us consider a graph corresponding to the following extended forward-star array:

Arc Name (a_i)	From	To	A_i^c	B_i^c
a_1	1	2	10	0
a_2	2	1	10	1

with unit arc cost functions

$$c_{a_i} = A_i^c + B_i^c f_{a_i} \quad i = 1, 2 \tag{9.48}$$

The nodal inverse supply and inverse demand functions are of the form

$$\Psi_\ell = A_\ell^\psi + B_\ell^\psi S_\ell \quad \ell = 1, 2$$

$$\Theta_\ell = A_\ell^\theta - B_\ell^\theta D_\ell \quad \ell = 1, 2$$

with parameters given by the following table:

Node (ℓ)	A_ℓ^ψ	B_ℓ^ψ	A_ℓ^θ	B_ℓ^θ
1	10	1	10	1
2	10	1	100	1

These data describe two spatially separated markets. The inverse supply functions for the two markets are identical, but the inverse demand functions are rather different. For market 1, inverse supply (supply price) exceeds inverse demand (demand price) for all positive quantities. Thus, we expect no consumption of the commodity at node 1. Hence, if there is production at node 1, it will all flow from node 1 to node 2. Furthermore, given the unit arc cost functions, the shipments will be at a unit cost of 10, regardless of the flow.

Applying the Frank-Wolfe algorithm to this simple example, the objective function takes the form

$$\begin{aligned} Z(f, S, D) &= \sum_{i=1}^{2} \left[A_i^c f_{a_i} + \frac{1}{2} B_i^c (f_{a_i})^2 \right] \\ &\quad - \sum_{\ell=1}^{2} \left[A_\ell^\theta D_\ell - \frac{1}{2} B_\ell^\theta (D_\ell)^2 \right] \\ &\quad + \sum_{\ell=1}^{2} \left[A_\ell^\psi S_\ell + \frac{1}{2} B_\ell^\psi (S_\ell)^2 \right] \end{aligned}$$

Despite the fact that there are only two nodes and two arcs for this example, there are six decision variables, and the notation can become quite confusing. As an aid in our calculations, it is useful to rename the variables and parameters according to the following scheme:

$$x = \begin{pmatrix} x_1 \\ x_2 \\ x_3 \\ x_4 \\ x_5 \\ x_6 \end{pmatrix} = \begin{pmatrix} f_{a_1} \\ f_{a_2} \\ D_1 \\ D_2 \\ S_1 \\ S_2 \end{pmatrix} \tag{9.49}$$

and associate with each such variable the function

$$V_i(x_i) = \alpha_i x_i + \beta_i (x_i)^2 \tag{9.50}$$

where the parameters are defined by

$$\begin{pmatrix} \alpha_1 \\ \alpha_2 \\ \alpha_3 \\ \alpha_4 \\ \alpha_5 \\ \alpha_6 \end{pmatrix} = \begin{pmatrix} A_1^c \\ A_2^c \\ -A_1^\theta \\ -A_2^\theta \\ A_1^\psi \\ A_2^\psi \end{pmatrix} = \begin{pmatrix} 10 \\ 10 \\ -10 \\ -100 \\ 10 \\ 10 \end{pmatrix}$$

$$\begin{pmatrix} \beta_1 \\ \beta_2 \\ \beta_3 \\ \beta_4 \\ \beta_5 \\ \beta_6 \end{pmatrix} = \begin{pmatrix} \frac{1}{2}B_1^c \\ \frac{1}{2}B_2^c \\ \frac{1}{2}B_1^\theta \\ \frac{1}{2}B_2^\theta \\ \frac{1}{2}B_1^\psi \\ \frac{1}{2}B_2^\psi \end{pmatrix} = \begin{pmatrix} 0 \\ \frac{1}{2} \\ \frac{1}{2} \\ \frac{1}{2} \\ \frac{1}{2} \\ \frac{1}{2} \end{pmatrix}$$

The objective function, consequently, has the form

$$Z(x) = \sum_{i=1}^{6} V_i(x_i) = \sum_{i=1}^{6} \left[\alpha_i x_i + \beta_i (x_i)^2 \right] \tag{9.51}$$

It is now relatively simple to determine an optimal step size rule by noting that the act of taking a step θ along the current direction vector means we wish to solve

$$\min_{\theta \in [0,1]} Z(\theta) = \sum_{i=1}^{6} \left[\alpha_i \left(x_i^j + \theta d_i^j \right) + \beta_i \left(x_i^j + \theta d_i^j \right)^2 \right] \tag{9.52}$$

$$= \sum_{i=1}^{6} \left[\alpha_i x_i^j + \alpha_i \theta d_i^j + \beta_i \left(x_i^j \right)^2 + 2\beta_i x_i^j \theta d_i^j + \beta_i \theta^2 \left(d_i^j \right)^2 \right] \tag{9.53}$$

which is a line search problem for the interval $[0,1]$.

We note that

$$\frac{dZ(\theta)}{d\theta} = \sum_{i=1}^{6}\left[\left(\alpha_i d_i^j + 2\beta_i x_i^j d_i^j\right) + 2\beta_i \left(d_i^j\right)^2 \theta\right] = 0 \tag{9.54}$$

leads directly to

$$\theta_j = \frac{-\sum_{i=1}^{6}\left(\alpha_i d_i^j + 2\beta_i x_i^j d_i^j\right)}{\sum_{i=1}^{6}\left[2\beta_i \left(d_i^j\right)^2\right]} \tag{9.55}$$

so that the optimal step size rule is

$$\theta_j = \left[\frac{-\sum_{i=1}^{6}\left(\alpha_i d_i^j + 2\beta_i x_i^j d_i^j\right)}{\sum_{i=1}^{6}\left[2\beta_i \left(d_i^j\right)^2\right]}\right]_0^1 \tag{9.56}$$

where $[.]_0^1$ is the usual elementary projection operator. We also note that linearization of the objective function at the current iterate leads to the problem:

$$\begin{aligned}
\min\left[\nabla_x Z\left(x^j\right)\right]^T y &= \sum_{i=1}^{6}\left(\alpha_i + 2\beta_i x_i^j\right) y_j \\
&= \left(10 + 0\cdot x_1^j\right) y_1 + \left(10 + x_2^j\right) y_2 + \left(-10 + x_3^j\right) y_3 \\
&\quad + \left(-100 + x_4^j\right) y_4 + \left(10 + x_5^j\right) y_5 \\
&\quad + \left(10 + x_6^j\right) y_6 && (9.57) \\
\text{subject to} \quad & y_3 - y_5 = y_1 - y_2 && (9.58) \\
& y_4 - y_6 = y_2 - y_1 && (9.59) \\
& y_i \geq 0 \quad i = 1,2,3,4,5,6 && (9.60)
\end{aligned}$$

the last of which are recognized as market clearing and non-negativity constraints.

The iterations of the Frank-Wolfe algorithm for this example are:

Step 0. *(Initialization, $k = 0$)* Let

$$\begin{aligned}
x^0 &= \left(x_1^0, x_2^0, x_3^0, x_4^0, x_5^0, x_6^0\right)^T \\
&= (10, 10, 10, 10, 10, 10)^T
\end{aligned}$$

and set $j = 0$.

Step 1. *(Solve approximating linear program ALP^0, $k = 0$)* Based on (9.57), we note that the objective function of ALP^0 is

$$\begin{aligned} Z^0 = & \quad (10 + (0)\,10)\,y_1 + (10 + 10)\,y_2 + (-10 + 10)\,y_3 + (-100 + 10)\,y_4 \\ + & \quad (10 + 10)\,y_5 + (10 + 10)\,y_6 \end{aligned}$$

We note that there are bounds on y_3 and y_4, arising from the fact that the demands obey

$$\begin{aligned} D_1 &= 10 - \Theta_1 \\ D_2 &= 100 - \Theta_2 \end{aligned}$$

Consequently, we must enforce

$$y_3 \equiv D_1 \leq 10 \tag{9.61}$$

$$y_4 \equiv D_2 \leq 100 \tag{9.62}$$

So ALP^0 is

$$\begin{aligned} &\min Z^0 = 10y_1 + 20y_2 + 0y_3 - 90y_4 + 20y_5 + 20y_6 \\ &\text{subject to (9.58), (9.59), (9.60), (9.61), and (9.62)} \end{aligned}$$

A solution of this LP is

$$y^0 = (0, 0, 0, 100, 0, 100)^T$$

We may now form the direction vector

$$\begin{aligned} d^0 &= y^0 - x^0 \\ &= (0, 0, 0, 100, 0, 100)^T - (10, 10, 10, 10, 10, 10)^T \\ &= (-10, -10, -10, 90, -10, 90)^T \end{aligned}$$

Step 2. *(Determine optimal step size, $k = 0$)* Note that the numerator of the ratio that determines step size is

$$
\begin{aligned}
&\sum_{i=1}^{6}\left(\alpha_i d_i^0 + \beta_i x_i^0 d_i^0\right) \\
= \; & \left[(10)(-10) + (0)(10)(-10)\right] + \left[(10)(-10) + \left(\frac{1}{2}\right)(10)(-10)\right] \\
& + \left[(-10)(-10) + \left(\frac{1}{2}\right)(10)(-10)\right] + \left[(-100)(90) + \left(\frac{1}{2}\right)(10)(90)\right] \\
& + \left[(10)(-10) + \left(\frac{1}{2}\right)(10)(-10)\right] + \left[(10)(90) + \left(\frac{1}{2}\right)(10)(90)\right] \\
= \; & -250 - 8,500 + 1,200 = -7,550
\end{aligned}
$$

while the denominator is

$$
\begin{aligned}
&\sum_{i=1}^{6}\left[\beta_i \left(d_i^0\right)^2\right] \\
= \; & (0)(-10)^2 + \left(\frac{1}{2}\right)(-10)^2 + \left(\frac{1}{2}\right)(-10)^2 \\
& + \left(\frac{1}{2}\right)(90)^2 + \left(\frac{1}{2}\right)(-10)^2 + \left(\frac{1}{2}\right)(90)^2 \\
= \; & 8,250
\end{aligned}
$$

Thus, we have

$$
\theta_0 = \left[\frac{-\sum_{i=1}^{6}\left(\alpha_i d_i^0 + 2\beta_i x_i^0 d_i^0\right)}{\sum_{i=1}^{6}\left[2\beta_i \left(d_i^0\right)^2\right]}\right]_0^1 = \left[\frac{7,550}{8,250}\right]_0^1 = 0.9152
$$

Step 3. *(Updating and stopping, $k = 0$)* The new iterate is

$$
\begin{aligned}
x^1 &= x^0 + \theta_0 d^0 \\
&= (10, 10, 10, 10, 10, 10)^T + (0.9152)(-10, -10, -10, 90, -10, 90)^T \\
&= (0.848, 0.848, 0.848, 92.368, 0.848, 92.368)^T
\end{aligned}
$$

Set $k = 1$, and go to Step 1.

Continuing in the above fashion generates the following solution: $f_{a_1}^* = 23.345$, $f_{a_2}^* = 0.0$, $D_1^* = 0.0$, $D_2^* = 56.655$, $S_1^* = 23.345$, $S_2^* = 33.345$. Note that the total demand at node 2 is (approximately) equal to the quantity produced at node 1 and shipped to node 2 plus the quantity produced at node 2. Substituting into the inverse demand and supply functions at node 2, we see that the price is given by $\Psi_2 = \Theta_2 = 43.345$. Furthermore, substituting into the inverse supply function at node 1, we see that the price at node 1 is given by $\Psi_1 = 33.345$. As should be the case, $\Psi_1 + c_{a_1} = \Psi_2 = \Theta_2$ since $c_{a_1} = 10$.

9.3 Sensitivity Analysis for STJ Network Spatial Price Equilibrium

We now consider the sensitivity analysis of the spatial price network equilibrium problem. Sensitivity analysis can be used to determine variations of a solution in response to changes in the input data without re-solving the problem, allowing one to explore the implications of changes in parameters. Here, we present a sensitivity analysis perspective originally developed in Chao and Friesz (1984) which requires the inversion of a matrix with a full rank equal to only the number of regions, rather than to the number of decision variables. The method facilitates sensitivity analyses of very large network spatial price equilibrium problems.

9.3.1 Perturbation Analysis

Using the notation $\xi = (\xi_1, \ldots, \xi_q)^T$ for the vector of parameter perturbations, the perturbed version of (9.30) we shall study is

$$\min Z(f, D, S, \xi) =$$

$$\sum_{a \in \mathcal{A}} \int_0^{f_a} c_a(f_a, \xi) dx_a - \sum_{\ell \in \mathcal{N}} \int_0^{D_\ell} \theta_l(D_l, \xi) dy_\ell + \sum_{\ell \in \mathcal{N}} \int_0^{S_\ell} \psi_l(S_l, \xi) dz_\ell \quad (9.63)$$

subject to

$$G_\ell = D_\ell - S_\ell + \sum_{a \in \mathcal{T}(\ell)} f_a - \sum_{a \in \mathcal{H}(\ell)} f_a = 0 \;\; \forall \ell \in \mathcal{N} \quad (\pi) \quad (9.64)$$

$$f \geq 0 \quad (\gamma) \quad (9.65)$$

$$D \geq 0 \quad (\alpha) \quad (9.66)$$

$$S \geq 0 \quad (\beta) \quad (9.67)$$

where

$$G : \Re^{|\mathcal{A}|} \times \Re^{|\mathcal{N}|} \times \Re^{|q|} \longrightarrow \Re^{|\mathcal{N}|}$$

is the vector of individual G_ℓ defined in (9.64). Note that in (9.63) for the above formulation we do not consider perturbations of the constraints, since these constraints are behaviorally motivated and must be enforced at all times. We will refer to the perturbed equivalent optimization problem as $EOP(\xi)$.

We make the following assumptions regarding $EOP(\xi)$:

(A1) the functions $c_a(f_a, \xi), \theta_l(D_l, \xi)$ and $\psi_l(S_l, \xi)$, for all $a \in \mathcal{A}$ and $\ell \in \mathcal{N}$ are once continuously differentiable in f, D, S and twice continuously differentiable in ξ;

(A2) the functions $c_a(f_a, 0)$, $-\theta_l(D_l, 0)$ and $\psi_l(S_l, 0)$ are strictly increasing in f_a, D_l, and S_l respectively, for all $a \in \mathcal{A}$ and $\ell \in \mathcal{N}$;

(A3) strict complementary slackness holds for the nonnegativity constraints; and

(A4) there are nonzero supplies and demands at every node (market) in the network.

If we define

$$w = \begin{pmatrix} \gamma \\ \alpha \\ \beta \end{pmatrix}$$

a key result is the following:

Lemma 9.4 *If $EOP(0)$ has a solution $(f^*, D^*, S^*, \pi^*, w^*)$ and obeys assumptions A1, A2, A3, and A4, then $EOP(\xi)$ is regular in the sense of satisfying assumptions (i)–(iv) of Theorem 2.22.*

Proof. It is convenient to use the shorthand

$$\begin{aligned} n &= |\mathcal{N}| \\ m &= |\mathcal{A}| \end{aligned}$$

Assumption A2 ensures that the Hessian $\nabla^2 L$ for $EOP\,(0)$ is positive definite, where

$$L = Z\,(f, D, S, 0) + \sum_{\ell \in \mathcal{N}} \pi_\ell G_\ell\,(f, D, S)$$

is the relevant Lagrangian. Hence, we know property (ii) of Theorem 2.22 is satisfied.

Clearly assumption A1 implies Z in (9.65) is twice continuously differentiable. By inspection the constraint functions are also twice continuously differentiable. Thus, condition (i) of Theorem 2.22 is satisfied. Evidently assumption A3 and condition (iii) of Theorem 2.22 are identical. It remains for us to establish that the gradients of binding constraints in (9.65) are linearly independent. To do this, observe that the matrix $A = \nabla_{f,D,S} G(f, D, S)$ has exactly one $+1$ or -1 in each of the last $2n$ columns. Because of assumption A4, the matrix of gradients of binding constraints is a subset of the rows of

$B = \nabla_{f,D,S} f$. This matrix has only zeros in the last $2n$ columns and exactly one $+1$ in each of the first m columns. In particular

$$\begin{pmatrix} A \\ B \end{pmatrix} = \begin{pmatrix} \nabla_{f,D,S} G(f,D,S) \\ \nabla_{f,D,S} f \end{pmatrix} = \begin{matrix} \\ n \\ m \end{matrix} \begin{matrix} m & n & n \\ \left(\begin{matrix} \nabla_f G \\ I \end{matrix}\right. & \begin{matrix} I \\ 0 \end{matrix} & \left.\begin{matrix} -I \\ 0 \end{matrix}\right) \end{matrix}$$

By inspection the rows of $\begin{pmatrix} A \\ B \end{pmatrix}$ are linearly independent regardless of the nature of $\nabla_f G$. Thus, condition (iv) of Theorem 2.22 is satisfied. ∎

Lemma 9.4 tells us that, provided assumptions A1-A4 hold, we may develop estimates for the partial derivatives needed in sensitivity analysis. To this end we first observe that, if we let

$$w = \begin{pmatrix} \gamma \\ \alpha \\ \beta \end{pmatrix}$$

and

$$x = \begin{pmatrix} f \\ D \\ S \end{pmatrix},$$

then the relevant Lagrangian may be expressed as

$$L(x, \pi, w, \xi) = Z(x, \xi) + \pi^T G(x) - w^T x \tag{9.68}$$

The corresponding Kuhn-Tucker conditions may be expressed as:

$$\left.\begin{aligned} \nabla L(x, \pi, w, \xi) = 0 \\ G_\ell(x) = 0 \;\; \ell = 1, \ldots, n \\ w_i x_i = 0 \;\; i = 1, \ldots, m + 2n \end{aligned}\right\} \tag{9.69}$$

In (9.69), and henceforth, we take ∇ to denote ∇_x for simplicity of notation.

We now set the total derivatives with respect to ξ of system (9.69) to zero in order to develop expressions for the desired partial derivatives. In particular, by using the chain rule, we have:

$$\frac{d}{d\xi_j}(\nabla L) = \sum_{i=1}^{m} \frac{\partial(\nabla L)}{\partial f_i} \frac{\partial f_i}{\partial \xi_j} + \sum_{i=1}^{n} \frac{\partial(\nabla L)}{\partial D_i} \frac{\partial D_i}{\partial \xi_j} + \sum_{i=1}^{n} \frac{\partial(\nabla L)}{\partial S_i} \frac{\partial S_i}{\partial \xi_j}$$

$$+ \sum_{i=1}^{n} \frac{\partial(\nabla L)}{\partial \pi_i} \frac{\partial \pi_i}{\partial \xi_j} + \sum_{i=1}^{m+2n} \frac{\partial(\nabla L)}{\partial w_i} \frac{\partial w_i}{\partial \xi_j} + \frac{\partial(\nabla L)}{\partial \xi_j} = 0 \tag{9.70}$$

$$j = 1, \ldots, q$$

$$\frac{dG_l}{d\xi_j} = \sum_{i=1}^{m} \frac{\partial G_l}{\partial f_i} \frac{\partial f_i}{\partial \xi_j} + \sum_{i=1}^{n} \frac{\partial G_l}{\partial D_i} \frac{\partial D_i}{\partial \xi_j}$$

$$+ \sum_{i=1}^{n} \frac{\partial G_l}{\partial S_i} \frac{\partial S_i}{\partial \xi_j} = 0 \quad j = 1, \ldots, q \; l = 1, \ldots, m \tag{9.71}$$

$$\begin{aligned}
\frac{d(w_i x_i)}{d\xi_j} &= x_i \frac{\partial w_i}{\partial \xi_j} + w_i \frac{dx_i}{d\xi_j} \\
&= x_i \frac{\partial w_i}{\partial \xi_j} + w_i \left\{ \sum_{k=1}^{m} \frac{\partial x_i}{\partial f_k} \frac{\partial f_k}{\partial \xi_j} + \sum_{k=1}^{n} \frac{\partial x_i}{\partial D_k} \frac{\partial D_k}{\partial \xi_j} + \sum_{k=1}^{n} \frac{\partial x_i}{\partial S_k} \frac{\partial S_k}{\partial \xi_j} \right\} \\
&= 0
\end{aligned} \tag{9.72}$$

$$j = 1, \ldots, q \quad i = 1, \ldots, m + 2n$$

Expressions (9.70)–(9.72) may be put in their following respective matrix forms:

$$(\nabla^2 L) \left[\nabla_\pi (f, D, S) \right] + (\nabla G)^t (\nabla_\xi \pi) - (\nabla x)^t (\nabla_\xi w) + \nabla_\xi (\nabla L) = 0 \tag{9.73}$$

$$(\nabla G) \left[\nabla_\xi (f, D, S) \right] = 0 \tag{9.74}$$

$$(\operatorname{diag} x)(\nabla_\xi w) + (\operatorname{diag} w)(\nabla x) \left[\nabla_\xi (f, D, S) \right] = 0 \tag{9.75}$$

where it is understood that the zeros on the right hand sides of (9.73)–(9.75) are appropriately dimensioned matrices of zeros.

By complementary slackness we know that $x_i > 0$ implies $w_i = 0$. Using this fact together with (9.72) we conclude that for all i and j

$$x_i > 0 \longrightarrow \frac{\partial w_i}{\partial \xi_j} = 0 \tag{9.76}$$

From (9.76) we obtain

$$(\operatorname{diag} x)(\nabla_\xi w) = \left\{ x_i \frac{\partial w_i}{\partial \xi_j} \right\}_{(m+2n) \times q} = 0 \tag{9.77}$$

since either $x_i = 0$ or $\partial w_i / \partial \xi_j = 0$.

Let x be an r-component vector comprised of all *active* nonnegativity constraints (inactive nonnegativity constraints are excluded) and w an r-component vector of associated dual variables. Without loss of generality, we may assume x consists of the first r entries of the original vector from which it is derived. When strict complementary slackness holds (assumption A3), we know $w > 0$. In this case it follows immediately from (9.77) that the nontrivial portion of (9.75) is

$$(\operatorname{diag} w)(\nabla x) \left[\nabla_\xi (f, D, S) \right] = 0 \tag{9.78}$$

Furthermore, (9.76) provides the following result:

$$(\nabla x)^T (\nabla_\xi w) = \left\{ \sum_{k=1}^{m+2n} \frac{\partial x_k}{\partial x_i} \frac{\partial w_k}{\partial \xi_j} \right\}_{(m+2n)\times q}$$

$$= \left\{ \sum_{k=1}^{r} \frac{\partial x_k}{\partial x_i} \frac{\partial w_k}{\partial \xi_j} \right\}_{(m+2n)\times q} = (\nabla x)^T (\nabla_\xi w) \tag{9.79}$$

Using (9.78) and (9.79) we may restate the system of equations (9.73)–(9.75) as follows:

$$(\nabla^2 L)\,[\nabla_\xi (f, D, S)] + (\nabla G)^T (\nabla_\xi \pi) - (\nabla x)^T (\nabla_\xi w) + \nabla_\xi (\nabla L) = 0 \tag{9.80}$$

$$(\nabla G)\,[\nabla_\xi (f, D, S)] = 0 \tag{9.81}$$

$$(\nabla x)\,[\nabla_\xi (f, D, S)] = 0 \tag{9.82}$$

Note that (9.82) is made possible by using the fact $(\operatorname{diag} w)$ is invertible (since $w > 0$) and premultiplying (9.78) by $(\operatorname{diag} w)^{-1}$. System (9.80)–(9.82) may be written as

$$\begin{pmatrix} \nabla^2 L & (\nabla G)^T & -(\nabla x) \\ \nabla G & 0 & 0 \\ \nabla x & 0 & 0 \end{pmatrix} \begin{pmatrix} \nabla_\xi (f, D, S) \\ \nabla_\xi \pi \\ \nabla_\xi w \end{pmatrix} = \begin{pmatrix} -\nabla_\xi (\nabla L) \\ 0 \\ 0 \end{pmatrix} \tag{9.83}$$

The desired partial derivatives may be calculated by multiplying both sides of (9.83) by the inverse of

$$M(\xi) = \begin{pmatrix} \nabla^2 L & (\nabla G)^T & -(\nabla x)^T \\ \nabla G & 0 & 0 \\ \nabla x & 0 & 0 \end{pmatrix} \tag{9.84}$$

By Lemma 9.4, $M(\xi)$ will be invertible provided assumptions A1, A2, A3, and A4 hold.

Formally, we may state

Theorem 9.6 *(Derivatives with respect to perturbations) If $EOP(0)$ has a solution and assumptions A1, A2, A3, and A4 hold, then for problem (9.65)*

$$\begin{pmatrix} \nabla_\xi (f, D, S) \\ \nabla_\xi \pi \\ \nabla_\xi w \end{pmatrix} = M(\xi)^{-1} \begin{pmatrix} -\nabla_\xi (\nabla L) \\ 0 \\ 0 \end{pmatrix} \tag{9.85}$$

where $M(\xi)$ is given by (9.84).

Proof. By Lemma 9.4, $EOP(\xi)$ is regular. Hence, the total derivative with respect to ξ of the Kuhn-Tucker system (9.69) vanishes, that is, (9.83) obtains. Further, $M(\xi)^{-1}$ exists and (9.85) follows immediately. ■

Unfortunately (9.85) will not generally be of practical significance. To see this note that $M(\xi)$ is an $(m+3n+r) \times (m+3n+r)$ matrix. For a realistic network the number of arcs (m) might be a few thousand, the number of nodes (n) a few hundred, and the number of binding nonnegativity constraints (r) several hundred, making $M(\xi)$ far too large for direct computer storage and inversion. In the next section we show that (9.80)–(9.82) may be manipulated to yield an expression for the desired partial derivatives which requires the inversion of significantly smaller matrices.

9.3.2 Efficient Computation of Partial Derivatives with Respect to Perturbations

In this section we exploit the special structure of (9.80)–(9.82) to develop expressions for $\nabla_\xi(f, D, S)$ and $\nabla_\xi \pi$ which require the inversion of matrices significantly smaller than the matrix $M(\xi)$ in (9.84). This is done through a series of substitutions and manipulations involving (9.80)–(9.82) which are designed to isolate the partial derivatives with respect to parameter perturbations.

We begin by introducing the following matrices which relate to problem (9.65):

$$\eta = (\nabla x)(\nabla^2 L)^{-1}(\nabla x)^T \tag{9.86}$$

$$\rho = (\nabla G)(\nabla^2 L)^{-1}(\nabla G)^T \tag{9.87}$$

$$\zeta = (\nabla^2 L)^{-1}(\nabla x)^T(\nabla x) \tag{9.88}$$

$$J = \rho - (\nabla G)\zeta(\nabla G)^T \tag{9.89}$$

The results cataloged below facilitate development of the desired sensitivity analysis result.

Lemma 9.5 *For problem (9.63)–(9.67) the Hessian matrix $\nabla^2 L$ is positive definite (and invertible) under assumption A2.*

Proof. The demonstration of this result is left as an exercise for the reader. ■

Lemma 9.6 *The matrix η defined by (9.86) obeys*

$$\eta^{-1}(\nabla x)(v^2 L)^{-1} = \nabla x \tag{9.90}$$

Proof. See Chao and Friesz (1984). ■

Lemma 9.7 *The matrix J defined by (9.89) is positive definite (and invertible) under assumption A2.*

Proof. See Chao and Friesz (1984). ■

In light of Assumption A2, we know from Lemma 9.5 that (9.80) may be rewritten as

$$\nabla_\xi(f,D,S) = (\nabla^2 L)^{-1}\left[(\nabla x)^T(\nabla_\xi w) - (\nabla G)^T\nabla_\xi\pi - \nabla_\xi(\nabla L)\right] \quad (9.91)$$

Multiplying (9.91) on the left by (∇x), substituting into (9.82), and rearranging terms yields

$$(\nabla x)(\nabla^2 L)^{-1}(\nabla x)^T(\nabla_\xi w) = (\nabla x)(\nabla^2 L)^{-1}(\nabla G)(\nabla_\xi\pi)+(\nabla x)(\nabla^2 L)^{-1}\nabla_\xi(\nabla L) \quad (9.92)$$

Result (9.90) of Lemma 9.6 together with definition (9.86) allows (9.92) to be simplified to

$$\nabla_\xi w = (\nabla x)\left[(\nabla G)^T(\nabla_\xi\pi) + \nabla_\xi(\nabla L)\right] \quad (9.93)$$

We may multiply both sides of (9.91) on the left by (∇G) and substitute the result into (9.81) to obtain

$$\nabla G(\nabla^2 L)^{-1}(\nabla G)^T(\nabla_\xi\pi) = (\nabla G)(\nabla^2 L)^{-1}(\nabla x)^T(\nabla_\xi w) - (\nabla G)(\nabla^2 L)^{-1}\nabla_\xi(\nabla L) \quad (9.94)$$

Upon substituting (9.93) into (9.94) and employing definitions (9.87)–(9.89), it is easy to show

$$(\nabla_\xi)J = \nabla G\left[\zeta - (\nabla^2 L)^{-1}\right]\nabla_\xi(\nabla L) \quad (9.95)$$

Because of Assumption A2, we know by Lemma 9.7 that (9.63)–(9.67) may be solved for $\nabla_\xi\pi$:

$$\nabla_\xi\pi = J^{-1}\nabla G\left[\zeta - (\nabla^2 L)^{-1}\right]\nabla_\xi(\nabla L) \quad (9.96)$$

Substituting (9.93) and (9.96) into (9.63)–(9.67) and rearranging terms yields

$$\begin{aligned}\nabla_\xi(f,D,S) &= \zeta(\nabla G)^T J^{-1}(\nabla G)\left[\zeta - (\nabla^2 L)^{-1}\right]\nabla_\xi(\nabla L)\\ &\quad + \zeta\nabla_\xi(\nabla L) - (\nabla^2 L)^{-1}(\nabla G)^T\\ &\quad \cdot\left\{J^{-1}(\nabla G)\left[\zeta - (\nabla^2 L)^{-1}\right]\right\}\nabla_\xi(\nabla L) - (\nabla^2 L)^{-1}\nabla_\xi(\nabla L) \quad (9.97)\end{aligned}$$

Expressions (9.96) and (9.97) provide a means of calculating the desired partial derivatives $\nabla_\xi\pi$ and $\nabla_\xi(f,D,S)$. A substitution of (9.96) into (9.93) also provides a means of calculating $\nabla_\xi w$.

In summary, we may state the following result:

Theorem 9.7 *(Efficient computation of derivatives with respect to perturbations) If EOP(0) has a solution and assumptions A1, A2, A3, and A4 hold, then for problem (9.63)–(9.67) the partial derivatives of primal and dual variables with respect to parameter perturbations may be calculated from (9.96) and (9.97).*

Proof. By Lemma 9.4 $EOP(\xi)$ is regular. Hence, (9.80)–(9.82) obtain. The algebraic manipulations (9.91)–(9.95) are made possible by assumption A2 (see Lemma 9.5 and Lemma 9.7) and yield (9.96) and (9.97). ■

Let us now consider the computational implications of (9.96) and (9.97). The matrices J and $\nabla^2 L$ must be inverted in order to apply these formulae. Note that the Hessian matrix $\nabla^2 L$ is an $(m+2n)\times(m+2n)$ matrix; it is, however, a diagonal matrix with positive elements along the diagonal and, consequently, very easy to invert. We may say without exaggeration that the calculation of $(\nabla^2 L)^{-1}$ in general poses no computational difficulties. The matrix J is an $n \times n$ matrix, where n is the number of regions (nodes) considered. If n is, for example, 50, then J may be stored and inverted without difficulty.

At this point it is worth recalling how the partial derivatives calculated from (9.96) and (9.97) will be used. In particular, we will estimate a solution of $EOP(\xi)$ for a given ξ from

$$[f(\xi), D(\xi), S(\xi)] \approx (f^*, D^*, S^*) + \nabla_\xi \left[f(0), D(0), S(0)\right]^T \xi$$

$$\pi(\xi) \simeq \pi^* + \nabla_\xi \pi(0)^T \xi$$

$$w(\xi) \simeq w^* + \nabla_\xi w(0)^T \xi$$

where $(f^*, D^*, S^*, \pi^*, w^*)$ is a solution of $EOP(0)$. Hence, the expressions on the right of (9.96) and (9.97) need only be calculated *once* at $\xi = 0$ for sensitivity analysis. This means the inverse matrices $(\nabla^2 L)^{-1}$ and J^{-1} need only be calculated once. These matrices are completely determined by the network topology and knowledge of the solution (f^*, D^*, S^*). Thus, even if $[J(\xi)=0]^{-1}$ is relatively difficult to calculate in a particular case, it may be reasonable to perform that calculation, since it will literally allow the solutions of an infinite number of perturbed problems to be estimated so long as the underlying network topology is unchanged.

9.3.3 A Numerical Example

In this section we consider a numerical example based on the network depicted in Fig. 9.1. This network has 16 nodes and 50 links (25 bi-directional links). All functions employed in this example are separable second-order polynomials and defined as follows:

(i) link cost functions:

$$c_a(f_a) = A_a^c + B_a^c f_a + K_a^c f_a^2$$

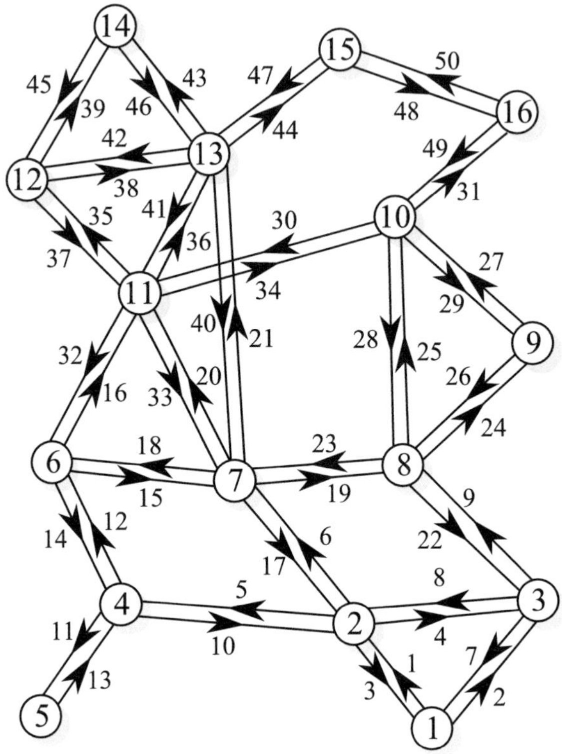

FIGURE 9.1: A NETWORK WITH 16 NODES AND 50 LINKS

(ii) inverse commodity demand functions:

$$\theta_\ell(D_\ell) = A_\ell^\theta - B_\ell^\theta D_\ell - K_\ell^\theta D_\ell^2$$

(iii) inverse commodity supply functions:

$$\Psi_l(S_\ell) = A_\ell^\Psi + B_\ell^\Psi + K_\ell^\Psi S_\ell^2$$

where values of the parameters employed for cost, inverse demand, and inverse supply functions must be specified. The values of the parameters used in the example are listed in Tables 9.1 and 9.2.

The equivalent optimization problem was solved with $\xi = 0$ and then again with K_s^Ψ increased by 30 %. The two solutions are compared in Tables 9.3–9.6. These same tables also contain the differences between the exact variables and perturbed variables estimated using the sensitivity analysis formulae we have presented above.

Note that the differences between exact and approximate solutions are generally very small. The largest differences occur for selected arc flows, but these are limited to about 5 %. The differences between exact and approximate demands, supplies, and prices tend to be quite small, usually well below 1 %.

Link	A^c	B^c	K^c	Link	A^c	B^c	K^c
1	0.120	0.120	0.014	26	0.130	0.130	0.012
2	0.130	0.130	0.013	27	0.140	0.120	0.011
3	0.140	0.140	0.012	28	0.130	0.130	0.012
4	0.130	0.130	0.013	29	0.120	0.120	0.013
5	0.150	0.150	0.011	30	0.113	0.113	0.013
6	0.130	0.130	0.012	31	0.120	0.120	0.014
7	0.140	0.140	0.010	32	0.130	0.130	0.013
8	0.130	0.130	0.012	33	0.140	0.140	0.012
9	0.120	0.120	0.013	34	0.130	0.130	0.013
10	0.113	0.113	0.013	35	0.150	0.150	0.011
11	0.120	0.120	0.014	36	0.130	0.130	0.010
12	0.130	0.130	0.013	37	0.140	0.140	0.010
13	0.140	0.140	0.012	38	0.130	0.130	0.012
14	0.130	0.130	0.013	39	0.120	0.120	0.013
15	0.150	0.150	0.011	40	0.0113	0.0113	0.013
16	0.130	0.130	0.012	41	0.120	0.120	0.014
17	0.140	0.140	0.010	42	0.130	0.130	0.013
18	0.130	0.130	0.012	43	0.140	0.140	0.012
19	0.120	0.120	0.013	44	0.130	0.130	0.013
20	0.113	0.113	0.013	45	0.150	0.150	0.011
21	0.120	0.120	0.014	46	0.130	0.130	0.012
22	0.130	0.130	0.013	47	0.140	0.140	0.010
23	0.140	0.140	0.012	48	0.130	0.130	0.012
24	0.130	0.130	0.013	49	0.110	0.110	0.012
25	0.150	0.150	0.011	50	0.120	0.120	0.013

TABLE 9.1: TRANSPORTATION COST FUNCTIONS

9.4 Oligopolistic Network Competition

We now wish to consider a small number of firms competing in the output market for a single homogeneous good. In particular, we formulate a statement of a Nash network oligopoly model that is similar in spirit to the models of Harker (1985, 1986), Weskamp (1985), and Dafermos and Nagurney (1987).

We assume that at each node, $i \in \mathcal{N}$, there is exactly one firm, and that this firm can sell in every market, $j \in \mathcal{N}$. To simplify the exposition, we assume that the network is completely connected and that every node corresponds to a market (i.e., there are no transshipment nodes). Hence, we need only consider arcs (and arc flows) and can ignore paths (and path flows).

The quantity supplied by firm i to market j is represented by f_{ij}, and $f = (f_{ij} : (i,j) \in \mathcal{N} \times \mathcal{N})$ denotes the complete vector of commodity shipments. The firm bears the unit transportation cost which is a function $c_{ij}(f)$ of the complete vector of commodity shipments; and the price at each market $j \in \mathcal{N}$

Region	A^θ	B^θ	K^θ	A^Ψ	B^Ψ	K^Ψ
1	150	0.120	1.20	5.0	0.01	0.11
2	220	0.150	1.76	1.3	0.04	0.44
3	210	0.150	1.68	1.3	0.05	0.77
4	250	0.210	2.00	1.4	0.80	1.54
5	200	0.160	1.60	1.1	0.03	1.32
6	200	0.150	1.60	1.2	0.30	1.32
7	260	0.200	2.08	1.0	0.40	1.10
8	280	0.230	2.24	0.5	0.80	1.10
9	250	0.200	2.00	1.0	0.70	1.21
10	290	0.023	2.32	0.8	0.90	1.32
11	260	0.220	2.16	1.1	0.71	1.21
12	200	0.200	1.60	1.0	0.60	1.10
13	310	0.240	2.48	1.4	0.90	1.54
14	340	0.270	2.72	1.5	0.70	1.65
15	300	0.230	2.40	1.7	1.00	1.87
16	310	0.250	2.48	1.1	0.90	1.21

TABLE 9.2: INVERSE DEMAND AND SUPPLY FUNCTIONS

is given by a decreasing inverse demand function $\Theta_j(f)$ of the form

$$\Theta_j = \Theta_j\left(\sum_{i\in\mathcal{N}} f_{ij}\right) \tag{9.98}$$

for all $i \in \mathcal{N}$.

Further, the firm located at i has an increasing total production *cost function* $e_i(f)$ given by

$$e_i = e_i\left(\sum_{j\in\mathcal{N}} f_{ij}\right) \tag{9.99}$$

for all $i \in \mathcal{N}$. Since firm i assumes that the quantity supplied to j by all firms other than i, $\sum_{k\neq i} f_{kj}$, is fixed, it is useful to rewrite (9.98) as:

$$\Theta_j = \Theta_j\left(f_{ij} + \sum_{k\neq i} f_{kj}\right) \tag{9.100}$$

Hence, the profit function for firm i can be defined as

$$J_i = \sum_{j\in\mathcal{N}}\left\{f_{ij}\cdot\left[\Theta_j\left(f_{ij} + \sum_{k\neq i} f_{kj}\right) - c_{ij}(f)\right]\right\} - e_i\cdot\left(\sum_{j\in\mathcal{N}} f_{ij}\right) \tag{9.101}$$

Link	Exact	Approx.	|Error|	% Error
1	6.8293	6.9334	0.1041	1.52
2	6.4522	6.7867	0.3345	5.18
5	4.9648	5.0169	0.0521	1.05
6	6.5005	6.5513	0.0508	0.78
8	0.6152	0.6402	0.0250	4.06
9	6.7807	6.8342	0.0535	0.79
12	3.5436	3.5663	0.0227	0.64
13	0.8399	0.8234	0.0165	1.96
16	2.7171	2.7263	0.0092	0.34
20	2.9846	3.0081	0.0235	0.79
21	3.0755	3.0960	0.0205	0.67
23	0.3511	0.3649	0.0138	3.93
24	2.5108	2.5292	0.0184	0.73
25	2.8024	2.8189	0.0165	0.59
27	1.3594	1.3655	0.0061	0.45
31	2.2949	2.3065	0.0116	0.51
35	1.0166	1.0193	0.0037	0.27
36	3.6350	3.6533	0.0183	0.50
39	1.2793	1.2839	0.0046	0.36
42	0.3433	0.3588	0.0155	4.52
43	1.5221	1.5268	0.0047	0.31
44	2.3407	2.3491	0.0084	0.36
50	0.7136	0.7148	0.0012	0.17

TABLE 9.3: COMPARISON OF EXACT AND APPROXIMATE FLOWS FOR A 30 % INCREASE IN K_1^{Ψ}

Each firm is a price-taker in the transportation market. Hence, the *total revenue* accruing to firm i as a result of sales to j is

$$R_{ij}(f) = f_{ij} \cdot \left[\Theta_j \left(f_{ij} + \sum_{k \neq i} f_{kj} \right) \right] \tag{9.102}$$

and the profit maximization problem for firm i is given by

$$\left. \begin{array}{ll} & \max\limits_{(f_{ij}: j \in \mathcal{N})} J_i = \sum\limits_{j \in \mathcal{N}} R_{ij}(f) - c_{ij}(f) f_{ij} - e_i(f) \\ \text{subject to} & f_{ij} \geq 0 \quad \forall j \in \mathcal{N} \end{array} \right\} \tag{9.103}$$

The Kuhn-Tucker conditions for firm i's profit maximization problem are given by

$$[\partial e_i(f)/\partial f_{ij} + c_{ij}(f) - \partial R_{ij}(f)/\partial f_{ij}] - \lambda_{ij} = 0 \quad \forall\, j \in \mathcal{N} \tag{9.104}$$

Region	Exact	Approx.	|Error|	% Error
1	8.0086	9.1064	0.0178	0.22
2	8.9924	9.0000	0.0076	0.08
3	8.8804	8.8854	0.0081	0.09
4	9.1609	9.1658	0.0049	0.05
5	8.6110	8.5940	0.0170	0.20
6	8.5395	8.5243	0.0161	0.00
7	9.2020	9.2066	0.0046	0.05
8	9.3536	9.3427	0.0109	0.12
9	9.0920	9.0963	0.0043	0.05
10	9.4357	9.4393	0.0036	0.04
11	8.9983	9.0014	0.0041	0.05
12	8.4715	8.4773	0.0058	0.07
13	9.5120	9.5154	0.0034	0.04
14	9.6555	9.6583	0.0028	0.03
15	9.4366	9.4379	0.0033	0.04
16	9.4956	9.4987	0.0031	0.03

TABLE 9.4: COMPARISON OF EXACT AND APPROXIMATE DEMANDS FOR A 30 % INCREASE IN K_1^Ψ

$$\lambda_{ij} f_{ij} = 0 \quad \forall\, (i,j) \in \mathcal{N} \times \mathcal{N} \tag{9.105}$$

$$\lambda_{ij} \geq 0 \quad \forall\, j \in \mathcal{N} \tag{9.106}$$

$$f_{ij} \geq 0 \quad \forall\, j \in \mathcal{N} \tag{9.107}$$

where λ_{ij} is the dual variable associated with the constraint $f_{ij} \geq 0$.

Given this notation, we consider a Nash equilibrium for the present bipartite graph of interest:

Definition 9.3 A commodity production pattern $f^* = (f_{ij}^*,\ (i,j) \in \mathcal{N} \times \mathcal{N})^T$ is said to be a *Nash equilibrium* if and only if

$$J_i(f^*) \geq J_i(f) \tag{9.108}$$

for all i and all f with $f_{kj} = f_{kj}^*$ (when $k \neq i$).

That is, we say that the market is in equilibrium if and only if each firm is maximizing profits given the behavior of all other firms. Letting

$$E(f) = ((\partial e_i(f)/\partial f_{ij} + c_{ij}(f) - \partial R_{ij}(f)/\partial f_{ij}),\ \ (i,j) \in \mathcal{N} \times \mathcal{N}) \tag{9.109}$$

we can now demonstrate the following result:

Region	Exact	Approx.	|Error|	% Error
1	21.3701	21.5927	0.2226	1.04
2	13.0132	12.9943	0.0189	0.15
3	9.8241	9.8099	0.0142	0.14
4	6.8997	6.8918	0.0079	0.11
5	9.4509	9.4408	0.0101	0.11
6	7.7130	7.7012	0.0028	0.04
7	8.4030	8.3944	0.0086	0.10
8	9.2448	8.2364	0.0084	0.10
9	7.9406	7.9329	0.0077	0.10
10	7.5687	7.5615	0.0072	0.09
11	7.9472	7.9396	0.0076	0.09
12	8.3908	9.3830	0.0078	0.09
13	7.0076	7.0090	0.0067	0.10
14	6.8541	6.8477	0.0064	0.09
15	6.3803	6.3745	0.0580	0.09
16	7.9143	7.9069	0.0074	0.10

TABLE 9.5: COMPARISON OF EXACT AND APPROXIMATE SUPPLIES FOR A 30 % INCREASE IN K_1^Ψ

Theorem 9.8 *The vector $f \in \Re_+^{|\mathcal{N}|}$ is a Nash equilibrium if and only if it solves*

$$
\begin{aligned}
[E(f)]^T f &= 0 \\
E(f) &\geq 0 \\
f &\geq 0
\end{aligned}
$$

That is, $f \in \Re_+^{|\mathcal{N}|}$ is a Nash equilibrium if and only if it is an NCP-solution.

Proof. We begin by observing that we need only demonstrate this result for some arbitrary firm, i, since a sum of non-negative terms is zero if and only if each term is identically zero. Now, consider any firm i.

(i) $[NE(E, \Re^{|\mathcal{N}|})] \Longrightarrow [NCP(E, \Re^{|\mathcal{N}|})]$ First, since $\lambda_{ij} \geq 0$ for all $j \in \mathcal{N}$, we know from (9.104) that $[\partial e_i(f)/\partial f_{ij} + c_{ij}(f) - \partial R_{ij}(f)/\partial f_{ij}] \geq 0$ for all $j \in \mathcal{N}$, and from (9.107) we know immediately that $f_{ij} \geq 0$ for all $j \in \mathcal{N}$. Also, if $\lambda_{ij} > 0$ then by (9.105) and the nonnegativity of λ and f, we must have $f_{ij} = 0$. On the other hand, if $\lambda_{ij} = 0$ then by (9.104) it must be true that $[\partial e_i(f)/\partial f_{ij} + c_{ij}(f) - \partial R_{ij}(f)/\partial f_{ij}] = 0$. Thus, either $f_{ij} = 0$ or $[\partial e_i(f)/\partial f_{ij} + c_{ij}(f) - \partial R_{ij}(f)/\partial f_{ij}] = 0$ for all $j \in \mathcal{N}$.

(ii) $[NCP(E, \Re^{|\mathcal{N}|})] \Longrightarrow [NE(E, \Re^{|\mathcal{N}|})]$ First, observe that the non-negativity condition (9.107) follows immediately. Further, if $f_{ij} > 0$ then

Region	Exact	Approx.	|Error|	% Error
1	70.5190	70.2136	0.3054	0.43
2	76.3314	76.0997	0.2317	0.30
3	76.1449	76.1135	0.0314	0.04
4	80.2334	80.0535	0.1799	0.22
5	79.9845	79.8112	0.1733	0.22
6	82.0419	81.8796	0.1623	0.20
7	82.0327	81.8642	0.1685	0.21
8	81.8702	81.7023	0.1679	0.21
9	82.8524	82.6934	0.1590	0.19
10	83.2291	83.0721	0.1570	0.19
11	83.1642	93.0078	0.1564	0.19
12	83.4806	83.3247	0.1559	0.19
13	83.3307	83.1708	0.1599	0.19
14	83.8136	83.6951	0.1545	0.18
15	84.2036	84.0520	0.1516	0.18
16	84.0134	83.8616	0.1518	0.18

TABLE 9.6: COMPARISON OF EXACT AND APPROXIMATE PRICES OR A 30 % INCREASE IN K_1^{Ψ}

$[\partial e_i(f)/\partial f_{ij} + c_{ij}(f) - \partial R_{ij}(f)/\partial f_{ij}] = 0$, and hence (9.104) and (9.105) hold with $\lambda_{ij} = 0$. On the other hand, if $[\partial e_i(f)/\partial f_{ij} + c_{ij}(f) - \partial R_{ij}(f)/\partial f_{ij}] > 0$ then $f_{ij} = 0$, and hence (9.104) and (9.105) hold with $\lambda_{ij} = [\partial e_i(f)/\partial f_{ij} + c_{ij}(f) - \partial R_{ij}(f)/\partial f_{ij}] > 0$. In either case, $\lambda_{ij} \geq 0$ and hence (9.106) holds. ■

9.5 Inclusion of Arbitrageurs

The model of oligopoly described above might be used to describe a wide variety of arbitrageurs (e.g., traders in the New York and London oil markets). Hence, we now extend this model to explicitly include arbitrageurs (which includes consumers that travel to a foreign market to make purchases).[1]

First, let $\hat{f}_{ij}$ denote the quantity of the commodity shipped from i to j by arbitrageurs, and let $\hat{f} = (\hat{f}_{ij} : (i,j) \in \mathcal{N} \times \mathcal{N})$ denote the complete *arbitrage shipment pattern*. With this notation, we now assume that each firm is only aware of the total quantity supplied to each market by all other players. That is, each firm is unaware of the quantity that is being bought and sold specifically by arbitrageurs. Hence, the quantity "supplied" to j by all players other than i is now given by

$$\sum_{k \neq i} f_{kj} + \sum_{k \in \mathcal{N}} \hat{f}_{kj} - \sum_{k \in \mathcal{N}} \hat{f}_{jk} \tag{9.110}$$

[1] This section is highly similar to the original development in Friesz and Bernstein (1992).

and the inverse demand function in each market, $j \in \mathcal{N}$, is now defined by

$$\Theta_j \equiv \Theta_j(f, \hat{f}) = \Theta_j \left(\sum_{i \in \mathcal{N}} f_{ij} + \sum_{i \in \mathcal{N}} \hat{f}_{ij} - \sum_{i \in \mathcal{N}} \hat{f}_{ji} \right) \tag{9.111}$$

where the argument of this function again represents the local consumption at market $j \in \mathcal{N}$.

Of course, none of these changes significantly impact the model of firm behavior introduced in the previous section. However, we must now explicitly consider the equilibrium conditions for arbitrageurs. To begin, observe that any equilibrium flow pattern must be feasible. That is, the quantity being "demanded" by arbitrageurs at any given market must be less than the "supply" to that market. More formally, in equilibrium it must be true that

$$\sum_{j \in \mathcal{N}} \hat{f}_{ij} \leq \sum_{k \in \mathcal{N}} \left(f_{ki} + \hat{f}_{ki} \right) \quad \forall i \in \mathcal{N} \tag{9.112}$$

In addition, several other conditions are also needed.

First, observe that if

$$\sum_{j \in \mathcal{N}} \hat{f}_{ij} < \sum_{k \in \mathcal{N}} \left(f_{ki} + \hat{f}_{ki} \right) \text{ for some } i \in \mathcal{N}$$

then it must be true in equilibrium that $(f, \hat{f})$ satisfies the conditions that $\hat{f}_{ij} > 0 \Longrightarrow \Theta_j(f, \hat{f}) - \Theta_i(f, \hat{f}) - c_{ij}(f, \hat{f}) = 0$ and $\hat{f}_{ij} = 0 \Longrightarrow \Theta_j(f, \hat{f}) - \Theta_i(f, \hat{f}) - c_{ij}(f, \hat{f}) \leq 0$ where $c_{ij}(f, \hat{f})$ is the unit cost of shipping from node $i \in \mathcal{N}$ to node $j \in \mathcal{N}$ which is now a function of the vectors f and $\hat{f}$. In other words, whenever there is "unexhausted supply" in market i and there are no arbitrage flows to market j, then it must be true that there is no arbitrage opportunity at market j. Further, when there is "unexhausted supply" at market i and there are arbitrage flows to market j, then it must be true that the prices at i and j differ by exactly the cost of shipping between them. These conditions are identical to the standard spatial price equilibrium conditions.

On the other hand, if

$$\sum_{j \in \mathcal{N}} \hat{f}_{ij} = \sum_{k \in \mathcal{N}} \left(f_{ki} + \hat{f}_{ki} \right) \text{ for some } i \in \mathcal{N}$$

then the standard spatial price equilibrium conditions may be inappropriate for this market. In particular, there may not be sufficient "unexhausted supply" to ensure that prices are equilibrated. Further, it must be true that arbitrageurs are only shipping to markets in which the arbitrage profits to be made are maximal. Therefore, letting $\mu_i = \max\{0, \Theta_j(f, \hat{f}) - \Theta_i(f, \hat{f}) - c_{ij}(f, \hat{f}) \ \forall\, j \in \mathcal{N}\}$ denote the maximum arbitrage profit that can be earned [for a given $(f, \hat{f})$] making purchases at i, it follows that in equilibrium it must be true that $(f, \hat{f})$ satisfies the conditions that $\hat{f}_{ij} > 0 \Longrightarrow \Theta_j(f, \hat{f}) - \Theta_i(f, \hat{f}) - c_{ij}(f, \hat{f}) = \mu_i$ and $\hat{f}_{ij} = 0 \Longrightarrow \Theta_j(f, \hat{f}) - \Theta_i(f, \hat{f}) - c_{ij}(f, \hat{f}) \leq \mu_i$.

Combining these two sets of conditions and letting $\mu = (\mu_i,\ i \in \mathcal{N})$ we introduce the following terminology:

Definition 9.4 A (non-negative) vector, $(f, \hat{f}, \mu) \in \Re_+^{|\mathcal{N}|\times|\mathcal{N}|\times 2+|\mathcal{N}|}$, is a *Nash equilibrium in the presence of arbitrageurs* if and only if it satisfies the Kuhn-Tucker conditions (9.104)–(9.107) [with $\partial e_i(f)/\partial f_{ij}$ replaced by $\partial e_i(f,\hat{f})/\partial f_{ij}$, $c_{ij}(f)$ replaced by $c_{ij}(f,\hat{f})$ and $\partial R_{ij}(f)/\partial f_{ij}$ replaced by $\partial R_{ij}(f,\hat{f})/\partial f_{ij}$], the feasibility condition (9.112), and the following conditions

$$\sum_{k\in\mathcal{N}} f_{ki} - \sum_{j\in\mathcal{N}} \hat{f}_{ij} + \sum_{k\in\mathcal{N}} \hat{f}_{ki} \geq 0, \quad \hat{f}_{ij} > 0 \Longrightarrow$$

$$\Psi_j(f,\hat{f}) - \Psi_i(f,\hat{f}) - c_{ij}(f,\hat{f}) = \mu_i \tag{9.113}$$

$$\sum_{k\in\mathcal{N}} f_{ki} - \sum_{j\in\mathcal{N}} \hat{f}_{ij} + \sum_{k\in\mathcal{N}} \hat{f}_{ki} \geq 0, \quad \hat{f}_{ij} = 0 \Longrightarrow$$

$$\Psi_j(f,\hat{f}) - \Psi_i(f,\hat{f}) - c_{ij}(f,\hat{f}) \leq \mu_i \tag{9.114}$$

$$\sum_{k\in\mathcal{N}} f_{ki} - \sum_{j\in\mathcal{N}} \hat{f}_{ij} + \sum_{k\in\mathcal{N}} \hat{f}_{ki} > 0, \quad \hat{f}_{ij} > 0 \Longrightarrow$$

$$\Psi_j(f,\hat{f}) - \Psi_i(f,\hat{f}) - c_{ij}(f,\hat{f}) = 0 \tag{9.115}$$

$$\sum_{k\in\mathcal{N}} f_{ki} - \sum_{j\in\mathcal{N}} \hat{f}_{ij} + \sum_{k\in\mathcal{N}} \hat{f}_{ki} > 0, \quad \hat{f}_{ij} = 0 \Longrightarrow$$

$$\Psi_j(f,\hat{f}) - \Psi_i(f,\hat{f}) - c_{ij}(f,\hat{f}) \leq 0 \tag{9.116}$$

for all $(i,j) \in \mathcal{N} \times \mathcal{N}$ with $i \neq j$.

While these conditions are considerably more complicated than the classical spatial price equilibrium conditions and the Nash conditions given above, we can nonetheless express them as a nonlinear complementarity problem. To see this, we use the following notation:

$$E = ([\partial e_i(f,\hat{f})/\partial f_{ij} + c_{ij}(f,\hat{f}) - \partial R_{ij}(f,\hat{f})/\partial f_{ij}] : \quad (i,j) \in |\mathcal{N}| \times |\mathcal{N}|) \tag{9.117}$$

$$G = ([\Theta_i(f,\hat{f}) + c_{ij}(f,\hat{f}) - \Theta_j(f,\hat{f}) + \mu_i],\ (i,j) \in |\mathcal{N}| \times |\mathcal{N}|) \tag{9.118}$$

and

$$H = \left(\sum_{k \in \mathcal{N}} f_{ki} - \sum_{j \in \mathcal{N}} \hat{f}_{ij} + \sum_{k \in \mathcal{N}} \hat{f}_{ki},\ i \in |\mathcal{N}| \right) \tag{9.119}$$

As a consequence, we can now present the following result:

Theorem 9.9 *A vector*

$$(\ f \ \hat{f} \ \mu \ ) \in \Re_{+}^{|\mathcal{N}| \times |\mathcal{N}| \times 2 + |\mathcal{N}|}$$

is a Nash equilibrium in the presence of arbitrageurs if and only if it is a solution of the following NCP:

$$(\ f \ \hat{f} \ \mu \ ) \in \Re_{+}^{|\mathcal{N}| \times |\mathcal{N}| \times 2 + |\mathcal{N}|} \tag{9.120}$$

$$\begin{pmatrix} E(f, \hat{f}, \mu) \\ G(f, \hat{f}, \mu) \\ H(f, \hat{f}, \mu) \end{pmatrix} \in \Re_{+}^{|\mathcal{N}| \times |\mathcal{N}| \times 2 + |\mathcal{N}|} \tag{9.121}$$

$$(f \ \hat{f} \ \mu) \begin{pmatrix} E(f, \hat{f}, \mu) \\ G(f, \hat{f}, \mu) \\ H(f, \hat{f}, \mu) \end{pmatrix} = 0 \tag{9.122}$$

for E as defined in (9.117), G as defined in (9.118) and H as defined in (9.119).

Proof. To begin, observe that the arguments in the proof of Theorem 9.8 continue to hold. Also observe that the feasibility condition (9.112) is subsumed by the nonlinear complementarity problem (NCP) expressed by (9.120)–(9.122). Hence it only remains to demonstrate equivalence for the arbitrage profit conditions (APC), (9.113)–(9.116).

(i) $[ACP] \Longrightarrow [NCP]$ First, observe that $\mu_i H_i(f, \hat{f}, \mu) = 0$ for all i with $H_i(f, \hat{f}, \mu) = 0$. Also, observe from (9.116) that if $H_i(f, \hat{f}, \mu) > 0$ and $\hat{f}_{ij} = 0$ for all $j \in \mathcal{N}$ then $\Theta_j(f, \hat{f}) - \Theta_i(f, \hat{f}) - c_{ij}(f, \hat{f}) = 0$ and it follows by definition that $\mu_i = 0$. On the other hand, observe from (9.115) that, if $H_i(f, \hat{f}, \mu) > 0$ and $\hat{f}_{ij} > 0$ for any j then $\Theta_j(f, \hat{f}) - \Theta_i(f, \hat{f}) - c_{ij}(f, \hat{f}) = 0$ and it follows from (9.113) that $\mu_i = 0$. Hence, $H(f, t, \mu)^T \mu = 0$.

Similarly, if $\hat{f}_{ij} = 0$ it follows that $\hat{f}_{ij} G_{ij}(f, \hat{f}, \mu) = 0$. Further, if $\hat{f}_{ij} > 0$ and $H_i(f, \hat{f}, \mu) > 0$ it follows from (9.115) that $\Theta_j(f, \hat{f}) - \Theta_i(f, \hat{f}) - c_{ij}(f, \hat{f}) = 0$ and from (9.113) that $\mu_i = 0$. On the other hand, if $\hat{f}_{ij} \geq 0$ and $H_i(f, \hat{f}, \mu) = 0$ it follows from (9.113) than $\Theta_j - \Theta_i - c_{ij} = \mu_i$. Hence, $G(f, \hat{f}, \mu)^T \hat{f} = 0$.

Finally, it follows from the definition of μ that $\mu_i \geq 0$ and $\mu_j - [\Theta_j(f,\hat{f}) - \Theta_i(f,\hat{f}) + c_{ij}(f,\hat{f})] \geq 0$, and it follows from the definition of feasibility that $\hat{f}_{ij} \geq 0$ for all $(i,j) \in \mathcal{N} \times \mathcal{N}$ and that $H_i(f,\hat{f},\mu) \geq 0$ for all $i \in \mathcal{N}$.

(ii) $[NCP \Longrightarrow APC]$ First observe that for any solution to the NCP, $\mu_i \geq 0$ for all $(i,j) \in \mathcal{N}\times\mathcal{N}$ and $\Theta_i(f,\hat{f}) + c_{ij}(f,\hat{f}) - \Theta_j(f,\hat{f}) + \mu_i \geq 0$ for all $i \in \mathcal{N}$. Hence, it follows that $\mu_i = \max\{0, \Theta_j(f,\hat{f}) - \Theta_i(f,\hat{f}) - c_{ij}(f,\hat{f}) \ \forall\, j \in \mathcal{N}\}$.

Now, observe that for any solution of the NCP, if $\hat{f}_{ij} > 0$ then it follows that $\Theta_i(f,\hat{f}) + c_{ij}(f,\hat{f}) - \Theta_j(f,\hat{f}) + \mu_i = 0$ and hence that (9.113) must hold. Further, if $H_i(f,\hat{f},\mu) > 0$ it follows that $\mu_i = 0$ and hence that $\Theta_i(f,\hat{f}) + c_{ij}(f,\hat{f}) - \Theta_j(f,\hat{f}) = 0$ and that (9.115) holds.

If, on the other hand, $\hat{f}_{ij} = 0$ it follows that $\Theta_i(f,\hat{f}) + c_{ij}(f,\hat{f}) - \Theta_j(f,\hat{f}) + \mu_i \geq 0$ and that (9.114) holds. Further, if $H_i(f,\hat{f},\mu) > 0$ it follows that $\mu_i = 0$ and, hence, that $\Theta_i(f,\hat{f}) + c_{ij}(f,\hat{f}) - \Theta_j(f,\hat{f}) \leq 0$, that (9.116) holds, and that $\hat{f}_{ij} = 0$. ■

Before concluding this section, it is worth pointing out that our arbitrage model can also be formulated as a "variational inequality".

Theorem 9.10 *A vector*

$$y^* = \begin{pmatrix} f^* \\ \hat{f}^* \\ \mu^* \end{pmatrix} \in \Re^{|\mathcal{N}|\times|\mathcal{N}|\times 2+|\mathcal{N}|}$$

is a Nash equilibrium in the presence of arbitrageurs if and only if it is a solution of the following variational inequality:

$$E(y^*)^T(f - f^*) + G(y^*)^T(\hat{f} - \hat{f}^*) + H(y^*)^T(\mu - \mu^*) \geq 0 \tag{9.123}$$

for all $f \in \Re^{|\mathcal{N}|\times|\mathcal{N}|}$, $\hat{f} \in \Re^{|\mathcal{N}|\times|\mathcal{N}|}$, and $\mu \in \Re^{|\mathcal{N}|}$, with E as defined in (9.117), G as defined in (9.118) and H as defined in (9.119). We denote this variational inequality by $VI(F,G,H;\Re^{|\mathcal{N}|\times|\mathcal{N}|\times 2+|\mathcal{N}|})$.

Proof. Trivial. ■

Given the above nonlinear complementarity formulation, it is a relatively straightforward task to establish conditions that ensure the existence of an equilibrium. Specifically, we assume inverse demand functions are bounded from above (i.e., demand is driven to zero at some finite price) and below. That is:

$$\left.\begin{array}{ll} \Theta_j(\cdot) < \infty & \forall j \in \mathcal{N} \\ \Theta_j(\cdot) \geq 0 & \forall j \in \mathcal{N} \end{array}\right\} \text{A1}$$

We also assume the unit cost of transporting an infinite flow between any two nodes is infinite and all transportation costs are positive. That is:

$$\left.\begin{array}{c}[f_{ij} \longrightarrow \infty \Longrightarrow c_{ij}(f_{ij}) \longrightarrow \infty] \Longrightarrow \left[c_{ij}\left(\hat{f}_{ij}\right) \longrightarrow \infty\right] \quad \forall (i,j) \in \mathcal{N} \times \mathcal{N} \\ c_{ij}(\cdot) \geq 0 \quad \forall (i,j) \in \mathcal{N} \times \mathcal{N}\end{array}\right\} \text{A2}$$

With these assumptions, we can demonstrate the following existence result:

Theorem 9.11 *For any continuous, decreasing inverse demand functions satisfying A1, and continuous transportation cost functions satisfying A2, there exists a Nash equilibrium in the presence of arbitrageurs.*

Proof. We proceed by demonstrating that there are no exceptional sequences for $(E \ G \ H)$ of the type obeying Definition 9.2. To do so, let us assume to the contrary that there exists an exceptional sequence $\{x^n = (f^n, \hat{f}^n, \mu^n)\}$.

First, observe that $\mu_i \geq 0 \ \forall i \in \mathcal{N}$ and hence that $\mu_i \not\longrightarrow -\infty \ \forall i \in \mathcal{N}$. Further observe that since $\Theta_j(f, \hat{f})$ is bounded it also follows that $\mu_i \not\longrightarrow \infty \ \forall i \in \mathcal{N}$.

Also, observe that $\hat{f}^n_{ij} > 0$ implies from (9.25) that $G_{ij}(f, \hat{f}, \mu) < 0$. But, if we assume that $\hat{f}_{ij} \longrightarrow \infty$ then it follows from A2 that $c_{ij}(\hat{f}_{ij}) \longrightarrow \infty$, which, together with $\mu_i \geq 0$ and the boundedness of $\Theta_i(f, \hat{f})$ and $\Theta_j(f, \hat{f})$, implies that $G_{ij}(f, \hat{f}, \mu) \geq 0$, which is a contradiction. Hence, it must be the case that $\hat{f}_{ij} \not\longrightarrow \infty \ \forall (i,j) \in \mathcal{N} \times \mathcal{N}$.

Now, if we let $\|x^n\| \longrightarrow \infty$ it must be the case that $x^n_i \longrightarrow \infty$ for some $i \in \mathcal{N}$. But, since A1, A2, and (9.117) together imply that $[E(x^n)]^T x^n \longrightarrow \infty$, it follows from Lemma 9.3 that $\{x^n\}$ cannot be an exceptional sequence and from Lemma 9.2 that an equilibrium exists. ■

9.6 Modeling Freight Networks

In this section we describe a model of commodity flows arising from consideration of freight shippers and carriers within a multimodal network. The computational tractability of the predictive network model reported in this section is due to its sequential nature: shippers are assumed to select commodity origins and carriers based on their perceptions of the transportation network, thereby determining transportation demands; carriers then respond to these transportation demands by routing freight over those portions of the actual transportation network under their control. Such a sequential perspective, of course, prevents a true shipper-carrier equilibrium from being reached, since the levels of service provided by carriers may differ from the perceived levels of service which are the basis of the shippers' transportation demand. Despite this limitation of a sequential shipper-carrier model, such a model is the obvious first step from a pure shipper (or pure carrier) model toward a behaviorally realistic shipper-carrier model, and its effectiveness in forecasting freight network flows requires careful assessment before one turns to formulations which are likely to be more demanding computationally.

9.6.1 Model Description

The model is constructed in such a way that consignees (the recipients of transported commodities) make decisions about where to purchase and how to ship freight (mode choice, transshipment, interlining, and general routing). These consignees are the shippers of the model. Said differently, a shipper is a particular entity requiring a particular transportable commodity at a specific destination node of the physical network, although the shipper will not generally possess complete control over the routing possibilities on the physical network.

A carrier, on the other hand is one of several freight transportation companies providing transportation services to the shippers; each carrier controls a specific subnetwork of the actual physical network. To represent the behavior of shippers and carriers and their interaction, the model is divided into three components that are applied sequentially. The first, the shippers' submodel, is a simultaneous generation, distribution, modal split and traffic assignment model. It is applied first to predict a user optimized flow pattern corresponding to the noncooperative minimization of delivered commodity prices by the shippers.

The aforementioned user optimized flow pattern defines a set of origin-destination transportation demands and a general routing pattern, which are then used as inputs to the second component, the decomposition algorithm. The decomposition algorithm simply translates the shipper path flow configuration into modal specific origin-destination transportation demands. In the case of railroads, it further subdivides the modal origin-destination information into carrier specific information.

Such information is then input to the third component, termed the carriers' submodel. As a first approximation to the complex set of decisions carriers make with respect to their activities, we assume here that each carrier optimizes the routing of traffic within its own system, considering total own-system cost. Thus, the carriers' submodel determines a system-optimized flow pattern for each carrier. An overview of this procedure is given in Fig. 9.2. Descriptions of each model component are presented below.

Shippers' Submodel

The shippers' submodel routes traffic over an aggregate representation of the real transportation network. This aggregate network includes only those origin, destination, route and mode choice options that might realistically he considered by shippers. Although this might vary from application to application, the nodes of the aggregate network would include all potential origins, destinations and transshipment sites. In addition, locations such as inter-railroad transfer

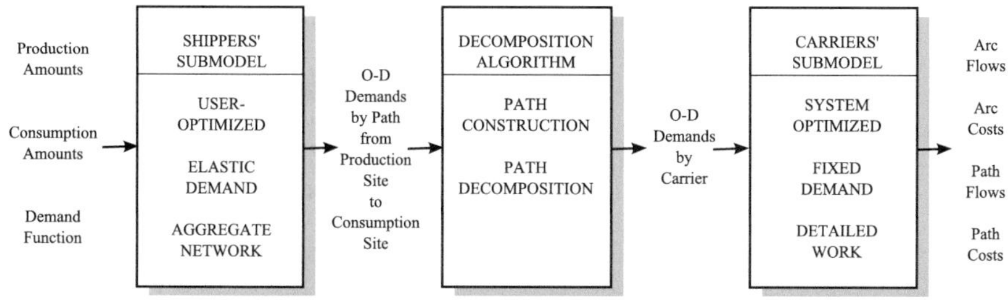

FIGURE 9.2: MODEL OVERVIEW

points (gateways) and major points of transportation activity that might he of special interest can be added. This aggregate network is used instead of the physical network because it is this representation of the transportation system that the shippers actually "see" when making routing choices. Shippers are concerned with, and have the power to determine, the origin-destination pairs, modes used, the location of transshipments (if any) and, to some extent, a general routing pattern. Unless private carriage is used, they neither have information about, nor control over, the detailed routing choices with which the carriers are faced. An example of this aggregation is given in Fig. 9.3.

We turn now to the notation necessary for creating a mathematical version of the shippers' submodel. We begin by defining the following sets reminiscent of prior models in this and other chapters:

$\mathcal{W}$ the set of all origin-destination (OD) pairs of the shippers' network

$\mathcal{A}$ the set of all network arcs of the shippers' network

$\mathcal{N}$ the set of all nodes of the shippers' network

$\mathcal{R}$ the set of commodities for which freight services are needed

$\mathcal{S}$ the set of all modes considered

$\mathcal{P}$ the set of all network paths

We shall consistently use the index $a \in \mathcal{A}$ to denote an arc, the index $p \in \mathcal{P}$ to identify a path, and the indices $i, j \in \mathcal{N}$ to denote nodes. In addition the superscript $r \in \mathcal{R}$ will refer to a specific commodity and the superscript $s \in \mathcal{S}$ to a specific mode. Thus, t_a^{rs} will denote the unit travel time on arc a for commodity r transported by mode s. Similarly, c_a^{rs} is the unit cost of transporting commodity r over arc a by mode s. Furthermore, f_a^{rs} is the flow on arc a of commodity r transported by mode s.

Other necessary notation includes the set $\mathcal{P}_{ij}^{rs}$ of paths between origin-destination (OD) pair $(i,\ j) \in \mathcal{W}$ over which commodity $r \in \mathcal{R}$ may be transported by mode $s \in \mathcal{S}$. The entity h_p^{rs} will signify the flow on path $p \in \mathcal{P}_{ij}^{rs}$ of

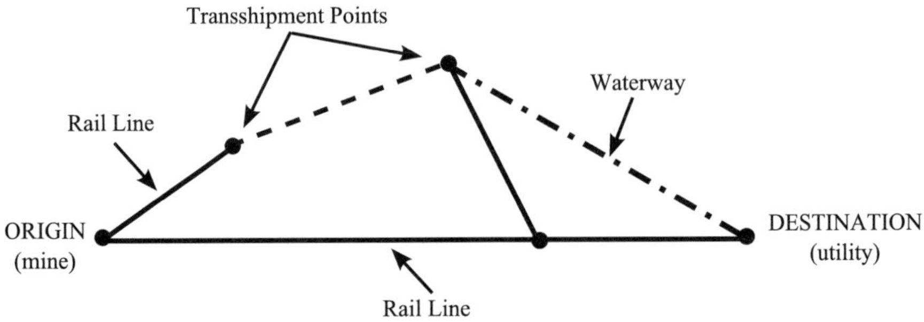

AGGREGATE NETWORK

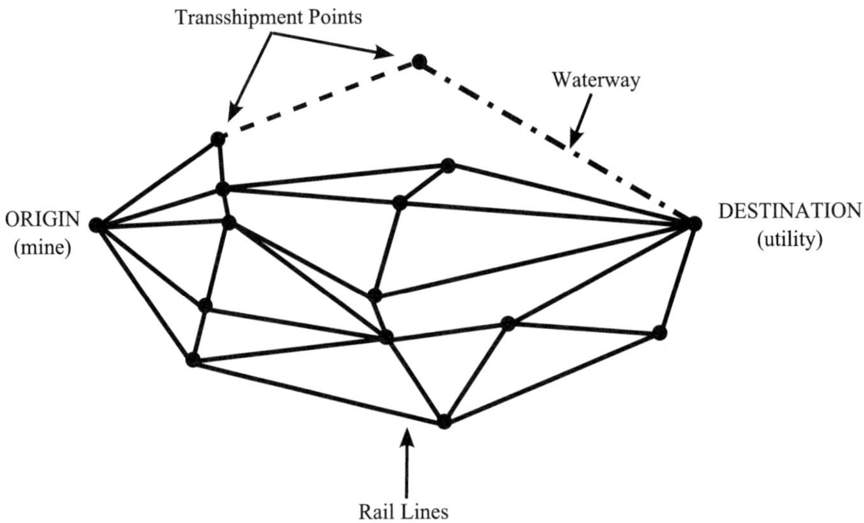

DETAILED NETWORK

Figure 9.3: Network Aggregation

commodity $r \in \mathcal{R}$ transported by mode $s \in \mathcal{S}$. Path flows are related to arc flows through the usual arc-path incidence matrix, an element of which is

$$\delta_{ap}^{rs} = \begin{cases} 1 & \text{if arc } a \text{ is on path } p \text{ and allows commodity } r \text{ by mode } s \\ 0 & \text{otherwise} \end{cases}$$

Consequently $f_a^{rs} = \sum_p \delta_{ap}^{rs} h_p^{rs}$. We may also speak of the unit travel time on path p for commodity r transported by mode s; we denote this by t_p^{rs} and observe that $t_p^{rs} = \sum_a \delta_{ap}^{rs} t_a^{rs}$. Similarly, c_p^{rs} is the unit cost of transporting commodity r over path p by mode s and $c_p^{rs} = \sum_p \delta_{ap}^{rs} c_a^{rs}$.

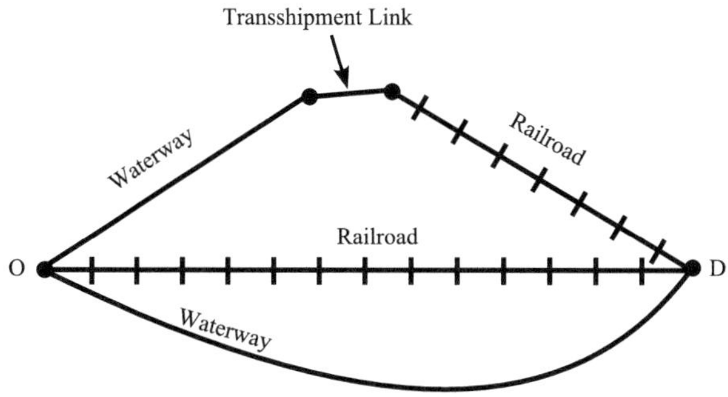

FIGURE 9.4: NETWORK SHOWING POSSIBLE OD MODES

A quantity central to the shippers' decision making is the delivered price of commodity r transported between OD pair (i,j) over path p by mode s, which we denote by $DP_{ij,p}^{rs}$. The minimum delivered price of commodity r transported between OD pair (i,j) by mode s is denoted by DP_{ij}^{rs}. Necessary to the construction of expressions for delivered price are the price of commodity r at origin i, denoted by m^{ir}; the value of time to the shippers for the transport of commodity r, denoted by q^r; and the fraction of the carriers' costs passed on to shippers for commodity r transported by mode s, denoted by ϵ^{rs}. We shall refer to ϵ^{rs} as the permeability for commodity r transported by mode s. The above notation makes it possible to completely describe the assumptions made about individual shipper behavior and the basic relationships which a flow pattern must obey. Note that in the shippers' submodel combinations of modes resulting from transshipment are treated as distinct modes. That is, for the example depicted in Fig. 9.4 the possible modes from O to D are rail, water and water/rail. Thus, in the discussion of the shippers' submodel which follows, a mode for purposes of the submodel may be a combination of modes occurring in the real world. Note also that, where necessary, yards are modeled as appropriately connected sets of links, and yard impedances (costs and delays) are articulated as arc impedances on such yard links: in this way no nodal delay or cost functions need by employed.

It is assumed that:

(1) Within each OD pair shippers compete with one another for limited transportation facilities while trying to minimize their own delivered price. A Wardropian user equilibrium among shippers in terms of delivered price exists when no shipper acting unilaterally can decrease its delivered price (Wardrop, 1952); and

(2) The final delivered price to the shipper is determined by the combination of commodity, origin, mode, and path selected, and can be expressed as

$$DP_{ij,p}^{rs} = q^r t_p^{rs} + m_i^r + z_{ij}^{rs} + \epsilon^{rs} c_p^{rs} \quad \forall (i,j) \in \mathcal{W}, r \in \mathcal{R}, s \in \mathcal{S}, p \in \mathcal{P}_{ij}^{rs} \tag{9.124}$$

It should be noted that the actual money expended on transportation is expressed by the third and fourth terms only. It is assumed here that this amount is equal to same base rate plus a specified percentage of the actual cost of shipment. The term z_{ij}^{rs} can be considered to be the posted tariff between OD pair (i, j) for commodity r transported by mode s. The ϵ^{rs} multipliers can then be adjusted to represent the degree of freedom that carriers are permitted in varying from this tariff, given the costs incurred in making these shipments. If the transportation industry is tightly regulated the multiplier is set equal to zero. If a market situation exists, the ϵ^{rs} multiplier can he reinterpreted as a profit multiplier, and the z_{ij}^{rs} term can then be deleted

(3) The arc costs and delays are separable functions of their own flows:

$$t_a^{rs} = t_a^{rs}(f_a^{rs}) \quad \forall a \in \mathcal{A}, r \in \mathcal{R}, s \in \mathcal{S}$$

$$c_a^{rs} = c_a^{rs}(f_a^{rs}) \quad \forall a \in \mathcal{A}, r \in \mathcal{R}, s \in \mathcal{S}$$

(4) Transportation demands are separable, negative exponential functions of the form:

$$Q_{ij}^{rs} = A_i^r B_j^r O_i^r expD_j^r(-\theta^r DP_{ij^*}^{rs}) \quad \forall (i,j) \in \mathcal{W}, r \in \mathcal{R}, s \in \mathcal{S} \qquad (9.125)$$

where A_i^r, B_j^r and θ^r are parameters that must be calibrated to ensure (9.125) accurately describes transportation demand for the situation being analyzed. We note that demand functions like (9.125) have been derived by Wilson (1970) by maximizing the entropy of the commodity flow pattern subject to appropriate constraints.

Keeping the above assumptions in mind we formulate the following mathematical programming problem:

$$\min Z = \sum_{a \in \mathcal{A}} \sum_{r \in \mathcal{R}} \sum_{s \in \mathcal{S}} \int_0^{t_a^{rs}} [q^r t_a^{rs}(x) + \epsilon^{rs} c_a^{rs}(x)] dx$$

$$+ \sum_{(i,j) \in \mathcal{W}} \sum_{r \in \mathcal{R}} \sum_{s \in \mathcal{S}} \sum_{p \in \mathcal{P}} (m_i^r + z_{ij}^{rs}) h_{\mathcal{P}}^{rs}$$

$$+ \sum_{(i,j) \in \mathcal{W}} \sum_{r \in \mathcal{R}} \sum_{s \in \mathcal{S}} (lnQ_{ij}^{rs} - 1) Q_{ij}^{rs} / \theta^r \qquad (9.126)$$

subject to

$$f_a^{rs} = \sum_p \delta_{ap}^{rs} h_p^{rs} \qquad \forall a \in \mathcal{A}, r \in \mathcal{R}, s \in \mathcal{S} \tag{9.127}$$

$$G_{ij}^{rs} = Q_{ij}^{rs} - \sum_{p \in P_{ij}^{rs}} h_p^{rs} = 0 \qquad (u_{ij}^{rs})\ \forall (i,j) \in \mathcal{W}, r \in \mathcal{R}, s \in \mathcal{S} \tag{9.128}$$

$$E_i^r = \sum_{s \in \mathcal{S}} \sum_j Q_{ij}^{rs} - O_i^r = 0 \qquad (\alpha_i^r)\ \forall i, r \tag{9.129}$$

$$F_j^r = \sum_{s \in \mathcal{S}} \sum_j Q_{ij}^{rs} - D_j^r = 0 \qquad (\beta_j^r)\ \forall j, r \tag{9.130}$$

$$Q_{ij}^{rs} \geq 0 \qquad (\rho_{ij}^{rs})\ \forall (i,j) \in \mathcal{W}, r \in \mathcal{R}, s \in \mathcal{S} \tag{9.131}$$

$$h_p^{rs} \geq 0 \qquad (\mu_p^{rs})\ \forall p \in \mathcal{P}^{rs}, r \in \nabla, s \in \mathcal{S} \tag{9.132}$$

The constraints (9.127)–(9.132) specify various relationships that must be maintained for a feasible shippers' flow pattern. In particular (9.127) specifies the relationship between path and arc flows, while (9.128) relates path flows and OD transportation demands. Equations (9.129) and (9.130), respectively, state the relevant trip production and consumption constraints. Inequalities (9.131) and (9.132) ensure nonnegativity of the decision variables. It is important to note that only the Q_{ij}^{rs} and h_p^{rs} are considered primal decision variables in the mathematical program (9.125)–(9.132). The f_a^{rs} variables are derived from the h_p^{rs} variables. Such quantities as the O_i^r and D_j^r are fixed numbers supplied exogenously. The variables to the right of constraints (9.128)–(9.130) are the dual variables associated with them.

The mathematical program (9.126)–(9.132) has been specially constructed to ensure that any solution obeys the assumptions regarding shippers' behavior made previously. It is motivated by the work of Evans (1976) on combined distribution and assignment models. In particular any solution of (9.126)–(9.132) must obey the KT conditions for (9.126)–(9.132), which are equivalent to the minimization of delivered price and to negative exponential transportation demand. To see this observe that the KT conditions for (9.126)–(9.132) are

$$\frac{\partial Z}{\partial h_p} + \sum_{(i,j) \in \mathcal{W}} \sum_{r \in \mathcal{R}} \sum_{s \in \mathcal{S}} u_{ij}^{rs} \frac{\partial G_{ij}^{rs}}{\partial h_p} - \mu_p^{rs} = 0 \quad \forall p \in \mathcal{P}^{rs}, r \in \mathcal{R}, s \in \mathcal{S} \tag{9.133}$$

$$\frac{\partial Z}{\partial Q_{ij}^{rs}} \sum_k \sum_v \alpha_k^v \frac{\partial E_k^v}{\partial Q_{ij}^{rs}} + \sum_k \sum_v \beta_k^v \frac{\partial F_k^v}{\partial Q_{ij}^{rs}} - \rho_{ij}^{rs} = 0 \quad \forall (i,j) \in \mathcal{W}, r \in \mathcal{R}, s \in \mathcal{S} \tag{9.134}$$

$$\mu_p^{rs} h_p^{rs} = 0 \quad \forall p \in \mathcal{P}^{rs}, r \in \mathcal{R}, s \in \mathcal{S} \tag{9.135}$$

$$\rho_{ij}^{rs} Q_{ij}^{rs} = 0 \quad \forall (i,j) \in \mathcal{W}, r \in \mathcal{R}, s \in \mathcal{S} \tag{9.136}$$

$$\mu_p^{rs} \geq 0 \quad \forall p \in \mathcal{P}^{rs}, r \in \mathcal{R}, s \in \mathcal{S} \tag{9.137}$$

$$\rho_{ij}^{rs} \geq 0 \quad \forall (i,j) \in \mathcal{W}, r \in \mathcal{R}, s \in \mathcal{S} \tag{9.138}$$

It follows immediately for all $(i,j) \in \mathcal{W}, r \in \mathcal{R}, s \in \mathcal{S}, p \in \mathcal{P}_{ij}^{rs}$ that

$$h_p^{rs} > 0 \Longrightarrow DP_{ij,p}^{rs} = q^r t_p^{rs} + m_i^r + z_{ij}^{rs} + \epsilon^{rs} c_p^{rs} = u_{ij}^{rs}$$

$$DP_{ij,p}^{rs} = q^r t_p^{rs} + m_i^r + z_{ij}^{rs} + \epsilon^{rs} c_p^{rs} > u_{ij}^{rs} \Longrightarrow h_p^{rs} = 0 \tag{9.139}$$

When we identify u_{ij}^{rs} as the minimum delivered price DP_{ij*}^{rs}, it is clear that (9.139) corresponds to the desired Wardropian user equilibrium for shippers in terms of delivered price. Furthermore, it follows that for all $(i,j) \in \mathcal{W}$, $r \in \mathcal{R}, s \in \mathcal{S}, p \in \mathcal{P}_{ij}^{rs}$:

$$Q_{ij}^{rs} > 0 \Longrightarrow Q_{ij}^{rs} = A_i^r B_j^r O_i^r D_j^r exp(-\theta^r u_{ij}^{rs}) \tag{9.140}$$

where

$$A_i^r = exp(-\alpha_i^r \theta^r)/O_j^r \tag{9.141}$$

$$B_i^r = exp(-\beta_j^r \theta^r)/D_j^r \tag{9.142}$$

Since u_{ij}^{rs} is equal to the minimum delivered price DP_{ij}^{rs} for all paths with positive flows, (9.140) is identical to (9.125). Therefore for all nontrivial demands the desired negative exponential demand function is obtained. Note that modal split is given by a logic modal since (9.140) leads to

$$M_{ij}^{rs} = \frac{Q_{ij}^{rs}}{\sum_m Q_{ij}^{rm}} = K_{ij}^{rs} \frac{\exp\left(-\theta^r DP_{ij*}^{rs}\right)}{\sum_m \exp\left(-\theta^r DP_{ij*}^{rm}\right)}$$

which holds for all $(i,j) \in \mathcal{W}, r \in \mathcal{R}$ and $s \in \mathcal{S}$; furthermore, each constant K_{ij}^{rs} is determined from (9.142) and (9.143).

Without further assumptions the mathematical program (9.126)–(9.132) may have multiple local optima and nonunique global optima; we reiterate that each of these optima will be a shippers' equilibrium obeying the behavioral conditions previously stipulated. Uniqueness of the shippers' equilibrium may be ensured by requiring that the $t_a^{rs}(\cdot)$ and the $c_a^{rs}(\cdot)$ functions be strictly increasing, for then Z in (9.126) will be strictly convex.

The shippers' sub-model (9.126)–(9.132) may be solved using the Frank-Wolfe algorithm originally proposed by LeBlanc et al. (1975), and discussed by Gartner (1977), for the Wardropian user equilibrium problem. The linear programming subproblems may be solved by out-of-kilter or network simplex algorithms. Evans (1976) has pointed out that the Q_{ij} may also be found by solving an appropriate doubly constrained gravity model by standard iterative methods; Frank (1978) has demonstrated that solution of the doubly constrained gravity model is more efficient in practice than solution of the Hitchcock problem. Consequently in the model validations reported in Sect. 9.6.2, the Evans (1976) algorithm was employed. Such algorithms may be employed to solve (9.126)–(9.132) even when the objective function (9.126) is not convex. In this case, the algorithm will determine a local optimum, which – as we have shown – will be one of the non unique equilibria of the problem. The only modification of the Frank-Wolfe algorithm needed in order to apply it to nonconvex problems is a modification of the procedure used to determine the optimal step size at each iteration; step-size rules for applying the Frank-Wolfe algorithm to nonconvex problems in order to determine local optima are discussed by Avriel (1976).

Decomposition Algorithm

Given the OD pairings and demands produced by the shippers' submodel, it remains to translate these into the carrier-specific OD information that is needed by the carriers' submodel. This is done in a two-step procedure. First the modal specific OD information is determined. For those models which are characterized by a large number of rights-of-way they do not control, such as barges on inland waterways and trucks on highways, the model assumes that the individual carriers which comprise each mode behave as a single carrier and no further decomposition is performed. For modes that control their own right-of-way, such as railroads, the modal information is further decomposed into carrier-specific OD information.

To determine modal-specific OD pairs, the intermodal paths generated in the shippers' submodel are examined for transshipment points. A typical shipper path is comprised of a production origin, sequences of nodes that reflect transshipments between carriers and/or modes, and a consumption destination. Careful bookkeeping described by Friesz et al. (1986) allows carrier-specific freight demands to be constructed.

In fact the following relationship couples the shippers' network and the carriers' networks:

$$V_{ik}^{rk} = \sum_{p \in \mathcal{I}_{ij}^{rk}} \hat{h}_p^{rk} \quad \forall i \in \mathcal{N}, k \in \mathcal{K},$$

where

V_{ij}^{rk} the demand for transporting commodity r by carrier k between OD pair (i, j)

$\hat{h}_p^{rk}$ the flow of commodity r by carrier k over intermodal path p of the shippers' network

I_{ij}^{rk} the set of intermodal paths of the shippers' network for commodity r, carrier k, and OD pair $(i,j) \in \mathcal{K}$ the set of carriers

Carriers' Submodel

As indicated previously, our primary behavioral assumptions regarding carriers are that they individually minimize their operating costs while satisfying the fixed demands for transportation established by the shippers. Recall that carriers operate over individual carrier networks, the union of all of which constitutes the detailed (physical) network. To mathematically articulate the carriers' submodel we must introduce some additional notation pertaining to the carrier subnetworks. In particular the indices a, p and r will respectively refer to arcs, paths and commodities, as in the shippers' submodel. The index k will refer to a specific carrier. We shall denote the arcs of the subnetwork associated with carrier k by $\mathcal{A}_k$; the OD pairs of this same network will be denoted by $\mathcal{W}_k$.

The arc flows on the carrier subnetworks will be denoted as e_a^{rk}, the flow on arc a of commodity r transported by carrier k. The unit operating costs to carrier k of transporting commodity r over arc a will be denoted as $\phi_a^{rk}(e_a^{rk})$. We assume for simplicity that these arc cost functions are separable. Other necessary notation includes g_p^{rk}, the flow on path p of commodity r transported by carrier k. Path flows are related to arc flows through the carrier arc-path incidence matrix, an element of which is

$$\Delta_{ap}^{rk} = \begin{cases} 1 & \text{if arc } a \text{ is on path } p \text{ and allows commodity } r \text{ by carrier } k \\ 0 & \text{otherwise} \end{cases}$$

Consequently $e_a^{rk} = \sum_p \delta_{ap}^{rk} g_p^{rk}$.

The above notation and the behavioral assumption of individual operating cost minimization leads immediately to the following mathematical program for each carrier k:

$$\min Z^k = \sum_{a \in A_k} \sum_r \phi_a^{rk}(e_a^{rk}) e_a^{rk} \tag{9.143}$$

subject to

$$e_a^{rk} = \sum_p \Delta_{ap}^{rk} g_p^{rk} \quad \forall a \in \mathcal{A}, r \in \mathcal{R} \tag{9.144}$$

$$\sum_{p \in R_{ij}^{rk}} g_p^{rk} = V_{ij}^{rk} \quad \forall r \in \mathcal{R}, (i,j) \in \mathcal{W}_k \tag{9.145}$$

$$g_p^{rk} \geq 0 \quad \forall p \in \mathcal{P}, r \in \mathcal{R}. \tag{9.146}$$

Note that (9.143)–(9.146) is a fixed demand system-optimal traffic assignment problem. As such it may be efficiently solved using the Frank-Wolfe algorithm (see LeBlanc et al. (1975) and Gartner (1977)). Again economies of scale may prevent Z^k in (9.143) from being convex; appropriate modifications of the Frank-Wolfe algorithm mentioned previously allow it to still be used to nonunique system optimal flow patterns.

Other Considerations

Backhauling or more generally, the movement of empty vehicles, is accommodated in the preceding theoretical structure through adjustment of the cost and delay measures reflecting the congestion impacts of backhauling, under the assumption that empty backhauls face an effective capacity equal to the forehaul capacity on every link. Another important consideration not dealt with explicitly in the preceding theoretical structure is the question of fleet capacity constraints. As the model is presented here, carriers are assumed to possess or to be able to bring on line whatever rolling stock and motive power is necessary to meet shippers' demands. For circumstances in which fleet capacity constraints are expected to be binding, such constraints would need to be introduced into the shippers' submodel and into the decomposition algorithm. Also important is the relationship between the cost and delay measures used for the shippers' aggregate network and those used for the detailed network. Clearly the impedance measures used on the shippers network should reflect the costs and delays on the detailed (carrier) network through an explicit aggregation. However, such aggregation requires an a priori knowledge of the flow volumes on the carriers' network, something which cannot be achieved with the sequential methodology described here. Rather, as Friesz, Tobin and Harker (1983) point out, such endogenous aggregation requires a simultaneous model structure. All that can be done in the sequential perspective employed here is to use impedance functions for arcs which are based on arc attributes (grade, curvature, operating speed, etc.).

9.6.2 Model Validation

In order to study pricing and operating policies with the freight network equilibrium model described above, it is first necessary to determine whether the model can reliably replicate observed freight flow patterns. We refer to the comparison of historical and model flow patterns as model "validation." Validation tests of the model were conducted for three network data bases: (1) a highly detailed railway-waterway network data base of the Northeastern United States with a single aggregate commodity and 5 rail carriers; (2) a somewhat more aggregate railway network data base of the entire United States with 15 commodities and a single aggregate rail carrier; and (3) a combined railway-waterway network data base of the entire United States with 15 commodities and 17 rail carriers. The results of such validation tests are reported by Friesz et al. (1983) and Friesz and Harker (1985).

9.7 References and Additional Reading

Avriel, M. (1976). *Nonlinear programming: Analysis and methods.* Englewood Cliffs, NJ: Prentice-Hall.

Beckmann, M., McGuire, C. B., & Winsten, C. B. (1956). *Studies in the economics of transportation.* New Haven, CT: Yale University Press.

Carey, M. (1980). Stability of competitive regional trade with monotone demand/supply functions. *Journal of Regional Science, 20*, 489–501.

Chao, G. S., & Friesz, T. L. (1984). Spatial price equilibrium sensitivity analysis. *Transportation Research B, 18*(6), 423–440.

Cournot, A. A. (1838). *Mathematical principles of the theory of wealth* (N. T. Bacon, Trans., 1960). New York: Kelley.

Dafermos, S. C., & McKelvey, S. C. (1992). Partitionable variational inequalities with applications to network and economic equilibria. *Journal of Optimization Theory and Applications, 73*(2), 243–268.

Dafermos, S., & Nagurney, A. (1987). Oligopolistic and competitive behavior of spatially separated markets. *Regional Science and Urban Economics, 17*, 245–254.

Evans, S. (1976). Derivation and analysis of some models for combining trip distribution and assignment. *Transportation Research, 10*, 37–57.

Fernandez, J. E., & Friesz, T. L. (1983). Travel market equilibrium: The state of the art. *Transportation Research, 17B*(2), 155–172.

Florian, M., & Hearn, D. (1995). Network equilibrium models and algorithms. In M. O. Ball, et al. (Eds.) *Network routing* (chapter 6, pp. 485–550). Elsevier: Oxford.

Florian, M., & Los, M. (1982). A new look at static spatial price equilibrium models. *Regional Science and Urban Economics, 12*, 579–597.

Frank, C. (1978). *A study of alternative approaches to combined trip distribution-assignment modeling.* Ph.D. dissertation, University of Pennsylvania, Philadelphia, PA.

Friesz, T. L., & Bernstein, D. (1992). Imperfect competition and arbitrage in spatially separated markets. *Readings in econometric theory and practice* (pp. 357–374). New York: North-Holland.

Friesz, T. L., & Harker, P. T. (1985). Freight network equilibrium: A review of the state of the art. In A. F. Daughety (Ed.) *Analytical studies in transportation economics* (chapter 7). New York: Cambridge University Press.

Friesz, T. L., Gottfried, J. A., & Tobin, R. L. (1983). Analyzing the transportation impacts of increased coal haulage: Two case studies. *Transportation Research A, 17*(6), 505–525.

Friesz, T. L., Harker, P. T., & Tobin, R. L. (1984). Alternative algorithms for the general network spatial price equilibrium problem. *Journal of Regional Science, 24*(3), 475–507.

Friesz, T. L., Tobin, R. L., & Harker, P. T. (1981). Variational Inequalities and Consequences of Diagonalization Algorithms for Derived demand Network Equilibrium Problems, Report CUE - FNEM - 1981 - 10 - 1, Department of Civil and Urban Engineering, University of Pennsylvania, Philadelphia, PA.

Friesz, T. L., Tobin, R. L., & Harker, P. T. (1983). Predictive inter city freight network models: The state of the art. *Transportation Research, 17A*, 409–417.

Friesz, T. L., Tobin, R. L., Smith, T. E., & Harker, P. T. (1983). A nonlinear complementarity formulation and solution procedure for the general derived demand network equilibrium problem. *Journal of Regional Science, 23*(3), 337–359.

Friesz, T. L., Viton, P. A., & Tobin, R. L. (1985). Economic and computational aspects of freight network equilibrium models: A synthesis. *Journal of Regional Science, 25*(1), 29–49.

Friesz, T. L., Gottfried, J. A., & Morlok, E. K. (1986). A sequential shipper-carrier network model for predicting freight flows. *Transportation Science, 20*(2), 80–91.

Gabay, D., & Moulin, H. (1980). On the uniqueness and stability of nash-equilibria in noncooperative games. In A. Bensoussan, et al. (Eds.), *Applied stochastic control in econometrics and management science*. New York: North-Holland.

Gartner, N. H. (1977). Analysis and control of transportation networks by Frank-Wolfe decomposition. In *Proceedings of the 7th international symposium on transportation and traffic theory* (pp. 591–623), Kyoto.

Harker, P. T. (1985). Investigating the use of the core as a solution concept in spatial price equilibrium games. *Lecture Notes in Economics and Mathematical Systems, 249*, 41–72.

Harker, P. T. (1986). Alternative models of spatial competition. *Operations Research, 34*, 410–425.

Harker, P. T., & Friesz, T. L. (1986a). Prediction of intercity freight flows, I: Theory, *Transportation Research B, 20*(2), 139–153.

Harker, P. T., & Friesz, T. L. (1986b). Prediction of intercity freight flows, II: Mathematical formulations. *Transportation Research B, 20*(2), 155–174.

LeBlanc, L. J., Morlok, E. K., & Pierskalla, W. P. (1975). An efficient approach to solving the road network equilibrium traffic assignment problem. *Transportation Research, 9*, 309–318.

Nagurney, A. (1987a). Competitive equilibrium problems, variational inequalities and regional science. *Journal of Regional Science, 27*(4), 503–517.

Nagurney, A. (1987b). Computational comparisons of spatial price equilibrium methods. *Journal of Regional Science, 27*(1), 55–76.

Pang, J. -S. (1984). Solution of the general multicommodity spatial equilibrium problem by variational and complementarity methods. *Journal of Regional Science, 24*(3), 403–414.

Pang, J. S., & Yu, C. S. (1984). Linearized simplicial decomposition methods for computing traffic equilibria on networks. *Networks, 14*(3), 427–438.

Samuelson, P. A. (1952). Spatial price equilibrium and linear programming. *American Economic Review, 42*, 283–303.

Smith, T. E. (1984). A solution condition for complementarity problems: With an application to spatial price equilibrium. *Applied Mathematics and Computation, 15*, 61–69.

Smith, T. E., & Friesz, T. L. (1985). Spatial market equilibria with flow dependent supply and demand. *Regional Science and Urban Economics, 15*(2), 181–198.

Takayama, T., & Judge, G. C. (1971). *Spatial and temporal price and allocation models.* New York: North Holland.

Tobin, R. L., & Friesz, T. L. (1983). Formulating and solving the network spatial price equilibrium problem with transshipment in terms of arc variables. *Journal of Regional Science, 23*(2), 187–198.

Varian, H. R. (1984). *Microeconomic analysis.* New York: W. W. Norton.

Wardrop, J. G. (1952). Some theoretical aspects of road traffic research. In *ICE proceedings: Engineering divisions, 1(3)*, 325–362. Thomas Telford.

Weskamp, A. (1985). Existence of spatial cournot equilibria. *Regional Science and Urban Economics, 15*, 219–227.

Wilson, A. G. (1970). *Entropy in urban and regional modelling.* New York: Pion.

10

Network Stackelberg Games and Mathematical Programs with Equilibrium Constraints

In this chapter we are concerned with the problem known as a *mathematical program with equilibrium constraints* (MPEC) and with its game theoretic counterpart – the Stackelberg game. MPECs and Stackelberg games arise in many branches of engineering, science, and economics. MPEC network applications include certain network design, plant location, congestion pricing, and tolling problems formulated so that a fixed-point, nonlinear complementarity, variational inequality, or other mathematical representation of an equilibrium acts as a set of constraints on the optimizing intentions of a central authority. In particular, an MPEC is based on a partition of decision variables into two sets: those variables that are directly determined by a "leader" or omniscient agent, and those variables that are determined by a noncooperative Nash game among so-called "followers" who take the leader's strategy as given. That is, the leader's actions are beyond the followers' influence.

The notion of an MPEC acknowledges an inherent truth concerning nonlinear Nash games on networks, known as the Braess paradox. For the time being, suffice it to say that the Braess paradox recognizes that local congestion mitigation may produce a global congestion increase for nonlinear networks in user equilibrium. Indeed it is the potential for the Braess paradox to arise that compels us to undertake the very challenging task of numerically solving certain MPECs that describe the topological design, capacity enhancement, or congestion pricing of vehicular networks by a central authority. Furthermore, it has now become commonplace to refer to metrics for the intrinsic conflict of Nash network agents with efficient flow control by a central authority as the *price of anarchy*. As such, it is the very existence of a price of anarchy that motivates conception and solution of MPECs for topological design, capacity enhancement, or congestion pricing of vehicular networks. Accordingly, the next section is devoted to defining and bounding the most commonly employed definition of the price of anarchy.

T.L. Friesz, D. Bernstein, *Foundations of Network Optimization and Games*,
Complex Networks and Dynamic Systems 3,
DOI 10.1007/978-1-4899-7594-2_10

When discussing Nash equilibria, our sole concern in this chapter, as in previous chapters, is atomic Nash games. This means that a very large number of Nash agents is active on the network, and no Nash agent has significant power to determine non-own flows or costs. All Nash agents employ current average (or unit) costs in making decisions.

Here is a summary of the content of this chapter:

Section 10.1: Defining the Price of Anarchy. This section discusses the "price of anarchy", which captures the inefficiency associated with a Nash equilibrium among network users.

Section 10.2: Bounding the Price of Anarchy. This section considers whether the price of anarchy may be bounded.

Section 10.3: The Braess Paradox and Equilibrium Network Design. This section considers an interesting phenomenon that can arise when adding capacity to a network. In particular, it demonstrates that adding capacity can actually make users worse off.

Section 10.4: MPECs and Their Relationship to Stackelberg Games. This section provides a general statement of a finite-dimensional mathematical program with equilibrium constraints (MPEC) and considers how this problem is related to Stackelberg games.

Section 10.5: Alternative Formulations of Equilibrium Network Design. This section considers some alternative formulations of the network design problem.

Section 10.6: Algorithms for Continuous Equilibrium Network Design. This section begins with a discussion of whether the continuous equilibrium network design problem can be solved using traditional nonlinear programming algorithms. It then considers other algorithms for solving this important problem.

Section 10.7: Numerical Comparison of Algorithms. This section compares the numerical performance of select algorithms for solving the continuous equilibrium network design problem.

Section 10.8: Electric Power Markets. This chapter concludes with a section that describes the use of MPECs in modeling the market for electric power.

10.1 Defining the Price of Anarchy

The *price of anarchy* is the name given by Roughgarden (2002) to the ratio of total congestion arising from user equilibrium traffic assignment to minimum total congestion, where the latter arises from a system optimal traffic assignment. As such the price of anarchy captures the inefficiency associated with a Nash equilibrium among network users. It is helpful to review and somewhat augment the notation we have introduced in previous chapters for traffic assignment. In particular, we will employ the following by now familiar set notation:

$\mathcal{W}$ the set of origin-destination (OD) pairs of the network of interest

$\mathcal{N}$ the set of nodes of the network of interest

$\mathcal{A}$ the set of arcs of the network of interest

$\mathcal{P}$ the set of paths of the network of interest

$\mathcal{P}_{ij}$ the set of paths connecting OD pair $(i, j) \in \mathcal{W}$

We will also employ the following matrix notation

$$\delta_{ap} = \begin{cases} 1 & \text{if } a \in p \\ 0 & \text{if } a \notin p \end{cases}$$

$$\Delta = (\delta_{ap} : a \in \mathcal{A},\ p \in \mathcal{P}) \text{ is the arc-path incidence matrix}$$

$$\gamma_{ij}^{p} = \begin{cases} 1 & \text{if } p \in \mathcal{P} \text{ connects } (i, j) \in \mathcal{W} \\ 0 & \text{otherwise} \end{cases}$$

$$\Gamma = \left(\gamma_{ij}^{p} : (i, j) \in \mathcal{W},\ p \in \mathcal{P}\right) \text{ is the path-OD incidence matrix}$$

Other key notation is the following:

$h \in \Re_{+}^{|\mathcal{P}|}$ a vector of path flows

$f \in \Re_{+}^{|\mathcal{A}|}$ a vector of arc flows

$Q \in \Re_{++}^{|\mathcal{W}|}$ a vector of fixed travel demands

$c(f) \in \Re_{++}^{|\mathcal{A}|}$ a vector of arc cost functions

$c(h) \in \Re_{++}^{|\mathcal{A}|}$ a vector of path cost functions

In fact, the network of interest associates the graph $\mathcal{G}(\mathcal{N}, \mathcal{A})$ with the fixed vector of demands Q and the arc cost function vector $c(f)$; it is denoted by $[\mathcal{G}(\mathcal{N}, \mathcal{A}), Q, c(f)]$ or simply $[\mathcal{G}, Q, c(f)]$ when no confusion will result. We also define the set of feasible solutions in the obvious way, familiar from Chap. 8:

$$\Omega_1 = \{f : \Gamma h = Q,\ f = \Delta h,\ \ h \geq 0\} \tag{10.1}$$

As a consequence of the above notation, it is possible to now offer the following formal definition of the price of anarchy:

Definition 10.1 (Price of anarchy) The price of anarchy for network $[\mathcal{G}, Q, c(f)]$ is

$$\rho\left[\mathcal{G}, Q, c(f)\right] = \frac{\sum_{a\in\mathcal{A}} c_a\left(f_a^{ue}\right) f_a^{ue}}{\sum_{a\in\mathcal{A}} c_a\left(f_a^{so}\right) f_a^{so}} \tag{10.2}$$

where $f^{ue} \in \Omega_1$ and $f^{so} \in \Omega_1$ are, respectively, the user equilibrium flow vector and the system optimal flow vector.

Clearly the price of anarchy may never be less than unity.

10.2 Bounding the Price of Anarchy

In this section we closely follow the exposition in Roughgarden (2002) and Roughgarden and Tardos (2004). A central question in the price of anarchy literature is whether the price of anarchy may be bounded. If a bound exists, then the inefficiency associated with a Nash equilibrium is bounded. Moreover, if that bound is not too large, one may elect to provide no centralized control of flow for the network of interest and yet be confident that the global cost of congestion will not grow to unpalatable levels.

10.2.1 Linear, Separable Arc Costs

Following Roughgarden (2002) and Roughgarden and Tardos (2004), we now seek a bound on the price of anarchy for the case of linear separable unit arc cost functions; that is, we now consider unit arc cost functions of the form

$$c_a = A_a + B_a f_a \quad \forall a \in \mathcal{A} \tag{10.3}$$

where each A_a and B_a is a known, positive constant. To establish a bound, we will need certain preliminary results; these are presented and proven below.

Lemma 10.1 *(Necessary and sufficient conditions for system optimal and user equilibrium flows) If $f^{ue} \in \Omega_1$ is a user equilibrium for $[\mathcal{G}, Q, c(f)]$ with separable linear cost functions (10.3), then*

$$h_p > 0 \Longrightarrow \sum_{a\in\mathcal{A}} \left(A_a + B_a f_a^{ue}\right)\delta_{ap} \leq \sum_{a\in\mathcal{A}} \left(A_a + B_a f_a\right)\delta_{ap} \quad \forall f \in \Omega_1 \tag{10.4}$$

If $f^{so} \in \Omega_1$ is a system optimal flow pattern for $[\mathcal{G}, Q, c(f)]$ with separable linear cost functions (10.3), then

$$h_p > 0 \Longrightarrow \sum_{a\in\mathcal{A}} \left(A_a + 2B_a f_a^{so}\right)\delta_{ap} \leq \sum_{a\in\mathcal{A}} \left(A_a + 2B_a f_a\right)\delta_{ap} \quad \forall f \in \Omega_1 \tag{10.5}$$

Proof. For a system optimized flow pattern f^{so}, we know the marginal cost for path $p \in \mathcal{P}$ obeys

$$MP_p(h^{so}) = \sum_{a \in \mathcal{A}} \delta_{ap} MC_a(f_a^{so}) \;\; \forall (i,j) \in \mathcal{W}, p \in \mathcal{P}_{ij}$$

where $f^{so} = \Delta h^{so}$ and

$$MC_a(f_a^{so}) = \frac{\partial \left[A_a f_a^{so} + B_a \left(f_a^{so}\right)^2 \right]}{\partial f_a}$$

so that

$$MP_p(h^{so}) = \sum_{a \in \mathcal{A}} \delta_{ap} \left(A_a + 2B_a f_a^{so}\right) \quad \forall (i,j) \in \mathcal{W}, p \in \mathcal{P}_{ij} \tag{10.6}$$

We have previously shown that the Kuhn-Tucker conditions require that marginal path costs be at their minimum values for each OD pair when path flow is strictly positive; moreover the Kuhn-Tucker conditions are necessary and sufficient owing to the convexity of the system optimal objective function

$$\sum_{a \in \mathcal{A}} \left[A_a f_a^{so} + B_a \left(f_a^{so}\right)^2 \right]$$

Consequently, result (10.5) follows immediately. We next note that the unit cost of flow on path p is

$$c_p(h^{ue}) = \sum_{a \in \mathcal{A}} \left(A_a + B_a f_a^{ue}\right) \delta_{ap} \quad \forall (i,j) \in \mathcal{W}, p \in \mathcal{P}_{ij} \tag{10.7}$$

where $f^{ue} = \Delta h^{ue}$. For user equilibrium, we have previously shown the Kuhn-Tucker conditions require that unit path costs be at their minimum values for each OD pair when path flow is positive; again the Kuhn-Tucker conditions are necessary and sufficient; and relationship (10.4) follows immediately. ■

Lemma 10.2 *(Relation of user equilibrium and system optimized flows for $[\mathcal{G}, Q, c(f)]$ with separable linear arc costs) If $f^{ue} \in \Omega_1$ is a user equilibrium flow for $[\mathcal{G}, Q, c(f)]$ with separable linear cost functions (10.3), then*

(1) $MC_a(\frac{1}{2} f_a^{ue}) = c_a(f_a^{ue})$ for all $a \in \mathcal{A}$; and

(2) $\frac{1}{2} f^{ue}$ is system optimal for $\left[\mathcal{G}, \frac{Q}{2}, c(f)\right]$

Proof. The result follows immediately from (10.4) and (10.5) upon inspection of (10.6) and (10.7). ■

Lemma 10.3 *(Total cost lower bound) Consider any feasible flow vector $f \in \Omega_1$ for $[\mathcal{G}, Q, c(f)]$ with separable linear arc costs, and let total cost be denoted by*

$$Z(f) = \sum_{a \in \mathcal{A}} (A_a + B_a f_a) f_a \tag{10.8}$$

Then

$$Z\left(\frac{f}{2}\right) \geq \frac{1}{4} Z(f)$$

Proof. Note that

$$Z\left(\frac{f}{2}\right) = \sum_{a \in \mathcal{A}} \left(A_a + B_a \frac{f_a}{2}\right) \frac{f_a}{2} = \sum_{a \in \mathcal{A}} \left(\frac{A_a}{2} + B_a \frac{f_a}{4}\right) f_a$$

$$= \frac{1}{4} \sum_{a \in \mathcal{A}} (2A_a + B_a f_a) f_a \geq \frac{1}{4} \sum_{a \in \mathcal{A}} (A_a + B_a f_a) f_a = \frac{1}{4} Z(f)$$

■

Lemma 10.4 *(System optimal variational inequality) A necessary and sufficient condition that $f^{so} \in \Omega_1$ be optimal for $[\mathcal{G}, Q, c(f)]$ is*

$$\sum_{a \in \mathcal{A}} MC_a(f_a^{so}) (f_a - f_a^{so}) \geq 0 \ \forall f \in \Omega_1 \tag{10.9}$$

Proof. We know that the Kuhn-Tucker conditions for $[\mathcal{G}, Q, c(f)]$ with separable arc cost functions are both necessary and sufficient. As we also know from prior discussions, the Kuhn-Tucker conditions require that

$$MC_p(h^{so}) - u_{ij} = \rho_p$$

$$\rho_p h_p^{so} = 0$$

$$\rho_p \geq 0$$

$$u_{ij} = \min_{p \in \mathcal{P}_{ij}} c_p(h^{so})$$

for all $(i, j) \in \mathcal{W}$ and all $p \in \mathcal{P}_{ij}$. Therefore, for every path p

$$MC_p(h^{so}) \geq u_{ij} \tag{10.10}$$

from which we obtain

$$MC_p(h^{so})\left(h_p - h_p^{so}\right) \geq u_{ij}\left(h_p - h_p^{so}\right) \tag{10.11}$$

because (10.10) holds as an equality when $\left(h_p - h_p^{so}\right) < 0$. Recalling that

$$MC_p(h) = \sum_{a \in \mathcal{A}} \delta_{ap} MC_a(f_a)$$

for $f = \Delta h$ and summing both sides of (10.11) over all paths, we obtain

$$\sum_{p \in \mathcal{P}} \delta_{ap} MC_a(f_a^{so})\left(h_p - h_p^{so}\right) \geq \sum_{(i,j) \in \mathcal{W}} \sum_{p \in \mathcal{P}_{ij}} u_{ij}\left(h_p - h_p^{so}\right) \tag{10.12}$$

or

$$\sum_{a \in \mathcal{A}} MC_a(f_a^{so})\left(\sum_{p \in \mathcal{P}} \delta_{ap} h_p - \sum_{p \in \mathcal{P}} \delta_{ap} h_p^{so}\right) \geq$$

$$\sum_{(i,j) \in \mathcal{W}} u_{ij}\left(\sum_{p \in \mathcal{P}_{ij}} h_p - \sum_{p \in \mathcal{P}_{ij}} h_p^{so}\right) \tag{10.13}$$

Because

$$f_a = \sum_{p \in \mathcal{P}} \delta_{ap} h_p \quad \text{and} \quad f_a^{so} = \sum_{p \in \mathcal{P}} \delta_{ap} h_p^{so}$$

$$Q_{ij} = \sum_{p \in \mathcal{P}_{ij}} h_p = \sum_{p \in \mathcal{P}_{ij}} h_p^{so}$$

expression (10.13) yields the desired result. ■

Lemma 10.5 *(Another total cost lower bound) Consider* $[\mathcal{G}, Q, c(f)]$ *with separable linear arc costs, and let* $f^{so} \in \Omega_1$ *be a feasible system optimal flow. Then, for every scalar* $\kappa > 0$, *any feasible flow for* $[\mathcal{G}, (1+\kappa)Q, c(f)]$ *will have at least the following cost:*

$$Z(f^{so}) + \kappa \sum_{a \in \mathcal{A}} MC_a(f^{so}) f_a^{so} \tag{10.14}$$

Proof. Note that

$$Z(f) = \sum_{a \in \mathcal{A}} Z_a$$

The total cost of flow

$$Z_a(f_a) = (A_a + B_a f_a) f_a = A_a f_a + B_a (f_a)^2$$

on any arc $a \in \mathcal{A}$ is a differentiable convex function of its own flow; therefore

$$Z_a(f_a) \geq Z(f_a^{so}) + MC_a(f_a^{so})\,(f_a - f_a^{so}) \tag{10.15}$$

where

$$MC_a(f_a^{so}) = \frac{dZ(f_a^{so})}{df_a}$$

and $f^{so} \in \Omega_1$ is optimal for $[\mathcal{G}, Q, c(f)]$. Summing (10.15) over all arcs, we obtain

$$\sum_{a\in\mathcal{A}} Z_a(f_a) \geq \sum_{a\in\mathcal{A}} Z(f_a^{so}) + \sum_{a\in\mathcal{A}} MC_a(f_a^{so})\,(f_a - f_a^{so})$$

or

$$Z(f) \geq Z(f^{so}) + \sum_{a\in\mathcal{A}} MC_a(f_a^{so})\,(f_a - f_a^{so}) \tag{10.16}$$

Suppose now that the flow f is feasible to $[\mathcal{G}, (1+\kappa)Q, c(f)]$; then $f\cdot(1+\kappa)^{-1}$ will be feasible to $[\mathcal{G}, Q, c(f)]$. Therefore, by Lemma 10.4, we have

$$\sum_{a\in\mathcal{A}} MC_a(f_a^{so})\left(\frac{f_a}{1+\kappa} - f_a^{so}\right) \geq 0$$

which may be restated as

$$\sum_{a\in\mathcal{A}} MC_a(f_a^{so})f_a \geq (1+\kappa)\sum_{a\in\mathcal{A}} MC_a(f_a^{so})f_a^{so} \tag{10.17}$$

From (10.16) and (10.17) we have

$$\begin{aligned} Z(f) &\geq Z(f^{so}) + \sum_{a\in\mathcal{A}} MC_a(f_a^{so})f_a - \sum_{a\in\mathcal{A}} MC_a(f_a^{so})f_a^{so} \\ &\geq Z(f^{so}) + (1+\kappa)\sum_{a\in\mathcal{A}} MC_a(f_a^{so})f_a^{so} - \sum_{a\in\mathcal{A}} MC_a(f_a^{so})f_a^{so} \\ &= Z(f^{so}) + \kappa\sum_{a\in\mathcal{A}} MC_a(f_a^{so})f_a^{so} \end{aligned}$$

The proof is complete. ■

Now we are ready to prove the following theorem that provides a bound on the price of anarchy for networks with separable linear arc costs:

Theorem 10.1 *(Price of anarchy for $[\mathcal{G}, Q, c(f)]$ with separable linear arc costs) Let $f \in \Omega_1$ and $f^{so} \in \Omega_1$, where f^{so} is optimal for $[\mathcal{G}, Q, c(f)]$. Then*

$$\rho\left[\mathcal{G}, Q, c(f)\right] = \frac{\sum_{a\in\mathcal{A}} c_a\left(f_a^{ue}\right) f_a^{ue}}{\sum_{a\in\mathcal{A}} c_a\left(f_a^{so}\right) f_a^{so}} \leq \frac{4}{3} \tag{10.18}$$

Proof. Let $f^{ue} \in \Omega_1$ be a user equilibrium and $f^{so} \in \Omega_1$ a system optimal flow for $[\mathcal{G}, Q, c(f)]$. By Lemma 10.2, we know that $\frac{1}{2}f^{ue}$ is system optimal for $\left[\mathcal{G}, \frac{Q}{2}, c(f)\right]$ with $MC_a(\frac{1}{2}f_a^{ue}) = c_a(f_a^{ue})$ for all $a \in \mathcal{A}$. Setting $\kappa = 1$ in Lemma 10.5, we have for $\left[\mathcal{G}, \frac{Q}{2}, c(f)\right]$ the following:

$$Z(f^{so}) \geq Z\left(\frac{1}{2}f^{ue}\right) + \sum_{a\in\mathcal{A}} MC_a\left(\frac{1}{2}f_a^{ue}\right)\cdot\frac{f_a^{ue}}{2} \tag{10.19}$$

Next note that

$$\begin{aligned} MC_a\left(\frac{1}{2}f_a^{ue}\right)\cdot\frac{f_a^{ue}}{2} &= \frac{1}{2}f_a\cdot\left[\frac{d}{dx}\left(A_a + B_a x\right)x\right]_{x=f_a^{ue}/2} \\ &= \frac{1}{2}f_a^{ue}\cdot\left(A_a + 2B_a\frac{f_a^{ue}}{2}\right) \\ &= \frac{1}{2}f_a^{ue}c_a(f_a^{ue}) \end{aligned} \tag{10.20}$$

Using Lemma 10.3 and result (10.20) together with (10.19), we obtain

$$Z(f^{so}) \geq \frac{1}{4}Z(f^{ue}) + \frac{1}{2}\sum_{a\in\mathcal{A}} c_a(f_a^{ue})f_a^{ue} = \frac{3}{4}Z(f^{ue}) \tag{10.21}$$

■

10.2.2 When a Potential Function Exists

When a user equilibrium may be computed by minimizing a well-defined objective function subject to the usual flow conservation and non-negativity constraints, that objective function is sometimes called a *potential function.* Thus, Beckmann's objective function, denoted by $V(f)$, for $[\mathcal{G}, Q, c(f)]$ with separable, but not necessarily linear, cost functions is a potential function. Recall that the nonlinear program based on Beckmann's objective function is

$$\min V(f) = \sum_{a\in\mathcal{A}} \int_0^{f_a} c_a(x_a)dx_a \quad \text{subject to} \quad f \in \Omega_1 \tag{10.22}$$

when Ω_1 is given by (10.1). The following result obtains:

Theorem 10.2 *(Potential function upper bound on the price of anarchy for $[\mathcal{G}, Q, c(f)]$ with separable arc costs) Let $f^{ue} \in \Omega_1$ be a user equilibrium flow and $f^{so} \in \Omega_1$ a system optimal flow for $[\mathcal{G}, Q, c(f)]$. Assume that both f^{ue} and f^{so} exist. Also assume that $c(f)$ is strictly monotone increasing for all $f \in \Omega_1$, and let $V(f^{ue})$ denote the global minimum of (10.22). Further assume that for any feasible $f \in \Omega_1$*

$$c_a(f_a)f_a \leq \beta \int_0^{f_a} c_a(x_a)dx_a \quad \forall a \in \mathcal{A} \tag{10.23}$$

where $\beta \in \Re^1_{++}$. Then

$$\rho\left[\mathcal{G}, Q, c(f)\right] = \frac{\sum_{a\in\mathcal{A}} c_a\left(f_a^{ue}\right) f_a^{ue}}{\sum_{a\in\mathcal{A}} c_a\left(f_a^{so}\right) f_a^{so}} \leq \beta \tag{10.24}$$

Proof. We have shown in Chap. 8 that any solution of the nonlinear program (10.22) is unique, owing to the assumed strictly monotone increasing nature of the arc cost functions. Thus f^{ue} is a unique global minimizer and, consequently, we know

$$\sum_{a\in\mathcal{A}} \int_0^{f_a^{ue}} c_a(x_a)dx_a \leq \sum_{a\in\mathcal{A}} \int_0^{f_a^{so}} c_a(x_a)dx_a \tag{10.25}$$

Setting $f = f^{ue}$ and summing (10.23), we obtain

$$\sum_{a\in\mathcal{A}} c_a(f_a^{ue})f_a^{ue} \leq \beta \sum_{a\in\mathcal{A}} \int_0^{f_a^{ue}} c_a(x_a)dx_a \tag{10.26}$$

Note that the strictly monotone increasing nature of the separable arc cost functions requires that

$$\frac{dc_a(f_a)}{df_a} > 0 \quad \forall a \in \mathcal{A}$$

Therefore, using integration by parts, we have

$$\sum_{a\in\mathcal{A}} \int_0^{f_a} c_a(x_a)dx_a - \sum_{a\in\mathcal{A}} c_a(f_a)f_a = -\int_{c_a(0)}^{c_a(f_a)} f_a(y_a)dy_a$$

$$= -\int_0^{f_a} x_a \frac{dc_a(x_a)}{dx_a}dx_a \leq 0 \tag{10.27}$$

Setting $f = f^{so}$ in (10.23) and using (10.27), we obtain

$$\beta \sum_{a\in\mathcal{A}} \int_0^{f_a^{so}} c_a(x_a)dx_a \leq \beta \sum_{a\in\mathcal{A}} c_a(f_a^{so})f_a^{so} \tag{10.28}$$

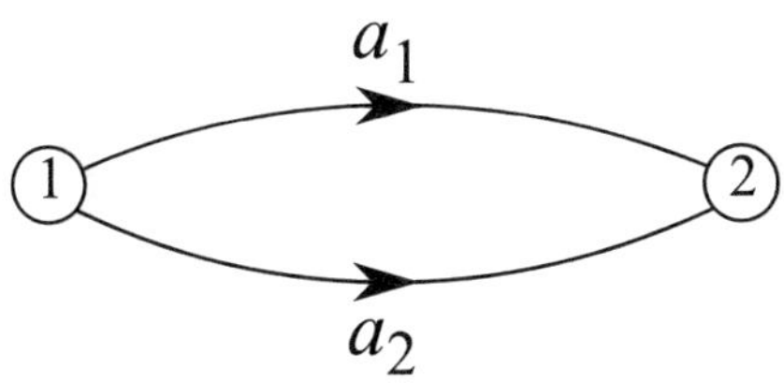

FIGURE 10.1: THE PIGOU/ROUGHGARDEN EXAMPLE NETWORK

From (10.25), (10.26) and (10.28), we have

$$\sum_{a\in\mathcal{A}} c_a(f_a^{ue})f_a^{ue} \leq \beta \sum_{a\in\mathcal{A}} \int_0^{f_a^{ue}} c_a(x_a)dx_a \leq \beta \sum_{a\in\mathcal{A}} \int_0^{f_a^{so}} c_a(x_a)dx_a$$

$$\leq \beta \sum_{a\in\mathcal{A}} c_a(f_a^{so})f_a^{so}$$

■

10.2.3 Importance of Bounding the Price of Anarchy

Shortly, we will introduce the so-called equilibrium network design problem, which seeks to create networks whose configurations and characteristics minimize congestion while recognizing agents obey a user equilibrium. All varieties of the equilibrium network design problem are challenging to solve numerically. If the price of anarchy has an upper bound that is not "too bad", we may very well elect not to solve the equilibrium network design problem. That is, we might let a flow pattern based on unfettered Nash-like competition emerge naturally. Consequently, a bound on the price of anarchy for a general network would indeed be especially valuable. Unfortunately, examples may be given for which the price of anarchy is unbounded. One such example is associated with Pigou (1920), although we employ the exposition due to Roughgarden (2005, 2007) to present it.

Consider the two-arc graph of Fig. 10.1, whose origin (source) is node 1 and whose destination (sink) is node 2. Let the cost per unit of flow on the two arcs a_1 and a_2 be f_{a_1} and f_{a_2}, respectively. Furthermore, take the unit cost of flow on arc a_1 to be constant and equal to unity; that is, $c_{a_1} = 1$. Let the unit cost of flow on arc a_2 be equal to its own flow; that is, $c_{a_2} = f_{a_2}$. Travel demand between node 1 and node 2 is unity. We want to calculate the price of anarchy. The system optimal flow must obey

$$MC_{a_1} = MC_{a_2}$$

In other words

$$\frac{\partial (1 \cdot f_{a_1})}{\partial f_{a_1}} = \frac{\partial (f_{a_2} \cdot f_{a_2})}{\partial f_{a_2}}$$

from which it is apparent that

$$1 = 2f_{a_2}^{so} \Longrightarrow f_{a_2}^{so} = \frac{1}{2} \tag{10.29}$$

Flow conservation, of course, requires

$$f_{a_1}^{so} + f_{a_2}^{so} = 1 \tag{10.30}$$

It is clear from (10.29) and (10.30) that

$$f_{a_1}^{so} = f_{a_2}^{so} = \frac{1}{2}$$

Naturally, the user equilibrium for the same network requires

$$c_{a_1} = c_{a_2}$$

$$f_{a_1}^{ue} + f_{a_2}^{ue} = 1$$

from which we conclude that

$$f_{a_1}^{ue} = 0 \quad f_{a_2}^{ue} = 1$$

Consequently, the price of anarchy is

$$\rho = \frac{\sum_{i=1}^{2} c_{a_i}\left(f_{a_i}^{ue}\right) f_{a_i}^{ue}}{\sum_{i=1}^{2} c_{a_i}\left(f_{a_i}^{so}\right) f_{a_i}^{so}} \tag{10.31}$$

$$= \frac{1 \cdot (0) + (1)(1)}{1 \cdot \left(\frac{1}{2}\right) + \left(\frac{1}{2}\right)\left(\frac{1}{2}\right)} = \frac{4}{3} \tag{10.32}$$

in agreement with the theoretical bound established by Theorem 10.1.

As noted in Roughgarden (2005, 2007), by changing the unit cost of arc a_2 from a linear to an appropriate nonlinear function, it is possible to create a network whose price of anarchy is unbounded. To that end, let the unit cost on arc a_2 be

$$c_{a_2} = (f_{a_2})^{\sigma}$$

where $\sigma \in \Re_{++}^1$ is a fixed, positive parameter. In this case, the relevant marginal costs are

$$MC_{a_1} = \frac{\partial (1 \cdot f_{a_1})}{\partial f_{a_1}} = \frac{\partial \left[(f_{a_2})^{\sigma} \cdot f_{a_2}\right]}{\partial f_{a_2}} = MC_{a_2}$$

from which we obtain

$$1 = (\sigma + 1)\left(f_{a_2}^{so}\right)^{\sigma}$$

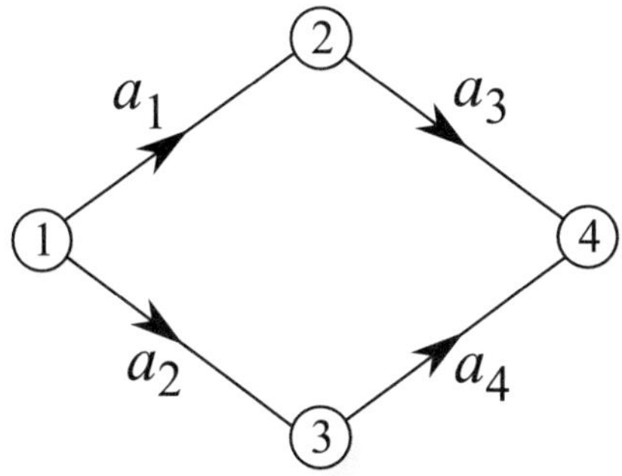

FIGURE 10.2: A FOUR-ARC NETWORK

Therefore, it is immediate that

$$\begin{aligned} f_{a_1}^{so} &= 1 - f_{a_2}^{so} = 1 - (1+\sigma)^{-\left(\frac{1}{\sigma}\right)} \equiv \varepsilon \\ f_{a_2}^{so} &= (1+\sigma)^{-\left(\frac{1}{\sigma}\right)} = 1 - \varepsilon \end{aligned}$$

Moreover

$$\begin{aligned} c_{a_1}\left(f_{a_1}^{so}\right) f_{a_1}^{so} + c_{a_2}\left(f_{a_2}^{so}\right) f_{a_2}^{so} &= 1 \cdot f_{a_1}^{so} + \left(f_{a_2}^{so}\right)^{\sigma} \cdot f_{a_2}^{so} \\ &= f_{a_1}^{so} + \left(f_{a_2}^{so}\right)^{\sigma+1} \\ &= \varepsilon + (1-\varepsilon)^{\sigma+1} \end{aligned}$$

We next observe that

$$\lim_{\sigma \longrightarrow \infty} \varepsilon = 0$$

so that

$$\lim_{\sigma \longrightarrow \infty} c_{a_1}\left(f_{a_1}^{so}\right) f_{a_1}^{so} + c_{a_2}\left(f_{a_2}^{so}\right) f_{a_2}^{so} = 0 \tag{10.33}$$

Because (10.33) is, as $\sigma \longrightarrow \infty$, the denominator of the price of anarchy as stated in (10.31), ρ becomes unbounded.

10.3 The Braess Paradox and Equilibrium Network Design

Let us consider road traffic on the simple network of Fig. 10.2, which is the foundation for a simple example of the Braess paradox presented in LeBlanc (1975) and repeated here. Specifically, we want to study the four arc network described by Fig. 10.2 and the following forward star array:

Arc	From Node	To Node	A_{a_i}	B_{a_i}
a_1	1	2	40	0.5
a_2	1	3	185	0.9
a_3	2	4	185	0.9
a_4	3	4	40	0.5

with the following cost functions:

$$c_{a_i}(f_{a_i}) = A_{a_i} + B_{a_i}(f_{a_i})^4$$

It is a relatively simple matter to compute, or obtain from symmetry arguments, the user equilibrium flows on this network, when node 1 is the origin and node 2 is the destination and demand obeys

$$h_{p_1} + h_{p_2} = 6 \tag{10.34}$$

In (10.34) h_{p_1} and h_{p_2} are the flows on the two paths connecting the single origin-destination pair $(1, 4)$ defined by

$$p_1 = \{a_1, a_3\}$$

$$p_2 = \{a_2, a_4\}$$

In fact the user equilibrium flows for this network configuration, which we call the *before* configuration, are

$$\text{before flow pattern } h^*_{p_1} = h^*_{p_2} = 3$$

$$\Longrightarrow f^*_{a_i} = 3 \quad i = 1, 2, 3, 4$$

so that the equilibrium unit path costs are

$$c^*_{p_1} = c^*_{p_2} = 338.4$$

and the total system wide congestion costs for this four-arc configuration are

$$TC_{\text{before}} = 6\,(338.4) = 2030.4$$

Now we consider improving the network by adding a fifth arc a_5 that directly connects node 2 to node 3. This means that the new network configuration, which we call the *after* configuration, is that given by Fig. 10.3 and the following forward star array:

The generalized unit cost for arc a_5 is

$$c_{a_5} = 15.4 + f_{a_5}$$

There is now a third path open between the origin and destination, namely

$$p_3 = \{a_1, a_5, a_4\}$$

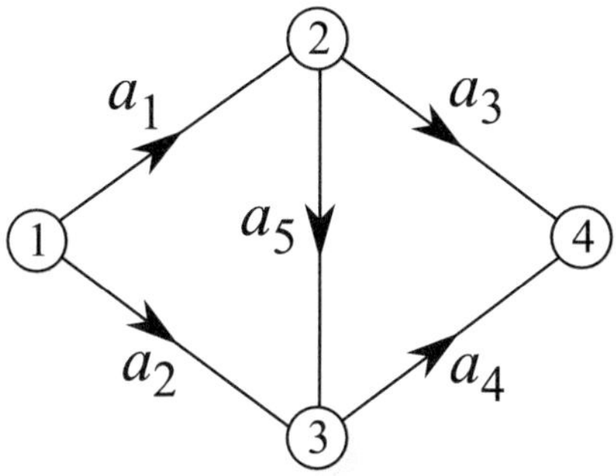

FIGURE 10.3: A FIVE-ARC NETWORK

Arc	From Node	To Node
a_1	1	2
a_2	1	3
a_3	2	4
a_4	3	4
a_5	2	3

The user equilibrium flows for the *after* configuration are

$$\text{\textit{after} flow pattern } h^*_{p_1} = h^*_{p_2} = h^*_{p_3} = 2$$
$$\Longrightarrow f^*_{a_i} = 2 \quad i = 1, 2, 3, 4, 5$$

since the unit path flow costs are now

$$c^*_{p_1} = c^*_{p_2} = c^*_{p_3} = 367.4,$$

which of course means a user equilibrium has been attained; the associated total congestion costs are

$$TC_{\text{after}} = 6\,(367.4) = 2204.4$$

The following conclusion is inescapable: addition of a new arc to this network in the manner described above has increased total system wide congestion. This phenomenon of increasing global congestion when adding to local capacity is known as *the Braess' paradox.*

An immediate consequence of the Braess' paradox is that we must include user equilibrium constraints among the constraints of any mathematical formulation of the optimal network design problem when network agents are empowered to make their own selfish routing decisions. That is, such *equilibrium network design models* must have the following mathematical structure:

$$\min \quad Z\,(f,y) \tag{10.35}$$

subject to

$$f = \Phi(y) \tag{10.36}$$

$$y \in \Lambda \tag{10.37}$$

where $Z(.,.)$ is a system-wide disutility measure (such as total congestion costs) and

$$f = (f_a : a \in \mathcal{A})$$

and

$$y = (y_a : a \in \mathcal{I})$$

are, respectively, vectors of network arc flows and logical variables indicating whether to add specific arcs. Furthermore, $\mathcal{I}$ is the set of arcs being considered for insertion into the network, $\Phi(y)$ denotes a mapping that identifies equilibrium flows for any given vector of arc additions y, and the constraints $f = \Phi(y)$ are stylized *equilibrium constraints*. Note that

$$I \cap \mathcal{A} = \emptyset$$

Furthermore, Λ is the set of constraints directly imposed on the capacity additions and includes a budget constraint. As such, problem (10.35)–(10.37) is a model for topological equilibrium network design. We shall see in subsequent discussions that other types of equilibrium network design models may be constructed.

We know from discussions of network user equilibrium in Chap. 8 that there are both extremal and nonextremal formulations of the network user equilibrium problem. For the sake of illustration, let us presume that we are dealing with discrete capacity additions (one variety of topological design) and that the arc cost functions are separable and strictly monotone increasing while travel demand is fixed. Then the user equilibrium problem may be stated as the convex mathematical program (10.22). Thus, we may write

$$\Phi(y) = \arg \left\{ \begin{array}{ll} \min & \displaystyle\sum_{a \in \mathcal{A} \cup \mathcal{I}} \int_0^{f_a} c_a(x_a)\, dx_a \\ \text{subject to} & \\ & f = \Delta h \\ & \Gamma h = Q \\ & My \geq f \\ & h \geq 0 \end{array} \right\} \tag{10.38}$$

where

Δ	the arc-path incidence matrix (δ_{ap})
δ_{ap}	equals 1 if $a \in p$ and 0 otherwise
Γ	the OD-path incidence matrix (γ_w^p)
γ_{ij}^p	equals 1 if $p \in \mathcal{P}_{ij}$ and 0 otherwise
M	$(M_a : a \in \mathcal{I})$ where $M_a > 1 \quad \forall a \in \mathcal{I}$
$\mathcal{A}$	set of all existing network arcs
$\mathcal{W}$	set of all origin-destination (OD) pairs
$\mathcal{P}_{ij}$	set of paths connecting OD pair $(i, j) \in \mathcal{W}$
$\mathcal{P}$	the set of all paths
$\mathcal{I}$	set of arcs being considered for insertion into the network
y_a	equals 1 if arc $a \in \mathcal{I}$ is added to the network and 0 otherwise
y	$(y_a : a \in \mathcal{A})$
Q_{ij}	travel demand between OD pair $(i, j) \in \mathcal{W}$
Q	$(Q_{ij} : (i, j) \in \mathcal{W})$

Even though we have considered the simplest of all user equilibrium problems, namely fixed demand and separable cost functions, it is apparent that the equilibrium constraints (10.38) cause the model (10.35)–(10.37) to take the form of a bi-level mathematical program. Moreover, (10.35)–(10.37) is a specific instance of a mathematical program with equilibrium constraints (MPEC) and is most commonly referred to as the *discrete equilibrium network design problem.*

Although we have presented the Braess paradox in the context of road network improvements, it should be clear that the paradox may arise for any situation wherein network agents are empowered to make decisions affecting flows that are potentially in conflict with a central authority and with localized efforts to enhance capacity. We also point out that at no time in the above presentation has it been said that the Braess paradox must occur. In fact, there is presently no reliable mathematical test that can be carried out to ascertain whether the paradox will or will not occur for a general network.

10.4 MPECs and Their Relationship to Stackelberg Games

We can give the following rather general statement of a finite-dimensional mathematical program with equilibrium constraints (MPEC):

$$\min_{y} \quad F(x, y) \tag{10.39}$$

subject to

$$x \in X(y) \subseteq \Re^n \tag{10.40}$$

$$y \in Y(x) \subseteq \Re^q \tag{10.41}$$

$$\left[G(x, y)\right]^T (x' - x) \geq 0 \quad \forall x' \in X(y) \tag{10.42}$$

where we have expressed the notion of an equilibrium as a quasivariational inequality in x whose principal operator, $F(\cdot, y)$, depends parametrically on y. Furthermore, in problem (10.39)–(10.42), the key mappings are

$$F(x, y) \quad : \quad \Re^n \times \Re^q \longrightarrow \Re^1$$

$$G(x, y) \quad : \quad \Re^n \times \Re^q \longrightarrow \Re^n,$$

and at this point no assumptions regarding differentiability or convexity have been made.

An MPEC of the form (10.39)–(10.42) has a one-to-one correspondence with the key features of a *generalized Stackelberg game*. In particular, a Stackelberg game is a type of noncooperative game wherein one of the agents is identifiable as a *leader*, meaning that he/she has the ability to anticipate the reactions of the other agents to his/her strategic decisions. Only the leader is capable of this omniscience; all the other agents are Nash agents whose strategies are nonanticipatory. The objective (10.39) of our MPEC of course corresponds to the leader's noncooperative play, and it is additionally constrained by considerations (10.41). Similarly, the Nash followers face constraints (10.40). Finally, we note that the leader's play is, to reiterate, explicitly constrained by the play of the followers, as represented by (10.42).

There are at least three principal types of Stackelberg games that are related to a broad interpretation of equilibrium network design as the identification of investments and mechanisms that alleviate congestion while taking into account the Braess paradox; these are:

(1) **Topological equilibrium network design.** The leader of such games minimizes global congestion, subject to budget and equilibrium constraints, by inserting individual arcs or nodes into existing networks. In principle, such games can also be used to design entirely new networks that have not previously existed. Examples of topological equilibrium network design models are: (a) the arc addition model (10.39)–(10.42) discussed above, whose flows are constrained to be a user equilibrium; and (b) the equilibrium facility location models developed by Miller et al. (1996) to optimally determine the location, production, and shipment activities of a new firm within an existing network economy described by an oligopolistic spatial price equilibrium.

(2) **Capacity enhancement equilibrium network design.** In such games, the leader minimizes global congestion, subject to budget and equilibrium constraints, by increasing the effective capacity of certain existing arcs of the network of interest. We shall discuss the mathematical formulation and numerical solution of capacity enhancement design models in subsequent sections of this chapter.

(3) **Equilibrium congestion pricing.** Such Stackelberg games differ from the two types described above in that the leader is concerned with

mechanism design rather than capital or maintenance investments. In particular, congestion pricing employs tolls to redistribute traffic in a fashion that diminishes congestion and avoids the Braess paradox. However, such games do employ explicit user equilibrium constraints and have a mathematical structure quite similar to capacity enhancement equilibrium design models. We shall also discuss the mathematical formulation and numerical solution of congestion pricing models in subsequent sections of this chapter.

10.5 Alternative Formulations of Network Equilibrium Design

In this section and the remainder of this chapter, we use the notation introduced in Chap. 8 augmented by certain new definitions introduced as needed. We initially consider a generalization the discrete equilibrium network design model presented in Sect. 10.3 for arc-only topological design.

10.5.1 The Discrete Equilibrium Network Design Model

Let us here provide some more detail regarding the model of Sect. 10.3. In particular, the complete mathematical formulation of the discrete equilibrium network design model under the assumptions of fixed travel demand and separable arc unit cost functions is the following:

$$\min \quad \sum_{a\in\mathcal{A}\cup\mathcal{I}} c_a\left(f_a\right) f_a \tag{10.43}$$

subject to

$$f = \arg\left\{\begin{array}{c} \min \sum_{a\in\mathcal{A}\cup\mathcal{I}} \int_0^{f_a} c_a\left(x_a\right) dx_a \\ \text{subject to} \\ f = \mathbf{\Delta} h \\ My \geq f \\ \Gamma h = Q \\ h \geq 0 \end{array}\right\} \tag{10.44}$$

$$y \in \Lambda \equiv \left\{y : \sum_{a\in\mathcal{I}} \beta_a y_a \leq B,\ y_a = (0,1)\ \forall a \in \mathcal{I}\right\} \tag{10.45}$$

where B is the budget available for improvements, β_a is the known cost of adding arc $a \in \mathcal{I}$ to the network, and $\mathcal{I}$ is a set of arcs considered for insertion. The selected arcs obey the budget constraint

$$\sum_{a\in\mathcal{I}} \beta_a y_a \leq B \tag{10.46}$$

and integrality restrictions on the logical variables. Clearly, the above formulation can be easily extended to accommodate nonseparable cost functions by replacing the equilibrium constraints with one of the nonextremal (complementarity or variational inequality) formulations introduced in our discussions of network equilibrium in Chap. 8.

In fact, the extension to nonseparable costs is the following:

$$\min \quad \sum_{a\in\mathcal{A}\cup\mathcal{I}} c_a(f)\, f_a \tag{10.47}$$

subject to

$$[c(f)]^T (g - f) \geq 0 \quad \forall g \in \Omega_1 \tag{10.48}$$

$$y \in \Lambda \equiv \left\{ y : \sum_{a\in\mathcal{I}} \beta_a y_a \leq B,\; y_a = (0,1)\; \forall a \in \mathcal{I} \right\} \tag{10.49}$$

where we recall that

$$\Omega_1 \equiv \{f : f = \Delta h,\; Q = \Gamma h,\; h \geq 0\}$$

Extension to accommodate elastic (variable) travel demand is more involved and requires some additional mathematical apparatus. In the interest of brevity we provide the relevant insights for constructing an elastic demand network design model in the next section in the context of continuous equilibrium network design. We believe it will be evident to the reader how to employ the ideas of the next section to fashion an elastic demand discrete equilibrium network design model.

As a final remark for this section, we comment that, by employing the corresponding system optimal problem to form a lower bound for any given discrete equilibrium network design problem, LeBlanc (1975) develops a branch-and-bound algorithm of considerable utility. The LeBlanc branch-and-bound algorithm may be employed for discrete equilibrium network design with either separable or nonseparable arc cost functions.

10.5.2 The Continuous Equilibrium Network Design Problem

Let us turn now to the so-called continuous equilibrium network design model and consider how to include elastic travel demand in its formulation. The functions $c_a(f)$ and $Q_{ij}(u)$ are, respectively, the nonseparable unit cost of flow on arc $a \in \mathcal{A}$ and the nonseparable travel demand for origin-destination pair $(i, j) \in \mathcal{W}$. Note that these functions are assumed to be continuous and differentiable. Of course, f continues to denote the full vector of arc flows. The vector u is the vector formed by concatenating the minimum travel costs u_{ij} between all origin-destination pairs $(i, j) \in \mathcal{W}$ of the network. These minimum origin-destination travel costs play the role of prices in that we imagine the demand for travel to rise and fall as own minimum origin-destination travel costs fall and rise, respectively.

Our immediate aim is to develop a means of expressing the notion of a user equilibrium as constraints of a mathematical program. Of course, we can always use the complementarity version of the user equilibrium conditions as constraints. That is, we can append the statements

$$\begin{aligned}[c_p(h) - u_{ij}]\, h_p &= 0 \\ c_p(h) - u_{ij} &\geq 0\end{aligned}$$

for every $(i, j) \in \mathcal{W}$ and $p \in \mathcal{P}_{ij}$ to the mathematical program for network design. Alternatively, one can append a variational inequality describing user equilibrium. Note that there are an infinite (uncountable) number of such constraints, as the user-equilibrium variational inequality holds for every flow pattern that is nonnegative and satisfies flow conservation. Consequently, the explicit use of variational inequality constraints carries computational challenges with it.

10.5.3 User Equilibrium Constraints

Tan et al. (1979) showed that flows obeying Wardrop's First Principle (user equilibrium) can be viewed as satisfying a finite set of inequality constraints in standard mathematical programming form. These constraints are discussed in depth in Friesz (1981b); because we make extensive use of them herein, they are reviewed below.

However, because the subsequent discussion hinges on some subtle properties of a user optimized flow pattern, we first restate the formal definition of user equilibrium, in a somewhat more verbose form than found in Chap. 8:

Definition 10.2 A vector of path flows h is a user equilibrium or user optimized flow pattern if and only if h satisfies the following:

(a) every path flow is non-negative:

$$h \geq 0 \tag{10.50}$$

(b) all path flows of the same origin-destination (OD) pair sum to the travel demand:

$$\sum_{p \in P_{ij}} h_p = Q_{ij} \quad \forall (i, j) \in \mathcal{W} \tag{10.51}$$

(c) utilized paths have the same perceived cost of travel, namely the minimum cost:

$$h_p > 0 \Longrightarrow c_p = u_{ij} = \min\{c_q : q \in \mathcal{P}_{ij}\} \quad \forall (i,j) \in \mathcal{W},\, p \in \mathcal{P}_{ij} \tag{10.52}$$

(d) paths with greater than the minimum cost carry no flow:

$$c_p > u_{ij} = \min\{c_q : q \in \mathcal{P}_{ij}\} \Longrightarrow h_p = 0 \quad \forall (i,j) \in \mathcal{W}, p \in \mathcal{P}_{ij} \tag{10.53}$$

The following theorem presents a mathematical characterization equivalent to Definition 10.2:

Theorem 10.3 *(User equilibrium expressed as a finite set of inequalities) A non-negative path flow $h \geq 0$ is a user equilibrium if and only if (10.51) together with*

$$c_p \geq \frac{\left(\sum_{q \in P_{ij}} h_q c_q\right)}{Q_{ij}} \quad \forall (i,j) \in \mathcal{W},\, p \in \mathcal{P}_{ij} \tag{10.54}$$

are satisfied.

Proof. The proof is in two parts:

(i) [user equilibrium $\Longrightarrow$ (10.54)] Recall that a user equilibrium satisfies

$$(c_q - u_{ij})\, h_q = 0$$

where

$$u_{ij} = \min(c_q : q \in \mathcal{P}_{ij}) \tag{10.55}$$

for all $(i,j) \in \mathcal{W}$ and $q \in \mathcal{P}_{ij}$. Thus, we have

$$\sum_{q \in \mathcal{P}_{ij}} c_q h_q = u_{ij} \sum_{q \in \mathcal{P}_{ij}} h_q \Longrightarrow u_{ij} = \frac{\sum_{q \in \mathcal{P}_{ij}} c_q h_q}{Q_{ij}} \leq c_p$$

for all $(i,j) \in \mathcal{W}$ and $p \in \mathcal{P}_{ij}$. Thus, necessity is proven.

(ii) [(10.54) $\Longrightarrow$ user equilibrium] Now define

$$u_{ij} = \frac{\sum_{q \in \mathcal{P}_{ij}} c_q h_q}{Q_{ij}} \quad (i,j) \in \mathcal{W}, p \in \mathcal{P}_{ij} \tag{10.56}$$

so that (10.54) may be stated as

$$c_p \geq u_{ij} \quad (i,j) \in \mathcal{W}, p \in \mathcal{P}_{ij}$$

keeping in mind we do not yet know that each u_{ij} is the minimum travel cost of OD pair $(i,j) \in \mathcal{W}$. As a consequence, of the above observations, we also have that

$$u_{ij} \leq \min(c_p : p \in \mathcal{P}_{ij}) \tag{10.57}$$

Using (10.56), we have

$$\begin{aligned}
\sum_{p\in\mathcal{P}_{ij}} (c_p - u_{ij})\, h_p &= \sum_{p\in\mathcal{P}_{ij}} \left(c_p - \frac{\left(\sum_{q\in P_{ij}} h_q c_q\right)}{Q_{ij}} \right) h_p \\
&= \sum_{p\in\mathcal{P}_{ij}} c_p h_p - \frac{\left(\sum_{q\in P_{ij}} h_q c_q\right)}{Q_{ij}} \sum_{p\in\mathcal{P}_{ij}} h_p \\
&= \sum_{p\in\mathcal{P}_{ij}} c_p h_p - \sum_{q\in\mathcal{P}_{ij}} c_q h_q = 0 \\
\Longrightarrow (c_p - u_{ij})\, h_p &= 0 \quad \forall\, (i,j) \in \mathcal{W}, p \in \mathcal{P}_{ij} \qquad (10.58)
\end{aligned}$$

which is recognized as equivalent to Wardrop's first principle, were we able to establish that (10.57) holds as an equality. To that end, note that, since $Q_{ij} > 0$ for each $(i,j) \in \mathcal{W}$, there is some path $p \in \mathcal{P}_{ij}$ such that $h_p > 0$; then, by (10.58), $c_p = u_{ij}$. Therefore, by (10.57), we have

$$u_{ij} = \min(c_p : p \in \mathcal{P}_{ij}) \quad \forall\, (i,j) \in \mathcal{W}$$

Thus, sufficiency is proven. ■

Note that in Theorem 10.3 demand may be either elastic (variable) or inelastic (fixed). The usual conservation constraints

$$\sum_{p\in\mathcal{P}_{ij}} h_p - Q_{ij}(u) = 0 \tag{10.59}$$

allow (10.54) to be written as

$$u_{ij} = \frac{\sum_{q\in\mathcal{P}_{ij}} h_q \;\; c_j(h,y)}{\sum_{p\in\mathcal{P}_{ij}} h_p} \equiv g_{ij}\,(h,y) \tag{10.60}$$

Theorem 10.3 and result (10.60) are important because they allow, as we shall see, a single-level conventional mathematical programming representation of the elastic demand equilibrium network design problem entirely in terms of path flows and improvement variables. Other efforts to achieve a single-level formulation have tended to rely on variational inequality constraints, nonlinear complementarity constraints, or gap functions. As we have once already commented, variational inequality constraints representing the user equilibrium are infinite in number Consequently variational inequality constraints require a cumbersome and somewhat arbitrary constraint accumulation process. Nonlinear complementarity constraints representing the user equilibrium are, by contrast, finite in number, but may result in nonconvexity of the feasible region. Single-level formulations based on gap functions involve substantially more mathematical overhead than a formulation based on Theorem 10.3 and (10.60), and their exposition is tedious. Moreover, gap function formulations do not necessarily enhance computational efficiency.

Theorem 10.3 above allows any need to enforce a Wardropian static user equilibrium to be expressed by constraints (10.54), together with flow conservation and nonnegativity. Note that these constraints:

(1) are in standard mathematical programming form;

(2) are finite in number;

(3) require explicit use of path variables; and

(4) generally make the feasible region nonconvex.

These path variable and nonconvexity properties may at first glance seem daunting, but they must viewed in light of the known nonconvexity of the equilibrium network design problem which arises regardless of the formulation employed. Viewed in that way, constraints (10.54) introduce only one new problematic feature: namely, the explicit use of path variables. We argue below, both by prose and appeal to previously published numerical results, that this supposed "difficulty" in fact poses no significant obstacle if appropriate use of path generation techniques and computational intelligence search algorithms is made.

10.5.4 The Consumers' Surplus Line Integral

To our knowledge, nearly all previous equilibrium network design models reported in the literature deal either with constant (inelastic) travel demand or presume travel demand functions are separable. Yang and Bell (1998) and Huang and Bell (1998) are among the few to have considered network design in the presence of elastic demand, and they employ separable demand functions. By contrast, we employ in the development which follows nonseparable, elastic transportation demand functions and use as an objective the maximization of change in net economic surplus. To understand how to formulate such an objective, we let

$$\Theta_{ij}(Q) = \text{the inverse travel demand corresponding to } Q \in \Re_+^{|\mathcal{W}|}$$

$$\Theta(Q) = \left(\Theta_{ij}(Q) : (i,j) \in \mathcal{W}\right)$$

Next we note that the net benefits associated with price-quantity pair $(\Theta(Q), Q)$ are given by a line integral for consumers' surplus net of congestion costs; that is, we have

$$CS(Q) = \sum_{(i,j)\in\mathcal{W}} \left[\oint_0^Q \Theta_{ij}(v)\, dv_{ij} - \Theta_{ij}(Q)\, Q_{ij} \right], \tag{10.61}$$

as is easily verified for the separable case by looking at Fig. 10.4 and/or Fig. 10.5.

The first term of (10.61) measures gross economic benefits and the second term is the payment made for benefits, expressed in terms of congestion costs. Note that a line integral *must* be employed in order to give an exact representation of net economic benefits in the presence of elastic, nonseparable demand functions. This is because consumers' surplus necessarily involves the integration of functions of several variables when demand functions are not separable. This is problematic because it is well known that a line integral does not have an unique, unambiguous value unless the Jacobian matrix formed from its integrand is symmetric. Such symmetry restrictions amount to a requirement that cross price elasticities of demand be proportional to one another, which is unlikely in any real-world setting. See Jara-Diaz and Friesz (1982) for a discussion of these subtleties.

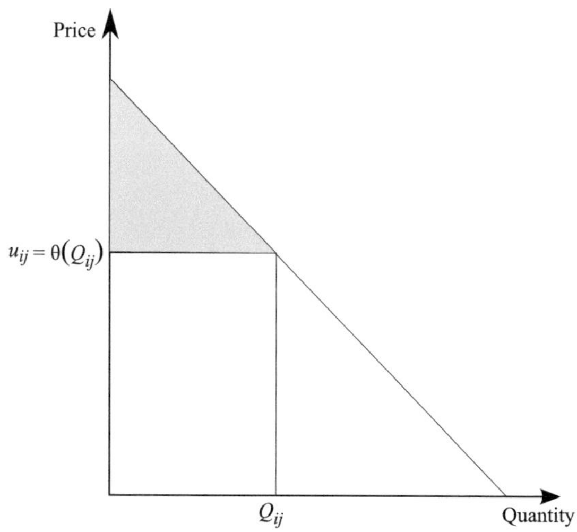

FIGURE 10.4: CONSUMERS' SURPLUS (SHADED AREA) $= \int_0^{Q_{ij}} \theta_{ij}(v)\, dv_{ij} - \theta_{ij}(T)\, T_{ij}$

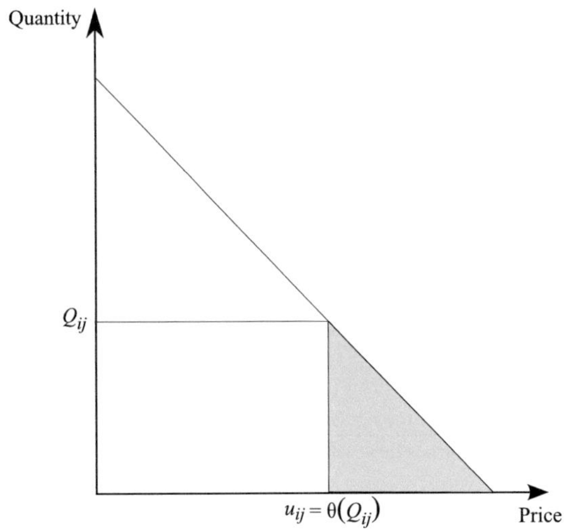

FIGURE 10.5: CONSUMER'S SURPLUS (SHADED AREA) $= \int_{u_{ij}}^{\tilde{u}_{ij}} Q_{ij}(x)\, dx_{ij}$

Expression (10.61) may be re-stated using the formula $\int v dw = wv - \int w dv$ for integration by parts to obtain:

$$
\begin{aligned}
CS(u) &= \sum_{(i,j)\in\mathcal{W}} \left\{ \left[\Theta_{ij}(u)\, u_{ij} \right]_0^{Q(u)} - \oint_{\tilde{u}}^{u} Q_{ij}(x)\, dx_{ij} - \Theta_{ij}[Q(u)]\, Q_{ij}(u) \right\} \\
&= \sum_{(i,j)\in\mathcal{W}} \oint_{u}^{\tilde{u}} Q_w(x)\, dx_{ij} \qquad (10.62)
\end{aligned}
$$

where

$$
\tilde{u} = \Theta(0) = \text{vector of price axis intercepts (maximal prices)} \qquad (10.63)
$$

Line integral (10.62) can also be constructed directly for the separable case by using the usual rules of integration to express the shaded area in Fig. 10.5. Our objective will be the maximization of the *change* in consumers' surplus resulting from alterations of arc capacities. A change in the capacity of a given arc will be manifest as a change in the minimum travel costs on paths using that arc. As such our objective is

$$
\max \Delta CS\left(u, u^0\right) = CS(u) - CS\left(u^0\right)
$$

when the minimum travel costs change from u^0 to u. It is evident from (10.62) that this objective takes the form

$$\max \Delta CS\left(u,u^0\right) = \sum_{(i,j)\in\mathcal{W}} \oint_u^{\tilde{u}} Q_{ij}(x)\,dx_{ij} - \sum_{(i,j)\in\mathcal{W}} \oint_{u^0}^{\tilde{u}} Q_{ij}(x)\,dx_{ij} \quad (10.64)$$

$$= \sum_{(i,j)\in\mathcal{W}} \left\{ \oint_u^{u^0} Q_{ij}(x)\,dx_{ij} + \oint_{u^0}^{\tilde{u}} Q_{ij}(x)\,dx_{ij} \right\}$$

$$- \sum_{(i,j)\in\mathcal{W}} \oint_{u^0}^{\tilde{u}} Q_{ij}(x)\,dx_{ij}$$

$$= \sum_{(i,j)\in\mathcal{W}} \oint_u^{u^0} Q_{ij}(x)\,dx_{ij} \quad (10.65)$$

It is interesting to note that, for the separable case, (10.65) can be obtained directly from Fig. 10.6 which shows how the consumers' surplus change depicted in Fig. 10.7 for the inverse demand function is mapped to the corresponding trapezoidal area under the demand curve. Furthermore, by using identity (10.60), we may express (10.65) in terms of h and y variables:

$$\max \Delta CS\left(h,y,u^0\right) = \sum_{(i,j)\in\mathcal{W}} \left[\oint_u^{u^0} Q_{ij}(x)\,dx_{ij} \right]_{u=g(h,y)} \quad (10.66)$$

where $g = (g_{ij} : (i,j) \in \mathcal{W})$ is defined in (10.60) and u^0 is the known initial vector of minimum travel costs prior to capacity alterations. It is the form (10.66) that we use as our objective for optimal design when demand is elastic.

The pertinent constraints are:

$$\sum_{p\in\mathcal{P}_{ij}} h_p - Q_{ij}(h,y) = 0 \quad \forall\,(i,j) \in \mathcal{W} \quad (10.67)$$

$$\sum_{q\in\mathcal{P}_{ij}} h_q c_q(h,y) - c_p(h,y) Q_{ij}(h,y) \leq 0 \quad \forall\,(i,j) \in \mathcal{W}, p \in \mathcal{P}_{ij} \quad (10.68)$$

$$c_p(h,y) - \sum_{a\in\mathcal{A}} c_a(\Delta h, y)\delta_{ap} = 0 \quad \forall\,(i,j) \in \mathcal{W}, p \in \mathcal{P}_{ij} \quad (10.69)$$

$$\sum_{a\in\mathcal{I}} \psi_a(y_a) \leq B \quad (10.70)$$

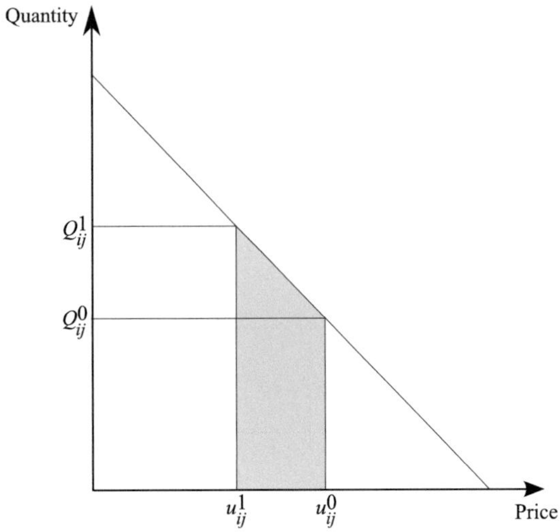

FIGURE 10.6: CHANGE IN CONSUMERS' SURPLUS (SHADED AREA)

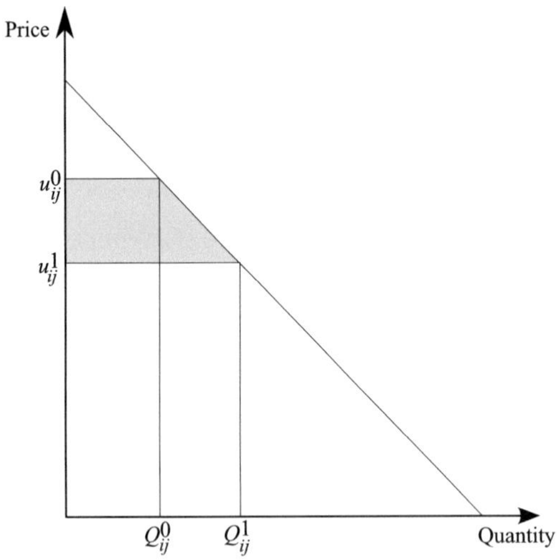

FIGURE 10.7: CHANGE IN CONSUMERS' SURPLUS (SHADED AREA)

$$h \geq 0 \tag{10.71}$$

$$y \geq 0 \tag{10.72}$$

where now $\mathcal{I}$ is the set of arcs being considered for improvement.

Furthermore, (10.67) describes flow conservation, (10.68) are the user equilibrium constraints, (10.71) and (10.72) are nonnegativity restrictions, (10.69) are the equilibrium definitions of path costs, and (10.70) is the budget constraint. Note that, in (10.66), we have recognized that at equilibrium $u = g(h, y)$ to achieve a formulation entirely in terms of path flows and improvement variables.

To refer to the aforementioned constraints, we introduce the notation

$$\Upsilon = \{(h, y) \geq 0 : \ (67) - -(72) \text{ hold}\} \tag{10.73}$$

which recognizes that the decision variables are h and y. The arc flows f are not included as decision variables since their values are completely determined by the path variables h. Our formulation may be stated in succinct form as

$$\left.\begin{array}{l} \max \ \Delta CS\left(h{,}y, u^0\right) = \displaystyle\sum_{(i,j)\in\mathcal{W}} \left[\oint_u^{u^0} Q_{ij}\left(x\right) dx_{ij}\right]_{u=g(h,y)} \\ \text{subject to} \\ \qquad (h, y) \in \Upsilon \end{array}\right\} \tag{10.74}$$

which is clearly a *single-level mathematical program.* We reiterate that constraints (10.68) are inherently nonconvex, making Υ a nonconvex set. Thus, formulation (10.74) is nonconvex regardless of the nature of the expenditure functions $\psi_a(y_a)$. The single-level formulation is an alternative to a bi-level formulation of equilibrium network design for which the inner (or lower-level) problem is either a mathematical program or a variational inequality or some other problem whose solution is an user equilibrium.

When demand is inelastic, constraints (67) and (68) become

$$\sum_{p\in\mathcal{P}_{ij}} h_p - Q_{ij} \quad = \quad 0 \ \forall\, (i, j) \in \mathcal{W} \tag{10.75}$$

$$\sum_{j\in\mathcal{P}_{ij}} h_j c_j(h, y) - c_p(h, y) Q_{ij} \quad \leq \quad 0 \ \forall\, (i, j) \in \mathcal{W}, p \in \mathcal{P}_{ij} \tag{10.76}$$

where the Q_{ij} are fixed for all $(i, j) \in \mathcal{W}$. Thus, model (10.74) yields the following formulation first proposed by Tan et al. (1979):

$$\left.\begin{array}{l} \min \ \displaystyle\sum_{(i,j)\in\mathcal{W}} \sum_{p\in\mathcal{P}_{ij}} c_p\left(h_p\right) h_p \\ \text{subject to} \\ \qquad (h, y) \in \Upsilon_0 \end{array}\right\} \tag{10.77}$$

where

$$\Upsilon_0 = \{(h, y) : (10.69), (10.70), (10.71), (10.72), (10.75), \text{and } (10.76) \text{ hold}\} \tag{10.78}$$

is the relevant set of feasible solutions when demand is fixed.

We reiterate that in (10.74) there is a need to evaluate a line integral in order to correctly consider user net benefits. In a static setting, this line integral may only be evaluated if transportation demand functions satisfy a symmetry restriction [see Jara-Diaz and Friesz (1982)] which is tantamount to requiring that all cross elasticities of demand be proportional to one another, an assumption which is unrealistic except for very unusual and nongeneral circumstances. Note also that such a symmetry restriction arises regardless of how the inner (lower-level) equilibrium problem is formulated. As such, it would appear that (10.74) *cannot be solved* since we have no guidance about what path of integration to employ in evaluating the consumers' surplus line integral intrinsic to its formulation. This suggests that the present state of theory regarding equilibrium network design cannot treat fully general elastic transportation demands. This is a significant shortcoming, yet knowledge of it and its implications is not widely recognized. So long as our modeling is confined to a static world view, there is no way around this difficulty. However, (10.74) can be specialized to the case of fixed demand, for which the consumers' surplus line integral is dropped from the formulation. As we have previously remarked, the result is the continuous equilibrium network design model (10.77) which determines capacity enhancements of individual arcs when there is a fixed trip table.

It is tempting, in light of the difficulties cited above, to somehow approximate the consumers' surplus line integral. However, Jara-Diaz and Friesz (1982) show that the available techniques for approximating this line integral may involve unacceptably large errors and are without any theoretical foundation. Only if one enters the realm of dynamics, may a means for evaluating the consumers' surplus line integral be given, as noted by Friesz et al. (1996).

10.5.5 Generating Paths

Some popular misconceptions have developed regarding the obstacle posed by the explicit use of path variables in formulations like (10.74) or (10.77). More specifically, many practitioners have the mistaken belief that the presence of explicit path variables in a model formulation makes that model numerically intractable because of the potential for extraordinarily large numbers of paths in networks of realistic size. This point of view has always been incorrect and only recently has the fear of path variables begun to subside among network model builders. Path variables are handled in all successful algorithms by path generation schemes which only calculate paths as they are needed; this philosophy – which is essentially the technique of column generation well known to mathematical programmers – is at the heart of the very popular Frank-Wolfe algorithm when it is employed to solve static network equilibrium problems.

What many do not realize is that although the Frank-Wolfe algorithm is usually implemented in a way that discards path information and saves only arc flows at the end of each iteration, it is straightforward to develop and implement

Frank-Wolfe type software which generates and saves path identities. Such software is no less intrinsically computationally efficient than Frank-Wolfe software that saves only arc information; the main additional computational burden is the storage of the chains of arcs defining paths. When the number of paths becomes large enough that some kind of virtual storage is needed to save paths, there can in principle be processing delays when paths are retrieved from memory. Yet even this is not very significant, since paths are typically associated with origin-destination pairs and there are typically only a handful of meaningful paths for each origin-destination pair, a situation that allows the rapid retrieval of path information. Moreover, Friesz et al. (1992, 1993) have shown how the Frank-Wolfe algorithm can be used very effectively as an a priori path generator. This is done by making the network increasingly congested through demand increases and saving paths that do not exceed a pre-established circuitousness threshold.

10.6 Algorithms for Continuous Equilibrium Network Design

Formulation (10.77) of the continuous equilibrium network design problem can in principle be solved by appealing to the traditional methods of nonlinear programming owing to its single-level nature. For example, one might proceed by using a barrier function or Lagrangean relaxation to lift the user equilibrium and budget constraints up into the objective function. This, of course, has the pleasant effect of leaving behind constraints for which we have established descent/feasible direction techniques (in particular, the Frank-Wolfe, gradient projection, affine scaling, and Lagrangean relaxation algorithms). However, such an approach must recognize that the line search step is potentially complicated by the nonconvexity of the objective function resulting from barriers, projections, and relaxations. In particular, one must take care not to take steps that degrade the objective function. This can be assured by use of the Armijo step size rule or other step size heuristics, although these may increase computation time. Furthermore, the great unsolved problem of mathematical programming – our inability to provide an a priori count of the number of local optima of a general nonconvex mathematical program – prevents us from finding a global solution with certainty.

10.6.1 Simulated Annealing

Formulation (10.77) is well-suited for the application of computational intelligence methods as demonstrated by Friesz et al. (1993), who employ simulated annealing. Of the four main categories of computational intelligence (CI) techniques – simulated annealing (SA), swarm optimization, neural networks, and genetic algorithms – SA may in specific cases offer the analyst the best compromise among ease of understanding, ease of software code development, and effectiveness in discovering global optima for equilibrium constrained optimization problems. SA has its roots in statistical mechanics and is, in effect, a kind of probabilistic search method. SA was originally developed by Kirkpatrick et al. (1983) to solve combinatorial or discrete optimization problems. Vanderbilt and Louie (1984) showed how this method can be employed to obtain global solutions for continuous optimization problems. In fact, SA has proven to be an effective technique for virtually any continuous nonconvex optimization problem when rapid response times are not mandated by the decision setting; see Anandalingam et al. (1989) for a more in depth discussion of this last point.

When SA, as well as more recent CI algorithms are employed to solve mathematical programs there are a lot of parameters under the control of the analyst. This gives the analyst freedom to tailor the computational intelligence algorithm of choice to a particular application. Sometimes, however, there is a price to be paid for this extra freedom; namely, in some problems, the selection of the various parameters can initially pose a serious challenge, mandating a systematic and sometimes tedious search for parameter ranges that allow convergence. This drawback, however, needs to be weighed against the relative simplicity of computational intelligence software code for solving optimization problems. In fact, our experience in training students and professionals indicates that most individuals with knowledge of a programming language can write adequate SA software code after a single lecture. This contrasts sharply with sophisticated decomposition algorithms and other techniques traditionally favored by mathematical programmers for large network problems that can require substantial mathematical sophistication and careful software engineering to fully understand and implement.

For a description of the details of applying SA to formulations such as (10.77), see Friesz et al. (1992, 1993). In fact, previously unknown equilibrium network design solutions were found by Friesz et al. (1992) using this approach for the much studied Sioux-Falls network; these local solutions were superior to any previously calculated for the same numerical example. The numerical results reported by Friesz et al. (1992, 1993) demonstrate unequivocally that simulated annealing is a viable and effective algorithmic approach to the continuous equilibrium network design problem (10.77).

10.6.2 The Equilibrium Decomposed Optimization Heuristic

Suwansirikul and Friesz (1987) proposed a heuristic algorithm for continuous equilibrium network design that often produces good results. Their algorithm is referred to as equilibrium decomposed optimization (EDO). To explain the algorithm, let us introduce the notation

$$Z_a(y) \equiv c_a(f_a(y), y_a)\, f_a(y) + \nu\psi_a(y_a) \tag{10.79}$$

and consider the continuous equilibrium network design model with fixed demand in the following form:

$$\min Z(y) = \sum_{a \in \mathcal{A}} Z_a \left(f_a(y), y_a \right) \tag{10.80}$$

subject to

$$\sum_{p \in \mathcal{P}_{ij}} h_p = Q_{ij} \quad \forall \, (i,j) \in \mathcal{W} \tag{10.81}$$

$$f = \Delta h \tag{10.82}$$

$$h \geq 0 \tag{10.83}$$

$$y \geq 0 \tag{10.84}$$

where $\nu \in \Re^1_+$ is now a dual variable corresponding to the budget constraint

$$\sum_{a \in \mathcal{A}} \psi_a(y_a) \leq B$$

and $\psi_a(y_a)$ is the cost of increasing the effective capacity of arc a by the amount y_a, a continuous variable. For this discussion, we take ν to be a known constant. Note that for any arc $a \in \mathcal{A}$

$$\frac{\partial Z_a}{\partial y_a} = f_a(y) \frac{\partial c_a}{\partial y_a} + c_a \frac{\partial f_a(y)}{\partial y_a} + \nu \frac{\partial \psi_a}{\partial y_a} \tag{10.85}$$

In general, the right hand side of (10.85) cannot be evaluated since $f_a(y)$ is not known explicitly. However, the aforementioned terms may be ignored when

$$\left| \nu \frac{\partial \psi_a}{\partial y_a} + f_a(y) \left[\frac{\partial c_a}{\partial y_a} \right]_f \right| \gg \left| c_a \frac{\partial f_a(y)}{\partial y_a} + \phi \right| \tag{10.86}$$

where

$$\left[\frac{\partial c_a}{\partial y_a} \right]_f$$

indicates that the partial derivative $\partial c_a / \partial f_a$ is calculated holding all flow variables fixed, and ϕ represents the difference

$$f_a \frac{\partial c_a}{\partial y_a} - f_a \left[\frac{\partial c_a}{\partial y_a} \right]_f \tag{10.87}$$

If (10.86) holds, then $\partial Z_a / \partial y$ is well approximated by

$$\nu \frac{\partial \psi_a}{\partial y_a} + f_a \left[\frac{\partial c_a}{\partial y_a} \right]_f \tag{10.88}$$

The preceding discussion is meant merely to suggest that calculating the gradient of $Z(h, y)$ by considering only those partial derivatives that one can determine without knowledge of the reaction function $f(y)$ may result in a good approximation.

Using the observations made above, together with a Bolzano line search scheme, one my express the EDO heuristic algorithm as follows:

EDO Heuristic Algorithm

Step 0. *(Initialization)* Determine a closed form approximation of the gradient by forming:

$$Z'_a = \nu \frac{\partial \psi_a}{\partial y_a} + f_a \left[\frac{\partial c_a}{\partial y_a} \right]_f$$

for all arcs $a \in \mathcal{I}$, where $\mathcal{I}$ denotes the list of arcs being considered for improvement. Let $\mathcal{S} \subseteq \mathcal{I}$ denote the set of arcs whose optimal improvements have been determined. Select vectors $L^0 \in \Re^{|\mathcal{I}|}_{++}$ and $U^0 \in \Re^{|\mathcal{I}|}_{++}$ such that

$$\begin{aligned} Z'_a(L^0) &< 0 \\ Z'_a(U^0) &> 0 \end{aligned}$$

for each arc $a \in \mathcal{I}$. Set $\mathcal{S} = \emptyset$. Set $j = 1$.

Step 1. *(Calculate user equilibrium)* Using the costs

$$\begin{aligned} c_a(f_a) \quad a &\in \mathcal{A} \backslash (\mathcal{I} \cup \mathcal{S}) \\ c_a(f, y^*) \quad a &\in \mathcal{S} \\ c_a(f, y^j) \quad a &\in \mathcal{I} \end{aligned}$$

where

$$y^j = \frac{L^{j-1} + U^{j-1}}{2} \in \Re^{|\mathcal{I}|}_{+}$$

find the user equilibrium flow vector

$$f(y^j)$$

Step 2. *(Perform line search)* For each arc $a \in \mathcal{I}$, calculate $Z'_a\left(y^j\right)$. Furthermore, for the same arcs $a \in \mathcal{I}$, carry out the following operations:

(i) If $Z'_a\left(y^j\right) < 0$, set $L^j_a = y^j_a$ and $U^j_a = U^{j-1}_a$.

(ii) If $Z'_a > 0$, set $L^j_a = L^{j-1}_a$ and $U^j_a = y^j_a$.

(iii) If $Z'_a = 0$, record the approximate optimal solution $y_a^* = y_a^j$, add arc a to $\mathcal{S}$, and remove arc a from $\mathcal{I}$.

Step 3. *(Stopping test)* For each arc $a \in \mathcal{I}$, check whether

$$U_a^j - L_a^j \leq \varepsilon, \tag{10.89}$$

where ε is a preset tolerance. For each arc $a \in \mathcal{I}$ satisfying inequality (10.89), remove that arc from $\mathcal{I}$, and add it to $\mathcal{S}$, while recording its approximate optimal value

$$y_a^* = \frac{L_a^j + U_a^j}{2}$$

If the improvement set $\mathcal{I}$ is not empty, set $j = j + 1$ and go to Step 1.

10.6.3 Computing When a Complementarity Formulation Is Employed

Despite a great deal of research, no "breakthrough" exact algorithm has been devised for general MPECs or for equilibrium network design. Although many intricate and highly original algorithms have been proposed, none is broadly better than the conversion of an MPEC to a single-level program that is then solved by traditional nonlinear programming algorithms or probabilistic search methods to identify local optima. In Sect. 10.5.3 we introduced the Tan et al. (1979) user equilibrium constraints, which were subsequently used to create the single-level formulation (10.77).

In fact, transformation of MPEC (10.39)–(10.42) to a single-level formulation involving a finite number of constraints may be accomplished in a number of other ways that are applicable to continuous equilibrium network design. One of the most obvious is to restate the variational inequality (10.42) as a nonlinear complementarity problem (NCP):

$$\left.\begin{array}{c} [G(x,u,y)]^T \begin{pmatrix} x \\ u \end{pmatrix} = 0 \\ \\ G(x,u,y) \geq 0 \\ x \geq 0 \\ u \geq 0 \end{array}\right\} \tag{10.90}$$

where $G(.,.,.)$ is created from the equilibrium problem of the MPEC of interest, while u is a vector of dual variables the details of such a formulation are provided in Chap. 7. Note that it is completely equivalent to state (10.90) as

$$\left.\begin{array}{c} [G(x,u,y)]^T \begin{pmatrix} x \\ u \end{pmatrix} \leq 0 \\ \\ G(x,u,y) \geq 0 \\ x \geq 0 \\ u \geq 0 \end{array}\right\} \tag{10.91}$$

As a consequence the MPEC structure (10.39)–(10.42) becomes

$$\left.\begin{array}{c} \min_y F(x,y) \\ \text{subject to} \\ [G(x,u,y)]^T \begin{pmatrix} x \\ u \end{pmatrix} \leq 0 \\ \\ G(x,u,y) \geq 0 \\ x \geq 0 \\ u \geq 0 \\ y \in Y \end{array}\right\} \tag{10.92}$$

This allows us a single-level formulation of an MPEC, which may be solved by conventional numerical methods for nonconvex mathematical programming problems; of course, applying such algorithms to (10.92) will not find a global optimum with certainty.

10.6.4 Computing When a Gap Function Is Employed

The gap function perspective, discussed in Chap. 7, for solving variational inequalities provides another means for creating a single-level mathematical program whose solutions are also solutions of MPEC (10.39)–(10.42). In particular, if we replace the variational inequality constraint in (10.39)–(10.42) with an appropriate gap function, we will obtain a single-level mathematical program with an additional equality constraint of a special structure. For a given $y \in Y$, using the Fukushima-Auchmuty gap function, the variational inequality subproblem

$$x = \arg VI(F, X, y)$$

(10.42), may be replaced by

$$\zeta_\alpha(x,y) = 0$$

where α is a positive constant and

$$\zeta_\alpha(x,y) = \max_{z \in X} \left\{ [F(z,y)]^T (x - z) - \frac{\alpha}{2} \|x - z\|^2 \right\}$$

This leads to a single-level reformulation of MPEC (10.39)–(10.42):

$$\left.\begin{array}{rc} & \min_y F(x,y) \\ \text{subject to} & \\ & \zeta_\alpha(x,y)=0 \\ & x\geq 0 \\ & x\in X \\ & y\in Y \end{array}\right\} \tag{10.93}$$

We leave as an exercise for the reader the formal statement of an algorithm for the continuous equilibrium network design problem based on the reformulation (10.93). Note that other gap functions may be employed. However, the Fukushima-Auchmuty gap function is continuously differentiable and, hence, computationally attractive.

Meng et al. (2001) were among the first to note the usefulness of gap functions in formulating and solving MPECs. They studied a problem with fixed demand and separable arc costs. For those circumstances, they employ a gap function related to the objective function of Beckmann's equivalent program. They employ an augmented Lagrangean method to solve their single-level reformulation.

10.6.5 An Algorithm Based on Sensitivity Analysis

The abstract MPEC of interest in this section is a variant of (10.39)–(10.42). Specifically, we are interested in the following problem:

$$\min_y \quad F(x,y) \tag{10.94}$$

subject to

$$L \leq y \leq U \tag{10.95}$$

$$y \in \Re^q \tag{10.96}$$

$$x \in X(y) \subseteq \Re^n \tag{10.97}$$

$$[G(x,y)]^T(x'-x) \geq 0 \quad \forall x' \in X(y) \tag{10.98}$$

where $L \in \Re^q_+$ and $U \in \Re^q_+$ are known fixed vectors. Friesz et al. (1990) proposed and tested a family of heuristic algorithms for the above MPEC, that employ variational inequality sensitivity analysis. One such algorithm, for MPEC formulation (10.94)–(10.98) that may be adapted to the continuous equilibrium network design problem is the following:

Approximate Reaction Function Algorithm

Step 0. *(Initialization)* Determine an initial solution y^0; set $k=0$. Select a value of β.

Step 1. *(Solve variational inequality)* Solve

$$\left[G\left(x, y^k\right)\right]^T \left(x' - x\right) \geq 0 \quad \forall x' \in X$$

Step 2. *(Calculate derivatives)* Based on sensitivity analysis calculate

$$\nabla_y x^k(y^k) = \left(\frac{\partial x_j\left(y^k\right)}{\partial y_i} : i \in [1, q], j \in [1, n] \right)$$

Step 3. *(Calculate direction)* Calculate

$$d^k = \nabla_y M(y^k) = \left(\frac{\partial M\left(y^k\right)}{\partial y_i} : i \in [1, q] \right)$$

where

$$\begin{aligned} M(y) &= F\left[x(y), y\right] \\ \frac{\partial M}{\partial y_i} &= \sum_{j=1}^{n} \frac{\partial F}{\partial x_i} \frac{\partial x_j}{\partial y_i} + \frac{\partial F}{\partial y_i} \quad i \in [1, q] \end{aligned}$$

Step 4. *(Determine step size)* Calculate

$$\alpha_k = \frac{\beta}{k+1} \tag{10.99}$$

Step 5. *(Updating and stopping)* Calculate

$$y^{k+1} = \left[y^k - \alpha_k \nabla_y M(y^k) \right]_L^U \tag{10.100}$$

where the right hand side of (10.100) is a projection of each $y_i^k - \alpha_k \left[\nabla_y M(y^k)\right]_i$ onto the real interval $[L_i, U_i]$. If

$$\left\| y^{k+1} - y^k \right\| \leq \varepsilon$$

stop and declare

$$y^* \approx y^{k+1}$$

Otherwise, set $k = k + 1$ and go to Step 1.

Note that the step size rule (10.99) is only meant to be illustrative; other rules are discussed in Friesz et al. (1990).

Variable	HJ	HJ	EDO	SA	GFAL	ARF
Initial value of each y-component	2.0	1.0	12.5	6.25	12.5	12.5
y_{16}	4.8	3.8	4.59	5.38	5.5728	5.55
y_{17}	1.2	3.6	1.52	2.26	1.6343	5.26
y_{19}	4.8	3.8	5.45	5.50	5.6228	5.55
y_{20}	0.8	2.4	2.33	2.01	1.6443	2.25
y_{25}	2.0	2.8	1.27	2.64	3.1437	4.53
y_{26}	2.6	1.4	2.33	2.47	3.2837	4.56
y_{29}	4.8	3.2	0.41	4.54	7.6519	4.74
y_{39}	4.4	4.0	4.59	4.45	3.8035	4.52
y_{48}	4.8	4.0	2.71	4.21	7.3820	4.82
y_{74}	4.4	4.0	2.71	4.67	3.6935	4.51
Value of objective function	81.25	81.77	83.47	80.87	81.752	83.79
Number of equilibrium solutions	58	108	12	3,900	2,700	15

TABLE 10.1: NUMERICAL COMPARISON OF ALGORITHMS

10.7 Numerical Comparison of Algorithms

Most papers proposing and testing new algorithms for equilibrium network design employ the well-known Sioux Fall network. See Suwansirikul and Friesz (1987) or Meng et al. (2001) for a complete presentation of the Sioux Falls data set. Table 10.1 compares the performance of the following algorithms as reported by Suwansirikul and Friesz (1987), Friesz et al. (1990), and Meng et al. (2001). These algorithms are identified as follows:

- Hooke-Jeeves pattern search (HJ);
- equilibrium decomposed optimization (EDO);
- simulated annealing (SA);
- gap function/augmented Lagrangean (GFAL); and
- approximate reaction function (ARF).

It must be noted that Table 10.1 is of limited value in accessing accuracy, since the algorithms tested may discover distinct local solutions due to the nonconvex nature of the problem being studied.

10.8 Electric Power Markets

We now develop a network model of the market for electric power.

10.8.1 Modeling the Firms That Generate Power

For this model we need the notion of an inverse demand function for electric power. An inverse demand function determines price when demand is specified. For the circumstance considered here, we take the inverse demand function for market $i \in \mathcal{N}$ during period t to be

$$\pi_{it}\left(\sum_{g \in \mathcal{F}} s_i^g\right)$$

where π_{it} is the price of power per MWatt-hour at node $i \in \mathcal{N}_f$ and s_{it}^f is the flow of power sold at the same node during period t. Naturally $\mathcal{N}_f$ is the set of nodes populated by firm f. The complete set of all nodes, when needed, will be referred to as $\mathcal{N}$. Therefore, the expression

$$\sum_{i \in \mathcal{N}_f} \pi_{it}\left(\sum_{g \in \mathcal{F}} s_{it}^g\right) \cdot s_{it}^f \cdot \Delta$$

is the *revenue* that firm f generates during period t, where Δ is the length of each time period, as described in Sect. 1.4.

The costs that a generating firm $f \in \mathcal{F}$ bears are:

(1) *Generation cost* for power generation unit $j \in G(i, f)$, denoted by,

$$V_{jt}^f\left(q_{jt}^f\right)$$

where q_{jt}^f is the rate at which generator unit $j \in G(i, f)$, located at node $i \in \mathcal{N}_f$, produces power. Generation cost typically has a fixed component and a variable component. For example, generation cost may be quadratic and take the form

$$V_{jt}^f\left(q_j^f\right) = \mu_j^f + \tilde{\mu}_j^f \cdot q_j^f + \frac{1}{2}\hat{\mu}_j^f \cdot \left(q_{jt}^f\right)^2$$

where $\mu_j^f, \tilde{\mu}_j^f, \hat{\mu}_j^f \in \Re_{++}^1$ for all $f \in \mathcal{F}$ and all $j \in G(i, f)$ are exogenous parameters.

(2) *Ramping cost* obtained from a generation unit's rotor fatigue, impacting rotor life span. Ramping cost is negligible if the magnitude of power change is less than some elastic range; that is, there is a range in which the generation rate can be adjusted that causes minimal wear on the rotors and is thus considered cost free. Therefore, in general we may use the function

$$\Phi_{jt}^f\left(r_{jt}^f\right) = \frac{1}{2}\gamma_j^f\left[\max\left(0, \left|r_{jt}^f\right| - \xi_j^f\right)\right]^2$$

to represent the ramping cost associated with some generation unit $j \in G(i,f)$ whose ramping rate is r_{jt}^f during period t, with corresponding elastic threshold $\xi_j^f \in \Re_{++}^1$ and cost coefficient γ_j^f. In general, there will be asymmetric ramp-up and ramp-down costs, causing the ramping cost to be expressed as

$$\Phi_{jt}^f\left(r_{jt}^f\right) = \frac{1}{2}\gamma_j^{f+}\left[\max\left(0, r_{jt}^f - \xi_j^{f+}\right)\right]^2 + \frac{1}{2}\gamma_j^{f-}\left[\max\left(0, -r_{jt}^f + \xi_j^{f-}\right)\right]^2$$

where γ_j^{f-} and γ_j^{f+} are the cost coefficients during ramp-up and ramp-down, respectively; naturally, ξ_j^{f+} and ξ_j^{f-} are the respective ramp-up and ramp-down elastic thresholds.

(3) *Wheeling fee* w_{it} paid to the so-called independent service operator (ISO) for transmitting 1 MWatt-hour of power from its hub, through which all power flows, to market i in period t. The wheeling fee is set by the ISO to enforce market clearing (supply of power equal to demand for power).

In light of the above, we may express the profits of each power generating firm $f \in \mathcal{F}$ as

$$\begin{aligned} J_f\left(s^f, q^f; s^{-f}\right) \;=\; & \sum_{t=0}^{N-1}\left\{\sum_{i\in\mathcal{N}_f}\pi_{it}\left(\sum_{g\in\mathcal{F}} s_{it}^g\right)\cdot s_{it}^f\right. \\ & -\sum_{i\in\mathcal{N}_f}\sum_{j\in G(i,f)}\left[V_j^f\left(q_{jt}^f\right)+\Phi_j^f\left(r_{jt}^f\right)\right] \\ & \left.-\sum_{i\in\mathcal{N}_f} w_{it}\cdot\left(s_{it}^f - \sum_{j\in G(i,f)} q_{jt}^f\right)\right\}\cdot\Delta \qquad (10.101) \end{aligned}$$

where the following vector notation is employed:

$$\begin{aligned} s^f &= \left(s_{it}^f : i \in \mathcal{N}_f, t \in [0, N-1]\right) \\ s^{-f} &= \left(s_{it}^g : i \in \mathcal{N}\backslash\mathcal{N}_f, g \in \mathcal{F}\backslash f, t \in [0, N-1]\right) \\ q^f &= \left(q_{it}^f : i \in \mathcal{N}_f, t \in [0, N-1]\right) \\ w &= \left(w_{it} : i \in \mathcal{N}_f, t \in [0, N-1]\right) \end{aligned}$$

We naturally assume that (10.101) is meant to be maximized by firm $f \in \mathcal{F}$ using those variables within its control.

There are also constraints that must be satisfied by each firm $f \in \mathcal{F}$. In particular:

(1) Each firm must balance sales and generation for all time periods, since we do not here consider the storage of electricity; therefore

$$\sum_{i\in\mathcal{N}} s_{it}^f = \sum_{i\in\mathcal{N}_f} \sum_{j\in G(i,f)} q_{jt}^f \qquad \forall t \in [0, N-1] \tag{10.102}$$

(2) The sales of power at every market must be nonnegative in each time period; thus

$$s_{it}^f \geq 0 \qquad \forall i \in \mathcal{N}_f, t \in [0, N-1] \tag{10.103}$$

(3) The output level of each generating unit is bounded from above and below for each time period; thus

$$0 \leq q_{jt}^f \leq CAP_j^f \qquad \forall i \in \mathcal{N}_f, j \in G(i,f), t \in [0, N-1] \tag{10.104}$$

where $CAP_j^f \in \Re_{++}^1$ is the relevant upper bound on output from generator $j \in G(i,f)$. Each such bound is a physical characteristic of the corresponding generator.

(4) Total sales by all the firms at a particular market are bounded from above by a regulatory authority. This feature is represented by the following constraint that holds for each node and each time period:

$$\sum_{f\in\mathcal{F}} s_{it}^f \leq \sigma_i \qquad \forall i \in \mathcal{N}, t \in [0, N-1] \tag{10.105}$$

where $\sigma_i \in \Re_{++}^1$ is an exogenous market sales cap for every node $i \in \mathcal{N}$.

(5) The ramping rate for every generation unit is bounded from above and below, which again expresses a physical characteristic of the unit; consequently, we write

$$R_j^{f-} \leq r_j^f(t) \leq R_j^{f+} \qquad \forall i \in \mathcal{N}_f, j \in G(i,f), t \in [0, N-1] \tag{10.106}$$

where R_j^{f+} and R_j^{f-} are, respectively, the upper and lower bounds on the ramping rate of generation unit $j \in G(i,f)$.

We may now state the set of feasible solutions for each firm $f \in \mathcal{F}$ as

$$\Omega_f(s^{-f}) = \left\{\left(s^f, q^f\right) : \text{(10.102)–(10.106) hold}\right\} \tag{10.107}$$

Note that the set of feasible solutions for each firm depends on the power flows sold by its competitors.

If we take the wheeling fees as exogenous, we have a collection of simultaneous, coupled mathematical programs that represent oligopolistic competition among power providing firms. With w and s^{-f} exogenous and using s^f and q^f as decision variables, each firm $f \in \mathcal{F}$ seeks to solve

$$\left.\begin{array}{c} \max J_f\left(s^f, q^f; s^{-f}\right) \\ \text{subject to} \qquad (s^f, q^f) \in \Omega_f(s^{-f}) \end{array}\right\} \tag{10.108}$$

We will subsequently learn how to reformulate (10.108) as a variational inequality in order to facilitate its analysis and computation.

10.8.2 Modeling the ISO

We turn now to modeling the independent service operator (ISO). For the simplistic view of electric power network markets we are now taking, the sole job of the ISO is to clear the market for power transmission by serving as auctioneer to facilitate transactions between sellers and buyers of electric power. Let us assume w is exogenous so that, in every period $t \in [0, N-1]$, the ISO solves a linear program to determine the transmission flow vector

$$y = (y_{it} : i \in \mathcal{N}, t \in [0, N-1])$$

where y_{it} denotes an actual power flow from a specific hub to node $i \in \mathcal{N}$ for period $t \in [0, N-1]$. The ISO's linear program for period $t \in [0, N-1]$ is

$$\max J_0 = \sum_{i \in \mathcal{N}} y_{it} w_{it} \tag{10.109}$$

subject to

$$\sum_{i \in \mathcal{N}} PTDF_{ia} \cdot y_{it} \leq T_a \ \forall a \in \mathcal{A} \tag{10.110}$$

where $\mathcal{A}$ is the arc set of the electric power network, the T_a are transmission capacities for each arc $a \in \mathcal{A}$, and the $PTDF_{ia}$ are power transmission distribution factors (PTDFs) that determine the flow on each arc $a \in \mathcal{A}$ as the result of a unit MW injection at the hub node and a unit withdrawal at node $i \in \mathcal{N}$. The PTDFs allow us to employ a linearized DC approximation for which every $PTDF_{ia}$, where $i \in \mathcal{N}$ and $t \in [0, N-1]$, to be considered is constant and unaffected by the transmission line loads. The DC approximation employed here means that the principle of superposition applies to arc and path flows, thereby dramatically simplifying the model. In the ISO formulation presented above, we ignore transmission loss, although such could be introduced without any complication other than increased notational detail.

To clear the market, the transmission flows y must balance the net sales at each node (market); thus

$$y_{it} = \sum_{f \in \mathcal{F}} \left(s_{it}^f - \sum_{j \in G(i,f)} q_{jt}^f \right) \qquad \forall i \in \mathcal{N}, t \in [0, N-1] \tag{10.111}$$

It is immediate that the ISO's set of feasible solutions is

$$\Omega_0(s) = \left\{ y : \sum_{i \in \mathcal{N}} PTDF_{ia} \cdot \sum_{f \in \mathcal{F}} \left(s_{it}^f - \sum_{j \in G(i,f)} q_{jt}^f \right) \leq T_a \ \forall a \in \mathcal{A} \right\}$$

As a consequence, the ISO's linear program may be restated as

$$\max_{y} J_{\text{ISO}}\left(y;s,q\right)=\sum_{t=0}^{N-1}\sum_{i\in\mathcal{N}}\sum_{f\in\mathcal{F}}\left(s_{it}^{f}-\sum_{j\in G(i,f)}q_{jt}^{f}\right)\cdot w_{it}\ \text{ s.t. }\ y\in\Omega_0 \tag{10.112}$$

The maximization in (10.112) is with respect to y, for given s and q solving the variational inequality introduced in Sect. 10.8.3, which follows immediately. Note that in this formulation the wheeling fee vector

$$w=\left(w_{it}:i\in\mathcal{N},t\in[0,N-1]\right)$$

is fixed and exogenous.

10.8.3 The Generalized Nash Game Among the Producers

The reader may easily verify that the generalized Nash game (10.108) may be expressed as the following variational inequality:

$$\text{find}\begin{pmatrix}s^*\\ q^*\end{pmatrix}\in\Omega\left(s\right) \tag{10.113}$$

such that

$$\sum_{f\in\mathcal{F}}\nabla_{s^f}\left[J_f\left(s^{f*},q^{f*};s^{-f*}\right)\right]^T\left(s^f-s^{f*}\right)+$$

$$\nabla_{q^f}\left[J_f\left(s^{f*},q^{f*};s^{-f*}\right)\right]^T\left(q^f-q^{f*}\right)\geq 0\quad\forall\begin{pmatrix}s\\ q\end{pmatrix}\in\Omega(s) \tag{10.114}$$

where

$$\Omega(s)\equiv\prod_{f\in\mathcal{F}}\Omega_f(s^{-f}) \tag{10.115}$$

and $\Omega_f(s^{-f})$ was previously defined by expression (10.107). For convenience let us refer to variational inequality (10.114) as $VI\left(\nabla J,\Omega\right)$ where

$$\nabla J\left(s,q\right)\equiv\begin{pmatrix}\nabla_{s^f}\left[J_f\left(s^{f*},q^{f*};s^{-f*}\right)\right]:f\in\mathcal{F}\\ \nabla_{q^f}\left[J_f\left(s^{f*},q^{f*};s^{-f*}\right)\right]:f\in\mathcal{F}\end{pmatrix} \tag{10.116}$$

10.8.4 The Stackelberg Game with the ISO as Leader

An alternative to the Nash and generalized Nash formulations previously discussed in this book in the context of diverse applications is one for which the ISO is the leader of a Stackelberg game; thereby the model formulation becomes a *mathematical program with equilibrium constraints* (MPEC). In fact, taken together, (10.108) and (10.112) constitute a Stackelberg game for which the individual power producers compete with one another according to the generalized Nash game and the ISO, as described by (10.112), is the leader. The Stackelberg game thusly formed will determine the power generated and sold by each oligopolistic power producer, as well as the power flows facilitated by the ISO. Through the inverse demand functions, the retail price of power is also determined. We are cognizant of the fact that the ISO in actual power markets does not presently have the complete powers of a Stackelberg leader. However, designating the ISO as a leader creates optimal pricing policies and optimal network designs that suggest desirable market operational and organizational enhancements.

In light of preceding remarks, the Stackelberg model of interest has the following form:

$$\left.\begin{array}{ll} & \max\limits_{y} J_{\text{ISO}} = \displaystyle\sum_{t=0}^{N-1} \sum_{i\in\mathcal{N}} \sum_{f\in\mathcal{F}} \left(s_{it}^{f} - \sum_{j\in G(i,f)} q_{jt}^{f} \right) \cdot w_{it} \\ & y \in \Omega_0(s) \\ \text{subject to} & \\ & \begin{pmatrix} s \\ q \end{pmatrix} = \arg VI(\nabla J, \Omega) \end{array}\right\} \qquad (10.117)$$

10.8.5 Solved Numerical Example of the MPEC Formulation

We now want to construct and solve a numerical example of the electrical power MPEC presented above as (10.117). In particular, we will solve an example of the electric power distribution and pricing problem presented in Sect. 10.8.4 using the notion of swarm optimization.

Description of the Network and Choice of Parameters

We assume that each firm has 2 generation units at each of three nodes ($i = 1, 2, 3$) with different capacities and ramping rates. Therefore, each firm has a total of 6 generation units which are geographically separated. We consider inverse demands having the following form:

$$\pi_i \left(\sum_{g\in\mathcal{F}} s_i^g, t \right) = P_{0,i}(t) - \frac{Q_{0,i}(t)}{P_{0,i}(t)} \cdot \left[\sum_{g\in\mathcal{F}} c_i^g \right]$$

where the parameters $P_{0,i}$ and $Q_{0,i}$ are market dependent according to the following table:

Market (i)	1	2	3
$P_{0,i}$	40	35	32
$Q_{0,i}$	5,000	4,000	6,200

The relevant PTDF values associated with the network are the following:

Arc	$(1,2)$	$(1,3)$	$(2,3)$
Node 1	0.33	0.67	0.33
Node 2	−0.33	0.33	0.67
Node 3	0	0	0

Generation capacities, CAP_j^f (in MWatt) of different generation units given in the following table:

	Firm 1		Firm 2		Firm 3	
	Unit 1	Unit 2	Unit 1	Unit 2	Unit 1	Unit 2
Node 1	1,000	500	750	500	600	500
Node 2	750	500	500	600	1,000	400
Node 3	800	400	400	500	1,200	400

It is evident from the above tables that each firm has a combination of high capacity and low capacity generators. The unit-specific and time-specific ramping rates, r_j^f, are bounded from above and below. We assume these bounds are symmetric, so that

$$R_j^{f+} = -R_j^{f-}$$

for all $f \in \mathcal{F}$, $i \in \mathcal{N}_f$, and $j \in \mathcal{G}(i, f)$. The upper bounds on ramping rates for the generation units are

	Firm 1		Firm 2		Firm 3	
	Unit 1	Unit 2	Unit 1	Unit 2	Unit 1	Unit 2
Node 1	58	336	84	330	290	340
Node 2	84	340	336	290	58	380
Node 3	70	400	400	340	35	365

If we compare ramping rate bounds and generation capacities, it is evident that units having higher capacity typically have slower ramping capability and vice versa. Also, ramping costs ($/MWatt-hour) associated with the faster ramping machines are higher compared to their slower counterparts. Unit ramping costs γ_j^f for all $f \in \mathcal{F}$ and $j \in \mathcal{G}(i, f)$ are presented in the following table:

	Firm 1		Firm 2		Firm 3	
	Unit 1	Unit 2	Unit 1	Unit 2	Unit 1	Unit 2
Node 1	2.14	6.82	4.50	6.72	6.00	6.90
Node 2	4.50	6.75	6.75	5.93	2.20	8.60
Node 3	5.50	8.70	8.74	6.80	1.54	8.65

Elastic limits for the generators, ξ_j^f, are usually not very dependent on the capacities of the generators, which is also evident from below where we list values of ξ_j^f (in MWatt) for all $f \in \mathcal{F}$ and $j \in \mathcal{G}(i, f)$:

	Firm 1		Firm 2		Firm 3	
	Unit 1	Unit 2	Unit 1	Unit 2	Unit 1	Unit 2
Node 1	65	57	60	55	55	53
Node 2	60	54	61	59	65	51
Node 3	62	52	51	55	67	52

The regional sales capacities in each of the three markets are assumed to be:

Market (i)	1	2	3
Market CAP, σ_i (MWatt)	3,000	3,200	2,900

Coefficients associated with the linear component of generation costs of the units, μ_j^f (\$/MWatt) are the following for all $f \in \mathcal{F}$ and $j \in \mathcal{G}(i, f)$:

	Firm 1		Firm 2		Firm 3	
	Unit 1	Unit 2	Unit 1	Unit 2	Unit 1	Unit 2
Node 1	15	15	15.2	14.7	15	15
Node 2	14.5	15	15.1	14.9	14.8	14.8
Node 3	14.7	15.2	15	15.1	15.3	15

We typically assume all coefficients associated with the quadratic component of generation costs of units belonging to a firm to be the same:

$$\hat{\mu}_j^1 = 0.08 \text{ for all } i \in \mathcal{N}_1, j \in \mathcal{G}(i, 1)$$

$$\hat{\mu}_j^2 = 0.07 \text{ for all } i \in \mathcal{N}_2, j \in \mathcal{G}(i, 2)$$

$$\hat{\mu}_j^3 = 0.075 \text{ for all } i \in \mathcal{N}_3, j \in \mathcal{G}(i, 3)$$

Transmission capacities of the arcs are assumed to be the following

Arc (a)	1	2	3
T_a (MWatt)	130	150	160

Our planning horizon in this example is 24 h with $t_0 = 0$ and $t_1 = 24$. The initial generation rates at $t_0 = 0$ are

$$
\begin{aligned}
q^1_{j,0} &= 150 \text{ for all } i \in \mathcal{N}_1, j \in \mathcal{G}(i,1) \\
q^2_{j,0} &= 175 \text{ for all } i \in \mathcal{N}_2, j \in \mathcal{G}(i,2) \\
q^3_{j,0} &= 160 \text{ for all } i \in \mathcal{N}_3, j \in \mathcal{G}(i,3),
\end{aligned}
$$

which implies that at the beginning all the generators for a firm were operating at the same level. This choice is intentional, as we want to study the impact of ramping rates on the generators. In the next section, we solve the proposed example using particle swarm optimization (PSO).

10.8.6 A PSO for MPEC

We apply particle swarm optimization to solve the power market model. In Chung et al. (2012) a PSO-based algorithm is applied to solve an MPEC model for dynamic congestion pricing, where the central control seeks to mitigate traffic congestion via adjusting the individual marginal cost of the traffic user on certain arcs. Differently here, the central control (leader) does not immediately affect the utility of the followers. Instead, one constraint in the strategy set is imposed by the leader. Thus, the PSO-based algorithm in Chung et al. (2012) is not immediately applicable here. To solve the MPEC problem of interest here, we set a penalty for any dissatisfaction of the relevant variational inequality and append that penalty to the objective function. To define a valid penalty function we employ the Auslender gap function described in Sect. 7.13.2. Specifically, the gap function is

$$\zeta(s^*, q^*) = \inf_{s,q\in\Omega} V(s^*, q^*, s, q)$$

where

$$V(s^*, q^*, s, q) = \sum_{f\in\mathcal{F}} \nabla_{s^f} \left[J_f\left(s^{f*}, q^{f*}; s^{-f*}\right)\right]^T \left(s^f - s^{f*}\right) + \nabla_{q^f} \left[J_f\left(s^{f*}, q^{f*}; s^{-f*}\right)\right]^T \left(q^f - q^{f*}\right)$$

The gap function can be a natural penalty function as it has the property that:

$$\zeta(s,q) = 0 \text{ if and only if } (s,q) \text{ is a solution of } VI(\nabla J, \Omega)$$

$$\zeta(s,\ q) \geq 0,\ \forall (s,\ q) \in \Omega$$

Therefore, we define the following penalty function:

$$P(s^*, q^*) = -M\zeta(s^*, q^*)$$

where $M \in \Re^1_+$ is properly large.

This leads to the problem

$$\left.\begin{array}{l} \displaystyle\max_y \sum_{t=0}^{N-1} \sum_{i \in \mathcal{N}} \sum_{f \in \mathcal{F}} \left(s_{it}^{f*} - \sum_{j \in G(i,f)} q_{jt}^{f*} \right) \cdot w_{it} + P(s^*, q^*) \\ \text{subject to} \\ \qquad y \in \Omega_0(s^*) \end{array}\right\} \tag{10.118}$$

A PSO algorithm for solving (10.118) is given in the pseudo-code that follows. Due to the PSO philosophy of random exploration of the feasible region, different interim solutions and even a different final solution may be obtained if one attempts to repeat the illustrative iteration presented below.

Step 0. *(Initialization)* Let $k = 0$. Randomly initialize 50 particle locations X_i^k, $i = 1, \ldots, 50$. Each particle is a representation of a candidate solution. Specifically, in our implementation, we have

$$X_i^k \equiv \left((y)^T, (s^*)^T, (q^*)^T\right) \tag{10.119}$$

For example, the first particle location is randomly generated as:

$$X_1^0 = [193.89 \quad 74.92 \quad \ldots \quad 72.11 \quad 232.56]^T \tag{10.120}$$

We also randomly initialize the velocity V_i^k as well as P_i^k (the so-called *pbest)* and G^k (the so-called *gbest*) for each given iteration k and all $i = 1, \ldots, 50$. The velocity V_i^k determines what step to employ for location updates, while P_i^k records the best location of X_i^k reached by iteration k. Furthermore G^k is best solution among the $\{X_i^k : i = 1, \ldots, 50\}$. In particular, let us select

$$V_1^0 = \begin{bmatrix} 1.99 & -2.84 & \ldots & -1.19 & -2.00 \end{bmatrix}^T \tag{10.121}$$

and imagine that

$$G^0 = \begin{bmatrix} 1.35 & 4.20 & \ldots & 122.37 & 101.26 \end{bmatrix}^T$$

When $k = 0$ it it is transparent that $P_i^k = X_i^k$.

Step 1. *(Update velocities and positions)* we employ these updating formula:

$$V_i^{k+1} = \omega_k V_i^k + c_1 r_1 (P_i^k - X_i^k) + c_2 r_2 (G^k - X_i^k), \ \forall i,$$

$$\hat{X}_i^{k+1} = X_i^k + V_i^{k+1}, \ \forall i,$$

In our implementation, we set $c_1 = c_2 = 2$, and $\omega_k = 0.98$. We randomly generate $r_1 = 0.13$ and $r_2 = 0.58$. Then

$$V_1^1 = 0.98 \cdot \begin{bmatrix} 1.99 \\ -2.84 \\ \dots \\ -1.39 \\ -2.00 \end{bmatrix} + 2 \cdot 0.13 \cdot \left(\begin{bmatrix} 193.89 \\ 74.92 \\ \dots \\ 72.11 \\ 232.56 \end{bmatrix} - \begin{bmatrix} 193.89 \\ 74.92 \\ \dots \\ 72.11 \\ 232.56 \end{bmatrix} \right)$$

$$+ 2 \cdot 0.58 \cdot \left(\begin{bmatrix} 1.35 \\ 4.20 \\ \dots \\ 122.37 \\ 101.26 \end{bmatrix} - \begin{bmatrix} 193.89 \\ 74.92 \\ \dots \\ 72.11 \\ 232.56 \end{bmatrix} \right) = \begin{bmatrix} -221.39 \\ -84.82 \\ \dots \\ 56.94 \\ -154.2680 \end{bmatrix} \tag{10.122}$$

$$\hat{X}_1^1 = \begin{bmatrix} -27.51 & -9.90 & \dots & 129.05 & 78.29 \end{bmatrix}^T \tag{10.123}$$

Then

$$X_1^1 = \arg\min_{X \in C} \|X - \hat{X}_1^1\|_2^2 = \begin{bmatrix} -27.51 & -9.90 & \dots & 129.05 & 78.29 \end{bmatrix}^T \tag{10.124}$$

where

$$C = \left\{ y : y_{it} = \sum_{f \in \mathcal{F}} \left(s_{it}^f - \sum_{j \in G(i,f)} q_{jt}^f \right), \right.$$
$$\left. \sum_{i \in \mathcal{N}} PTDF_{ia} \cdot \sum_{f \in \mathcal{F}} \left(s_{it}^f - \sum_{j \in G(i,f)} q_{jt}^f \right) \leq T_a \right\} \tag{10.125}$$

Step 2. *(Update "pbest" and "gbest")*

$$P_i^{k+1} = \begin{cases} P_i^k & \text{If } f(X^k) \leq f(P_i^{k-1}) \\ X_i^k & \text{Otherwise.} \end{cases}$$

$$G^{k+1} = \begin{cases} G^k & \text{If } f(G^k) \leq \max_i f(P_i^{k-1}) \\ P_{i*}^k & \text{Otherwise,} \end{cases}$$

where $i* = \arg\max_i f(P_i^k)$, and $f(\cdot) = J_{\text{ISO}}^P(\cdot, s^*, q^*)$. In our implementation, since X_1^1 improves the objective value over X_1^0, we have $P_1^1 = X_1^1$. Moreover, the gbest G^1 is set to the pbest solution of the current iteration, which turns out to be

$$G^1 = \begin{bmatrix} -1.21 & -7.64 & \dots & 50.53 & 100.09 \end{bmatrix}^T \tag{10.126}$$

Step 3. *(Iterate)* Check the termination criteria. If the value of gbest has recently been improved after 20 more iterations, then let $k = k + 1$, and go to Step 2.

Figure 10.8 depicts convergence of the algorithm. The solution is then given in Table 10.2. For comparison, we also present the solution of a pure Nash game model without the ISO using the complementarity problem reformulation for a Nash equilibrium discussed previously.

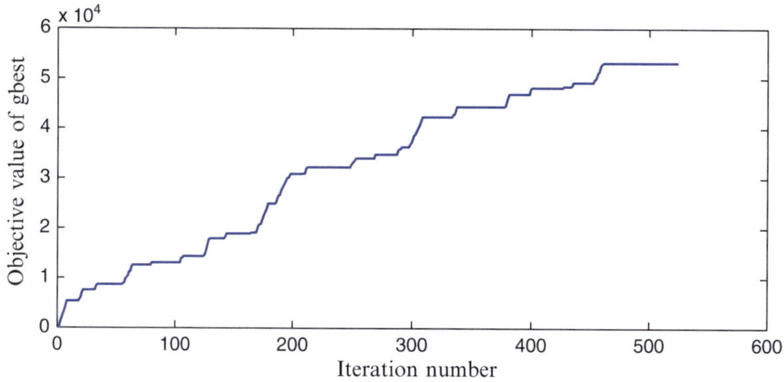

FIGURE 10.8: CONVERGENCE PLOT OF THE PSO

		t_1	t_2	t_3	t_4	t_5	t_6	t_7	Obj
	y_{1t}	0.19	0.16	-0.08	130.02	129.95	130.16	129.96	
MPEC solution	y_{2t}	-0.47	-0.17	-0.25	149.93	149.99	149.96	139.81	53,201.51
	y_{3t}	0.39	0.29	-0.03	-280.02	-279.85	-283.20	-273.81	
	y_{1t}	0.00	0.00	0.00	0.00	0.00	0.00	0.00	
Nash equilibrium	y_{2t}	0.00	0.00	0.00	0.00	0.00	0.00	0.00	0.00
	y_{3t}	0.00	0.00	0.00	0.00	0.00	0.00	0.00	

Table 10.2: Transmission Flow of ISO and its utility

10.9 References and Additional Reading

Abdulaal, M., & LeBlanc, L. (1979). The continuous equilibrium network design problem. *Transportation Research, 13B*(1), 19–32.

Anandalingam, G., Mathieu, R., Pittard, L., & Sinha, N. (1989). Artificial intelligence based approaches for hierarchical optimization problems. In R. Sharda (Ed.), *Impact of recent computer advances on operations research.* New York: North-Holland.

Chen, Y., Hobbs, B. F., Leyffer, S., & Munson, T. S. (2006). Leader-follower equilibria for electric power and NO_x allowances markets. *Computational Management Sciences, 3*, 307–330.

Chung, B. D., Yao, T., Friesz, T. L., & Liu, H. (2012). Dynamic congestion pricing with demand uncertainty: A robust optimization approach. *Transportation Research Part B, 46*, 1504–1518.

Dupuis P., & Nagurney, A. (1993). Dynamical systems and variational inequalities. *Annals of Operations Research, 44*, 9–42.

Friesz, T. L. (1981a). An equivalent optimization problem with combined multiclass distribution, assignment and modal split which obviates symmetry restrictions. *Transportation Research, 15B*, 361–369.

Friesz, T. L. (1981b). Multiobjective optimization in transportation: The case of equilibrium network design. In (Lecture notes in economics and mathematical systems, Vol. 190, pp. 116–127). New York: Springer.

Friesz, T. L., & Shah, S. (1999). Foundations of a theory of disequilibrium network design. In M. Bell (Ed.), *Transportation networks: Recent methodological advances* (pp. 143–162). Oxford: Elsevier.

Friesz, T. L., Tobin, R. L., Cho, H.-J., & Mehta, N. J. (1990). Sensitivity analysis based heuristic algorithms for mathematical programs with variational inequality constraints. *Mathematical Programming, 48B*, 265–284

Friesz, T. L., Cho, H.-J., Mehta, N. J., & Tobin, R. L. (1992). Simulated annealing methods for network design problems with variational inequality constraints. *Transportation Science, 26*(1), 18–26.

Friesz, T. L., Tobin, R. L., Shah, S. J., Mehta, N. J., & Anandalingam, G. (1993). The multiobjective equilibrium network design problem revisited: A simulated annealing approach. *European Journal of Operations Research, 65*, 44–57.

Friesz, T. L., Bernstein, D., Mehta, N. J., Tobin, R. L., & Ganjalizadeh, S. (1995). Day-to-day dynamic network disequilibrium and idealized driver information systems. *Operations Research, 43*, 1120–1136.

Friesz, T. L., Bernstein, D., & Stough, R. (1996). Dynamic systems, variational inequalities and control theoretic models for predicting urban network flows. *Transportation Science, 30*(1), 14–31.

Friesz, T. L., Shah, S., & Bernstein, D. (1998). Disequilibrium network design: A new paradigm for transportation planning an control. In *Network infrastructure and the urban environment* (pp. 99–112). New York: Springer.

Harker, P. T., & Friesz, T. L. (1982). A simultaneous freight network equilibrium model. *Congressus Numerantium, 36*, 365–402.

Hobbs, B. F., & Pang, J. S. (2007). Nash-cournot equilbria in electric power markets with piecewise linear demand functions and joint constraints. *Operations Research, 55*(1), 113–127.

Huang, H. J., & Bell, M. G. H. (1998). Continuous equilibrium network design with elastic demand: Derivative-free solution methods. In *Transportation networks: Recent methodological advances* (pp. 175–193). Oxford: Elsevier.

Jara-Diaz, S. R., & Friesz, T. L. (1982). Measuring the benefits derived from a transportation investment. *Transportation Research B, 16B*(1), 57–77.

Kirkpatrick, S., Gelatt, C. D., & Vecchi, M. P. (1983). Optimization by simulated annealing. *Science, 220*, 671–680.

LeBlanc, L. J. (1975). An Algorithm for the discrete network design problem. *Transportation Science, 9*, 183–199.

Meng, Q., Yang, H., & Bell, M. G. H. (2001). An equivalent continuously differentiable model and a locally convergent algorithm for the continuous network design problem. *Transportation Research Part B, 35*, 83–105.

Metzler, C., Hobbs, B. F. & Pang, J.-S. (2003). Nash-cournot equilibria in power markets on a linearized DC network with arbitrage: Formulations and properties. *Networks and Spatial Economics, 3*(2), 123–150.

Miller, T., Friesz, T. L., & Tobin, R. L. (1996). *Equilibrium facility location on networks*. New York: Springer.

Mookherjee, R., Hobbs, B. F. Friesz, T. L., & Rigdon, M. (2008). Dynamic oligopolistic competition on an electric power network with ramping costs and sales constraints. *Journal of Industrial and Management Optimization, 4*(3), 425–452.

Murchland, J. D. (1970). Braess's paradox of traffic flow. *Transportation Research, 4*(4), 391–394.

Nagurney, A. (1994). Comments during *The conference on network infrastructure and the urban environment – Recent advances in land-use and transportation modeling*, Sweden.

Nisan, N., Roughgarden, T., Tardos, É., & Vazirani, V. V. (2007). *Algorithmic game theory*. Cambridge: Cambridge University Press.

Pigou, A. C. (1920). *The economics of welfare*. London: Macmillan.

Ramos, F. (1979). *Formulations and computational considerations for a general irrigation network planning model*. S.M. thesis, Massachusetts Institute of Technology.

Ramos, F. (1981). *Capacity expansion of regional urban water supply networks*. Ph.D. dissertation, Massachusetts Institute of Technology.

Rigdon, M. A., Mookherjee, R., & Friesz, T. L. (2008). Multiperiod competition in an electric power network and impacts of infrastructure disruptions. *Journal of Infrastructure Systems, 14*(4), 3–11.

Roughgarden, T. (2002). *Selfish routing*. PhD thesis, Cornell University, Ithaca.

Roughgarden, T. (2005). *Selfish routing and the price of anarchy* (196 pp.). Cambridge, MA: MIT.

Roughgarden, T. (2007). Routing games. In N. Nisan, T. Roughgarden, É. Tardos, & V. V. Vazirani (Eds.), *Algorithmic game theory*. New York: Cambridge University Press.

Roughgarden, T., & Tardos É. (2002). How bad is selfish routing? *Journal of the ACM, 49*(2), 236–259.

Roughgarden, T., & Tardos É. (2004). Bounding the inefficiency of equilibria in nonatomic congestion games. *Games and Economic Behavior, 47*(2), 389–403.

Smith, T. E., Friesz, T. L., Bernstein, D., & Suo, Z. (1997). A comparative analysis of two minimum-norm projective dynamics and their relationship to variational inequalities. In M. Ferris & J.-S. Pang (Eds.), *Complementarity and variational problems: State of the art* (pp. 405–424). Philadelphia: SIAM.

Suwansirikul, C., & Friesz, T. L. (1987). A heuristic algorithm for continuous equilibrium network design: Equilibrium decomposed optimization. *Transportation Science, 21*(4), 254–263.

Tan, H.-N., Gershwin, S., & Athans, M. (1979). *Hybrid optimization in urban traffic networks*. LIDS Technical Report. Cambridge, MA: MIT.

Vanderbilt, D., & Louie, S. G. (1984). A Monte Carlo simulated annealing approach to optimization over continuous variables. *Journal of Computational Physics, 56*, 259–271.

Wardrop, J. G. (1952). Some theoretical aspects of road traffic research. *Proceedings of the Institute of Civil Engineers, Part II, 1*, 278–325.

Yang, H., & Bell, M. G. H. (1998). Models and algorithms for road network design: A review and some new developments. *Transport Review, 18*, 257–278.

Index

T.L. Friesz, D. Bernstein, *Foundations of Network Optimization and Games*,
Complex Networks and Dynamic Systems 3,
DOI 10.1007/978-1-4899-7594-2

D

E

MIX
Papier aus verantwortungsvollen Quellen
Paper from responsible sources
FSC® C105338

If you have any concerns about our products,
you can contact us on
ProductSafety@springernature.com

In case Publisher is established outside the EU,
the EU authorized representative is:
Springer Nature Customer Service Center GmbH
Europaplatz 3, 69115 Heidelberg, Germany

Printed by Libri Plureos GmbH
in Hamburg, Germany